11-1-91

Foundations of
Business Systems

Foundations of Business Systems

Andersen Consulting Arthur Andersen & Co.
Per O. Flaatten
Donald J. McCubbrey
P. Declan O'Riordan
Keith Burgess

The Dryden Press
Chicago   Fort Worth   San Francisco   Philadelphia
Montreal   Toronto   London   Sydney   Tokyo

Acquisitions Editor: DeVilla Williams
Project Editor: Karen Hill
Design Director: Alan Wendt
Production Manager: Barb Bahnsen
Director of Editing, Design, and Production: Jane Perkins

Cover Designer: Richard Stalzer Associates, Ltd.
Copy Editor: Kathy Pruno
Indexer: Sheila Ary
Compositor: HBJ ImageTypesetting
Text Type: 10/12 Garamond Light

Library of Congress Cataloging-in-Publication Data

Foundations of business systems/Per O. Flaatten . . . [et al.], Arthur
  Andersen & Co.
    p. cm.
Bibliography: p.
Includes index.
ISBN 0-03-021628-1
1. Management information systems.   I. Flaatten, Per O.
II. Arthur Andersen & Co.
T58.6.F68   1989   88-38685
658.4'038—dc19   CIP

Printed in the United States of America
901-016-987654321
Copyright © 1989 by The Dryden Press, a division of
Holt, Rinehart and Winston, Inc.

Address orders:
The Dryden Press
Orlando, Florida 32887

Address editorial correspondence:
The Dryden Press
908 N. Elm St.
Hinsdale, IL 60521

The Dryden Press
Holt, Rinehart and Winston
Saunders College Publishing

To our wives and families

The Dryden Press Series in Information Systems

FOREWORD

Since the 1960s, virtually every industry worldwide has become increasingly competitive. Various reasons are cited for this, including the changing economics of transportation (both goods and information) as well as deregulation. In the late 1970s and early 1980s, Michael Porter and then others developed new approaches and methods of strategic planning that shifted the focus from internal concerns to issues of competition. In the early to mid-1980s, these approaches and methods were extended to consider the use of information and information technology to gain competitive advantage.

Porter's approaches have gained wide use and have driven many organizations to understand that information systems development is a critical organizational activity. We have witnessed not only a change in the amount of systems development activity but also a change in the nature of the systems being developed for business.

In the past, most data processing applications were limited to a single organizational unit or department. Today's systems often cross organizational lines and sometimes even reach to other enterprises—customers and suppliers. Second, these systems are at the heart of the business, such as order processing and plant scheduling, and they have significant performance, security, and control requirements. Third, these new systems have an increased requirement to be responsive to change beause they tend to be part of the enterprise's competitive posture and therefore will be duplicated by competitiors. Last, these systems are developed by very large project teams of sophisticated, seasoned information systems professionals.

This book is intended to assist in the education of college-level students who are interested in studying how business information systems are planned, built, and implemented. Andersen Consulting has been performing these activities for clients since the mid-1950s, when we assisted in the first business application of computers, a payroll system for General Electric in their Louisville plant on a UNIVAC machine. Since then, we have planned, built, and implemented thousands of business systems for clients in every industry, in virtually every country, on all sorts of hardware and software platforms, and to perform every business function imaginable. Andersen Consulting, which at the time of printing numbers some 15,000 people, is considered to be the leading provider of these services in the world.

We have witnessed through the years the metamorphosis of the information system's developer from eccentric scientist to egocentric artist to organizational neophyte to professional contributor to the strategic health of the enterprise he or she serves.

Our interest in writing this book is to share our experience and the resulting methods with students who are interested in the rewarding field of information systems. Few fields of endeavor are as important, as challenging, and as open to opportunity.

Melvyn E. Bergstein
Managing Partner—Technical Competence
Andersen Consulting

Preface

Systems analysis and design are the fundamental skills required by information systems professionals who are to develop, implement, and maintain computer-based business systems. Systems analysis is deciding what a system is to do; systems design is deciding how it is to do its work.

For some years—the late 1970s and early 1980s—systems analysis and design were de-emphasized in favor of end-user computing using fourth-generation languages and application software package installation. Since then, however, the increased use of information technology as a strategic weapon in the competitive arsenal of large corporations has redirected the focus on the custom development of applications by information systems professionals. This textbook recognizes that trend: it applies current theory about systems development to today's competitive environment, emphasizing teamwork, change management, and usability and giving a wealth of practical examples and advice. The book also attempts to update some of the techniques traditionally taught in systems analysis and design so that they more closely resemble current practice in information systems departments.

ABOUT THE TEXTBOOK

Foundations of Business Systems is about the initial phases of the systems development life cycle, systems analysis and design. It focuses on day-to-day transaction processing and management information systems in businesses and similar organizations. It meets the guidelines for the first course in systems analysis and design set by the Data Processing Management Association (DPMA) and those by the Association for Computing Machinery (ACM).

The book is divided into seven sections:

- Section I, "Information Systems in the Business," is an introduction to the environment in which today's systems are being built: the competitive motivation for building or extending systems, the management of the change process implied by systems implementation, and the organization of the information systems (IS) department.

- Section II, "Systems Planning," describes how systems development projects originate: one at a time through feasibility studies or in a coordinated whole through an enterprisewide systems plan.

- Section III, "Requirements Analysis," covers the first part of the analysis and design curriculum. The emphasis is on how to understand and document the functions of the system to be designed, either by interviewing users about the present system, its shortcomings, and the users' desiderata or by eliciting the requirements more directly by a group interviewing technique such as Joint Application Design (JAD).

- Sections IV to VI cover the design part of the curriculum. Section IV, "User Interface Design," emphasizes the current focus on users, whether they are dedicated clerks or end users such as financial analysts, marketing professionals, and engineers.

- Section V, "Data Design," covers recent developments in data modeling, which is increasingly recognized as one of the most important tools of the system designer. The coverage stops short of data base design, concentrating on the functional aspects of the data structures manipulated by typical transaction processing and management information systems.

- Section VI, "Process Design,"concentrates on proven elements of technical architectures for on-line and batch processing: single-exchange and multi-exchange conversations, recovery and restart, and batch updating and reporting. Also covered are controls and performance. The final chapter in this section, "Installation Planning, Economic Analysis, and Management Approval," describes the synthesis of the results of the three design activities: user interface, data, and processes.

- Section VII, "Implementation," rounds out the description of the systems development life cycle by covering the remaining activities: programming, testing, installation, and maintenance.

The core of the book is constituted by Sections III to VI, which are designed to give the student majoring in information systems knowledge of and skills in analysis and design. The remaining sections give useful background information. It is not expected that the student will single-handedly be able to apply Michael Porter's approach to the use of information technology for competitive advantage, manage technology insertion, reorganize an information systems department, or even complete a systems planning project: all these activities require a team approach, led by seasoned professionals. Nor is the book designed to cover programming, testing, and maintenance in depth: the student is assumed to have knowledge in at least one commercial programming language and to have written, tested, debugged, and possibly modified at least one program.

It is hoped that the book, including the initial and final sections, can also be helpful to students majoring in subjects other than information processing. And although the book is primarily directed to undergraduates, there is sufficient substance to justify its use in selected graduate courses.

FLEXIBLE ORGANIZATION

Each section of the book is essentially autonomous and can be taught in any sequence. The book follows the generic systems development life cycle chronologically; however, it is possible to teach implementation before design,

design before analysis, and analysis before strategic systems planning, conforming to the conventional wisdom that the objectives and deliverables of an activity are best understood by those who have had a chance to use those deliverables as input to a subsequent activity.

There is one exception to the book's flexibility: the techniques at the end of each section are best taught in the sequence in which they appear in the book.

The boxed vignette appearing at the beginning of each section may be used to introduce a topic and thus make it more lively, or it may be used at the end of teaching the section to illustrate applications of the concepts taught. In addition, the techniques may be taught before, during, or after the detailed chapters in the section.

As for the sequence of the chapters within each section, there is also some flexibility. For instance, "Joint Application Design" (Chapter 8) may be taught before "Interviewing" (Chapter 7) if desired. The sequence may be varied in other ways as the instructor deems appropriate.

PEDAGOGICAL HIGHLIGHTS

A boxed vignette opens each section. The vignettes illustrate modern systems design practice in actual companies. Each chapter begins with learning objectives and chapter overviews to prepare the student for the topic and closes with review and discussion questions to reinforce the material presented. In addition, several features support the text discussion: Real-world perspectives, highlighted in color in the text, realistically relate the strategy described in the section-opening vignette to the relevant management concerns, placing particular emphasis on competitive advantage and current systems development practice. Boxed features enhance textual material with real-world examples and applications of concepts, plus examinations of special interest topics. Mini-Cases link business issues and chapter contents through real-world cases with questions. Selected readings provided a capsule summary of major works in the subject area.

PACKAGE

Software/Case Tools Casebook

Foundations of Business Systems: Projects and Cases
By Andrew C. Boynton, *The Darden School of the University of Virginia*
Michael E. Shank, *University of North Carolina at Chapel Hill*

An ideal companion to *Foundations of Business Systems,* this realistic casebook utilizes the same seven-section organization as the text. The cases simulate the real-world business environment, covering the entire systems development life cycle. The integration between the ongoing cases and exercises allows your students to work independently or in groups.

The "projects" section of the casebook corresponds to the end-of-section techniques found in the main text. Projects incorporate the use of a special educational version Andersen Consulting's *Foundation®* software.

Foundation® Software

Adopters of *Foundations of Business Systems: Projects and Cases* will have access to a special educational version of Andersen Consulting's *Foundation®*, a CASE tool that covers the entire systems development life cycle. The software includes techniques from the text such as Data Flow Diagrams, Hierarchical Diagramming, Entity-Relationship Diagrams, and more.

Ancillaries

A complete instructional support package is offered with *Foundations of Business Systems:*

- Instructor's Manual
- Test Bank
- Computerized Test Bank
- Transparency Acetates

ACKNOWLEGMENTS

The writing of *Foundations of Business Systems* has been a team effort, and the authors wish to thank all of those who have contributed to it. Particular thanks are due to Bob Evanson, Senior Vice-President of Harcourt Brace Jovanovich, Inc., for the idea for this book and Mel Bergstein, Managing Partner, Technical Services, Andersen Consulting, for his enthusiastic reception and support for the idea. Thanks are also due to the following, for contributing, reviewing, and critiquing substantial contents of various portions of the book: Bill Bramer, Glover Ferguson, Carl Longnecker, Jill Smith, Peter Wenzlick, Will Zachman. Special thanks go to the members of the Editorial Review Board, who reviewed the entire manuscript and whose suggestions have immeasurably improved the text.

The development of *Foundations of Business Systems* would not have been possible without the input and responsiveness of those in the marketplace. Robert Ashenhurt, University of Chicago; Don Amoroso, University of Colorado, Colorado Springs; Roger Hayen, Central Michigan University; Khaleeb Hussain, New Mexico State University; William Konn, University of Wisconsin, Eau Claire; Khris McAlister, University of Alabama, Birmingham; William Moates, Indiana State University; Tarun Sen, Virginia Polytechnic & State University; Robert Trent, University of Virginia; and Ira Weiss, University of Houston, University Park are to be thanked for their participation in our focus groups. Marketing research also played a critical role in the production of this text. The following are to be thanked for their time, information, and ideas:

Joyce Abler
Central Michigan University

Joseph Adamski
Grand Valley State College

Robert Ader
Middle Tennessee State University

Gary Baram
Temple University

William Beidler
University of Southern Mississippi

Virginia Bender
*William Rainey Harper
Community College*

Charles Bilbrey
James Madison University

David A. Bird
University of Missouri—St. Louis

Stephen Bird
New Mexico State University

James Blaisdoll
Humboldt State University

Mark Blank
San Francisco State University

Roy Boggs
University of South Florida

Michael Brendler
Louisiana State University—Shreveport

Elias Callahan
Mississippi State University

Jan Carey
Texas A & M University

Carol Chrisman
Illinois State University

Frank David
Bloomsburg University

Sasa Dekleva
DePaul University

E.Reed Doke
Southwest Missouri State

Peter Duchessi
State University of New York at Albany

John Durham
Fort Harris State

Henry Etlinger
Rochester Institute of Technology

Robert Fleck
Columbus College

Jack Fuller
West Virginia University

Jack Gilman
Florida International University

Carol Grimm
Palm Beach Community College

Ted Grossman
Babson College

Patricia Guinan
Boston University

Dennis Guster
St. Louis Meramec Community College

Maurice Halloday
Suffolk University

Fred Harold
Florida Atlantic University

Brian Honess
University of South Carolina

Jeretha Horn
Oklahoma State University

Wallace Jewell
Edinboro State University

Ernest Kallman
Bentley College

Dale Kewitz
Marshall University

Chuck Litecky
University of Missouri

Rebecca Litner
St. Joseph's University

Thomas MacBeth
University of Lowell

Roy Martin
Southwest Texas State University

Thomas Mason
Florida A & M University

M. Khris McAlister
University of Alabama—Birmingham

Roger McGrath
University of South Florida

William McHenry
Georgetown University

Bruce McLaren
Indiana State University

Rich Montague
Western Connecticut State University

Lewis Myers
Texas A & M University

Lowell Needham
Pittsburg State University

Ronald Norman
San Diego State University

Shailendra Palvia
Babson College

Gehrhard Plenert
California State University, Chico

David Russell
Western New England College

Bruce Saulrigs
Quinnipiac College

Carol Saunders
Texas Christian University

Valerie Schmeider
Western Connecticut State University

Tarun Sen
Virginia Polytechnic & State University

Jerri Frances Sitek
*Southern Illinois University—
Edwardsville*

Craig Slinkman
University of Texas—Arlington

Ralph Stair
Florida State University

Fred Stiner
University of Delaware

Stephen Strane
Western Illinois University

Joel Stutz
University of Miami

Madjid Tavana
LaSalle University

James Teng
University of Pittsburgh

Robert Trent
University of Virginia

Michael Varano
Villanova University

Lawig Weathe
University of Texas—Austin

John Willhardt
Alabama State University

Mustafa Yilmiz
Northeastern University

Ron Zigli
Memphis State University

Great improvements were also brought to the book by Mark Fitzgerald, Bonnie Carter, and Craig Skates.

Heartfelt thanks are due to the people at Harcourt Brace Jovanovich, Inc., at Holt, Rinehart and Winston, at The Dryden Press, and at Andersen Consulting who helped with design, production, and marketing: David Bassin, Mike Brown, Ted Buchholz, Manuel Castro, Ben Elderd, Leng Eng, Butch Gemin, David Hall, MaryEllen McKee, John Sulzycki, Chuck Wahrhaftig, Alan Wendt, and Shari Wenker. Karen Hill kept tireless track of where each part of the book stood and what remained due: without her, chapters, vignettes, techniques, and figures would be a hopeless jumble today, rather than a whole book. We also thank all our friends and colleagues at Andersen Consulting and at the University of Denver College of Business Administration for their contributions and support, in the small and in the large.

Last but not least, we wish to thank DeVilla Williams, our beloved editor and Chief Whip. This book is as much hers as it is ours.

ABOUT THE AUTHORS

Per O. Flaatten is Manager at Andersen Consulting in Chicago. He has more than twenty years of experience developing information systems in the United States and Europe and has taught several courses in Systems Development and Methodology. Mr. Flaatten is presently responsible for Andersen Consulting's methodology development.

Donald J. McCubbrey is Chairman of the Management Information Systems Department at the University of Denver. Before joining the University of Denver staff in 1984, he served as a partner in Andersen Consulting, Arthur Andersen & Co., where he was responsible for a large number of Information Systems planning, design, and installation engagements throughout the United States, Canada, and Latin America.

P. Declan O'Riordan, who is now located in the Washington, D.C., office of Andersen Consulting, has twenty-six years of experience in information systems design and installation at both IBM and Andersen Consulting. He is currently a member of the firm's Technology Advisory Committee and has previously served as a Director of Information Technology Research for the firm. He has also served as the firm's representative on the Sponsor's Advisory Board of the Center for Information System Research at the Sloan School of Management, Massachusetts Institute of Technology.

Keith Burgess is Division Head of the Advanced Information Technology and Industrial, Commercial, and Public Enterprises Division of Andersen Consulting in the United Kingdom. He is currently chairman of the Technical Advisory Committee, which is responsible for overseeing the technical direction of the firm's practice.

Contents in Brief

Contents

Chapter 6

IS Resource Planning

Technique

Entity-Relationship Diagrams

Section III

REQUIREMENTS ANALYSIS

Chapter 7

Study of Present System (Interviewing)

| Chapter 8 | **Joint Application Design** | 215 |

| Technique | **Data Flow Diagrams** | 227 |

| Section IV | **USER INTERFACE DESIGN** | 241 |

| Chapter 9 | **Designing Dialogs and Document Flows** | 251 |

Chapter 20   **Installing the System**   661

Chapter 21   **Maintenance**   683

Technique   **Writing User Documentation in Playscript**   699

Appendix 1 **Value Chain Analysis**   713

Appendix 2 **Typical Job Descriptions**   727

Appendix 3 **State Transition Diagrams**   731

Appendix 4 **Computer Graphics**   737

Index   746

Section I

Information Systems in the Business

The purpose of Section I is, not to teach the practice of systems analysis and design, but to show how successful organizations view today's information technology and information systems professionals in relation to the rest of the enterprise—executive management and information systems users.

Chapter 1 describes how information technology is increasingly used by creative organizations to achieve competitive advantage. For the past few years, the use of information technology has been shifting from transaction recording and management reporting systems, which process information about business activities after the fact, to transaction processing and management information systems, which use information technology to actually help carry out the business activity. This shift has taken place against the backdrop of an increasingly competitive economic environment. One approach to the use of information technology—that of Michael Porter of Harvard—has been effective in achieving success in this environment, as described in Chapter 1.

As information systems have become both more pervasive and more strategic, they are used by more and more people as an integral part of their work. As a result, new information systems introduce deep changes in the way the work is done. Chapter 2 points out some of the factors causing resistance to change and suggests how proper systems development practices can help overcome this resistance.

Chapter 3 examines the place of the information systems (IS) department in the organization and the way the department is organized internally. Because of the increasing importance of information systems in most companies, it is only to be expected that the organizational environment in which the information systems professionals work would change. This change is emphasized by the greater complexity of the technology and the greater demands that users place on systems. The chapter introduces forms of systems development projects that are responsive to user demands and to the process of change.

The Hospitals of Kalamazoo

Kalamazoo, Michigan, is a city of 125,000 people located in the southwestern part of the state, about midway between Detroit and Chicago. It is the site of Western Michigan University and the home office of such companies as Upjohn. It is known as a pleasant place in which to live and raise a family.

The health care market in Kalamazoo is dominated by two major acute-care hospitals, both close in size. In early 1985, the competition between Borgess Medical Center and Bronson Methodist Hospital intensified. Because of increased outpatient treatment and early patient discharges, both hospitals found that a greater percentage of their beds were unoccupied at any point in time. An empty bed in a hospital is like an empty seat in an airplane or at a concert. It is capacity underutilized and revenue lost. The question both hospitals were asking themselves was "How can we get an increasing share of a decreasing market?" Because patients would travel only so far for hospital care, the market for both hospitals was limited to the city of Kalamazoo and the surrounding areas. Clearly, if one hospital were to find a way to increase its inpatient population, it could only do so by taking patients away from the other.

One hospital, Borgess Medical Center, developed an information system that enabled it to increase its inpatient population at the expense of its crosstown rival, Bronson Methodist Hospital. The project to achieve a competitive advantage began when planners realized that the customers of hospitals were physicians, not patients. In a market such as Kalamazoo, physicians tended to be on the medical staffs of both major hospitals, which meant they were permitted to admit their patients to either one. Hospitals that find themselves in such a position generally try to make themselves the more attractive alternative to physicians by offering the latest in medical technology, building medical office buildings nearby, and generally offering amenities such as attractively furnished lounges and preferred parking. All other things being equal, the physicians would tend to suggest the hospital he or she preferred when it came time to discuss hospitalization with the patient.

The planners at Borgess also realized that a physician's time was valuable. If a way could be found to both make Borgess a more attractive facility and save the physicians' time, physicians would be more likely to admit their patients to Borgess instead of its rival.

The solution they developed involved the creative use of information technology. They offered to place personal computers in the physicians' offices at no cost. Software was provided to perform routine office management functions such as patient billing and accounts receivable, appointment scheduling, and patient records. More important, the personal computers were able to connect with the hospital's computer over telecommunications lines.

The telecommunications capability made it much easier for the physicians to communicate with the hospital for such purposes as scheduling admissions and operating rooms, and also for scheduling patients for laboratory and radiology examinations administered to outpatients. Previously, making such arrangements was often a frustrating and time-consuming process for physicians and their office support personnel. When results of laboratory tests or radiology exams were needed, they could be obtained in the physicians' offices through computer-to-computer links, avoiding the same frustrations.

In addition, Borgess offered physicians who signed up for the program membership in a physicians' referral service operated by the hospital. Advertising programs for the service were developed for television and newspapers, giving people a telephone number to call when they needed a physician but did not know whom to call. Most physicians welcomed this service, particularly those just starting their practices, because the same pressures that made hospitals compete also exerted themselves on the physicians. Moreover, the number of physicians was on the increase. This meant that physicians were competing for patient volumes as well.

Physicians soon discovered the many advantages to the new service provided by Borgess Medical Center:

- They began seeing more patients as a result of the referral service.

- They saved time, as did their office staffs, by making appointments and receiving results through computer-to-computer communications rather than by using the telephone. In addition, there was much less aggravation associated with the new system.

- Their cash flow increased because of an increased patient volume and the more effective billing and accounts receivable operations provided by the software.

Consequently, the physicians sent more of their patients to Borgess and Borgess filled more of its beds.

The success of the system was described in *Modern Healthcare* as follows:

"Frank Tiedemann, vice president for marketing at Borgess, said the network is largely responsible for 'our most profitable year in history.' In the year ended June 30, Borgess had more than $14 million in net income, double projections and up about 40% from the previous year. Net operating revenues were up 18% to $130 million.

"The financial success was attributable largely to a 3% increase in admissions during the first nine months the network was operating, Mr. Tiedemann said. In the year since the network began, admissions have risen about 5% at a time when most of the state's hospitals are experiencing declines in admissions, he said."[1]

Thus, Borgess Medical Center achieved its goal of increasing its share of a decreasing market through the innovative use of information technology, at the expense of its chief competitor, Bronson Methodist Hospital.

SYSTEMS DEVELOPMENT LIFE CYCLE

The first section is an overview of the classical systems development life cycle and shows how the various parts fit together. Each subsequent section of the book deals with one phase of the systems development life cycle.

The systems development life cycle is an approach to developing systems in an organized and disciplined manner. In its most general form, the approach consists of four components:

- Define the objectives of the system to be developed.

- Define indicators of success that will measure whether the objectives have been met.

- Generate alternative strategies.

- Select and implement a strategy.

Although this approach appears simple and almost self-evident, many systems efforts flounder, especially through failing to address the first two steps. If the objectives are not clear or not universally accepted, the systems developers will be in the position of Alice in Wonderland: "Cheshire-Puss," she began, "Would you tell me, please, where I ought to go from here?" "That depends a great deal on where you want to get to," said the Cat.

As an IS professional, if you have not established measurable indicators of success, you may know where you are going, but you will never know whether you are there yet. You may meet your own expectations and those of some others; you will have exceeded those of some users and fallen short of those of others. You will be criticized for doing too much and not doing enough. The system will fail because disappointed users will not make the necessary effort to make the system work.

The Phases of the Systems Development Life Cycle

All systems development life cycle variations in use today divide the life of a system into phases, from the initial idea to its full implementation, followed by enhancements and possibly replacement by a new system based on a fresh idea. Not only is the cycle of defining objectives, defining indicators of success, generating alternatives, and developing an operational plan applicable to a system as a whole, but it is also applicable to each successive development phase.

The Waterfall Life Cycle

The basic life cycle is called the waterfall life cycle. It is adapted to both custom development and implementation of packaged application software. However, the waterfall life cycle has some problems. More recently developed life cycles— iterative development and prototyping—have addressed some of these problems.

The waterfall life cycle arose from the difficulty that systems developers had in accurately predicting the cost of a system and how long implementation would take, without first having to do a substantial part of the work. Because the cost of a system is usually the single most important success factor, the use of the systems approach led to subdividing the whole systems development effort into successive phases, each with its own cycle of defining objectives, defining success factors, generating alternatives, and implementing the selected alternative.

In this approach, each successive phase can be started only after the previous phase has been completed and a formal decision has been made by management whether the results obtained so far justify continuing the project. The name *Waterfall Life Cycle* stems from the way the life cycle was often depicted (see Figure I–1).

There are a great number of versions of the waterfall life cycle on the market. They generally differ in how many phases are recognized, typically from two to ten. The number of phases need not always be the same. For example, it is sometimes possible to combine phases on a small systems project, when time is short. The

Figure I–1 **Waterfall Systems Development Life-Cycle**

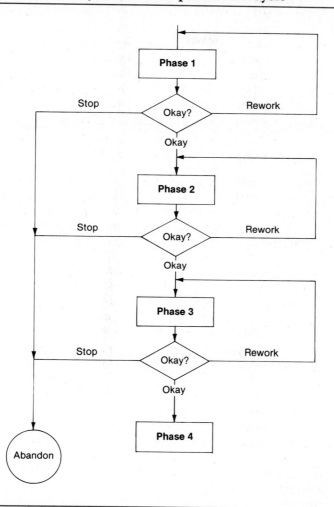

generic life cycle used in this book has five phases: systems planning, requirements, design, implementation, and maintenance (see Figure I–2).

As shown in Figure I–3, each phase has an overall objective and an end product (often called deliverable), which serves as the measure of success: when the deliverable is ready and approved by all interested parties, the phase is finished. In addition, each phase has generally accepted methods and techniques for selecting and implementing the alternatives. This process is what this book is all about.

Figure I–2 **Generic Systems Development Life Cycle Used in This Book**

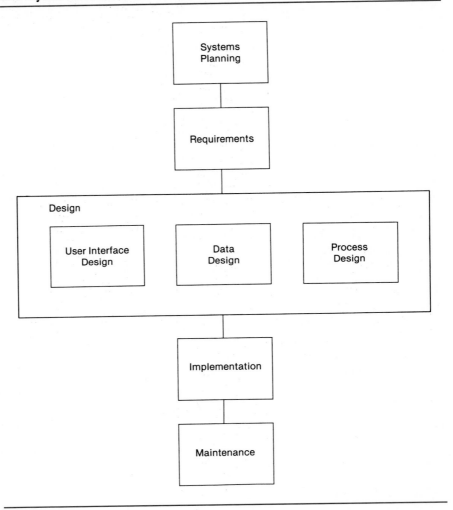

Figure I–4 shows typical relative costs of each phase of the waterfall life cycle. These costs assume that the system is to be installed in one location only. Multilocation systems require an additional phase, often called rollout, which can easily surpass the cost of all the other phases combined. Imagine, for instance, a new mail sorting and delivery system to be installed in every post office in an entire country.

Figure I-3 **Phases, Objectives, and Deliverables**

Phase	Objective	Deliverable
Systems Planning	Identify projects and resources required over next 3–5 years	Systems Plan
Requirements	Determine the scope of a system and its success factors	Requirements Specification
User Interface Design	Design the external behavior of the system	Dialog and Document Flow Design
Data Design	Design the logical structure of the data bases and files	Entity, Relationship, and Attribute Descriptions
Process Design	Design the internal behavior of the system	Program/Module Descriptions
Implementation	Program and test the system; prepare the users; convert	Operational System
Maintenance	Correct and enhance the system	Operational System

Figure I–5 shows how the figures vary when an application software package is to be installed. Here, requirements analysis is a much higher proportion of the total; in fact, its cost remains almost constant while the costs of other phases are lower.

Problems with the Waterfall Life Cycle. The waterfall life cycle has fallen into disrepute over the last few years. The main problem is the length of time that it can take to go through the life cycle. In particular, once a design is approved, it may typically be 18 months before the system is actually implemented. By that time, requirements have changed and users have forgotten why a design decision was adopted. On the other hand, if new requirements are incorporated into the design throughout the implementation phase, programmers and analysts must work towards a moving target, and the implementation effort becomes difficult or impossible to manage.

Another problem associated with the length of time it takes to implement systems in large chunks is that users have not been sufficiently involved in the development of systems. The IS department often has the reputation of working on its own, concentrating only on technical issues, and out of touch with the real world of the users.

Contributing to this perception of IS departments is that, until recently, the cost of the technology was so high that IS departments concentrated on maximizing the use of the equipment and neglected human factors. Users, typically clerical workers, were trained to conform to the demands of the system instead of the system being designed to conform to the needs of the users. This attitude is rapidly giving way to the opposite. Today, good designers recognize that humans are inherently conservative and do not particularly want to change. Modern methods therefore encourage designing systems in such a way that users will respond positively to the changes that the systems require.

Figure I–4 **Relative Development Costs by Phase**

Phase	Percentage Range of Effort
Requirements	2–5%
User Interface Design	5–10
Data Design	5–10
Process Design	5–15
Total Design	15–40
Program Specification	10–20
Program Coding and Unit Test	15–50
User Procedures and Training	5–25
Conversion	5–30
System Test	5–25
Total	100%

This attention to the user has resulted in a major and a minor change in methodology. The minor change is the added emphasis on user interface design. This added emphasis is apparent in so-called heart-of-the-business systems, where the computer technology is used to help carry out an organization's main tasks, rather than to record data about those tasks after the fact. The change is reinforced by the emergence of personal computers and computer literacy. Users who are accustomed to good interfaces such as those of spreadsheets, graphics, and mice do not readily accept black-and-white terminals with high response times and cryptic or missing instructions.

The major shift in methodology is towards a much more participative style of systems development. Two modern approaches illustrate this shift: iterative development and prototyping.

Iterative Development

With the iterative approach, the development team can avoid long projects and make sure something of value is delivered to the users of an application every few weeks. For example, as soon as a report is found to be required, it can be designed, programmed, tested, and implemented, perhaps in less than two weeks. The development team then goes on to diagnose the next requirement (see Figure I–6).

The iterative development approach has both merits and problems. The merits of the approach are obvious—increased user involvement and returns on investment. Users remain involved because very little time goes by between being promised something and seeing it actually delivered. Returns on investment are increased because the average time to implement a given function is roughly divided in half for the same total cost. Therefore, the breakeven point of the application, the moment when accumulated benefits or savings overtake accumulated costs, can easily come several months or a year earlier than with the waterfall style.

Figure I–5 **Relative Development Costs by Phase Using Packaged Software**

Phase	Percentage Range of Effort
Requirements	10–20%
User Interface Design	0–5
Data Design	0–2
Process Design	0–5
Total Design	10–30
Program Specification	20–30
Program Coding and Unit Test	10–30
User Procedures and Training	5–20
Conversion	15–40
System Test	5–25
Total	100%

To people who are used to the waterfall methodology, the problems with this approach seem equally obvious. One problem is that it is difficult to evaluate the total economics of an entire system before implementation starts. This objection is often met by the argument that each step must pay for itself, thus ensuring that the entire system will achieve at least the sum of the savings of each individual deliverable.

In practice, some systems functions that are a prerequisite for others may not pay for themselves, may take long to implement, and may consequently make the iterative approach impossible. Although invoicing cannot be implemented before a customer data base is established, the customer data base may not pay for itself, especially if the full-fledged, integrated, total customer data base is implemented. It only pays in terms of the applications—order entry, invoicing, marketing, and so on—that it makes possible. If only the small part of the data base actually required for invoicing were implemented in an initial step, and then the other applications were added as they were implemented, an unstable data structure with difficult maintenance problems would result. This problem is getting easier to solve with relational data bases, but it is by no means negligible.

As a consequence, iterative development is much more difficult to apply to transaction processing systems than to management information systems and decision support systems. Transaction processing systems tend to be integrated and operate as a whole. Management information and decision support systems are much easier to subdivide into smaller units and tend to use already existing data bases.

For transaction processing systems, iterative development requires an initial phase of fairly detailed systems planning. The plan lays out the overall data structure and the technical architecture of the system as well as a general sequence of implementation. Then, both infrastructure systems (e.g., data base management, utilities, report distribution, security) and business applications

Figure I–6   **Impact of Iterative Development on the Life Cycle**

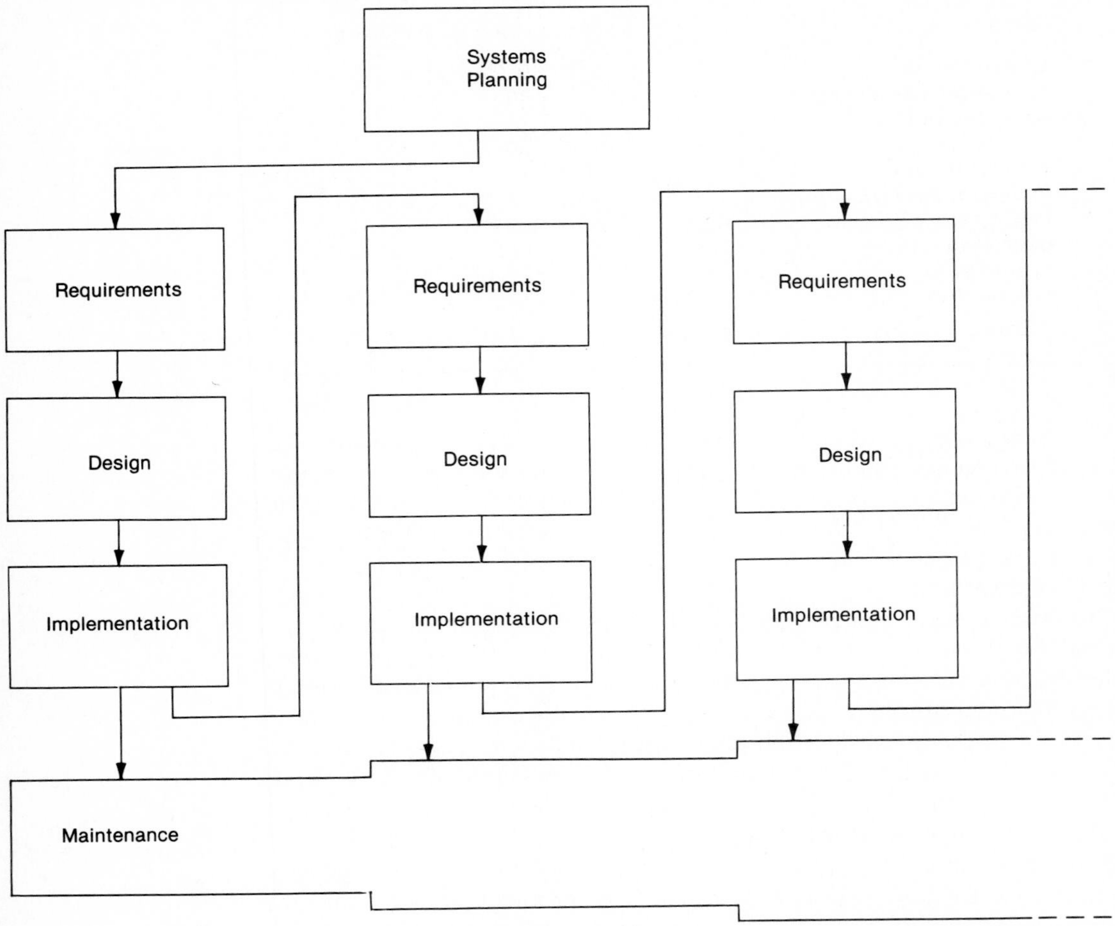

can be implemented in small chunks. The systems plan must also be constantly maintained, and changes must be communicated to the systems developers so that they can continue to aim for the right target, even though it keeps moving.

In summary, iterative development is difficult and requires experienced planners and excellent project leaders, but its rewards can be immense.

Prototyping

In addition to iterative development, another style of participative development has emerged—prototyping. Prototyping is creating a working design rather than

Figure I-7 **Impact of Prototyping on the Life Cycle**

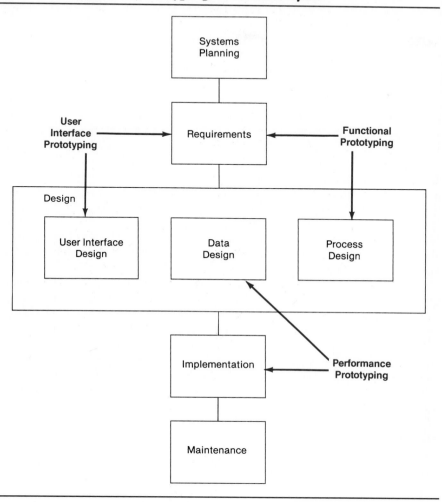

a design on paper. As shown in Figure I-7, this approach does not modify the flow of the life cycle as does iterative development. Rather, it changes how the work is done in some of the classical life cycle phases.

One of the great difficulties of designs on paper—screen layouts, English language descriptions of procedures, flowcharts, and data flow diagrams—is that the users, who are generally required to sign off on a design before implementation starts, tend to object to the implementation later on, saying that what they had approved was different or that they had understood the design differently. Sometimes, the users approve something they would have objected to had they read the specification more carefully. Often, however, there is a genuine difference of interpretation that can only be resolved when the actual system is seen.

Instead of a design on paper, prototyping creates a demonstration model of the part of the design that the users are interested in. The prototype is analogous to the clay model of automobile stylists, the scale model that airplane engineers use for wind-tunnel tests, and the cardboard replicas that architects use.

Prototyping is found in three distinct areas: user interface design, performance design, and functional requirements determination. In practice, it is most often used to demonstrate the flow of human-computer interactions. In particular, it can demonstrate the layout of a screen on an actual display and the succession of operator actions—menu choices, data entry, function keys—together with typical system responses.

The second most frequent use of prototyping is to simulate a system under conditions that are close to real volumes. A prototype data base can be developed, and a program can then simulate a large number of simultaneous users. This process is usually applied to the evaluation of a technical design or the suitability of a piece of hardware. It generally only involves the technical part of the team, not the users.

Finally, prototyping is proving useful when users have difficulty formulating requirements. The main symptom of this difficulty is when someone says, "I don't know what I want, but I will know it when I see it." Another typical indication is when a user states a processing rule and then never seems to run out of exceptions to the rule. When this problem occurs, artificial intelligence techniques and tools can often be used to develop a working prototype that gives satisfactory results. The requirements analysis process can then pull the prototype apart to ascertain which rules actually made the result come out right. Prototyping is explored in more detail in Section IV.

References

1. Anderson, Howard J., "Physician Computer Network Moves into New Markets after Michigan Test." *Modern Healthcare*, (November 21, 1986): 50.

Chapter 1

Information Technology and Competitive Advantage

After a brief historical perspective, Chapter 1 describes the impact of today's rapidly changing and highly competitive environment on the use of information technology. The framework for strategic business planning in this environment is built on Professor Michael Porter's approach: the five forces model, the three generic strategies, and the value chain analysis. Described next are two areas in which work has been done to complete this framework. The first is the strategic grid. This grid enables planners to analyze how important information technology is to a specific organization. The second area is that it may not always be advantageous to pioneer, even when the objective is to achieve an advantage over the competition. Finally, the notion of competitive advantage, which applies mainly to profit-oriented businesses, is extended to not-for-profit organizations.

Learning Objectives

- Describe how management attitudes towards information technology are changing from the view that the technology is useful for recording routine business transactions to the view that information is a valuable corporate resource.

- Recognize how information technology supports the management and use of the information resource.

- Understand how strategic planning is used to anticipate and instigate change.

- Become aware of how Michael Porter's model can be used as a framework for thinking about ways to use information technology to achieve a competitive advantage.

- Understand how the model developed by Cash, McFarlan, and McKenney—

the strategic grid—can be used to evaluate the strategic significance of an organization's existing and projected information technology applications.

- Recognize that an organization should consider possible repercussions before introducing a system designed to yield a competitive advantage.
- Realize that applications to achieve a competitive advantage are applicable to the not-for-profit sector as well.

A BRIEF HISTORICAL PERSPECTIVE

Business managers today are much more concerned about the effects of competition than they were even a few short years ago. They must react to competitive threats not only from local sources but also from regional, national, and international sources. Deregulation in such industries as airlines and banking in the United States has also increased competitive pressure. For organizations to survive, much less grow and prosper, in such a competitive environment, managers must employ all of the resources at their command as efficiently and effectively as possible. They, the managers, are responsible for their organizations being better than the competition.

One potentially powerful resource available to managers is information technology. More and more stories tell how information technology has successfully given some companies an advantage over their competitors. Also, companies that are forced to react to a competitor's innovative use of information technology are at a disadvantage.

Computers have been available for business use since 1954, when a Univac 1 was installed at General Electric's Appliance Park facility in Louisville, Kentucky. If computers have been around this long, why is it that the use of information technology for competitive advantage is a relatively recent phenomenon? Several factors help explain why:

- Early applications focused on the mechanization of existing procedures.
- A gap between technicians and users emerged in many organizations.
- The environment has only recently become more changing, more competitive.

application focus

At Appliance Park, the first computer was used to prepare the plant's payroll. In the early years of computer systems, the **application focus** of most companies that used computers was to mechanize existing manual or punched-card transaction processing systems such as payroll, billing and accounts receivable, and general ledger. Most often the data processing group reported to the accounting function. This tended to keep them focused on the development of accounting and related applications in all but the most enlightened of environments.

In addition, because the technology was changing so rapidly, data processing professionals were hard pressed to keep up. As a result, more and more data processing specialists emerged. They were experts in such areas as computer operating systems, data base, telecommunications, and higher-level languages. In many companies, the specialization caused a **technician-user gap**; information systems specialists spoke a language all their own, unintelligible to all but other specialists. They placed a higher value on competence in information technology than on company or industry expertise and tended to change employers frequently to work with the latest technology. Thus, a gap developed between the IS professionals and the users they were supposed to support. In extreme situations, users' needs for information systems remained unmet while the information systems department specialists struggled with backlogs of many years of work or pursued technical adventures of their own.

technician-user gap

Many companies are now discovering the contribution that information technology can make to overall corporate effectiveness by developing innovative systems themselves, by reading about systems developed by others, or by experiencing the sting of a system developed by one of their competitors. The **change in the nature of applications**, from routine back-office systems such as payroll and billing to systems such as the airline reservation systems that increase competitiveness, makes a profound contribution to an organization's strategic goals. Information has been added to the traditional physical, human, and financial resources available to organizations. In the words of one prominent practitioner: "The relative performance of companies in the future will increasingly depend on how effectively they use information."

change in the nature of applications

The competitive use of information technology will affect national economies as well, for nations compete with each other in today's global economy. Michael Blumenthal, chairman of UNISYS Corporation, stated it this way: "Increasingly, then, a country's comparative advantage lies in its ability to utilize effectively the new information technology, in the speed of its absorption into the productive process, and in the relative efficiency with which it is applied. Less and less it is the other factor endowments, the availability of raw materials or the cost of labor, that determines which country has the advantage and which has the lowest cost."[1]

An ancient Chinese proverb states that change is the only constant. Not only is this truth as valid as ever, but the pace of **change in the business environment** is more rapid than before and seems to be constantly increasing. All businesses have to be prepared to operate in an environment of accelerating change. For example, computer-aided design and manufacturing (CAD/CAM) techniques have shortened product development life cycles by several years in some cases. Technological advances have created new products where none existed before. One such new product is the facsimile machine, which transmits copies of documents from one location to another using the dial-up telephone network. Facsimile transmission will no doubt continue to force change in the overnight express delivery industry, and existing players in that industry will have to react willy-nilly.

change in the business environment

Although traditional uses of information technology still exist, including clerical personnel cost reductions and reduction of paperwork turnaround

BOX 1–1

Top Management's Understanding of Information Technology

Top management's understanding of information technology varies. In many organizations, top management views information technology as useful for getting out the payroll or for processing payments, but fails to appreciate the potential it has for doing much more: for leveraging management talent through decision support and expert systems, for information systems tailored for top executives, and for information systems designed to be used as competitive weapons. Part of the explanation for this failure is that information technology is still a young field compared with other areas of business such as manufacturing or marketing. As a result, the techniques for managing information technology effectively are still evolving. Many of today's top managers were not exposed to information technology in their formal training or when they were rising through the ranks except for its use in basic transaction processing systems. Thus, there is little in their backgrounds that prepares them to view information and information technology as a valuable corporate resource.

times, achieving a competitive edge has become the single most powerful motivation for the creation of new systems. Those organizations that recognize information as a resource to achieve their strategic goals are the ones where new application development is the most vigorous.

INFORMATION TECHNOLOGY'S ROLE TODAY

information resource management

As just noted, increased recognition is being given to information as a valuable corporate resource, one that must be managed as carefully as other corporate resources. A new domain has appeared, **information resource management,** whose purpose is to find ways to ensure that corporations are making the most effective use of this increasingly valuable resource. In some organizations a new executive position, the chief information officer (CIO), has been created to make sure that the information resource receives the appropriate level of executive attention.

supportive role of information systems

At a more fundamental level, management must recognize the **supportive role of information systems**, enabling the organization to operate smoothly and economically. In this role, the information systems function must be properly channeled and directed by senior management in pursuit of overall corporate goals. However, in many organizations top management has not understood the potential of information technology. Many examples exist of a business moving in one direction and its information systems function moving in a direction all its own, almost oblivious that it was supposed to contribute to corporate goals.

For information systems to support overall organizational goals, these goals must be defined and expressed. This process is typically labeled strategic business planning or long-range planning. Strategic business planning is particularly important in a rapidly changing competitive environment. Without it, companies might not be able to survive and prosper.

A FRAMEWORK FOR STRATEGIC BUSINESS PLANNING

Change is inevitable. If an organization does not change on its own, the competitive environment will force it to. Strategic business planning can help companies anticipate change. More important, planning can help companies instigate change rather than be its victims. Instead of letting unexpected change threaten its stability, an organization can capitalize on the opportunities that change presents. To anticipate or, even better, to plan for change, a company can use the traditional strategic planning model, which involves three steps:

- Defining the mission of the organization.
- Identifying strategic goals and objectives in support of the mission.
- Developing strategies to achieve these goals and strategies.

These three steps constitute the strategic planning process itself. Further steps are required to put the strategy into action: development of tactical measures and monitoring results.

One of the challenges of strategic planning is to develop alternative views, or scenarios, of what the future business environment will be like and then to plan corporate strategies appropriate for each scenario. Without the aid of information technology, only a small number of alternative scenarios can be evaluated. For some time, computer-based corporate models and other forecasting techniques have been available to assist organizations in strategic planning and in monitoring progress towards the plan's goals and objectives.

Professor Michael Porter has created a conceptual model for strategic planning that planners can use as a framework for thinking about ways to use information systems to achieve competitive advantage. This model uses information technology not just for planning the strategy, but also for implementing the strategy that is being planned. The three key concepts in Michael Porter's approach are the five forces model, the three generic strategies, and the value chain.

Five Forces Model

Porter defines five competitive forces that collectively determine an industry's overall attractiveness. The opportunities for growth and investment return will vary by industry. Hence, planners first evaluate the areas of attractiveness before committing resources to any particular strategy.

Figure 1–1 **The Five Forces Model**

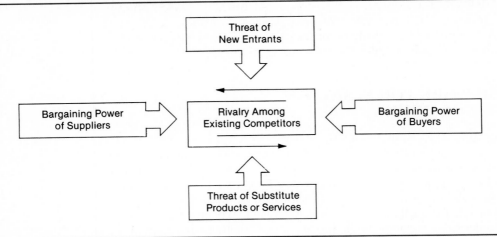

Source: Reprinted with permission of The Free Press, a Division of Macmillan, Inc. from *Competitive Advantage: Creating and Sustaining Superior Performance* by Michael E. Porter, p. 5. Copyright © 1985 by Michael E. Porter.

As illustrated in Figure 1–1, the five forces are:

- Threat of New Entrants

    An industry is deemed less attractive if it is relatively easy for new competitors to enter, more attractive if existing competitors can raise barriers against potential new entrants.

- Threat of Substitute Products or Services

    An industry's attractiveness is diminished if substitute products or services are easy for its customers to obtain.

- Bargaining Power of Buyers

    An industry becomes less attractive when the bargaining power of its buyers increases, more attractive when the bargaining power of its buyers decreases.

- Bargaining Power of Suppliers

    As with buyers, the attractiveness of an industry decreases as the bargaining power of its suppliers increases, and vice versa.

- Rivalry Among Existing Competitors

    A slow-growth industry with many vigorous competitors and high exit barriers, for example, is inherently less attractive than a high-growth industry with a few relatively courteous competitors.

Let us examine each of the five forces and their interaction in greater detail.

Threat of New Entrants. Members of a particular industry will find it advantageous to erect entry barriers against potential new entrants, thus keeping the number of competitors to a minimum. Traditional barriers to entry have been such factors as economies of scale, large capital requirements, high switching costs, and proprietary technology. For example, an entry barrier exists if large volumes or heavy investments are necessary for new entrants to be cost-efficient producers, because their fixed costs will be very high. It is not until they have reached a sufficient volume of production that the total revenue will be sufficient to cover both variable and fixed costs, thus achieving the required economies of scale. Companies such as Sears that have attempted to enter the credit card market have had to face formidable entry barriers based on economies of scale. Another example of a barrier is the switching costs associated with changing from one supplier to another. For example, if a large organization were to switch from using Lotus 1–2–3 to another spreadsheet package with different layouts and key usage, it would incur large costs in retraining its personnel to use the new spreadsheet. Some of Lotus's competitors have attempted to make Lotus look-alike spreadsheets. No doubt Lotus Development Corporation was aware that the barriers to entry were being lowered when it sued a competitor for having created a look-alike.

Threat of Substitute Products or Services. The availability of substitute products or services may make an industry less attractive. For example, someone wishing to open a restaurant would do well to consider potential competition not only from other restaurants in the market area but also from establishments that offer consumers alternative ways to spend an evening out, such as theaters, athletic clubs, and cultural and sporting events.

Bargaining Power of Buyers. Buyers are likely to have an advantage when negotiating for prices and terms with their suppliers if the product they are purchasing is a highly standardized one. Then they can fairly easily switch to other sources. They also have the advantage if their purchases constitute a major portion of a supplier's business. For example, in the automobile industry, automotive manufacturers ask much from their parts suppliers. A GM, Ford, or Chrysler is often so important to parts suppliers that the suppliers are willing to do whatever is asked of them. The manufacturers typically ask for such things as just-in-time inventory systems (transferring some of the costs of carrying inventory to the supplier) and electronic data interchange systems in formats compatible with the manufacturers' internal systems. The seller is dependent on the buyer, and because moving from one supplier to another is inexpensive, the buyer has the advantage.

Bargaining Power of Suppliers. When there are relatively few suppliers and few substitute products, and when the threat of forward integration (the supplier entering the business of the customer) exists, the supplier has an advantage. When OPEC was at the height of its power and influence during the energy crisis of the mid-1970s, the advantage in the oil industry tilted heavily towards the suppliers and against buyers. Even though the power of OPEC subsequently waned, primarily because of increased supplies and a greater reliance on substitute products, a few OPEC members such as Kuwait and Saudi Arabia seized the opportunity to pursue a strategy of forward integration by entering the petroleum refining and retail distribution businesses.

Rivalry Among Existing Competitors. Intensely competitive industries have many competitors, relatively slow growth, high fixed costs, significant exit costs, a lack of buyer switching costs, and diverse competitors. For example, acute-care hospitals in large metropolitan areas are in an intensely competitive industry. In most cases, the nature of the health care industry changed when the government imposed greater cost controls and third-party insurers insisted on lower costs. The challenge to hospitals has become to find ways to get an increasing share of a decreasing market for inpatients.

Interaction of the Five Forces. The way in which the five forces interact determines the overall attractiveness of an industry. The strategic plan of an organization takes into account both the basic attractiveness of its industry and its individual performance. The attractiveness of companies that compete in several industries depends on the performance of its component strategic business units, or SBUs, in their respective industries. The overall performance of the corporation will be the sum of the performances of the SBUs it controls.

Three Generic Strategies

According to Porter, there are three generic strategies an organization can use to create a sustainable competitive advantage for itself: it can alter the structure of the industry; it can improve its position; or it can create a new product.

Altering the Industry Structure. Recall that an industry's basic attractiveness results from the interaction of the five forces in Porter's model. An organization can attempt to improve its position by altering the industry structure in its favor by creating entry barriers or by creating stronger linkages between an organization and its suppliers or customers. The creative use of information technology can make the structural alteration possible.

Improving a Position in Existing Lines of Business. A company that sets out to enhance its existing position without changing the industry structure can strive either to become the low-cost producer or to produce a differentiated product. Within both of these strategies a company can choose to focus on broad or narrow market segments. As illustrated in Figure 1–2, the choices are to become an overall cost leader, an overall provider of differentiated products or services, or a more narrowly focused cost leader or differentiator.

Creating New Products. The third strategy is to move to another product or a new market altogether. Information technology can be used to develop and

BOX 1-2

Systems That Have Changed an Industry Structure

Cash Management Accounts in the Securities Industry

Merrill-Lynch introduced its innovative Cash Management Account (CMA) a few years ago. The CMA automatically placed customers' cash balances resulting from securities sales into money market interest accounts and also gave the customers limited check-writing privileges. All activity during a given month was shown on an easy-to-read statement that also summarized the customers' holdings placed with the firm. The CMA met such success that it soon became a prerequisite for any firm who wished to compete for the individual investor's business. It was not too long before Merrill-Lynch's competitors had similar products of their own, but Merrill-Lynch gained market share during the intervening period. A product such as the Cash Management Account would have been impossible without information technology. It also raised an entry barrier to any other firm that wished to enter the industry. Any new entrant would have to create its own version of the information technology-based Cash Management Account.

Automatic Teller Machines

Automatic teller machines (ATMs) are an example of a substitute product created with the help of information technology. Many routine banking transactions can be handled directly by the ATMs with no need for human interaction. Moreover, the ATMs are available 24 hours per day. Their acceptance by consumers has been so dramatic that in 1988 there were over 40,000 ATMs installed in the United States. Two competing nationwide (soon to be worldwide) networks permit a customer of a bank located in Lincoln, Nebraska, to obtain cash from an ATM in Orlando, Florida. Banks that were slow to install ATMs ran the risk of losing their customers as a result. Banks that failed to anticipate the wide acceptance of ATMs and that built traditional branches may be burdened today with unwanted real estate. A secondary effect of the use of ATMs has been to make bank tellers' jobs more challenging as, increasingly, machines handle the more routine transactions.

American Hospital Supply's ASAP System

American Hospital Supply's ASAP system is one of the most oft-cited examples of a use of information technology for competitive advantage. The system evolved over many years, but its main purpose has always been to tie hospitals, the company's primary customers, more closely to American Hospital Supply by making ordering faster and more convenient. ASAP permits hospital purchasing agents to place orders using computer-to-computer communication. It also transmits confirmations back and suggests substitute products if a desired item is not in stock. Hospital purchasing agents can also inquire to determine the status of open orders and back orders and can have certain materials management functions performed for them as well. The system has changed the traditional buyer-supplier relationships by making satisfied customers more reluctant to order from competitors. The system tends to decrease the buyers' power and increase the power of the supplier.

Figure 1–2 **The Strategic Options**

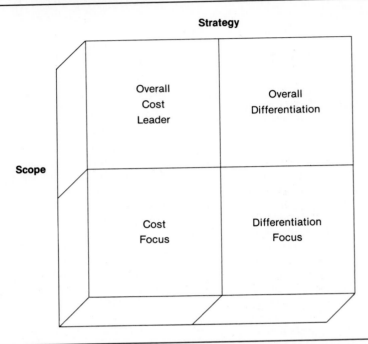

Source: Reprinted with permission of The Free Press, a Division of Macmillan, Inc. from *Competitive Advantage: Creating and Sustaining Superior Performance* by Michael E. Porter, p. 37. Copyright © 1985 by Michael E. Porter.

offer entirely new products. Quite often, this can be done simply by delivering and using information that is already available in the organization.

The Value Chain

Porter's framework includes an analytical tool called the value chain, an aid in highlighting the role of information technology in achieving a sustainable competitive advantage (see Figure 1–3). The value chain, a diagram of the functional activities performed by a strategic business unit, highlights the contribution of both direct and supportive activities to the delivery of a product or service to the buyers. A generic value chain, as shown in Figure 1–3, consists of the direct functions of inbound logistics, operations, outbound logistics, sales and marketing, and service. Support functions consist of procurement, technology development, human resource management, and firm infrastructure. Added value represents the difference between the product cost determined as the sum of the value chain functions and the price the buyer is willing to pay. Detailed coverage of the way systems analysts use the value chain concept and related analytical tools is presented in Appendix 1.

BOX 1–3

Companies That Have Improved Existing Products or Services

To reduce costs, *Deere & Company* created a computerized parts data base system for the 300,000 parts it uses in production. Having information on existing parts available in an easily accessible form enables the company to determine quickly if needed parts are available, thus avoiding unnecessary duplication in design and production. In two recent years, the company estimated that the system saved it over $9 million.

Aetna Life & Casualty developed a system called AECLAIMS, which automatically maintains insurance contracts and processes claims and insurance premiums. The system has significantly reduced the time and clerical effort required to process claims.

An example of the use of information technology in marketing and sales is the computerized bridal gift registry developed by the *Dayton-Hudson Department Stores*. Previously, a prospective bride would register in a single store, making it difficult to keep track of gifts purchased at other stores. The new system main-

tains a chainwide data base that records all purchases in a computer record. Store sales of wedding gifts increased 20 percent annually in the first two years after the system was installed. Dayton-Hudson is presently applying the same concept to baby gifts, calling it "The Stork Club." The company plans to use information about what newlyweds and new parents have been given through the registry to improve their marketing to these prospective customers.

In the highly competitive credit card industry, *American Express* used information technology to create a differentiated product, the Year-End Summary of Charges, first offered to GoldCard members. The computer-prepared report showed each charge the cardholder made during the year in many categories such as airline tickets, lodging, restaurants, car rentals, and merchandise. The report provided the detail of each charge and also summarized the charges in each category by month for the entire year. Many cardholders found the documentation useful for tax purposes.

In analyzing the value chain for a strategic business unit, it is important to remember that the value chain is, indeed, a chain, with linkages between its various functions. For example, increasing the quality (and cost) of raw materials may reduce manufacturing (i.e., operations) costs and reduce the overall cost of the SBU's product. If the market price remains return, to the SBU will increase. Similarly, costly technological development may create a differentiated product for which the market may be willing to pay a premium. The systems analyst's challenge is to search for ways to use information technology to decrease costs or increase product differentiation, thereby increasing the added value segment of the value chain.

The five forces model, the three generic strategies, and the value chain are analytical tools that can help an organization create and sustain a competitive advantage for itself. Firms that fail to do this will have to settle for average returns at best. Superior performers will generate the profit margins necessary

Figure 1–3 **The Value Chain**

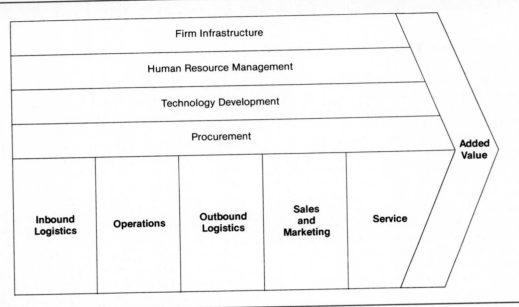

Source: Reprinted with permission of The Free Press, a Division of Macmillan, Inc. from *Competitive Advantage: Creating and Sustaining Superior Performance* by Michael E. Porter, p. 12. Copyright © 1985 by Michael E. Porter.

to sustain themselves. Some will also generate the additional capital required to flourish in their existing industry or to expand into other, more attractive ones.

THE STRATEGIC GRID

In most businesses, information technology does not contribute nearly as much to create a competitive advantage as it could. The examples cited in this chapter are clearly occurring in companies that are on the leading edge. Others have not nearly tapped the potential of the information technology resource. This potential will vary from company to company, depending on individual industry or company circumstances. A useful framework for the analysis of a company's potential is the strategic grid developed by Cash, McFarlan, and McKenney, which describes four different environments (see Figure 1–4).

An organization belongs in one of the four quadrants as a function of the strategic significance of its existing applications and applications development plan, or portfolio.

strategic quadrant A company is in the **strategic quadrant** if both its existing and planned applications are of strategic importance. An example might be a bank that depends on the smooth functioning of existing applications for doing business and that is currently working on a new loan approval system that will use expert

BOX 1–4

Companies That Have Created New Products or Services

Dow Jones News/Retrieval offers subscribers access to many data bases through a dial-up connection from a personal computer located at a business office, a home, or even the subscriber's resort condominium. In addition to company and industry news from such sources as back issues of *The Wall Street Journal* and *Barron's*, the service offers current stock quotes and general services such as news, sports, and weather and on-line shopping, travel, and mail.

Often, a new product is spawned through the creative use of information a company already has available. TRW, the largest credit rating service in the United States, maintains credit histories on millions of people. The credit histories are maintained on a large computer system that is updated by businesses to reflect experiences they have had with consumers and accessed by businesses to obtain a credit report on individuals to whom they are considering granting credit.

TRW developed a differentiated product called TRW CREDENTIALS, which it is marketing to consumers. For a fee of $35 per year, individuals who sign up for the service can review their own credit report, receive notification when a third party receives a copy of their credit report, add supplemental information to their credit history, apply for credit or financing through an electronic network, and finally, register their credit cards in case of loss or theft.

One of TRW's choices was whether to focus on a market segment or on a broad market. It could have made other choices: bundling more services with the product, charging a higher price, or directing its marketing toward high-income individuals. (TRW should certainly know who they are!) TRW apparently decided that its best returns would come from a product-pricing strategy aimed at the broader market.

---

systems technology to give it an edge over the competition by approving more loans more quickly at reduced risks.

A company is in the **factory quadrant** if its existing applications are of strategic significance but it does not have any applications of strategic importance in its development plans. An example might be an airline that depends on its on-line reservation system to do business but has only nonstrategic systems currently under development.

factory quadrant

A company in the **support quadrant** has no systems of strategic importance in its applications development portfolio and its existing systems are noncritical data processing applications. The company would not be severely damaged even if the application suffered deterioration or breakdown of service. An example might be a high-fashion retailer that has mechanized customer billing and accounts receivable but has no significant systems development projects under way. The difference between good and bad years depends on the expertise of the store's buyers in anticipating which merchandise will appeal to customers, not on the quality of the information technology used.

support quadrant

Figure 1–4 **The Strategic Grid**

Categories of Strategic Relevance and Impact

Strategic Impact
of Existing Systems

	Low	High
High	Factory	Strategic
Low	Support	Turnaround

Low   High

Strategic Impact of Applications Development Portfolio

Source: Cash, James I., McFarlan, F. Warren, and McKenney, James L. *Corporate Information Systems Management—The Issues Facing Senior Executives*, 2nd ed. Homewood, Illinois: Irwin, 1988.

turnaround quadrant

A company in the **turnaround quadrant** has existing applications similar to a company in the support quadrant and development plans similar to a company in the strategic quadrant. An example might be a retailer developing a computer system to track sales of high-fashion items on a daily basis. With this system, managers can determine optimal times either to order more merchandise (if an item is moving faster than expected) or to mark down the prices (on items that are moving too slowly). Waiting too long to reorder may cause lost sales from unavailable merchandise. Waiting too long to reduce prices may result in large inventories of unsold items that must be sold at even lower prices or possibly held until the next season.

Information technology should be managed differently in companies in each of the four quadrants. Companies in the strategic quadrant should manage computer operations as efficiently as companies in the factory quadrant, should have the applications development resources to create innovative systems using leading-edge technologies, and should have the support and attention of top management. Similar comments apply to the operations of firms in the factory quadrant and to the applications development function for firms in the turnaround quadrant. For firms in the support quadrant, corporate priorities are likely to lie in areas other than information technology.

Although information technology will vary from company to company in its actual or potential strategic significance, its potential should not be dismissed too easily lest a company be taken by surprise by a competitor who suddenly introduces a system giving a competitive advantage, as is typically the case.

FIRST-MOVER DISADVANTAGES

Michael Vitale, in an article entitled "The Growing Risks of Information Systems Success,"[2] introduced a note of caution when he suggested that companies would be well advised to consider certain undesirable repercussions if they are the first to introduce a system designed to give them a sustainable competitive advantage. Certain events could keep a competitive advantage, if achieved at all, from being sustainable. Vitale identified the following events as the kind that could cause undesirable results:

- Systems that change the basis of competition to a company's disadvantage.

   A company could introduce an information technology-based product to permit its customers to enter orders on-line. It might find that the competition reacts by lowering prices and that the lower prices are more appealing to the market than the added value of the system.

- Systems that lower entry barriers.

   A health and casualty insurance company that markets its policies primarily to smaller businesses discovered that the bookkeepers of potential customers were reluctant to process another payroll deduction. The company considered offering a computerized payroll service as a way of getting over this obstacle but decided that this new service would open up the sale of insurance policies by the much more entrenched companies that already offer computerized payroll preparation services.

- Systems that bring on litigation or regulation.

   The airline reservation systems developed by American and United were so effective that they eventually brought on charges of unfair competition. Eleven competing airlines that purchased services from the two airlines claimed that the prices they had to pay and the treatment they received put them at a competitive disadvantage. The competitors sued and asked that the reservation systems be spun off into separate subsidiaries. As of this writing, the suit has not been settled.

- Systems that increase the power of buyers or suppliers.

   An order entry system that permits buyers to examine a company's inventory files prior to placing an order may place too much power in the hands of the buyer. The knowledge of item availability may give the buyer a bargaining advantage: a buyer who sees that an item is in short supply may choose to negotiate for a price break in exchange for a longer delivery time.

As in any planning process, possible outcomes must be analyzed before initiating a change to be sure that the change does not bring about undesirable side effects.

APPLICABILITY TO THE NOT-FOR-PROFIT SECTOR

Up to this point, the discussion of the use of information technology for competitive advantage has applied to a profit-seeking environment. The approaches can apply in the not-for-profit and public sectors as well. In the story of the two competing hospitals in Kalamazoo, the hospitals were not competing to make a profit but rather to reduce the deleterious effect of high fixed costs when volumes were dwindling. In the not-for-profit sector, the measures of success tend to be whether the application of information technology leads to greater efficiency or effectiveness in an organization rather than whether an organization achieves a sustainable competitive advantage. The following examples illustrate the successful use of information technology in this sector:

- Law enforcement officials in many countries have access to data bases containing records of drivers and vehicles. If a driver is stopped for a traffic violation, a police officer can determine if there are outstanding arrest warrants for the driver or if the car is stolen or has recently been used in a crime. By using the driver's license number and the vehicle's license plate number, a police officer can use a terminal in the police vehicle that is connected by short wave radio to the computer where the records are stored.

- Several universities have devised systems that permit students to register for classes by using a touch-tone telephone, thereby avoiding the long lines, stress, and inconvenience associated with traditional registration processes.

Thus, the innovative use of information technology is not confined to profit-oriented businesses. Although not-for-profit organizations are not subject to the same competitive forces as business firms, they have to compete for scarce resources such as qualified personnel and financial grants. Therefore, the use of information technology for competitive advantage is just as relevant as in the business sector.

Summary

Increased competition and the pace of technological change have combined to give organizations unprecedented opportunities to achieve a competitive advantage through the creative application of information technology. Although information technology has long been used to support the strategic planning process, Michael Porter's recently developed analytical framework composed of the five forces, the three generic strategies, and the value chain have proved particularly useful in helping organizations identify applications that can have a significant strategic impact.

The strategic grid designed by Cash, McFarlan, and McKenney can also help organizations analyze their needs. The four quadrants of the grid indicate the different levels of significance that information technology may have for different kinds of organizations.

In addition, the work of Michael Vitale points out certain disadvantages that may be associated with being the first organization to introduce an application intended to have strategic impact.

Finally, examples of creative uses of information technology in the public and not-for-profit sectors point out that the concepts in this chapter can be applied in those areas as well as in the profit-making sector.

Selected Readings

Porter, Michael E. *Competitive Strategy*. New York: Free Press, 1981.

Porter, Michael E. *Competitive Advantage: Creating and Sustaining Superior Performance*. New York: Free Press, 1985.
Michael Porter's books have had enormous influence on management thinking in the 1980s. They are indispensable reading for systems analysts who want to understand how the information systems department can support executive management's objectives.

Cash, James I., McFarlan, F. Warren, and McKenney, James L. *Corporate Information Systems Management—The Issues Facing Senior Executives*. 2d ed. Homewood, Illinois: Irwin, 1988.
This book extends the theories created by Michael Porter and others. It is representative of the lines of thought that have led to the emergence of the chief information officer as a member of the executive leadership of organizations.

Wiseman, Charles. *Strategic Information Systems*. Homewood, Illinois: Irwin: 1988.
A thorough review of the subject including implementation techniques. In addition, this text is rich with examples culled from the author's extensive collection of successful and unsuccessful examples of strategic information systems.

Review Questions

Traditionally, the management of many organizations has thought that information technology was useful for transaction processing systems such as payroll or billing, but not much else. This attitude is now changing.

1. Explain the emerging management attitude towards information technology.

2. Describe how the rapidly changing business environment has stimulated the change in attitude.

3. What are the responsibilities of the information resource management function?

4. Explain why aiming to achieve a sustainable competitive advantage has become a major preoccupation in most organizations.

5. What role does information technology play in the management of an organization's information resource?

6. What are the five competitive forces that collectively define an industry's overall attractiveness? Describe the forces that make an industry more or less attractive.

7. Summarize the three strategies that managers can use to find ways for information systems to give their organization a sustainable competitive advantage.

8. Why should management consider the first-mover disadvantages described by Michael Vitale before introducing an information system that may give their organization a competitive advantage?

9. Differentiate between the measures of success used for information technology applications in the for-profit and not-for-profit sectors.

Discussion Questions

1. Electronic data interchange (EDI) is a technology whereby purchase orders, invoices, and other order-related documents are exchanged electronically between purchaser and supplier. How might a supplier use EDI to improve its business position?

2. Not all organizations are ready to use information technology to achieve a competitive advantage. Select an industry of interest to you. Explain how Cash, McFarlan, and McKenney's strategic grid may aid a company within that industry to examine its readiness to use information technology for competitive advantage.

Mini-Case

The following excerpt is from an article in *The Wall Street Journal*.

Electronic Price Labels Tested in Supermarkets

Prices of more than 500 items will change today at Bauersfeld's supermarket in Topeka, Kansas, but the clerks won't have to peel outdated labels off the shelves.

Instead, they will change the prices electronically, plugging a hand-held computer into programmable labels clipped to the store's shelves. The computer sends a signal to a microchip in the molded plastic label, which then displays the new price in half-inch-high liquid crystal numbers.

Such devices are part of the grocery industry's continuing effort to reduce overhead with technology. Already more than half of the nation's supermarkets have electronic scanners at check-outs to ring up prices of bar-coded packages. Programmable shelf labeling promises to trim labor costs further and allow quicker price changes than are now possible.

Last week, a big scanner company acquired North American distribution rights for one of two electronic labels on the market. Datachecker Systems, Inc., a unit of National Semiconductor Corp., signed a five-year agreement to sell labels made by Telepanel, Inc., a Canadian concern.

Its rival is Graphic Technology, Inc., of Olathe, Kansas, which makes the labels being tested in Bauersfeld's store. While Graphic Technology's labels must be touched by hand-held computer, Telepanel's labels needn't be. They contain FM transceivers and can be programmed in virtually no time by a store computer sending out a different radio signal to each of the potentially thousands of shelf labels.

Source: "Electronic Price Labels Tested in Supermarkets," by Richard Gibson *The Wall Street Journal* (March 31, 1988), p. 25. Reprinted by permission of *The Wall Street Journal*, © Dow Jones & Company, Inc. 1988. All Rights Reserved.

Questions for Discussion

1. In what ways could the technology be used to give supermarket operators a competitive advantage?

2. What are some potential first-mover disadvantages?

3. In what other industries could the technology be applied?

References

1. Blumenthal, Michael. "Change and Technology." *Foreign Affairs Special issue:* America and the World 1987/1988 (March 1988): 529–550.

2. Vitale, Michael R. "The Growing Risks of Information Systems Success." *MIS Quarterly* (December 1986): 327–334.

Chapter 2

Technology Insertion and the Management of Change

Chapter 1 covered the use of information technology to give businesses a competitive edge in a rapidly changing environment. This chapter covers the changes in an organization made necessary by the very introduction of information technology-based solutions to those problems. The first part describes the nature and depth of these changes. The second part describes the challenges in implementing changes caused by new technology, users' resistance to such change, and some approaches to overcome this resistance.

Learning Objectives

- Realize that systems and systems developers are agents of change.
- Understand the Lewin three-stage model of social change.
- Describe four common reasons that people resist computer-based innovation.
- Acquire an understanding of the roles of management, users, and information systems professionals in implementing change in organizations.

NATURE OF CHANGES INTRODUCED BY INFORMATION TECHNOLOGY

The changes brought about by information technology in recent years have been both pervasive and deep. Their effects have been compared to those of both the invention of printing and the industrial revolution. In fact, the terms *information revolution* and *information economy* have been widely used. Whether or not these terms are justified can best be judged by future generations, but there is no doubt that information technology lies at the very heart of more and more businesses.

BOX 2–1

The Need for Change

Top management in any organization is only too familiar with the challenge of introducing change. The pressure of competition together with advances in technology has made doing "business as usual" a thing of the past. As one top executive in a fast-changing industry said, "Nothing's easy anymore."

Examples can be found in many industries, but here are two:

Automobile manufacturers in the United States used to take five years to bring out a new model car, from the time a development project was approved until the time new models were on the dealers' floors. International competition, particularly from the Japanese, has forced U.S. manufacturers to shorten the product development cycle from five to three years in order to stay competitive. Information technology has helped by using computers to support human efforts in every step of the cycle, from computer-aided design through automated inventory control, factory robotics, and marketing. Even after-sale service is improved with information technology: microchip processors in the automobile yield diagnostic readouts to assist the service mechanics.

Airlines have been among the most creative users of information technology to force change in their industry. Those entering the airline business today must offer not only a computerized reservation system, but also:

- A frequent-flier awards program.

- An advanced seat selection service.

- An advanced special menu selection service.

- A locator system for lost baggage.

All of these computer-based systems are used in U.S. airlines today; none were in existence a few years ago. An airline operating without such systems would be at a clear disadvantage compared to its competitors.

Changing the direction of a large corporation has been likened to turning an aircraft carrier around: it is not as easy as turning a smaller vessel. Likewise, smaller corporations have had the advantage of being able to adapt more quickly to changes in their industries while larger organizations have struggled to catch up. We have come to expect more innovation from smaller, more nimble companies.

Competition has changed this, however, and large companies have discovered that they must adapt to change more quickly because their competitors have managed to do so. Some of the techniques used have been based on "intrapreneurship," a technique designed to foster within a corporate giant the entrepreneurial spirit so typical of smaller companies. The IBM PC was developed by a team of IBM "intrapreneurs," who were left to organize their own work autonomously in an organization known for its high degree of central control. The normal product planning and investment cycles were bypassed and management reporting was reduced to a minimum. As a result, the IBM PC was created in approximately 11 months and was introduced on the market in a very timely fashion. This timing contributed for a large part to its success.

The normal resistance so often experienced when managers attempt to implement change can no longer be condoned in the competitive environment of today. Information technology holds great promise as a powerful change agent if properly and creatively applied. To be effective, IS professionals must realize that the bottom line is to get human beings to change. If that does not happen, the systems they attempt to implement will not meet their objectives of improving the way the business is conducted.

Let us first consider the process of change caused by any technology, and then apply that process to information technology.

The use of technology progresses through three stages. In the first stage, technology is used to do the same thing as before, only better. The earliest automobiles, for example, were little more than "horseless carriages." In the second stage, the technology is used for major improvements. For example, during the Henry Ford era of the automobile, private transportation was much improved. In the third stage, the technology is used to effect radical change. Today, the automobile, together with a network of highways and streets, has changed the very pattern of urbanization, with workers often living in residential suburbs far away from the workplace. The automobile has also changed the social fabric of rural communities by eliminating isolation. Moreover, the availability of a network of highways has created a highly competitive alternative to rail transport for goods and passengers.

Another way to think of the three stages of technology is that if the technology were suddenly to disappear, we would be affected differently in each stage. In the first stage, the disappearance would hardly be noticed. In the second stage, it would create inconvenience and increase cost. In the third, society—or large sectors of it—would come to a grinding halt.

Technologies that have achieved the third stage within the last century include the automobile, modern medicine, electric power, the telephone, radio and television, aviation, and the new kid on the block—information technology.

The first use of what is now called information technology was to do computations by electronic computers that were once done by hand. In fact, any dictionary published before World War II will contain a definition of a computer as a person who makes mathematical computations for actuarial, statistical, or military purposes. (In 1964, one dictionary still put man before machine: "Computer: a person who computes or a device used for computing."[1]) An electronic computer was a machine to do the human computer's job electronically, just as the earliest automobile motors pulled the carriage that a horse used to pull. This stage lasted for a short while only.

In the second stage of information technology, computers were used to cut costs. Not only did they displace clerical workers filling out forms, preparing invoices, and preparing financial statements, but they also made better use of other resources. For instance, the cost of carrying inventory could be reduced by using a computerized system to supervise inventory levels and adjust them according to demand. Most of the applications developed in this context are what might be termed *record keeping*. The computer is used to track and report on some activity or object that continues to exist independently of the computer system. The application is largely backed up by paper. A typical sign of this stage is that manual backup systems were designed to take over should the computer fail for an extended period of time.

The third stage, reached by many firms today, is the integration of the technology into the heart of the business. The computer is used to help conduct the actual business rather than just to record facts about how the business is conducted. Travel reservations, frequent-flier programs, insurance claims processing, direct deposit of payroll checks, automatic teller machines, supermarket checkout equipment, numerical control of machine tools, computer-aided design are all business activities, not merely clerical tasks. Even when the product of the business is a physical object, or the transportation of a physical object, information technology is at the heart of the production process. Information technology is all the more essential to businesses or organizations (such as banks, insurance companies, and many government services) that deal almost exclusively in information.

SYSTEMS DEVELOPMENT AS AN AGENT OF CHANGE

We have seen in Chapter 1 that creatively designed information systems have often given organizations a competitive advantage. Information systems alone, however, do not yield an advantage to an organization. Instead, information systems leverage the human resources of an organization to make them more effective in carrying out their responsibilities. In some cases we find that a department (inventory control, for example) can manage a large amount of information more effectively with a computerized system. In other cases we find that the quality and timeliness of executive decisions are improved if they are supported by a computer-based executive information system. Expert systems used to support, rather than replace, human knowledge are good examples of how human talent can be leveraged with the support of well-designed and accepted information systems.

Information systems are installed in an organizational setting, composed of people with their own sets of values and goals and with their own understanding of the organization with its set of values and goals. It is not enough to develop an information system that supports an organization's objectives. The people who will use the information system must also understand the organization's objectives and the way the new system will help them play their parts in achieving these objectives. Information systems are tools. Just as with other tools, people must want to use them and often must be trained to use them in the most effective manner. IS professionals must be aware that the most brilliantly conceived system is of little value to the organization if it is not accepted and used by the people for whom it was designed.

THE NATURE OF CHANGE

People are generally reluctant to leave the comfort of the status quo for the unknowns associated with a new way of doing things. This resistance to change, while quite normal, must be managed in the interest of permitting the organization to compete. To know how to manage change, an IS professional must understand the nature of the change process itself.

The most widely accepted model of social change is that of Kurt Lewin, who postulated a model with three stages: unfreezing, changing, and refreezing, as

A View of Tomorrow

Figure 1

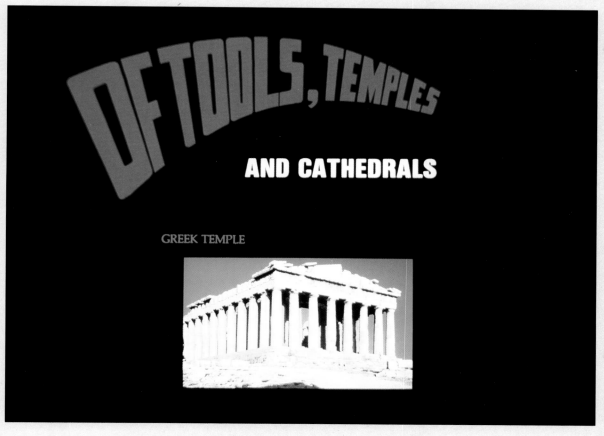

It has been observed that the marble columns of Greek temples are really surrogates for tree trunks. Before the Greek civilization was advanced enough to carve stone, temples were built with raised tree trunks, logs for rafters, and a roof covering of branches, twigs, and leaves.

Figure 2

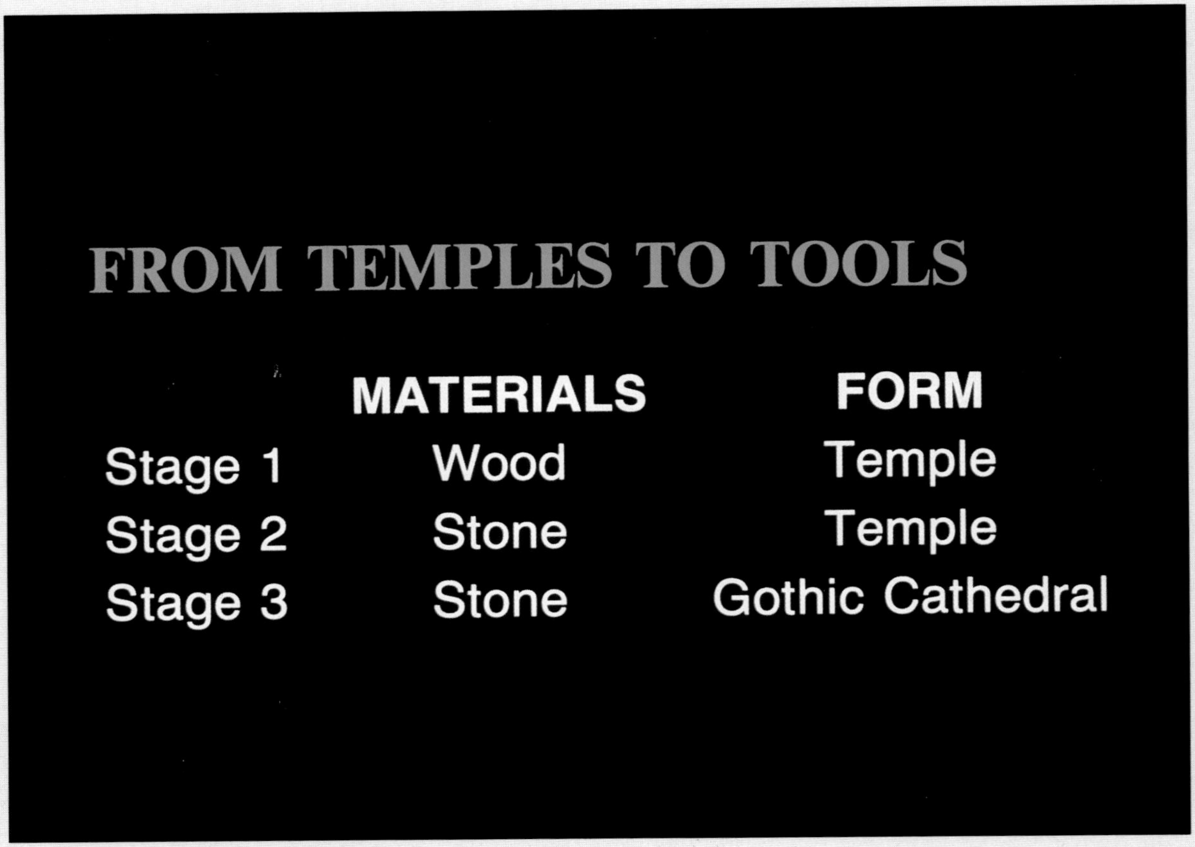

FROM TEMPLES TO TOOLS

	MATERIALS	FORM
Stage 1	Wood	Temple
Stage 2	Stone	Temple
Stage 3	Stone	Gothic Cathedral

The explanation for continuing to build stone temples in the same form as wooden temples is that change takes time, and it is nearly impossible to change both the materials for building and the forms of what is built simultaneously.

Figure 3

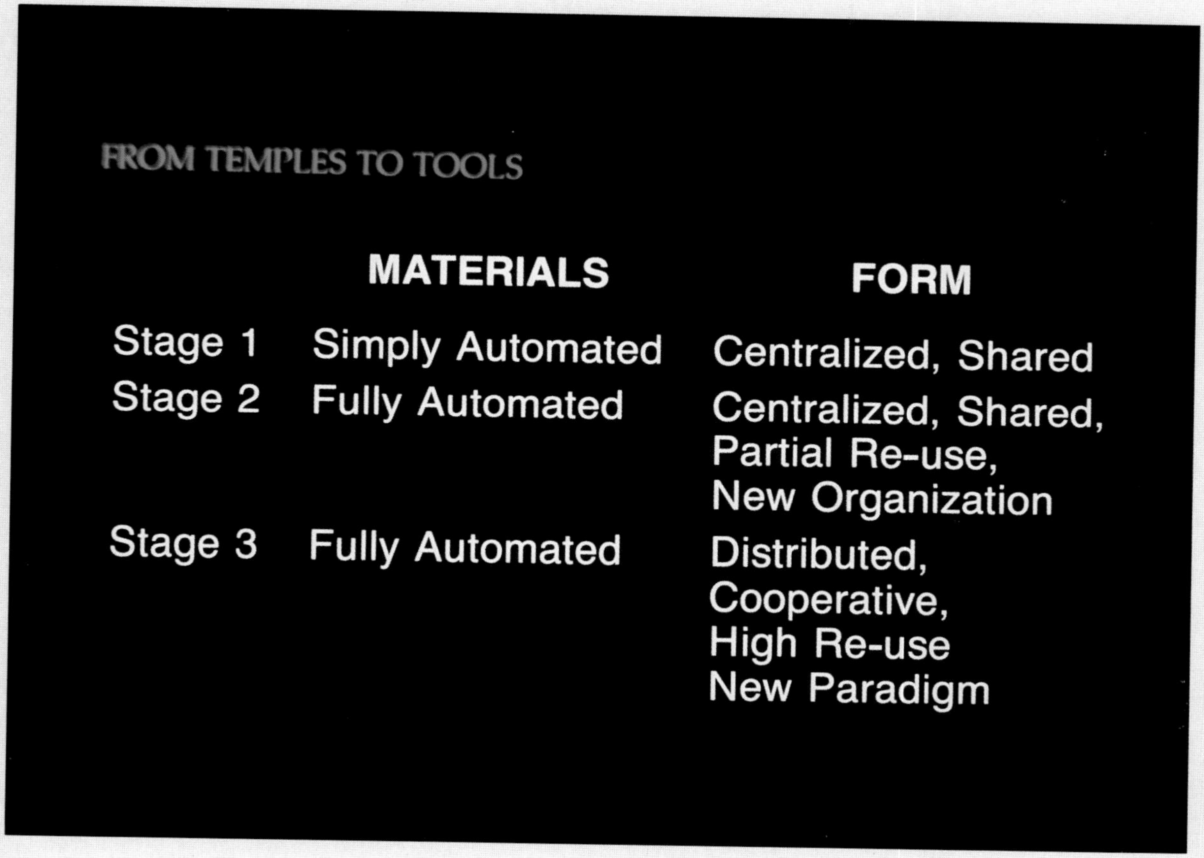

FROM TEMPLES TO TOOLS

	MATERIALS	FORM
Stage 1	Simply Automated	Centralized, Shared
Stage 2	Fully Automated	Centralized, Shared, Partial Re-use, New Organization
Stage 3	Fully Automated	Distributed, Cooperative, High Re-use New Paradigm

This phenomenon of gradual change is paralleled in the evolution of systems development. The evolution takes place in three stages separated by two major shifts: tools first, then application styles.

Figure 4

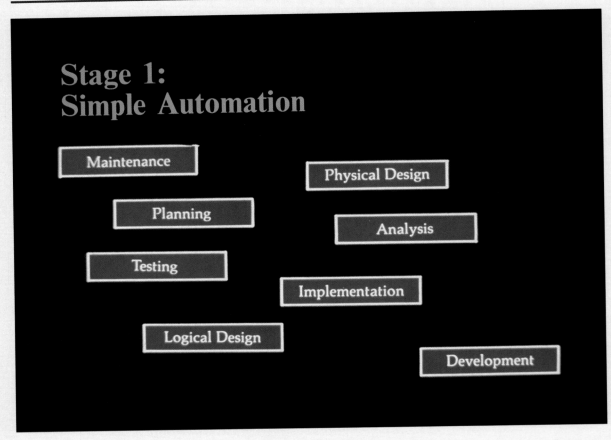

The tools that were initially used for systems development were isolated from each other and had limited scope. Examples were compilers, program editors, and, more recently, graphical editors. The scope of automation was an individual's job.

Figure 5

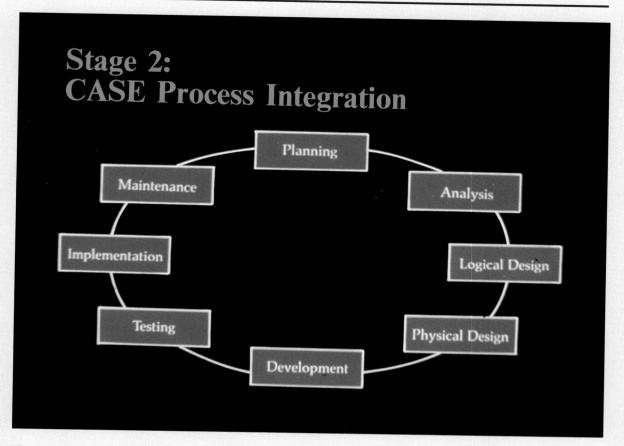

The second stage of change, that of tools integration, is currently well under way. Many of today's CASE tools use as input the output from some other tool. The scope of automation is becoming that of an entire team.

Figure 6

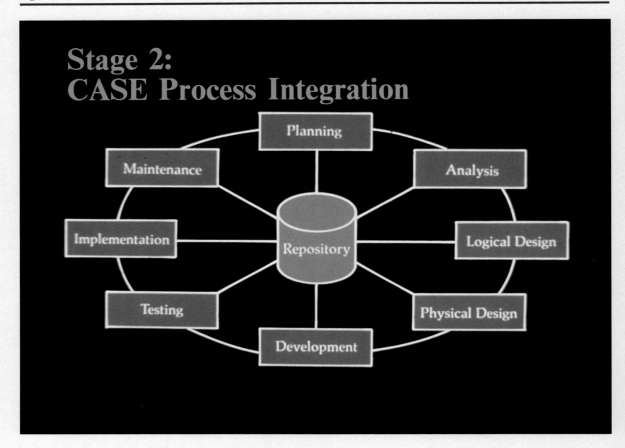

Still lacking from most CASE tools is a central repository of design objects, such as data structures and processing flows, where different tools can refer to the same underlying entities. When these tools become available, Stage 2 will be complete.

Figure 2–1 **Lewin's Three Stages of Organizational Change**

Stage	Description
Unfreezing	Increasing the receptivity of the organization to a possible change.
Moving	Choosing a course of action and following it.
Refreezing	Reinforcing the "equilibrium" of the organization at a new level after the change has occurred.

Source: G. Davis and M. Olson. *Management Information Systems*. New York: McGraw-Hill, 1985.

illustrated in Figure 2–1.[2] Groups of people (for example, members of a department in a business organization) are accustomed to performing their daily assignments in a certain way. They have been trained to do so and have become comfortable with their abilities to carry out their assigned duties. To introduce a new way of carrying out their tasks, it is first necessary to prepare them to accept a change. This is the "unfreezing" step. Attempting to impose a change on people unprepared for the change in advance is almost always a mistake. Once the group members have been prepared, the change can be introduced, but it should be followed by a "refreezing" step in which their understanding of the new methods is solidified.

RESISTANCE TO CHANGE

Systems professionals are often considered change agents because they cause changes to the organization. As change agents, they must expect to encounter resistance and be prepared to deal with it. Niccolò Machiavelli, an astute observer of human behavior, said it well some 400 years ago:

> It must be considered that there is nothing more difficult to carry out, nor more doubtful of success, nor more dangerous to handle, than to initiate a new order of things. For the reformer has enemies in all those who profit by the old order, and only lukewarm defenders in all those who could profit by the new order. This lukewarmness arises partly from fear of their adversaries, who have the laws in their favor, and partly from the incredulity of mankind, who do not truly believe in anything new until they have had an actual experience of it.[3]

Diagnosing and Dealing with Resistance to Change

The first step in overcoming resistance to change is to understand the reasons for it. Peter G. W. Keen identified four specific reasons in an article in *Computerworld*:

- Resistance to computer personnel.
- A feeling that the project is not good, that the cost/benefit assumptions are invalid.

- A lack of felt need: things are satisfactory as they are and this innovation simply disturbs the situation.
- A fear of social uncertainty, which is sometimes mistaken for a fear of computers.[4]

We will add a fifth reason, not so apparent at the time Keen wrote his article, but which is now significant:

- An unwillingness to bend to the requirements of poorly designed systems.

Depending on the situation, some or all of these reasons for resistance to change may apply, and the reason for resistance usually affects the choice of remedy to deal with it.

resistance to computer personnel

Resistance to computer personnel can be diagnosed by observing the interactions between users and IS personnel. A good working relationship between the two groups is characterized by feelings of mutual trust and understanding. A poor working relationship is often marked by recriminations for past failures and statements implying that one side does not understand the other's problems. The following techniques have proven useful in overcoming resistance to computer personnel:

- A good working relationship between the higher levels of management to whom the IS department and the affected user department report. Higher levels of management can be role models for cooperative action among subordinates.
- Joint project teams of information systems and user personnel to undertake systems projects. As will be discussed, bringing users and information systems professionals together to work towards a common goal can be very helpful in overcoming gaps in understanding.
- Support and understanding of the user's perspective by IS personnel. It is the IS professional's responsibility to adopt the user's viewpoint, not vice versa.
- Training for the users in computer concepts and the role that information technology can play in modern organizations. This training removes much of the mystique of the technology and helps close the gap between user and technician. Often, hands-on experience can also convert a user from skepticism to acceptance.

feel that the project is not good

Users often resist a systems proposal because they **feel that the project is not good** or that the cost/benefit analysis is inaccurate. In such cases, they have usually been insufficiently involved in determining the feasibility, the scope, or the requirements of the system. Users must be significantly involved in developing the systems proposal as a part of a project team, and they must accept the assumptions and the conclusions of the cost/benefit analysis. As we will discuss in Chapter 17, one of the steps in the systems development process is to

Figure 7

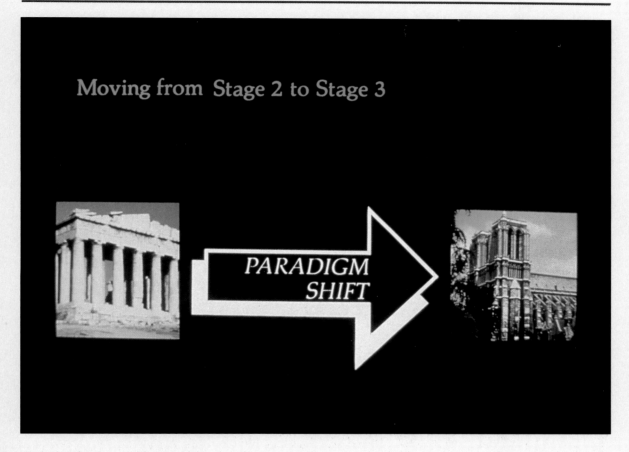

Once the change in tools is completed, a change in application styles (Stage 3), will become possible. Just as the ancient Greeks of the fifth century B.C. could not imagine a structure such as Notre Dame cathedral, which was built in Paris around 1250 A.D., we cannot imagine the full impact of today's tools on tomorrow's systems.

Figure 8

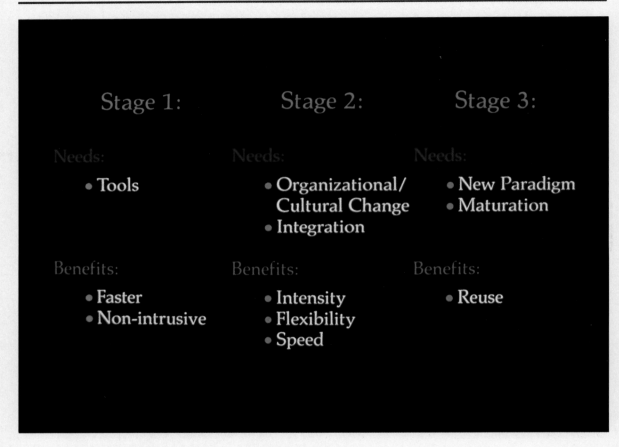

We know, however, that there will emerge a new paradigm for systems development. We will be able to build highly distributed or cooperative systems. We believe that these systems will become possible through new modes of reuse of requirements specifications, designs, and codes.

Figure 2–2 **Resistance to Computer Personnel**

put together a project proposal for management approval before proceeding with a project. A cost/benefit analysis is usually a part of the proposal. It is much more convincing to have a representative of the user department describe the system concept and the benefits to be derived from its installation. This technique lets management know that the users understand what the system will do for them and will attest to a set of expected benefits offsetting the cost of installing the system.

We often hear the phrase "If it ain't broke, don't fix it." This is essentially what users are saying when they resist a proposed change because of the

lack of a felt need

lack of a felt need. They see no reason to change because they are comfortable with the status quo. Viewing a situation this way has been called the "problem of no problem." Rather than saying "if it ain't broke, don't fix it," users should be saying "fix it before it breaks." This insight is particularly important in today's environment when organizations can expect their competition to be constantly seeking to improve current ways of doing things. In addition to using the techniques mentioned in the previous paragraph, we can best deal with resistance due to lack of a felt need by demonstrating that a proposed systems change will aid the users in meeting goals and objectives in accordance with the organization's strategic plan.

fear of social uncertainty

Resistance to change often arises because users **fear social uncertainty** about how the change will affect existing relationships between members of a given department, the roles assigned to members of the affected department, and the power and influence they currently possess. For example, Peter F. Drucker says that a company's organization structure is affected when it begins to concentrate its information technology resources on producing information rather than merely crunching numbers:

> Almost immediately, it becomes clear that both the number of management levels and the number of managers can be sharply cut. The reason is straightforward: it turns out that whole layers of management neither make decisions nor lead. Instead, their main, if not their only, function is to serve as "relays"—human boosters for the faint, unfocused signals that pass for communication in the traditional pre-information organization.[5]

Middle managers are all too conscious of the corporate penchant for becoming "lean and mean" by eliminating white-collar workers. A week rarely goes by without at least one story of a large corporation streamlining operations out of competitive necessity by eliminating staff positions. User resistance is understandable in this type of environment.

It is critical to address this problem because changes can scarcely be implemented without the support of middle management, even if the changes do not affect them directly.

When a user is unsure of the way a proposed change will affect him or her personally, the change is often resisted. However, the concern may be expressed as a fear of computers rather than as the underlying, more personal, concern. The systems professional acting as the change agent must be able to listen to objections and isolate the real reasons for resistance.

systems with poor human factors

Finally, another reason for resistance to change is that users have seen too many **systems with poor human factors**. Before the so-called microcomputer revolution, systems were generally designed to optimize use of technology rather than human resources. Job descriptions and clerical procedures were designed to fit the system requirements rather than the system being designed to fit the human requirements. With the advent of reasonably priced personal computers and widely available, well-designed software, users have come to expect more. The nature of the applications themselves have changed, partly

Figure 2–3 **A Comparison of the Kolb/Frohman and Lewin/Schein Models of Organizational Change**

Kolb/Frohman Stage	Activities	Underlying Lewin/Schein Stage
Scouting	Client and Consultant assess each other's needs and abilities; entry point is chosen	Unfreezing
Entry	Initial statement of problem, goals, and objectives; develop mutual commitment and trust; establish "felt need" for change	Unfreezing
Diagnosis	Data gathering to define Client's felt problem and goals; assessment of available resources (Client's and Consultant's)	Unfreezing
Planning	Defining specific operational objectives; examination of alternative routes to those objectives and their impact on the organization; developing action plan	Moving
Action	Putting "best" alternative solution into practice; modifying action plan if unanticipated consequences occur	Moving
Evaluation	Assessing how well objectives were met; deciding to evolve or terminate	Moving and Refreezing
Termination	Confirming new behavior patterns; completing transfer of system "ownership" and responsibility to the Client	Refreezing

Source: M. Ginzberg. "A Study of the Implementation Process." *TIMS Studies in the Management Sciences* 13, 1979, quoted in Davis and Olson.

because of the availability of workstation technology and partly because of competitive pressures. Computer-based applications are now much more integrated into the operation of the business, rather than being simple back-office transaction recording systems.

Users who do not believe that IS personnel have absorbed the lessons of this revolution may very well resist change out of skepticism over the quality of the resulting design.

In summary, IS professionals can expect to encounter resistance to change. They can overcome the resistance only by understanding its nature and developing a plan for dealing with it.

PREPARING USERS FOR CHANGE

Once the users seem likely to accept the changes anticipated with a new system, the IS professionals must develop a plan to prepare users for the specific changes that will occur.

Figure 2–3 illustrates how a plan for effecting change can be put together. The figure compares the Lewin three-stage model (as later elaborated by Schein) with a seven-stage model proposed by Kolb and Frohman. In the Kolb/Frohman model, the process for effecting change is accomplished through a series of seven steps. In their terminology, the "client" is the user and the "consultant" is the systems professional acting as the change agent. The figure

Figure 2–4 **Responsibilities for Preparing Users for Change**

Primarily Management's Responsibility:
- Decide that change is necessary in support of strategy
- Communicate need to the organization
- Determine when timing is right to introduce change
- Approve plan for effecting change
- Monitor progress of implementation
- Assist in resolving problems that may arise

Primarily the Users' Responsibility:
- Commit to making the change
- Participate in the design of the new system
- Demand creative solutions

Primarily the IS Department's Responsibility:
- Understand the role of the change agent
- Understand the nature of the change process in organizations
- Ensure creativity and quality of system design
- Deal with problems as they arise

shows some of the tasks and end products associated with each step as well as their relationship to the unfreezing, moving, and refreezing steps of Lewin/Schein.

Three participants, each with roles to play, are involved in the preparation for change: management, the users themselves, and the IS professional. The primary responsibilities for each are illustrated in Figure 2–4 and discussed in the following paragraphs. At the end of this discussion, the need for the three categories of participants to coordinate their actions is reviewed.

Role of Management

Top management is responsible for deciding that a proposed change is necessary and that the timing for its introduction is right. Beyond that, management should approve the plan for implementing the change, monitor its progress, and stand ready to assist in resolving problems as they arise.

One of the reasons for resistance is that users have low tolerance for change. Often, changes occur too frequently and management gets a reputation for operating by "slot-machine management," constantly introducing changes that are not well thought out in hopes of hitting the jackpot. For this reason, management must be sure a change is necessary before disrupting the organization. Management's criterion for deciding to implement a change is that the change should be essential in achieving the organizational unit's goals and objectives.

Management is also responsible for ensuring that the need for the change is understood by the personnel in the organization who will be affected by it and who will participate in the change process. For example, the U.S. market share captured by foreign car manufacturers was high enough to convince workers and management alike that the existing methods of operation must be changed if American companies were to compete or even survive. It was this acceptance of change that permitted the introduction of such techniques as computer-integrated manufacturing, robotics, just-in-time inventory control, and quality circles.

In other countries, radical steps have been taken to ensure that management adopts a participative style of systems development. In Norway, for example, legislation mandates that unions participate in all systems development projects. This legislation has been remarkably successful in improving management-worker relationships without adversely affecting the use of information technology.

Role of Users

Just as executive management must believe the changes are necessary, so must the users. The commitment of the users to change is a fundamental requirement for a system to be successful. Experience shows that the most successful systems are those where the strongest champion of the system is someone from the user department. User management must make the project their own rather than watching, as passive spectators, a change designed and implemented by outsiders and imposed on their organization. Users should play a key role in the design of a new system, combining their knowledge of industry and operating problems with the information technology knowledge of systems professionals to arrive at creative solutions.

Ideally, if a change is to be made, it should be a lasting one, to avoid having to introduce another change too soon. Techniques for lasting change include significant user involvement and a creative process that includes seeking out and trying to improve on the state of the art in similar applications. Users must demand creative solutions to their business problems and should not settle for less. Pedestrian solutions are not likely to last long, nor are they likely to contribute to sustained competitive advantage.

Role of Information Systems Professionals

IS professionals must understand that they serve as catalysts for change, change agents, and that a key requirement to be effective in this role is gaining the acceptance and trust of the users. Professionals should understand the nature of change and should expect a natural resistance to change. This resistance does not mean that users are ignorant, uncooperative, obstructionist, or even wrong. Resistance comes from human beings who have honest disagreements or concerns that must be diagnosed and dealt with. The biggest mistake an IS professional can make is to try to brush disagreements under the rug. They do not disappear. They remain and grow, eventually emerging as much larger problems, possibly impinging on the IS professional's own career.

Users are more comfortable if they help to effect change by working as part of a project team composed of both users and IS professionals (see Chapter 3). A work plan that clearly delineates the project's goals, end products, timetable, tasks to be performed, and responsibility for each is useful for achieving an understanding of objectives, roles, and expectations.

Training users in operating a new system is an important step that frequently receives too little attention. Users must be trained in the new procedures and supported by the project team until they are comfortable with operating on their own. The place of training in the implementation process receives complete coverage in Chapter 20.

To ensure that systems are well designed, some organizations have implemented a usability laboratory. In such a laboratory, users test a system under realistic conditions, and trained industrial psychologists observe the tests. The sessions are recorded on videotape so that difficulties in learning or using the system can be analyzed in depth and the user interface modified where necessary. Experience shows that systems tested in this way have had a much higher rate of acceptance than those that have not. This concept has proven itself in situations where there will be a large number of users of different backgrounds and in situations where the provider of the system has little control over its users.

Coordination Between User, IS Department, and Executive Management

Each of the three areas—user, IS department, and executive management—has an individual role in the change process. But the three areas must also coordinate their work to ensure the successful introduction of change.

Executive management must identify a sponsor in its ranks to ensure that the organization is committed to the project and that the project is supportive of broad organizational goals and objectives. This sponsor's authority must be acknowledged by both users and the IS department.

Users must avoid putting departmental goals (such as maintaining the status quo) above corporate goals. In other words, users must accept or, ideally, initiate changes that will help their departments contribute more to organizational objectives.

The IS department must make a serious effort to empathize with the users, to understand their business problems, to provide ideas for information technology solutions, to understand users' fears and concerns, and to be supportive in overcoming them. Management, users, and IS department efforts are best coordinated through the project team approach discussed in Chapter 3.

Summary

Information technology is becoming increasingly mature. Many of the strategic information systems being implemented now touch the very heart of the business. The work done by the users of the system is changing deeply, and more and more users are affected by these changes.

A new information system will not be successful unless it is accepted by the people for which it is designed. Human beings have a natural resistance to change, which has been well studied in its organizational setting. Resistance to change must be diagnosed and overcome if the introduction of new technology is to work. For these reasons, information systems professionals must understand the nature of the change process and ways to overcome resistance.

Lewin's three-stage model of change illustrates the need to prepare the organization and to solidify changes once they are made. A plan for overcoming resistance should be developed once the nature of resistance has been diagnosed. Peter Keen cited four reasons for resistance to computer-based innovations. This analysis is a useful framework for diagnosing reasons for resistance to change.

Executive management, users, and the IS department have roles in facilitating the successful introduction of change as well as in supporting the project team approach. A key role of executive management is to ensure that the proposed change supports overall strategic goals and objectives and that the nature of this support is communicated to and understood by members of the organization charged with its implementation, both users and information systems professionals.

Selected Readings

Gildersleeve, Thomas R. *Successful Data Processing System Analysis,* 2nd ed. Englewood Cliffs, New Jersey: Prentice-Hall, Inc., 1985.
Gildersleeve is the proponent of "fix it before it breaks."

Mumford, Enid, and Weir, Mary. *Computer Systems in Work Design: The ETHICS Method,* Ch. 3. New York: Halsted, 1979.
This work describes the socio-technical approach to systems development and the implementation of change. This method is particularly appropriate in environments where change will affect multiple categories of users (for instance, sales personnel, accounting clerks, and data entry operators) or where substantial changes are anticipated (goals and objectives as well as environment and procedures).

Review Questions

1. What is the role of information technology in the ever-increasing pace of change in the business environment?

2. What are four specific reasons for human resistance to computer-based innovations? If these reasons apply to a given situation, there are often clues to determine if people feel resistant as well as countermeasures available to information systems personnel. What are the clues and countermeasures for each reason cited above?

3. Managers and users should be equal partners with information systems personnel in the introduction of technological change. What is the role of each in the process?

Discussion Questions

1. Innovations made by airline companies for competitive advantage (or for survival) were discussed in this chapter. Expand the discussion by describing innovations made in other industries.

2. Why does the success of organizational change pivot on human acceptance of the change?

3. What techniques might information systems personnel employ to overcome resistance to change in a situation where users express discontent with past projects and an unwillingness to work with project team personnel?

4. IS personnel have educational backgrounds and experience that are primarily technical. Explain how this background might hinder them in dealing with user resistance to change.

Mini-Case

Avion Corporation, a major credit corporation in the southwestern United States, recently automated its customer service and credit authorization procedures. Benefits included reduced clerical costs and more effective use of management time. Clerks, aided by computer terminals, are now able to handle considerably more customer inquiries and credit authorizations without management assistance than they could with the previous system.

One expensive technological innovation at Avion, however, did not fare as well. The innovation, voice mail, was implemented by information systems professionals at the same time as the customer service and credit authorization system. It seems that whenever anyone telephoned an Avion employee directly and had to leave a message because the employee was unavailable, the caller was forced to leave a voice message. Complaints soared as callers claimed they were never able to speak to a human being. There were other technical problems, and the system was eventually scrapped.

Questions for Discussion

1. What was the probable rationale for the voice mail system?

2. Recall the suggested roles of management, users, and information systems professionals in preparing the organization for change discussed in the chapter. What are some possible reasons the customer service and credit authorization system was successful but the voice mail was not?

References

1. *Webster's New World Dictionary*, College Edition, 1964.
2. Lewin, Kurt. "The Coming of the New Organization." *Human Frontiers* 1 (1947).

3. Machiavelli, Niccolò. *The Prince*. Translated by Luigi Rice, Rev. E. R. P. Vincent. New York: New American Library, 1952.

4. Keen, Peter G. W. "Introducing Change," *Computerworld* (September 29, 1982): p. 10.

5. Drucker, Peter F. "The Coming of the New Organization." *Harvard Business Review* (January-February 1988): pp. 45–53.

Chapter 3

Systems Projects and the Information Systems Department

The charge of the information systems department is to design, install, operate, and maintain information systems that truly meet the needs of users. This chapter covers the principal organizational factors that determine how effectively an IS department discharges its responsibilities:

- The placement of the IS department in an organization's hierarchy.
- The internal organization of the IS department.
- The organization of project teams for development of new applications.
- Career path planning for IS personnel.

Learning Objectives

- Understand the traditional placement of the information systems (IS) department in organizations and the trends promoting a change in placement.

- Realize the impact on IS of the merging islands of technology—data processing, telecommunications, and office automation.

- Review three common forms of IS department organization—functional, product line, and matrix.

- Recognize issues affecting the degree of centralization or decentralization of an organization's IS resources (hardware, data, and personnel).

- Recognize the rapid emergence of two trends in systems development—end-user computing and advanced systems development.

- Describe the purpose, process, and personnel involved in the project team approach to systems development.

- Become aware of alternatives to the project team approach and the possible shortcomings of each alternative.

- Understand key points for management control of project teams.
- Describe the importance of effective career path planning for IS personnel.

THE PLACE OF THE IS DEPARTMENT IN THE ORGANIZATION

This chapter explains how to set up and manage projects involving the design and installation of new systems. First, however, two broader topics will be discussed: where the IS department fits in the overall organization and how an IS department is organized internally.

An IS department can have the following responsibilities:

- Designing, installing, operating, and maintaining infrastructure applications (i.e., those that provide data and services to the entire organization).
- In most cases, providing resources and support to end users, functional departments, and other organizational units, so that the information technology needs of smaller groups can be satisfied.
- Increasingly, managing other information technology areas such as telecommunications and office automation.

Which of these responsibilities are actually in the province of the IS department depends on the degree of evolution reached by the organization. In turn, the function to which the IS department reports most often depends on the extent of its responsibilities.

Since the first business-oriented computer was installed at General Electric in 1954, there has been a continuous evolution in the perception of information technology and of its proper place within an organization. As previously mentioned, businesses initially used computers for accounting and related applications, thus reducing costs by substituting computers for clerks. Examples of early computer applications are customer billing, demand deposit accounting, policyholder accounting, payroll, and general accounting. Organizations typically delegated the responsibility for these applications to the chief accounting officer (i.e., the controller or financial vice-president). In many organizations, the responsibility remains there today. A high-level organization chart of such a company is pictured in Figure 3–1.

Two recent trends are changing the way top managers view information technology and where they place the IS function for maximum effectiveness:

- The IS department increasingly encompasses not only data processing but also all information technology functions, including office automation and telecommunications.
- The IS department has the potential to support many parts of the organization at all levels of its hierarchy.

Figure 3–1 **Organization Chart Showing Traditional Placement of Data Processing**

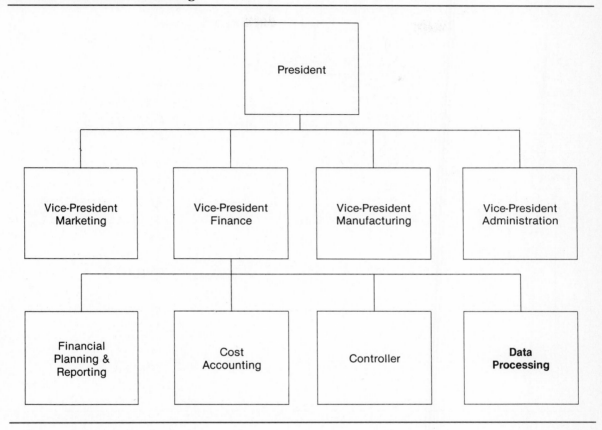

Merging the Islands of Technology

In 1982, James McKenney and F. Warren McFarlan proposed that the three separate "islands of technology" (data processing, telecommunications, and office automation) be placed under integrated control because they were likely to converge in advanced information systems.[1] Under integrated control, the three technologies would be more likely to be managed in a coordinated fashion to the benefit of the organization. For example, a computerized payroll system in the 1960s most probably operated as illustrated in Figure 3–2. Payroll time cards and other transactions needed to produce a paycheck were collected from user areas and sent to the corporate data center. The transactions were converted from paper forms into media readable by the computers of that time, most probably punched cards. These transactions on punched cards were then read by the computer. Through a series of related programs, employees' pay was

Figure 3–2 **Payroll System (ca. 1960)**

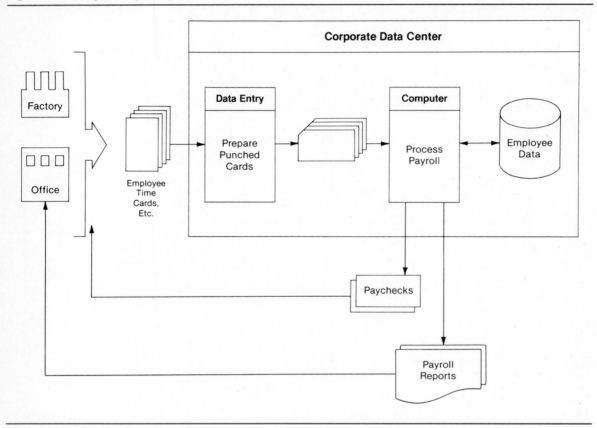

calculated, employee computer records were updated, and checks were printed along with reports such as the payroll register.

If that same payroll system were to be installed using today's technology, it might appear as in Figure 3–3. Payroll transactions would be entered through computer terminals located in user departments and sent over communications lines directly to the computer in the corporate data center. The payroll transactions would be processed, pay would be calculated, and the employees' records would be updated. Checks would be prepared along with the payroll register and other reports. In this system, employees could request that their checks be deposited directly into their checking accounts. For these employees, deposit data would be sent to their bank over telecommunications lines. Various departments needing access to payroll information could inquire against the computer records. Extracts from the payroll data base could be transmitted to

Figure 3–3 **Payroll System (ca. 1990)**

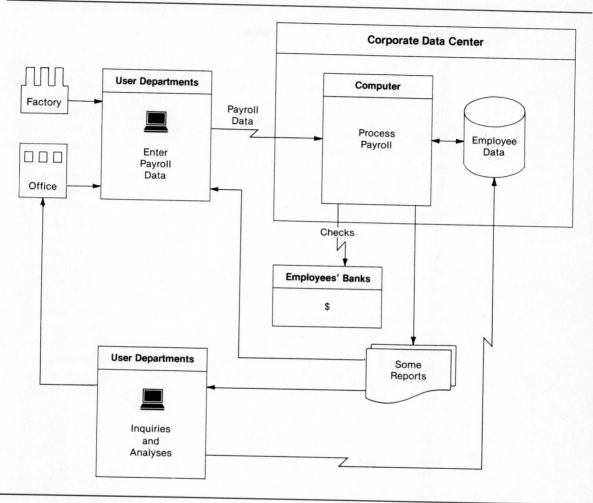

departmental microcomputers where analysis could be performed using spreadsheet software. Exhibits such as tables and graphs thus created could be incorporated into reports prepared with office automation software such as a word processor or in-house publishing software.

At the time of payroll systems such as the one in Figure 3–2, there were corporate functions labeled data processing, telecommunications, and office automation. However, these functions were not interconnected as they are in the second example. Data processing took place exclusively at the corporate data center; telecommunications consisted of the public telephone service, internal telephones, and perhaps a telex machine; and office automation consisted of electric typewriters and photocopiers.

In the second example, the design of the payroll system uses today's technology to improve service to the users. Personal computers in user departments perform many office functions such as word processing and spreadsheet applications. Some of these computers are also connected over telecommunications networks to a large computer in the corporate data center. Systems taking advantage of office automation, telecommunications technology, and data processing technology are becoming the norm rather than the exception. Accordingly, in many organizations the responsibility for managing the three areas is given to the IS department.

Systems integration is the name given to a strategy that formally recognizes the convergence of data processing, telecommunications, office automation, and where applicable, process control. The objective is organization-wide integration of systems. Because an organization's many systems were typically installed over a period of years, they use different vendors and serve different users. However, many users need the same information. To satisfy them, information is frequently moved manually from one system to another. Unfortunately, manual interfaces are inefficient and error-prone. As a result, secondary users of the information (in many cases management personnel) receive outdated or inaccurate data. To overcome this problem, organizations are recognizing the convergence of these branches of information systems and beginning to integrate them. A successful integration strategy requires the development of organization-wide standards for information resource management and communications. The strategy also requires IS personnel to recognize that formerly disparate systems must fit together if the organization is to be well served.

The Supportive Role of the IS Department

Information technology applications have expanded to include all functional areas of an organization. A new information system being installed today could be one that improves operations on the factory floor, permitting better utilization of raw materials and factory resources through better production scheduling and control. It could be a marketing information system that permits precise identification of sales prospects. Or it could be a system tailored to meet the specific information requirements of a top executive.

The specific location of IS in the organization and the level at which it reports varies from company to company. In some, it reports to the chief financial officer, in keeping with tradition. In others, it reports directly to the chief executive officer (CEO) or to an administrative vice-president.

In searching for guidelines for positioning the IS department, the CEO must recognize the supportive role of IS within the organization: it renders service to other functional areas of the organization. The IS department should be placed so that it can provide its services according to organizational priorities rather than the priorities of the vice-president to whom it happens to report. Thus, in many cases the IS executive should be part of the management team.

In practice, however, many IS directors have risen through the technical ranks and lack the interpersonal and managerial skills expected from a high-level executive. Effective communication and good personal relationships between IS personnel and their counterparts in user departments are as important to the effective delivery of information technology services as more concrete measures of performance. Management should consider this fact when deciding where to place the IS department. Often, the IS director reports to someone who can serve as an ambassador to improve relations with the rest of the organization. This ambassador is often a vice-president with other operational or functional responsibilities and a good working relationship with contemporaries throughout the organization.

Increasingly, organizations are establishing a new executive position called the *chief information officer* (CIO). We referred briefly to this trend in Chapter 1. The CIO is most likely to be found in organizations that recognize the strategic value of information and manage it accordingly. The CIO is most often positioned at the vice-presidential level, on a par with executive managers of other key functional areas. The charge of the CIO is to see that the available information resources are managed in a manner consistent with their importance to the organization. Usually, the CIO is not a technician, although he or she should understand the technology well enough to manage the IS professionals. In addition, the CIO should possess broad management skills and an understanding of the business so that information technology is appropriately used throughout the organization. The CIO should also have the political and interpersonal skills to serve as the liaison for the IS technicians as previously discussed.

The strategic grid discussed in Chapter 1 provides additional guidelines for determining the level to which the IS department should report. The more important information technology is to an organization, the more attention it should receive from top management and the higher up it should report. Therefore, if an organization places itself in the strategic or turnaround quadrants, the IS department would report to an executive such as a CIO. If an organization is in the factory quadrant, IS would report to an executive who can ensure delivery of high-quality, uninterrupted service. If an organization is in the support quadrant, IS can safely report to a lower level of the organization, since other matters will be of a higher priority to top management (see Figure 3–4).

ORGANIZATION OF THE IS DEPARTMENT

Form of Organization

As pointed out by Davis and Olson, the three major variations in the organization of IS departments are by function, by product line, or as a matrix.

Figure 3–4 **How IS Departments Report**

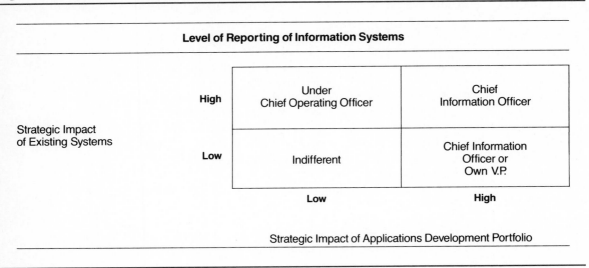

Functional Organization. The IS department is usually organized along functional lines, as illustrated in Figure 3–5. The three primary tasks of the IS department are development of new applications, maintenance and enhancement of existing applications, and computer operations. In the functional organization, these functions are typically headed by managers who report to the director of information systems. Applications development is responsible for performing the tasks necessary to design and install a new computer system from the project approval through its subsequent conversion and acceptance by the users. At that time, computer operations assumes responsibility for the operation of the system. The program maintenance group performs subsequent changes or enhancements.

New applications are typically developed by project teams composed of users and IS personnel formed specifically to design and install an application. The formation and management of project teams are discussed in a later section of this chapter.

Product Line Organization. An IS department organized along product lines commonly has groups of IS personnel devoted to particular user departments or to types of IS products. For example, Figure 3–6 shows an IS department with groups of personnel dedicated to financial systems, manufacturing systems, and marketing systems. One portion of the personnel in each product group is devoted to building new applications and another portion to maintaining existing systems. Frequently this division can prevent politically difficult resource allocation problems with the user departments. A specific level of IS

Figure 3-5 **IS Department Organized along Functional Lines**

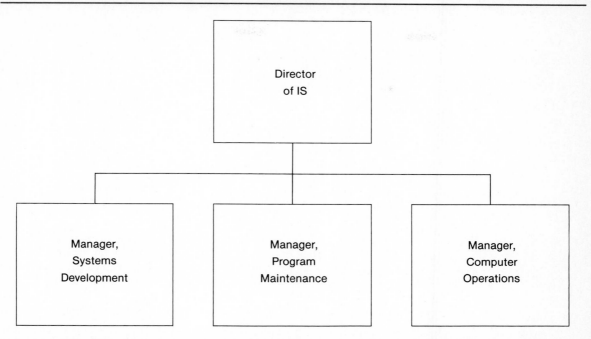

personnel is dedicated to each product line, and user personnel are deeply involved in deciding which new applications and which existing applications should be worked on. This arrangement is often used by decentralized organizations. It dedicates resources to functional areas or operating groups which are themselves decentralized. (The next section of this chapter contains a more complete discussion of considerations regarding the centralization and decentralization of IS resources.) The product line approach to organizing IS departments illustrated in Figure 3-6 shows that a single computer center operates existing systems for all product groups, although as an alternative, each product group can have its own computer center as well.

Matrix Organization. In a matrix organization, IS resources are dispersed to various organizational units on a product group basis, a geographical basis, or some other basis. The dispersed IS groups report hierarchically to the operational head of the unit to which they are attached and functionally to an IS director, who is responsible for maintaining technical competence, tools, and infrastructure. An example of an IS function organized on a matrix basis is shown in Figure 3-7. In a manner similar to the product group form of organization, the purpose of the matrix approach is to give users more control

Figure 3–6   IS Department Organized along Product Lines

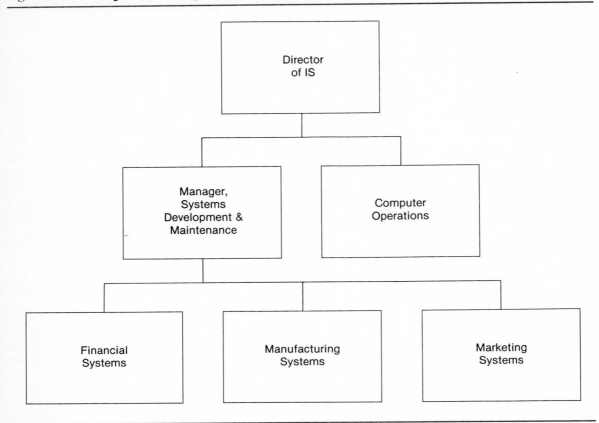

over information systems resources. Again, there are many options regarding which functions are retained by the IS director. In the example shown in Figure 3–7, all major functions are dispersed. The IS director retains responsibility for overall coordination and such corporate-level functions as standards setting, long-range systems planning, and IS research and development.

Centralization versus Decentralization

When Chinese party leader Deng Xiaoping began to introduce economic and social reforms that opposed the established dogmas of the time, he was fond of saying to his critics: "It doesn't matter if a cat is black or white as long as it catches mice." The same view applies to issues of centralization versus decentralization of IS resources. It does not matter whether resources are highly centralized or highly decentralized as long as the choice permits the IS resource to serve the entire organization as effectively as possible. In other words, the IS

Figure 3–7 **Matrix Organization of IS**

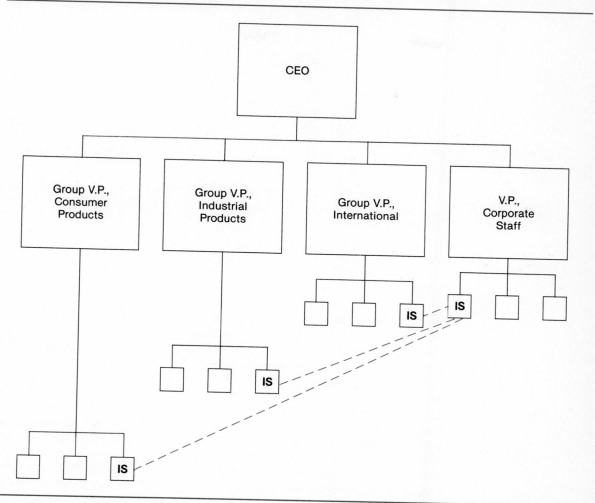

department should fit the company that it serves—its organization, management style, geographical distribution, channels of communications, and culture.

When organizations review their options in deciding the degree of centralization or decentralization of IS resources, they normally take three resources into consideration: hardware, data, and systems development personnel.

Hardware and Data Considerations. Hardware (processing power) and data may be centralized or decentralized. Figure 3–8 shows that both may be centralized or both decentralized. It is also possible to decentralize processing

Figure 3–8 **Centralization vs. Decentralization**

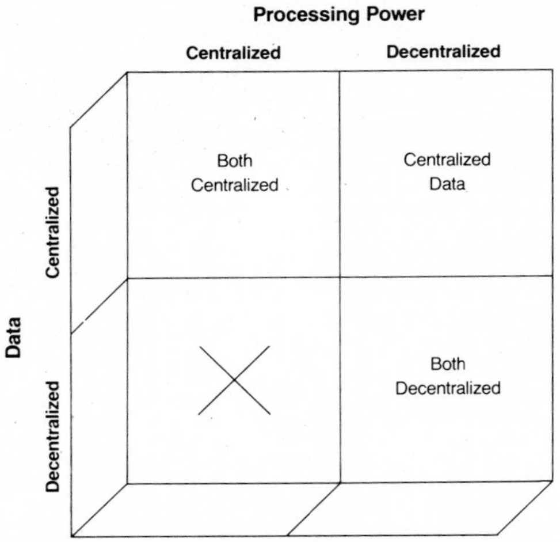

Processing Power

	Centralized	Decentralized
Centralized	Both Centralized	Centralized Data
Decentralized	✕	Both Decentralized

power while keeping data centralized. In this case, some centralized hardware must be available to manage that data; thus, the processing power cannot be totally distributed. The converse—distributing the data while keeping the processing power centralized—is not possible.

Initially, organizations using computers tended towards a centralized approach for computer operations, largely because a central site permitted them to realize economies of scale. (The cost per unit of processing power tended to decrease as the size of the processor increased.) A centralized approach also permitted experts in computer operations, telecommunications, and systems software to be concentrated at a single site. In recent years, advances in technology have permitted organizations more options in the way they distribute their computer processing resources. The economies of scale once so generally accepted no longer apply to computer hardware, and the price and range of options with telecommunications is increasing. For example, many large organizations have created private telecommunications networks for their own use at significant cost savings. Such trends in technology have allowed organizations considerably more flexibility in placing hardware and data for a given cost.

The development of minicomputers and microcomputers has permitted the placement of powerful computers close to the users. In raw computing power, the personal computers of today rival the mainframes of ten years ago. Telecommunications capabilities and networking techniques permit computers to be tied together in local, regional, or international networks, public and private, enabling users to access and use data stored in computer files thousands of miles away.

Figure 3–9 **Three Patterns of Overall Technical Architecture**

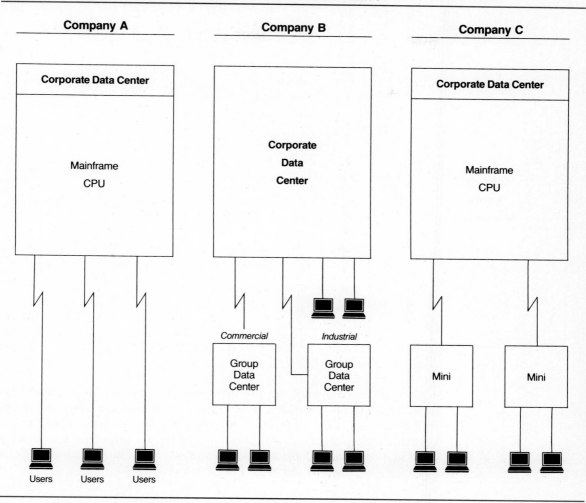

Three common patterns of technical architecture are illustrated in Figure 3–9. Company A has chosen a centralized approach built around a large mainframe computer. All applications for the organization are run on this mainframe. Company B has chosen to establish several data centers located near key user concentrations. Each data center serves a specified community of users. Company C has chosen to combine a large mainframe computer with departmental minicomputers located in certain departments. In each case, terminals and desktop personal computers are in place throughout the organization. In most cases, the specific resource configuration derives from the organization's

Figure 3–10 **Three Patterns of Organizing Systems Development Personnel**

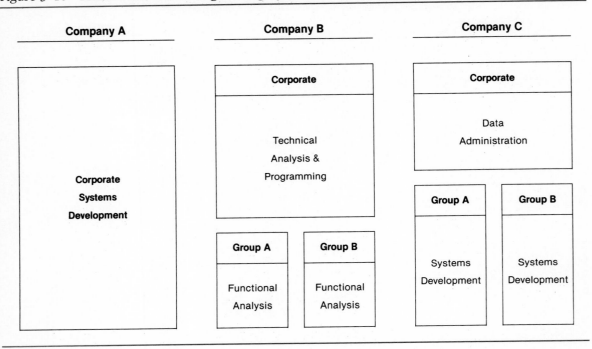

application requirements and the users' requirements for data access. Once these requirements are known, the cost and performance of alternative patterns of hardware and data distribution are analyzed, and a specific alternative is selected. Backup, security, and personnel issues are additional factors to be taken into consideration. Additional information on this subject can be found in the selected readings listed at the end of this chapter.

Systems Development Personnel Considerations. As with hardware and data, most companies initially had a single systems development group, centrally located to serve the needs of the entire organization. Later, some organizations decentralized the group along divisional or geographic lines. Usually, the purpose of decentralization was to place systems development resources more closely under user control or to make them more responsive to user demands for service. Also, when the organization itself operates on a highly decentralized basis, a decentralized IS development function is more consistent with the prevailing corporate culture. Here, too, an organization may choose from a wide spectrum of solutions, ranging from complete centralization to complete decentralization (see Figure 3–10).

Summary of Centralization/Decentralization Issues. Alternative ways of organizing resources range from highly centralized to highly decentralized. All can work well if the alternative chosen is right for a specific organization. Even if an organization chooses a decentralized model, some tasks could be handled either by a small central staff or by a coordinating body representing each of the decentralized locations. These tasks include recommending standards for hardware, software, and documentation; recommending systems development methodologies; planning cooperative development projects; overseeing information technology research and development; and coordinating personnel policies and training programs. The final task relates to controlling the corporate data resource. Regardless of the degree of decentralization, procedures should be in place to ensure the integrity of corporate data no matter who is responsible for updating or changing records on computer files. Cash, McFarlan, and McKenney refer to this fundamental responsibility as long-term data hygiene.

More Recent Trends

When computers were first used, one person could often perform all of the functions necessary to bring an application to operating status and then operate the computer as well. In other words, a single individual could (and often did) perform the tasks of systems analysis and design, programming, testing, conversion, and maintenance. Today, with the introduction of more complex computers and operating systems, one person is rarely capable of performing all such tasks in a mainframe computer environment. The tasks of the IS department have continually subdivided into specialized areas. Two recent advances in technology are creating another subdivision, with predictions that two new specialized groups will arise in application development: end-user computing specialists and advanced systems developers.

End-User Computing Specialists. The rise in end-user computing has profoundly affected computing within most organizations. End-user computing in business started in the mid-1970s with IBM Canada's creation of the Information Center concept and gathered momentum in 1981 with the introduction of the personal computer and business-oriented software packages such as spreadsheets, word processors, and data base management systems.

In the early days, end-user computing took place on mainframes separated from the transaction processing applications run by the IS department. In general, the IS department procured hardware and software for the Information Center (or Infocenter, for short). The IS department also supplied specialists to help novice users with product and methodology training and troubleshooting. But because the environment was hardly less hostile to novices than traditional computing and because sharing a large machine invariably causes conflicts about priorities, the Infocenter initially caught on only in a small number of organizations.

The availability of personal computers and associated friendly, easy-to-learn, easy-to-use software provided the real impetus to end-user computing. At first, the trend had a mixed reception by the IS community, which had grown up developing custom systems to run on a mainframe computer. Some IS directors perceived end-user computing as a threat to their turf and attempted to regain control from the users by insisting on a heavy IS involvement in building systems and in procuring all hardware and software. Fortunately, IS departments with this perspective are in the minority.

The more enlightened IS departments have come to believe that properly supported end-user computing benefits them and the organization. It benefits IS departments because they need not devote limited resources to smaller systems, when there is typically a multiyear backlog of large project requests that only the IS department can handle.

End-user computing benefits users because they need not go through the centralized IS department priority-setting process and wait in line to get a small project approved; instead, they can build it themselves. On the other hand, users often lack expertise in development and operations. Some of the problems often cited with systems developed by end users are lack of adequate documentation, poor controls, and the choice of unstable vendors.

Many IS departments have now adopted the Information Center approach to supply some professional guidance to end-user computing. For example, some IS departments are providing users with a way to manage the variety of hardware and software products. Others provide users with a quality control function that can help evaluate whether an end-user application is likely to cause data integrity or maintenance problems in the future.

Box 3–1 illustrates the Information Center concept as it has been applied at XYZ Company. It is staffed with end-user computing specialists who guide and assist users in building applications and steer them to other resources, including data resources, that are available to help in the process.

Advanced Systems Developers. In recent years, the number of tools to streamline systems analysis, design, and programming tasks has greatly increased. Prototyping, application generators, and computer-aided software engineering (CASE) tools are the most important of these. In combination with modern development methods, these tools enable IS departments to build systems that are more complex and highly integrated and that are used by more people than before. The complexity of these systems and the use of high-technology tools require a new type of personnel, called advanced systems developers.

Although most new corporate systems will be developed with the new technologies, there will still be the need for IS personnel who can maintain and enhance systems developed with the old technologies. James Martin's view of the IS development group of the future is illustrated in Figure 3–11. The group has an Information Center, devoted to the support of end-user computing; an Advanced Development Group, using the new tools to develop systems; and a

BOX 3–1

The Information Support Center at Sterling Drug Co.

The staff at Sterling Drug Co.'s Information Support Center in New York consists of a project manager and three information consultants—two seniors, who do the initial consultation and evaluate the user's job request to see if it is suitable for "doing-it-yourself," and another, who gives training and hands-on support.

The IC is part of Sterling's management information services group, and project manager Valerie Martin reports to the director of corporate MIS. As with any successful policy implementation, top management support has been vital. Last year, at the request of the company president, her group held a series of lunchtime seminars on microcomputers for top executives, underlining that support.

About 300 people have used the training, applications development or general consulting services of Sterling's Center, which is located within the management information services group and equipped with color terminals for personal computing on the mainframe, a printer, videotape equipment and projectors. There is a microcomputer room with an IBM PC, an Apple II and a Compaq Portable, which Martin expects to expand.

End-users who do a lot of work on the mainframe usually have their own terminals in their departments; those with an occasional project can use the Center's equipment. The micros are used for evaluation by users.

Also critical to the Center's success is a good working relationship between the IC and the other data processing departments. To avoid being regarded as an "upstart" group out to step on other departmental toes, Sterling's IC staff meets periodically with the other groups to keep them aware of what projects are being done and also offers them training and program support in their use of the Center's mainframe applications.[2]

Traditional Development Group, doing things in the old way and phasing out, as the systems they maintain are replaced by newer ones.

PROJECT TEAMS FOR DEVELOPMENT OF INFORMATION SYSTEMS

Regardless of how the IS department is organized internally and to whom it reports, some way must be found to develop a system from the resources of the IS department itself, the users, and executive management. The project team approach, the most frequently used, consists of a team of individuals with the combination of skills required to accomplish a specific set of tasks. The team usually includes users, personnel from the IS department, and often consultants or contract programmers from outside the organization. The approach is particularly well suited to the development of large to medium-sized systems and rather less so to the smaller systems typically found in an end-user

Figure 3–11 **Three Separate Channels of Development**

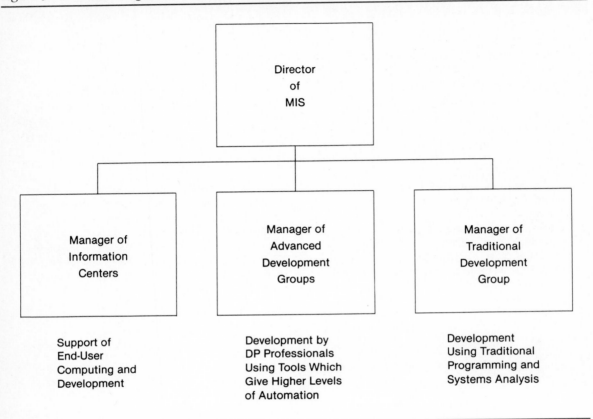

Director of MIS		
Manager of Information Centers	Manager of Advanced Development Groups	Manager of Traditional Development Group
Support of End-User Computing and Development	Development by DP Professionals Using Tools Which Give Higher Levels of Automation	Development Using Traditional Programming and Systems Analysis

computing environment. The project team approach has gained such wide acceptance because it is the most effective way of securing a commitment from the key groups: users, management, and IS personnel.

It is a management imperative to support IS projects, because they are designed to help users pursue organizational goals more effectively and efficiently. One way to insure user management commitment is to have the project sponsored by the highest possible level of user management. A formal announcement of a project's initiation is often written and circulated to personnel expected to assist the project team in some way during the course of the project. Figure 3–12 shows an example of the announcement of a project to design a new order entry and billing system.

Figure 3–13, a project organization chart, shows the major organizational units in a typical IS development project. A project steering committee made up of management representatives from the user community, IS representatives,

Figure 3–12 **Sample Project Announcement**

```
PERSONNEL                       SUBURBAN PUMPS                    CD-20
SYSTEM                                                           PRANN
                             PROJECT ANNOUNCEMENT

 ┌─────────────────────────────────────────────────────────────────────┐
 │ PREPARED BY: PIERRE FAVIER    DATE:   24MAR90    VERSION:  1.1  PAGE 1│
 │ APPROVED BY:                  DATE:   28MAR90    STATUS :  D          │
 └─────────────────────────────────────────────────────────────────────┘
```

OVERVIEW

Suburban Pumps is in the process of redeveloping a number of systems to support our present and future information needs. Our present personnel and payroll systems, while providing excellent payroll processing, has shortcomings in its ability to provide timely answers to management's information needs and to accommodate the constant improvements in benefits programs that it is our policy to implement.

I have selected Jack Ham, one of the senior project managers in the Information Systems Services department, to lead this effort. He will be assisted by a project team representing a cross-section of key management, user, and ISS personnel. This team will report their progress to my staff on a periodic basis to ensure that the system developed is responsive to our particular requirements.

SCOPE

The new personnel system will cover the needs of our Human Resources department as well as the needs of all the line managers throughout the company, in the following functional areas:

o   Job classifications and descriptions

o   Skills needs

o   Personnel evaluations and skills inventory

o   Outside sources of training

Because of the wide variety of needs, we have decided to use a phased approach to the implementation of the system. Initially, we will concentrate on managerial and professional positions. Later projects will cover clerical, technical, and production personnel.

REQUIREMENTS

As part of this effort, the project team will be interviewing various members of Suburban Pumps management during the next few months. These discussions will provide the basis for documenting the information needs of management. We recognize that the time required of you may put additional pressure on your schedule. However, your assistance and cooperation are critical to the success of this project and we thank you in advance for your support.

Figure 3–13 **Organization Chart for Typical Systems Project**

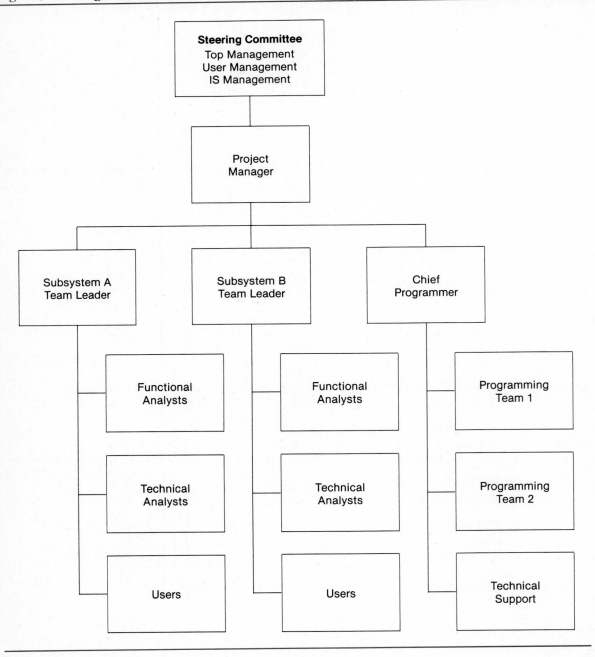

and representatives from any outside consultants. The purpose of the project steering committee is to set the overall project direction and to serve as a review committee, sounding board, and arbitrating committee for the project. The steering committee meets at the beginning of the project to make sure that everyone agrees on the project scope and expectations of results. Thereafter, it meets periodically, often monthly, to review progress and direct the project team.

The project manager, who reports to the project steering committee, is assigned full time to the project. This person is responsible for planning and controlling the work of the project team members. Most practitioners prefer that the project manager be selected from among the user community, usually a middle-level manager who is too valuable to be spared from current assignments. (People in this category are usually the most competent and are therefore most likely to be wise choices.) A project manager chosen from the user community is also further evidence of user commitment to the project. An IS department representative is often designated as co-project manager or assistant to the project manager to add the necessary technical expertise.

Project team members are selected according to the requirements for time and skills as set out in a project work plan. The work plan, prepared by the project managers, lists all the tasks and their target completion dates. The functions of the team members, illustrated on the project organization chart in Figure 3–13, are described in Appendix 2.

The number of project team members and their required skills vary from project to project. Project managers are well advised to insist on the right mix of skills in the personnel assigned to them if they expect to deliver a quality end product. If personnel with the right skills are not available when called for by the work plan, the project manager should either ask management to supply them from an outside source or adjust the project work plan to compensate for the skill deficiency.

Alternatives to the Project Team Approach

Several alternative approaches can establish a project team to develop a new information system. However, each of these alternatives has shortcomings when compared with a project team approach.

Independent Effort. There have been examples in which large, complex systems have been built by a very small group of highly qualified individuals. The best example is an information system developed at the *New York Times* in one year by two developers, Harlan Mills and Terry Baker, with assistance from a third person who checked their code, all 87,000 lines of it! An IBM executive close to the project was quoted as saying: "Baker was supported in a way similar to a great surgeon in an operating room." An example such as this one, however, is the exception rather than the rule. Usually a development project undertaken by one or two persons results in slow progress and greater risk because a small team does not possess the expertise in all necessary areas.

Permanent IS Team. A second alternative is a permanent team of IS professionals assigned to a broad application area. The major problem with this approach is that all too often users are not sufficiently involved. In addition, little cross training within the IS department takes place and there can be resistance to change within each permanent group. Finally, permanent teams frequently find themselves bogged down with maintenance requests with little time left to devote to new systems development.

User Department Team. In some cases, a user department may set up its own development team. The main difficulties with this approach are the lack of technical expertise, lack of awareness of opportunities for systems integration, lack of systems project management skill, and the like.

Part-Time IS Team. All too often, usually due to the press of other matters and limited resources, an IS department will have its personnel work on projects part time. This approach makes project management difficult because of the lack of a focused effort, a formalized approach, and a project plan that identifies what is to be delivered and when.

Nonproject Approach. A final alternative to the project team approach is an unorganized, nonproject approach in which individuals in a company do systems work as time is available. This approach combines the drawbacks of the others with no appreciable advantages.

PROJECT CONTROL

Control of IS projects is in itself a subject worthy of a text. The key points from a management perspective are as follows:

- A framework for planning, estimating, and scheduling the project, most commonly one of the various systems development life cycle methodologies.
- A method for having each member of the project team report actual time spent on tasks to which he or she has been assigned.
- Periodic review sessions with each project team member to review progress. Periodic review sessions with the entire team should also be scheduled so that team members get a project-wide perspective, something easy to miss when working on detailed tasks within a subsystem.
- Periodic review sessions with the project steering committee. A typical agenda follows:

    Summary of work performed to date, including conclusions reached and project status compared with estimates of effort and target dates in the work plan.
    Discussion of items needing input from the steering committee.

Discussion of tasks planned until the next scheduled meeting of the steering committee. This step allows the steering committee to guide the project team on tasks before they are performed. At this time, steering committee members can warn the project team of certain political sensitivities in parts of the organization they may plan to visit.

Discussion of any changes to the original work plan, including target dates.

Minutes of the meeting should be distributed to all committee members—to those attending as well as to those unable to attend. This latter step prevents members of the committee from complaining later that they disagree with a project-related decision and were not informed about it.

CAREER PATHS

Career path planning is particularly important in the IS field because there are forecasts of a continuing shortage of qualified personnel in all job categories. IS personnel have always tended to have more loyalty towards their profession than towards their employers, and thus turnover is a constant threat. Turnover among analysts and programmers was reported to be as high as 20 percent in 1985. Losing a key member of a project team at a critical juncture can create serious problems for a systems project.

To analyze how to avert these problems, let us look at the main reasons for turnover. IS professionals usually leave because they do not feel they are advancing professionally and that a new position will offer them greater professional growth. Often, turnover can be reduced by providing training and motivation on the job.

For example, systems project managers should take the time to develop learning objectives for each project team member and ensure that each receives maximum training from the project experience. The project manager should also review the training objectives with each team member to emphasize the training that results from working on the project.

In a larger sense, a well-managed IS department will have a career plan for each member of the department. As a part of an annual performance appraisal, managers should discuss this career plan with each individual to be sure that he or she understands the path to professional advancement—the skills to be acquired and demonstrated.

In practice, most IS departments have two distinct career paths for systems development personnel, one more technical than the other, but both having associated managerial positions, as illustrated in Figure 3–14. The common entry-level position is that of programmer. The next level is programming group leader. After that, depending on individual aptitudes and interests, the paths diverge: one path places a greater premium on technical computer skills and the other on general business skills such as communications ability, team leadership

Figure 3–14 **Alternative IS Career Paths**

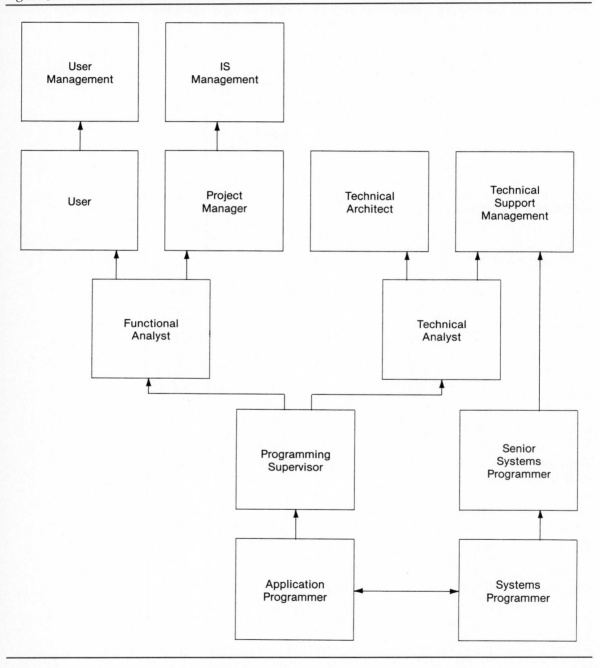

skills, and business perspective. Additional career path considerations are necessary where the trend is towards advanced systems developers and end-user computing.

The need to develop ever more advanced and responsive systems for basic transaction processing (e.g., airline reservation systems) will be here for some time. As we have already seen, an organization capable of designing and installing such systems has an edge on the competition. The number of these systems to be installed, however, will not grow as fast as those designed to leverage management talent (decision support systems, executive information systems, etc.). Many of these systems are relatively small and will be developed in an end-user computing environment using fourth-generation languages. Analysts working in these areas must possess skills different from those of their counterparts working with larger transaction systems. To gain the confidence of high-level users, they will need strong interpersonal and communications skills and an ability to understand higher management needs. A greater premium will be placed on knowledge of industry and company issues as well as on alternative sources of data to meet systems requirements. For a systems professional aspiring to a general management position, this career path could be promising.

Conversely, end-user computing has spawned a new sort of professional, the so-called power user or peer expert. The power user is someone within the user department who has developed stronger information technology skills than his or her peers. The main advantage of having a peer expert is that he or she quite naturally becomes the champion of the department's applications and a natural liaison between the users and the IS department. There are some dangers, however. The power user may develop strong professional loyalties outside the department. Moreover, because power users tend to develop an exclusive interest in information technology, they may block their normal career paths within their original departments. On the other hand, they are usually not professional enough, at least not without considerable retraining, to find an attractive future in a transfer to the IS department.

Summary

The IS function in most organizations originally consisted of a data processing department reporting to the chief accounting officer. With the advances in office automation, telecommunications technology, and data processing, today's information systems take advantage of all three. Because all three areas are technology-based and often require project management skills, the management of office automation, telecommunications, and data processing is increasingly consolidated under the director of IS.

The IS department can now be found reporting to functions other than accounting, as organizations have realized the potential of information technology to serve all areas. In organizations where information technology is valued as a competitive weapon, the IS function is more likely to report to higher levels, even to the CEO. The chief information officer position is gaining increasing favor as an executive-level officer responsible for managing an organization's information resources.

The IS department can be organized in many different ways to serve the rest of the organization. The three most common patterns are according to function, product, or a matrix. The IS function can be centralized or decentralized with respect to hardware, data, and personnel resources. The constantly changing environment has seen two new groups emerge in some IS departments, an Information Center to support end-user computing and an Advanced Systems Development Group composed of specialists trained in the use of new development tools.

The most effective method of designing and installing information systems is the project team made up of full-time, dedicated individuals with the requisite skills. A typical project organization consists of team members drawn from IS and the user community, a project manager, and a project steering committee. Executive-level support for the project is helpful in smoothing the project team's contacts with the rest of the organization.

Finally, alternative career paths for the IS professional are available. They range from the very technical to the business or user oriented. All are important in today's environment. Because turnover can be high among IS professionals, IS departments must develop and communicate tailored career path plans for their professional personnel.

Selected Readings

Davis, Gordon B., and Olson, Margrethe H. *Management Information Systems, Conceptual Foundations, Structure and Development,* 2nd ed. New York: McGraw-Hill, 1985.
This book contains a complete description of the organization of a typical IS department.

Martin, James. *The Information Systems Manifesto.* Englewood, NJ: Prentice-Hall, 1984.
This book is a plea for end-user computing and information centers. It contains the story of how the Santa Fe Railway end users successfully implemented a complex system with a fourth-generation language. The book's weakness is that it does not sufficiently recognize the dangers and shortcomings of end-user computing.

Review Questions

1. What is the fundamental mission of the IS department in a typical organization?

2. Why did organizational responsibility for early information systems most often lie with the accounting department?

3. Explain why the management of telecommunications and office automation has been or is being transferred to the IS department in many organizations.

4. Why is it so important that the IS department be placed where it can provide service according to overall organizational priorities?

5. How can the strategic grid be used to help decide the proper organizational placement of the IS department?

6. What are the key considerations for management in deciding whether to centralize or decentralize IS hardware, data, and personnel?

7. What skills will be important for personnel working in end-user computing? In advanced systems development?

8. What measures can be taken to ensure management commitment to a systems project?

9. Summarize the job functions of the following project team members:

    a. Functional Analyst

    b. Technical Analyst

    c. Programmers and Programming Supervisor

    d. Data Administrator

    e. Data Base Administrator

    f. Systems Software Specialist

    g. User Personnel

    h. Computer Operations Personnel

10. Explain the shortcomings of the alternative approaches to the project team approach for systems development.

11. What are the key project management and control considerations described in the chapter?

12. Describe the two career paths for systems development personnel.

Discussion Questions

1. Identify and describe two or three IS applications used in organizations today that combine functions of office automation, telecommunications, and data processing.

2. Obtain an organization chart of an IS department of a local company. Compare and contrast the organization chart of the selected firm with the IS organizations described in this chapter—functional, product line, and matrix.

3. Discuss the possible repercussions to an organization without adequate career path plans for its IS personnel.

Mini-Case

Assume you are an independent consultant specializing in information systems. The vice-president of finance of Midwestern Insurance (to whom the internal information systems department reports) calls and asks you to come to his office. When you arrive, he asks you to help him deal with the following problem.

The vice-president of marketing has proposed to purchase a microcomputer for each one of the company's agencies located across the United States and put policyholder information on them so that agents can answer policyholder inquiries better. The vice-president of marketing feels that the present method of having agents telephone the home office is inadequate. Agents tell him that sometimes they can not get through. When they do, they often have to talk with clerks in the policyholder service department (which also reports to the vice-president of finance) who are ill-trained and rude. Several agents have already purchased microcomputers on their own and have placed policyholder data on them. These agents find that because most changes originate in the field, they can keep their own files current, reducing their aggravation levels enormously. Some have purchased IBM PCs, while others have purchased Apples or Macintoshes. Various other manufacturers are also represented.

The director of IS is violently opposed to the proposal. He was just in the final stages of preparing a proposal for a distributed data system that would link personal computers in the agents' offices to the home office computer. He maintains that his approach would be best in the long run even though it will probably require about two years to get it off the ground. In the meantime, he wants all microcomputer purchases to be approved by his department because MIS has responsibility for computer hardware purchases. The vice-president of marketing has said he can not wait two years for action; he wants results now. Furthermore, he maintains that microcomputers cost so little that they should be considered office equipment and not come under the purchase supervision of IS.

Question for Discussion

1. The vice-president of finance has asked for your help. What advice can you give him?

References

1. McKenney, James, and McFarlan, F. Warren. "The Information Archipelago—Maps and Bridges." *Harvard Business Review* (September 1982): pp. 109–120.

2. Friedman, Selma. "The Information Center: Taking Control." *Micro Manager* (May 1984): pp. 22–24.

Technique

Hierarchical Diagramming

DEFINITION

One of the most frequently used documentation techniques is the hierarchy chart. A hierarchy chart depicts relationships between entities or concepts as a tree-like structure, where each entity or concept is related to one and only one higher-level entity. A higher-level entity may have several lower-level entities attached to it. Some entities have no lower-level entities related to them, and are considered the leaves of the tree. The highest-level entity is the root, and the intermediate entities are nodes. The number of nodes between a node and the root, including the root itself, represents the level of the node. Thus, the root has a level of zero. The highest level of any node is called the depth of the hierarchy. The number of nodes at a given level characterizes the breadth of the hierarchy, also called fan-out. A node is often called a child and its next higher level node is called a parent. The root is a parent only. Leaves are children only.

EXAMPLES

As Figures 1 through 11 illustrate, relationships expressed by hierarchy charts are quite common.

- Figure 1. A family tree is a hierarchy with the person whose family tree is being traced placed at the root (the left side of the figure), with that person's mother and father at level 1, the grandparents at level 2, and so on.

- Figure 2. The line of succession of English kings from 1327 to 1499 shows a hierarchy with Edward III at the root.

- Figure 3. The table of contents of this book is a hierarchy: the entire book (the root) is subdivided into sections, chapters, and paragraphs (the nodes).

Figure 1 **Family Tree**

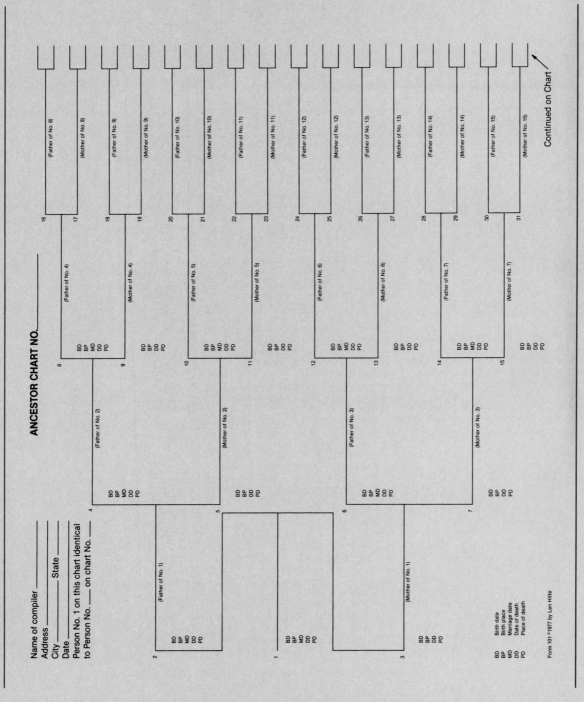

Form 101 ©1977 by Len Hitte

Figure 2   **Line of Succession to the Throne of England**

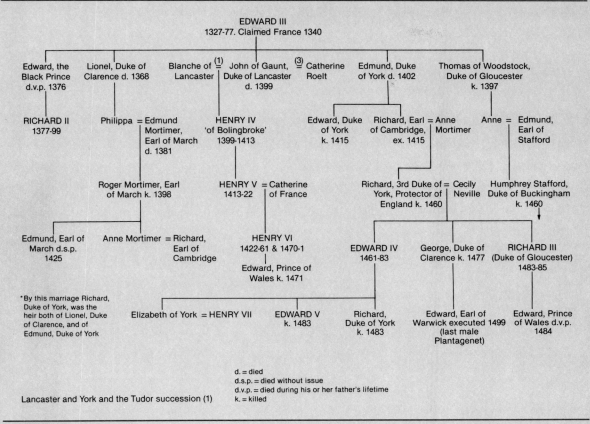

EDWARD III
1327-77. Claimed France 1340

Edward, the Black Prince d.v.p. 1376 — Lionel, Duke of Clarence d. 1368 — Blanche of Lancaster =(1) John of Gaunt, Duke of Lancaster d. 1399 =(3) Catherine Roelt — Edmund, Duke of York d. 1402 — Thomas of Woodstock, Duke of Gloucester k. 1397

RICHARD II 1377-99 — Philippa = Edmund Mortimer, Earl of March d. 1381 — HENRY IV 'of Bolingbroke' 1399-1413 — Edward, Duke of York k. 1415 — Richard, Earl of Cambridge, ex. 1415 = Anne Mortimer — Anne = Edmund, Earl of Stafford

Roger Mortimer, Earl of March k. 1398 — HENRY V = Catherine 1413-22 of France — Richard, 3rd Duke of York, Protector of England k. 1460 = Cecily Neville — Humphrey Stafford, Duke of Buckingham k. 1460

Edmund, Earl of March d.s.p. 1425 — Anne Mortimer = Richard, Earl of Cambridge — HENRY VI 1422-61 & 1470-1 — EDWARD IV 1461-83 — George, Duke of Clarence k. 1477 — RICHARD III (Duke of Gloucester) 1483-85

Edward, Prince of Wales k. 1471

*By this marriage Richard, Duke of York, was the heir both of Lionel, Duke of Clarence, and of Edmund, Duke of York

Elizabeth of York = HENRY VII — EDWARD V k. 1483 — Richard, Duke of York k. 1483 — Edward, Earl of Warwick executed 1499 (last male Plantagenet) — Edward, Prince of Wales d.v.p. 1484

d. = died
d.s.p. = died without issue
d.v.p. = died during his or her father's lifetime
k. = killed

Lancaster and York and the Tudor succession (1)

- Figure 4. The structure of this book is an abstraction of its table of contents, with the same number of levels, but fewer nodes at each level.

- Figure 5. A program structure chart is a hierarchy of modules with the program name at the root.

- Figure 6. In the hierarchy of the pseudo-code of a structured module, the module is the root and each statement is a node. Indentation of the code indicates the level of the node.

- Figure 7. A COBOL program is a hierarchy in which the first levels are the divisions and the sections. The next levels are paragraphs and the text of the program (except in the data division, where level numbers are used to denote further levels of the hierarchy).

- Figure 8. French schoolchildren learn that an essay has a hierarchical structure.

Figure 3 **Partial Table of Contents of This Book**

- Figure 9. In the hierarchy of military ranks, the general is at the root and the soldier is the leaf.

- Figure 10. The order of battle is a hierarchy—the breakdown of the armed forces into armies, divisions, battalions, and so on.

- Figure 11. A corporation's organization chart is a hierarchy similar to that of the order of battle.

WHERE USED IN THE LIFE CYCLE

Hierarchical charts are primarily used in two places in systems development. One is the program structure chart, for example, the VTOC (Visual Table of Contents), which is part of IBM's approach to structured program design (Figure 5); the Warnier chart (Figure 12); or the Jackson chart (Figure 13). The other place is in functional decomposition, an alternative to data flow diagramming

Figure 4 **Structure of This Book**

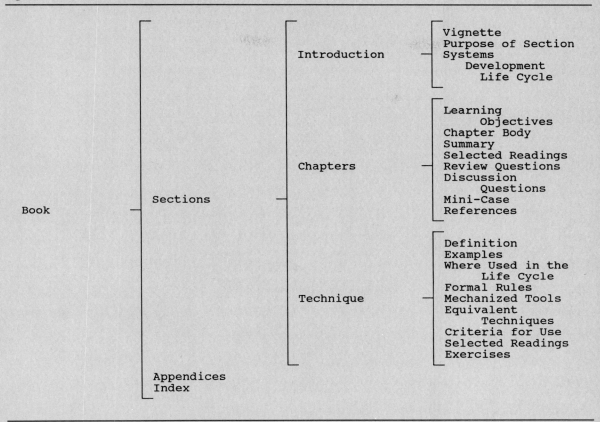

(Figure 14). Function charts are easier to establish than data flow diagrams, but they are a less powerful mode of representation.

Hierarchical techniques are used whenever a top-down approach is appropriate, although the documentation technique may not reflect the approach directly. For instance, data flow diagrams (DFDs) can be leveled. Each subdivision of an entire domain may be detailed on a different page. Further divisions appear on other pages. These pages have an obvious hierarchical relationship that may be clearer in a numbering scheme or in a table of contents (see Figure 15). (The DFD is further explained at the end of Section III.)

Another illustration of the concept of leveling is a world atlas, which contains a world map, maps of each continent, and detailed maps of countries, regions, and even cities.

Figure 5 **Program Structure Chart**

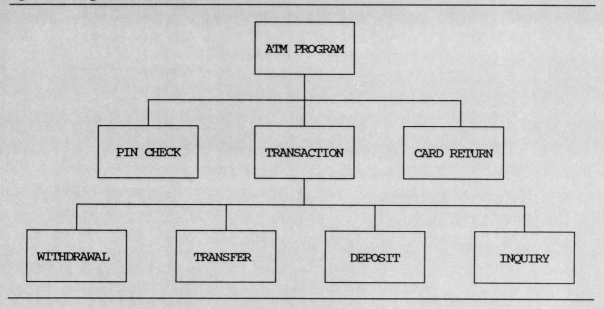

FORMAL RULES

Hierarchies can be depicted in any of three ways—top to bottom, left to right, and bottom to top—according to where the root is. Generally, the bottom-to-top representation is chosen only when a tree effect is aimed for; it is seldom used in business charts.

Top to bottom is the best representation for deep hierarchies with little fan-out, as in Figure 9. Left to right is best for shallow hierarchies with high fan-out, as in Figure 4. The indented representation used for book outlines and pseudo-code are also suitable for high fan-out (Figures 3 and 6).

In a hierarchy chart, only a single type of relationship between nodes should appear. The relationship between military ranks is Ranks-Higher-Than. The relationship between military units in the order of battle is Is-Made-Up-Of. A specialized hierarchy is the taxonomy, or classification, scheme. Here, the nodes are classes or sets of individuals, and the relationship is called Is-A. The most frequently encountered hierarchy relationship in data processing is Is-Made-Up-Of. (The process of documenting Is-Made-Up-Of is called decomposition; hence the name functional decomposition has been given to the process of documenting the hierarchy of functions or processes during the user requirements phase.)

The family tree contains two types of relationships, Has-Mother and Has-Father. These are symmetrical forms of the same, more general relationship. Hierarchies that mix two truly different types of relationships are problematic

Figure 6 **Pseudo-Code**

```
get Card_Stripe_Content
get User_Entered_PIN
if User_Entered_PIN = Card_Stripe_Pin
then
        dountil Trans_Code_Done
                get Trans_Code
                case
                        Trans_Code = Withdrawal
                                perform Withdrawal_Process
                        Trans_Code = Transfer
                                perform Transfer_Process
                        Trans_Code = Deposit
                                perform Deposit_Process
                        Trans_Code = Inquiry
                                perform Inquiry_Process
                endcase
        enddo
        put Return_Card
else
        perform Confiscate_Card
        print Error_Message
endif
```

and should be avoided. For instance, the taxonomy of animals, an Is-A hierarchy, could be mixed with notations that each animal has a head, a body, limbs, and possibly a tail, an Is-Made-Up-Of hierarchy. However, to mix these two independent hierarchies, the Is-A and the Is-Made-Up-Of would be extremely confusing. If mixing is required, it should only occur either at the root or at the leaves, never at intermediate nodes.

Implied relationships of another nature may be incorporated into the hierarchical diagrams. Both the Warnier and Jackson program structure charts generally incorporate the main three programming structures—sequence, iteration, and alternative. Sequence is implied by the physical disposition of the diagrams; alternatives and iterations must be represented by special conventions (Figures 12 and 13).

A hierarchy chart produced by functional decomposition can be read in different sequences. Consider the example in Figure 14. If it is read from the top of the page down (at the lowest level in the hierarchy), it answers the question "What?" If it is read from left to right, it answers the question "How?" If it is read from right to left, it answers the question "Why?"

Often a numbering scheme for the nodes in a hierarchy helps reflect that hierarchy. There are two main types of numbering schemes. The first is suitable

Figure 7 **COBOL Program Structure**

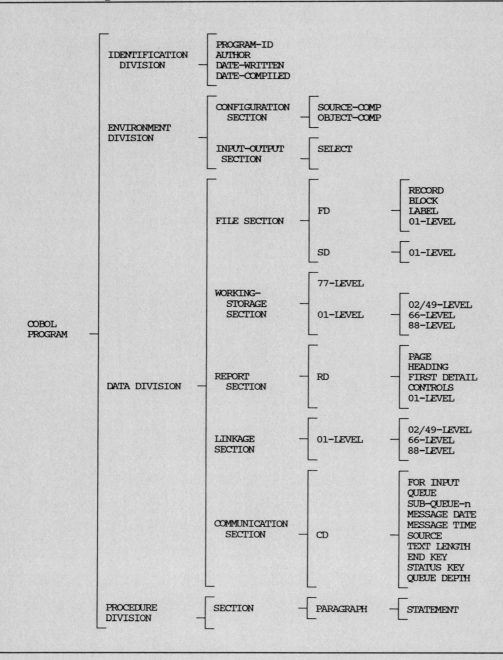

Figure 8 **Structure of an Essay**

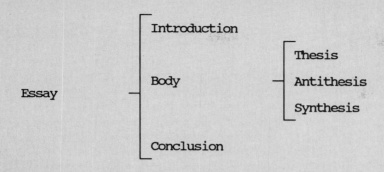

for shallow hierarchies with high fan-out. The root node number is 0, and each of the children of the root is numbered from 1 to n. Then, each entity within node 1 is numbered 1.1 through 1.x. Each additional level adds another level of numbering. For three or four levels, this system is manageable; the most complex number might look like 4.13.2.7. With 10 levels, one of the nodes would awkwardly be numbered 1.1.1.1.1.1.1.1.1.2 and another one 1.1.1.1.1.1.1.1.2.1. This powerful numbering scheme actually contains all the information about the hierarchy; in theory, no diagram is required. (A diagram is still useful since a pictorial representation is a superior way of communicating.)

A useful device, often used in business reports, is to alternate numbers and letters, roman and arabic numerals, upper and lower case, so that a section of a report might be numbered I.A.1.a.iii. This scheme is useful when each level has a different name, such as section, chapter, paragraph, and the number of levels is fairly homogeneous. It is less useful when the levels are not distinguishable and the depth of the hierarchy varies according to the branch.

The second approach, suitable for deep hierarchies with little fan-out, is to number the levels and then number the nodes across the entire level. The number would then combine the two components. This method is less powerful than the previous one, because it does not show exactly where in a hierarchy the numbered node is located. For a deep hierarchy with high fan-out, combinations of the two approaches can often be devised.

Many authors recommend reducing the fan-out at each node to some number bearing a relationship to the magical number seven plus or minus two. This system is especially useful during analysis. One of the purposes of leveling structure charts is to present a manageable amount of information at a time. In addition, a criterion for grouping functions under a more general label is that this label be understandable—logical, if you will—to the reader of the chart. Thus, at a given level functions and their relationships can be discussed without

Figure 9 **United States Army Ranks**

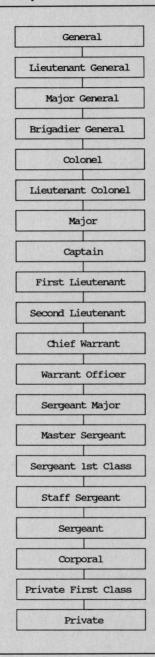

Figure 10 **Order of Battle**

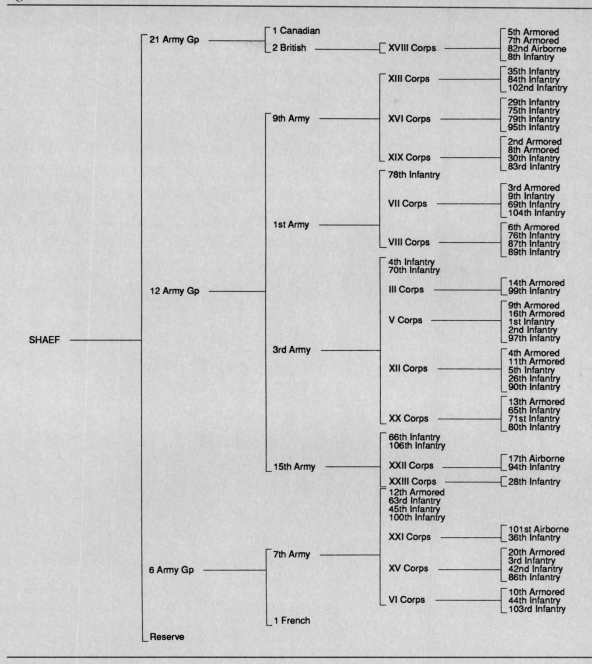

Figure 11   **Organization Chart**

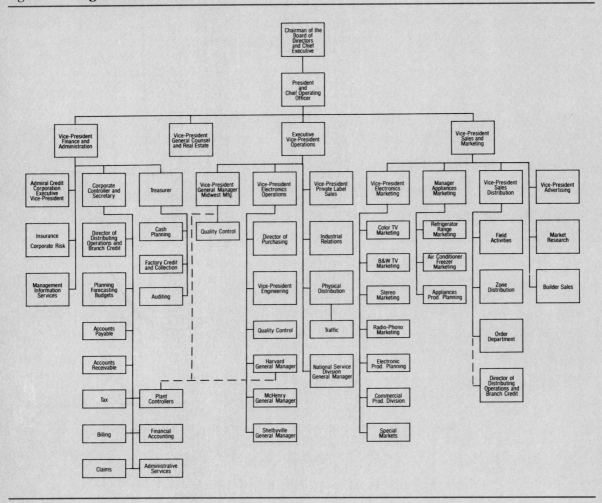

worrying about the details of each. Only if there is uncertainty about how functions documented at a lower level affect higher levels is it necessary to explore the depths of the hierarchy.

Reducing fan-out does not have any adverse effects in the analysis stage because the only purpose of the intermediate levels is to organize and communicate ideas. Reducing fan-out merely for the sake of reducing fan-out in a program structure chart is another matter altogether. If the documentation is of modules that will be developed, called, and maintained as independent entities, the rules of good module design take precedence over the rules of

Figure 12 **Warnier Diagram of a Program Structure**

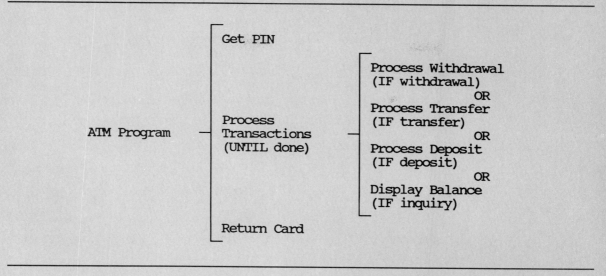

Figure 13 **Jackson Diagram of a Program Structure**

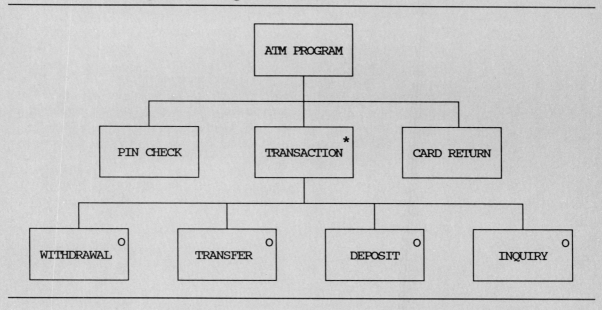

Figure 14 Function Chart

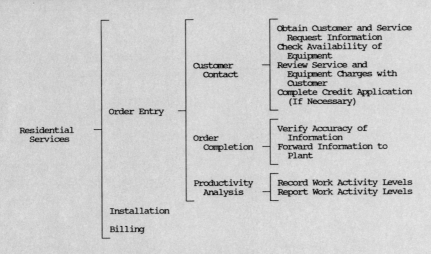

presentation. Arbitrarily increasing the number of levels in a program hierarchy increases execution overhead unnecessarily. More seriously, module cohesion and coupling may suffer. The increase can in turn add to maintenance and destroy reusability of components that could otherwise be standardized.

MECHANIZED TOOLS

Most CASE tools support the creation of hierarchical diagrams in appropriate places of the life cycle, especially program structure charts and equivalent forms such as pseudo-code. In addition, hierarchical data base design tools have facilities for preparing charts representing the data base structure. These specialized tools, however, cannot readily be used to create general-purpose hierarchies.

Some CASE tools incorporate a general-purpose facility that can be used to prepare any hierarchical documentation from function decomposition to report outlines. An outliner such as ThinkTank or Idea Processor is a useful adjunct if the CASE tool does not have a general-purpose hierarchy diagrammer.

CRITERIA FOR USE

The main criterion for using hierarchical charts is that they depict what is really a hierarchy. To force nonhierarchical structures such as entity-relationship diagrams or data flow diagrams into the mold of a hierarchy is counterproductive.

Figure 15 **Leveling of Data Flow Diagrams**

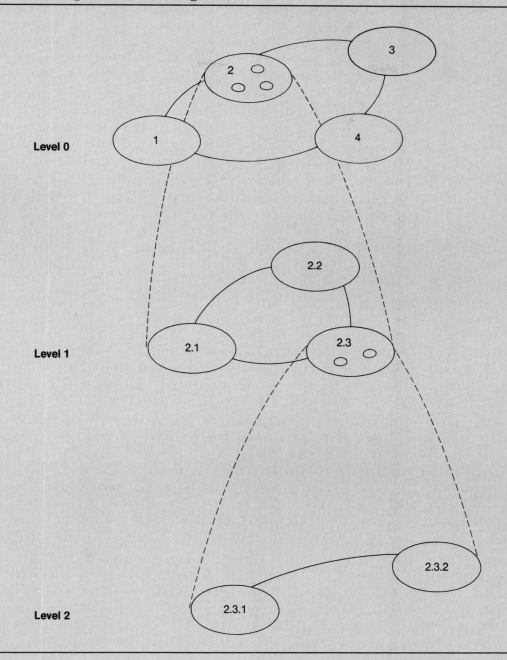

Also, it is not much use to prepare multiple levels in hierarchical diagrams unless the levels contribute additional information or clarity. If each component of the system is independent of the others and can be reviewed with each user separately, then multiple levels should not be created. For instance, if a new code is being created to designate geographical areas and there is no organizational entity that groups these areas, it is useless to create a regional level.

EXERCISES

1. Create a hierarchical chart depicting:

- The organization of the university you are attending.
- The curriculum that will lead to your bachelor's or master's degree.
- The outline of an editorial or in-depth article that you have recently read.
- The Dewey classification scheme.

2. Search other textbooks for examples of hierarchies. Critique their presentation and content. Do they mix different types of concepts and relationships?

3. Examine the geopolitical subdivisions of your state—counties, townships, cities, villages, wards, school districts, and so on. Can these divisions be represented in a single hierarchy? If not, discuss whether it would be opportune to restructure the subdivisions.

4. If you play chess, discuss the requirements for a hierarchy representing chess openings with their main variations. What is the theoretical fan-out at 10 moves on the part of each opponent? What is the practical fan-out? Can the problem be solved by creating catch-all categories? How do you treat openings that transpose into one another?

 5. Imagine that you were to create your own family tree going back 930 years (to William the Conqueror or thereabouts). Assume that each successive generation has its children at the average age of 30. How many forebears would you have in the year 1066? Estimate what percentage of the world's population is represented by your ancestors. What does this prove?

Section II

Systems Planning

There are two possible approaches to planning systems projects. The first approach, covered in Chapter 4, Feasibility Studies, is to evaluate each project in isolation, as the need for it is realized. The second approach is to create a global plan. Systems planners consider in a single study all the applications that the organization is likely to require over the next few years. This approach is covered in Chapter 5, Establishing the Systems Plan, and Chapter 6, IS Resource Planning.

Social Security Administration Revamps Software, Data Structures

The Social Security Administration's director of system modernization requirements spoke of some of the daunting problems his agency has faced in bringing its software up to date, as well as the methods used to launch the improvement, during a speech at the recent Federal Office Systems Expo in Washington, D.C.

Richard Gonzalez said at the session on "Strategic Information Systems Planning and Implementation" that after initial analysis of the agency's long-standing software systems, SSA determined none of the software in place at the time was acceptable. Estimates were that 38 percent of the software could be kept with modifications, but that 62 percent needed replacement.

Gonzalez said the review and documentation of existing software asked what pieces of data exist and how they are used and what functions are performed by which software modules. He said the process is a labor-intensive activity.

He also said although strides have been made, full results are "still not there."

Data content and structure analysis has been another important part of the modernization process. "The critical thing in building information systems is having data that everybody understands," Gonzalez said. He said for the purpose of understanding the 1.2 trillion bytes of data in SSA's systems, "we're trying to separate the data from the functions for which it is used." He said different modules of the old software contain nominally duplicative data items that often don't agree, compounding the modernization problem.

Unvalidated Data

The example he gave was birth dates. He said the modular, non-relational system of data in place virtually guarantees that many people's data will include multiple birth dates, with obviously only one being objectively correct. He said this has come about because of different requirements for proving birth date, depending on whether someone is applying for a Social Security number or applying for benefits, for example.

The lack of a central data repository and validation point has conspired with variant data collection policies to corrupt the data base. Gonzalez said, "When I ask for a birth date, the data base administrator is going to say, 'I have three or four. Which one do you want?'"

This problem has led to a data purification project. "We had to somehow look at the existing data and define a logical equivalent for it. We looked at 5,000 elements and were able to reduce that to 600 logical equivalents," Gonzalez said. He said this would expand, but the data analysis requires as few logical equivalents as possible initially. Each logical equivalent could point to up to 10 individual elements. An example would be a client's mailing address. If this is in five old files, it's at least five elements and probably more. The paring down effort would make it one unit, possibly with subcomponents for its identifiable parts.

Gonzalez said this smorgasbord of data is going to be a huge problem.

Gonzalez said the magnitude of the project, encompassing a system tracking 350 million Social Security numbers, past and present, with the attendant payroll tax records and claims, and using 12 million lines of code and 1,500 processing locations to do it, required a proven methodology for planning and mapping requirements. He said the agency chose IBM Corp.'s Business Systems Planning methodology, because it is comprehensive and people in the industry have experience with it.

Gonzalez and SSA also got references. "We asked the Postal Service. They said, 'Yes, it's good.'"

He said the methodology, as its name suggests, relies on defining the business of the agency and the information needed to carry out the business of the agency. The major steps, according to Gonzalez, include analysis of the business and the data used; development of an application architecture, which outlines the applications that will be applied to the functions of the organization's basic business; and the assessment of current systems.

Interdisciplinary Teams

A core tactic in the BSP process is forming an interdisciplinary team of users and systems personnel "as senior as you can get," said Gonzalez. IBM recommends 10 on the team, but SSA went with 25 to ensure all the major players would be included, helping to ensure the success of the plan.

An advantage SSA found was that "we are centralized in terms of our management and software development," Gonzalez said. He said the constant coordination of diverse interests takes a great deal of organizational perseverance. He added, "I am now convinced planning is not so much planning as doing."

The most difficult part of keeping a large-scale planning process on track in a federal agency is the broad consensus required, and understanding that managers must maintain, even though it doesn't yield short-term, immediate payoffs, he said.[1]

PURPOSE OF SECTION

This section describes how systems development projects come into being and how organizations try to ensure that the right project gets done at the right time.

When most systems were developed to automate some existing manual system, systems planning was done system by system. The cost of each system was justified based on its own merit. Its scope was generally reduced to a single department, and the hardware and software architecture was chosen without regard to existing technical environments in other departments. The initial phase of systems development was the feasibility study. It was designed to provide an overview of costs and benefits for a single system. If there was a greater plan, it was usually reduced to a sequence of development projects based on the ranking of the anticipated return on investment of the various projects.

When more integrated systems became possible with the advent of hardware and systems software that could be shared among several applications, large centralized data processing equipment became the rule, dictated by the economies of scale. It was then realized that additional benefits could be drawn from sharing the technical architecture, the systems software platforms (such as access methods, data base management systems, on-line transaction monitors), and above all the data.

In nonintegrated systems, the same data is partly duplicated in many systems. The source of the data, although theoretically the same, is viewed as distinct for each application; therefore, data collection is duplicated. As a result, the integrity of the data—its consistency in all the different places where it appears—is difficult or impossible to ensure.

These problems gave rise to more sophisticated methods of systems planning. Most of the methods in use today emphasize two aspects of overall planning: planning for the sharing of data across applications and organizational units (Chapter 5), and planning for the sharing of technology, both hardware and software (Chapter 6).

KEY TASKS AND DELIVERABLES

The purpose of systems planning is twofold: to identify and assign priorities to development projects to be undertaken in the next few years and to make sure that the resources to implement the plan are available. Systems planning, therefore, typically includes the following steps.

The first step, which is the responsibility of IS management and executive management, is to ensure that the systems plan will support the strategy of the business. Unless a well-understood business plan already exists, the planning team establishes lines of communication and defines the criteria for deciding on the systems to develop first.

Then, the planners study the business processes, the information needs of management, and the data required to support the processes and fulfill the needs. As a result of this study, high-level functions are grouped into systems according to data usage and the ideal applications of the organization are identified.

The current status of existing applications must be assessed to identify how close they are to this ideal. Also, the costs, benefits, and risks associated with enhancing or redeveloping the applications to make them closer to the ideal are weighed. This analysis forms the basis for the application development plan, which identifies projects, development resources, migration strategies, and the preferred sequence of development. The deliverable from this stage is an application and data plan.

Next, the resources required to develop and operate the applications are analyzed. This includes personnel, development tools (such as CASE, application generators, and data dictionary), and the operating environment (including the data base management system, the transaction processing monitor, communications software, network equipment, and central and departmental hardware). The deliverable from this stage is the resource plan (or the technology plan).

Finally, required compromises are made among the speed of development, the level of ambition of the projects, and the resources that are likely to be available. The resulting deliverable is a time line for project development and for the acquisition of resources: hiring and training personnel, acquiring software, and procuring hardware.

In many corporations, the systems plan is much less formal. In practically every IS department, the IS manager has a fairly explicit strategy. Increasingly, this strategy is in tune with the strategic thinking of top management. However, the strategy is rarely formally documented. One of the main drawbacks of this lack of documentation is that neither users nor top management can know precisely what the IS department will achieve over the next few years.

When there is no formal plan or when an unanticipated application is suddenly needed, the project must be reviewed before starting the development cycle. The review defines the project's scope, the order of magnitude of benefits that can be expected, and the resources that management is willing to commit to achieve these expectations. The steps to perform such a feasibility study, as it is called, are much the same as for the systems plan, but the scope of the study is reduced to a single project.

At this point, the requirements, features, and functions do not determine the cost. It is rather the other way around; only those functions and features that can be implemented within the overall budget of the project will be incorporated into the system, which may therefore fall somewhat short of the description in the feasibility study or the systems plan. At such an early stage, the development cost cannot be predicted accurately based on the functions of the system. Management generally prefers to set a budget constraint and leave some uncertainty about the functions and features of the system, rather than decide on all the functions and be uncertain about the cost.

Reference

1. "SSA Revamps Software, Data Structures," *Government Computer News* (April 10, 1987): pp. 65–67.

Chapter 4

Feasibility Studies

Chapter 4 first describes the objectives of a feasibility study and gives examples of situations where feasibility studies are appropriate. It then describes the criteria for deciding whether a project is feasible and explains how to evaluate whether those criteria are met. A detailed section on cost/benefit analysis, the most important criterion of feasibility, concludes the chapter.

Learning Objectives

- Understand how management uses the feasibility study early in the systems development life cycle for a quick evaluation of the potential costs and benefits of a proposed system.

- Become aware that the feasibility study is particularly appropriate for organizations that consider projects one at a time and have not yet adopted an enterprise-wide approach to systems planning.

- Describe four common reasons for initiating a feasibility study and understand the specific approach to be followed for conducting each type of study.

- Identify five types of feasibility that should be addressed in a feasibility study.

- Understand those aspects of a cost/benefit analysis important to management at the feasibility study stage.

OBJECTIVES AND ORGANIZATION OF A FEASIBILITY STUDY

The feasibility study is a quick review of a proposed information systems development project. The study determines whether it makes sense to allocate resources to a project, whether the project is worth doing but should be postponed, or whether the project is worth doing at all. A feasibility study refines a system's concept to the point where the benefits to the organization are more clearly understood. In addition, the study predicts the costs associated with proceeding with the project's development and installation with a degree of accuracy appropriate for this stage of the life cycle, i.e., well enough for management to decide whether continuing is worthwhile, and if so, when.

To understand how a feasibility study is conducted, you should know when it is done, by whom, and with what result.

One common characteristic of the life-cycle methodologies used in the design and installation of information systems is the *phased approach* concept described in Section I. In this approach, the steps necessary to design and install an information system are divided into natural phases, with management approval of the end products of one phase being required before continuing on to the next phase. Gildersleeve calls this approach the *creeping commitment* approach.[1] Management commits resources to a large information systems project little by little, as the project team presents evidence at the conclusion of each phase in the life cycle that the project continues to be viable.

A feasibility study is the first phase of a project to which resources are committed. It occurs at the beginning of the life cycle. Figure 4–1 shows how the feasibility study fits in with the generic life cycle introduced in Section I. It generally substitutes for the systems planning phase; in some cases, when a project was omitted from the systems plan or was studied in insufficient detail, a separate feasibility study may be done in addition to what was done during the preparation of the systems plan.

The feasibility study is best prepared by a project team consisting of users and IS personnel. In practice, however, one group may have the primary responsibility for the study.

The end product of a feasibility study is a report that outlines the concept of a proposed system with sufficient clarity that a distinction can be made between the proposed system and the present system. Costs and benefits of moving to the proposed system are presented in enough detail to permit management to decide whether it is worthwhile to move on to the analysis and design phases. Typically, a management group making the decision is described as an executive steering committee. However, the decision could be, and often is, made by other types of management groups or by individual executives.

When systems planning is performed in an organization, as will be discussed in Chapter 5, steps similar to those performed in a feasibility study are performed for projects identified as part of the planning process. The difference is that in systems planning the team takes an overall view of the organization's requirements. In contrast, those who perform a feasibility study view one project at a time.

EXAMPLES OF THE USE OF FEASIBILITY STUDIES

IS departments usually have more requests for new applications and maintenance of existing systems than they can handle immediately. The list of approved projects waiting for IS resources to become available is called the application development backlog. Some observers estimate the extent of the application

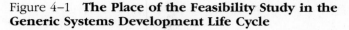

Figure 4–1 **The Place of the Feasibility Study in the
Generic Systems Development Life Cycle**

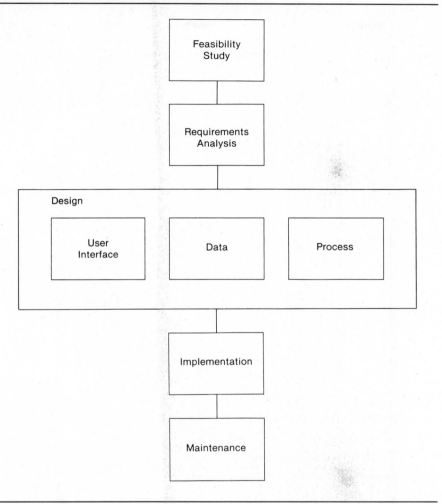

development backlog in a typical large IS department at two to four years with
an additional "invisible backlog" on top of that.[2] The invisible backlog is work
that would be requested by users if the visible backlog were not so high. The
size of the application development backlog is a major reason for the rise in
popularity of end-user computing, CASE technology, code generators, and other
tools to shorten the time required to implement systems.

An organization with a large application development backlog and with no
formal long-range systems planning approach might use feasibility studies to

Figure 4–2 **The Feasibility Study Approach for Selecting and Assigning Priorities to Projects**

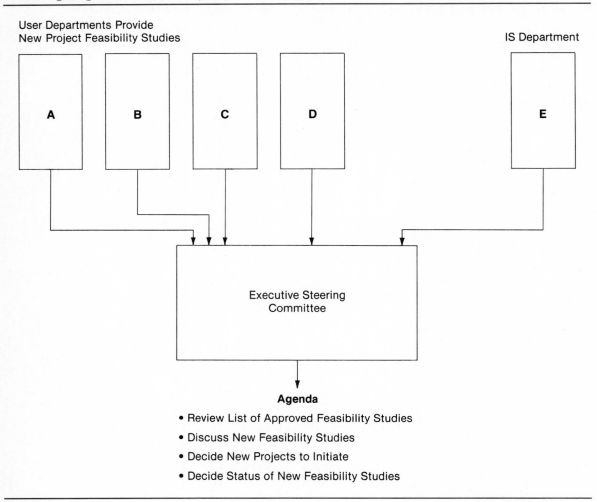

User Departments Provide
New Project Feasibility Studies

IS Department

A   B   C   D

E

Executive Steering
Committee

Agenda

• Review List of Approved Feasibility Studies

• Discuss New Feasibility Studies

• Decide New Projects to Initiate

• Decide Status of New Feasibility Studies

select and assign priorities to projects in a manner similar to that illustrated in Figure 4–2. The key components in the organization are user departments, the IS department, and an executive steering committee, made up of the vice-presidents to whom the heads of each user department report. The executive steering committee meets with the director of information systems once a month to review the list of approved feasibility studies for projects in the backlog, to discuss new feasibility studies that have been received in the current month, and to decide (after considering availability of IS resources) which projects should be initiated in the current month. The executive steering committee, after discussing a new feasibility study, either approves it for placement in the backlog queue in its proper priority sequence or decides that it is currently not worthy of further consideration.

Ideas for new projects (or for major enhancements to existing applications) are almost always initiated by a user department in response to a business problem or opportunity. If a department head thinks that a suggestion from a department member has merit, a feasibility study will be prepared and submitted to the executive steering committee at its next monthly meeting.

One of the shortcomings of a process such as the one illustrated in Figure 4–2 is that the executive steering committee considers only projects for which feasibility studies have been prepared. If a project is not suggested by a user department, it may never be considered by the executive steering committee. Another issue is that politically powerful members of the executive steering committee may find that they are able to get projects approved for their departments even though other projects may be more beneficial to the organization. (In some cases, the idea for a project comes from a member of the executive steering committee, who then asks someone in one of his or her departments to prepare the necessary feasibility study.) Organizations following this approach often fail to communicate organizational objectives very far down in the organization. Therefore, while members of the executive steering committee may have a good understanding of the objectives, other members of the organization who initiate most of the ideas do not. These members cannot be expected to suggest projects that clearly support organizational objectives.

Even though the preceding process for determining project priorities has shortcomings, it is still often encountered in practice today. In such environments, the preparation of feasibility studies is a generally accepted method for reviewing projects that arise one at a time rather than as the result of an overall systems planning process. Feasibility studies are useful tools for management decision making in such environments.

TYPES OF FEASIBILITY

Five types of feasibility should be evaluated in a feasibility study, according to Davis and Olson:

- Technical
- Operational
- Economic
- Schedule
- Motivational[3]

Most authors only consider the first three, but all five are important.

Technical Feasibility

Technical feasibility addresses the issue of whether the technical aspects of a proposal are practical and achievable. Usually this feasibility is more of an issue if the technology involved in the proposal is generally new or new to the organization. For example, suppose an organization is considering the installation of a computer integrated manufacturing system that depends for part of its data input on quality control readings from automatic sensors. The feasibility study would have to present evidence that the sensor technology was sufficiently accurate and reliable to use as a component of the proposed system. Some of the ways this evidence could be presented include representations (and guarantees, if possible) by the sensor equipment manufacturer, site visits to other installations using the same equipment for similar applications, and pilot tests in the environment where the equipment will be expected to operate.

In addition, technical feasibility is lacking when problems have no known algorithms, or when the algorithm is not efficient enough. Some scheduling problems and many problems currently being researched in artificial intelligence have this characteristic. For example, unconstrained natural language cannot be used to communicate between a user and a program.

Operational Feasibility

Operational feasibility involves whether the system concept is appropriate for the operating environment for which it is proposed. For example, a feasibility study for a system to support student registration by touch-tone telephone would have to show the university executive steering committee some evidence that the system was operationally feasible. The committee might question not only whether the system would be accepted by the students (almost certainly), but also whether security features could be built into the system to deter mischievous tampering by creative minds. Without such controls, the system would probably fail in actual operation.

Economic Feasibility

Economic feasibility addresses the issue of whether the resources needed to develop and operate the proposed system can be justified by the returns from installing it. A section on costs and benefits is included as an important part of the feasibility study. This inclusion, however, does not imply that all systems should have direct cost savings as a part of their justification. Whether the potential benefits from a system's installation justify its cost is a matter of management judgment. Increasingly, economic feasibility has to be determined by intangible elements such as an increase in the quality of managerial decision making or an increase in customer satisfaction. Placing a value on these intangible elements is difficult. In these cases, decisions to proceed with a system's installation may be based on management's opinion that the system is in the long-term interest of the organization, regardless of immediate payback. Cost/benefit analyses will be covered in more detail later in this chapter.

Schedule Feasibility

The executive steering committee will want assurance that the schedule for developing and installing the proposed system is realistic and reasonable in the light of the business requirements. There are certain times of the year that are natural conversion dates. For example, financial planning and reporting systems are usually scheduled to convert at the beginning of the organization's fiscal year. A feasibility study normally does not identify a specific changeover date because the installation effort cannot be identified precisely until after analysis and design have been completed. The feasibility study should give a realistic estimate of the time required to perform the next phase and should present a range of possible conversion dates with a target date to be established when the necessary analysis and design tasks are completed. The executive steering committee will expect to see the target dates supported.

Motivational Feasibility

Finally, the feasibility study should assure the executive steering committee that the users want the proposed system badly enough that they are willing to participate in a development project and undergo disruption in their daily routines to absorb the changes introduced by the new system. The best evidence of user support is active user participation in preparing the feasibility study.

APPROACHES TO DETERMINING PROJECT FEASIBILITY

Projects are commonly instigated for one of four reasons:

- To solve operational problems
- To replace existing technology
- To mechanize a manual system
- To create a new activity

The preparation of the feasibility study will often vary according to the reason it is undertaken. But all studies have in common the need for a precise definition of the business problem being addressed. Without this definition, management cannot evaluate whether the proposed project adequately addresses the problem. A useful technique is to contrast the current operations with the proposed operations to convey their differences. How this contrast might be portrayed is exemplified in the case of a billing system in Figure 4–3.

Solving Operational Problems

With the passage of time, operational problems often occur in even the best of systems. Such problems are typically associated with costs, volumes, speed, or errors, individually or in combination. For example, many hospitals have

Figure 4–3 **Example of Comparison between Current and
Proposed System for a Hospital Billing System**

Problems: **Accounts receivable balances are too high relative to the level of billing activity.
Uncollectible accounts receivable are too high.**

Current Operations	Proposed Operations
1. Four days between patient discharge and bill preparation.	1. One day between patient discharge and bill preparation.
2. Maximum of 3 percent charge error rate.	2. Maximum of 1 percent charge error rate.
3. No reports generated for management follow-up activity on delinquent accounts.	3. Two reports prepared: Aged analysis of open patient accounts. Adjustments to patient account.

problems with their patient billing and accounts receivable systems. The accounts receivable balances are too high and, consequently, an unacceptably large number of receivables must be written off as uncollectible. The problem can usually be traced to several causes: billing systems that take too long to prepare bills once a patient is discharged, charge collection systems that are inaccurate, and accounts receivable systems that do not provide the necessary management reports for an effective follow-up on delinquent accounts. A proposal to solve these problems should specifically identify the problems to be addressed by the proposed changes and should describe in detail the way the solutions will eliminate the problems. A proposal to solve the hospitals' problem, for example, might show how the number of days between patient discharge and preparation of the bill could be reduced by three days and how controls could be established to reduce the number of errors in charges by a specified percentage. Also, the proposal might include sample accounts receivable reports containing information needed for follow-up of delinquent accounts. Other examples of operational problems that feasibility studies might address are shown in Figure 4–4.

Replacing Existing Technology

Existing systems have to be replaced from time to time. Systems grow old and have been changed so often that proper maintenance becomes almost impossible. For example, an inventory control system installed in the early 1960s contains the technology available at that time. If it was installed on a large IBM mainframe, the computer was probably a second-generation computer, and the language an assembly-level programming language or perhaps an early version of COBOL. Vendor support for both hardware and software is likely to have been long since withdrawn. The expertise that the IS department once had in this technology has almost certainly disappeared, although both the machine and the programs may continue to function. Machines that were technologically outdated more than 20 years ago may still be operational today. A system's functions

Figure 4–4 **Examples of Operational Problems that May Warrant a Feasibility Study**

Over 25 percent return rate on mail order catalogs.
Over 30 days wait on back orders.
Excess inventory to store.
Inventory shortage on customer requests.
Long lines for banking service, student registration, fast-food service, grocery checkout lanes.
High error rate in entering customer orders.
Excessive time between requisition and receipt of raw materials.

may have been well thought out and advanced for its time, with meaningful user involvement in setting the system's requirements. In a situation such as this, the user may be satisfied with the system as it was originally designed, perhaps with minor enhancements made during the intervening years.

A feasibility study to replace the existing technology with current technology must make the change clear to the user. The study must show that the technology will be changed to bring the system up to date so that it can be more easily maintained and perhaps operate more efficiently. The user may be unaware that the technology has changed because the existing system continues to function as it always has. In this situation, the existing system should, in fact, be moved to the current technology even if the user is satisfied. The study should compare the out-of-date system with state-of-the-art systems to make sure that the user understands that technological changes or upgrades have occurred. In addition, a feasibility study to replace existing technology should point out the shortest and simplest way to move to the new technology with the least disruption of user department operations. Examples of systems that might need replacing are shown in Figure 4–5.

Mechanizing a Manual System

Feasibility studies that consider the mechanization of a manual system often involve dealing with users who have little experience with information technology. Some users may need to be educated on the technology so that they can contribute to the study. And personnel at all levels may need their fears about the effect of a change put to rest (see some of the techniques discussed in Chapter 2). For this type of feasibility study, acquiring a good understanding of the current system is more important than in the two previous types. Because management will be asked to decide whether to approve the mechanized system or to stay with the present manual system, a comparison of the alternative modes of operation is the basis for the decision. In the two previous types of studies, the existing system is likely to be already understood, because it is already mechanized. Where the present system is a manual system, system characteristics are often not well documented. They must be analyzed by the team

Figure 4–5 **Examples of Systems where Existing Technology May Need Replacement without Change in User Function**

General ledger
Billing
Accounts receivable
Accounts payable
Payroll
Order entry
Inventory control

performing the feasibility study. At this time, the team needs to gather only those details necessary to compare the present system with alternative proposed systems for management's understanding. Because one of management's options is to decide to stay with the present system, knowledge of the present system is required for an informed decision.

With the status of technology today, most large companies have long since mechanized their routine transaction processing systems such as payroll, order entry, billing, and accounts receivable. As illustrated in Figure 4–5, it is just such systems that are the most likely candidates for replacement with current technologies. As computer processing capability has dropped in price, the technology is now practical for very small companies. Physicians' offices now have mechanized patient records, attorneys have systems for time accounting and client billing, and small retailers or distributors have inventory control systems.

Other manual applications being mechanized for the first time are systems to support high levels of management, often in very personal ways and on a one-on-one basis. Examples of such systems are an expert system that aids physicians in forming diagnoses, a decision support system that helps an associate dean schedule classes, and an executive information system that is tailored to the specific needs of top management and often contains both internal and external information. Additional examples of systems for high-level users are illustrated in Figure 4–6.

Creating a New Activity

New activities are created when a business is just beginning or when an activity is added to an existing organization. Feasibility studies analyzing a proposed new activity typically require more creativity by the project team than most of the previous examples because no present system exists that can be used as a basis for developing the proposed system. Creative solutions are also important in the other situations; however, creative solutions are even more important when a new activity must be planned, because they can help an organization meet its goals. As a result, the organization is more likely to accept the solution. In

Figure 4–6 **Examples of New Activities that May Require a Feasibility Study**

> Debt restructuring
> Financial planning
> Cash-flow management
> Pricing strategy analysis
> Group decision support
> Revenue optimization

addition, a creative solution will take longer to become obsolete. Thus, the organization will get a better return on its investment in the system's development.

There are many examples of creative new systems that have brought organizations a competitive advantage. One example of such a system is the Care Monitoring System developed at Providence Hospital in Southfield, Michigan, over ten years ago.[4] At that time, hospitals were not overly concerned about cost control because they were being reimbursed on what was, in effect, a cost-plus basis. Providence Hospital officials, however, were able to foresee the time when reimbursement policies would be changed to put more pressure on hospitals to control costs. The officials also realized that the people most responsible for cost control were the physicians, not the heads of hospital departments such as nursing, laboratory, and radiology. Physicians admitted patients, ordered tests and procedures, performed operations, ordered medications, and decided on the times for discharging patients. Yet, even though physicians were becoming aware of the rising public concern over increases in health care costs, they were receiving no feedback on the cost consequences of their actions. The Care Monitoring System changed that by gathering cost information and presenting it to physicians in a series of reports that gave them the information they needed to seek out ways to reduce costs without compromising the quality of care delivered to patients. A technique adapted from manufacturing was used to determine costs according to a particular patient diagnosis. Historical information on the costs of treating patients with specific diagnoses proved to be very useful, especially after the federal government changed the method for reimbursing hospitals for Medicare and Medicaid patients. Hospitals without similar systems (the majority by far) had to find a way to generate similar information. Otherwise, they would be handicapped by the lack of it. Additional examples of systems created to support new activities are shown in Figure 4–7.

Project teams conducting feasibility studies for creating a new activity often benefit from visiting other organizations that have recently added a similar activity. In other words, the team learns from the experiences of early users. For example, Providence Hospital found itself entertaining visitors from hospitals around the United States. The visitors had heard of Providence's system and were interested in seeing it firsthand and talking to the physicians, administra-

Figure 4–7 **Examples of Systems Created To Support New Activities**

Hotel Reservations   Using a system developed by Eloquent Systems Corporation of Manchester, New Hampshire, the Balsams Grand Resort Hotel at Dixville, New Hampshire, has added new functions to its hotel reservation systems. When a guest calls for a reservation, the system will match available rooms with guest preferences. Much of this is done automatically by the system, which has information on up to a million customers stored on optical disk. Other systems capabilities include (1) a faster reservation process, (2) special arrangements for guest activities, (3) automatic generation of confirmation, correspondence, and management reports, (4) reduction of occupancy gaps, and (5) easy modification of rates, hotel policies, and guidelines.

Flight Scheduling   United Airlines and Texas Instruments have developed the Gate Assignment Display System (GADS), a knowledge-based system to handle irregularities in the flight scheduling process. Gate scheduling may become a quagmire when the weather or other operational problems require schedule adjustments affecting hundreds of aircraft using a limited number of gates. GADS facilitates and optimizes United's scheduling process for Chicago O'Hare and Denver Stapleton airports. GADS is also used to aid in scheduling aircraft maintenance, enabling the airline to effectively reduce the aircraft downtime for maintenance, thereby allowing more aircraft to be scheduled for revenue-producing flights.

tors, and IS professionals involved in its development. Project teams can also benefit from industry symposia, consultants, software vendors, equipment manufacturers, and literature searches that can uncover examples of state-of-the-art systems.

COST/BENEFIT ANALYSIS

The purpose of the cost/benefit analysis in a feasibility study is to summarize the relevant costs and benefits of the proposed project in sufficient detail to permit management to decide whether to proceed any further with the project.

In the feasibility study, many of the estimates are probable ranges of costs and benefits. Management should not expect precise estimates at this stage because there is still much that is not yet known about the costs of installing and operating a proposed system. Each additional phase of the development allows a more accurate cost/benefit analysis as more detail is gathered. Estimating has been likened to "trying to guess what the core of an onion will look like as you peel off its outside layers."[5]

The general format of a cost/benefit analysis is illustrated in Figure 4–8. The following information is needed before the analysis can be prepared:

- An estimate of the cost of operating the current system.
- An estimate of the cost of operating the proposed system.
- An estimate of costs for subsequent phases of the development project.
- A description of intangible benefits.

Figure 4–8 **Typical Cost/Benefit Analysis Worksheet**

```
PERSONNEL                    SUBURBAN PUMPS                    CD-20
SKILLS SYSTEM                                                 CBSUM
                         COST/BENEFIT SUMMARY

┌─────────────────────────────────────────────────────────────────────┐
│ PREPARED BY:  RON TURNER    DATE:  27NOV88    VERSION:  1    PAGE 1   │
│ APPROVED BY:  JOE DAVIS     DATE:  05DEC88    STATUS :  F            │
└─────────────────────────────────────────────────────────────────────┘

                                                      Amount
                                                      ------
        1.   One-time Change Costs
        -------------------------------------------------

                Personnel expense -

                    50 workdays analyst               6,000
                   100 workdays programmer            8,000
                    30 workdays clerical                960

                Machine hours cost -

                    20 CPU hours                      12,250

                Equipment and supplies -

                    Paper and office supplies           100
                 25 reels magnetic tape                 625
                                                    ----------
                         Subtotal                    27,935
                                                    ----------


        2.   Recurring Costs and Savings
        -------------------------------------------------

                Clerical savings - Annual -

                    25 workdays/month                (9,600)

                Supplies                               (100)


        3.   Intangible Costs and Benefits
        -------------------------------------------------

                Information available earlier (not
                    quantified)                          (0)

                                                    ----------
                         Subtotal                    (9,700)
                                                    ----------

        4.   Payback Period
        -------------------------------------------------

            27,935/9,700 = less than 3 years
```

- A basis for estimating how the above costs and benefits will change over the next few years (e.g., assumptions regarding volume increases, inflation).
- An identification of the risks associated with either doing or not doing the project.

Different organizational units should assume primary responsibility for the various components of the cost/benefit analysis under the overall coordination of the project team.

Economic analyses prepared at the completion of the design phase are much more comprehensive than this analysis though the format is essentially the same (see Chapter 17). The following characteristics apply to feasibility study cost/benefit analyses:

- State the cost/benefit analysis conservatively.

    In subsequent stages of the systems development life cycle, experience has shown that costs of installing and operating a new system tend to exceed estimates made in feasibility studies while realized benefits tend to be less than what was estimated. The project team should present ranges of probable costs and benefits; however, if an error is made, it should err on the side of conservatism. An effective technique is to assign the user responsibility for estimating savings and benefits from installation of the new system and be sure this responsibility is noted in the feasibility study document. When users are made aware that they will subsequently be held accountable for achieving savings or benefits, they will tend towards conservative estimates. The IS department should be responsible for estimating the cost of developing the system and of the information technology to be used when the system is in operation.

    One risk of trying to be conservative in a cost/benefit analysis is that users and IS departments may be so overconservative that nothing gets done. The executive steering committee must make sure this does not occur. Periodic reviews by qualified outsiders, for example, will give the steering committee assurance that internal estimates are in line.

- Make assumptions for financial projections.

    Feasibility study cost/benefit analyses require that certain assumptions be made about the behavior of future costs and/or activities. Assumptions can be made about inflation, interest rates, growth projections, volume increases, wage increases, and the like. In most organizations, similar assumptions are made as a routine matter in medium- and long-range financial plans. The project team's best strategy is to use the same assumptions in its cost/benefit analysis as are used in an organization's financial plans. Thus, assumptions in the cost/benefit analysis will be consistent with the other financial projections that members of the executive steering committee review when they carry out their other responsibilities.

- Assess the elements of project risk.

    Some proposed projects are inherently more risky than others. Risky projects are likely to exceed their estimated costs of installation and operation; they may take much longer to install than predicted; the technology suggested may not be appropriate or work effectively; users may not accept the system once it has been installed; and business operations may be disrupted. Such a list could go on and on, and unfortunately, many real-life examples could be furnished for each item on the list. Often, IS professionals in particular are aware that a proposed project carries a higher-than-normal degree of risk, but they have not found a way to convey that awareness to the executive steering committee at the feasibility study stage.

F. Warren McFarlan developed a framework for assessing project risk that consists of three components:

1. The familiarity of the company with the technology proposed for the project.

2. The project "structure," i.e., the extent to which user requirements are known at the outset.

3. The size of the project relative to those normally undertaken.[6]

Figure 4–9 illustrates the way these three factors can interrelate to create an overall project risk profile. McFarlan also discusses techniques for managing projects with differing risk profiles. Project risk is an important concept to consider in the feasibility study not only because it can be an important element in evaluating whether to proceed, but also because it puts the executive steering committee on notice that this particular project will require close scrutiny as it goes forward.

The concept of project risk also applies to a group of projects. As pointed out by McFarlan, a group of systems development projects can be examined for the collective risk when all the projects are considered at one time.

Different companies will respond differently to risk. For example, companies in the strategic or turnaround quadrants of the strategic grid would be expected to assume a greater degree of risk than companies in the factory or support quadrants. If a company places itself in the strategic quadrant and yet has a low risk profile, the executive steering committee would do well to inquire why. The inquiry may be just the catalyst needed to convince the company that it is time to undertake a systematic approach to systems planning, the subject of the next two chapters.

Summary

A feasibility study, a quick assessment of a proposed system, is performed as one of the first steps in the systems development life cycle, particularly for an organization that does not use a systematic approach to systems planning. The study's purpose is to determine whether a project should be pursued or rejected.

Figure 4–9 **Project Implementation Risk**

	High Structure	Low Structure
Low Company-Relative Technology	Large size– low risk	Large size– low risk (very susceptible to mismanagement)
	Small size– very low risk	Small size– very low risk (very susceptible to mismanagement)
High Company-Relative Technology	Large size– medium risk	Large size– very high risk
	Small size– medium-low risk	Small size– high risk

Source: McFarlan, F. Warren, "Portfolio Approach to Information Systems." *Harvard Business Review* (September–October 1981): pp. 142–150.

A feasibility study is normally performed by a project team consisting of users and IS professionals. The team's findings are put into a report that is presented to an executive steering committee or its equivalent so that a decision can be made.

Five types of feasibility should be evaluated: technical, operational, economic, schedule, and motivational.

The focus of a feasibility study can vary depending on the reason the study is performed. Feasibility studies are most frequently done for the following four reasons:

- To solve operational problems
- To replace existing technology
- To mechanize a manual activity
- To create a new activity

The cost/benefit analysis section of a feasibility study should contain a conservative treatment of costs and benefits, should include assumptions consistent with those typically used for making projections, and should assess project risk.

Selected Readings

Biggs, Charles L., Birks, Evan G., and Atkins, William. *Managing the Systems Development Process*. Englewood Cliffs, New Jersey: Prentice-Hall, 1980.

Written by practicing information systems consultants, this book is a practical guide to the tasks performed in each phase of the systems development life cycle. Deliverables expected at the end of each phase are described, and many sample forms used in documenting a systems project, including a feasibility study, are illustrated.

Davis, Gordon B., and Olson, Margrethe H. *Management Information Systems: Conceptual Foundations, Structure and Development*, 2d ed. New York: McGraw-Hill, 1985.

This book is one of the most complete and influential textbooks on management information systems. It contains a concise description of feasibility studies. It correctly adds schedule and motivational feasibility to the more commonly listed factors of technical, operational, and economic feasibility.

Gildersleeve, Thomas R. *Successful Data Processing Systems Analysis*, 2d ed. Englewood Cliffs, New Jersey: Prentice-Hall, 1985.

This book contains a lengthy chapter on cost/benefit analysis from an investment standpoint. For example, it covers such concepts as differential costs, payback, cash flow, and net present value as applied to a feasibility study. It also discusses techniques systems analysts can use to place a value on intangible benefits.

McFarlan, F. Warren, "Portfolio Approach to Information Systems." *Harvard Business Review* (September-October 1981): 142–150.

This article notes that traditional feasibility studies fail to consider certain risks that are usually present in computer systems projects. It discusses the consequences of risk as well as the dimensions influencing risk. It suggests that companies develop an aggregate risk profile of their systems development projects.

Review Questions

1. What factors may prompt an organization to use feasibility studies for selecting and assigning priorities to projects?

2. Describe the shortcomings of the executive steering committee approach to IS project selection.

3. Explain the five types of feasibility that should be evaluated in a feasibility study.

4. Provide examples of how the following organizational problems may lead to the initiation of a feasibility study:
  a. A recognized operational problem
  b. A need to replace an existing system
  c. A desire to mechanize a manual system
  d. A strategy to create a new activity

5. Describe the kinds of information needed to prepare a cost/benefit analysis. Who is responsible for providing the information?

6. Why should the cost/benefit analysis be stated conservatively?

7. Explain McFarlan's framework for assessing project risk.

Discussion Questions

1. Do feasibility studies necessarily have to include a cost/benefit analysis in those cases where management is certain it will proceed with a project?

2. Consider the five types of feasibility (technical, operational, economic, schedule and motivational) in relation to the following proposed projects:
  a. An expert system to make hotel reservations.
  b. A replacement order entry system that would require operators to telephone prospective customers and read a tailored sales message directly from a CRT screen.
  c. A personal income tax software package that will be available on March 1.
  d. A quality control system to be used to reduce the number of defective gaskets on newly manufactured engines.

Mini-Case

Dunlop State University. Dunlop State University is considering a new system that would computerize all student transcripts. Presently, all transcripts are filed, updated, and copied manually. In the proposed system, current transcripts would be updated at the end of each semester. Corrections, inquiries, and printing would be handled on-line.

Advocates predict a significantly lower error rate for updating and correcting procedures. They also believe goodwill with students and alumni will increase.

With proper identification and fee payment, a student or alumnus would be able to have a transcript immediately, as opposed to the five-day delay with the present system.

The university's executive steering committee will meet in one month to consider the feasibility study for the transcript project along with other prospective projects. You are on the project team and are responsible for drafting the feasibility study for the transcript project.

Questions for Discussion

1. How would you classify the reason for initiating this feasibility study? What approach would you use for conducting the study?

2. Consider each type of feasibility for the proposed transcript system.

3. What specific kinds of information would be included in the cost/ benefit analysis? Who would supply this information?

References

1. Gildersleeve, Thomas R. *Successful Data Processing Systems Analysis*, 2d ed. Englewood Cliffs, New Jersey: Prentice-Hall, 1985.

2. Martin, James. *An Information Systems Manifesto*. Englewood Cliffs, New Jersey: Prentice-Hall, 1984.

3. Davis, Gordon B., and Olson, Margrethe H. *Management Information Systems: Conceptual Foundations, Structure and Development*, 2d. ed. New York: McGraw-Hill, 1985.

4. Rinaldo, J. A. Jr., McCubbrey, D. J., and Shryock, J. R. "The Care Monitoring, Cost Forecasting and Cost Monitoring System." *Journal of Clinical Computing*, vol. IX, no. 3, 1981.

5. Biggs, Charles L., Birks, Evans G., and Atkins, William. *Managing the Systems Development Process*. Englewood Cliffs, New Jersey: Prentice-Hall, 1980.

6. McFarlan, F. Warren. "Portfolio Approach to Information Systems." *Harvard Business Review* (September-October 1981): 142–150.

Chapter 5

Establishing the Systems Plan

After describing the benefits of a formal systems plan, this chapter explains the relationship between the strategic business plan of an organization and its systems plan. Then, the development of a systems plan is described: identifying application selection criteria, understanding how the business operates, analyzing data requirements, and identifying and evaluating systems projects. The chapter concludes with some advice on how to organize a systems planning project.

Learning Objectives

- Describe the benefits of preparing a formal systems plan.

- Understand the relationship between a strategic business plan and a systems plan.

- Be aware of the steps required to identify and assign priorities to the applications of an entire organization or a strategic business unit.

- Describe the three dimensions of analysis of systems requirements: information needs, processing requirements, and data structure.

- Recognize how a systems planning effort can be organized to maximize its impact on management and to ensure that its results actually are used.

- Understand the level of documentation typically produced in a systems plan.

BENEFITS OF SYSTEMS PLANNING

A formal systems plan has three benefits. First, a systems plan that covers multiple applications within an organization has technical merit. The plan enables applications to share data, thereby minimizing redundant acquisition and storage, reducing systems development and operations costs, and lowering the costs associated with inconsistent versions of the same data stored in different places. Second, the systems plan serves to promote harmony between the corporate strategy set by top management and the tactical and operational plans of both users and the IS department. Finally, the systems plan helps reduce costs.

Shared Data

Most of the data maintained by a company's information systems are of interest to multiple departments. Experience has shown that data sharing across organizational boundaries does not come naturally. The requirement to share must be explicitly recognized and addressed in the systems design. If this requirement is not explicit, each application will tend to be limited to a single department. The data of the application could then be duplicated in other departments' systems; the result will be higher costs.

Shared Strategy

Another merit of a formal systems plan is that it will help middle management understand the organization's objectives, and it will minimize the effect of the interdepartmental rivalries that usually exist. It will show how top management views the contribution to overall goals made by each user department and by the IS department. Thus, the plan can increase users' understanding and acceptance of the sequence assigned to applications development.

The systems plan can also help explain corporate policies on hardware, software, and systems procurement. User management can understand why there must be limits to departmental autonomy in hardware selection and in end-user development.

IS departments have in the past come under heavy fire for being technocratic, unresponsive to the real needs of users, and out of touch with reality. By establishing a systems plan, an IS department can demonstrate that it understands top management's strategies as thoroughly as do the users.

Cost Reduction

Finally, the systems plan is a valuable cost-containment tool because organizations can plan ahead for the resources required, in particular the development resources. An IS department can use a systems plan to avoid hiring people to meet a peak in demand, who will later go idle or underutilized because of a slowdown in development. The next chapter treats resource planning in depth.

Despite all of these benefits, many organizations do not put together a formal systems plan. Some organizations have not yet reached the stage where the plan is necessary; others believe that the strategy is so well understood that there is no need for a formal document. The following types of organizations— those that would fit in the support quadrant of the strategic grid (see Chapter 1)—might not need a systems plan:

- Small organizations, where information can be obtained and communicated informally.

- Organizations where the bulk of mechanization so far has concentrated on automating labor-intensive applications.
- Organizations where end users are only superficially involved in computing.

For other organizations, a coherent strategy is required. Often, a strategy does exist; however, it did not result from a formal study and it has not been documented in a single report. Rather, the strategy resulted from a consensus of a tightly knit management team, of which the IS department head is a part. If enough mutual trust exists among the IS department, top management, and user departments, most of the objectives of systems planning can be met without a formal document. This hinges on mutual trust and on a certain permanence of the management team. The lack of a formal plan is probably reasonable only in a medium-sized company; and even in such a company, not preparing a formal plan has its risks. Many assumptions could go unchallenged, and many important issues could remain hidden. There is also a technical risk: the data architecture might not be the best and could ultimately cause higher maintenance costs than necessary.

Although the absence of a systems plan increases the risks, an organization may successfully implement systems without one. On the other hand, a systems plan is no panacea. In many cases, systems plans have been created only to remain on paper. The value of a systems plan is in its implementation. The systems identified in the plan, and the data and network architecture that it describes, must serve as the focus for all applications development. This is not to say that the plan must be followed slavishly. New requirements may crop up through technological innovation, competitive pressure, or regulatory changes. The systems plan must not be so rigid as to forbid the creation of applications that are not in the plan.

UNDERSTANDING THE STRATEGIC BUSINESS PLAN

The first requirement for a systems planning project is to understand the value system, the culture, and the strategies of the organization for which the systems plan is being developed. How easy this understanding is depends very much on how explicitly top management has stated its strategy. In those comparatively rare instances where a strategic business plan has been established, understanding is no problem. In fact, for companies in the strategic or turnaround quadrants as defined by Cash, McFarlan, and McKenney, the existence of a strategic business plan usually implies the existence of a systems plan; the two are almost inseparable.

Most organizations, however, have no formal business strategy. In this case, two solutions are possible: the systems planning effort can be suspended until a strategic business plan has been developed, or the systems planning team can attempt to articulate enough guiding principles within the systems plan itself to ensure that top management and the IS department are in step.

Figure 5–1 **Schematic Representation of the BSP Methodology**

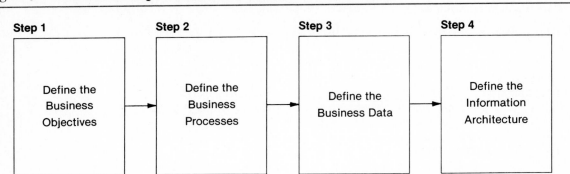

Source: *Business Systems Planning: Information Systems Planning Guide,* IBM Manual No. GE20-0527.

Most systems planning methodologies in use today realistically take this approach, as strategic business planning is not yet in general use. Among the first to realize the importance of tying the systems plan to the business strategy was IBM's Business Systems Planning (BSP) methodology, created in 1970 (see Figure 5–1). The first step in a BSP study is to determine the business objectives and environment. The study team determines these by interviewing top executives to determine the corporation's view on such topics as the following:

- Industry trends
- Business strategies
- Critical success factors
- Current problem areas
- Forecast of where the organization is going over the next few years

A number of business planning tools have emerged in recent years. Some examples were covered in Chapter 1. Others include the use of critical success factors described by John F. Rockart[1] and the six stages of growth in data processing described by Richard L. Nolan[2]. Which of these tools is the best depends on the circumstances. The project team should pick the tool that is most likely to strike some responsive chord in top management, thereby contributing to both management commitment and insight. In fact, it may well be appropriate to combine several of these tools to obtain the best result.

In addition to these tools, which are business rather than system related, many systems planners include the analysis of information needs. Information needs can be viewed as the most critical output of the enterprise-wide information system. Each information need can be tied to a critical success factor which it helps satisfy. A matrix of typical information needs in the discrete manufacturing industry is depicted in Figure 5–2.

IDENTIFYING CRITERIA FOR EVALUATING APPLICATION DEVELOPMENT PROJECTS

The next step of the systems planning project is to identify a specific set of measurable criteria by which the merit of proposed application development projects can be judged. It is not enough to enumerate benefit-oriented criteria, as shown in Figure 5–3. It is also necessary to consider the risk factors: uncertainty about how much the project it will cost, whether it will actually achieve the benefits, and whether it might turn out to counteract some other project (lack of synergy). The main risk factors are summarized in Figure 5–4.

Most of the criteria will naturally fall out from the study of the strategic business plan. Others may come from well-documented corporate policies, for example, the required return on investment that any project must achieve to be approved. Yet other criteria, such as the willingness of the corporation to take technological risks, are less likely to be explicitly stated on paper and can only be ascertained by someone who understands the corporate culture.

These factors may be tied together in a rating system that defines measures and assigns weights to the factors, so that each project will have a numerical score. In most cases, however, the additional precision gained with this method is not required (and it is somewhat illusory because the measuring systems and the weights are assigned in a fairly arbitrary manner). Projects will naturally tend to fall into three or four categories, as shown in Figure 5–5.

Once the criteria have been tentatively identified, they should be presented to all the interested parties to obtain consensus on the criteria and the weights attached to them. The acceptance of these criteria by the entire management team, top executives, and middle management alike is a powerful way to ensure consensus about which projects get the most attention during the implementation of the systems plan. It also provides an excellent tool for updating the systems plan when unanticipated needs arise that require priorities to be reassigned. Obtaining acceptance of the project evaluation criteria, although not specifically described in the BSP methodology, is nevertheless a required step.

UNDERSTANDING THE OPERATION OF THE BUSINESS

Most systems planning methodologies follow BSP in advocating the identification of business processes and decision-making activities executed by middle management. Each process must be defined and analyzed to determine which part of the organization has responsibility for it. A matrix such as the one represented in Figure 5–6 documents the results of this kind of analysis.

An important framework for the analysis is the classical pyramid of strategic, tactical, and operational activities (see Figure 5–7). Transaction processing appears at the operational level. Transaction processing includes applications such as order entry and billing, payroll, and purchasing—applications that support an organization's day-to-day operations. At the tactical level are man-

Figure 5–2   **Sample Information Needs Matrix**

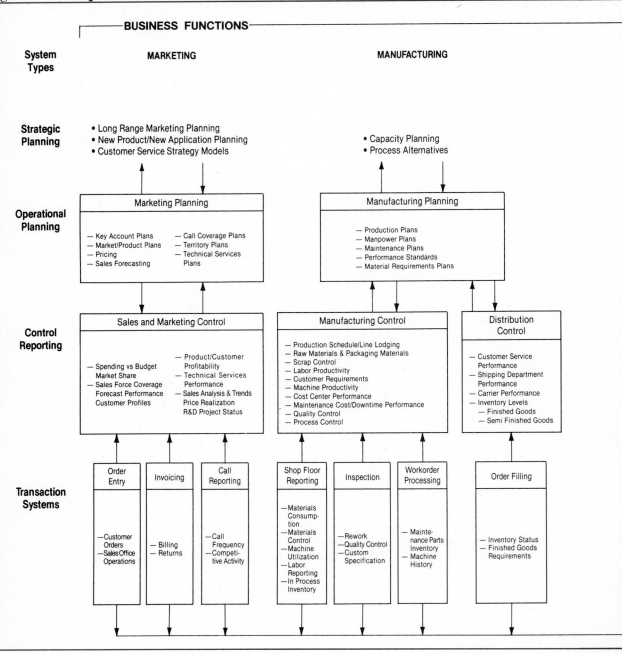

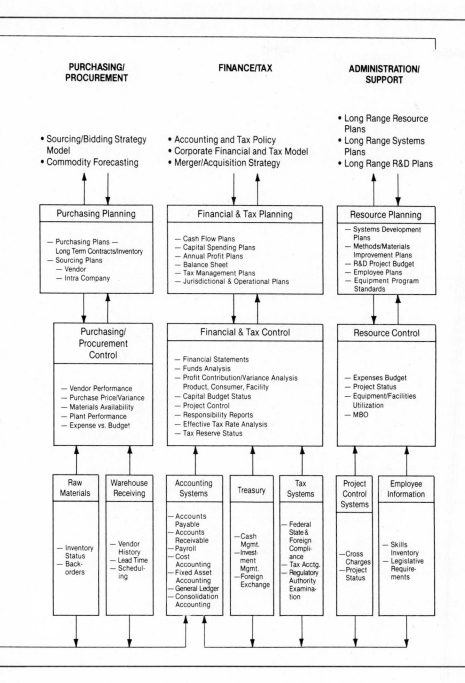

PURCHASING/ PROCUREMENT

- Sourcing/Bidding Strategy Model
- Commodity Forecasting

Purchasing Planning

— Purchasing Plans —
Long Term Contracts/Inventory
— Sourcing Plans
— Vendor
— Intra Company

Purchasing/ Procurement Control

— Vendor Performance
— Purchase Price/Variance
— Materials Availability
— Plant Performance
— Expense vs. Budget

Raw Materials

— Inventory Status
— Back-orders

Warehouse Receiving

— Vendor History
— Lead Time
— Schedul-ing

FINANCE/TAX

- Accounting and Tax Policy
- Corporate Financial and Tax Model
- Merger/Acquisition Strategy

Financial & Tax Planning

— Cash Flow Plans
— Capital Spending Plans
— Annual Profit Plans
— Balance Sheet
— Tax Management Plans
— Jurisdictional & Operational Plans

Financial & Tax Control

— Financial Statements
— Funds Analysis
— Profit Contribution/Variance Analysis Product, Consumer, Facility
— Capital Budget Status
— Project Control
— Responsibility Reports
— Effective Tax Rate Analysis
— Tax Reserve Status

Accounting Systems

— Accounts Payable
— Accounts Receivable
— Payroll
— Cost Accounting
— Fixed Asset Accounting
— General Ledger
— Consolidation Accounting

Treasury

—Cash Mgmt.
—Invest-ment Mgmt.
—Foreign Exchange

Tax Systems

— Federal State & Foreign Compli-ance
— Tax Acctg.
— Regulatory Authority Examina-tion

ADMINISTRATION/ SUPPORT

- Long Range Resource Plans
- Long Range Systems Plans
- Long Range R&D Plans

Resource Planning

— Systems Development Plans
— Methods/Materials Improvement Plans
— R&D Project Budget
— Employee Plans
— Equipment Program Standards

Resource Control

— Expenses Budget
— Project Status
— Equipment/Facilities Utilization
— MBO

Project Control Systems

—Cross Charges
—Project Status

Employee Information

— Skills Inventory
— Legislative Requires-ments

Figure 5–3 **Benefits-related Criteria for Evaluating Systems Projects**

```
SYSTEMS                    CONDOR TELEPHONE COMPANY              CD-20
PLAN                                                            BCRIT
                           BENEFITS-RELATED CRITERIA
┌──────────────────────────────────────────────────────────────────────┐
│ PREPARED BY:  J. WEBER        DATE:  27AUG88   VERSION:  1.1   PAGE 1   │
│ APPROVED BY:  JACK CROFT      DATE:  05SEP88   STATUS :  D             │
└──────────────────────────────────────────────────────────────────────┘
```

    I.   Increase Profits/Avoid or Reduce Costs

        A.   To satisfy this criterion, a prospective systems development project must result in a measurable increase in earnings brought on by:

            1.   An increase in product sales
            2.   A cost reduction
            3.   A favorable change in asset levels

            A prospective project satisfies this criterion to the extent that the source of earnings can be identified and the magnitude and timing of the earnings can be quantified.

            Where a prospective project's primary benefit criterion is increased profits, cost avoidance or reduced costs, it must also meet the normal financial justification screens imposed on all other investments (A&FM Policy #19, sections IV, V and VI).

    II.   Improve Information Available for Decision Making

        A.   To satisfy this criterion, a prospective systems development project must produce a management support system structured to provide immediately accessible information for decision making.

            A prospective project satisfies this criterion to the extent that it provides:

            1.   Data collected and arrayed on a comparable basis together with pertinent analysis; or
            2.   Sophisticated data management, communications, and processing techniques to meet an immediate "need to know"; or
            3.   Environmental and/or competitive information in a form useful for decision making.

   III. Support Strategic/Tactical/Operational Objectives

        A.   To satisfy this criterion, a prospective systems development project must directly support business objectives of a Corporate function or Division business organization.

Figure 5–4 **Risk-related Criteria for Evaluating Systems Projects**

```
SYSTEMS                        CONDOR TELEPHONE COMPANY              CD-20
PLAN                                                                 RCRIT
                                 RISK-RELATED CRITERIA

PREPARED BY:   J. WEBER      DATE:   27AUG88    VERSION:  1.1     PAGE 1
APPROVED BY:   JACK CROFT    DATE:   05SEP88    STATUS :  D
```

A.   Factors

   1.   Implementation Risk

        a.   Level of internal experience
        b.   Degree of design complexity
        c.   Degree of technical complexity
        d.   Magnitude of effort required for implementation
        e.   Time constraints for implementation
        f.   Degree of management support

   2.   Benefits Risk

        a.   Possibility that anticipated benefits will not be
             achieved
        b.   Ease of measurement of benefits actually attained
        c.   Quality of estimating assumptions

   3.   Synergistic Risk

        a.   Interrelationship within the portfolio of
             proposed systems development projects
        b.   Interface within the organization of different
             projects in development

B.   Definition of Process

   1.   Systems projects differ in their difficulty of
        implementation.

   2.   This perceived difficulty puts the achievement of
        benefits at risk.

   3.   A measure of this perceived difficulty of implementation
        may be expressed in degrees of risk that can significantly
        affect achieving benefits.

Figure 5–5 Groups into which Systems Projects Tend To Fall

Benefits	Risk	Priority	Comment
Quick	Low	1–2	Need at least one such project
High	High	1	Mainstay of strategic systems plan
Slow	Low	2	Second tier
Low	Low	3	Should be considered for elimination
Medium	High	3	Should be considered for elimination

agement information systems (accounting and responsibility reporting, for example), which use data from operational systems to keep management informed about how well the organization is operating. Also, tactical planning applications such as budgeting and forecasting, which communicate objectives and plans to the operational level, are included at the tactical level. The strategic level typically contains executive support systems. In many cases, these systems rely more on external data sources than on summarized data from the enterprise itself. Top management is usually more interested in analyzing the possible impact of outside events—changes in regulations, in the economic climate, and in specific competitors, suppliers, and customers—than in the daily running of the business, which has been delegated to middle management.

Let us consider how a representative methodology, BSP, advocates understanding and documenting how the business operates. BSP prescribes the following six steps:

Identify Products (or Services) and Supporting Resources

For each basic group of products or resources (in many cases there is only one), the project identifies how the product is planned for, how it is developed and manufactured (or otherwise created), how it is stored, and how it is disposed of (sold or scrapped). This analysis is done for:

- Products
- Services
- Materials
- Money
- Facilities and equipment
- Personnel

Identify Strategic Planning and Management Control Processes

These processes should be easily identifiable from the previous stage, which identified management's strategies and critical success factors. The strategic

Figure 5–6 **Sample Organization/Function Matrix**

						VERSION: 1.1 PAGE 1
PREPARED BY:	J. WEBER	DATE: 27AUG88				VERSION: 1.1 PAGE 1
APPROVED BY:	JACK CROFT	DATE: 05SEP88				STATUS : D

ORGANIZATION

BUSINESS FUNCTION	VP Manufacturing	VP Marketing	VP International	VP Financial	VP I/S	Managing Director	Sales Manager	Advertising Manager	Market Research Manager	Corporate Planner	Controller	Budgeting Director	Internal Audit Director	Operations	Materials	Equipment Control	Quality Control	Information Services	Personnel	Office Support
	SENIOR MANAGEMENT						MARKETING			FINANCIAL				MANUFACTURING				SUPPORT		
Strategic Planning	1	1	1	1	1					1	2	1	3							
Financial Planning	2	2	2	1	2					2	1									
Information Systems Planning	2	2	2	2	1	2				3								1		
Research & Development	1																			
Payroll											2								1	
Employee Relations																			1	
Employee Benefits																			1	
Government Relations																			1	
Employee Development																			1	
Recruiting																			1	
Operations														1						
Process Engineering														1						
Equipment Control															3	1				
Quality Control																3	1			
Purchasing															1					
Materials Requirements Planning														1	1					
Inventory Control														1	1					
Distribution							3							1	1					
Market Intelligence		2							1											
Sales		2					1		3											
Advertising		2					3	1												
Budgeting				2						3	1									
General Financial Administration						2					1									
Reports										1	1	1								
Accounting											1									
Information Processing					2							3						1		
Property Management					2									1						1
Security					3								2							2

1 Major Responsibility
2 Significant Involvement
3 Some Involvement

Figure 5-7   **Pyramid of Strategic, Tactical, and Operational Systems**

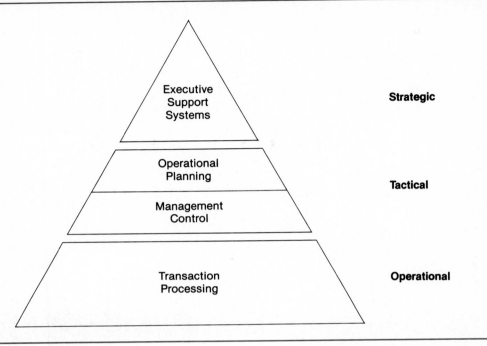

planning process concerns the corporation as a whole and usually has a horizon of several years. The management control processes can often be determined by reviewing a corporation's operating plan or budget system; its scope is usually a department or a product group; its horizon is one year or less.

Identify Operational Processes

Identifying operational processes consists of taking each of the products, services, and resources defined in the first step and identifying the business functions required to perform each of the four stages in its life—planning, acquiring, storing, and disposing. An example of the result of this process for a men's apparel manufacturer is shown in Figure 5-8.

Other methodologies use different techniques. Some advocate tying the processes together by using a data flow diagram (see Section III). This approach generally takes longer than the simple identification of functions. Others use hierarchical representations such as Warnier charts or boxes such as organization charts (see Section I); the result may then be less structured than the BSP matrix. These differences are not material and are not likely to have a bearing on the quality of the systems plan.

BOX 5–1

Types of Systems

The types of systems that fall into the framework of the pyramid of operational, tactical, and strategic uses of information can be analyzed somewhat more precisely. The most frequently used categories of systems are:

- Transaction processing systems
- Management information systems
- Decision support systems
- Office automation systems
- Departmental systems
- Expert systems
- Executive information systems

Transaction processing systems are the successors of the initial payroll system at General Electric. In the era of batch, these systems were designed to mechanize the work of clerical personnel such as payroll and invoicing clerks. A side effect was to create a new class of less specialized clerks for data entry (then called keypunch).

The advent of on-line systems has reversed the trend. Now, the users of transaction processing systems are increasingly qualified to make decisions or otherwise contribute to corporate goals as they operate the system. For example, order entry is increasingly done by people who have a marketing function as well, suggesting substitutes, upgrades, and promotional offerings.

The increasing integration of transaction processing systems has also brought about a trend towards so-called subject data bases. These are data bases that centralize all the data about a single entity and are shared across all the departments of an organization.

Management information systems have their roots in budgeting and cost accounting systems. In the past, these systems produced large amounts of printed output. A typical example

would be responsibility reports, made up of a series of detailed reports about budgeted amounts versus actual spending at the lowest levels of the organization's hierarchy, then rolled up into summary reports by section, department, division, and so on. The recipient of these reports would use them to find action items and as a detailed reference.

The trend here is twofold. Actual reports are less and less frequently produced on paper. Instead, they are stored in electronic form so that users can query the data on-line, choosing their own data content, sequence, and level of detail. If on-line query is impractical from a cost-effectiveness standpoint, ad hoc reports can be requested, most often overnight.

In addition, many users receive periodic extracts from the activity files of the management information system and can use these extracts for their own analysis purposes. This is described in detail under decision support systems.

Although the trend is towards integration of data, these management information systems do not necessarily use the subject data bases of the transaction processing system. Subject data bases are generally reserved for operational use. An inquiry against a subject data base is about a subject or a list of subjects satisfying a number of criteria, for example, the list of customers served by the Phoenix branch who have a particular item on order.

Subject data bases, and more generally transaction processing data bases, are not suitable for management information systems for two reasons. First, they are volatile, since they are updated as the business activity is conducted. Second, they reflect the current state of affairs rather than the historical figures. To solve these problems, a periodical (monthly, weekly, or even daily) program reviews activity records and creates management information that is properly cut off, i.e., assigned to a definite period in time. Generally, the information is also summarized to some extent, so that the system does not need to carry full details of every single business event over the period that management may want to analyze—often several years.

This summarization poses a problem because the criteria that appear appropriate for what is retained can vary over the years. As a result, the historical and statistical data that a corporation accumulates can become useless because it does not correspond to the categories of analysis that are of current interest to management.

Decision support systems are in reality an outgrowth of management information systems. These systems are capable of providing varying analyses of the same data without programming effort. It becomes possible to search for correlations between data without rewriting part of the management information system for every new idea to be tested. Often, these systems also have graphics capabilities, making both trend analysis and reporting on the analysis to top executives much easier. Finally, modeling capabilities make it possible to explore many alternative scenarios, answering management's "what-if" questions.

When decision support tools are used on management information data (such as the data supplied by the various cut-off processes in the organization), they support tactical decisions. They can also support strategic decisions. In that case, they will usually be based on different data, as described under executive information systems.

A problem with decision support systems is that they are often PC-based and the mechanism for distributing cut-off data to a large number of PCs is usually lacking today. As a bypass, many decision support users have to rekey data off management reports onto a spreadsheet of their choice. This is obviously inefficient, error-prone, and, one hopes, temporary.

A more serious problem is that conclusions drawn by manipulating data in a decision support system are not always warranted. There are statistical traps that are known to trained statisticians but not necessarily to financial analysts.

The use, or misuse, of graphics is another source of erroneous conclusions. Worst are clerical mistakes such as those that can arise when a row on a spreadsheet is set to total some of the rows above, and an additional row is inserted outside the scope of the total. The impeccable presentation that can be obtained on workstation printers and the reputation for hardware reliability can make management rely excessively on corrupted data.

Office automation systems have emerged as a vehicle for processing documents. They are neither transaction processing systems, since they do not recognize business transactions and rules that apply to them, nor management information systems in the usual sense. They may seem to have little to do with our purpose, but they are of interest in two domains.

First, the desktop metaphor of user interfaces was primarily invented as an office automation system. This metaphor, which is incorporated in Apple's Macintosh and expected to be implemented on the IBM PS/2 under the name Presentation Manager, has been tremendously influential and will probably be the basis for standard user interface design in all types of systems in the future. (Standard does not mean invariable. Rather, the standard approach is defined as the one taken unless you can justify that some other approach meets your particular requirements better.)

Second, the distinction between transaction processing, done by clerks, and office work, done by secretaries, is beginning to fade. With the help of information technology, professionals can now do some of both. Many transaction processing systems today incorporate elements of correspondence management. Examples are claims processing in the insurance industry, mortgage applications in the banking industry, and benefits systems in government and health care.

Departmental systems are often distinguished as a separate category. In truth, departmental systems are often a mix of transaction processing, decision support, and office automation, but with a scope that is reduced to a single department (most often a single location). An example today might be a lab system in a hospital, tracking requests for work and communicating results back. Similar systems might be in the X-ray department, the pharmacy, and the operating room of a large hospital. Each of these departments has requirements for processing and data storage that are distinct from other departments.

This example is intentionally defective. In fact, all the information is about patients, and it is all being produced for the same persons: physicians, nurses, and hospital administrators (billing and accounts receivable, in particular). There is already a growing demand for integration of all these partial systems.

A better example of departmental systems is when a department performs a differentiated support function which is only incidental to the main purpose of the organization, such as facilities management in a large legal firm or the hospital cafeteria. Here, departmental systems may well be justified because the need for integration will remain much lower.

Expert systems are often also mentioned as a separate category. Expert systems are usually rule-based systems that help the not-so-expert perform tasks, often of a diagnostic nature. Thus, the terminology designates both a technology and a goal for the system. The goal is to leverage knowledge that is possessed by a small number of experts, often only one. The technology is artificial intelligence (AI).

The use of AI technology implies that knowledge is not embodied in programs on the one hand and data on the other, but that both the procedural part and the data part are united in a knowledge representation scheme, most often of the Post production rule type. This consists in maintaining a set of facts in memory, for example: "The patient has a temperature of 103 degrees" and "the bacteria isolated are gram-positive." A so-called rule base, a collection of If-Then phrases, is then reviewed. For each rule whose If-part is true, the Then-part is added as an assertion in memory. For example: "If the patient has no fever, then the infection may be bacterial"

is not acted on; "If the bacteria is gram-positive, then there is evidence for such-such an illness" is acted on and the evidence of the illness is added as a fact. At the end of this process, if there is enough data and the rule base is correct, a more or less tentative diagnosis is derived.

This type of system has been applied in the medical field, in the maintenance of steam locomotives, in troubleshooting oil drilling bits, in configuring computer hardware, and in analyzing chemical compounds among many others.

Expert systems can have a deep impact on the business environment. We have just seen that information technology can tend to displace unskilled personnel such as data entry operators and typists, transferring work to above-average employees. This has an obvious limit: not everybody can be above average. It therefore becomes important to find applications where expertise—the high competence and reliable judgment that comes from years of experience—can be leveraged, i.e., used by people who are younger or less gifted.

Increasingly, there will be scope for integrating expert systems approaches with mainstream transaction processing and decision support.

Of almost equal importance is that AI technology, in expert systems and elsewhere, is breaking down the dichotomy between programs and data, preferring to see both as aspects of knowledge. This is already enriching our repertoire of systems development techniques. Although the results are not yet generally embodied into commercially available tools and generally adopted methodologies, the next decade should see considerable progress. The earliest concrete embodiment of this trend may be object-oriented design and programming, which is described in Section VI.

Executive information systems or executive support systems are the current terms for the top of the pyramid. Executive information systems are distinguished from management information systems because top executives are generally much more interested in information generated outside the organization, about the industry, the competition, and technical innovations. As a result, executive information systems tend to be designed to give executives access to external data bases and to a top-level summary of internal enterprise information.

Executive information systems have been slow to take off, both because the IS department tended not to realize that top management was mainly interested in outside information and because most top executives had keyboard fright. Both of these factors will be overcome with time.

Some interesting experiments with user interfaces have taken place in the efforts to sell information systems to top executives. In one case, a corporation founded by ex-Air Force pilots used a set of dials, reminiscent of a cockpit layout, to display the key indicators of the business. Another scheme which has been successfully used is to display a matrix of green, amber, and red squares, highlighting the areas that need management attention.

Group/Split the Processes

Once the processes have been identified, they are grouped or split so as to be understandable to all concerned, to reduce inconsistencies in levels, or to combine processes that are similar (for instance, purchasing materials might be the same process as purchasing equipment).

Write a Description of Each Process

Each process is then described, usually on one-half page to two pages. A guideline is that each process should be decomposed into three to seven components and a paragraph defining each should be written. These descriptions ensure that everyone has the same understanding of what a given process does and does not include. It is particularly valuable for team members who have not been involved with the analysis of a particular area. The write-up is less useful to users, who usually understand each process under their control on the basis of a process name. They typically do not need a detailed description.

If hierarchical representation techniques are used, the written descriptions may be replaced by adding one or two levels of detail to the hierarchical chart.

Relate the Business Process to the Organization

Each business process is then reviewed to determine which parts of the organization play a role in it. The usual technique is to create a matrix such as the one in Figure 5–6.

ANALYZING DATA REQUIREMENTS

The next stage in the planning process is to group data into what has been called *subject data bases* (because each data base is devoted to a single subject of

Figure 5–8 **Sample Process Identification**

```
SYSTEMS                    SUBURBAN PUMPS
PLAN
                         PROCESS IDENTIFICATION                              CD-20
                                                                            PID

PREPARED BY:  J. WEBER       DATE:  27AUG88      VERSION:  1.1     PAGE 1
APPROVED BY:  JACK CROFT     DATE:  05SEP88      STATUS :  D
```

	PRODUCT/SERVICE	SUPPORTING RESOURCES			
	Pumping Equipment	Raw Materials			
Requirements	Forecast Product Requirements; Analyze Marketplace; Design Product	Plan Seasonal Production	Establish Business Direction; Comply With Legal Requirements	Determine Facilities and Equipment Requirements	Determine Control and Financial Requirements; Determine Personnel Requirements
Acquisition	Schedule and Control Production	Purchase Raw Materials		Acquire Facilities and Equipment	Manage Cash Receipts; Hire Personnel
Stewardship	Control Product Inventory; Ship Product	Control Raw Materials Inventory		Maintain Equipment; Manage Facilities	Determine Product Profitability; Manage Accounts; Manage Personnel
Disposition	Advertise and Promote Product; Market Product; Enter and Control Customer Order; Schedule and Control Production			Dispose of Facilities and Equipment	Manage Cash Disbursements; Terminate Personnel

interest to the corporation, rather than to serving a single group of users). Again, the methodology used by BSP can serve as a model for understanding the process. Typically, four steps are involved: identify business entities, determine data usage by process, identify data classes, and develop a process/data matrix.

Identify Business Entities

The business entities are those persons, things, or concepts that are of lasting interest to the business and about which data needs to be stored. Examples range from customers to warehouses, departments, products, and shipments. There are several strategies for defining these entities:

- By using an iterative approach, through group discussions. (An initial list of, say, 10 to 20 entities is proposed and is then gradually refined until the group feels comfortable.)

- By analyzing present mechanized systems and assuming that one record type in an existing file represents one entity, then factoring similar entities to reduce their number.

- By analyzing existing documents exchanged with the outside world (customers, suppliers, government, etc.) to develop an understanding of the primary entities and the type of data to be stored about them.

- By using checklists available from suppliers or colleagues in professional associations. (Such checklists are usually specific to a given industry.)

The approach selected is not critical. In practical terms, the only risk is to identify too many entities, so that the output becomes unwieldy. In a large organization, it is usually possible to identify several hundred of them; this number is in all probability too large, and related entities should be consolidated to provide a higher level of abstraction.

If too few entities have been proposed, the lack will be discovered in the next step, and it is fairly easy to complete the list.

Determine Data Usage by Process

The next step is to determine which entities are required by each process and which entities the process creates or updates. Not only is the entity identified, but the type of data that is involved is also identified. In general, each process only requires part of the data about an entity. For instance, the data about the employee entity might be divided into several categories such as vital statistics, status, employment history, skills, salary and withholding data, and so on. Each process might use only one or two of these categories.

Identify Data Classes

From the data types for each process, the data classes are defined. A data class is a category of information about an entity with a single source of creation. If a data class is created by several processes rather than just one, then the data class must be decomposed, or the processes must be factored or combined.

Develop a Process/Data Diagram

The result of the above analysis is documented in matrix form (see Figure 5–9). For each process, the data that it uses is marked with an A (for "access only"), and that which it creates or updates with a U (for "update"). The matrix is manipulated until natural groupings fall out. This is fairly easy to do with a spreadsheet, but is much more painful by hand. If the matrix is drawn by someone with good knowledge of the industry and previous BSP experience, this grouping will tend to become apparent after the first attempt (see Figure 5–10).

In addition, data/organization matrices (see Figure 5–11) showing the responsibility and use of data across organizational and geographical boundaries should be established whenever there is considerable sharing of data across organizational boundaries or whenever there may be a case for implementing distributed systems. It is fairly easy to see the need for this additional analysis based on comparing the process/organization matrix developed earlier with the data/process matrix in Figure 5–10.

Both processes and data groupings are relatively standard within an industry. Identifying the categories listed along the rows and columns of the matrix is usually not extremely difficult. Some practitioners recommend establishing a corporate data model before doing the data/process matrix. The model is created by enumerating all the external entities of interest to the organization, such as customers, suppliers, and third parties. Internal entities such as products, parts, and employees that are of interest to the external entities are then added. Then, the relationships between all these entities are charted according to the rules of a data modeling technique—usually entity-relationship modeling. This modeling technique, related to the approach by products, services, markets, and channels, is most useful for transaction processing systems. In contrast, management planning and reporting are more related to the internal activities and processes than to the data entities (see Figure 5–12). Regardless of when such a corporate data model is undertaken, it is a part of the end product of the systems planning process.

The data/process matrix designed here is the essential component of the systems architecture that BSP establishes. It identifies how data entities are grouped into logically coherent data bases and how groups of processes make up systems and subsystems that maintain and use the data.

Some Practical Considerations

Two refinements, not explicitly covered in BSP, tend to cause difficulties later if glossed over now. One is the identification of data ownership. The problem involves who is responsible for defining the meaning of data and authorizing others to use it, on one hand, and who is responsible for data integrity on the

Figure 5–9 **Sample Process/Data Matrix—Initial Version**

SYSTEMS
PLAN

SUBURBAN PUMPS

PROCESS/DATA MATRIX

CD-20
PDMTX

PREPARED BY: J. WEBER	DATE: 27AUG88	VERSION: 1.1	PAGE 1
APPROVED BY: JACK CROFT	DATE: 05SEP88	STATUS : D	

DATA ENTITIES

BUSINESS FUNCTION	Strategic Plans	Annual Plans	Vendor	Raw Materials — Materials Inventory	Purchase Order	Finished Goods — Inventory	Finished Goods Warehouse	Competitor	Market Sector	Product	Product Structure — Mfg. Process	Work Center	Plant	Department	Employee	Process Type — Equipment Type	Sales Region	Salesperson	Customer	Order	Agent	Financial
Strategic Planning	U	U						A	A	A	A		A				A	A	A		A	A
Financial Planning	A	A						A	A	A	A		A				A	A				A
Research & Development								A		A	A	A										U
Payroll													U		U							
Employee Relations												U	U	U	U							
Employee Benefits												U	U	U	U							
Government Relations													U	U	U							
Employee Development													U	U	U							
Recruiting																						
Operations						U					U	U	U			U	U					U
Process Engineering											U	U				U	U					
Equipment Control												A	A			A	A					
Quality Control										A	A	A	A			A						U
Purchasing			U	U	U											U	A					U
Materials Requirements Planning																						
Inventory Control				A	A	U	U			A	A	A				U	A					U
Distribution						U	U									U	A		U	U		
Market Intelligence			U					U	U	A									U	U		U
Sales									A	A								A	A	A	A	U
Advertising										A								U	A	U	A	
Budgeting				A									U									U
General Financial Administration																			U		A	U U
Reports																						
Accounting																						U
Administrative Reporting						U							U	U	U		U					U

A Access Only
U Update

Figure 5–10 Sample Process/Data Matrix—Final Version

SYSTEMS PLAN SUBURBAN PUMPS CD-20 / PDMTX

PROCESS/DATA MATRIX

PREPARED BY: J. WEBER	DATE: 27OCT88	VERSION: 3	PAGE 1
APPROVED BY: JACK CROFT	DATE: 28OCT88	STATUS : F	

SUBJECT DATA BASES / DATA ENTITIES

APPLICATION SYSTEMS

System	EMPLOYEE — Department	Employee	Benefits	Payroll	Training	MANUFACTURING — Product	Product Structure	Mfg. Process	Work Center	Plant	Process Type	Equip. Type	MARKETING/CUSTOMER — Competitor	Sector	Region	Salesperson	Customer	Order	Agent	MATERIALS — Warehouse	Vendor	Raw Materials	Raw Materials Inventory	Purchase Order	Finished Goods Inventory	FINANCIAL	PLANNING — Strategic	Annual
FINANCIAL																												
Purchasing						A														A	A			A				
Accounts Payable																					U			U				
Accounts Receivable																	U								U			
General Ledger						U	A	A																				
Cost Accounting						U	A	A												A	A	U	A					
MANUFACTURING																												
Production Scheduling						U	U		U	U	U	U																
Plant Process Control									A	A																		
Inventory Control						A														U	U							
ADMINISTRATION																												
Personnel Planning	U	U	A	A	A																							
Payroll/Personnel	A	U	U	U	U																							
Training		A	A																									
MARKETING																												
Sales Analysis						A							A	A	U	A	A	A	A									
Profitability						A								U												A		
Reporting			A			A											A									A		
Order Entry						A	A								U	U	U	U		A					A			
DECISION SUPPORT																												
Strategic Planning														A	A											A	A	U
Budgeting														A	A											A	U	A

A Access Only
U Update

Figure 5-11 **Sample Organization/Data Matrix**

```
SYSTEMS                  SUBURBAN PUMPS                    CD-20
PLAN                                                       ODMTX
                   ORGANIZATION/DATA MATRIX

PREPARED BY: J. WEBER      DATE: 27AUG88    VERSION: 1.1   PAGE 1
APPROVED BY: JACK CROFT    DATE: 05SEP88    STATUS : D
```

Column headers (hierarchical):

```
Strategic Plans
: Annual Plans
: : Vendor
: : : Raw Materials
: : : : Materials
: : : : : Inventory
: : : : : : Purchase
: : : : : : : Order

Finished Goods
: Inventory
: : Finished Goods
: : : Warehouse
: : : : Competitor
: : : : : Market
: : : : : : Sector
: : : : : : : Product

Product Structure
: Mfg. Process
: : Work Center
: : : Plant
: : : : Department
: : : : : Employee

Process Type
: Equipment Type
: : Sales Region
: : : Salesperson
: : : : Customer
: : : : : Order
: : : : : : Agent
: : : : : : : Financial
```

DATA ENTITIES

BUSINESS LOCATION

```
Headquarters            D D S     S         S S S   S S S S S   S S S P S D D
Plants                  D D D D D   P D P   D D P   D D D D     D D
Regional Sales Offices  D D P P     D D D D         P           D D D
Finished Goods
  Warehouses            D D         P           P             P D P

-----------------------------------------------------------------------------

Data Volumes            L L M H H   H L L M   M L L L H   L L L M H H H M
```

```
D  Detailed Data
P  Partial Copy of Detailed Data
S  Summary Only

L  Low
M  Medium  Volumes
H  High
```

other. Because subject data bases tend to cross organizational boundaries, often the data in one part of the data base is maintained by one group, and the data in another part by another group. In that case, who has responsibility for seeing that the data in the two parts are coherent? For instance, if a human resources department has the responsibility for maintaining personnel records—date of hire, job experience, and so on—and a separate payroll department maintains payroll data—salary, deductions, and so on—who is responsible for ensuring that each employee qualifies for each benefit? What happens if the human resources department changes some characteristic, such as age (because of a previous error), and does not check whether the employee is still eligible for age-related benefits?

A similar difficulty arises when one organizational group is responsible for maintaining data that is used exclusively by another group. One of Murphy's laws pertaining to data is the following: "Data not used by the persons who maintain it becomes erroneous."

The second problem, not generally addressed explicitly by most methodologies, is that transaction processing systems do not view data in the same way as do tactical or strategic systems. The difference is that transaction processing needs the most recently known value of each piece of data; this value changes as transactions are processed. Other types of systems contain data that has been *cut off*, i.e., assigned to a specific period. In addition, the historical data may go back several years. Generally, this difference implies the use of separate data bases because it is technically quite difficult to store both current and cut-off data on the same data bases. Moreover, it implies a cut-off function, or information-delivery function, in each transaction processing system.

IDENTIFYING SYSTEMS PROJECTS

At this stage of the systems planning project, the identification of new systems to be developed can be based on two sources: a natural grouping of processes and data and a list of unsatisfied information needs of top and middle management. Most systems planning methodologies do not prescribe that one source should be used rather than another. The practical consequences of preferring one or the other are described below.

Systems plans have historically relied heavily on the information needs analysis. The information needs approach appeals to top management (it is the one that results naturally if Porter and Rockart are followed) and tends to yield more immediate payback. It also corresponds best to the earlier stages in Nolan's analysis. The systems identified in this way are usually implemented by using data from existing transaction processing systems and data bases, thus requiring few infrastructure modifications. These systems are usually either management information systems or data delivery systems for decision support.

The systems plans that rely more on the concept of subject data bases tend to be more comprehensive. Most of the data bases identified during this process already exist in the form of nonintegrated, partially redundant files serving

Figure 5–12 **Sample Corporate Data Model**

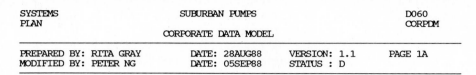

SYSTEMS PLAN	SUBURBAN PUMPS	D060 CORPDM
	CORPORATE DATA MODEL	

| PREPARED BY: RITA GRAY | DATE: 28AUG88 | VERSION: 1.1 | PAGE 1A |
| MODIFIED BY: PETER NG | DATE: 05SEP88 | STATUS : D | |

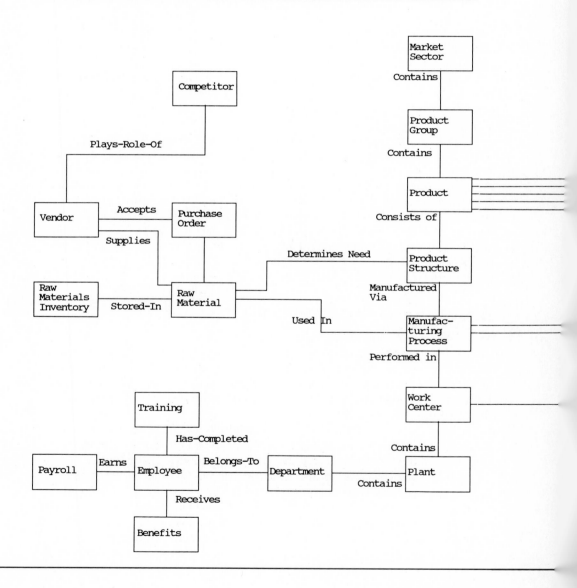

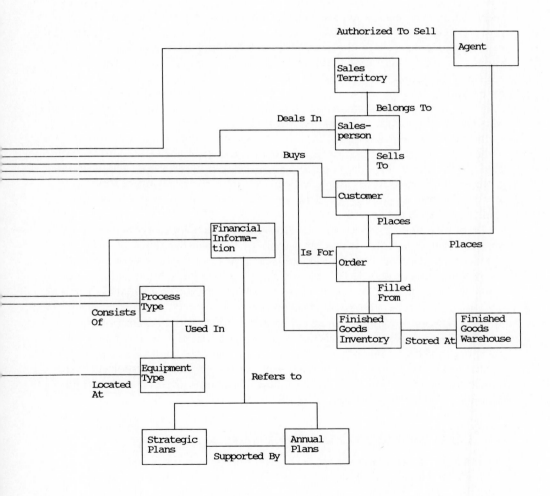

current transaction processing systems. To implement the subject data base approach usually means replacing, little by little, most or all of the existing transaction processing applications. As a result, these plans are more costly, take longer to implement, and have a higher degree of risk because they present a higher degree of integration. However, the promised benefits are greater than in the previous approach because the systems developed under this approach will have an architecture that lends itself better to maintenance and evolution, while maintaining the proper degree of data integration. So far, few success stories have been associated with this type of systems planning, both because it is more recent (and fewer companies have used it) and because it takes longer to show positive results.

A great danger with the subject data base approach is that too much attention is paid to the target that is aimed for, and not enough to the strategy for reaching the target. Any organization has systems today, and these systems cannot all be instantaneously replaced by the new systems. The plan for migrating towards the ideal architecture represented by the future subject data bases and integrated applications must take into account that, while an application is being developed, its predecessor has to make do. In particular, when the first new application is installed, it has to interface to all the old applications that it does not replace. As more applications are developed and replace older ones, these interfaces will continue to be changed. Finding a workable, low-cost strategy to deal with this problem is one of the main challenges to the systems planner.

Most planning methodologies do not specify which approach to use. Some implicitly favor one over the other, simply by the way the different tasks are executed. The fact that information needs analysis leads to short-term improvements and subject data base analysis leads to long-term integration is not explicitly recognized. (We are indebted to John Zachman, from IBM Corporation, for pointing out this essential difference.)

The obvious recommendation is to combine the best of both approaches— to solve the most glaring operational and informational problems immediately while undertaking a longer-term, deeper renovation of the application structure. In fact, it may be a good idea to start some of the shorter-term projects even before the systems plan is completed, so as to demonstrate conclusively the benefits of the systems plan at a very early stage.

EVALUATING SYSTEMS PROJECTS

The final step in preparing the application part of the systems plan is to evaluate the benefits, risks, and possible sources for each of the systems projects just identified. This evaluation serves as the basis for assigning priorities and developing an initial phased plan with development schedules.

Once the new systems or groups of systems have been identified, the analysis of how well the objectives of these systems are carried out by today's applications will identify which systems, groups of systems, and subsystems are candidates for development projects. The benefits and risks of those that are candidates must then be evaluated, using the criteria agreed upon earlier. If required, a brief study akin to the feasibility study described in the previous chapter is conducted. Once a project's benefits have been evaluated, the amount of resource to be allocated to it is estimated. This estimate is partly based on the systems planners' perception of the probable development and running costs, but also, more realistically, it is based on what the organization is willing to invest to achieve the benefit. The analysis determines the orders of magnitude of the benefits and risks; the analysis is not a rigorous economic analysis using net present value techniques, for example.

As a simplified illustration, suppose an electronic mail system is estimated to save $5 million in postage over the next four years. (This period was evaluated to be the economic life of the required hardware.) The hardware cost is estimated not to exceed $3 million. Thus, $2 million is left as the upper limit on development cost. The question then becomes whether, in the planners' judgment, there is a strong chance of developing the system for, say, $1.5 million. The experience of the systems planners will usually tell them whether the risk of exceeding the benefit is very high or very low. (Gray areas are, by definition, high-risk.)

At this point, the probable source for each system is initially evaluated. In particular, all those systems that qualify for application software packages are identified. Systems for which no application software package is known to exist and those heart-of-the-business systems that are being deployed for a competitive edge are normally excluded.

Systems that are to be entirely developed by the users themselves are also identified at this point. The criteria for end-user development are the following:

- The application should not be on a critical path.
- The application should be limited in scope to the department or division that develops it.
- Data integrity and privacy should not be a major issue.
- The system should preferably use proven technology.

The result of this phase is a document for each identified system, depicting its general principles, its use of subject data bases, and its score against the criteria identified earlier.

When logical constraints are added—no system can use a subject data base until that data base exists—this document forms the basis for assigning priorities to the application development projects according to the policy set out at the beginning of the planning project.

ORGANIZING THE SYSTEMS PLANNING EFFORT

Little has been said so far about how the systems planning project itself is set up, who should participate, how long it is likely to last, and what practical problems have to be resolved.

BOX 5–2

Sources of Systems

In Section I, the discussion of the systems development life cycle assumed tacitly that all systems were developed by the personnel of the organization, working either in the IS department or in user departments. There are other sources of systems. The two main alternatives to the classical approach are packaged application software and turnkey systems.

Packaged application software consists of prewritten programs that perform a function that is similar from one organization to another, in the same industry (for example, materials requirements planning for discrete manufacturing) or across industries (for example, project control, general accounting, and payroll systems).

The advantages of packages are obvious: the cost and time of preparing detailed programming specifications, coding, and testing is replaced by a lump sum. The application software vendor can afford to charge much less per copy of the system because many copies will be sold.

Application software packages cannot be installed overnight. The life cycle activities associated with packages are requirements analysis, application software selection, interfacing to other systems, creation of data bases, and installation (user training and system test). In addition, the package may require customization when the specifications of the software do not meet those of the organization exactly. For instance, a user may prefer a different report sequence than the standard one or request that an additional piece of information be included.

In general, the more options the package has and the more flexible it is, the longer it may take to install, but the better it will ultimately meet the specific requirements of the users. There are no hard-and-fast guidelines; whether you select a no-frills, no-options product which can be installed quickly (but may force solutions that you may not be completely happy with) or a more sophisticated and difficult to install product is an individual decision for each new application.

When are application packages appropriate? In general, packaged application software is a good solution for nonstrategic systems. Payroll and general accounting are two examples of functions which generally do not provide strategic competitive advantage to an organization. For a retail chain, purchasing is a very important function and may not be appropriately filled by a package. For a firm of architects, purchasing is not critical, and application software is likely to be adequate. The reason behind this analysis is that if one firm can buy application software, then so can all its competitors. It is therefore difficult to differentiate based on application software. Moreover, the installation time of application software is short, so the possible competitive edge gained from installing it is not sustainable over the long run.

End-user computing has been mentioned as a source of departmental systems. It is difficult to have end users develop heart-of-the-business systems because the scale and scope of such systems generally require full-time IS professionals. End users can be expected to develop smaller systems, such as those that are to be used within their own departments and do not have the strong data integrity requirements of major transactions processing applications. End users who develop systems could be compared to do-it-yourself carpenters, who may be expected to build a set or garage on their own, but not a house.

Turnkey systems, or systems specified by the organization and developed exclusively for it by third parties, are generally chosen as a solution to the lack of personnel to develop the system in-house. The requirements specifications and the final integration testing must remain with the organization itself, just as with application software. In fact, custom-developed turnkey systems have a lot in common with application software, but they are more costly and take longer to implement. They are perhaps most appropriate where an application software package would have been a good solution had one existed.

The greatest disadvantage of turnkey development is that the organization may lose touch with the project during the development stage (which may last for many months, sometimes years). The result is the loss of the sense of ownership that comes from continuing user participation.

In-house custom development, the classical approach, is likely to continue to be the choice for implementing critical systems in large organizations. If the organization does not have a

sufficient number of developers or lacks experience in some of the fields, the team can be completed with temporary resources, be they programmers, analysts, or project leaders. In some cases, the leadership of the whole effort may be delegated to a systems integrator who can command all the hardware, software, and personnel resources required. However, it is prudent to insist on substantial participation of the client organization's personnel—top management (on a steering committee), users, and IS department personnel, who will run the system and maintain it.

Even though the proportion of systems coming from in-house development is likely to diminish relative to other sources, end-user computing and application software in particular, its total volume will continue to increase.

First, it should be apparent that a systems plan always covers multiple systems and multiple organizational units. For most medium-sized businesses, the plan covers the entire business. For very large enterprises, the plan may only cover a single strategic business unit (SBU). The requirement is that the SBU be quite independent, both in its operation and in its management, from the rest of the enterprise.

For a systems plan to be successful, it must first and foremost have the full **support of top management**. For example, IBM's BSP methodology recommends devoting a substantial part of the effort to gaining executive commitment. Perhaps as much as one-third of the elapsed time is spent up front planning and preparing the study. IBM also gives several types of briefings and courses to non-IS executives to prepare them for a BSP study by training them in the uses of information technology, discussing potential uses to solve the executives' day-to-day problems, and developing techniques to evaluate whether an information technology investment is worthwhile. IBM has recently been offering Information Systems Investment Strategy sessions as an addendum to BSP.

IBM recommends that the BSP team be led by an "executive with broad business perspective," who is supported by two to five managers from various functional areas and by one representative from the IS department. The **ideal user representative** on any project is the user who is absolutely indispensable in his or her own department and has no time available. To secure the cooperation of such an individual, it is all the more important to have executive commitment to the systems planning project.

support of top management

ideal user representative

**a project of six to
eight weeks**

IBM's BSP methodology aims at **a project of six to eight weeks**. Other methodologies tend to take more time, often as much as six months. A great deal of the value of systems planning lies in doing it quickly. If it lasts for longer than a few months, there is a significant risk that top management support will flag, as will user interest.

Three practical problems have to be addressed in planning and executing a systems planning project. The first is related to what has just been said about BSP, which prescribes the participation of about a half dozen high-level users for several weeks. Although this participation is an ideal to strive for, it is practically impossible to achieve. Compromises usually have to be made on the level and degree of involvement of the users. The compromises must then be compensated for by making sure that the best possible resources from the IS department are assigned to the project. Another partial solution is to hire consultants with good knowledge of the industry. It may also be necessary to exceed the eight-week guideline.

The second problem is that it is very difficult for the systems planners to stay at a general enough level of analysis. The criticism that has been leveled at some methodologies is that they encourage the team to go into too much detail. There are not enough firm guidelines on when to stop analyzing and start doing. A good indicator is that the project should under no circumstance exceed six months in duration. The tendency to generate excessive details is tied to the previous problem: it is much easier for high-level people to stay at a high level of abstraction. People with less experience and perspective need a deeper level of detail before they can be satisfied that they have understood all the critical aspects of a problem.

Finally, any successful systems planning project must result almost immediately in the implementation of some of the high-priority opportunities. How to translate the systems plan into a usable project plan for the IS department is one of the themes of the next chapter. Here suffice it to say that if the IS department is not ready to start delivering almost as soon as the systems plan is ready, the planning effort may well turn out to have been wasted.

Summary

Management's first goal in establishing a systems plan is to create systems that serve the organization better through the sharing of data across the entire organization. The second goal is to ensure better communications, understanding, and support among the three principal actors in information technology: top management, the users, and IS professionals. Harmony can be achieved by increasing the users' understanding of corporate goals and information technology policies and by making sure that the IS department takes the business view of the systems it develops rather than the technocrats'.

The first requirement of a systems planning project is therefore to ascertain the corporation's goals and strategies, either by reviewing the strategic business plan, if it exists, or by interviewing top management to develop the guiding principles that can help direct the study.

The knowledge of these goals and strategies enables the systems planning team to identify the commonly accepted criteria by which a proposed project's merits will be evaluated. Both potential paybacks and risks associated with the projects should be incorporated in these criteria.

When criteria are identified, the analysis of the organization's systems needs can proceed. Although this analysis can be undertaken in several ways, BSP is an effective example.

Most formal methodologies group data and functions around a fairly small number of subject data bases. These groups make up the ideal architecture towards which future systems development will attempt to evolve. Depending on how far the present systems are from this architecture and how much the organization is willing to spend on long-term versus short-term improvements, the systems actually identified in the systems plan will vary from situation to situation.

Some of the factors that will make a systems planning project successful are to keep the duration of the project short, to obtain sufficient top management commitment and user involvement, and to identify projects with quick payback that should be undertaken immediately following the conclusion of the systems planning project, or even earlier if possible.

Selected Readings

IBM Corporation, *Business Systems Planning: Information Systems Planning Guide* (Order No. GE20–0527), IBM, White Plains.
This manual is IBM's description of BSP. The current edition can be obtained through local IBM branch offices.

Zachman, John. "Business Systems Planning and Business Information Control Study: A Comparison," *IBM Systems Journal*, Vol. 21, No. 1, 1982.
In this article, John Zachman, who is IBM's foremost authority on systems planning, compares BSP and BICS, another methodology researched by IBM in the 1970s. This issue also contains interesting articles on information requirements analysis by Gordon Davis and on cost-benefit analysis by M. M. Parker. The best way to obtain a copy of the entire issue is from University Microfilms, Inc., Ann Arbor, Michigan.

Martin, James. *Strategic Data-Planning Methodologies*. Englewood Cliffs, New Jersey: Prentice-Hall, 1982.
This book justifies top management involvement, the subject data base approach, and the analysis of processes to get at the data structure. It refers to BSP and extends the planning process to distributed environments.

Martin, James, and Finkelstein, Clive. *Information Engineering*. Savant Institute, London, UK, 1979, 2 vols.
This is more a monograph than a book. It is much more theoretical than Martin's book, Strategic Data-Planning Methodologies. *It is of interest to students who wish to explore data analysis and entity-relationship modeling in depth.*

Cotterman, W. W., Couger, J. D., Enger, N. L., and Harold, F., eds. *Systems Analysis and Design: A Foundation for the 1980s*. New York: North Holland, 1980. *This collection of papers was presented at a symposium at Georgia State University in 1980. It contains a number of thought-provoking articles that still have a great deal of interest ten years later, although some of the technical discussions are outdated.*

Review Questions

1. Enumerate the steps that lead to the establishment of a systems plan. Which steps can be omitted and under what conditions?

2. What are the two main benefits of a formal systems plan? What are the risks inherent in not having one?

3. List some typical criteria that are used to evaluate systems projects in a systems plan. Why are these criteria not identical from one organization to another?

4. What are the two main sources for identifying systems projects? Explain why both sources are necessary for a balanced view.

5. How can a systems planning study team best ensure top management commitment to the study and to the resulting plan?

Discussion Questions

1. The text implies that methods based on the analysis of management information needs tend to result in short-term improvements and that methods that use a subject data base approach have a more long-term perspective. Discuss how these approaches are likely to affect the search for the use of information technology to competitive advantage.

Mini-Case

The First Mercantile Bank & Trust is a large bank with $20 billion in assets and 700,000 customers, individuals and corporations alike. Cynthia Kline, Vice-President of Information Systems, tells you that First Mercantile does not have a formally documented systems plan. She explains that it is not really necessary, because:

- She attends meetings with top management regularly, at least once a month if not more frequently. Information technology is a regular topic in these meetings, and she feels she has top management's support in the current direction of the IS department.

- All IS analysts and programmers are currently busy either with maintenance or with one of the two very large development projects currently under way: branch banking and commercial loans.

- Any additional need must be met with minimal assistance from the IS department, a case in point being the mortgage application approval system being developed by the user department with assistance from an artificial intelligence firm and outside consultants, analysts, and programmers.

- Subject data bases are not yet implemented, except for a shared Customer Information File, which uses hierarchical data base technology. However, account and balance information is maintained by separate systems for checking, savings, NOW, commercial loans, mortgages, and consumer loans.

- There is a hardware acquisition plan based on a capacity planning study first done two years ago with the help of the hardware vendor and updated every six months. The plan covers the next three years and takes into account the central mainframe, computing equipment in branches, office automation and departmental computing, and teleprocessing network needs.

The IS department has about 140 programmers, analysts, and project managers. Of these, approximately 105 are full-time on maintenance, and the rest are doing development work.

Questions for Discussion

1. How would you try to convince Ms. Kline to do a formal systems planning study?

2. If you succeeded in convincing her, what overall approach to the study would you recommend to her?

References

1. Rockart, John F. "Critical Success Factors." *Harvard Business Review* 57, no. 2 (March–April 1979): 81–91.

2. Nolan, Richard L. "Managing the Crises in Data Processing." *Harvard Business Review* 57, no. 2 (March–April 1979): 115–126.

Chapter 6

IS Resource Planning

IS management can use the systems planning process to plan for the IS department's organization and resources. The process will ensure that the systems plan can actually be implemented and will eliminate some of the pitfalls that result if one project is done at a time.

The chapter first outlines the advantages of the resource planning process. Next, it describes the process of planning for technology. This process is divided into two parts: planning for the resources used to develop applications and planning for the resources used to run the applications, once they are developed. The chapter concludes with sections on planning the personnel requirements and the organization of the IS department. Throughout the chapter, less emphasis is placed on describing the management planning process itself than on describing practical, real-world choices that need to be made.

Learning Objectives

- Understand the need to plan for the availability of personnel, software, and hardware resources required to implement a systems plan.
- Describe the main considerations in establishing the plan for a development hardware and software environment.
- Recognize the factors that preside over planning for the operating environment.
- Evaluate personnel planning requirements.
- Understand how resource planning considerations can affect the implementation strategy for the systems plan.

PROBLEMS SOLVED BY PROPER RESOURCE PLANNING

Many of the problems facing IS departments in the 1980s could have been avoided, or at least minimized, by better resource planning in the 1960s and

1970s. Three of these problems are described more fully here: the lack of availability of development resources due to excessive maintenance, the consequences of disparity in hardware and software, and the information technology needs of the IS department.

Lack of Development Resources

This problem manifests itself in the reputation of IS departments for not being able to take on new projects in a timely manner. The reputation for untimeliness is partly due to the nature of systems projects, which are more difficult and take longer to implement than most users realize. But it is also partly due to poor personnel planning. Maintenance tends to take up more than 50 percent—often up to 80 percent—of the IS department's personnel, leaving few resources available to cope with new development. Planning for maintenance has been inadequate. Improvements in this area would contribute to resolving several problems: unreasonable expectations about development speed, a lack of quality in the systems developed, and an unrealistic view of the benefits of end-user computing.

Good planning probably does not reduce the requirement for maintenance, but it can point out to top management the need for more staff if new development is to take place (with consequently higher budgets), or alternatively the need for lower expectations on the users' part. In other words, user and management expectations for the speed with which new projects can be developed could be better managed with effective planning.

Planning for realistic levels of maintenance could also help management realize the need for higher quality in the initial development of projects. Many IS departments tend to skimp on design, documentation, and reviews under the pressure of both top management and users to produce operational applications quickly and within the initial budget.

This problem is not easy to solve because of today's imperfect techniques for reducing maintenance by increasing the quality of the systems design and implementation techniques and tools. Moreover, IS professionals do not yet have reliable mechanisms for predicting maintenance efforts as a percentage of development effort or as a function of system size.

In the early days of end-user computing, the cost of maintenance of user-developed systems was even less well recognized than that of applications developed by the IS department. In many organizations, this is still the case.

There are two common results of this lack of recognition. First, many end users who develop their own applications because the IS department does not have sufficient resources find the development project to be challenging and rewarding, but they run out of steam when it comes to maintenance. In other words, they commit the same mistakes as early IS departments in failing to plan for high maintenance levels. Some of these user departments ask the IS department to take over the responsibility for the application, thus adding to the maintenance burden of the IS department.

A more frequent cause of added maintenance is that end-user computing usually places demands for data delivery systems on the central IS facility. Analysts and programmers have to be assigned to writing programs to cut off, extract, format, and deliver data to Infocenters, departmental computers, or PCs.

Even though proper planning does not by itself reduce the levels of maintenance in an organization, the systems plan should be the first step towards recognizing the problem and bringing it under control.

Equipment and Software Disparity

Equipment and software disparity occurs when multiple types of hardware and software coexist within an organization. Some of the resources may be incompatible. For instance, an IBM 3270 terminal cannot be attached to a Digital VAX or a Tandem computer. Other resources may be compatible, for instance, multiple programming languages such as COBOL, PL/I, Fortran, Assembler, and C. These languages may all be compatible; they can usually all be intermixed in the same application. Nevertheless, having too many products with the same purpose can cause problems.

The most frequent reason for disparity is that applications have been developed in isolation, and each application development team has chosen the hardware and software that suited the particular application, without regard to other applications. Another reason for disparity is that an IS department may be the result of a merger between firms and has therefore inherited multiple environments.

The two major difficulties associated with disparity are the lack of integration and the fragmentation of expertise. A minor problem is software cost: having five compilers instead of two is bound to be more costly.

The lack of integration caused by disparity is usually found when each application has been developed with its own tools and architecture, without regard to other applications. It will then be difficult to make Application A deliver data to or use data from Application B.

The fragmentation of expertise results because each developer can only be proficient in a small number of products and techniques. When developers or maintainers are moved from one application to another with different tools and techniques, their productivity is greatly reduced for substantial time periods. The alternative is to assign developers to specific applications and avoid moving them. This alternative is frequently unacceptable because it reduces personnel planning flexibility too much.

The proper planning for software and hardware environments can force the systems planners to choose the environment that best suits the organization over the long term. Properly done, the plan also stresses that the technological environment is going to change and that these changes are independent of the requirements of the applications that are identified today. As a result, it can become somewhat easier to design applications that are less intimately coupled with the technical environment and that will therefore cause fewer maintenance and integration problems in the future. As an example, most on-line data base applications today are designed with a specific teleprocessing (TP) monitor and data base management system (DBMS) in mind. If recognition is given to the fact that the choices made today may not be appropriate three, five, or ten years hence, the development team may try to design these applications so that the functional part—what the user sees—is less intimately tied to the technical part—the specific DBMS and TP monitor.

This kind of design is just as difficult to achieve as the proper planning for maintenance, but if the effort is not made, it is certain that progress will not be achieved.

Information Technology for the Developers

Finally, resource planning can also point out the information technology needs of the development teams themselves, long treated as shoemakers' children. Traditionally, IS departments have concentrated on satisfying the customers, i.e., the users, first and their own employees second. Most programmers continued to maintain their source programs on cards long after their users had started converting to on-line transaction processing.

This situation can be alleviated today with the widespread availability of intelligent workstations and reasonably priced CASE tools. An additional condition is necessary. For productivity tools to be effective, their installation must be treated just like any other application. The analysts' and programmers' requirements must be analyzed, the tools selected, the users (IS professionals) trained, and the process of change managed. In too many cases, tool selection is left to individual project leaders. As a result, the tools are adopted only by the members of that project. Other project leaders, partly suffering from the "not-invented-here" syndrome, may select other tools, thus creating a tools proliferation problem.

Frequently, the impact of tools on methodology is neglected. The use of some tools practically forces the use of a methodology. Tool proliferation then also leads to methodology proliferation, which, in turn, causes integration, management, and quality problems. The choice should be made the other way around: select and implement a department-wide methodology first, then pick the tools to support it.

PLANNING FOR THE DEVELOPMENT ENVIRONMENT

The objective of planning for the development environment is to avoid, as much as possible, the disparity problem described above. During the systems planning project, the main activity is to select those components of the development environment that are the most critical and that will contribute the most to high productivity (including the avoidance of disparity). A second important consideration is software costs. The components to be selected typically include the following:

- The data base management system (DBMS).
- The transaction processing monitor.
- Methods and tools such as programming languages, CASE tools, application generators, and fourth-generation languages.

The first critical choice for the technology planners is probably that of a **data base management system** (DBMS). This has an impact on all the other development tools and on the production environment.

In the late 1980s, the situation is often that an organization is committed to relational data base technology for its management information systems, end-user computing, departmental systems, and decision support data base. There are numerous merits to relational technology, one of which is flexibility in selecting and presenting information.

The question that often arises is that of transaction processing data bases. Is relational technology efficient enough to accommodate the volumes of transaction processing? Do end users need access to the production data bases as well as the information data bases? Does the organization already have a nonrelational DBMS, and if so, how can existing data bases migrate to relational technology? Can the organization afford to support multiple DBMS products?

Many of these questions, in particular those concerning performance, will be resolved in time, as relational technology grows more efficient and hardware becomes less costly. A strong indicator of the tendency toward relational DBMS as a generally accepted choice is that SQL, the premier relational data manipulation language, has been standardized by the American National Standards Institute. It therefore has the required stability and industry-wide support.

If data need to be shared across geographical boundaries, distributed data base becomes an issue. Distributed DBMS products are barely emerging on the market, and although distributed systems are becoming more widespread, they are still difficult to plan and implement. Distributing information to end users from a central clearinghouse for data is difficult enough to manage. On-demand access to data located in another part of the network, possibly with the intention to update it, requires a great deal of computing and communications power as well as considerable design expertise.

A final question to be addressed concerning DBMS is that of how well the DBMS is supported by the main application software packages that the organization uses or is planning to implement in the future. Is there a requirement for the application software to access existing subject data bases? Will end users be able to get the required data from the application software transparently? Are batch file interfaces needed between the application software and the rest of the organization's systems?

Once the DBMS has been chosen, the next choice is usually the **transaction processing monitor** to be used for operational systems. This is an easier question to resolve, because it has an impact only on the IS department professionals who will be developing transaction systems. Even here, the

data base management system

transaction processing monitor

choices are not as simple as a few years ago: new solutions for high-volume transaction processing are appearing with front-end, fault-tolerant machines with operating systems specifically designed for easy transaction processing. More importantly, these systems facilitate distributed processing and gradual, modular growth. As their name indicates, fault-tolerant machines can continue to operate even in the presence of failing components. (Nonspecialized processors can increasingly do this, but not quite to the full extent of the fault-tolerant alternatives.)

methods and tools

The next question concerns development **methods and tools** such as programming languages, application generators, fourth-generation languages, and CASE. A large number of tools claim to increase programming productivity and enable end users to develop systems. The contingency approach applied to the choice of style and language weighs project size, degree of integration, and processing volumes against the use of high-level tools.

The general guideline is that the larger the project, the less time is spent, in proportion, on programming and the more on other tasks. The need for communicating specifications and design documents between project members grows exponentially with the size of the project team. It becomes necessary to make sure of the coherence of design choices in different parts of the system. Much time is also spent on integration testing, i.e., testing to see that all the parts of the application fit together as planned. As a result, extremely large projects (say 500,000 lines of code and up) do not benefit nearly as much from advanced tools such as fourth-generation languages or application generators. The tendency today is to choose third-generation languages for very large systems, because the toolset that covers activities outside the coding effort tends to be much better established than for more recent tools. Because third-generation languages have been in existence for a long time and are highly standardized, tools working in this environment are easier to leverage.

Choosing a third-generation language as the core development language should not preclude the IS department from using a report writer, a query processor, or a program generator for low-volume, nonintegrated tasks such as ad hoc query.

A psychological factor to take into account is that fourth-generation languages and application generators are usually associated with prototyping and iterative development because of the speed with which code can be written. The temptation can then be to curtail design. This is fine if the prototype developed is truly a prototype with the objective of experimenting with a specific aspect of the application—the user interface, the data base performance, the functional rules—and if the intention is to throw the prototype out in favor of a designed solution. It is more of a problem if the prototype becomes the operational system, as sometimes happens. In iterative development, care should be taken that the design phase that precedes the first of the iterations is solid enough.

It may prove easy to code an insufficiently designed application the first time. The problem comes with maintaining it and trying to integrate it with other applications. The lack of design and the ease with which code is produced and modified can easily produce such a large number of different successive or even parallel versions of the same program that all control is lost.

In a number of instances, the use of a fourth-generation language has been unsuccessful in handling high volumes. The cause is not necessarily that fourth-generation languages are inherently inefficient. Rather, the trade-off between development productivity and flexibility has been made to favor development productivity. As a result, more architectural decisions have already been made and are embedded in the product. These can easily be incompatible with the volume requirements of the application.

An example of this problem occurs in one of the oldest types of productivity tools, report writers. A report writer generally reads a sequential file and produces a printout of selected parts of the file, possibly in a different sequence, with totals and summaries where required. A good report writer can easily save 80 percent of the coding effort that would be required to write the corresponding program in COBOL. The problem is that many report writers can only produce a single output report in each pass of the file. If this report writer is used to produce ten or more daily reports, the file will be read ten or more times in a day. A custom-written program or a more perfected (but less easy-to-use) report writer could read the file once, extracting all the data required as each record is read, do all the required manipulations, and print the reports, thus eliminating nine passes of the file.

The range is wide from application generators and fourth-generation languages to third-generation languages with tools concentrating on documentation, testing, integration, and design. Most large installations will require both categories of products.

An IS department with multiple tools needs guidelines on which tool to use under which circumstances and on the acquisition of new tools when they are required. The degree of end-user computing; the balance of centralized, integrated versus departmental systems; and the corporate culture should determine how stringently these guidelines are enforced.

Once the development tools and methodology strategy have been determined, a **plan for implementing** them must be devised. This plan includes a schedule for acquiring the tools and provisions for training the users, building up expertise, and gradually extending the use of the tool throughout the IS organization. The effort to implement new methods and tools is no different from any other project aiming to change the way people work. As outlined in Chapter 2, this change must be managed; it cannot be implemented at breakneck speed, and it requires absolute management commitment and support.

plan for implementing

PLANNING FOR THE PRODUCTION ENVIRONMENT

This book is mainly about development; planning for a production environment is not its central theme. However, many production issues have an impact on design and implementation, and they therefore affect the maintenance, disparity, and technology problems indirectly. Two areas are covered here: planning for capacity and planning the communications network.

Capacity

The main role of planning for production resources is to match hardware and software to processing volumes and characteristics. The planning for capacity is quite different for production systems and for end-user computing.

Production. Most production applications run on centralized mainframes or departmental minicomputers. For transaction processing, there are fairly well-developed capacity planning tools, especially on the more popular mainframes, that can help predict hardware requirements.

Because the trend has been towards on-line processing, batch problems have been largely glossed over. However, in most transaction processing systems, batch processing still plays a large role. With most of the working day devoted to on-line activity, the so-called batch window, the time frame in which the day's batch processing must be done, must be strictly respected. Within this time frame, the day's activities must be cut off, interface files to other systems created, data bases backed up and possibly reorganized, daily reports produced (possibly in time for a postal deadline to be met), and any other ad hoc or periodic processing completed.

All these processes may be easy to complete if nothing goes wrong. If anything does, there must be sufficient time for the night shift personnel to find out what the problem is, get the solution, implement it, and redo the work before the on-line program is started in the morning. Ideally, the batch window should contain provisions for such incidents and the time required to recover from them. In other words, the night work should probably be scheduled to be over around 2 or 3 A.M. Despite appearances, the entire night is not available for batch work. Also, for centralized systems that process transactions from several different time zones, the batch window may have to be further contracted.

Historically, most on-line systems have been designed to be stopped at the end of the day to let the batch system take over. A serious problem occurs if the batch window gets too small. A recent trend has been to design applications that can operate continuously, continuing to process transactions while the day's processing is being cut off and the data bases are unloaded.

The requirement for continuous operations must be diagnosed early so that operating systems, TP monitors, and DBMS can be selected to support this requirement.

End-User Computing. End-user computing is increasingly done on personal computers or intelligent workstations, connected by local area networks that give the PCs access to local data bases and telecommunications networks. The required capacity of shared central resources, local networks, telecommunications facilities, and data base machines is difficult to predict because the architecture and the offerings are newer. If end-user computing is done from terminals on a departmental computer or a central mainframe, the difficulty stems from the fact that some users tend to consume a great deal of resources while others are much more modest in their demands. An "average" user cannot be reliably defined when the extremes range so far.

The best approach is probably to use historical data to estimate the needs of various classes of users and to extrapolate growth trends. If the cost of end-user computing thus estimated is substantial, top management should be informed that there is a high risk of the actual need being quite different from the plan after a few years.

Data Communications

In addition to the plan for processors and operating systems, planning for the operating environment requires that consideration be given to the communications network and the related software. In general, the communications software selected is the proprietary software of the main hardware vendor, such as SNA for IBM and DECNet for Digital.

Special considerations apply when multiple systems from different vendors need to communicate. If these systems are all within the organization, it is usually feasible either to standardize on one communications standard that can be accommodated by all the equipment or to provide protocol converters, which can enable two incompatible pieces of equipment to converse through a translator.

The network itself must be designed. Because network design is the work of telecommunications specialists, it will not be covered in detail here. The technology is changing very fast, as are the offerings of the various vendors. Basically, the planning activity consists of anticipating peak and average data transmission volumes between different sites. The planners then decide whether to install leased communications lines (unlike switched telephone lines, these lines are always available and do not require one site to dial up the other in order to connect), to use the switched (or dial-up) public telephone network, or to use a dedicated data network offered by a third party such as Tymnet, Telenet, Autonet, General Electric, or IBM. With increasing frequency, the question concerns not only the network for transmitting data between locations but also intracompany telephone conversations, image (as in facsimile), and electronic mail.

Within each of these options, the many choices of capacity, quality, and reliability of service make decisions extremely complex. In those cases where the organization routinely exchanges large volumes of data with its suppliers, vendors, or competitors, the choices are more limited, because they must be negotiated and agreed upon by several independent organizations. For instance, a bank that wishes to execute international funds transfers to its correspondent banks abroad has little choice but to connect to the S.W. I.F.T. network, based in Brussels, Belgium. This network has its own well-defined transmission disciplines. Most vendors of communications software to the banking industry offer an interface to S.W. I.F.T. Another emerging example of intercompany data transfer is electronic data interchange (EDI), which enables corporate customers and suppliers to transmit ordering, invoicing, and shipping data among themselves. EDI data is usually transmitted over either a third-party network or the switched telephone network.

Distributed data processing offers even more alternatives than telecommunications networks. Box 6–1 details some considerations that apply when planning for distributed data processing.

PLANNING FOR PERSONNEL REQUIREMENTS

Given the applications to be developed and the development environment (methodology and tools), overall personnel requirements to implement the systems plan can be estimated. The best way to plan the level and sources of personnel required is a spreadsheet such as the one in Figure 6–1. This spreadsheet shows the required level of staffing by project and by category for each month of the plan. Analyst and programmer are the two main categories; if personnel from user departments is to be assigned full time to the project, user analysts may make up a third category. The lower part of the spreadsheet shows gross and net available personnel, the unfulfilled requirement, and the proposed solution to this requirement.

The technique used is that of resource loading. For large projects, mechanized tools can help. For smaller projects, the steps are as follows:

- Identify the amount of resource required per project (divided into design and programming) and personnel type.

- Summarize the resource required for the period of the plan by adding up all the projects.

- Summarize the available personnel and identify the net personnel requirement (the difference between the gross requirement and the available resource). Remember to subtract the requirement for maintenance.

- Prepare a strategy for filling the net requirement: recruiting and temporary personnel.

- Add the recruited personnel to existing available personnel and distribute it over the duration of the plan on a spreadsheet.

- Start loading the highest-priority projects by spreading the available personnel evenly over these projects, from the start of the plan. Adjust this loading by adding temporary personnel, if that strategy is to be used, wherever needed.

- Add second-priority projects to the spreadsheet when resources become available from higher-priority projects. Adjust as required with temporary personnel.

Figure 6–1 **Personnel Requirements Plan**

PREPARED BY: J. WEBER	DATE: 27AUG88	VERSION: 1.1
APPROVED BY: JACK CROFT	DATE: 05SEP88	STATUS : D

PAGE 1

Legend: each quarter has two sub-columns — PM and AP.

APPLICATION	1989 Q4 PM AP	1990 Q1 PM AP	1990 Q2 PM AP	1990 Q3 PM AP	1990 Q4 PM AP	1991 Q1 PM AP	1991 Q2 PM AP	1991 Q3 PM AP	1991 Q4 PM AP	1992 Q1 PM AP	1992 Q2 PM AP	1992 Q3 PM AP	1992 Q4 PM AP
Document Existing Systems	1 3												
Automate Delivery Tickets	1	1 2	1 2										
Develop Procedures and Training	1 1	1 2											
Develop Purchased Products			1 1	1 2	1 5	1 5	1 5						
Rewrite and Enhance Batch			1 1	1 1	1 2	1 3	1 3	1 3					
Major Systems Enhancements													
Order Status Change			1 1	1 1									
Commit/Decommit Fabrication			1 1	1 1									
Inventory Improvements					1 1	1 1							
Production Scheduling						1 1	1 1						
Pricing Support							1 1	1 1					
Install New General Ledger								1	1 3	1 3	1 4	1 4	
Other													
Alpha Cargo		1 1	1 1	1 1	1								
Plant and Fleet Maintenance			1	1									
Payroll Data Collection	1 1	1 1											
Gross Requirement	4 5	4 6	6 7	5 5	4 8	4 10	3 9	3 4	1 3	1 3	1 4	1 4	
Available	4 5	4 6	5 7	5 5	5 8	5 8	5 8	5 8	5 8	5 8	5 8	5 8	
Net Requirement/(Excess)	0 0	0 0	1 0	0 (2)	(1) 0	(1) 2	(2) 1	(2) (4)	(4) (5)	(4) (5)	(4) (4)	(4) (4)	
Recruitment			1 1	1		2	1						
Temporary	1		1			2	1						

BOX 6–1

Distributed Data Processing

Distributed data processing (DDP) is the processing of a single application on more than one physically and logically separate computer. The distributed application is any set of programs that share data (even through a batch interface such as the transmission of files of extracted data from a production data base to a decision support system). The computers may be physically separated by distances requiring telecommunications links, or they may be close enough that channel-to-channel connections or sharing of disk peripherals are available, but they must be running under the control of multiple independent operating systems (logically separate).

Conceptually, DDP is not particularly desirable. Shared access to data is much easier to control if the data exists in only one copy at a central site. Whenever multiple copies exist, there is a loss of control because the copies may wind up with inconsistent values. Also, the more copies there are, the easier it is for an intruder to get access to one of them.

Science fiction stories from the 1950s illustrate the dream of a single centralized data base serving the entire population. For example, stories by Isaac Asimov depict a giant "Multivac" spreading out over multiple square miles underneath the Washington, D.C., area.

Why hasn't this dream materialized? Why do we need distributed data processing?

There are two technical reasons and one organizational reason for distributed data processing. First, telecommunications costs have not dropped as fast as hardware costs. In some cases, transporting a data file to a staging point closer to its main users is more economical than letting the users connect via telecommunications lines to a central facility.

Second, the maximum processing capacity of even the largest mainframe computer running under control of a single operating system is limited. Moreover, this maximum capacity has tended to grow more slowly than the aggregate need for computing capacity. Therefore, some applications must run on multiple computers. IBM's internal electronic mail, electronic messages, and information data base system is of this nature. In some cases, an organization has multiple brands of computers. For example, an application software package that is particularly desired may not run on the main computer because it requires a different brand. (Thus, DDP may be an issue even for single-site installations.)

Third, the organizational reason, which has been the main reason for distributed data processing in the past, is that the management at a remote site (such as a factory, a bank branch, or a regional agency) has wanted control of its computing resources. Consequently, when the network and the central computer are not 100 percent reliable, locally controlled computer resources can continue to function in degraded mode while the problem is being fixed. Also, when the demand exceeds the capacity, local management wants to be able to arbitrate, rather than be subjected to, the decision of a remote headquarters.

In the late 1970s, the trend towards DDP was accelerated by the perception that minicomputers (and later microcomputers) had a better price/performance ratio than large mainframes. This perception was only superficially true. When all factors were taken into account, distributed processing and centralized processing tended to even out. For example, it was not as easy to balance the processing load of a collection of smaller machines (the machine at Location A might be nearly idle while that at Location B might be overloaded); it was more costly to develop distributed systems; and data tended to be duplicated and therefore occupy more space.

As the technology evolved, the 1980s saw new applications, such as office automation and departmental systems, and new technologies, such as the personal computer. Now, the price of the personal computer has fallen so low that it is desirable to move as much processing to the PC, used as a workstation, as possible. Shared data must still be controlled at a more central point—a departmental file server or a central mainframe. However, an increasing number of systems that have user interaction are executed in what has been termed *cooperative processing* mode, partly on the PC, partly on the computer where the data resides.

In some cases, the PCs are attached directly, via a telecommunications link, to a single central mainframe. In other cases, the PCs are the workstations of a departmental minicomputer that maintains the communications link with the mainframe (three-tier computing). In most cas-

es, however, the PCs are attached locally to each other via a local area network. To this local area network is also attached a file server that controls the shared data. A communications server is used as a shared gateway to the central mainframe.

The systems planning study team must address which of these architectures is best adapted to the organization's need and culture. Next, within the selected architecture, the team must estimate which part of the main applications will be executed where, where the data will reside, whether it will be replicated at multiple sites, and so on. Then, the team must evaluate the consequences of these assumptions on the hardware, telecommunications, and development costs.

- Summarize temporary personnel requirements to check that the total does not exceed the need determined earlier.

- Adjust the schedule as necessary by varying recruiting dates and temporary personnel and by changing project time lines until a satisfactory result is obtained.

Described in this fashion, the process seems relatively simple. However, there are many practical difficulties. At such an early stage little if anything is known about the specific requirements of each of the applications identified in the systems plan and the personnel requirements can only be roughly estimated. A frequent strategy is to refer to similar projects done in the past or in other corporations in the same industry. Experience is more useful than analysis in this case.

The most frequent error in personnel planning for such an exercise is to assume that executing the plan can start immediately with the first project. Very often the systems plan is associated with a change in the technical direction of the IS department, for example, toward relational data base, distributed computing, or even simply a new operating system. The lead time to get all the support functions in place for the first project is on the order of a few weeks, perhaps even months. Software and equipment may have to be installed, standards developed, and IS professionals trained.

An additional factor requiring lead time is the possible reorganization of the IS department to cope with a period of high development activity. Reorganization is especially necessary in IS departments that have gotten into the rut of *creeping maintenance*, defined as the gradual encroachment of day-to-day activities on new projects until practically all personnel are assigned to maintenance.

Finally, recruiting new or temporary personnel also requires long lead times.

In practice, it is prudent to provide for a two- to three-month buildup for the initial projects. Failure to provide enough time may result in having to report to management after only three months or so that the implementation of the plan is already behind schedule. Such a report can have disastrous effects on the credibility of the plan and the future of top management support for it.

Meanwhile, the plan will probably have identified one or two areas of quick return. These should be undertaken as high-priority items immediately without waiting for the support activities to take place. Early successes will increase the credibility of the plan and enhance both top management and user support.

HANDLING ORGANIZATIONAL ISSUES

As mentioned earlier, the implementation of a systems plan is often preceded by a reorganization of the IS department. A systems plan is often a manifestation of fresh thinking about how to tackle the problem of developing new applications. This freshness often carries over to the organization of the development teams and, indeed, the entire department.

The main objective of such a reorganization is to ensure that the resources that are assigned to new development (both the development teams themselves and the required support functions such as data administration, data base administration, and software support) remain assigned to new development and do not gradually get frittered away on maintenance of existing systems.

Even if no reorganization takes place, the analysis of personnel require-ments described in the previous paragraph often leads information systems management to perform general personnel planning. Not only is it important to have the number of personnel available at the right times during the plan, but it is equally important that it should be the right personnel. Recruiting and training plans, career paths, and an assessment of existing personnel's manage-rial, professional, and technical qualifications should be undertaken during the development of the systems plan.

Summary

Poor resource planning is at the root of many of the IS department's problems in the 1980s. The maintenance workload, often not planned for, tends to stifle systems development projects and contribute to the IS department's reputation for unresponsiveness. The accumulation of disparate hardware and software causes duplication of effort and makes development personnel less interchange-able. Finally, only recently have IS departments started to treat the technology needs of their personnel with the attention the problem deserves.

If a systems plan, developed as described in the previous chapter, is to succeed, it must be accompanied by proper resource planning: for the development environment, for the production environment, and for personnel.

The decision that most affects the development environment is probably that of a data base management system. Today, the natural choice is a relational data base management system. Relational DBMS may not always be feasible in all environments, particularly those that already have a first-generation DBMS and those that rely heavily on application software.

The next decision is usually that of a teleprocessing monitor for transaction processing. Once the hardware and the DBMS are known, the TP monitor follows almost automatically.

Of more immediate importance to the development teams is the choice of methods and tools such as programming languages, application generators, fourth-generation languages, and CASE tools. All categories of tools are not equally suitable to all types of projects. For instance, the tools that shorten the coding cycle are less important on large projects where coding tends to be a smaller part of the total effort.

A plan for implementing these tools—a technology insertion plan—should accompany the choice of the actual tools.

Planning for production resources consists of making sure that the available hardware and software meet the needs of new systems as they are being implemented. Most of the capacity required is caused by on-line transaction processing and interactive end-user computing, but batch requirements cannot be neglected.

Teleprocessing network plans are also part of the production environment, both for in-house communications and for electronic data interchange with customers and suppliers.

The planners must analyze the personnel requirements for developing the new applications and identify the sources of personnel: internal resources (analysts and programmers who are not required for maintenance), user departments, new hires, or temporary external sources such as consultants and programming houses.

Finally, due consideration must be given to organizational issues such as the best organization of the IS department for the implementation of the plan as well as training and career planning for its personnel.

Review Questions

1. List the three main components of resource planning for a systems plan.

2. Why is the choice of a DBMS so critical?

3. Explain why tools that aim for programming efficiency are less important on large projects.

4. Discuss the relative importance of on-line and batch activities in determining the total hardware capacity required for the production environment.

5. Discuss the pros and cons of hiring new personnel, assigning user personnel as analysts, and using temporary personnel to fill personnel requirements for a systems plan.

Discussion Questions

1. What are the risks of trying to implement a systems plan without resource planning?

2. Discuss the pros and cons of having multiple data base management systems or transaction processing monitors in a single IS department.

3. What are some requirements for implementing a homogeneous set of analysis, design, and programming tools or workbench?

Mini-Case

You are preparing a systems plan for Mid-Continental Electric Company. The applications to be developed over the next five years have been identified, and the required development resources have been estimated. The applications are described in Figure 6–2. Figure 6–3 indicates which current applications are being replaced by new applications and the number of analysts and programmers that are currently maintaining these systems.

Prepare a proposed calendar of application development covering all the applications in the plan. Assume that, as soon as an application project is started, the maintenance level on the applications being replaced is reduced by half. In addition, as soon as the new application is implemented, the maintenance level of the applications being replaced drops to 0. Also assume that maintaining one of the new applications for a year will require 5 percent of the total initial development effort.

The calendar should stretch over no more than five years and require no more than a personnel increase of 15 percent in any given year.

Figure 6–2 **List of Applications in Mid-Continental
Electric Company's Portfolio**

```
SYSTEMS                 MID-CONTINENTAL ELECTRIC              CD-20
PLAN                                                         PSCHED
              PROJECT SCHEDULE AND PERSONNEL REQUIREMENTS
```

```
PREPARED BY:  ANNA TERHOOFT  DATE:  30APR89    VERSION:       PAGE 1
APPROVED BY:  H. B. WALKER   DATE:  30APR89    STATUS :
```

PROJECT DESCRIPTION		TOTAL WORKDAYS	PROJ MGR	ANAL	USER	PROG	DATE FROM	TO
Budget Preparation	M	200	30		170		03/90	07/90
Crew Time/Field Rept.	M	900	135		765		07/89	12/89
Trans. Doc. Prep.	M	800	120		680		10/89	01/90
On-Line Table Maint	M	1000	150		850		07/89	04/90
Job Closing	M	300	45		255		01/90	06/90
Forms & Report Review	M	1000	150		850		04/90	02/91
Enhanced On-Line Info.	D	300	45	255			12/89	02/90
	I	1400	210	420		770	03/90	09/90
Cooperative Proc. Arch.	D	200	30	170			09/90	10/90
	I	600	90	200		310	11/90	03/99
Training and Support		900	135	765			07/89	12/92
Detail Transaction DB	D	500	75	425			07/89	10/89
	I	1000	150	325		525	11/89	06/90
Work Reporting	D	1700	255	1445			07/89	01/90
	I	4900	735	1560		2605	02/90	02/91
Contract Management	D	700	105	595			03/91	05/91
	I	1500	225	400		875	06/91	12/91
Cost Accounting	D	650	100	550			01/90	05/90
	I	3450	500	1070		1880	06/90	03/91
Interim Commitment Rept.	D	100	15	85			07/89	09/89
	I	350	50	65		235	10/89	01/90
New FMIS Design	D	3450	525	2925			09/90	07/91
Source/Report Interface	I	11900	1785	3450		6665	01/91	08/92
Cost Acctg/Coding Block	I	600	90	230		280	01/92	08/92
Budgeting	I	2400	360	965		1075	10/91	06/92
General Ledger	I	7150	1050	3400		2700	09/91	12/92
Management Reporting	I	5950	890	2680		2380	10/91	12/92

```
KEY:  M=Manual System
      D=Design
      I=Installation
```

Figure 6–3 **List of Existing Applications To Be Displaced**

```
SYSTEMS                    MID-CONTINENTAL ELECTRIC              CD-20
PLAN                                                            RSCHED
                       SYSTEM REPLACEMENT SCHEDULE

┌────────────────────────────────────────────────────────────────────┐
│ PREPARED BY:  ANNA TERHOOFT  DATE:  30APR89   VERSION:      PAGE 1   │
│ APPROVED BY:  H. B. WALKER    DATE:  30APR89   STATUS :              │
└────────────────────────────────────────────────────────────────────┘


                                                    CURRENTLY
                                                    ASSIGNED
        SYSTEM BEING REPLACED     REPLACED BY    PM  ANAL  PROG

        Work and Contract Management  Work Reporting   1   10   13

        Cost Accounting           Cost Accounting    1   12    9

        Financial and G/L         New FMIS           1   14   25

        Budgeting                 New FMIS               2    3

        Responsibility Reporting  New FMIS               6   10



    Personnel currently unassigned to maintenance:

             Project Managers:   4

             Analysts:           6

             Programmers:       13


    User personnel can be assumed to be available as required.


    Available time calculation:

             Workdays/year:  5 * 52     =  260
             Less -
                  4 week's vacation     =  (20)
                  Absences              =   (5)
                  Training and depart-
                       mental           =  (25)
                                           -----
             Net available:            =  210   workdays/year/person
                                           =====
```

Technique

Entity-Relationship Diagrams

DEFINITION

An entity-relationship diagram depicts the types of objects about which data is maintained in the system, the types of relationships that hold among these objects, and in some cases, the types of attributes (data elements) that are stored about each object.

An entity-relationship diagram is one technique used to represent a model of the data base that stores the system's data. (There are other, usually less graphic techniques.)

EXAMPLES

A library lends books to its patrons. Each book is characterized by its title, author, publisher, edition, and ISBN number. Each book in the library may exist in several copies. Each patron can borrow a certain number of books. If a patron requests a book for which there are no copies available (all are out on loan), he or she is put on a waiting list. If a patron requests a book that the library does not have, the library may decide to order the book. The patron is to be notified when the book arrives (see Figure 1).

A university enrolls students in courses. Each course has a name and a number. Each course may be given several times in a given semester. Each course is given by a professor—not necessarily the same for the different schedules of a single course. For example, Professor McCarthy may give Accounting 101 on Tuesdays at 9A.M., and Professor O'Brien may give Accounting 101 on Thursdays at 3P.M. Courses have prerequisites; for instance, Accounting 210 requires that Accounting 101 have been taken previously. The system has registered the courses each student has already taken, together with the grades obtained (see Figure 2).

A manufacturing company manufactures washing machines from raw materials, stores the manufactured machines in one of several regional warehouses, and sells the machines to customers. Each customer order is delivered

Figure 1 **Entity-Relationship Diagram for a Lending Library**

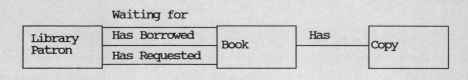

from the warehouse closest to the customer. Deliveries are always complete; there is no back-ordering system. Each order can request several different products. Payment on orders is due ten days after delivery.

Raw materials and parts are obtained from suppliers. For each type of raw material and for each different part, the company maintains a list of suppliers, with the prices that the supplier has quoted. Two suppliers may supply the same materials at different prices. Every time more materials are needed, the company calls one or more suppliers to find out the delivery lead time and places the order with the supplier who charges the least and who can deliver within a specified time.

The washing machines are made of parts that can be manufactured in-house, from raw materials (sheet metal for the body), or purchased (nuts, screws, washers, and bolts). A rough corporate data model for this manufacturer is shown in Figure 3.

WHERE USED IN THE LIFE CYCLE

Entity-relationship diagrams (ERDs) are initially created in the project identification phase. Depending on the methodology chosen for project identification, they may be more or less central to the process. In general, if systems planning (identification of a long-term strategy for implementing projects that have been identified early) is implemented, ERDs are a critical part of the phase. If project

Figure 2 **Entity-Relationship Diagram for a University**

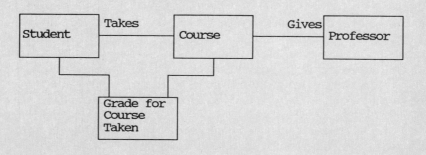

Figure 3 **Entity-Relationship Diagram for a Manufacturing Company**

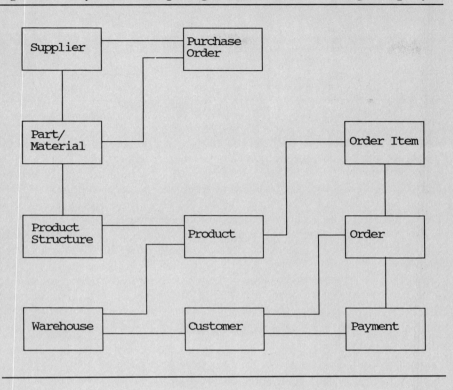

identification is ad hoc, with each project being identified as its need is felt by the users, the use of ERDs is more informal.

The ERDs established during project identification are refined and detailed during the requirements analysis phase to incorporate the different uses of the data that different users will make.

The updated ERDs established during requirements analysis are refined in the data design activity of the design phase. They are given their final form here; they are then communicated to the implementation phase where programmers and data base administrators use them as input to their work.

FORMAL RULES

Entities, representing the objects about which data is to be stored, are depicted as rectangular boxes. Straight lines between the boxes indicate the relationships among these entities. Each end of the relationship may have a symbol indicating the degree, or *cardinality*, of the relationship. For instance, some relationships

Figure 4 **One-to-One Relationship**

hold between one of each of the two entities. In a data base about universities, each university has one president and one only (see Figure 4).

Each university has many students registered. If students are not allowed to register in several universities at the same time, this would be represented by a crow's foot (indicating "many") on the student end of the relationship and a cross (indicating "one") on the university side (see Figure 5).

Each university delivers a number of different degrees. Some degrees (such as a B.S. in mechanical engineering) are delivered by many different institutions. This type of relationship is known as many-to-many (see Figure 6).

In the above examples, the name of the relationship has also been indicated. Each relationship can be read in either of two ways and has therefore two possible names. The name is always a verb; it is written closer to the subject of the verb than to the object. The relationship names in the last example can be read as:

"Each university delivers one or more degrees."
"Each degree is delivered by one or more universities."

In all these examples, the cardinality at either end is at least one. There is no university without a president, and there is no university president without a university. This may not always be the case. For instance, in the relationship between a customer and an order in the manufacturing example, each order is placed by a customer (and one only), but there may be customers who do not have an order. This situation may be represented by drawing a small circle at one end of the relationship (see Figure 7).

Figure 5 **One-to-Many Relationship**

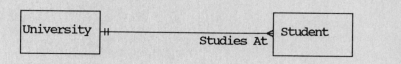

Figure 6 **Many-to-Many Relationship**

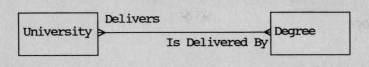

An entity may have a relationship to itself. In the real world, one instance of the entity type has the relationship to another entity of the same type. For instance, on a family tree, each person has a relationship to other persons in the same family, as illustrated in Figure 8.

In the manufacturing example, a part could have a relationship either to a number of suppliers or to materials from which the company makes it. This is an either-or relationship, and it could be represented in either of two ways.

The bracket encompassing the two relationships that the part has indicates an alternative (see Figure 9).

Figure 10 is slightly more complex, but it is a more powerful way of representing alternatives. In reality, this diagram states that what the finished product views as an entity (a part) is made up of two subentities, a purchased part and a manufactured part, each of which has a different set of relationships.

Simplifications may be made to the entity-relationship diagram. In the early stages, before a detailed analysis is made of the entities, the degree symbols may be suppressed. They may be evident or they may not be critical to the understanding of the diagram. The degree symbol can often be omitted early in the life of a project (especially during systems planning).

Usually, only one relationship exists between two given entities. In that case, it may be possible to omit the relationship name, especially where the nature of the relationship is evident from the context (as between customer and order, between order and order item, or between order item and product). If multiple relationships exist between two entities, they must be designated. In general, only one of the two possible names are given, to be read in the active voice and

Figure 7 **One-to-Many Relationship (Optional)**

Figure 8 **Entity with Relationship to Itself**

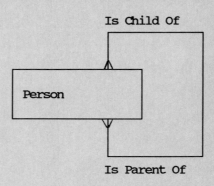

in the one-to-many direction (if it is a one-to-many relationship). An example of multiple relationships between two entities is given in the library example where a patron may have borrowed one book and be on the waiting list for another (see Figure 1).

MECHANIZED TOOLS

Most CASE tools on the market have some facility for drawing entity-relationship diagrams. Those tools that have the most powerful ERD features are the ones that adopt a data-driven development methodology; they may be somewhat weaker for data flow diagramming. This characteristic may be a deterrent to installations

Figure 9 **Either-Or Relationship**

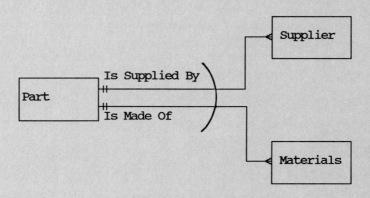

Figure 10 **Relationship with Entities and Sub-Entities**

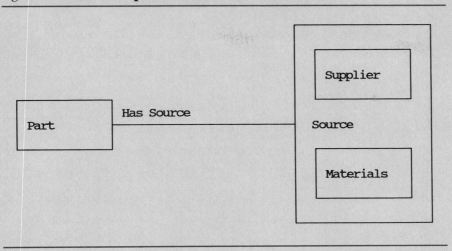

that have implemented other methodologies (process-driven or more classically structured, such as Gane & Sarson, DeMarco, or IBM's IPT).

The ideal facility would be able to store formal descriptions of entities, relationships, and attributes and transform these into diagrams for display. The tool should also store data descriptions for programming languages (such as COBOL) and data description language (for describing data base structure to a DBMS).

Ideally, the form used for storing the information about entities and relationships should be one that captures most of the structure. To capture structure, it is better to store the information as data rather than as schematics. However, most input and output should be in the form of schematics. Transforming a description into a schematic is not very difficult, whereas creating a formal description from a schematic is much more difficult. The process generally requires a fairly strict methodology. Thus, the products that rely on such a methodology are generally more powerful than general-purpose graphics tools.

The tool also needs to be able to download data descriptions from other tools such as data dictionaries or program libraries. Most tools that are interactively oriented only, with no batch facility, cannot do this.

Finally, the tool should provide support for both the informal, high-level diagrams established early in the development process and the detailed, formalized diagrams used in the design phase. It should support both bottom-up and top-down development.

None of the tools available on the market in 1987 had all these features.

EQUIVALENT TECHNIQUES

Many different conventions exist for drawing entity-relationship diagrams. The technique described in this section follows the majority, as exemplified by Chris Gane in *Rapid System Development*. Many of the minor variations (in particular on the incorporation of relationship names and degree symbols) have also been described.

Other variations are:

- Inclusion of attributes alongside each entity. (Some authors recommend including only the key to each entity—its identifying attribute, such as its Social Security number. Others recommend including all the known attributes or data elements.)

- Using ovals instead of rectangles.

- Using arrows and double arrows, or noting degrees with numbers, instead of the cross and crow's feet symbols.

- Distinguishing between different types of entities with different box shapes: entities that exist independently of others (customer, product), entities that cannot exist except in connection with some other entity on which it depends (order, depending on customer), and intersection product).

- Forbidding many-to-many relationships. (This is appropriate in the design stage where one of the design steps is to make sure that the relationships are either one-to-one or one-to-many. However, in earlier stages where the ERD is used to communicate with users rather than with data base designers, the many-to-many relationship is a useful form of shorthand.)

- Using data attribute names rather than verbs to designate relationships. (A relationship such as that of a customer and an order can be implemented by including the customer number of the owner of the order as an attribute of the order. Again, this technique is appropriate in later stages where the main purpose is to communicate with data base designers rather than with users.)

- Including narrative. (A useful guideline is to include enough narrative with the top-level models—before the design phase—that users can understand all the implications and conventions of the diagram without formal training. Typically, for a one-page diagram, this might be a one- to three-page typed narrative.)

- Letting relationships bear attributes.

- Using representations that depend on the data base management system being used. (This variation is obviously appropriate only when the physical data base design is done. To use the technique earlier is harmful, because it forces the designer to make implementation decisions before design decisions. The peculiarities of these representations are the strongest for the hierarchical type of data base, such as IBM's IMS.)

An obvious alternative is to use a nongraphic representation such as that provided by a DBMS data-definition language. Each entity is described by noting

Figure 11 Sample Non-Graphic Representation of Entities and Relationships

```
LIBRARY                    COUNTY OF DUSABLE                    CD-20
SYSTEM                                                          ERDESCR
                    ENTITY/RELATIONSHIP DESCRIPTION

┌──────────────────────────────────────────────────────────────────────┐
│ PREPARED BY:  ADS          DATE:   27NOV88    VERSION:        PAGE 1   │
│ APPROVED BY:  JCG          DATE:   06DEC88    STATUS :  D             │
└──────────────────────────────────────────────────────────────────────┘


    ENTITY             Patron
    KEY                Patron-Number
    ATTRIBUTES         Patron-Name
                       Patron-Address
                       Patron-Telephone-No

    ENTITY             Book
    KEY                ISBN-No
    ATTRIBUTES         Book-Title
                       Book-Author-Name
                       Book-Edition
                       Number-of-Copies

    RELATIONSHIP       Has-Borrowed
    ORIGIN             Patron
        DEGREE         {0,N}        N<=Number-of-Copies
    TARGET             Book
        DEGREE         {0,N}          N<=Lending-Limit
    REVERSE-NAME       Is-On-Loan-To

    RELATIONSHIP       Is-Waiting-For
    ORIGIN             Patron
        DEGREE         {0,N}
    TARGET             Book
        DEGREE         {0,N}
    REVERSE-NAME       Is-Reserved-By

    RELATIONSHIP       Has-Requested-Purchase
    ORIGIN             Patron
        DEGREE         {0,1}
    TARGET             Book
        DEGREE         {0,N}
    REVERSE-NAME       Is-Ordered-For
```

its name and data contents (attributes). Each relationship is described by noting the two entities that participate in it and the degrees at either end. An example of such a description for the library example is shown in Figure 11.

This technique is equivalent to the graphic technique: one can be generated from the other. However, it is much less effective in communicating the data design to a user or a programmer. ERDs represent a case where the cliché "A picture is worth a thousand words" actually holds true.

CRITERIA FOR USE

The use of entity-relationship diagrams is particularly helpful in two areas: communicating with users to make sure that the analyst understands the application area and serving as a basis for proper design.

The first goal is served by the graphic technique, by providing intelligible names for the entities, and by depicting relationships (and naming them wherever necessary).

The second goal is served by including the cardinality, or degree symbols, on the graph. The majority of bad design decisions come from inadequate analysis of many-to-many relationships and from the analysis of which attributes implement those relationships. As we shall see in Chapter 11, this activity constitutes the substance of data design.

Other items that would be useful for good design would tend to overload the diagrams and therefore make them less suitable for communicating with users. With appropriate CASE tools, a complex diagram could be maintained, showing only the simple parts of it to users. This is not, however, a feature of most current CASE tools.

EXERCISES

1. Make an ERD for the following application:

A bank has a number of customers of two types: individuals and companies. Each customer may have several accounts of various types: checking, savings, mortgage, consumer loans, trust. In addition, the bank can sell a customer certificates of deposit (redeemable only at the bank) and treasury bonds (redeemable in other banks and at designated federal facilities). Treasury bonds may be sold by the customer to some other person or company without the bank's being informed about it.

Other services that are offered are automatic transfers between accounts and automatic bill payment. An automatic transfer between two accounts can be, for example, transferring the amount of the monthly mortgage payment from the savings account every month or depositing the revenue from the trust account (bond interest and stock dividends) into the checking account. Automatic bill payment consists of the bank's transferring an amount of money to another customer in the same bank or a customer of another bank.

The trust account activity is different from the others because it contains stocks and bonds rather than money. For each trust account, the bank must keep track of which stocks and bonds the customer has and how many of each. Also, for tax purposes, the purchase price and the commissions paid must be tracked.

 2. Investigate the following applications and make the corresponding entity-relationship diagrams:

Municipal dog licensing.

Organized tours for groups of people—making arrangements for travel, hotels, and events.

Airline reservations.

3. Keep the ERDs developed above until after you have covered Chapter 13, then review, critique, and complete them.

Section III

Requirements Analysis

The four central sections of the book, Sections III through VI, describe the process of systems analysis and design. This section, Requirements Analysis, will help you understand how to start the systems development process. The section also introduces several tools and techniques helpful in collecting and documenting the facts that will serve as the basis for the analysis and, later, the design of a new system.

Lone Wolf Timber & Mining Company

The Lone Wolf Timber & Mining Company is a conglomerate established in Billings, Montana, with mining and forestry operations throughout the Rocky Mountains. Lone Wolf also has several sawmills and paper mills in Montana and Wyoming, as well as part interest in a building materials manufacturing company in Portland, Oregon.

In the late 1960s, each of the mines of Lone Wolf had developed its own information systems. A few years later, a central accounting system was created for all the forestry and sawmills operations, and the individual mine systems were consolidated into a corporate system separate from the forestry systems. The paper mills, a recent acquisition, continued to have their own systems.

In 1989, the information systems and services (ISS) department of Lone Wolf initiated a project to consolidate all the billing, collection, and accounts receivable systems of all the operations. The objectives of this consolidation were to reduce maintenance, to simplify administrative operations, and, most importantly, to speed up invoice collection by providing on-line access to the system.

ISS decided to use the joint application development (JAD) approach to determine user requirements and design the user interface of the new billing and collection system (BCS). JAD had already been used a few months earlier to design the user interface and the data structures of a forest management system after the manager of systems development had attended an information-processing conference where JAD was discussed. At the conference, JAD had been presented as a new method for systems analysis and design that consisted of work sessions grouping up to ten key users and two or three information systems professionals, to arrive at requirements and design specifications through group consensus, with most of the emphasis on user participation.

When planning for the JAD sessions, Jeff Hamilton, the BCS project manager, contacted the project manager and several users of the forestry project to try to learn from the earlier effort's successes and failures. He found that the main success of JAD on the forestry project had been to reduce the need for "selling" the users on the benefits of the system. All those who had participated in the group sessions were knowledgeable and enthusiastic about the new system and had communicated their enthusiasm to their colleagues in their respective departments. Another benefit of JAD had been to accelerate some very complex design decisions requiring the input from multiple departments and locations. This benefit had been harder to achieve, however, because of the JAD session leaders' lack of forestry systems expertise, which had hampered the group in articulating the issues.

Jeff Hamilton also found that the JAD process had presented some problems, and he tried to devise means to avoid some of these problems. First, the users in a group session had difficulties creating documents from scratch. Hamilton therefore decided to rely heavily on prepared starting points communicated to the group well beforehand. Thus, the group could concentrate on critiquing rather than creating. He also prepared multiple alternative suggestions so that the group would never feel unduly pressured.

Hamilton also found that some earlier sessions had moved very slowly because group members had difficulty agreeing on terminology. He decided to prepare a project glossary at the outset of the sessions and to maintain this glossary, with new terms being defined or old definitions changed as required. Although this would not prevent all misunderstandings and delays due to explanations, it would accelerate the process.

Another problem had been found in the earlier project when technical subjects were broached: the group could only move as fast as its least knowledgeable member. Hamilton decided to reduce the impact of this problem by avoiding, to the extent possible, technical topics. He also ensured that those sessions during which technical subjects were likely to be brought up would be attended by at least one person with both technical and functional expertise who would be able to explain the topic better to the others.

Last, the previous project had encountered a problem when users from some departments had brought up requirements that were either inconsistent with those expressed by other departments or simply too costly. The forestry system team had found it difficult to say no when working in a group. Hamilton felt that this problem would not arise to the same extent on his project because all the users of BCS were in the same department, albeit from different locations.

When the BCS project started, two more problems were found. Both could fortunately be addressed quickly. First, the BCS systems development strategy was to base the system on application software packages, which would be completed with additional functions and interfaces to other systems as required. The JAD sessions were planned mainly to select the best package and to determine which additional features were absolutely required. However, the users in the group sessions showed a tendency to add too many features that were embellishments rather than requirements. This problem was partly corrected by organizing a presentation on the cost of changing and adding features to packages.

The second problem was caused by the solution to an earlier problem. The administrative support required to prepare the written materials prior to a session was underestimated. The project team found that it was usually necessary to produce 10 or 12 packets consisting of 50 to 80 pages of materials per day of workshop. Then, after the workshop session, these documents had to be edited and a session report issued. As a result, one additional analyst and two secretaries had to be assigned to the project team.

The benefits achieved by the use of JAD on the BCS project were those hoped for: quick results, maximum user adhesion, and a high-quality design, although at a somewhat greater cost than anticipated. The comment of one user who had attended JAD sessions for both projects was: "The forestry project went well, but I sometimes felt that I was spending too much time in group sessions rather than at my normal activities. On the BCS project, I rarely had the impression of wasting time, although my normal activities probably suffered as much as on the previous project."

PURPOSE OF SECTION

Interviewing, the main focus of Chapter 7, is the most widely used fact-gathering technique in systems analysis. Analysts interview future users of the system individually to find out what the present system does and what changes are needed. The information gathered during the interviews enables the analysts to design a new system that will eliminate the shortcomings of the current one.

An increasingly popular alternative to interviewing individuals is the group interview conducted by an impartial leader. A representative method, described in Chapter 8, is Joint Application Design (JAD), developed and taught by IBM. The advantages of JAD are that the analysis phase of the life cycle is shortened and that the specifications document produced tends to be better accepted by the users.

The importance of documenting the results of interviews and JAD sessions can scarcely be overemphasized. The documentation serves as a reference for all subsequent phases of the systems development, directly (as the basis for design and acceptance testing) or indirectly, through the medium of design documentation, for coding, unit testing, integration testing, and implementation. The clarity and completeness of this documentation is critical to users and IS personnel alike. The most popular technique for documenting the findings of the analysis phase is data flow diagramming, described at the end of this section.

Definition of Analysis

The term *analysis* applied to the first phase of systems development is somewhat of a misnomer. To analyze a system means to break it down into component parts and to study each part in isolation as well as in its interactions with other parts. To be useful, analysis must generally be followed by synthesis, that is, putting the parts together and determining how the system functions as a whole. Analysis consists of finding out *how* a system works, synthesis in *what* it does (and possibly why, how well, etc.).

The analysis phase produces a requirements specifications document that describes what the future system is to do but not how. The how will be determined during the design phase. The analysis phase would therefore appear to require a stronger component of synthesis than analysis, and a better term for *requirements analysis* might perhaps be *requirements determination* or *problem determination*.

The emphasis on analysis stems from two factors. First, the implementers of systems have not traditionally been experts in the area of the application being developed; rather, they have been technology experts—computer programmers or information systems analysts. Analysis is a powerful technique for learning about the application. Second, when the project consists of replacing an existing system, the easiest way to produce a requirements specification for the new system is to proceed by difference. Document the old system, make only those changes required to improve performance and eliminate operational problems, and—whoosh!—you have the specification of the new system.

This technique is still widely applied today although it tends to be de-emphasized when the project objective is to provide competitive advantage by finding new uses of information technology rather than to perfect old methods and procedures. Joint Application Design (conducting requirements determination in an intensely concentrated workshop) emphasizes the requirements of the future system rather than the analysis of the existing system.

KEY TASKS AND DELIVERABLES

The team should not start the requirements analysis unless there is a clear statement of the scope and objectives of the project. The systems plan or a feasibility study normally provides this statement. If not, or if the statement requires additional detail, the scope of the system must be circumscribed before work can start. Ideally, this step will tell the systems developers with some precision how much they can question existing rules or habits so that the team will know to what degree of abstraction the requirements should be carried.

The next phase is to build a logical model of the system (one which does not depend on details of implementation), usually by one of the following methods:

- Interviewing users to build a physical model of the present system, abstracting this to a logical model of the present system, and then incorporating desirable changes so as to create the logical model of the future system.

- Organizing a workshop with group methods such as JAD to create the logical model of the new system directly, without the intermediate steps of the physical and logical models of the present system.

In either case, the logical model of the new system becomes the requirements specification. Typically, it contains:

- An introduction containing the scope, goals, and objectives of the system.
- Data flow diagrams depicting the workflow of the new system, including the clear identification of business transactions.
- A project data model (as described in Section V and in the technique for Section II).
- Information needs: which types of questions will be asked of the system and which data will support the answers.
- Interfaces with other systems.
- Sample report, screen, and form layouts, if required.
- Volume projections.
- Operational information such as processing frequencies and schedules, response time requirements, resource utilization constraints.
- Measurable criteria for judging the implementation.

The final test of the system, the user acceptance test, should be conducted as a benchmark against this document. Therefore, all those factors that will determine whether the users are satisfied with the system should be documented and agreed upon.

There may be a final step in the requirements analysis—to have the users and top management sign off on the specification document. In most cases, if sufficient contact is maintained with the users during the work, this step is not necessary. The requirements specification approval can then be bundled with the approval of the design (see Chapter 17).

Chapter 7

Study of Present System (Interviewing)

This chapter first examines why reviewing the present system is important and under what conditions it should be done. Next, the chapter describes interviewing, by far the most widely used technique for reviewing present systems and determining future requirements. Other techniques, such as questionnaires, observation, and sampling, are briefly discussed. The last part of the chapter describes how the information gathered during review is analyzed and documented to obtain a complete set of requirements for the application being developed.

Learning Objectives

- Recognize the value of reviewing the present system as a prelude to creating a new system.

- Understand the four techniques used in reviewing present systems (interviewing, questionnaire, sampling, and observation) and be aware that interviewing is the technique most commonly used.

- Acquire skill in the five steps of the interviewing process: (1) prepare for the interview, (2) plan and schedule the interview, (3) open and close the interview, (4) conduct the interview, and (5) follow up for clarification.

- Recognize the value of active listening and restatement at both the direct and emotional levels.

- Understand the methodologies available for documenting the results of interviews and other data-gathering techniques.

- Describe how the data gathered on the present system is used in analysis to determine (1) which parts of the current system are unnecessary, (2) which parts could be retained in the new system, (3) which information requirements are not served by the present system, and (4) what are the major performance problems in the current system.

- Identify techniques used to develop creative solutions and appreciate the value of combining knowledge of the business with knowledge of the technology.

APPLICABILITY

Reviewing the present system is usually the first step in designing a new system. Some practitioners maintain that reviewing the present system is an unnecessary step, one that can lead to repeating in the future system the deficiencies of the present system. These practitioners are in the minority, however. Most agree on the value of reviewing the present system as a prelude to further design work for the following reasons:

- Reviewing gives the design team a good grasp of the business problems to be addressed by a new system and of the strengths and weaknesses of the present system in addressing those problems.
- It enables the design team to understand the environment in which the new system will operate.
- It ensures that no operating requirement or process will be overlooked in the specification of requirements for the new system.
- It anchors the new design in the old one: often, users can more easily understand implications of new designs when they are expressed as being "similar to before, with the following exceptions." It may also permit reusing satisfactory parts of the existing system.
- It enhances the cooperation between the project team and the users.

Some practical advice follows on how to exploit these advantages of reviewing the present system.

Understanding the Business Problem

The better the design team understands the business problem being addressed, the better the chances of developing a solution that uses information technology creatively. In many cases, the underlying business problem is not well articulated or well understood by the user. If the user's underlying business problem will be addressed by a new system, it must be clearly stated and understood by the project team. Gildersleeve states that a good problem statement begins with two things:

- A description of the present situation.
- A standard of desired performance.[1]

Rockart's critical success factors referred to in Section II, can help define a standard of desired performance. Most business managers, at any level, monitor a relatively short list of items to assure them that their areas of responsibility are under control. For example, a supermarket store manager may monitor such items as sales per square foot, personnel cost per sales dollar, departmental margins, and this year's sales compared with last year's by day of the week. Such items would be the manager's critical success factors. If they are within a range of acceptability, the manager's mind is at ease. On the other hand, if margins in the produce department fall below the critical success factor target, the manager can initiate action to uncover the cause so that a correction can be made. Evaluating the quality of critical success factors can help analysts determine whether a particular manager has a good grasp of a unit's business problems. The approach also identifies information that a system must provide to satisfy a manager's information requirements.

Understanding the Operating Environment

One of the first things an experienced IS professional will do when beginning a new project is to take a plant tour—a tour of the relevant facilities that will be the subject of a review. It may be an actual plant in a manufacturing company, but it could also be an office, retail space, the registration desk of a resort hotel, or the emergency room of a city hospital on a busy Saturday night. The plant tour exposes the IS professional to the business environment that a new system will support. The professional is therefore more sensitive to which solutions will work and which will not. Understanding the business environment does not mean the internal environment only, because today's systems cast their nets much wider and include entities external to the organization. For example, imagine a project team member beginning a review of the department that handles customers' telephone inquiries for a large electric distribution company. The team member might sit beside a customer service clerk and listen to the types of questions customers ask and the information used by the clerk in responding to them.

Not all companies are ready to digest the latest in technology, and a project team sensitive to the operating environment can avoid expensive mistakes. For example, taking a tour of a bank's office in a lesser-developed country and seeing stacks of paper and disorganized files should sensitize a project team to two issues. First, such an organization might need to walk with the technology before running with it. In other words, a pilot test in a smaller unit may be wise; or improvements may have to be made to the manual procedures before mechanizing them. Second, if the project team were to recommend going ahead with a computerized system, they should realize that they may have serious problems with data conversion and should plan accordingly.

Considering All Requirements

A systematic review of the current system should identify all data used and all processes performed by the current system. This review will ensure that critical

Figure 7–1 **Checklist of Information Usually Gathered
during a Review of the Current System**

User responsibilities, priorities, goals, problems

Information sources
  Computerized/noncomputerized
  Reports/documents/screens
    Accuracy
    Timeliness
    Relevance
    Duplication
    Conciseness
    Uniformity
    Volumes

Information flow
  Action taken with information received
  Identification of bottlenecks and delays
  Identification of missing information
  Documentation of methods used to obtain information
    outside the formal system

User suggestions for improvements
  Responsibilities, work systems
  Information sources
  Information flows

minor processes are not overlooked when requirements for the new system are specified. In addition, the project team can develop a list of strengths and weaknesses of the present system in meeting the business needs of its users. This list will help ensure that the new system retains the strengths of the present system where appropriate and corrects its weaknesses. A checklist of information usually gathered during a review of the current system is shown in Figure 7–1.

Anchoring the New System in the Old

The approach usually chosen to determine the requirements of the future system consists of constructing a model of the present system, interviewing management and hands-on users, then modifying the system with those changes that the analysis team deems necessary.

The analysis team should document not only the required changes but also all the possible changes that might be made in the future. The art of systems analysis is in large part the capability to choose those aspects of the present system that are unchangeable, those that are likely to change over the long term, and those that can be changed immediately. Box 7–1 describes which functions and features of a system are the most permanent and which are the most likely to change.

BOX 7-1

Permanence versus Change

Any feature or function that depends on industry wide standards or customs is likely to be fairly permanent. For instance, in an airline reservation system, it is not likely that one airline would be able to charge for cancellations (except on discounted tickets) without a radical change of mood in the industry. Similarly, a single insurance company is not likely to implement no-fault insurance on its own.

The next most unlikely changes are those that are tied to national or corporate culture. For instance, a closed-shop factory is likely to continue considering union requirements in its personnel scheduling systems for a number of years.

Organizational change is next on the list of unlikely changes. Most companies prefer not to reorganize too frequently; however, if management is convinced that reorganization will solve a problem, it will happen. It is therefore generally better to make information systems flexible enough that different distributions of tasks can be supported. It is also obviously better not to code reporting relationships into the systems, thus avoiding heavy maintenance to cost centers, profit centers, and responsibility reporting if reorganizations do take place.

In contrast, management fiat is at relatively high risk of change. Rules such as the number of points charged for a mortgage loan, penalties for late payments, and cost-of-living salary raises are typical examples. A conscious effort should be made to avoid relying on these requirements as a permanent basis for the information system.

Finally, regulatory requirements are even more unstable than management decisions because the regulatory body, usually a federal or state government organization, often does not feel the effect of changing requirements with the same intensity as do the regulated companies. On the other hand, such changes tend to be unpredictable. In a heavily regulated industry such as electric utilities, considerable expertise is required to minimize future disruptions due to regulatory changes.

Enhancing User Relationship

Members of user departments may express some irritation at having their work interrupted, particularly if a project is perceived to be "yet another study." Usually, however, they welcome the opportunity to spend time familiarizing the project team with the present system. They like to have their problems taken seriously and are suspicious of analysts who jump to conclusions, in the same way we want to explain our symptoms to a physician before hearing the diagnosis. In addition, good ideas are often obtained from people who work with the present system every day. In many cases, they have had these ideas for a long time, but no one has ever taken the time to ask for them before.

INTERVIEWING

Of the various techniques employed for reviewing present systems, interviewing is by far the most common. Other techniques—questionnaires, sampling, and observation—will be discussed later in this chapter.

An interview is a systematic attempt to collect information from a person. Interviewing is an important skill for systems analysts because success depends on an ability to identify work flows, factors that influence the operations of systems, and the elements (documents, procedures, policies, etc.) that make up systems. Without accurate and complete information, the new system would probably not contain the necessary features to meet the needs of the organization. In addition, poorly performed interviews can affect the attitudes of the users and have a negative effect on the entire project effort.

As illustrated in Figure 7–2, the interview process has five steps:

- Preparing for the interview
- Planning and scheduling the interview
- Opening and closing the interview
- Conducting the interview
- Following up for clarification

Each step is discussed in more detail in the following paragraphs.

Preparing for the Interview

Adequate preparation is essential for successful interviewing. Before undertaking an interview, the analyst should first have a good understanding of the organization, its industry setting, and the project's scope and objectives. Analysts become familiar with the organization by reviewing organization charts, annual reports, long-range planning documents, statements of departmental goals, and the like. Existing procedure manuals and systems documentation should also be reviewed. Finally, a physical tour of the facilities, as discussed above, completed before the interviews, is helpful in giving the analyst a feel for the organization.

Analysts performing a project for the first time in a particular industry will find the interviewing process more effective if they first familiarize themselves with the industry. While first-time analysts should not pose as industry experts on the basis of their initial research, at least they will understand common industry terms and be somewhat familiar with the business problems of the industry. Users are more comfortable talking to analysts whom they do not have to educate in the problems of their industry. For example, in a banking setting, users would expect an analyst to understand that DDA refers to demand deposit accounting and that deregulation of the financial services industry and interstate banking are current items of concern in the United States.

Finally, as discussed in Chapter 3, management can pave the way for the interviewing process with an announcement that interviews will be taking place.

Planning and Scheduling the Interview

Analysts should plan interviews by preparing a list of topics and questions to be covered. This list will help ensure that important points are not overlooked and that the interview follows a logical progression. In some cases, a preinterview

Figure 7–2 **Five Steps of the Interviewing Process**

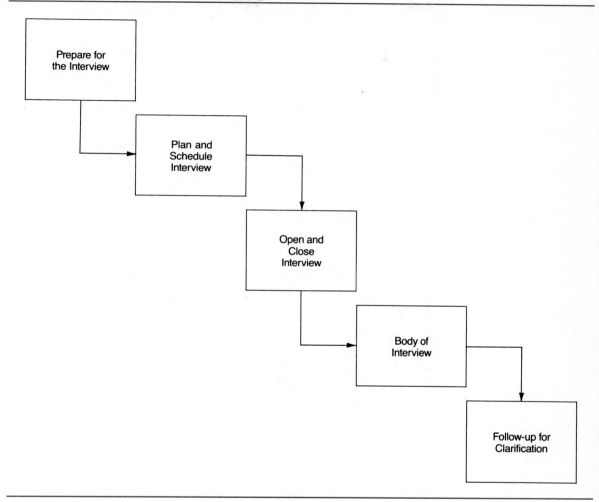

questionnaire (see Figure 7–3) is sent to the interviewee ahead of time. The questionnaire gives the interviewee time to consider the areas to be covered and, in many cases, to gather samples of documents and reports the analyst may wish to obtain.

The first task in scheduling interviews is to determine who should be interviewed. Most analysts will take a top-down approach to this task and start with higher-level user personnel. They may also use a copy of the organization chart when selecting personnel for interviews so that no critical areas or persons are inadvertently overlooked. Protocol also requires that interviews within

Figure 7–3 **Sample Preinterview Questionnaire for a Supervisor of Order Processing**

```
CIS                          SUBURBAN PUMPS                    CD-20
ORDERS                                                         PIQUE
                       PREINTERVIEW QUESTIONNAIRE

 ┌─────────────────────────────────────────────────────────────────────┐
 │ PREPARED BY:  RHONDA TURNER   DATE:  27FEB88   VERSION:      PAGE 1   │
 │ APPROVED BY:  SUSAN BAKER     DATE:  05MAR88   STATUS :               │
 └─────────────────────────────────────────────────────────────────────┘

Position:      Supervisor of Order Processing
--------


1.    What are the steps performed to process an order?


2.    Are there different order processing methods used according to type of
      order, customer classification, geographical area, etc.?


3.    What data are used during the order-taking process?  What data are
      generated?


4.    Are additional data needed?  Under what circumstances?


5.    How large is a typical order, in number of items and dollar value?  How
      large is the smallest order?  The largest?


6.    How many orders are processed per day or week?  What are the peaks and
      troughs?


7.    How often does a typical customer order?


8.    Are there ever difficulties with the workflow?  If so, identify problems,
      bottlenecks, delays, frequent errors.


9.    What documents and reports are created?  Who uses them?
```

departments or areas proceed from the top down. Heads of departments or sections are usually interviewed before employees who report to them. There may be a logical sequence for interviews that should be considered when the schedule is prepared. For example, analysts may get greater understanding of a process or transaction if they follow it from beginning to end, rather than starting in the middle. When time is short and many individuals must be interviewed, compromises are sometimes necessary to accommodate the individual schedules of the interviewees.

When contacting personnel to schedule interviews, team members should explain the purpose of the interview, the general areas to be covered, and the approximate amount of time required to cover all areas. In most cases, the interview takes place at the interviewee's work location. In some cases, however, another location must be found. For example, a work site may lack the necessary privacy or may be too noisy. An interview with a factory supervisor is probably best done in a location other than on the factory floor. An alternative location should be a relaxed environment conducive to a business discussion.

Opening and Closing the Interview

In addition to gathering targeted information, effective interviews are carefully opened and closed. Failure to open an interview properly may affect the body of the interview, and failure to close the interview properly may make a follow-up interview more difficult.

In opening an interview, an analyst will first introduce himself or herself, state the purpose of the interview, address any concerns sensed by the analyst or raised by the interviewee, and then explain that brief notes will be taken and shared with the interviewee after they have been organized. Often interviewees are concerned that an analyst is trying to find fault with the way they work. One way to set them at ease is to get them to talk about processes with which they are familiar. The analyst selects topics on the basis of an advanced questionnaire, if one was used, or on the basis of discussions with persons to whom the interviewees report.

The best interviews are those where the interviewees do most of the talking. Therefore, analysts look for ways to get interviewees to open up to them. With some interviewees, this is no problem; with others, it is. One of the most widely used approaches is active listening, which is described below. One technique to be avoided is a series of specific, closed questions. The result of this approach is usually that the interviewees give a brief answer to the question and then wait for the next one, almost as if they were being interrogated by a detective.

Note taking can become a distraction if not restricted to brief notations for later elaboration. The analyst's notepad is best kept out of the interviewee's line of vision. The purpose of an analyst's notes should be to help recall pertinent points and hypotheses formed during an interview. Many analysts will use broad headings for note taking rather than specific categories (see Figure 7–4).

Figure 7–4 **Note Headings for a Data-Gathering Interview**

```
                           SUBURBAN  PUMPS                        U716
                                                                 INOTE

 ┌──────────────────────────────────────────────────────────────────────┐
 │ PREPARED BY:            DATE:            VERSION:        PAGE          │
 │ APPROVED BY:            DATE:            STATUS :                      │
 └──────────────────────────────────────────────────────────────────────┘


 Key Interview Topics              │   Interviewee Response
 --------------------              │   --------------------
                                   │
                                   │
                                   │
                                   │
                                   │
                                   │
                                   │
                                   │
                                   │
                                   │
 ──────────────────────────────────┴─────────────────────────────────────
 New Ideas
 ---------



 ────────────────────────────────────────────────────────────────────────
 Interviewee Opinions
 --------------------
```

Taping an interview is usually not recommended. It tends to intimidate the interviewee; moreover, listening to the tape and culling pertinent information is very time consuming.

When all areas on the interview outline have been explored, analysts will often ask questions such as "Is there anything we've overlooked?" or "What other areas should I have asked you about?" This tactic encourages the interviewee to discuss issues that should have been covered. Another question often asked by analysts is "What one change would make your job easier or more effective?" This question elicits suggestions for improvement.

Closing the interview involves briefly summarizing the areas that have been discussed, highlighting the important facts and the analyst's understanding of them. This technique lets the interviewee know that the analyst has been listening carefully during the interview and also provides an opportunity for clarifying any misunderstandings. During the summary, as well as during the entire interview, the analyst should adopt a posture of objectivity and avoid personal comments, observations, or conclusions.

Finally, in closing, the analyst thanks the interviewee for the time and asks if a shorter follow-up interview can be scheduled at a later date if necessary.

Conducting the Interview

One of the main objectives of the analyst conducting an interview is to see that information flows easily from interviewee to analyst and is not shut off for any reason. The technique of active listening helps to maintain the information flow and facilitates adequate feedback from analyst to interviewee. The active listening technique has five key tools:

- Asking open-ended questions
- Using appropriate words and phrases
- Giving acceptance cues
- Restating the interviewee's responses
- Using silence effectively

Asking Open-Ended Questions. Open-ended questions cannot be answered with a simple yes or no response and thus encourage the interviewee to provide more information. Open-ended questions begin with such words as *what, how* or *tell me* rather than such words as *can, does,* or *when*. For example, more information is likely to flow from a question such as "Tell me what happens when a customer calls" than a series of questions such as "Does your department handle customer calls? Can they be answered by any clerk sitting at a terminal? Do you expect the customers to have their account numbers ready?"

Some questions are best answered by a yes or no, so not all questions should be open ended. Experienced analysts try to find the right balance appropriate to each situation. An approach with no open-ended questions is almost never appropriate, however, and should be avoided.

Using Appropriate Words and Phrases. The analyst should avoid using words or phrases that are emotionally charged, distracting, or difficult to understand. For example, such emotional expressions as *problem area, cumbersome process,* or *poorly controlled* imply a foregone conclusion. Distracting statements contain excessive abbreviations or acronyms, name dropping, or controversial words and phrases. Finally, analysts should avoid colloquialisms, slang, and jargon unless the interviewee is certain to understand them. IS professionals are notorious for peppering their speech with the jargon of their profession, using such words or acronyms as data models, DFDs, DASD, and connectivity.

Giving Acceptance Cues. Humans communicate with more than words; they use body language as well, sending messages by tone of voice, posture, eye contact, facial expressions, and body movements. Such nonverbal cues play a critical role in the interviewing process. When used properly, they encourage an interviewee to provide information. When used poorly, they can have the opposite effect.

For example, failure to make eye contact in an interview can be interpreted as a lack of interest or concern for the other person. Good eye contact can communicate interest, attention, openness, and a regard for the other person's worth. On the other hand, too much eye contact can be misinterpreted as staring. In U.S. culture, for example, eye contact between strangers for more than a brief moment is considered a challenge. In some cultures, eye contact is considered an invasion of privacy.

Nodding the head to indicate understanding is an acceptance cue, as is a posture of attentiveness: sitting straight and leaning slightly forward. Contrast this posture with a person slouching in a chair with one arm flung over the back of the chair or leaning back with both hands folded behind the head. The following are other errors commonly made by inexperienced analysts:

- Sitting back in a chair with arms folded across the chest (This posture implies a lack of openness to what is being said and may also indicate that the analyst is ill at ease.)

- Looking at objects in the room or staring out the window instead of looking at the interviewee. (Because this behavior suggests that the analyst would rather be somewhere else doing other things, the interviewee will often cut the interview short.)

- Taking excessive notes or visually reviewing notes. (An analyst who records rather than listening may arouse interviewee concerns over what is being written.)

- Sitting too far away or too close. (Sitting too far away often communicates that the analyst is intimidated by the interviewee, while sitting too close may communicate an inappropriate level of intimacy and make the interviewee uncomfortable.)

Acceptance cues are used to convey understanding, not agreement. The communication of agreement that does not exist can cause future misunderstandings. Furthermore, the analyst must maintain an air of objectivity and neutrality throughout the interview.

Restating the Interviewee's Responses. Restatement is the most difficult of the active listening skills to master. It involves repeating something the interviewee has said in the analyst's own words as an indication that effective communication has occurred and that the analyst understands what the interviewee has said. Restatement must be made in such a way that the interviewee will acknowledge it and keep on talking. Effective restatements will encourage the interviewee to elaborate; ineffective restatements will create an unintended pause or halt in the interview process (see Figure 7–5).

Restatement is normally used under the following circumstances:

- When the interviewee is describing a problem. (At such times, the analyst's restatement communicates that the interviewee's problem has been heard and understood.)

- When the analyst wants to check his or her understanding of what has been said. (This technique is often used in response to complex statements or in group situations where several persons have commented on the same issue.)

- When the analyst wants to encourage the interviewee. (Restatement can prompt the interviewee to expand or elaborate on what has been said.)

Restatement can also overcome emotional barriers set up by interviewees who, for some reason, are uncooperative. Perhaps they feel that the interview squanders valuable time they could spend on more important tasks. Or perhaps they had negative experiences with systems analysts in the past. Whatever the reason, the challenge for the analyst is to establish rapport—to make the interviewees confident that their feelings are understood. This confidence, in turn, helps to break down emotional barriers and thus produce successful interviews. Figure 7–6 illustrates restatements at the emotional level. Although restatement at the emotional level is a powerful technique, it must be used judiciously. First, it should be used only when the analyst senses that the interviewee's strong feelings might jeopardize the interview. Second, even after restatement, the analyst will sometimes sense that the interviewee's attitude still does not permit effective communication. In such cases, the interview should probably be rescheduled at a later date. Third, the analyst should restate with such phrases as "it sounds as if" or "it seems as if" to avoid misinterpreting or misstating the interviewee's feelings. Finally, the analyst must remain neutral. For example, if the interviewee is critical of management, the analyst should neither agree with the criticism nor attempt to defend management. Instead, the analyst should simply convey that the interviewee's feelings are understood.

Figure 7–5 **Effective vs. Ineffective Restatements of an Interviewee Response**

Interviewee Response:	We continue to sell products to customers who have not paid their bills.
Effective Restatement:	The system processes orders to customers who are bad credit risks. (Encourages interviewee to expand.)
Ineffective Restatement:	Why don't you check the customer's credit status before processing the order? (Distorts interviewee's meaning.)

When using restatement the analyst must try to avoid the following common errors:

- Echoing the interviewee, i.e., repeating exactly what the interviewee has said rather than restating in different words. (Echoing becomes very obvious after the first few times it occurs and can make the interviewee uncomfortable.)

- Overusing restatement, which can be distracting to the interviewee.

- Altering or distorting the meaning intended by the interviewee. (A restatement should be as close to the interviewee's meaning as possible.)

- Raising the pitch of the voice at the end of a restatement. (This habit converts a restatement into a question answerable by yes or no instead of an invitation for the interviewee to expand on his or her comments.)

Figure 7–6 **Examples of Restatements at the Emotional Level**

Interviewee Statement:	The last time I was interviewed, the result was that I got this report that I cannot use without literally weeding it.
Restatement:	It seems as though you feel that some analysts do not listen carefully enough to your requirements and ideas.
Interviewee Statement:	I do not have the typing skills to become an on-line data entry operator in the new system.
Restatement:	You seem to feel that the new system might take away some of the challenge and excitement of your job.
Restatement Alternative (if the restatement does not evoke a response):	You do not appear to have been exposed to terminals or personal computers in your work.

Using Silence Effectively. Silence as an interviewing technique is employed in two situations: either just after a question or after an answer that the analyst considers incomplete. Silence after a question gives the interviewee a chance to speak. Some people require longer periods of time to formulate an answer and become disconcerted if interrupted by another question or comment from the analyst. Silence following an incomplete answer can encourage the interviewee to elaborate as long as the analyst continues to maintain a posture of interest and receptivity. Long silences should be avoided, however; if the interviewee does not respond, the conversation should be resumed by the analyst.

Following Up for Clarification

After the initial rounds of interviews are completed and documented, analysis of the findings almost always results in the need to clarify certain aspects. For example, the analyst may have obtained conflicting information from two interviewees or may not have completely understood the way information on a particular report is used or by whom. If follow-up interviews are necessary, they are usually brief, consisting primarily of closed questions. Frequently, simple points can be settled by a telephone call or informal visit.

OTHER INFORMATION-GATHERING TECHNIQUES

Although interviews with user personnel are by far the most common way of gathering information on the present system, questionnaires, observation, and sampling can be effective in certain situations.

Questionnaires

As mentioned previously, questionnaires are often sent to users prior to scheduling an interview. In some cases, a questionnaire is used without an interview—most often when analysts need to contact users in remote locations but cannot justify the travel and when the information needed is more than what can be obtained in a telephone conversation. In such cases, the combination of a questionnaire with telephone or mail follow-up for clarification is often appropriate.

Observation

Observation of the present system is often a fertile source of new ideas. For example, all of us have been frustrated at one time or another by choosing the incorrect line at a bank or an airline counter. Some of us even switch to another line when the one we originally chose seems to be moving too slowly, only to find that we would have been better off staying with our original choice. Many businesses now have a single waiting line for all customers so that all are served in arrival sequence. The new approach may well have been the result of someone who observed the lines with a fresh perspective and concluded that multiple waiting lines do not treat customers fairly. According to a recent article in *Fortune*, "the best intelligence is usually gathered in the field. Stephen Moss, of the Arthur D. Little consulting firm, an expert in streamlining factory operations . . . once tried to limit his staff's travel by having videotapes showing troubled factories sent to his office in Cambridge, Massachusetts. Unfortunately, he says, 'We couldn't see on the tape how workers were feeling or where the dust was piling up. Some of the most telling evidence just wasn't visible.' "[2]

Sampling

Sampling techniques are used when the population is too large to permit all members to be interviewed, given questionnaires, or observed. Conclusions on the attributes of the population as a whole are then drawn based on the results of a sample. When selecting the sample, analysts must take care that the sample is truly representative of the entire population. Otherwise, they may draw erroneous conclusions.

DOCUMENTING AND ANALYZING THE PRESENT SYSTEM

Documenting and analyzing the results of interviews or alternative data-gathering techniques is the primary means of communicating to other project team members the information obtained.

Documentation

The larger the project team, the more important it is to document information in a standard format. Many IS departments have adopted documentation standards as a part of their systems development methodologies. In such cases, documentation guidelines are readily available. Where standard documentation guidelines have not been established, the project team should adopt a standard format.

Three of the most frequently used documentation formats are memoranda, sample forms and reports, and data flow diagrams (or flowcharts). The formality and content of a memorandum can vary widely in practice. The most important attribute of a systems review memorandum, and of all forms of documentation for that matter, is accuracy. (Figure 7–7 illustrates an interview memorandum.)

Lists are most often used as an index to copies of forms, reports, screens, and so forth obtained during the interviews. Members of the project team use these lists to search for documents that contain additional details. Forms that contain actual data are preferable to blank forms, which do not indicate realistically how they are used. When forms contain confidential data (salary information, for example), it is better to illustrate with fabricated rather than actual data.

Figure 7–7 **Documenting the Results of an Interview**

```
PERSONNEL                    SUBURBAN PUMPS                    CD-20
TIME REPORTING                                                 IWRUP
                          INTERVIEW WRITE-UP

PREPARED BY:  RON TURNER    DATE:  13OCT90    VERSION:     PAGE 1/2
APPROVED BY:  JOE DAVIS     DATE:  15OCT90    STATUS :
```

Interviewee: Hector Diaz; Manager--Employee Time Reports

Functions Reporting to Interviewee:

          Supervisors of Employee Time Reporting and Payroll

X-Ref.   Notes
------   -----

          1.   Scope of Operations, Characteristics of Environment
                ----

                Hector is responsible for all employee time reporting.
                Presently, time reports are collected by each of the three
                area supervisors.

                Although Hector sets company-wide time reporting policies,
                several factors complicate the consistent implementation of
                these policies. The lack of a uniform centralized time
                reporting system that identifies variances by locality
                contributes to the less than efficient employee
                utilization.

                Hector feels that the proposed centralization of all time
                reporting at headquarters would provide significant
                improvements. This would include the timely identification
                of project variances among other benefits.

          2.   Business Objectives
                ----

                a. Timely reporting of project variances
                b. Establish effective control over intra-location
                    transfers

          3.   Information Needs
                ----

                a. Project variances
                    (i)   Standard Employee Time Report

                b. Intra-location Transfers
                    (i)   Projected Personnel Requirements
                    (ii) Standard Employee Time Report

          4.   System Features
                ----

                a. Monthly Budget/Actual Variance Reports
                b. Variance reports are restricted to supervisors and
                    above
                c. Time reports must be processed within two hours of
                    their submission

Volume information obtained during the data-gathering process can also be documented on such lists, or if appropriate, in two-dimensional tables (see Figure 7–8).

Data flow diagrams (DFDs) tie together the inputs, processes, outputs, and files into a visual representation of the flow of information through a system. DFDs are particularly useful in identifying missing or contradictory data and serving as the basis for review by users and project managers. DFDs are covered in depth in the Technique section following Chapter 8.

Sometimes the system documentation of the user organization contains elements usable in their present form. More often than not, the existing documentation is outdated. Therefore, the project team might be required to create some new elements and update the existing ones.

Analysis

After evaluating the overall and subsidiary objectives of the organization under review, the project team analyzes the data to summarize the strengths and weaknesses of the current system. The purpose of the analysis is to determine how well the present information system is helping to meet the organization's objectives and which of the current functions and features should be carried over to the new system.

Four steps are usually performed in analyzing the current system:

- Determining which parts of the current system are unnecessary.

   For example, the review may uncover similar processing steps repeated unknowingly or no longer needed. Many systems prepare reports month after month and distribute them to users who promptly discard them. Some IS departments try to find such unnecessary reports by preparing, but not distributing, suspect reports for a month or two to see if anyone complains about not receiving them. If no one complains, the reports are stopped.

- Determining information requirements not adequately served by the present system.

   A top-down approach to this step usually works best. To evaluate the effectiveness of the present system, the project team should understand the industry setting, the objectives of the entire organization, and the objectives of the organizational unit under review. To identify the requirements of the new system, the team should understand the kinds of decisions a manager must make, the critical success factors, and the support provided by the current information systems. Inexperienced analysts sometimes make the mistake of asking the user to tell them what additional information is needed. The usual response is either "I get more reports now than I know what to do with" or "You tell me. You're the expert."

Additional techniques to determine requirements are covered later in the next section.

Figure 7–8 **Volume Worksheet**

```
CIS                            SUBURBAN PUMPS                        CD-20
ORDERS                                                              VOLWS
                              VOLUME WORKSHEET

┌──────────────────────────────────────────────────────────────────────────┐
│ PREPARED BY:  J. M. LECLERC  DATE:  27MAR88     VERSION:          PAGE 1   │
│ APPROVED BY:  SUSAN BAKER    DATE:  31MAR88     STATUS : F                 │
└──────────────────────────────────────────────────────────────────────────┘
```

Location	Nash-ville	Denver	Kansas City	St. Louis	Louis-ville	Memphis
No. Orders	10000	1500	200	150	350	700
Avg. Value	1750	1650	2050	950	1500	1500
Avg. No. Items	22	25	21	33	24	17
Max. No. Items	65	77	78	45	53	40
No. Customers	23000	5400	500	100	900	1200

● Identifying major performance problems: timeliness, accuracy, flexibility, security, quality.

Working from the operational objectives of the organizational unit under review, the project team can establish departures from stated performance targets. If stated targets are not available, the team can derive them from interviews and use them as a standard of performance against which to measure the present system. For example, the standard of performance of an on-line computer system for entering customer orders might be as follows: it should be available (working) 98 percent of the time that it is scheduled to be available, and response time for simple transactions should be no longer than 5 seconds even in periods of peak demand. Actual performance is measured against the standards to determine if major problems exist.

- Determining which parts of the present system may be retained in the new system.

   Large computer systems are often designed and installed in subsystems relatively independent of each other so that one one subsystem may be replaced while another subsystem may remain unchanged. For example, an organization might have a personnel information system for the payroll department and another system to meet the needs of the human resources department. If the payroll subsystem was developed on a custom basis in 1980 and the human resources subsystem was added in 1985 by purchasing an application software package, a project team might conclude that the payroll subsystem should be replaced because it is increasingly difficult to maintain, but that the human resources subsystem has another few years of life.

DEDUCING PROCESSING AND INFORMATION REQUIREMENTS: LESSONS FROM PRACTICE

In an era when information technology can create a sustainable competitive advantage, a premium should be placed on creativity in systems work. Mundane, run-of-the-mill solutions can no longer be accepted if an organization expects to remain competitive. Creatively designed systems are much more likely to help an organization compete more effectively. They can also contribute by promoting greater acceptance among the user community and by yielding a longer useful life. Both of these contributions provide a more favorable return on the investment.

   The most creative systems result from a truly collaborative effort of users and IS personnel; a unique solution requires a deep knowledge of both the business problem and the capabilities of the technology. One of the values of the project team approach is that it encourages users and IS professionals to work together toward a solution. In the process, users learn more about the technology, and IS professionals come to understand the business problem from the user's perspective (see Figure 7–9).

   Applying this attitude to the way that information and processing requirements are deduced, certain techniques have proven to be effective:

- Understanding the business problem.

   Users often cannot express the business problem to an analyst in part because they tend to frame the problem statement according to what they believe the technology can handle. (Educating user members of the project team in the capabilities of the technology helps avoid this problem.) For example, a systems review with the executive vice-president of a small private bank catering to high-income individuals began with the vice-president's statement of the problem: getting monthly management reports prepared on a PC more efficiently. All of the bank's data processing was

Figure 7–9 "Primitive Sophistication on the Costa de Careyes"

The error of todays' architects is that
*   they work in offices with T-squares.*
They might as well be working in factories.
They plan houses as if they were making
*   the same Ford car over and over. . . .*

I cannot build a preconceived house . . .
I must understand the land . . .
feel the cold at night . . .
feel how the winds blow . . .
see how the sun moves and the birds fly . . .
think about the history of the place and the people. . . .

The personality of the owner is very important. . . .
I need someone who can help me—through
*   his personality—build a house.*
The owner must consider architecture a
*   work of art.*
He is my collaborator.

I find these ideas to be extremely relevant to our systems development efforts. While some might say, "It's just common sense," we tend to forget why we do the things we do. Perhaps more importantly, we lose track of what to emphasize among all our activities. An important theme of this book is that the analyst must "go to the land" to get really in touch with the users, their problems, and their objectives. Working in some back room using memos and the telephone, the analyst will get only a secondhand view of the problem.

The back-room approach is not a substitute for firsthand data gathering. The analyst must touch, feel, and have extensive, personal contact with the environment. By doing so, the analyst will be able to obtain sufficient information to test the validity of preconceived notions. Furthermore, he will open the lines of communication with the user community. *The most successful projects are truly joint efforts in which both analysts and users make significant contributions:* Users bring to the problem an indispensable business expertise; analysts bring objectivity, technical expertise, and analytical skills. They need each other's perspective and cooperation to do the best possible job.[3]

Source: Allen Carter, "Primitive Sophistication on the Costa de Careyes," *Architectural Digest*, Vol. 33, No. 1 (July/August 1976), pp. 45–48. Reprinted from *Architectural Digest*. Copyright © John C. Brasfield Publishing Corp., 1976.

performed by a service bureau, and approximately 20 reports were prepared once each month. The problem, according to the vice-president, was to avoid a manual keying of summary data from the service bureau reports to the PC for combining into a management report needed by the bank's officers. An analyst could have tackled the problem by visiting the service bureau to see if information could be downloaded or combined in some way to make the process easier at the bank.

In the actual situation, however, the analyst got the executive vice-president to talk about the business. The analyst learned that the bank had been operating for about three years and had successfully attracted high-income customers because of its personalized services. The officers were struggling to continue growth in the face of increasing competition in a geographic area experiencing only moderate economic expansion. The systems project was defined more broadly: discovering how the bank might acquire an increasing share of the market through information technology. The original problem was solved with little effort. The real payoff to the bank, however, came from systems ideas that addressed its marketing problem.

- Avoiding early constraints on system boundaries or on the capabilities of the technology.

  Early constraints can unnecessarily limit a systems solution to the detriment of the organization. For example, an analyst interviewing users of an aging inventory control system scheduled for replacement might find that users simply want the present system's features to be duplicated in the replacement system. If the study were constrained to inventory control, the users would end up simply getting a replica of the old system.

  If, however, the analyst and users recognize the interrelationships of inventory control, accounts payable, and purchasing as components of the procurement cycle, they could produce a much more efficient system. Communications between subsystems would be performed within the computer system rather than by passing paper documents back and forth. In addition, if instead of accepting a paper purchase order as an output of the purchasing module, the team recognized that the technology could transmit orders directly to suppliers and thereby reduce the procurement lead time (and inventory levels), they would produce a more effective system.

- Viewing the problem from another perspective.

  Large organizations, in particular, tend to determine systems requirements solely on the basis of an internal perspective. Some of the best examples of creative systems design, however, have resulted when the project team has viewed the system from another perspective, for example that of customers or suppliers. In other cases, creative design takes concepts from one industry and applies them to another. For example, the product costing approach so common in manufacturing can be applied to the health care industry. Figure 7–10 illustrates other examples of different perspectives that can help determine systems requirements.

- Determining the state of the art and attempting to extend it.

  A certain degree of similarity exists between the information and processing requirements for common applications in the same industry. (This similarity has made application software packages a commercial success.) Many experienced analysts prevent early obsolescence of their

Figure 7–10 **Viewing Problems from a Different Perspective**

External perspectives
Customers
Suppliers
Competitors
Regulatory agencies
Public

Transfer concepts from one industry to another
Product costing
Electronic data interchange (EDI)
Video games
Taking product view of services
Taking service view of products

New applications of technology
Bar coding
Facsimile
Optical disk and image processing
Expert systems

recommended systems by determining the state of the art for similar systems. Many will go further and attempt to extend the state of the art and establish a new standard. This technique is particularly useful for a company seeking a competitive advantage over its rivals. It is usually not enough simply to catch up with the competition; companies must attempt to surpass it.

The state of the art for a traditional application can be determined by performing a literature search, by attending trade shows and seminars, and by talking with industry or technical experts from consulting firms, equipment manufacturers, or academicians who have had exposure to a number of organizations.

As a rule, companies developing competitive systems do not publicize what they are doing. Therefore, analysts determining the state of the art typically focus on known systems and hypothesize on what the competition is doing.

On the other hand, excessive broadening of a project's scope is dangerous. A fairly mundane project with well-defined objectives may grow out of hand, raising false expectations, exceeding time limits and costs, and giving the IS department a reputation for blue-sky thinking. In particular, if a systems plan exists, the boundaries and the variety of perspectives may already have been studied by the systems planning team in sufficient depth.

Summary

Most practitioners agree that the benefits of reviewing the present system outweigh the costs. After the review, the project team will grasp the business problems of the organization under study and the effectiveness of the present information system. In addition, the project team will appreciate the operating environment of the new system and will not likely overlook critical processing requirements.

Of the four techniques used in reviewing a present system (interviewing, questionnaires, sampling, and observation), interviewing is by far the most common and most important. The five steps in the interviewing process are preparation, planning and scheduling, opening and closing, interviewing, and following up. Interviewing is an information-gathering technique, and analysts should learn such active listening skills as open-ended questions, appropriate words and phrases, acceptance cues, and restatement at both the direct and emotional level. Used properly, silence can also be effective. In most instances, not all information can be gathered during a single interview, and arrangements for follow-ups should be made.

The results of interviews and the other data-gathering techniques must be documented properly so that information thus obtained is easily accessible to all members of the project team. IS departments that have adopted one of the standard methodologies will have documentation formats available to them. Others will have to develop documentation standards applicable to the project.

By analyzing the information gathered during a review, a project team can determine which parts of the current system are unnecessary, which parts can be retained in a new system, which information requirements are not being served by the present system, and finally, which major performance problems result from the current system. A summary of strengths and weaknesses of the current system is the end product of the analysis.

Determination of the components of a new system, when done well, is a creative process; project team and user cooperate to develop a system that best meets the users' requirements. Some of the techniques used to find a creative solution include understanding the business problem, avoiding placing constraints on system boundaries or use of the technology too early, viewing the system from various perspectives, and attempting to extend the state of the art.

Selected Readings

Gildersleeve, Thomas R. *Successful Data Processing Systems Analysis*, 2d ed. Englewood Cliffs, New Jersey: Prentice-Hall, 1985.
    This text has good coverage of the topics of interpersonal relations and creative thinking with a chapter devoted to each. Gildersleeve is a practicing IS professional.

Rockart, J. F. "Critical Success Factors." *Harvard Business Review* (March-April 1979): 81–91.

The widely quoted article in which the critical success factors technique is described and discussed.

Wetherbe, James C. *Systems Analysis and Design*, 3d ed. St. Paul, Minnesota: West Publishing, 1988.

As part of its coverage of systems analysis and design, this text has a section devoted to a framework for studying problems and opportunities and good coverage of alternative data gathering techniques.

Review Questions

1. What are the advantages of reviewing the present system? Why do some practitioners maintain that this review is unnecessary?

2. How does an IS professional obtain an understanding of the current operating environment?

3. Why is interviewing such an important skill for IS professionals?

4. What are the five steps in the interview process?

5. Describe the recommended procedures for (1) preparing for the interview and (2) planning and scheduling the interview.

6. How may an analyst put the interviewee at ease?

7. What steps are involved in closing the interview?

8. Describe the four key techniques of active listening.

9. What are the information-gathering techniques other than interviewing? Under what circumstances are they likely to be most useful?

10. List the four steps in the analysis process.

11. What techniques can IS professionals use to design more creative systems?

Discussion Questions

1. Rockart's critical success factors can help define a standard of desired performance. Select an industry and develop critical success factors for a manager within that industry. Identify the information a system will need to satisfy the manager's reporting requirements for the critical success factors.

2. Note taking during an interview may distract, annoy, or even threaten the interviewee. How would you suggest the analyst overcome this problem? What do you think of tape recording the session?

3. In addition to the suggestions in the chapter, in what other ways could an analyst encourage an interviewee to do most of the talking?

4. The analyst walks a fine line between seeming to understand an interviewee's opinions and seeming to agree or disagree with them. Explain how an analyst can show understanding yet maintain neutrality.

5. The following questions have been outlined by a junior analyst for an initial user interview. Critique the questions and suggest ways in which they could be rephrased:

a. "What information do you need that you are not currently receiving?"

b. "I understand you are having trouble meeting deadlines. Is that true?"

c. "Do you agree with the vice-president of marketing that implementing this new technology will significantly improve sales?"

d. "What would you like the new system to do?"

e. "Do you have any problems with the present system?"

Mini-Case

Foothills Industrial Supply, Inc. You encountered the following situations during a project at Foothills Industrial Supply. The project objective is to determine whether the company should replace its ten-year-old order entry/inventory control computer system with a more up-to-date system.

- The inventory control manager has told you that he does not feel it is necessary to spend time with you personally or to make his people available for interviews. He has seen the system he wants—a software package used at his brother-in-law's company in Boston. He would like to quit wasting time, order a copy of the same package, and install it at Foothills.

- In your initial interview with the sales manager, you first asked him what information he needed to make him and his organization more effective. He responded that he thought he was pretty effective already, and besides, it was your job to tell him what information was needed, not the other way around.

- During your interview with the president, she confesses that data processing sends her several weekly and monthly reports but that she normally does not use them because they are too long. She tells you that she gets the information she needs by walking around the place and talking with people and by having the controller give her a hand-prepared summary of activity each day. She likes to find it on her desk the first thing every morning.

Question for Discussion

1. Describe how you would handle the situations at Foothills Industrial Supply.

References

1. Gildersleeve, Thomas R. *Successful Data Processing Systems Analysis*, 2d ed. Englewood Cliffs, New Jersey: Prentice-Hall, 1985.

2. Nulty, Peter. "Why Do We Travel So *#!?*! Much." *Fortune* (March 28, 1988): 84.

3. Weinberg, V. *Structured Analysis*. New York: Yourdon Press, 1980, pp. 3–4.

Chapter 8

Joint Application Design

After presenting the rationale for Joint Application Design (JAD), Chapter 8 describes the roles of the various participants and explains how to prepare, organize, conduct, and use the results of a JAD workshop. Finally, the benefits and the risks of JAD are analyzed.

Learning Objectives

- Understand the advantages of Joint Application Design (JAD) and other similar techniques for collecting facts about a current system and for determining the requirements of a system under development.
- List the participants in a JAD session and describe their respective roles.
- Describe the various steps to be taken to prepare for a JAD session.
- Understand the eight points about each application that should be covered in a JAD session.

RATIONALE FOR JOINT APPLICATION DESIGN (JAD)

As a method for analyzing system requirements, JAD is an alternative to interviewing. In place of interviews, JAD substitutes a two- to four-day workshop, in which several qualified users meet with IS personnel. The method is designed to produce the same end product as the more classic approaches but in a shorter period of time and at less cost.

JAD and related methods were developed in an attempt to reduce three of the problems associated with interviews, the more traditional approach to requirements analysis. First, interviewing—preparing for the interview, conducting it, documenting the results, and combining the results into a homogeneous set of requirements—was time consuming. On a medium or large project, this phase could easily occupy a number of analysts full time for several weeks. JAD was designed to shorten the requirements analysis phase by weeks and, consequently, reduce the cost of analyst personnel.

Second, in the 1970s it became more and more apparent that most difficulties with operational systems—bugs, user dissatisfaction, high maintenance—were due to the analysts' poor understanding of the systems requirements. Moreover, poorly understood requirements could lead to a mistake such as forgetting a transaction type or a special case of billing logic applied to a category of customers. This kind of mistake is much more difficult to correct than a mistake in coding the program. The group technique of JAD is likely to eliminate more requirements errors than the one-on-one technique of classic analysis methods.

Finally, JAD promotes a participatory style of systems development. Most users who have participated in a JAD session feel some ownership of the system when it is delivered. Also, participation in a JAD session increases the users' understanding of the systems development process and of the demands that are placed on IS professionals.

JAD is not a life-cycle activity as such; rather, it is a technique that supports a life-cycle activity. As such, it has primarily been used in two areas— requirements analysis and user interface design. It can also be used in systems planning and in data analysis with minimal adaptations. Although JAD has its own deliverables, it can easily be adopted or adapted.

Because JAD is used extensively in the requirements analysis phase, the technique is detailed in this section. JAD can also be used in both user interface design and data design, but with more limited benefits. For instance, JAD is adequate for those systems in which the user interface is a simple menu and forms structure with a reporting or ad hoc query system, but it is not well adapted to the design of more sophisticated user interfaces.

SIX TYPES OF PARTICIPANTS

users

A JAD session has six types of participants: users, IS analysts, observers, scribes, a session leader, and an executive sponsor. The key participants are the **users**, those whose views determine the bulk of the requirements. Normally, any user who would be interviewed in the classic process is eligible for participation in a JAD meeting. Users can come from the top-level user management through supervisory personnel to clerks. Usually, an effort to have personnel higher than a clerical level will help ensure that the participants are knowledgeable, that they can see the forests as well as the trees, and that they have the authority to make decisions.

Obviously, the group should have as many users as necessary for a balanced view. One of the advantages of group methods is that the participants usually feel deeply committed to the decisions made by the group. If consensus is important, as many users as possible should attend. However, too large a group becomes unmanageable and defeats the very purpose of group methods.

The users invited to attend should have some familiarity with computer systems. If they do not, their fear (or just their ignorance) of the technology may prevent them from communicating effectively with the rest of the group. The problem of lack of familiarity usually does not arise when the proposed system replaces an already mechanized system. Most of the participants then have a fairly good sense of what can be expected of the new system, and little time will be spent on unrealistic ideas or basic explanations.

An **IS analyst** from the project team should also be present. In contrast to the interviewing approach described in Chapter 7, the analyst primarily has a passive role, listening to the users state their requirements and making sure that these requirements are understood and achievable. This passive role is difficult for an analyst who is used to interviewing and taking the lead in the design phase.

IS analyst

The analyst's role becomes even more difficult if user expectations are too high and the probable cost of the proposed system becomes excessive. Ideally, the analyst should be able to explain why certain functions are likely to cost too much. For instance, if the users decide that they need a response time of less than a second for certain transactions that involve a great deal of processing and data base I/O, the analyst should immediately be able to explain that this requirement might mean spending more on additional hardware than the organization would save.

The alternative to an immediate explanation is to accept the requirement and wait for a later stage to document its cost and prove that it would not be cost effective. Waiting is acceptable as long as the number of unreasonable requirements is not very high. In other words, if the user requirements get out of hand during the JAD session, something must be done to moderate them on the spot.

In most cases, one analyst should suffice. If necessary, the analyst can be backed up by **observers** who are present to provide technical assistance and advice. There can also be observers from departments other than IS if the project calls for technical information from other sources.

observers

One or two **scribes** should attend the meeting to note everything that is said and to publish the results of the session within a week or two after it is over. Normally, the scribe is from the IS department; if there are two scribes, it is a good idea to have one scribe from the user department. The two scribes can then divide the tasks so that one notes functional requirements, process descriptions, and data definitions and the other notes technical requirements, volumes, and performance and schedule constraints.

scribes

The **session leader** conducts the session according to JAD methods. A good session leader often means the difference between a successful session and a failure.

session leader

Because the essence of group methods is free expression and consensus, the session leader is responsible for providing a climate in which this is possible. The session leader must therefore have several important qualifications:

- The session leader should not report hierarchically to anyone in the group.
- The session leader should not play the classic role of a meeting chairman, for instance, by casting the decisive vote in case of disagreement.
- The session leader should be capable of promoting consensus rather than majority or authority decisions in case of disagreements or conflicts within the group.

Other important characteristics and skills are described later in this chapter.

The session leader role is best a full-time one because of the training required and because of the time needed to sell the concept of a JAD workshop to users, the IS department, and top management. An organization that cannot assign a person full time may retain a consultant. Several consulting firms specialize in training and providing session leaders.

executive sponsor

Finally, an **executive sponsor** is required to kick off the meeting and to be present at its conclusion. The executive sponsor is a ranking user executive with some direct or moral authority over the IS personnel. The role of the executive sponsor is to assure the participants of top management commitment both to the project and to the JAD method.

PREPARING FOR THE WORKSHOP

The preparation for a JAD workshop, mainly under the direction of the session leader, can be divided into several steps. First, the session leader locates an executive sponsor and determines the workshop's scope. Then, the session leader helps identify the participants, becomes familiar with the application to be discussed during the workshop, and helps the participants gain familiarity. Finally, the session leader organizes the meeting. For a workshop to be successful, the session leader should perform each step in the following way:

- Locate an executive sponsor and determine scope.

    Once it has been decided to use JAD on a project, the session leader locates an executive sponsor. With the help of other management members, they determine the scope of the workshop. The scope is based on the systems plan or determined at the outset of the development project. The scope statement describes the areas (organizational, functional, geographical) to be covered, the business objectives of the system, the assumptions about future growth and other factors of change, and the general cost and performance constraints within which the system is to be developed.

    If the scope of the system is too broad to be covered in a single workshop or if the number of participants required to cover the entire ground is large, the system can be divided into several parts, each with its own JAD session. However, there is a risk of conflicting information or requirements arising from the several sessions. The most insidious of these risks is that terms may not have the same meaning for different groups of participants.

- Identify the participants.

    Next, the participants in the session are identified. Most experts recommend 8 to 12 users as the ideal number. The users should all be experts in some area of the business under study. In many cases, the best users to select are the people who user management feels can least be spared for the duration of the workshop. The role of the executive sponsor in negotiating their availability is likely to be critical. A useful plan is to ask hesitant user management personnel to get the opinion of some other company that has already practiced JAD. In general, testimonials tend to be glowing.

- Learn the application.

    Although the session leader does not need to be an expert on the application being discussed because he or she will not contribute content to the workshop, some familiarity with the application must be gained before the JAD session starts. In the method prescribed by IBM, the session leader interviews user personnel, focusing on the workflow within the area to be discussed at the workshop. An important difference from interviewing as presented in the previous chapter is that the interviewer makes no effort to critique or find areas for improvement; rather, he or she aims for a basic understanding of the business activity.

    Other methods can be used where applicable: studying existing procedure manuals and systems documentation, scanning general literature on the subject, and so on.

    IBM has a form called the Familiarization Guide for recording information from the interviews. One merit of filling in the guide is that its information can be communicated to the users and IS personnel in advance of the workshop. This information can solidify the common understanding of the area under study and serve as a guide to the discussions.

- Organize the meeting.

    The usual activities for organizing a meeting must take place. A **venue** must be identified, preferably off-site, so that there will be as few interruptions as possible. The room must be large enough to accommodate all the participants in reasonable comfort. The participants will have to spend two to four days in these quarters doing unfamiliar work, perhaps with an intensity not typical in their day-to-day activities. Plenty of refreshments should be provided, and it may be a good idea to relax the usual corporate dress code. **venue**

    Audiovisual aids must be available. The minimum aids required are two overhead projectors, a magnetic board or a white-board (if possible equipped with its own copier), and flipcharts. Slide projectors, PCs, and video projectors are also often used. See Figure 8–1 for the layout of a typical JAD room. **audiovisual aids**

    A convenient **date** for meeting must be found. Thus, the meeting should be planned well in advance—several weeks at least. If a critical participant cannot make the meeting, it should be postponed rather than held without him or her. **date**

    An **agenda** must be established and distributed in advance. **agenda**

    If possible, a half-day **orientation meeting** for the participants should be held some days in advance of the actual workshop. This meeting will help the participants understand their roles and adapt to them more quickly once the session starts. **orientation meeting**

Figure 8–1 **Typical Layout of a Room Suitable for JAD Sessions**

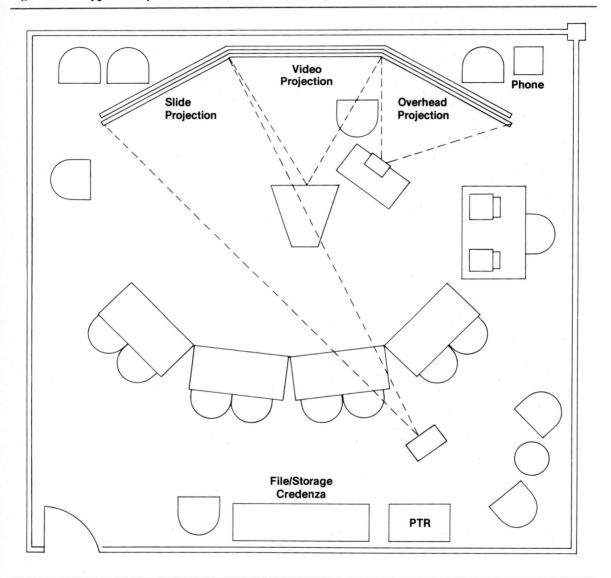

Video
Projection

Slide
Projection

Overhead
Projection

Phone

File/Storage
Credenza

PTR

CONDUCTING THE SESSION

At the beginning of the meeting, the executive sponsor briefly presents the objectives and expresses the interest of top management in the project. The session leader then conducts the meeting, guiding the participants through a structured analysis of the various activities identified earlier.

As taught by IBM, the analysis covers the following points of a proposed system:

- Planning

    What are the sources that tell users what work to expect and when?

- Receiving

    Where and how is work received? Where and how are resources (people, machines, materials, supplies) to do the work received?

- Receipt processing/tracking

    How are receipts reported and received work uniquely identified? Are other locations notified of receipts?

- Monitoring and assigning

    How will planned work be received, received work be processed, and priorities and resources monitored? What identification documents, instructions, and reports does the system provide?

- Processing

    How is the work done, by whom, on which machines? How does the system monitor and guide progress? How does it report?

- Recording

    How does the system record events about the work and notify clients, if required?

- Sending

    Where is the work sent after completion? What labels, directions, and other documents are required? Who is notified of completion? What billing or accounting data is produced?

- Evaluating

    What management information is required to indicate trends, summary data, measurements, or exceptions to plans, objectives, and budgets?

IBM's structured guide is well adapted to the automation of existing manual workflows or to the redeployment of aging systems. Used correctly, the guide can be helpful in integrating transaction systems with office automation—a major source of new systems development in the coming years.

The guide is perhaps less useful for analyzing new ways of using existing information (or identifying sources of new information) to gain competitive advantage. Also, management information systems and decision support systems are less amenable to any highly structured approach such as this one.

Value can be added to the approach if the session leader knows something about similar systems used by other corporations in the same industry and can tailor the questions accordingly.

During the workshop, the session leader should ensure that everybody is heard. The session leader can encourage less vocal participants to express their opinions and concerns, can stem the flow of discussion away from the more prolific participants, and can redirect the discussion back on track when it wanders.

The session leader should concentrate on how the meeting is conducted, not on the contents of the participants' remarks. The session leader should quickly gain everyone's respect. Finally, the session leader should be an effective negotiator, capable of devising satisfactory compromises or win-win solutions—those where no one loses.

DOCUMENTING THE RESULTS

After the meeting, the scribes organize the materials and deliver them to the IS analyst who attended the workshop. The analyst's responsibility is to prepare a specification document, which may include the following items:

- Management objectives
- Scope and limits
- Business questions the system will answer
- Information required to answer the questions
- Relationship with other systems
- Issues
- Data element definitions
- Screen and report layouts
- Menus
- Processing rules
- Operating procedures
- Performance and operational requirements

This list of items may be tailored to fit the organization's existing documentation standards.

ALTERNATIVE METHODS

Several firms have developed proprietary methods based on group techniques for requirements analysis. The best known are The Method, from Performance Resources, Inc; WISDM, from Western Institute of Software Engineering; and Rapid Analysis, from C&CE. The main difference between these methods is in the contents of the structured guides followed during the session. As described above, JAD's emphasis is on workflows, whereas WISDM emphasizes business functions and their associated inputs and outputs, and The Method emphasizes data analysis.

COSTS AND BENEFITS

The main costs of JAD are the extensive training required for the session leader and the substantial time commitment of key users. When compared with the benefits that can be obtained, these costs should be easily borne.

Many companies report that JAD can shorten the total life-cycle time up to 15 percent. Perhaps more critically, the high degree of user participation in the JAD approach can increase the quality of the system: less rework after implementation, higher user satisfaction, and better responsiveness to management goals.

Care must be taken, however, not to raise false expectations from the method. After all, JAD produces only what can be expected from a two- to four-day concentrated effort. The team approach is powerful; it cannot, however, solve all business problems by itself, nor can it solve the technical and implementation problems of later phases.

JAD has been used successfully in several large organizations such as Texas Instruments, The Travelers, IBM, CNA, American Airlines, and TWA. As more experience is gained, we can expect increased acceptance of JAD and its integration into most systems development life cycles.

Summary

JAD is a technique developed in the early 1980s to overcome some of the difficulties caused by the more classic approaches to requirements analysis. The two main difficulties addressed by JAD are the length of time taken up by interviewing and the lack of user participation and motivation generally associated with systems projects.

The technique itself consists of gathering highly competent users (about ten) for a two- to four-day workshop to discuss, conceptualize, and analyze. IS personnel are present, mainly to listen, to record what is being said, and to document the users' contributions. The workshop is led by an independent person to whom neither the users nor the IS personnel report. The role of the leader is twofold: to elicit decisions by consensus and compromise rather than by fiat or majority vote and to keep the meeting on track so that the system to be built is the one that is discussed.

JAD proposes a checklist of the following aspects that the participants should address: planning, receiving, receipt processing and tracking, monitoring and assigning, processing, recording, sending, and evaluating. This list is appropriate for systems that concern a workflow. It is less useful for innovative or unstructured systems.

The results of a JAD workshop need not be different from what they would have been with a classic approach. In general, each company can adapt JAD to fit into its own version of the systems development life cycle.

Several consulting firms have developed their own variations on the technique, all using the impartial session leader as a central theme, but varying the emphasis of the approach, for example, concentrating more on data analysis than on the workflow.

JAD has been used successfully in very large organizations, and its acceptance in the industry will probably increase.

Selected Readings

Joint Application Design, GUIDE Publication GPP-147, Chicago: GUIDE International, 1986.
  This publication is the main source on JAD and the competing methodologies. For more details, one must attend a course given either by IBM or by the various consultants who provide proprietary versions of the method.

Gane, C. *Rapid Systems Development*. New York: Rapid Systems Development, Inc., 1987.
  This book contains a chapter (8 pages) on impartial-leader group interviews. The chapter is concise, but points out all the essentials. This book contains a number of other topics of interest, and it is highly recommended reading.

Doyle, M., and Straus, D. *How to Make Meetings Work*. New York: Berkely/Jove, 1976.
  This book is not specifically about systems development, but it is very useful on how to make groups of people set and achieve common goals.

Review Questions

1. What are the two main reasons why group methods are superior to one-on-one interviewing?

2. Who should participate in a JAD session and what should the participants' roles be?

3. List the qualities needed by a session leader. What personal characteristics would eliminate someone from a job as session leader?

4. Describe the preparation steps for a JAD workshop.

5. Describe each of the eight points that IBM proposes be covered in a JAD workshop.

6. What is contained in the document prepared by the IS department after the JAD session? How does it differ from documentation that would be prepared after a series of interviews?

Discussion Questions

1. Discuss the use of JAD-like techniques in other parts of the life cycle.

2. What are the disadvantages of JAD?

3. Establish a list of points to be addressed (similar to the checklist in the chapter) for the following types of problems, rather than for problems that concern workflow:

a. Management information systems

b. Decision support systems

c. Subject data base design

d. Use of information technology for competitive advantage

Mini-Case

Lord's Chemicals and Drugs . Assume you are a newly hired project manager in the IS department of Lord's Chemicals and Drugs, a pharmaceutical distributor located in Charlotte, North Carolina. Your first assignment is to lead a project to develop a new payroll system. Your proposed strategy on the project is to use joint application design, but when you suggest this to colleagues and users, the reactions are negative. Here is a sampling:

- From the IS department:
  "Last time we tried JAD, it took us longer than interviewing would have."
  "Our users do not understand information systems, so they create requirements that are impossible to implement."
  "All JAD does is create paperwork."
  "It won't be any use since all we want to do is put in a payroll package."

- From the personnel department, where JAD was tried three years earlier when the current payroll system was upgraded to include flexible benefits:
  "We never understood what JAD was supposed to accomplish."
  "The session leader did not understand what most of us were saying. He only understood the representative from the accounting department, so they designed a system that is not very practical for us in the personnel department."
  "The sessions got out of control and only those who spoke louder than the others were heard."
  "Workshop sessions take too much time, and our daily work suffers."
  "All they produced were more forms that nobody could use."

Questions for Discussion

1. What went wrong?

2. How would you persuade your colleagues from IS and personnel to give JAD another try?

Technique

Data Flow Diagrams

DEFINITION

A data flow diagram (DFD) is a schematic representation of a complex process in as abstract a form as possible, disregarding material contingencies such as the media on which data is stored, the way the data is communicated, and the organizational unit or the computer that processes it. A DFD does not represent organizational structures or data relationships.

DFDs were developed in the 1970s by several authors more or less simultaneously and independently. Among the most influential are DeMarco, Gane and Sarson, and Yourdon and Constantine. As a result, several slightly different conventions have evolved.

DFDs were fairly quickly adopted by a large part of the IS community for two main reasons: DFDs are easy to prepare, and they force a certain level of abstraction, thus encouraging synthesis and innovation.

EXAMPLES

Figure 1 shows the data flow diagram for an order entry, shipping, and billing application. Orders arrive from customers. They are priced by referring to permanent product information. Availability of each product is checked against an inventory file. If the merchandise is available, it is reserved against the inventory and the order is stored for later processing. If the merchandise is not available, a back order is created. Back orders are reviewed periodically, and when the back-ordered merchandise becomes available, the back order is transformed into a regular order. Batches of orders are taken from the store of orders and scheduled for delivery, using truck fleet and geographical route information supplied by the transportation department. Pick lists are prepared to enable warehouse workers to traverse the warehouse once, picking out all the items of a certain type to be shipped together in the same truck. Any exceptions (items that could not be located) are noted on the pick list, which then serves to update the inventory. When picking for a route is completed, the truck is

Figure 1 **Sample Data Flow Diagram**

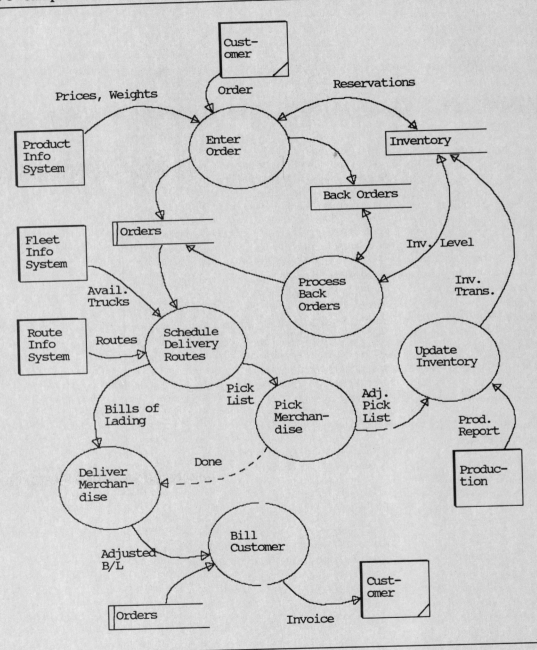

loaded and deliveries made, using bills of lading (a list of what is to be delivered to each customer). The customer checks the delivery. Any exceptions are noted on the bill of lading, which then serves to prepare customer invoices for the products that actually reached the customer and to post accounts receivable.

Figure 2 shows an expansion of the Schedule Delivery Routes process of the Order Entry DFD. Orders are sorted by general geographical area using the route information supplied by transportation. Next, trucks are scheduled using fleet information from transportation, which indicates which trucks are available and what their capacities are. Orders are batched by truck so that each truck is loaded as fully as possible while called to do the shortest route possible. For each truck, the order items are sorted into warehouse location sequence and pick lists are created. For each truck, a bill of lading is printed for each order, in delivery sequence.

WHERE USED IN THE LIFE CYCLE

DFDs are principally a tool for documenting the results of the requirements analysis phase and for verifying the closure of the analysis. They are created at the end of the interviewing process or after a Joint Application Design (JAD) session.

As an example, the interviewing process could lead to drawing a DFD of the application as it currently works, with most of the implementation consider-ations factored out, yielding a logical view of the present application. This view would be analyzed with respect to the operational and informational problems diagnosed during the analysis. The required changes to the DFD would then be made, transforming it into a logical representation of the view of the future application.

The DFDs of the logical view of the future application are used as input in all the various design stages. During user interface design, the DFDs are used to determine which parts of the processing are to be on-line, batch, and manual and to identify which reports and screens are needed. In data design, the DFDs are used to check that all the processes are supported by data, that all the data in the data bases can be entered, and that each data item is used by some process. During process design, the DFDs are used to determine which processes have to be designed and which functions have to be incorporated into the various programs.

DFDs are used again in the implementation phase when all the ancillary processes and interfaces (such as table updating processes and error reports) are designed. This use of DFDs is quite similar to that in the design phase.

One of the main merits of DFDs over other forms of process representations such as systems or procedure flowcharts is that DFDs force a certain level of abstraction. DFDs are therefore useful in those phases (such as requirements analysis) where abstraction is required and not so useful in later phases, where implementation decisions are documented.

Figure 2 **Expansion of a Process Box (Leveling)**

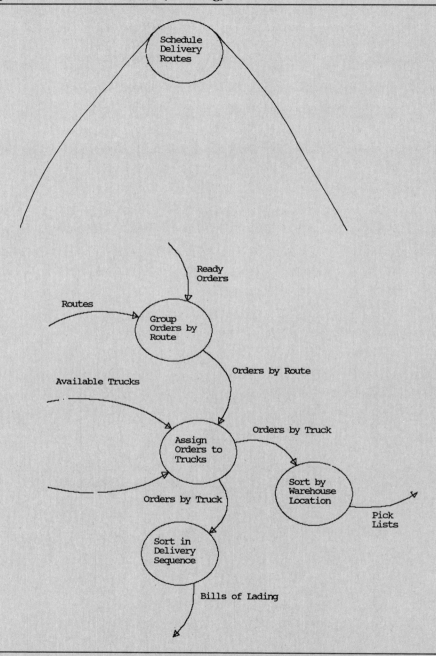

Figure 3 **Process Box**

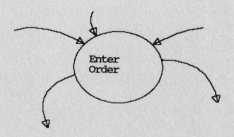

FORMAL RULES

Symbols

The main component of a DFD is the **process box** (see Figure 3). The process box is a bubble or a rectangle with rounded corners. It contains the name of the process, in the form of a verb followed by an object. The presence of multiple verbs or multiple objects is a sign that there should probably be multiple processes that communicate between them.   **process box**

Process boxes may be numbered. Numbering is useful for cross-referencing detailed DFDs to higher-level ones and to textual descriptions. In CASE tools that create and maintain DFDs, these cross-references can be maintained by the tool and do not necessarily appear on the DFD itself.

DFDs do not refer to the subject of the process verb, i.e., the person or program responsible for executing the function. Because responsibility for execution is an implementation decision, it is abstracted out of the DFD.

The next important component is the **data flow** (see Figure 4). A data flow is a line that connects a process to the rest of the system. Data flows carry the inputs and outputs of each process. A data flow is generally labeled (an exception will be noted later). Arrows indicate the direction of the flow; a double arrow indicates that the data is first retrieved, then updated.   **data flow**

Inputs to the system from the outside, and data from the system that is sent to the outside, originate or terminate in **external entities** (see Figure 5). These external entities are represented by square boxes, shaded on two sides. External entities can be persons, corporations, or other systems.   **external entities**

If the same external entity communicates with the system via several data flows (as the Customer in Figure 1), it may, for esthetic reasons, be represented several times on the chart. A useful convention is to note the number of occurrences of the entity beyond one by an oblique stroke in the corner of the external entity box, as illustrated in Figure 1.

Figure 4 **Data Flow**

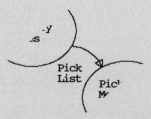

Some data flows connect two processes or a process and an external entity. Others connect a process and a **data store**(see Figure 6). A data store is represented by a rectangle that is open at one end and that has a name. Data stores are used whenever it is functionally necessary to store the output from a process before sending it on to the next process. For instance, because it is necessary to have a number of orders before delivery routes can be scheduled, an Orders data store is required between Enter Order and Schedule Delivery Routes. In contrast, although invoices may be stored in the mailroom before being sent to the customer, there is no functional need for storage. Therefore, no Invoices data store is necessary.

data store

Data stores provide the exception to the rule requiring that data flows be labeled. If the data flow between a process and a data store would carry the same label as the data store (in the singular instead of the plural), it is not strictly necessary to label the data flow. (see Figure 7.)

Figure 5 **External Entity**

Figure 6 **Data Store**

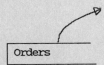

Some authors permit the representation of the same data store at several places in the data flow diagram, using the same convention as for external entities—one or more oblique strokes in the corner of the data store (see Figure 8). Others use a slightly different convention, multiplying the left side of the box (see Figure 9). Yet others insist that each data store can only figure once and that otherwise it becomes hard to check whether the DFD obeys the required set of formal rules. Our view is that imposing a single copy of each data store can make the DFD difficult to read. This difficulty arises especially when the data store represents a subject data base or part of a subject data base shared by many different processes.

Finally, some authors distinguish between data flow and control flow. Control information flows between processes and is represented by dotted arrows, as in Figure 10. Timing and other dependencies can thus be represented. Other authors do not distinguish control information, which must then be represented as an ordinary data flow.

Figure 7 **Unlabeled Data Flow**

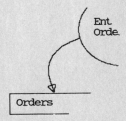

Figure 8 **Data Store Replicated in Several Places (Option 1)**

Orders

Orders

Figure 9 **Data Store Replicated in Several Places (Option 2)**

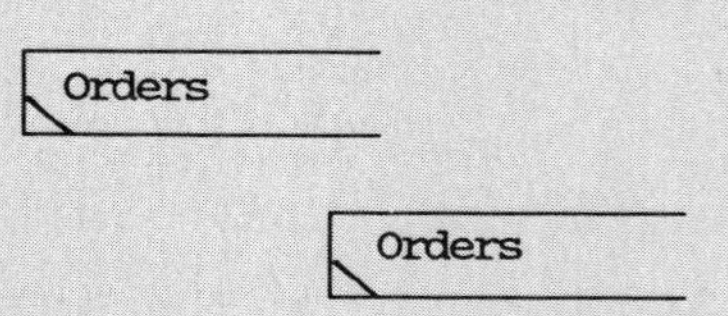

Orders

Orders

Figure 10 **Control Flow**

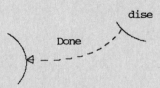

Constraints

A process must have at least one input data flow and one output data flow. If the process has only one of each, it should also be critically examined to see whether it might be combined with a preceding or following process.

A data flow has at least one end connected to a process. On a top-level DFD, the other end must be connected to one of the following:

- Another process
- A data store
- An external entity

(On a lower-level DFD, it may be left dangling—see the section on leveling below.)

A data store must have at least one input and one output data flow. A data store with only one of each should be examined to determine whether the store is a functional requirement or just a physical, temporary storage that is conceptually unnecessary.

Leveling

Some authors, such as DeMarco, recommend that a single DFD not hold more than about seven processes, because the human brain can attend to only about five to nine objects, concepts, or chunks of information simultaneously. Others, such as Gane, insist that it is possible to concentrate successively on various parts of a DFD and that subdividing the DFD is not necessary, and may indeed be harmful. But even Gane admits that there are physical limitations to a DFD, especially when prepared on a CASE tool and viewed on a screen or sent to a printer. Therefore, it may be necessary to subdivide the DFD into more manageable pieces.

Leveling a set of DFDs consists of preparing a top-level (or level 0) DFD that depicts only very high-level processes and data flows. Each process might require tens or even hundreds of pages of textual description to explain it completely.

For each process whose description would exceed a certain number of pages (which Gane puts at five on an average, ten at the most), a second-level DFD is prepared (see Figure 2). As the illustration shows, only the process box itself is expanded, not the surrounding processes, the external entities, or the data stores. Therefore, data flows that are disconnected at one end can arise. (If the data flow was not named on the higher-level chart, it must nevertheless be on the lower-level chart where the data store it is named after does not appear.)

A problem may arise when DFDs are developed top down. The analysis of a lower-level diagram may make new data flows appear to and from the outside of the process. These might typically be errors, exception reporting, and the like. Some authors advocate incorporating these data flows in the higher levels as necessary to make all the data flows balance. Others take the view that the higher-level diagrams are primarily planning and communication tools and that the system must balance downward, but not necessarily upward.

MECHANIZED TOOLS

Most CASE tools today have a facility for drawing DFDs. What differentiates the tools is mainly how the DFD diagramming facility ties in to other facilities. It should, for instance, be possible to cross-reference processes, data flows, and data stores to other components in the repository that give a more complete description (textual or lower-level DFD).

Another difference is the stringency with which the DFD diagramming tool will enforce the rules of data flow diagramming. The principal inventors of DFDs are far from agreeing on the rules; it is only to be expected that the tools should differ as well.

Today, the only rules that can be enforced relate to the internal syntax of the DFD. No convincing way of tying together data flow diagramming and data analysis has yet been developed. Therefore, no single tool exists that can analyze both data flows and data stores in terms of entities, access keys, integrity constraints, and processes using or updating these entities.

Finally, DFDs can be presented in many slightly different ways, as described below. The way chosen is largely a matter of preference and habit.

EQUIVALENT TECHNIQUES

The examples in this book use Yourdon and DeMarco's round or elliptical boxes for processes.

Gane and Sarson use a square or rectangular box with rounded corners (see Figure 11). The top of the box contains a process number, usually coded in some

Figure 11 **Alternative Process Box**

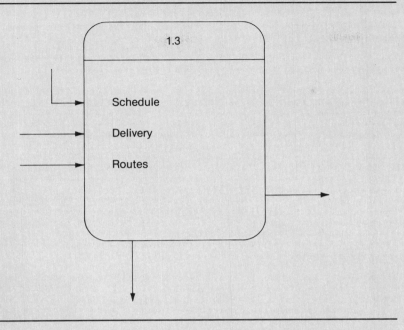

hierarchical form to reflect the level and cross-reference to the parent DFD. The bottom of the box may contain the name of the entity—person, organization, or program—that executes the process. The executing entity's name is only for use in making the DFD represent physical systems rather than logical ones. In his later works, Gane does not refer to this possibility.

SADT, a proprietary set of tools and techniques from Softech, Inc., adds the important concept of control information flow in addition to data flow. Also, SADT has been adapted for use in real-time systems, such as the ones used in industrial control or embedded weapons systems. Today, real-time features are not normally required for business systems, but as business systems become more integrated and more complex, such additions may become important.

Adaptations to all of these methods have been proposed to accommodate the flow of goods or materials as well as data. In the order entry, shipping, and billing example in Figure 1, adding the flow of goods would be a marked advantage, especially in explaining DFDs to users.

Other methods of documenting processes exist. Although these methods may appear quite different from DFDs, they have fundamentally the same expressive power. Systems and procedure flowcharting represent basically the same concepts as DFDs, but they tend to show much more implementation detail. They are therefore less likely to force the analysts to look at the forest as well as the trees. They also put excessive emphasis on forms and documents (for procedure flowcharts) or files and reports (for systems flowcharts). In other words, they overemphasize the vehicles of information and underemphasize the information itself.

The appearance of HIPO (hierarchical input-process-output) diagrams (see Figure 12) is quite different from DFDs, but there is a rough equivalence between the two. This equivalence can be illustrated as follows: the H in HIPO corresponds to the leveling of DFDs; the I and the O correspond to input and output data flows of DFDs; and the P corresponds to the processes of DFDs. HIPO documentation is less visual, but can easily be made more detailed because it contains more descriptive text and more data structure information. HIPO is essentially suitable for communicating program structures and specifications to programmers. DFDs are much more suitable for communicating with users and management. HIPO diagrams are not good tools for abstraction. They are good for program packaging, because they tend to decrease coupling and increase cohesiveness naturally.

CRITERIA FOR USE

When invented, data flow diagramming made a major contribution to analysis techniques: it forced analysts to increase their level of abstraction. DFDs have become almost universally accepted as the prime tool for documenting the processes of an application.

Because of the simplicity of the symbols, users have little difficulty understanding a DFD and pointing out mistaken assumptions, omissions, and even possible improvements to the flow.

The danger in DFDs lies in two directions. The first is the temptation to use them to represent physical implementations, for which other tools are better suited. In particular, the much maligned systems flowchart is still a better tool than the DFD to document a batch systems flow. Also, DFDs do not contribute to data analysis, data design, and data base design. A similar danger lies in the exclusive use of DFDs to represent unstructured problems where the data flow is not known or does not even exist, as in many office automation, personal computing, and decision support environments.

The other danger is to mistake the documentation tool for an analysis tool. The syntactical rules of data flow diagramming ensure that some glaring omissions will not be made. They do not, in themselves, ensure that the system being analyzed will meet its objectives, that the users will be happy, or that the project will come in under budget. The analysis techniques of interviewing and JAD are better tools for that purpose.

DFDs have shortcomings because the concept of a process is still ill-defined. In comparison, data analysis lends itself much better to mathematical treatment; it is therefore probably an inherently more powerful discipline today.

Despite its shortcomings, data flow diagramming is essential. No analyst can afford to be unfamiliar with the process. It is the best tool available for

Figure 12 **HIPO Diagram**

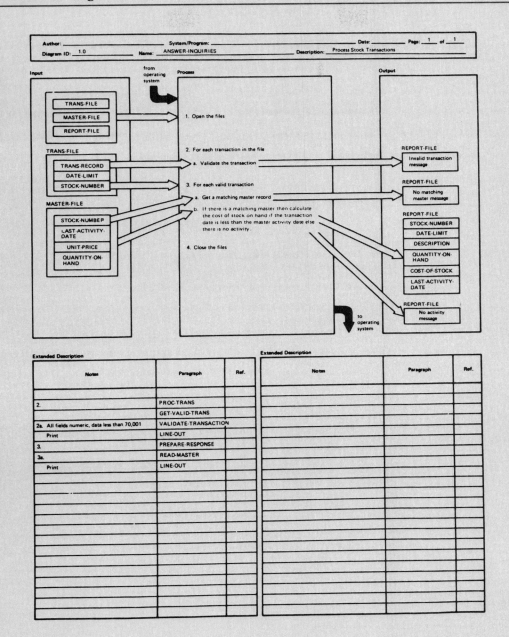

documenting a transaction processing system or a management information system at the desired level of abstraction.

Selected Readings

DeMarco, T. *Structured Analysis and System Specification*. New York: Yourdon Press, 1978.

Yourdon E. and Constantine L., *Structured Design*. New York: Yourdon Press, 1978.

Gane C. and Sarson T., *Structured Systems Analysis: Tools and Techniques*. New York: IST, Inc., 1977.

These three books make up the traditional view of structured analysis and design, which became popular in the late 1970s and which introduced the data flow diagram as an important analysis tool.

Gane, C. *Rapid Systems Development*. New York: Rapid Systems Development, Inc., 1977.

In this concise and to-the-point book, Chris Gane adds JAD-like techniques and entity-relationship modeling, thus extending the arsenal of analysis and design tools available to the systems professional.

EXERCISES

1. Draw a level-0 data flow diagram for the process of entering a university, completing its curriculum, and graduating with a bachelor's degree. Then draw a level-1 DFD for a student's view of the registration process, depicting the student's sources of information, the successive decisions to be made, and finally, the administrative steps.

2. Draw a DFD for the registration process from the viewpoint of the university administration. Contrast this view with the student's view in Exercise 1.

3. Draw a DFD for municipal dog licensing, tour organization, airline reservations. Choose the same domain that you analyzed in the entity-relationship diagramming exercise in Section II.

4. Draw a DFD for an application for which you have not already established an entity-relationship diagram. Is it easier to do entity-relationship diagramming first, then data flow diagramming (as in Exercise 3)? Or is it easier to do the DFDs first?

Section IV

User Interface Design

Section IV describes how to design user interfaces—those parts of the system that are on the boundary between humans and computers. User interfaces are designed in two steps. First, the flow of the interaction, or dialog, is designed, as described in Chapter 9: Designing Dialogs and Document Flows. Next, the detailed layouts of inputs and outputs are designed, as described in Chapter 10: Designing Forms, Screens, and Reports.

Videotex: A Success Story

In the early 1980s, Videotex was thought to be the magic medium by which the information revolution would reach into the home. At the touch of a button, users would be able to display the day's news, the weather forecast, the films playing at a nearby movie theater, the latest stock price quotations from Wall Street, and even bank balances.

Various systems were being experimented with before Videotex's full launch. Prestel in Britain, Télétel in France, and CAPTAIN in Japan were government-sponsored efforts; in the United States, Knight-Ridder, the Los Angeles Times, and Columbus-based Banc One were some of the prominent private corporations trying the concept.

Now, almost a decade later, only one of the efforts can truly be described as a success. In France, the system tested by the *Direction Générale des Télécommunications* (D.G.T.), the French telephone authority, went into production in 1984. At the end of 1987, more than 3 million Videotex terminals had been installed, with each terminal being used on the average of once every other day for a total of 90 minutes per month.

The technology that was initially developed for the Télétel system included a terminal that could be connected to standard television sets to provide color and graphic capabilities. The French authorities assumed that most people had television sets. With this terminal came a detachable keyboard that sent its signals via infrared waves—a sort of giant remote control. The keyboard had a full alphabet as well as a numeric keypad. Its special-purpose keys allowed users to sign on to the system, to leaf forward and backward in a sequence of related screens or pages, to back up one level and make another query, to retransmit garbled information, and to stop the session. Because the users of the system were presumed not to be trained typists, nor even computer literate, the keys were laid out in alphabetic sequence, instead of the more usual QWERTY style.

Later, the D.G.T. decided to add a low-cost choice of terminal. The so-called Minitel was a self-contained unit with a small (about 5 by 8 inches) black-and-white screen and the same keyboard layout as the larger terminals. Some models also had a handset so that they could double as telephone sets. This model was developed for the white and yellow pages application that was the telephone company's own principal motive for developing Videotex. This terminal has become the most popular, not least because of its low cost. In fact, in the initial stages, before the number of subscribers reached critical mass, the terminal was distributed free of charge. The telephone company was repaid by the success of the system: revenue from the increase in number of phone calls, revenue from the yellow pages advertisers, and reduced costs of printing directories and answering directory assistance calls.

After some resistance, the D.G.T. had to offer an additional option, that of a standard typewriter-layout keyboard, even though it meant reducing the benefits of mass production. But some of the most interesting initial applications were aimed at businesses and computer-literate people rather than the general public, and these users had an absolute need for standard keyboards.

Why was the French venture successful where the others were not? The main reason is probably that the technology and the initial applications were right for the users that the authorities had targeted. The low cost of the terminals, the reasonable response times, and the availability of transaction services such as home banking were crucial factors. In addition, the D.G.T. did not hesitate to invest large sums from which benefits would not be obtained for several years. The long term took precedence over quick profitability.

Some measure of serendipity was probably also present. One of the most popular applications initially, the so-called *carnet rose*, was a bulletin board dating service. It is improbable that the French government had counted on its success.

Initially, it was critical to provide a low-cost system, for instance by providing the Minitel terminal free of charge. Other endeavors did not succeed in reaching mass audiences, in part because they required expensive terminals or even personal computers and then relied on subscriptions to information services at an additional cost.

Another important factor was the availability of free transaction processing applications such as home banking. One of the initial service providers, the Crédit Commercial de France (France's ninth or tenth largest bank, with assets of $10 billion and 300,000 customers), converted its customer base from paper bank statements to electronic query. By avoiding the mailing of daily statements, it reduced its postage and paper handling costs so much that the home banking system was profitable even though it was free to the customers. Users had the perception that a system that processed their personal transactions was delivering much better value than a data base containing only generic information, such as the yellow pages, train timetables, and sports results. The home banking application, even more popular because it was free, contributed heavily to the early success of Videotex and gave the project momentum.

The Crédit Commercial de France was a precursor in another application. The first Videotex-based application that was operational in France, even before the experimental stage was over, was a cash management tool offered to corporate customers. The customers could obtain the detail of the previous day's activity via telephone first thing in the morning and transmit orders to the bank to transfer money from account to account as needed. The few hours' gained in getting the information was enough to make this system a success.

Another major factor in the success was that the user interface was well constructed. When subscribers called the system, they were given clear and simple instructions on what to do to select a service. A cascade of menus led them to the application of their choice by using clearly labeled keys on the keyboard. Whatever service was desired, the conventions of calling up menus, leaving applications, and recovering from errors were identical. In addition, advanced users were given the option of typing in the name of the service that they wanted, to avoid going through multiple menu choices every time. (Prestel, the British system that was experimented with at about the same time, had a much reduced keyboard, with only a numeric pad and special keys. This limited keyboard reduced the possibility of typing in names directly and may have been a factor in the slower acceptance of Prestel.)

During the trial periods, it also became clear that colors and graphics were valuable in some applications but that, in most cases, the cost of transmitting colors and graphics was too high. Response time suffered, and the profusion of colors was counterproductive. The most successful applications used only two or three colors—for background, text, and response, for example—and graphics were limited to the initial display of the service provider's logo. As it turned out, the popularity of the black-and-white Minitel terminal de-emphasized the role of color, which had initially been thought to be much more important than it actually was.

The French system had a primitive graphics facility, relying on so-called alphamosaics, little squares of color the size of one-quarter of a character. Putting these squares side by side, service providers could develop graphic effects that looked satisfactory and were pleasant when watched from afar but that strained the eye when seen close up. By contrast, the system adopted in the United States has far more sophisticated graphics capabilities. Unfortunately, this capability also makes transmission either slow (on slow phone lines) or expensive (on higher-quality lines). The equipment required to handle the U.S. graphics is also more expensive than the Minitel. The proponents of Videotex in the United States may have thought that most homes would have personal computers capable of handling the complex graphics at no added cost, but a personal computer is still not part of the average American home.

One technological trick that the French used to improve response time while maintaining low cost was different transmission rates for sending and receiving. The French telephone network would normally support only aggregate rates of less than 1500 bits per second at the time of the initial implementation. Therefore, sending and receiving would have taken place at 300 bits per second (about 30 characters per second) each way, the highest speed for which standard components could be found and which would not exceed the aggregate capacity available. Instead, the French system was designed to deliver information from the application to the user at 1200 bits per second (resulting in information being displayed on the screen faster than the human eye can read it) and only 75 bits per second from the user to the application (still more than twice as fast as most people can type).

Other mass market systems have been successful. Bulletin boards, publicly available data bases, electronic mail systems, and services such as those provided by CompuServe and the Source are good examples. Automatic bank tellers and pay phones that read the magnetic strip on the back of a credit card are other, more specialized applications. But the Télétel system is certainly the most successful system to deliver multiple applications from different vendors to a large number of private individuals.

PURPOSE OF SECTION

As the story of the French Videotex system illustrates, user acceptance is a large part of the success of a system. User acceptance takes on particular importance when the system reaches outside the boundaries of the organization (see Figure IV–1) or when new classes of users—managers, engineers, analysts, office principals, and other types of professionals—will be in day-to-day contact with it.

Yesterday's back-office systems were designed to be used by specially trained clerks. Deficiencies in the system could be made up for by additional training or, in some cases, by coercion. Data entry clerks, employed exclusively to transcribe data from forms to a CRT, did not really have a choice of whether or not to use the system that they worked on. Doctors in a hospital do have a choice; so do engineers and managers. Even more importantly, so do customers. If customers feel uncomfortable with the automatic teller machines (ATMs) provided by one bank, they may well go to another bank that has fewer ATMs but longer lobby hours.

The purpose of this section is to show how to design those parts of an application where the users are in direct contact with the computer. Good design will ensure that the users judge the system favorably and that the overall performance of the application meets the requirements set in the previous phase.

The user interface of an application is defined as the boundary between machines and persons. It includes all the points of interaction between the two,

Figure IV–1 **Systems that Reach beyond an Organization's Boundaries**

An airline places a reservation terminal in a travel agent's office.

A hospital-supplies vendor places an order entry terminal on customer's premises (in hospitals and clinics).

An automobile manufacturer requires its suppliers to process orders and engineering changes from electronically transmitted data.

The entire transportation industry in the United States is increasingly relying on electronic order processing and billing.

Computers perform self-diagnosis and, in case of a problem, send a message to the computer maker to provide replacement parts. The part arrives at the computer user's premises the following morning with installation instructions.

Quarterly filings of financial reports are submitted to the SEC electronically by publicly traded corporations.

---

and it always relies on some mechanism for transforming data between human-readable and machine-readable forms. The most frequent of these mechanisms are input forms, workstations, and output reports.

Chapter 9 describes the design of the flow of data between the users and the system, whether in batch or on-line. Input forms and output reports are batch-oriented mechanisms; workstations are generally interactive.

Chapter 10 describes how to design the format of the elements of the user interface: input forms, output reports, and workstation screen layouts.

KEY TASKS AND DELIVERABLES

User interface design activities take place both in the design and implementation phases of the life cycle. The general rule is that *all* the interfaces must be identified and described in general terms in the design phase so that the effort required in the implementation phase can be estimated and the work planned accordingly.

In addition, during design, all the *essential* interfaces must be designed in detail (mocked up for reports and forms, prototyped for screens and dialogs). The detailed design of *ancillary* interfaces can be postponed until the implementation phase. The detailed design of essential interfaces is required to make sure that users and management understand enough of the system to come to an informed decision on whether to approve the design and go ahead with the implementation.

The key tasks and corresponding deliverables in the **design phase** are depicted in Figure IV–2. The general flow of activity follows these steps. First, those activities that are on-line and those that are batch are marked off on the data flow diagrams that were prepared in the requirements analysis phase. Then, for each on-line activity, each logical unit of work (conversation, dialog, business transaction) is identified and briefly described.

design phase

Figure IV–2 **User Interface Design Activities in the Design Phase**

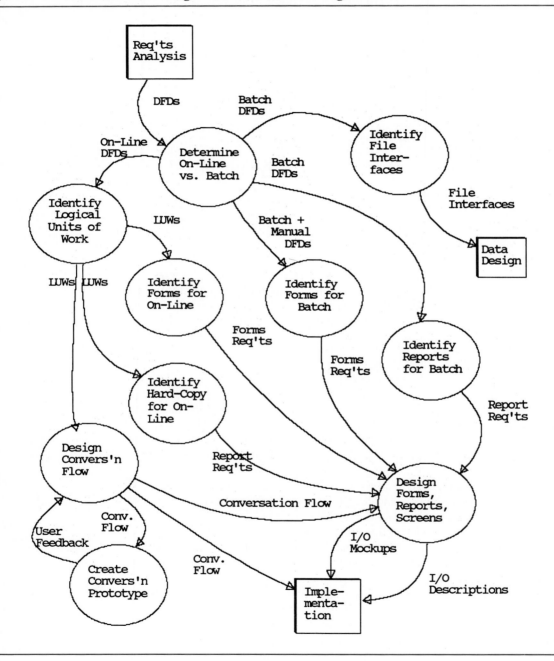

Required forms are identified for each batch activity as well as for those on-line activities that need forms. The forms are listed, and the purpose of each form is described. Generally, the purpose will be to support a business transaction or to provide updates to data stores.

For each logical unit of work, the analysis shows whether printed output (such as hard copy for audit trails, receipts, correspondence) is needed. Also, output reports from each batch process are identified. All outputs are listed, and the purpose of each output is described.

The analyst identifies and lists interface files, in particular those that will be sent to decision support and management reporting systems, and then describes the data contents of each in terms of entities, not attributes.

For each of the lists of logical units of work, forms, and reports, the analyst designs the detail of those elements that are essential in the sense described in Section III. For on-line conversations, the analyst describes the conversation flow fully, designs the screens, and creates a conversation prototype to show to the future users of the system. (If there are no tools for creating a prototype, the analyst may have to create screen mock-ups on paper.)

Next, form and report mock-ups for all essential forms and reports are created.

All of the deliverables in this phase have two destinations: printed out, they will become part of the design report that management and users will review and approve; in electronic form (by means of a CASE tool), they become part of the repository of design information that will be used by analysts and programmers to install the system. In addition, the interface file descriptions will be used in the data design segment of the design phase. Mock-ups of any preprinted forms and reports will be used in the forms procurement cycle of the implementation phase.

In the design phase, all of the interface design tasks described above are highly iterative. In addition, they are dependent on activities in parallel phases, data design and process design, which in turn depend on interface design. This lack of natural sequence among the tasks requires a high degree of coordination among the project members. The best approach for dividing the work is to assign subsystems to individuals or small teams, so that each individual can do all the design for a small part of the system. This approach is better than having some individuals specialize in report design and others in forms design or data element design, for example.

The key tasks in the **implementation phase** (see Figure IV–3) consist in completing the design of the nonessential, or ancillary, elements—reports, forms, and dialogs. The resulting documents will be shown to their users (but need not, in general, obtain management approval) and will also become part of the programming specifications. The reports and forms designed in this phase will in general not be preprinted, so they do not need to enter the forms procurement cycle.

implementation phase

The forms procurement cycle is generally performed during systems installation. It consists of communicating forms designs to one or more printers,

Figure IV–3 **User Interface Design Activities in the Installation Phase**

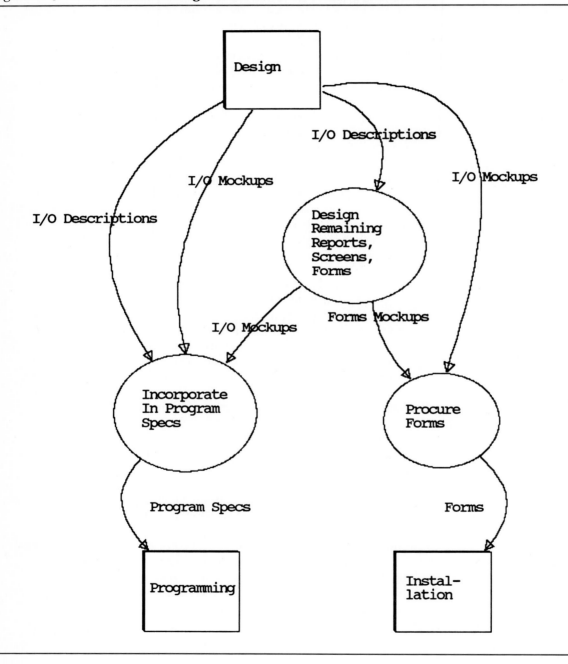

evaluating bids, approving the typeset layout of the form, placing a firm order, and monitoring its delivery. It must be carefully planned by starting from the deadline for delivery (usually for the system test) and working backwards, allowing slack for unanticipated problems along the way. If the installation phase is very short, the procurement process may need to be started before the design phase is over.

Chapter 9

Designing Dialogs and Document Flows

Chapter 9 describes the various steps in the design of document flows and on-line dialogs. First, data flow diagrams from the requirements analysis phase are analyzed to determine which activities are to be manual, on-line, and batch. Next, how to design document flows (which are batch-oriented) is described. Then, the design of human-computer dialogs is presented: how to determine the scope of a conversation and select the dialog style. Dialog design also requires an understanding of the impact of the terminal technology both on dialog style and, more especially, on the type of on-line help to be provided. Some practical advice on clarity, consistency, performance, and respect for the user follows; the chapter ends with a section on how to document the conversation design.

Learning Objectives

- Understand the criteria for choosing between batch and on-line implementations of data flows.
- Identify logical units of work.
- Understand the different modes of user-computer interaction that are available to the designer and the criteria for choosing the appropriate mode.
- Apply these criteria to the design of on-line conversation corresponding to logical units of work.
- Understand the impact of technological characteristics of workstations on the design of dialogs.

ON-LINE VERSUS BATCH

The first step in user interface design is to start transforming the logical data flow diagrams established during the requirements specifications phase into physical data flow diagrams. This step requires identifying who—user, computer, or a combination of both—performs each activity.

The cost-effectiveness of computer-based systems is based on the computer doing as much routine work as possible. Humans intervene in a system for two main reasons:

- Technical requirements

    Humans must make data available to the computer system in the first place, through batch data entry or on-line transaction processing.

- Nonroutine work

    Despite the promises of artificial intelligence, humans outperform computer systems in making decisions in unanticipated situations, in recognizing patterns (or deviations from normal patterns), and in applying common sense. Typical areas for manual and interactive activities will therefore be analysis and forecasting (in decision support activities), system controls (in transaction processing), and professional work generally (in situations where the computer system is a supporting tool rather than a vehicle for automating the activity).

With routine work mechanized, users spend more time on challenging, nonroutine work.

In addition to this general principle, certain cues on a data flow diagram can help determine whether an activity should be manual, interactive, or batch. The three main cases to be considered are data flows from an external entity, data flows to an external entity, and data flows in which no external entity appears. In addition, a special case may arise when a data flow cycles from one data store through one or more activities and external entities and returns to the same data store.

Data Flows from an External Entity

Any activity that takes a data flow from an external entity and sends it with little or no processing to a data store should probably be interactive to help prevent errors and to increase the effectiveness of the system in meeting business requirements.

Interactive data entry as close to the source as possible is helpful in preventing errors because of two factors. First, the person originating the information may be present, so that any question that arises can be resolved then and there. For example, a new customer opening a bank account can check the spelling of the name. Second, manual transcription of data, which increases the distance between the source of the information and the data store, is error-prone. Transcribing a telephone order onto a form, to be keypunched later by a different operator, gives rise to mistakes both when the first operator writes to the form (transposition of digits in the customer number or product codes, for instance) and when the second operator reads the form (misinterpretation such as mistaking a 1 for a 7).

BOX 9–1

Good Design

A good design is one that the user does not even notice. When someone uses a well-designed object—say a hammer or a pen—there is no conscious perception of the tool. An ill-designed tool makes the user more conscious by causing awkwardness or irritation. It is when a tool breaks or does not function properly that its user consciously perceives it. (Picture what happens when a ball-point pen runs out of ink or a pencil point breaks.) This theory of design is well described in *Understanding Computers and Cognition.*[1] The book concludes that "design constitutes [. . .] a committed attempt to anticipate future breakdowns."

This view applies directly to the design of user interfaces, in particular to interactive workstation interfaces. (It is also applicable to less interactive media, such as reports. A well-designed report is one that presents information so clearly that its readers do not need instructions to interpret it. The report never offends with its poor appearance such as pale ink, unaligned characters, too many colors, and so on.)

By far the most important factor in interface design is knowledge of which tasks the user is to accomplish and how they are accomplished. This knowledge enables the designer to create what is called a *metaphor*. Users very quickly form mental models of the system they work with: it is this mental model that prompts them to try various actions to perform their jobs or correct errors. If the mental model of a user is close to how the system actually operates, then that user will have few difficulties with the system. Another user, with a mental model that is very different from the system will have much greater difficulties in handling unanticipated situations. A good design strategy is to force a correct mental model on the user. Thus, the application should use as a metaphor something that the user already knows.

The best illustration of a useful metaphor is a spreadsheet package interface, such as that of Visicalc or Lotus 1–2–3. The reason the interfaces to these packages are said to be easy to learn, easy to use, friendly, and so on is that practically all the users understand the spreadsheet metaphor: "Lotus 1–2–3 is just like a paper spreadsheet, except for . . . ." The interfaces become totally invisible to the user as soon as he or she starts using them. The user acts as though there were a physical spreadsheet just behind the screen, on which figures and text can be written directly and which can be moved about behind the screen so that different parts of the spreadsheet become visible. The user "believes" that he or she is manipulating a concrete object directly.

The second reason for data entry at the source is to increase the effectiveness of the system in meeting the business requirements. For example, if the external entity is a customer, then interactive processing can often help in the sales process by indicating to the operator options to propose to the customer: special prices, new products or services, reminder of products that the customer usually purchases. This information can increase both sales and customer satisfaction.

Figure 9–1 **Examples of Applications of Electronic Data Interchange**

Industry	Applications
Automotive	Purchasing
Electronic Supplies	Order Entry
Textile Manufacturing	Shipping Information
Paper	Order Entry
Railroads	Order Entry and Invoicing; Bills of Lading
Trucking	Order Entry and Invoicing; Truckload Shipment Exchange
Ocean Shipping	Customs Paperwork; Shipment Brokerage
Pharmaceuticals	Order Entry and Invoicing
Medical Supplies	Order Entry
Optometry	Order Entry
Retail/Wholesale Distribution	Order Entry; Shipping
Health Insurance	Claims Processing
Insurance Underwriting	Policy Underwriting by Independent Agents
Internal Revenue Service	Electronic Filing of Tax Returns (Experimental)
Banks	Electronic Funds Transfer

An exception to the general rule that data flows from an external entity should be on-line is the possibility of obtaining the data in machine-readable form. The interface can then become batch. If the external entity is another system, passing data in a file (on tape, diskette, or via data communications) is effective. The rise of electronic data interchange (EDI) in the trucking industry is an example. Bills of lading and invoices are passed electronically between customers and suppliers. This cost-effective and safe way of entering data is extending beyond the trucking industry (see Figure 9–1.)

Batch-oriented input to the system is also effective in situations where more unconventional input technology can be used. Optical technology (mark reading, bar codes, image scanners, optical character recognition) is the most widely used today; magnetic and electrical (mark-sensing) techniques have also been used, but they tend to be associated with particular industries. Magnetic ink character recognition (MICR) is, for instance, widely used in banks to read data on checks. Optical mark reading and character recognition can be used for manual input; the other techniques require that the input documents be specially printed. They will therefore usually be turnaround documents, printed by a computer (or a specialized output device) and then read back in (see Figures 9–2 to 9–7).

Optical reading is usually operator-assisted. Someone must feed in the documents; more importantly, there will be occasions when the input device

Figure 9–2 **Handwritten OCR Form**

This is an example of a form that can be completely handwritten, requiring no special equipment. It does, however, require great care and is not suitable for form-filling by occasional users.

Order forms are probably the most popular application for this technology. To motivate and train its sales force in the use of OCR, one company used OCR in an initial application to reimburse the salespersons' travel expenses. When the sales force had gotten used to the technology, the order entry system was implemented, with a very low initial error rate.

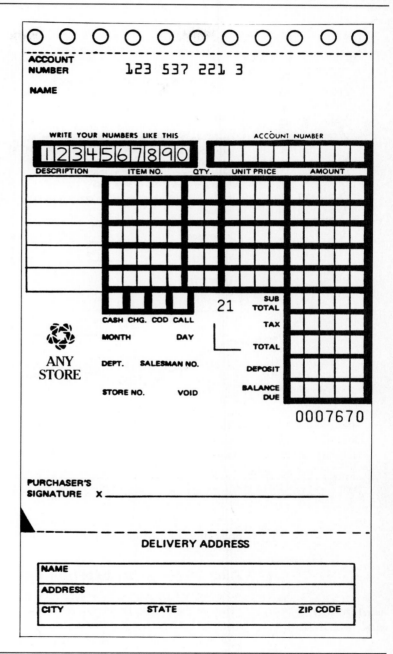

Figure 9–3 **Form for Mark-Sensing**

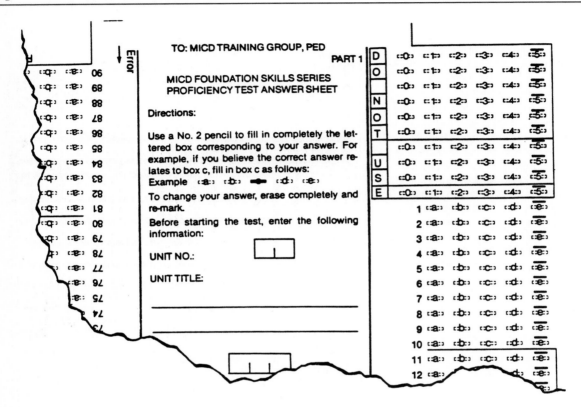

Here are some other special-purpose technologies that are quite popular. The first one is a vehicle for grading tests automatically. For each multiple choice question, the student fills in the box corresponding to the answer. Special mark-sensing (electrical or optical) equipment reads the marks and grades the student.

cannot recognize a character because it is malformed or smudged; the operator must then be present to interpret the character.

Data Flows to an External Entity

transaction documentation

An activity that prepares a data flow to an external entity will often be batch. Many of these data flows will be **transaction documentation** that goes with each individual transaction or that concerns each individual external entity—customer, supplier, employee. These data flows are called reports, although they do not have the characteristics of management reports. The volume for each transaction is usually modest, say one or two pages per customer. The number

Figure 9–4 **Printed OCR Form**

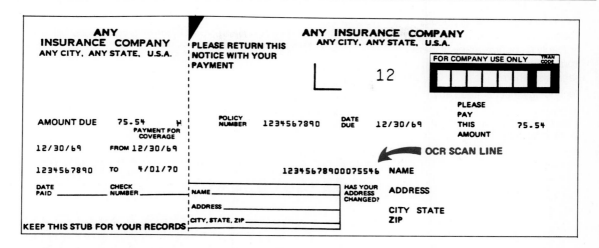

This is a typical turnaround document using OCR technology. To the left of the name is a line printed in machine-readable font, the so-called OCR A. In the upper right-hand corner is a field labeled "For company use only." This field is for entering handwritten machine-readable data.

of customers may be very large, however, and it is usually most cost-effective to print these reports in batch mode at the end of the day's processing. An exception to this rule arises when the data flow represents immediate feedback about the transaction, for example in the presence of a customer.

Often, the external entity to which data is sent is labeled **management.** Depending on the use that management is to make of the data, reports or data files may be the most appropriate. For control purposes, reports are usually the most appropriate. Such reports commonly contain exception data and overall totals that let management verify that the system—both mechanized and manual parts—is functioning correctly. The reports can also help determine whether management objectives for the application area are being met (comparing budgeted and actual sales or graphing statistics on customer satisfaction, for instance).

management

An example of another data flow to an external entity may be an **audit trail.** Audit trails are designed to enable users (or auditors, external or internal) to trace the chain of events leading from some event or events to a result, but traveling upstream, as it were, from result to event. For instance, an auditor may need to justify a customer's balance by reconciling it to all the transactions concerning that customer. Another example would be to justify that the prices applied to a given order (which may be months or even years old) were, at the

audit trail

Figure 9–5 **Popular OCR Fonts**

To the right are the most popular specialized OCR fonts. You will probably recognize many of them from documents that you have seen elsewhere.

Technology that can read any typed or printed font is emerging. This will decrease the reliance on OCR fonts in the future.

OCR-A
The OCR–A font is the standard approved by the American National Standards Institute. This style is available in three sizes.

OCR–A Size 1
for high-speed printers and typewriters
ABCDEFGHIJKLMNOPQRSTUVWXYZ 1234567890
Y5H$%|&*{} -+=ııı:;ⁿ'¬.?/

OCR–A Size 3
for cash registers and adding machine tapes
ABCDEFGHIJKLMNOPQRSTUVWXYZ
0123456789&*{}-+

OCR–A Size 4
for embossed plastic credit cards 0123456789
ABCDEFGHIJKLMNOPQRSTUVWX
Y5H$%|&*{} -+=ııı:;ⁿ'¬.?/

OCR–B
The OCR–B font is an international standard that was designed by the European Computer Manufacturers Assoc.
1234567890
ABCDEFGHIJKLMNOPQRSTUVWXYZ*"/@£_&'()[]¤↑$

FARRINGTON SELFCHEK®

Farrington 7B Selfcheck®
for embossed plastic credit cards
123 456 789 0

time of processing, in accordance with company policy. Audit trails may be contained in reports or on files, depending on volume and retention requirements.

The main choice for output is between computer-readable files and printed reports. This choice is analogous to the choice of input medium: magnetic files are the least error-prone of media and they are also highly cost-effective. Sending data on files should therefore be the first choice whenever the external entity can make use of files. The main drawback is that files cannot be read directly. Two computer tapes or two diskettes look exactly alike, and it is impossible to detect mislabeling or other errors of manipulation until the file is actually read by the receiving system.

Output flows to external entities within the system can often reside on a file to be called up and viewed through a screen-based terminal or workstation. This

Figure 9–6 **Magnetic Ink Character Recognition**

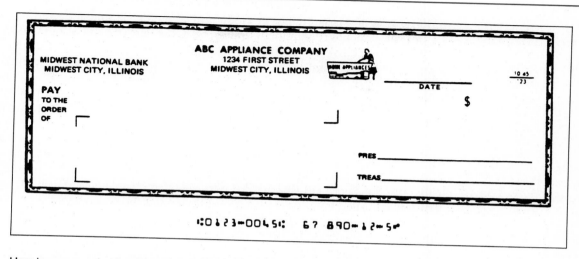

Here is an example of a check. The line at the bottom is printed in magnetic ink. It contains the customer's account number and the check number. Once the check is made out and deposited to the recipient's bank account, the amount of the check will be added, also in MICR characters. Thereafter, the clearing of the check (the processing that culminates with the issuer's account being debited and the check being returned) can be very largely automated.

Figure 9–7 **Universal Product Code**

The final example is this universal product code (UPC) bar code, universally adopted by the supermarkets, which is found on the labels of practically all packaged food.

arrangement simplifies the report flow. However, in some circumstances, it is unacceptable to the recipient, who may not have a terminal. Moreover, the report may be too large (either in width or in length) to be suited to a terminal.

If management's requirement is more related to analysis and planning than to day-to-day control, it is probable that an output file is more responsive than a report to management's real need. What is to be avoided is to create printed output that will be directly reentered into a spreadsheet on a PC. Lotus Development Corporation did a study in the mid-1980s that showed that 80 percent of all Lotus 1–2–3 spreadsheet data was copied from computer-printed output!

The general rule that an output data flow to an external entity should be batch has an exception. An example of **on-line transaction output** is provided in international banking, where the network called S.W.I.F.T. handles interbank transfers (see Chapter 5). Although many banks accumulate these transfers and send them out in batches at the end of the day, others have their computers connected to the S.W.I.F.T. network and can both send and receive funds on-line as the need arises.

Data Flows that Do Not Involve an External Entity

Activities that neither receive data from, nor send data to, external entities can be manual, on-line, or batch depending on their characteristics. The choice of processing mode for most activities within the system depends on when and where the activity is performed.

When the Activity is Performed. The general rule is that an activity set off by a transaction or an event is best processed on-line and that an activity set off by a schedule is best done in batch.

Event-driven activities are set off by transactions (external events such as a customer call) or by demands (internal events such as users deciding that they need certain information). Transactions are best processed on-line. Some demands are also best processed on-line, particularly inquiries that concern a single entity in a data base, such as the status of a shop floor work order or the schedule of a truck.

An exception to the general rule is that inquiries concerning more than one entity in the data base may sometimes best be performed in batch. Satisfying the request for information may require reading large portions of the data base. An illustration would be an auto dealer who is notified of a recall and who wants to find out how many customers may be affected (and the additional workload that the dealer may expect). The dealer might have to read the entire data base to find out the model and options purchased by each customer over the past several years. If several users make the same type of request every day, the file would have to be read multiple times in a 24-hour period to satisfy all the requests. Cost constraints may compel a batch solution, even though users would prefer to have the information immediately through on-line query.

User Interface Design

Figure 1   **Use of Colors To Enhance Screen Output**

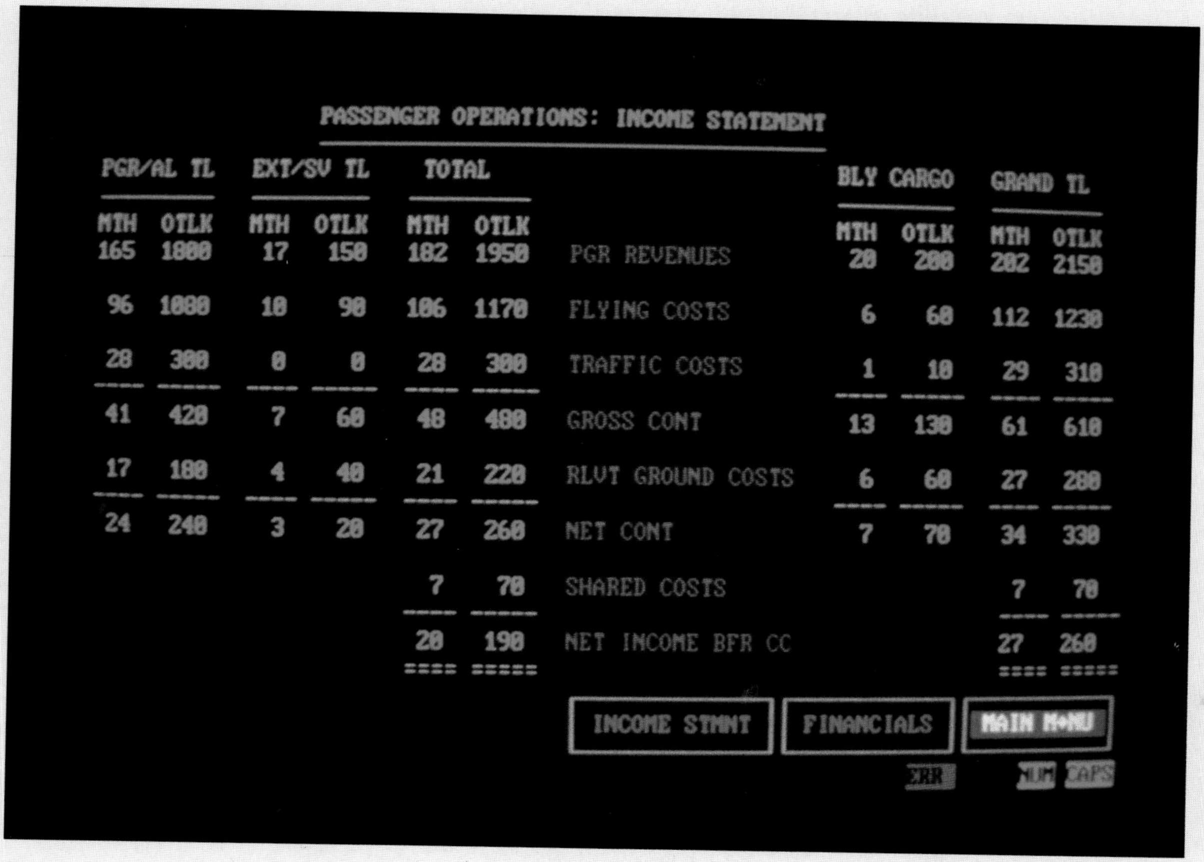

PASSENGER OPERATIONS: INCOME STATEMENT

PGR/AL TL		EXT/SV TL		TOTAL			BLY CARGO		GRAND TL	
MTH	OTLK	MTH	OTLK	MTH	OTLK		MTH	OTLK	MTH	OTLK
165	1800	17	150	182	1950	PGR REVENUES	20	200	202	2150
96	1000	10	90	106	1170	FLYING COSTS	6	60	112	1230
28	300	0	0	28	300	TRAFFIC COSTS	1	10	29	310
41	420	7	60	48	480	GROSS CONT	13	130	61	610
17	180	4	40	21	220	RLVT GROUND COSTS	6	60	27	280
24	240	3	20	27	260	NET CONT	7	70	34	330
				7	70	SHARED COSTS			7	70
				20	190	NET INCOME BFR CC			27	260

INCOME STMNT   FINANCIALS   MAIN MENU

ERR   NUM CAPS

Figure 2   **Pleasantly Designed Display Combining Color and Graphics**

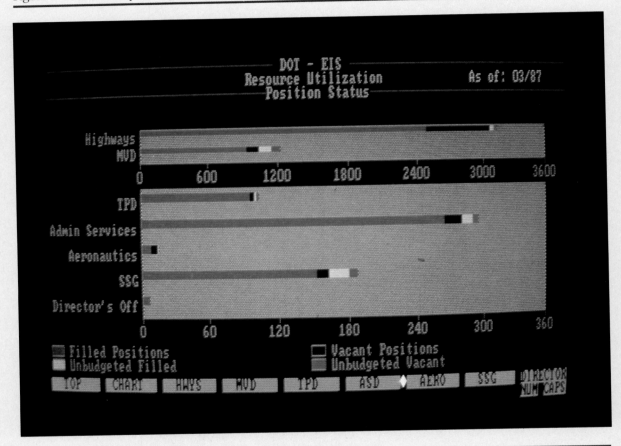

Figure 3   **Icon-based Menu on a Touch-Sensitive Screen**

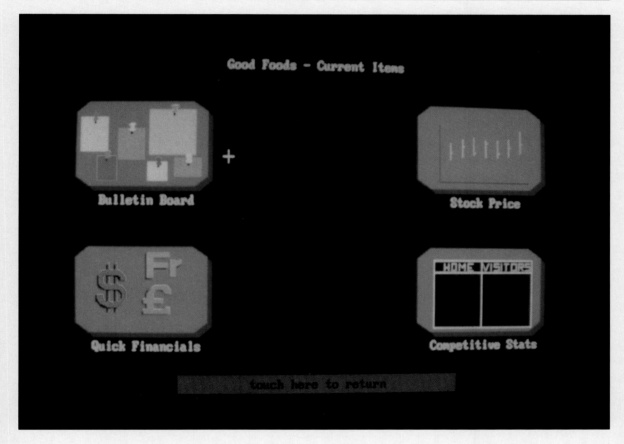

Touch-sensitive screens allow the user to select an option simply by touching an area of the screen. This technology appeals to beginning users. However, it often causes fatigue, especially in presbyopic users, who lean back to see better and then have to reach out farther to touch the screen.

Figure 4   **An Executive Support System Alert Screen**

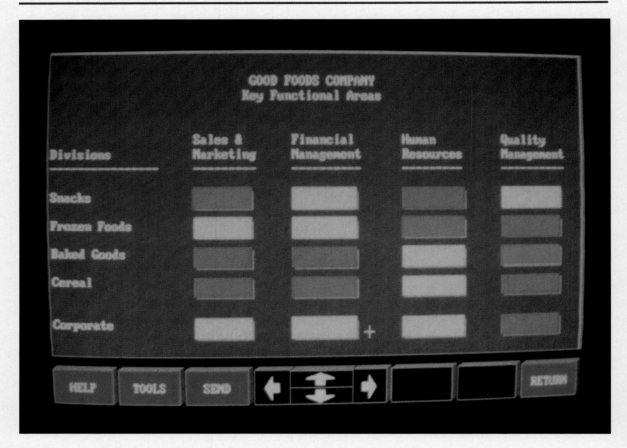

This screen, reached by touching one of the icons in the Figure 3 illustration, uses familiar color imagery to alert executives to problems. A red rectangle indicates that immediate action is required, a yellow one that the area needs watching, and a green one that all is well.

Figure 5   **A Screen Using Multiple Graphics and Colors**

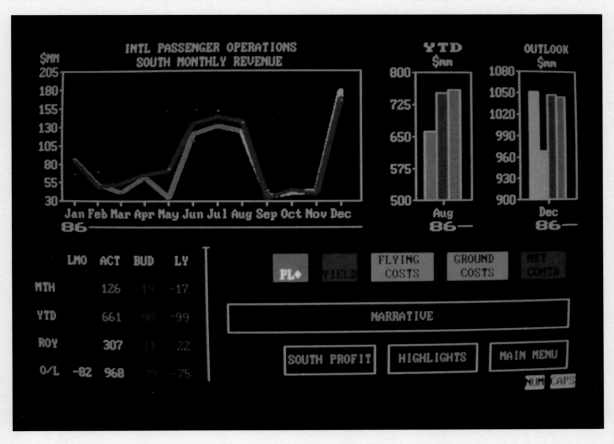

This screen is not particularly well designed – it is too busy. However, it has the merit of being exhaustive: all the information about a given area is on the screen. A less busy design would have required multiple interactions. In this case, esthetics and ergonomics were knowingly sacrificed for efficiency.

Figure 6 **A Map Used as a Top-Level Menu**

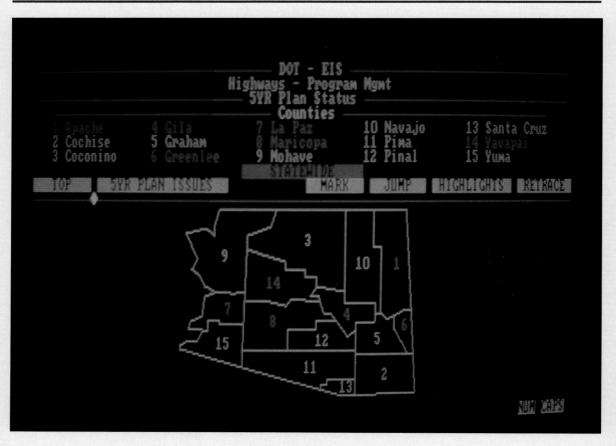

This map is used to summarize a number of construction projects throughout the state of Arizona. Pointing to one of the counties provides the user with a more detailed map.

Figure 7 **An Intermediate-Level Map-based Screen**

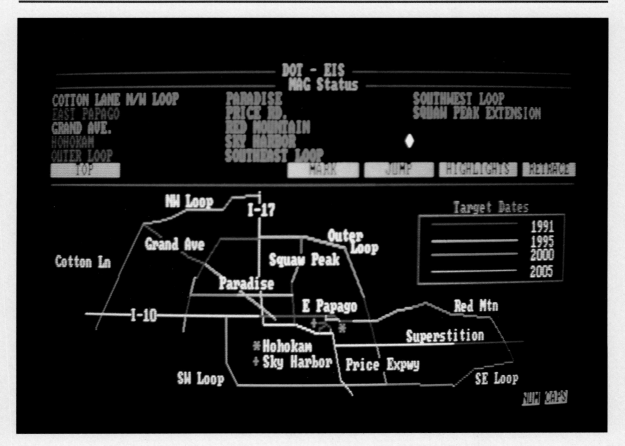

This map depicts the next level of detail from Figure 6. All projects within the county are represented on the map through a combination of textual data and color coding.

Figure 8 **The Lowest Level of Detail**

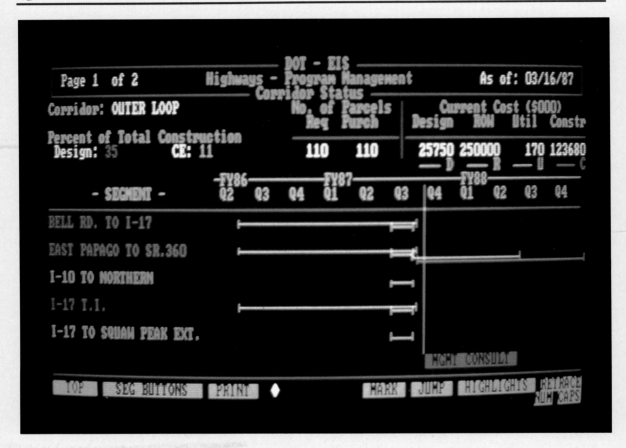

Each project can be examined in further detail. The color coding is consistent with that used at the higher levels (*see* Figures 6 and 7). One of the users of this system was color-blind, however, and an alternate interface, using different highlighting techniques, was devised for him.

Finally, processing that is driven by a schedule, such as the weekly payroll, the monthly closing of the accounts, the yearly renewal notices for magazine subscriptions, or periodic reporting to regulatory agencies, is practically always done in batch mode.

Where the Activity Is Performed. The location where the activity is performed may impose certain constraints on the technology and the processing mode. For example, an activity to be performed by a human agent in a place where there is no access to a workstation must obviously be done manually. This constraint is disappearing from many applications because of the increased availability of portable equipment, such as the laptop workstation where considerable progress has been, and is being, made. For instance, the Internal Revenue Service plans to equip IRS personnel with portable PCs to be used on location.

Another striking example is portable data entry equipment such as that used by Federal Express. This equipment can read bar codes that identify each individual package. Every time a package moves from one location to another, a hand-held scanner registers the fact. The package is thus tracked from the moment it is received until final delivery.

If a workstation is available at the location where the activity is performed, a choice still must be made between on-line and batch. If there is no on-line connection to the facility where the central application is run, the data flow must obviously be batch. In some cases, even if there is a possible communications link, it may not be cost-effective to use it on-line, for example, if response times are excessive.

Data Flow that Cycles through Several Activities

A turnaround document is one that is produced as output by a system, then completed manually, and reused as input to the same system. In many order entry and billing systems, the order is entered, then shipped, and only when the customer has actually received the order, is it billed. In this case, a turnaround document is often used. When the order is entered, a bill of lading is printed. The bill of lading goes with the shipment to the customer, who signs off that everything has been shipped or notes any exceptions on one of the copies of the bill of lading. This copy returns to the supplier, who can then call up the initial order, enter the modifications, and initiate the billing process.

This type of processing is indicated whenever the data flow diagram has flows with the same name or similar names flowing through several activities and returning finally to the same data store.

After the processing mode of each activity on the data flow diagram is identified, the data flow diagram is annotated as shown in Figure 9–8. During this analysis, some activities may need to be decomposed into several because there is a change of processing mode in the middle of the activity. (The annotated data flow diagram is an example of a work document used to help the analyst perform a specific task. It does not necessarily need to be stored as

BOX 9–2

Ad Hoc Inquiry and Data Storage

Ad hoc inquiry poses a problem. Because the inquiry is ad hoc, it is essentially unpredictable. (If it were predictable, it would become part of the exception reporting category.) It is therefore difficult to know the amount of detailed data to keep available for inquiry and the best form for the data. An extreme solution is to keep a trace of every single transaction that has entered the system ever since its beginning. This solution quickly becomes unmanageable for large systems. A credit card operation such as American Express, VISA, MasterCard, or Diner's Club can hardly be expected to keep records of individual purchases for much longer than it takes to bill them to customers. As an example, VISA processed 200,000,000—two hundred million—purchases between Thanksgiving and Christmas of 1986. If a marketing analyst in a credit card company wanted to track the buying habits of a customer over the past seven years by accumulating every purchase made in every store visited, the analyst would find that the data was not available. Some choice would have been made to accumulate statistical data by period, by customer category, or by category of expenditure, at the expense of losing the details.

This dilemma illustrates an important application of information theory, the so-called data processing theorem. This theorem states that the output of a data processing operation cannot contain more information than the input. There are two immediate consequences. "Garbage In, Garbage Out" is one. The other is that, whereas you can obtain a total if you have the details, you cannot deduce the details from the total alone.

Determining what to accumulate and what to keep in detailed form requires experience and judgment. Unfortunately, judgment is not always enough. Requirements change and unanticipated needs arise—particularly in the services business, where new products (new forms of bank accounts tailored to the individual, new insurance policies, new combinations of travel, hotel and leisure services) can be created without much difficulty. The problems are to ensure that these new products meet a demand and to market them to the right targets. This can only be done if the right level of detailed data is available to marketing analysts.

permanent project documentation, because the information that it contains will be reflected in other documents.)

At this point, the input/output medium for the data flowing in and out of the activity is selected. For on-line activities, it will usually be a CRT terminal; for batch or manual activities, forms, reports, or other technologies may be chosen. How to select the medium is described in more detail in Chapter 10.

DESIGN OF DOCUMENT FLOWS

Most of the system input and output flows identified above are likely to be paper-based. The overriding consideration for deciding how to implement these

Figure 9–8 **Data Flow Diagram Marked with Batch, On-Line, and Manual Domains**

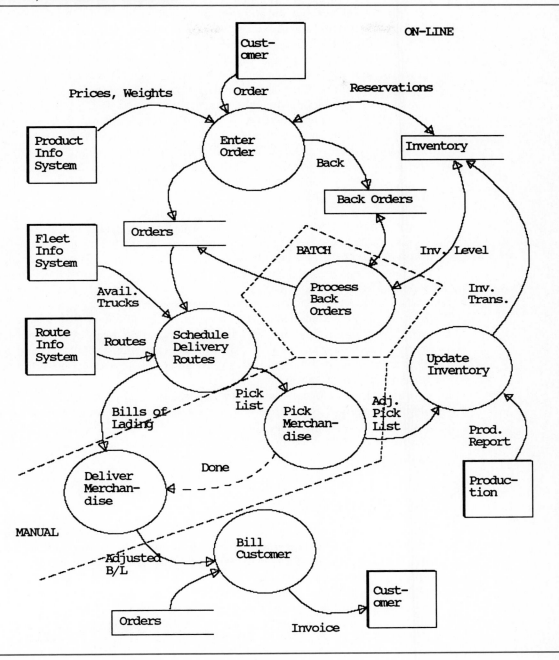

flows is that they should be as simple as possible. It is a good idea to distribute information—both files and reports—electronically.

All outputs (except turnaround documents) should go directly to their recipients. A turnaround document should ideally accompany the merchandise to which it pertains to avoid loss or delays. This is obviously impossible in those cases where physical goods are not involved, such as in financial services. However, in the example of a check, which is a turnaround document on which the account number and check number have been printed and to which the amount will be added when the check is deposited, the paper flow is the materialization of the transaction. This case is quite similar to the cases where the documents accompany the physical goods.

Some systems produce large amounts of printed output that must be distributed to a large number of individuals or organizations. Billing individuals for services is a typical example. Direct marketing based on mailing lists is another. A large bank or a utility may need to print and mail several million statements every month. Handling this type of output can be very costly because it may require multiple stages of processing: bursting and collating the output forms, folding and inserting them in envelopes, and adding promotional inserts or canceled checks. Special equipment that automates these activities is available but may be expensive and occupy precious square footage. In some cases, the report and the envelope that is to contain it can be printed in a single operation, using specially designed mailers that are assembled as continuous forms. If the process cannot be automated or if the additional equipment is very expensive, the cycle billing technique that utilities have used for many years may be the answer. This technique consists of dividing the customer base into as many parts as there are days in the month, say twenty, and only processing one-twentieth of the invoices on any given day.

Input flows of forms—again with the exception of turnaround documents—should be as short as possible. Whenever input forms are transmitted from one activity in the system to another, there must be some control procedure to ensure that all the forms that leave their source actually arrive at their destination.

DIALOG DESIGN

The design of human-computer dialogs, or conversations, starts with determining the scope of the conversation, the logical unit of work. The next step is to choose the type of dialog—whether the dialog is controlled mainly by the operator or by the system. This choice is influenced not only by the functional requirements and the users' preferences but also by the terminal technology to be used. Finally, the level and style of operator help during the interaction is chosen. This choice is even more influenced by the technology than the overall dialog style.

Determining the Logical Unit of Work

The first step in conversation design is to identify the logical units of work that make up an activity on the logical data flow diagrams. Usually, but not always, there is one logical unit of work for each activity. (If several activities make up a single logical unit of work, the logical data flow diagram may have been drawn to an excessive level of detail.)

In general, a logical unit of work is the processing of an elementary **business event**, that part of a business transaction that takes place within a single unit of time. Entering an order, entering modifications to a bill of lading so as to initiate billing, and entering the data on an accounting journal entry (making sure that debits and credits balance) are typical examples. The criteria for a good logical unit of work are that it must be a reasonably self-contained whole and that it must be completed within a short time span. The main characteristic of a unit of work is that, if the system should go down during the processing, the unit has either been completely processed or not at all. The unit of work is also the unit of data base update and the unit of recovery in case of incident.

business event

Generally, a logical unit of work concerns a single entity such as customer, product, supplier, account, employee—or at worst a very few entities. An exception might appear when a mass update is to take place, such as increasing the prices of a whole list of products by some percentage. Because this work does not involve a small number of entities, it is best processed in batch.

In many organizations, a new type of processing is emerging that is based on a much larger logical unit of work. The generic name for this type of logical unit of work is **case**. Examples of casework are the processing of an application (for life insurance, retirement benefits, or a mortgage loan); the design of a new product using computer-aided design and an expert system to estimate its manufacturing cost; and, closer to home, systems development activities such as the design of a conversation, the analysis of the impact of a request for maintenance, and the planning and conduct of a series of system test sessions.

case

Choosing the Type of Dialog

The choice of the type of dialog is mainly directed by the type of application and the degree of "user-friendliness" required (see Box 9–4.) There are two main types of dialog between a computer system and the operator:

- Program-directed dialogs

    The program has the overall initiative and directs the operator to enter commands and data in a predetermined sequence, leaving few, if any, choices to the operator. The sequence in which screens are processed can often be chosen by the operator, but each screen is usually fixed in format. Usually, the program is instrumental in determining whether the logical unit of work is completed.

BOX 9–3

Logical Units of Work

From the technical side of systems comes the need for a notion of a logical unit of work. A logical unit of work is that portion of an activity that stands on its own, that has a meaning independent of other units of work.

Take, for example, a customer calling the Hawthorne Pasta Company with an order for 144 cartons of spaghetti and 160 cartons of rotini. This order is a unit of business. Recording that there is an order for 160 cartons of something unspecified has no meaning; nor has recording an order of 160 cartons of rotini for some unspecified customer. It is the entire order that is the logical unit of work, not a number such as 160, nor a single line. (Obviously, if the Hawthorne Pasta Company is out of spaghetti, a partial order for rotini only could be recorded; this would still be a logical unit of work.)

There are three reasons for logical units of work. First, logical units of work provide *closure* for the operator. Closure provides the operator with answers to such questions as *Where am I in my work? What have I done? What remains to do? What is completed and what remains open?*

Second, precise guidelines are necessary for *recovery* from a system malfunction. Logical units of work provide a means to recover. In the days of sequential files, it was fairly easy to know how to recover from a system malfunction: the program was just started over. The logical unit of work was the program that processed an entire input file. With direct-access files and on-line systems, it is more productive to have smaller units of recovery. It would in fact be very inconvenient to have to redo the entire day's processing if the system went down at 4:30 P.M.

The third reason is the *sharing of data* in files and data bases among several users. To avoid losing data in certain cases, each user must block off data that has been read from the file or data base with the intention of modifying it, so that no one else can modify it until the logical unit of work has been completed (see Figure 9–9).

The user of any on-line system that records activity against a shared data base must know what constitutes a logical unit of work, because it is the user's responsibility to signal the end of a logical unit of work by some action at the terminal (for example, by pressing the *Enter* key or responding "OK") which is said to *commit* the transaction to the data base. Conversely, the user will then know that as long as the transaction has not been committed, there is always some way to back off, correct errors, or abandon the work without consequence.

Users of on-line systems must also be aware that if they pause for a long time in the middle of a logical unit of work, the corresponding records on the data base remain blocked; they cannot be unblocked until the transaction is either committed or abandoned. Blocked records cause problems for other operators who might be trying to get at the same data.

Transaction processing systems are the most sensitive to this type of constraint. Handling it has become a matter of routine programming discipline because most logical units of work, or *business events*, only take a few seconds or minutes to complete and because the risk of conflict is low. If a transaction requests a record that has been blocked, the user is not even notified; the system just suspends work on the transaction until the record is freed, and then proceeds. The operator notices nothing but a slight pause.

Decision support systems (DSS), where a given task of analysis can last for hours, usually provide the users with their own copies of the data, which they can then manipulate, update, or even destroy without consequence to others. In general, DSS users are not allowed to update the data base that they share; they must go back through the transaction processing system that created the DSS data in the first place.

New types of systems are emerging where the transaction processing component is present, yet the units of work last much longer. Updating a drawing of a manufactured part or adjusting an insurance claim, for instance, typically takes minutes to hours. This kind of processing has been termed *casework* to differentiate it from data base transaction processing. The logical unit of work is a case, by analogy to a case in the medical and legal professions. In this context, any operator who requests a record or set of records on which someone else is already working must be notified that the data is unavailable. The system must thus provide for each user to "check out" (as when borrowing a library book) a case for the time required to work on it, then "check it back in" (return the library book) when the work is done. This method is widely used in program development and maintenance when several analysts and programmers are working on the same project.

In summary, a logical unit of work is in general a business transaction that is accomplished or not as a unit. It can take several exchanges (or interactions) between the operator and the on-line program to accomplish. This collection of exchanges is often called a conversation. (The term *transaction* is better avoided, because it is ambiguous. Some system software products use it to mean an elementary exchange between the program and the operator The program sends a blank form, a prompt, or some other form of data, and the operator responds by filling in the form or pressing a function key. This meaning of the word *transaction* is not necessarily the same as in the phrase *business transaction*.)

- Operator-directed dialogs

    The operator directs the program to perform various tasks in the sequence which the operator has determined to be appropriate in the particular case. The sequence of entering commands and data is often arbitrary. The operator may be totally responsible for determining whether the logical unit of work is completed.

Historically, transaction processing systems have implemented a largely program-directed dialog. Office automation, decision support systems, and casework, on the other hand, tend to emphasize operator-directed dialogs. The choice between the two depends largely on how structured the operator's task is and how much decision power he or she has. The current trend is towards less specialized users with a wider range of options for performing their work and towards integration of computer systems in the tasks of knowledge workers. The trend is away from computers operated in the back office by data specialists.

As a result, transaction processing is also becoming more operator-directed, although it remains, in general, more structured than casework, office automation, and decision support.

Within program-directed dialogs, the following modes of interaction are the most frequently used:

- Menu choices

    The operator is given a small number of alternative actions and chooses one by pointing to it.

Figure 9–9 **Example of How Data Can Get Lost when Two Users Access the System Simultaneously**

	ATM 1		ATM 2
3:33	Smith requests a withdrawal of $90	3:33	
3:34	ATM 1 starts to deliver 9 ten-dollar bills	3:34	Jones requests a withdrawal of $90
3:35		3:35	ATM 2 starts to deliver 9 ten-dollar bills
3:36	ATM 1 completes delivery	3:36	
3:37	HQ updates balance	3:37	ATM 2 completes delivery
3:38		3:38	HQ updates balance

BOX 9–4

Ease of Use

User friendly, *easy to use*, and *easy to learn* are terms that appear in advertisements for nearly every software package. But little is said about how these qualities are actually achieved. To understand what constitutes ease of use (the term used here, because it encompasses ease of learning and user-friendliness), one must understand the characteristics of different kinds of users and different kinds of usage patterns.

First, it is a myth that a user-friendly computer program is one that imitates an outgoing, friendly human by responding to the user with such items as "Hi there! I am Hal, your friendly computer, and I will help you add numbers together! By the way, have you heard the one about . . . ." This style of interface entertains no one but the programmer who implemented it. Computers are not humans; they are still far from being able to duplicate even the most primitive of human thought processes; and even if they could, it is not at all certain that they should give the impression that they have human qualities.

In reality, to design an easy-to-use system, the designer needs to know something about the user—his or her prior knowledge of the application and of computers—and about the pattern of usage—daily, intermittent, or infrequent.

Perhaps the easiest interfaces to design are those that address themselves to "perpetual beginners," where the designer can assume that the user knows little about the application, little about computers, and will only use the system very infrequently. In this case, extensive guidance and explicit instructions must be offered all the way. This type of user is the exception, and very few systems designed by IS professionals in a business organization will be of this nature. In most systems, the users (such as middle-level managers, engineers, analysts, or other professionals) know the application area and use it intermittently or daily. Or the users may be people (such as clerks) with little knowledge of the application area who use the system all day (see Figure 9–10).

For instance, data entry clerks have little prior knowledge of the application domain. They will, however, use the system with great frequency. Therefore, the user interface for data entry need not be especially well guided. Training and experience will soon make up for beginners' difficulties. The main criterion for a user interface for data entry clerks must be performance—speed and accuracy. Interfaces for such users are fairly easy to design; it is mainly a technical or technological problem.

On the other hand, highly qualified professionals such as engineers, financial analysts, or foreign-exchange traders bring considerable prior knowledge of their own application domain, far more knowledge than the designer of the user interface. However, they may know little or nothing about computers. Very often, the systems used by such people must provide a lot of initial guidance. Once the hurdles of learning the system have been overcome, the users may become impatient with too much guidance (if they use the system frequently). They also become impatient when they perceive that the computer does not "understand." This impatience frequently results from sketchy or ambiguous instructions, which cause a gap between the user's mental model of how the system works and the reality. Users who leave the system for a few weeks or months and then start using it again may also need an intermediate level of help for a short while.

If the metaphor presented to these users is a good one, the users will find the initial learning fairly easy and relearning after a period of nonuse even easier. The user may not recall all the details of the interface, but with minimal prompting, he or she will recognize the correct course of action. (Think of the difference between recall (open-ended questions) and recognition (multiple-choice items) in a test.)

An important characteristic of the dialog between the user and the computer system is the degree of initiative left to the user. Data entry clerks or transaction processing operators usually have little to say about how the work is to be done. Generally, the interface is computer-directed: the on-line program directs the sequence of operations in an invariable (or at least deterministic) manner.

Decision support systems, professional support systems such as computer-aided design, and office automation systems are, in contrast, user-directed. At any point in time, the user may choose between many different courses of action. The types of interfaces for these two categories of systems are very different.

Figure 9–10 Users Classified According to Prior Knowledge and Frequency of Use

This figure shows what types of users can be expected to use systems frequently, intermittently, or rarely and what prior knowledge they may be expected to have of the application they are working with. An arrow from a category of user pointing towards the knowledge of computers column indicates that some individuals in the population are likely to acquire a good knowledge of computers and become so-called power users.

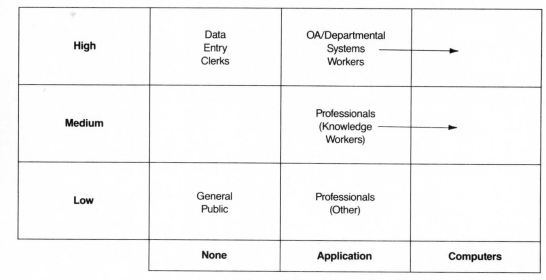

- Form filling

     The program displays the equivalent of a form, with captions and fields where the operator keys in the data indicated by the corresponding caption. The fields are filled in in fixed sequence, from left to right on each line and from top to bottom on the screen.

- Prompting

     The program displays a single question at a time and waits for the answer before displaying the next question.

In these types of dialog, operator help facilities are relatively easy to implement, because the program knows what the state of the processing is and because there are relatively few options at the operator's disposal. However, on-line help has often been absent from these systems in the past. A paper-based reference manual or operator training (with or without a manual) has usually taken the place of on-line guidance.

Operator-directed dialogs usually rely on one of the following methods:

- Command language

     Rather than ask a question, as in a prompted dialog, the computer indicates that it is ready, and the operator types in an activity description (usually in the form of a verb and one or more objects on which the verb is to act).

- Direct manipulation

     The prototype of this method is the Macintosh interface, where a number of objects are depicted on the screen; the operator selects the object to be manipulated and then indicates (by a menu choice or a command) the activity to be performed. (Another example of direct manipulation is the spreadsheet, where the operator points to a cell, then enters or modifies its content.)

Because the number of choices at any point is essentially the entire gamut of operator actions, providing focused help in a command-language based system is much more difficult. Even if complete help is provided, the user must usually remember either the exact form of each command or the topics along which the help facility is organized. Some systems do provide a menu-like table of contents for the help facility. This kind of help is tantamount to providing an on-line reference manual—not a bad solution, but not as helpful as more context-oriented help.

     One of the major motivations for the direct manipulation style of interfaces is to have the interface itself provide the help by using the underlying metaphor of the interface to display most of the possibilities for action on the screen. Then the user can just point to icons or other objects of interest, rather than have to remember command and object names.

     With the possible exception of direct manipulation, which has only recently become popular, all these techniques are well described in the literature, in particular by James Martin[2] and, more recently, by Ben Shneiderman.[3]

The choice between the different modes of dialog depends, as stated above, on the tasks that the user is expected to perform. It also depends on the technology that is to be used. For instance, a combination of menus and form filling is appropriate for simple transaction processing on traditional, so-called block-mode terminals (see Figure 9–11).

Prompting is most appropriate in two cases: either when the user is expected to be very naive (and the dialog short), as for an automatic teller machine (see Figure 9–12), or when the content of each question depends on the answer to a preceding question (see Figure 9–13).

A command language is appropriate in very few cases. Typical examples of such an interface are operating systems such as UNIX and MS-DOS (see Figure 9–14). The problem is that a command language does not help the user recall how to perform a task. Consequently, command languages have been universally decried as "unfriendly" and hard to learn. There are exceptions: some command interfaces are well-designed and reasonably easy to learn. Many word processing programs and programming editors use this technique, and those operators who use the interface frequently like it.

A simplified form of command language is appropriate for data entry when the sequence of data is unpredictable, for example, in airline reservation systems. The operator enters data in the sequence in which the customer specifies his or her request. Each piece of data is entered either with a prefix indicating what it means, such as *d* for departure time or *a* for arrival time, or in some unambiguous format, such as the standard three-letter abbreviation for the airport (see Figure 9–15).

Direct manipulation interfaces, created in reaction to the poor image of command language interfaces, tend to use technology that may not be available on older equipment—graphics, pointing devices (mouse, light-pen, tracking ball, graphic tablets), color, and local intelligence (see Figure 9–16). In fact, the very logic of these interfaces usually requires that every user action—moving the cursor, clicking the mouse, entering a single keystroke—result in a change to the display. On fixed-function terminals that are driven by central, shared computers, this requirement is not economically feasible.

Choosing the Technology, Dialog, and Help Styles

As mentioned previously, the type of terminal available to the user has an influence on dialog and help styles. The technology of terminals and workstations interacts with dialog styles and their associated help modes.

Types of Workstations. Three main types of workstations are available: unbuffered (character-mode) terminals, buffered (block-mode) terminals, and intelligent workstations.

unbuffered terminals

Unbuffered terminals send each character entered via the keyboard directly to the processor to which it is attached. The processor sends the character back, in so-called echoplex mode, to be displayed on the screen. Thus,

Figure 9–11a **Menu and Form Filling Conversation Example**

This is the main menu of a hospital patient care system. The operator has just chosen line 1 and entered it by the ? Line No prompt towards the bottom of the screen.

```
PICS  0010   CP2            CONVERSATIONS                 10/06/92    14:02
                                                          CCN 80432192




      01 ? Order Entry                        09 ? Review Messages
      02 ? Chart Review                       10 ? Signon
      03 ? Nursing Update
      04 ? Nursing Station Reporting
      05 ? Nursing Assignments
      06 ? PT Location
      07 ? PT Bed Swap
      08 ? PT Discharge




  _1   ? Line No

?SIGNOFF    ?CANCEL    PAGE:   ?P    ?B    ?01    ?COPY    ?HELP    ?DONE    ?ENTER
```

Figure 9–11b

The system has responded by displaying the names of all the patients for which the operator has responsibility. The operator has just picked patient No. 2, Reginald Heathcraft.

```
PICS  0060   CP2            ORDER ENTRY                   10/06/92    14:02
                                                          CCN 32587112



  No.    Room/Bed Name                   Sex Age SVC  C  Unit # I Physician

      01 ? CP203  1 Schwartzbinder, Malcolm  M 52  MED  S  123487 2 Knoll
      02 ? CP203  2 Heathcraft, Reginald      M 43  MED  S  218765 1 Grossman
      03 ? CP204  1 Smith, Joe                M 23  SUR  P  321862 2 Sampson
      04 ? CP205  1 Jones, John               M 28  MED  P  437906 1 Grossman
      05 ? CP206  1 Johnson, Cynthia          F 81  SUR  S  567215 2 Grant
      06 ? CP206  2 Wislon, Monica            F 77  SUR  S  286791 2 Sampson




  _2   ? Line No

?SIGNOFF    ?CANCEL    PAGE:   ?P    ?B    ?01    ?COPY    ?HELP    ?DONE    ?ENTER
```

Figure 9–11c

This panel enables the operator to enter the name of the health care professional who has authorized the order, again by choosing from several alternatives.

```
PICS 0444  CP2            ORDER ENTRY              10/06/92    14:02
                                                  CCN 38976332


218765 Heathcraft, Reginald D.              Attending:  Grossman, Alvin, M.D.
CP203-2 M 43Y Serious                       ***  PROVIDER IDENTIFICATION  ***

   01 ? Grossman, Alvin, M.D.
   02 ? Sampson, Stanley, M.D.
   03 ? Social Services
   04 ? Guerega, Barbara, R.N.




  _2   ? Line No

?SIGNOFF    ?CANCEL    PAGE:  ?P    ?B    ?01    ?COPY    ?HELP    ?DONE    ?ENTER
```

Figure 9–11d

The operator has selected line 2, Chemistry.

```
PICS 0420  CP2            ORDER ENTRY              10/06/92    14:03
                                                  CCN 44498762


218765 Heathcraft, Reginald D.

   01 ? Blood Service      08 ? Equipment          15 ? Pharmacy
   02 ? Chemistry          09 ? Gastroenterology    16 ? Physical Ther
   03 ? Coagulation        10 ? Hematology          17 ? Radioligand
   04 ? Coronary Care      11 ? Hemodialysis        18 ? Respiratory T
   05 ? Diagnostic Prog.   12 ? IV                  19 ? Serology
   06 ? Dietary            13 ? Microbiology        20 ? Urinalysis
   07 ? EKG, EEG           14 ? Nursing Care        21 ? X-Ray
                                                   22 ? Other




  _2   ? Line No

?SIGNOFF    ?CANCEL    PAGE:  ?P    ?B    ?01    ?COPY    ?HELP    ?DONE    ?ENTER
```

Figure 9–11e

The menu selection is Line 6—Potassium. The operator has also marked the ?Comments prompt with X, indicating that there is additional data to be entered.

```
PICS 04308 CP2              ORDER ENTRY               10/06/92    14:03
                                                     CCN 34587609


218765 Heathcraft, Reginald D.                   ***   CHEMISTRY   ***

   01 ? 2 Hr PP Glucose      08 ? Magnesium          15 ? COT
   02 ? Glucose              09 ? Uric Acid          16 ? Alk. P'tase
   03 ? Bun                  10 ? T. Protein         17 ? Cholesterol
   04 ? CO2                  11 ? Albumin/Globulin   18 ? CPK
   05 ? Chloride             12 ? Calcium            19 ? CPT
   06 ? Potassium            13 ? TID Bilirubin      20 ? CCTP
   07 ? Sodium               14 ? LDN                21 ? Acid P'tase



   _6  ? Line No

   X ?Comments   _ ?Stat   _ ?Today  _ ?Pre-Op  _ ?Label  _ ?Schedule

?SIGNOFF    ?CANCEL    PAGE:  ?P   ?B   ?01   ?COPY   ?HELP   ?DONE   ?ENTER
```

Figure 9–11f

The operator has completed the data entry of the comments and other indications such as the Frequency, Duration, Schedule, and Specimen requirements.

```
PICS 0421  CP2              ORDER ENTRY               10/06/92    14:03
                                                     CCN 04659633
218765     Heathcraft, Reginald D.             ***  PROCEDURE COMMENT  ***
           Procedure Potassium
           Comments: should precede x-ray at 11 am_____
           _____
           _____

OD_____  2 day___ 7:30_____                          3 Plasma_
Frequency Duration        Schedule     Start Date Stop Date Other  Specimen
?OD   ?Q1H ?1      ?M ?Mon   ?7    ?:15                       ?AC   ?Urine
?RID  ?Q2H ?2      ?H ?Tues  ?8    ?:30                       ?PC   ?SterUr
?TID  ?Q3H ?3      ?D ?Wed   ?9    ?:45                             ?24HrUrin
?QID  ?Q4H ?4         ?Thurs ?10                                    ?WndSwab
?QOD  ?Q6H ?5      ?15 ?Fri  ?11                                    ?Feces
?PRN  ?Q9H ?6      ?30 ?Sat  ?12                                    ?SpnlFl
?QOS      ?7          ?Sun   ?1
?Q12H     ?8                 ?2
?Q15H     ?9                 ?3
?Q30M     ?10                ?4   Back Procedure _____
?AD LIB                      ?5   Department _____

?SIGNOFF    ?CANCEL    PAGE:  ?P   ?B   ?01   ?COPY   ?HELP   ?DONE   ?ENTER
```

Figure 9–12a   **Example of a Prompted Conversation for Naive Users**

The customer inserts the card in the slot.

```
        WELCOME TO CASH NETWORK            7    8    9

          PLEASE INSERT YOUR               4    5    6

          CARD, STRIPE DOWN                1    2    3

                                          OK    0    .

                                          CANCEL

                        ========>
```

Figure 9–12b

The customer enters four numeric digits known only to himself or herself, and then presses the "OK" key. After three unsuccessful attempts, the transaction is canceled, and the card remains in the ATM. The customer must retrieve it from the bank the next day.

```
   ENTER YOUR PERSONAL                     7    8    9

   IDENTIFICATION NUMBER                   4    5    6

                                           1    2    3

        IF CORRECT, PRESS    ========>    OK    0    .

        IF ERROR, PRESS      ========>    CANCEL
```

Figure 9–12c

If the customer presses any of the 4, 5, or 6 keys, cash withdrawal is selected.

```
   SELECT TRANSACTION TYPE:                7    8    9

        CASH WITHDRAWAL     ========>      4    5    6

        DEPOSIT             ========>      1    2    3

        TRANSFER            ========>     OK    0    .

        BALANCE INQUIRY     ========>     CANCEL
```

Figure 9–12d

The customer enters the amount, in whole dollars with the decimal point or in cents without the decimal point. If the amount is incorrectly entered or if the customer pressed "Cash Withdrawal" in error, the "Cancel" key takes the conversation back to the Application Selection screen.

```
 -----------------------------------------          7    8    9
|                                           |
|   ENTER AMOUNT IN MULTIPLES OF $20        |        4    5    6
|                                           |
|   ****   $000.00   ****                   |        1    2    3
|                                           |
|                                           |        OK   0    .
|   WHEN CORRECT, PRESS ========>           |
|                                           |        CANCEL
|   TO START OVER, PRESS =======>           |
|                                           |        ===========
 -----------------------------------------
```

Figure 9–12e

The customer now can retrieve the cash. (In the meanwhile, a screen may have appeared, saying: "Please be patient. The transaction is being processed."

```
 -----------------------------------------          7    8    9
|                                           |
|   PLEASE OPEN DOOR AND TAKE CASH          |        4    5    6
|                                           |
|   ****   $160.00   ****                   |        1    2    3
|                                           |
|                                           |        OK   0    .
|   ANOTHER TRANSACTION? =======>           |
|                                           |        CANCEL
|   DONE?                 ========>         |
|                                           |        ===========
 -----------------------------------------
```

Figure 9–12f

The transaction is now ended. Should the customer wish to process another transaction, such as a deposit or a balance inquiry, the card must be inserted again.

```
 -----------------------------------------          7    8    9
|                                           |
|   PLEASE TAKE RECEIPT AND                 |        4    5    6
|                                           |
|   REMOVE YOUR CARD                        |        1    2    3
|                                           |
|                                           |        OK   0    .
|   THANK YOU FOR USING CASH NETWORK        |
|                                           |        CANCEL
|                                           |
|                                           |        ===========
 -----------------------------------------
```

Figure 9–13 **Example of Prompted Conversation where Questions Depend on Previous Answers**

This conversation is taken from a program that helps IBM customers obtain price information and configure equipment and software. It was originally created for internal use by professionals, with the assumption that the users would not necessarily know the system itself, but would know a great deal about the subject matter. However, since

```
*** Type of Configuration ***

                  This Aid may be used by Customer personnel according
                  to the terms and conditions of the Customer agreement.
6802)             What type of hardware configuration do you want?
CONFIG.TYPE  2          1=MES (Miscellaneous Equipment Specification)
                          Use MES to make changes to existing installed
                          or on-order hardware.
                       2=Create a hardware configuration
_____

*** System Overview Questions ***
22)*
PROCESSOR    4381      Select one processor from-
                       43XX      308X      3090
                       --------------      ---------------
                       4321      3081      3090
                       4331      3083
                       4341      3084
                       4361
                       4381
   Press the HELP PF key for information about configuring the 937X
   processor.
_____

*** System Overview Questions ***
8)                Full System Configuration-
CONFIGURECPU y         Will the CPU be configured ? (Y/N)
                       A 'Y' response will configure the CPU with
                       selected devices.
                       An 'N' response will allow the configuration
                       of selected devices.

_____

*** System Overview Questions ***
11)*              Select ALL types of peripherals wanted-
PERIPHERALS  0_____

0=None          4=Card I/O       8=Other Devices
1=DASD          5=Mass Storage    (Press HELP PF key for
2=Tape(s)       6=OCR               additional information.)
3=Printer(s)    7=MICR

NOTE: Subsequent questions will be based on selections entered here.
_____

*** Processor, Channel, and Console Questions ***
24)*              Select Console:
CONSOLE      1         0=None
                       1=3205 Color model 100
                       2=3278 model 2A
_____

*** Processor, Channel, and Console Questions ***
40)               For 3205-100 Color Console :
QUANTITY     2         Quantity of 3205-100 Color Consoles ? (1-4)
_____

*** Processor, Channel, and Console Questions ***

28)*              Select 4381 processor
MODEL        R92       Enter model desired-
                       L01 L02 L11
                       M01 M02 M03 M11 M12 M13 M21
                       P01 P02 P03 P11 P12 P13 P14 P21 P22 P23 P24 P91 P92
                       Q02 Q03 Q12 Q13 Q14
                       R02 R03 R12 R13 R14 R22 R23 R24 R91 R92
                       S23 S24 S91 S92
```

the information required to configure one model, such as the 4381, is radically different from that required for another model, such as the 3090, or the PC, or peripheral equipment, the approach needed to be very interactive. This is the reason for the prompt style of dialog.

```
Select PF1 for information on available memory sizes.
The model ranges for 91E and 92E are respectively
P91, R91, S91, T91, and P92, R92, S92, T92.
```

```
*** Processor, Channel, and Console Questions ***
3244)          Model group channels :
CHANNEL     1              0=Standard number of channels
                             Twelve channels are standard for Model Group 92E.
                           1=Additional Block Multiplexor
                             This provides the model groups with an
                             additional 6 channels.
```

```
*** Processor, Channel, and Console Questions ***
3348)          Model Group 24 and 92E channels-
CHANNEL     n              Additional Block Multiplexer ? (Y/N)
                           This provides the Model Group with another
                           additional six channels for a total of
                           twenty-four.
```

```
*** Processor, Channel, and Console Questions ***
3255)          Accessories-
CONSOLE.TBLE y             Console table ? (Y/N)
BOOK.RACK    y             Book rack and cable holder ? (Y/N)
```

Accessories are available on a purchase only basis.

```
*** Processor, Channel, and Console Questions ***
3335)*         Remote Support
SUPPORT     1              Remote support (RSF/ROCF)-
                           0=None
                           1=Integrated modem (no integrated coupler)
                           2=External modem interface
                           3=Integrated-modem, Protective-coupler
```

```
0) If NONE is selected, a feature code indicating "NO RSF" will be
   generated.
1) Integrated modem, 1200 bps, switched network, manual answer.
2) EIA interface, 1200 bps, switched network, manual answer.
3) Integrated-modem with integrated protective-coupler, 1200 BPS,
   Switched network, AUTO answer.
```

Your responses generated the following configuration:

FEB 26, 1988   IBM 4300 PROCESSOR MODEL 4381

| | | | MONTHLY | |
UNIT MDL/FC	DESCRIPTION	QTY	RENTAL	PURCHASE
4381-R92	DUAL PROCESSOR MG92E	1	129450.00	1000000.00
1480	BOOKRACK AND CABLE HOLDER +	1	N/O	25.00P
1550	CONSOLE TABLE	1	N/O	495.00P
1871	BLOCK MULTIPLEXER CHAN ADDL	1	3005.00	35580.00
3205-100	COLOR DISPLAY CONSOLE	2	N/O	5790.00P

Figure 9–14 **Sample Dialog Showing Use of a Command Language**

The dialog shown represents the initial steps in installing Lotus 1-2-3® on a personal computer under MS-DOS. The user's responses to the prompts are in bold type. Note the cryptic nature of the commands and the unhelpful error message when the command "copy" was misspelled. Also note that the last line contains the prompt "C>." It is the user's "turn," but there is nothing to indicate which courses of action are possible. (The correct course of action is spelled out in the Lotus 1-2-3 Installation Manual.)

```
Current date is  Sat 2-27-1988
Enter new date (mm-dd-yy):
Current time is 10:28:21.94
Enter new time:

C>md \123

C>cd \123

C>cpoy a:*.*
Bad command or file name

C>copy a:*.*
A:123.CMP
A:LOTUS.COM
A:123.COM
A:123.CNF
A:123.HLP
A:123.SET
        6 File(s) copied

C>
```

interfaces can be designed that are rich in function because they can respond to each elementary action performed at the keyboard. However, the price to be paid in number of instructions executed by the central computer to which the terminal is attached may be prohibitive.

buffered terminals

Buffered terminals have a storage element, called buffer, that contains as many characters as can be displayed on a screen. When the user presses a key on the keyboard, the character is sent to the buffer and is displayed on the screen at the location of the cursor (usually a blinking rectangle, the size of one character). To send the data to the processor, the operator has to press a particular key, usually labeled *Enter* or *Transmit*. The program in the central processor can then process all the data that was in the buffer. The data on the screen will stay there until the program sends its response, which will overwrite the buffer and change the contents of the screen.

intelligent workstations

Intelligent workstations such as PCs have not only a buffer but also a programmable processor in the workstation itself. Therefore, each character can be processed as it is keyed in (like unbuffered terminals). The workstation then sends a message, possibly already partly processed, to the central computer, where the rest of the processing (such as data base update) will take place.

Figure 9–15 **Sample Free-Form Dialog**

This is an example of a dialog on an airline reservation system. The operator enters cryptic input on an unformatted screen. The second screen shows the system response, which is in fixed form output but without captions or explanations. The third screen shows the operator's final action, actually reserving two seats in coach class on the 8:04 flight.

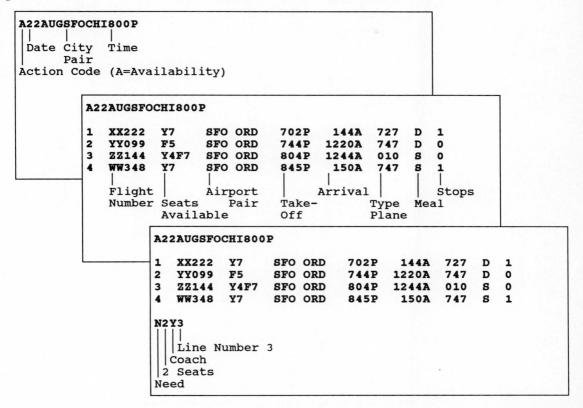

One advantage of an intelligent workstation is that the user interface can be enriched (by processing character by character, by adding graphics, by providing much more user help) without overloading the central processor. Another advantage is that when the workstation is not being used to access a central application, it can be used for personal computing purposes—word processing, spreadsheets, maintaining personal data bases—or for gaining access to external data bases.

Styles of Dialog and On-Line Help. Different styles of dialog are suited to different types of terminals. The main difference in style is that the buffered terminal encourages so-called full-screen processing, while the unbuffered

Figure 9–16 **Example of a Direct Manipulation Interface:
The Apple® Macintosh™ Finder Desktop**

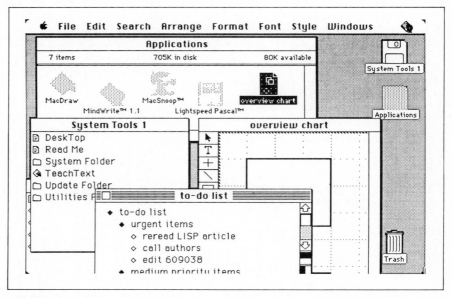

terminal is best for processing a line at a time. This makes the unbuffered terminal suitable for prompted (question-and-answer) and command-oriented dialogs. The buffered terminal is best suited to menu choices and form filling.

Fixed-function terminals, which include both buffered and unbuffered terminals, do not support on-line help very well. The text that is to help the user must be transmitted by the central computer to the terminal every time it is requested. This process is costly if the terminals are in a remote location, because it increases the load on the central computer and also on the communications network.

Intelligent workstations, on the other hand, can support on-line help of several kinds. In the most primitive kind, the user can invoke a **fixed help text** by pressing a function key. This text can fill more than one screen: all the help program needs to do is to provide *Next* and *Previous* function keys for the user to navigate within the help text. It can also provide a more elaborate menu system of its own, allowing the user to choose on a menu the subject where help is needed. When the help screen is no longer needed, the user can press an *Escape* key, returning to the place in the application where he or she left off.

A more elaborate form of on-line help is **context-sensitive help**. The program running in the intelligent workstation is capable of knowing where the user is and what he or she is trying to achieve at all times by sensing which field

fixed help text

context-sensitive help

BOX 9–5

User Dialog and Natural Language

All the dialog techniques described in this chapter require that their users undergo training or, at least, be given very specific directions. It has long been a goal of artificial intelligence research to reduce or eliminate this requirement by allowing users to communicate with computer systems in everyday English (or any other natural language, for that matter). The theory behind this research is that even top executives would use computers directly if they could communicate in their own language. The use of English would also reduce or obviate the need for programmers.

A number of reasonably successful products on the market use natural language technology. The two best known are Intellect from Artificial Intelligence Corporation and Clout from Microrim. Both are essentially capable of understanding loosely formulated queries against a data base, which must have been described to them previously. Intellect runs on large mainframes; Clout on personal computers.

A typical query to such a system might read:

"Print the names of all salespeople in New York who have sold more than $100,000 of widgets."

If appropriately instructed, the program might respond with:

"Do you mean New York City or New York State?"

A subsequent query might imply that the interest is still in salespeople in New York by asking:

"More than $50,000?"

Subsequent queries might be:

"How about Massachusetts?"
"How about gismos?"
"Print their addresses as well."

So far, only data base queries can be processed in this way. Other functions, such as decision support, office automation, or transaction processing, have not been addressed by natural language interfaces. The reason for concentrating on data base queries is that it is fairly easy to anticipate the sorts of questions that can be asked. Even so, these systems often fail to respond when users use unfamiliar terms, or they respond unexpectedly because the query was formulated imprecisely or erroneously. (For instance, if the query has to do with personnel who are outside the category "married, with children," the query should not be "not married *and* no children" but "not married *or* no children.")

Establishing a dictionary of terms for one of these systems can be a lengthy process. Extensive experimentation is usually required to ensure that the most common errors get caught. User training (to sign on to the system, to use the hardware, and to formulate queries correctly) is still required. Even so, the lexicon of the system is likely to be insufficient. It will lack the commonsense knowledge that is taken for granted in humans. An old chestnut is the story of the computer that was set to interpret results of physical examinations and rejected a draftee on the grounds that he was pregnant.

As for interfaces to other types of applications, it is probable that they will not be available for many years, if ever. The main problem seems to be that natural language is specifically adapted to communicating with humans, on human terms, about human problems. Human language is much more oriented towards negotiating an agreement between two individuals, one of whom, as a result of the exchange, commits to some course of action. (The negotiation may be pretty one-sided, as when a superior gives a direct order to a subordinate, but the subordinate will still make an explicit commitment, such as "Yes, sir!") Further conversations can then take place to follow up on the commitment, if the result is not delivered or is late.

The nature of a dialog with a computer is totally different. The computer is already committed to perform a certain range of services and needs no negotiation, explicit or implicit, to actually do so. It may be that the request is not within the possibility of the program; no matter how hard the user tries to persuade the computer to do what he or she wants, the result will still be an error message. The further away from the prearranged possibilities of the computer the request is, the more cryptic the message.

According to this view, it is futile to attempt to use natural language to address the computer, not because the computer cannot "understand" it, but because natural language is not a good vehicle for communicating what the user wishes the computer to do. If a human being were asked to deliver the same type of information, natural language would be used to make sure that the person understood and accepted the task. A very restricted and formalized subset of natural language would be used to specify the information content of the request. (A branch of logic called *first-order predicate logic* deals with this type of language.)

Even if all the knowledge of the world could be infused into a computer, natural language is not a good vehicle for communicating that knowledge.

the cursor is in, what has already been filled in, and the like. It is therefore possible to display a more specific help screen, directed at what the user's problem is likely to be. For instance, if help is invoked while the cursor is in a field where a dollar amount is expected, the help facility could display: "Type in the dollar amount without leading zeroes. The decimal point is not required for whole dollar amounts."

Context-sensitive help can be augmented by artificial intelligence techniques that use a knowledge base to infer what the user is attempting to do, explain to the user what the consequences of previous actions were, and deduce the explanation most likely to satisfy the user on what to do next.

data-dependent help

The most sophisticated form of help is **data-dependent help**. This kind of help enables the user to position the cursor in a field, press the *Help* key, and obtain a display of the possible data values in the field, for example, a list of legal two-letter airline codes (AA for American Airlines, UA for United, and so on). It is even better to provide a list of data values that are possible as a function of previously entered data. For instance, given a departure and an arrival airport, the help facility could display a list of those airlines and flight numbers that serve those airports. Or given the partial spelling of a customer name, the help facility could display the list of all those customers who match the partial spelling.

When this technique is adopted, the user should be able to point to the value that is to be entered and, with a function key, "escape" from the help facility back to the original screen, where the field for which help was invoked would be filled in with the selected value. With this technique, sometimes called the *sticky cursor,* the value on the help screen appears to stick to the cursor as one screen disappears and another one appears.

Even if data-dependent help cannot be implemented for every field, many transaction processing systems on buffered terminals can suspend a transaction, perform a query, and return to the original transaction. This technique, known as *suspend-and-resume*, should ideally be used with the sticky-cursor technique.

On intelligent terminals, a system could conceivably be built where it would not even be necessary to invoke the help screen. As soon as the number of possible choices is reduced to a certain number, the choices could all be displayed in a window to one side. If there is only one possible value, the operator could stop keying and let the program fill in the rest.

Again, for data-dependent help, artificial intelligence techniques can be useful.

Simple and context-sensitive help facilities are relatively straightforward to implement on intelligent workstations. Data-sensitive help is more difficult, both because the design is more difficult and because the data needed must be available instantaneously. The data must be stored either in the workstation or on a data server on a local area network to which the workstation is attached.

Coexistence of Multiple Terminal Types. It is not always possible to dictate that a given application will use a given type of terminal. Intelligent workstations, which are the most flexible, are also the most costly and, thus, may not be economically justified. The users may already be equipped with terminals, and it may not be possible, or desirable, to force the users to have multiple terminals of different types on their desks.

Some systems may therefore need to specify different classes of terminals for different users. Users may be at different locations or belong to different departments, and each location or department may have different types of terminals already installed. Sometimes, because the users are customers, the company cannot dictate which terminals they should equip themselves with.

This problem can be solved in two different ways: the application can be written for a fixed-function terminal, and the intelligent terminal only emulates, or imitates, a fixed-function terminal; or two different interfaces, one for fixed-function and the other for intelligent terminals, may be created. The first solution reduces the functionality available to intelligent workstation users. The second adds to the cost of the application.

ELEMENTS OF GOOD DIALOG DESIGN

The elements of good dialog design are clarity, consistency, performance, and respect for the user. The following practical guidelines were developed from experience with on-line business systems over the past two decades.

Clarity

The user should be given complete guidance on what the next permitted actions are by displaying menu bars (if the choices are not numerous) or pop-up/pull-down menus (if a menu bar is not sufficient or if space on the screen is scarce) or by invoking context- or data-dependent help. Menu bars and pop-up/pull-down menus are shown in Figure 9–16.

The current state of the user process should always be displayed on the screen (this is known as WYSIWYG—What You See Is What You Get). If a user action has resulted in a data value being changed on the data base, the new value should immediately be displayed.

The effect of learning should be taken into account. Novice users appreciate a great deal of guidance, but after a certain time, would like to be able to shortcut some frequently used sequences of operations. For example, a cascade of menus can be intermixed with a command language that enables the user to go directly to some activity whose name is known. Or a dialog can be designed with shorthand keystrokes, where some function keys are reserved for the user to define as standing for a longer sequence.

Consistency

Let the same commands or function keys should have the same effect even under dissimilar circumstances. So-called modes, where a sequence of keystrokes can be interpreted either as a piece of data or as a series of one-letter commands depending on the context, should be avoided. This problem is easy to avoid with today's workstations with many function keys and pointing devices. Committing the transaction (end of conversation) should be an identifiable step, different from simply changing screens within the conversation.

The cursor movement should be uniform. If all the fields on the screen are a fixed length and must be filled in entirely, the cursor can skip automatically to the next field when a field is completely filled in. When the length of the information in a field is variable, as with a name, an address, or an amount, automatic cursor skip is not possible. The operator must indicate that the end of the data in the field has been reached and that he or she is ready for the next field. For example, the operator presses a function key, the *Tab* key, or the *Enter* key, depending on conventions. Mixing the two modes—auto-skip and tabbing—on the same screen should be avoided, where possible. (There is not always a choice, particularly with buffered terminals.)

Performance

The response time, defined as the time elapsed between the operator taking an action and the terminal showing that the action has been recorded, is critical in two main categories of actions. The first is the need for the terminal to display instantaneously every data character that the operator types in. This need can be a problem for unbuffered terminals. On these terminals, there is no direct connection between the keyboard and the screen. A character typed on the keyboard travels over the communication line to the computer to which the terminal is attached. The computer then echoes it back to the screen. If the computer is heavily loaded, there may be a perceptible interval between keying and displaying on the screen. The effect is to slow down the operator. It also tends to cause irritability and impatience. On buffered (block-mode) and intelligent terminals this problem does not arise.

The more classical notion of response time is the time between the user signaling the program to begin a processing activity and the appearance on the screen of the first character of the program's response. (In some cases, it is the last character of the program's response that counts, rather than the first one, for example if the transmission is lengthy—more than 10 or so characters—and slow—under 30 characters per second. Then, the user can read the response faster than it appears on the screen and therefore has the impression of waiting for the system. If the response is short or it is displayed at a high rate, the user does not feel slowed down by the system.)

On a block-mode (buffered) terminal, the operator usually fills in the entire screen before pressing the *Enter* or *Transmit* key. This method, typical of form-filling applications, can require a large amount of data to be processed before the program can display the result, thus causing a potential response time problem. This problem has two solutions. The first is to cut up the activity into smaller subactivities, getting partial results back. If it were to take 10 seconds to process a 10-line order in one single operation and 1.5 seconds to process each line, the operator would probably be more productive with the second solution, even though 5 seconds appear to have been wasted. Another solution is to display some indication that the screen has been received and to continue displaying signs of progress every few seconds. This solution helps the operator by showing that the reason for the delay is not a malfunction.

Response time requirements are relative. It is important that the response time be about the same for similar activities. It is also important that response times for what the user perceives as easy tasks be shorter than for difficult tasks. For instance, a user would expect that the response to a query to display the inventory status of a given item, identified by a code, would be substantially less than the creation of a table of amortizations for a 30-year mortgage loan.

It is also important that response times remain relatively constant over time. In one case, where the implementation of the system was gradual, a few users being added at a time, the response times in the build-up phase would have been on the order of one-half second, whereas the fully loaded system was expected to have response times of nearly two seconds. It was necessary to introduce a routine to slow down the system during the initial phases to avoid high expectations followed by disappointments.

Respect for the User

Respect for the user requires adopting a neutral tone in messages and directions. Computer anthropomorphism—the attribution of human qualities to a computer or a program—should be avoided at all costs. Messages, in particular error messages, should avoid loaded terms, such as "You committed an error." Experience has shown that novice users can panic when they see a message such as "Fatal error—transaction aborted." Although it is difficult, an error message should incorporate information that is useful to the user, showing the cause of the error rather than the effect, and describing how to overcome the problem. For instance, "Order buffer overflow" is a poor error message. It should be replaced with something such as: "You can only enter 15 detail lines per order. If you have an order with more than 15 lines, please split it in two."

DOCUMENTING THE CONVERSATION FLOW

The best way to document a conversation flow is to prototype it. Prototyping entails designing each of the screens that can be used in the conversation and then adding indications on how to make the conversation progress from screen to screen. In most cases, a set of test data must also be specified so that the user can actually work the prototype with data that approximates real situations. This technique is described at the end of Section IV.

The main objective of such a prototype is to serve as a vehicle for showing users what a system will do. For subsequent phases of the analysis, additional documentation, in paper or electronic form, is required, in particular in the program design activity (see Chapter 14).

Most cases of transaction processing are based on a mix of menu selection and forms processing. From a menu, a user selects a form or set of forms; after processing the forms, the user returns to the menu to select the next form. In such a case, the conversation flow can be depicted as it would flow in normal sequence, if no errors are discovered and no on-line help is needed (see Figure 9–17). Exceptions to the linear flow can be noted on the side. Experience has proved that users understand a linear flow with exceptions much better than a flow chart with decision boxes and loops.

Another tool that can prove useful is the state transition network, which is used when it becomes difficult to keep track of the actions that are possible depending on where the user is in the dialog. The more operator-directed a dialog is, the better chance there is of the state transition diagram being appropriate. Figure 9–18 shows a state transition diagram for a bank teller clerk who has several ways of identifying the account number or numbers of the customer who is being served. This diagram looks somewhat like a data flow diagram, but the flow is between states, not activities, and the lines of flow do not represent data, but control information. More details on how to prepare transition networks appear in Appendix 3.

A cascade of menus, where a choice in a top-level menu causes a lower-level menu to be displayed, is best represented by a hierarchy such as the one depicted in Figure 9–19.

Summary

In the design of the overall flow of a user interface, event-driven processing is generally best implemented on-line. Typical examples are transaction process-

Figure 9–17 **Sample Conversation Flow Document**

The left part of the document shows the normal flow of a conversation to enter time cards for employees for payroll processing. The column ALTERNATE SCREEN shows what other screens than the one immediately below the operator can choose, and the FUNCTION KEY column shows the name of the function key to be pressed. (The assignment of these names to actual function keys such as PF1 through PF12 will take place later.) For each screen, the first function key listed (the one that does not have an alternate screen assigned to it) is the one that will cause normal flow (i.e., the next screen in sequence).

```
PERS                                                                CFLOW
PAYROL                                                              CNV311
                   CONVERSATION FLOW - Time Card Data Entry
_____
PREPARED BY: Jatdu Ilah      DATE: 08FebXX      VERSION:            PAGE 1
APPROVED BY:                 DATE:              STATUS :
_____


                      (PER CONV.)
  DEFAULT FLOW         OCCURS        SCREEN NAME      ALTERNATE SCREEN    FUNCTION KEY
  ------------         ------        -----------      ----------------    ------------

   SCR2101                          ┌─────────────┐                       Time Card
                                    │    Main     │
                                    │    Menu     │
                                    └──────┬──────┘
                                                                          Enter
   SCR2141               1          ┌──────┴──────┐   Employee Header     Start Over
                                    │  Employee   │   Employee Trailer    Done
                                    │   Header    │   Overtime Approval   OT Appr
                                    └──────┬──────┘
                                                                          Enter
   SCR2142               1          ┌──────┴──────┐   Employee Trailer    Done
                                    │ First Line  │
                                    └──────┬──────┘

                                                                          Done
   SCR2142              0-50        ┌──────┴──────┐   Next Line           Enter
                                    │  Next Line  │
                                    └──────┬──────┘

                                                                          Enter
   SCR2143               1          ┌──────┴──────┐   Employee Header     Start Over
                                    │  Employee   │   First Line          Correct
                                    │  Trailer    │   Employee Header      Enter
                                    └──────┬──────┘   Menu                 Menu

                                                                          Menu
   SCR2144              0-1         ┌──────┴──────┐   Employee Header     Start Over
                                    │  Overtime   │   First Line          Correct
                                    │  Approval   │   Employee Header      Enter
                                    └─────────────┘
_____
```

Figure 9–18 **Sample State Transition Diagram**

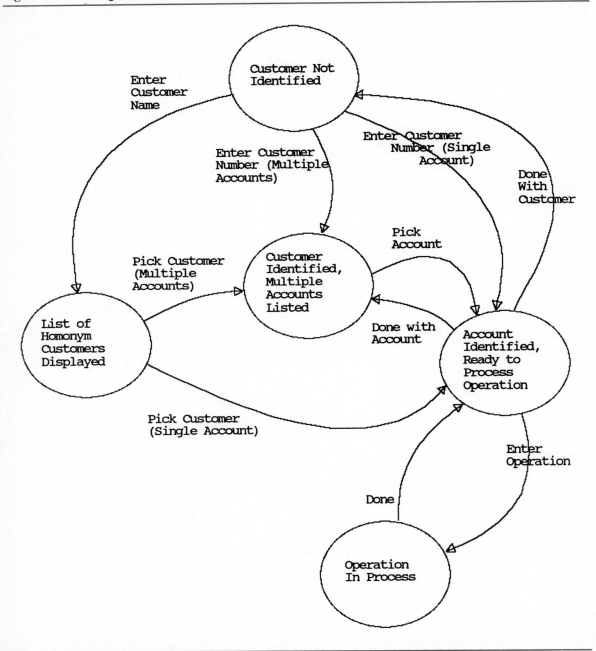

Figure 9–19 **Sample Hierarchical Chart
Representing a Menu Structure**

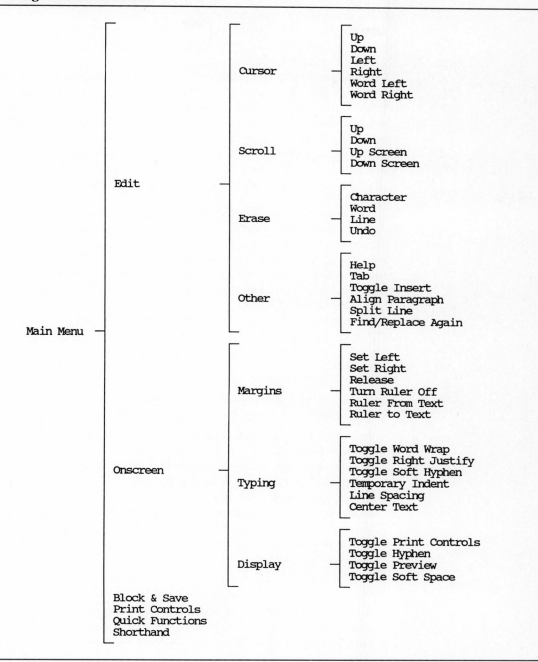

ing and ad hoc data base query. The main advantages of on-line processing are that it reduces error rates and may add value to the processing of transactions by making more information available to customers, suppliers, and employees.

Batch processing, on the other hand, is the best alternative for periodic processing such as management reporting and the preparation of activity files for decision support systems.

Forms and report flows should be as short and simple as possible to reduce the risk of manipulation errors. Because on-line work is more and more prevalent, the main emphasis of the chapter is on the design of conversations.

Conversation design consists in identifying logical units of work—business transactions or more extensive cases. Business transaction dialogs are usually program-driven. The conversations rely on menu selection and form filling. If the operator is not dedicated, on-line help is usually a major requirement. Buffered terminals or intelligent workstations are appropriate for this type of processing.

Casework, office automation, decision support, and other systems oriented towards professionals rather than clerks are usually operator-driven. Prompting, command languages, or more modern interfaces such as direct manipulation are usually appropriate. Context-sensitive help (and data-dependent help where possible) is usually required. Intelligent terminals are best for this type of work, with unbuffered terminals a possibility if the data traffic allows it without degrading response times.

Criteria for good on-line dialog design are clarity, consistency, performance, and respect for the user.

Selected Readings

IBM Corporation. *Systems Application Architecture: Common User Access Panel Design and User Interaction*, 1st ed. IBM Publication No. SC26–4351, 1987.

This document contains a detailed description of the standard that IBM recommends for screen and interaction design for developers of programs that are to run on IBM systems—whether mainframes, minis, or micros. The most striking characteristic of this book is that it illustrates how rich the intelligent terminal (or PC) environment is and how many choices are made explicitly or implicitly when designing even a very simple user interface. The problem with this manual is that it does not provide a high-level overview. This lack is partly made up for by the inclusion of demonstration diskettes.

Apple Computers, Inc. *Human Interface Guidelines: The Apple Desktop Interface*. Reading, Massachusetts: Addison-Wesley, 1987.

This document contains the same type of description as the IBM document above, but the description applies to Apple's Macintosh computers. The text is more concise and easier to read than the IBM document. It is, of course, mostly relevant to Apple users.

Figure 9–20 **Characteristics of Dialog Types**

| Dialog Type | Data | | | Operator | | | | | |
	Source	Volume	Sequence	Decision Maker	Casual/ Dedicated	Training Required	Objective	Technical Requirements	Preferred Technology
Menu	Operator	Low	Predictable	Yes	Casual	Low	Easy to learn	Fast response	Buffered Intelligent
Prompted	Operator	Low	Predictable	Yes	Casual	Low to Medium	Easy to learn/use Questions depend on context	Fast response	Unbuffered Intelligent
Form Filling	Customer Paper	Low to High	Predictable	Partly or No	Casual or Dedicated	Medium to High	Complete validation Assist business function	Fast response Good screen layout	Buffered Intelligent
Command Language	Customer	High	Random	Partly	Dedicated	Very High	Flexibility	High throughput	Intelligent Buffered
Direct Manipulation	Operator	Medium	Random	Yes	Casual	Medium	Flexibility Easy to learn/use	Good layout Graphics	Intelligent

Winograd, T., and Flores, F., eds. *Understanding Computers and Cognition.* Reading, Massachusetts: Addison-Wesley, 1987.

This book describes Terry Winograd's theory of design as well as some of the reasons that natural language is not the best medium for human-computer interaction. This book is difficult but very rewarding.

Review Questions

1. What are the main criteria for deciding whether an activity should be performed on-line or in batch mode?

2. What are the advantages of operating on-line when doing transaction processing?

3. Why are management reports generally prepared in batch mode?

4. Describe the differences between transaction processing and casework.

5. What are the four criteria for good conversation design? Describe the most commonly used ways of meeting these criteria.

6. Describe the differences between buffered, unbuffered, and intelligent workstations.

Discussion Questions

1. Relatively few executives have terminals in their offices. For those who do, discuss user interface and dialog design requirements.

2. Discuss the differences in dialog design for untrained (naive), fairly frequent, and full-time users. Suggest how systems can be designed to fulfill the needs of all three categories simultaneously.

3. Review examples of businesses and local government organizations and identify examples of casework versus transaction processing. Discuss the differences. Are there gray areas that could be classified in either category?

4. Review systems or programs with which you are familiar (MS-DOS, spreadsheet, word processing package, automated bank teller, tourist information panels). Classify the type of dialog. Review the help facility. Critique. Conclude what sort of users these applications were designed for. Were the designers successful?

Mini-Case

Suppose that a local pizza shop is so successful that it has decided to process its orders on-line. The requirements include telephone orders for take-out and delivery, as well as sit-down table service.

There are three sizes of pizza. Optional toppings are:

- Extra cheese
- Pepperoni
- Sausage
- Black olives
- Green peppers

Side orders are:

- Garlic bread
- Fried cheese

There are two sizes of the following beverages:

- Cola drink
- Diet cola
- Uncola drink
- Diet uncola
- Coffee

If the order is to be delivered, it must show the name, address, phone number, delivery time, and directions (e.g., Deliver to side door).

Question for Discussion

1. Design an interactive order entry dialog that will accommodate all the above requirements and handle multiple sizes, topping options, side orders, and beverages.

References

1. Winograd, T., and Flores, F., eds. *Understanding Computers and Cognition*. Reading, Massachusetts: Addison-Wesley, 1987.

2. Martin, James. *Design of Man-Computer Dialogues*. Englewood Cliffs, New Jersey: Prentice-Hall, 1973.

3. Shneiderman, Ben. *Designing the User Interface*. Reading, Massachusetts: Addison-Wesley, 1987.

Chapter 10

Designing Forms, Screens, and Reports

This chapter presents the general design factors that apply to forms, screens, and reports alike. The chapter then describes specifically the design criteria for input forms and reports—first, the overall format and then, the arrangement of component parts. The final section describes screen design and offers practical guidelines on specifics such as operator guidance, ergonomics, paging and scrolling, and attribute bytes.

Learning Objectives

- Understand the criteria for good form, screen, and report design.
- Critique examples of form, screen, and report designs according to these criteria.
- Apply the criteria to design forms, screens, and reports, given a set of specifications.
- Relate the activities of form, screen, and report design to the other activities in the life cycle.

SIGNIFICANCE OF FORM, SCREEN, AND REPORT DESIGN

Input forms, output reports, and input or output screens carry practically all the information between users and the computer system. Forms and reports are also the most important vehicles for transmitting information to and from the outside world—customers, suppliers, regulatory agencies, and the general public. More and more frequently, screens are used in communicating with the outside: automatic teller machines, reservation terminals placed by airlines in travel agencies, on-line data bases.

Good form, report, and screen design practices are crucial in determining how the system is perceived by its users, and ultimately, how successful the system will be. The designer should strive for forms that are easy to fill in and reports in which users can easily locate the data they are interested in.

Ease of use of forms, reports, and screen layouts depends greatly on consistency in both layout and content (such as consistent captions). The designer does not work in a vacuum; the documents must be consistent with those that the users may receive from other systems. If the organization does not have formal standards for screen and report design, there is still likely to be an informal standard, a certain consistency in style from system to system, to which the designer should conform.

Decreasing Emphasis on Reports and Forms

With on-line data entry and query and with the use of electronic files to communicate activity data from transaction systems to decision support or management information systems, the emphasis is moving away from report design by the systems analyst. Often, the recipient of data will get the information in electronic form and use a report generator or a spreadsheet package to manipulate the information and present it in the best format.

This technique solves a dilemma that once made report design difficult: should reports be designed for a function or for an individual? In early systems, it was assumed that the analyst could determine objectively the data required for a given purpose—say analyzing the trends in employee turnover and the reasons for it. In addition, this data would be independent of the personal tastes of whomever happened to be the manager in charge of performing the analysis.

Experience has shown, however, that different people have different styles and therefore need information presented differently. Some prefer graphic presentations, others a synthetic one-page summary, yet others a mass of details. When determining a user's information requirements, an analyst is influenced by the style of the individual who states the requirement. Consequently, many reports end up being designed for specific individuals rather than for an abstract, idealized function. Reports designed in this way work well until the person accomplishing the function is replaced by someone with a different style.

Many reports are designed to solve a specific problem and do not need to continue to be produced once the problem is solved. For example, a report that contains data analyzing the turnover of personnel has probably been requested because management has a problem with turnover. If the system meets its objective, then the report on turnover will become useless (or at least much less useful) as the turnover rate declines. The initial report will probably be replaced by a report on some other problem area masked by the previous problem (for instance, data helping management to analyze recruiting practices) or perhaps even caused by its resolution (for instance, data to analyze retraining requirements for experienced employees whose jobs change over time). Many of these problems can be solved by letting the users create their own reports from suitably prepared summary files.

The form and report design activities that continue to be required are for communication with the outside (order forms and invoices, for example) and for systems control purposes (error and exception reports, audit trails, control reports reconciling total inputs and outputs).

Increasing Emphasis on Screen Design

Conversely, screen design is taking on greater and greater importance. The most noteworthy consequence of this trend is that it greatly reduces the amount of information that can be presented simultaneously to a user—about 2,000 characters, including blanks (24 or 25 lines of 80 characters each). The designer may have to exercise considerable ingenuity to enable the user to leaf back and forth between multiple screens.

Another problem is that the contents of a screen are volatile and offer no audit trail. If erroneous information was presented on a screen, and later corrected, there may be no trace of what the erroneous information was or who used it to make what wrong decision.

On the plus side, more and more terminals have color and graphics capability, thus increasing the variety of information presentation techniques. To some, a picture is worth a thousand words, and a well-designed color graph can summarize large quantities of information. Most uses of graphics in business systems today are in the realm of decision support systems. In general, users design the graphics output that they want to produce themselves, and IS analysts are seldom involved. The main considerations on the use of computer graphics are covered in Appendix 4.

Graphs are not always suitable, however. They are more difficult to print and duplicate (especially if they are in color). They can also introduce bias. Disraeli, the nineteenth-century British prime minister, once said: "There are three kinds of lies: Lies, damned lies, and statistics." (The quote has also been attributed to at least three other, less illustrious individuals.) We can perhaps add graphics as a fourth kind: "reports inform, graphics convince."

THE CHOICE OF THE MEDIUM

This section will cover the four main categories of input/output media: reports, screens, forms, and special-purpose media. Each is appropriate in different situations. There are no hard-and-fast rules, however. The range of choices is increasing with the availability of new technological alternatives. The analyst should use creativity in meeting information needs and implementing information flows effectively.

Printed reports are the usual choice for output when one of three conditions occurs:

- The output is to be sent to an outside organization: customer, supplier, or regulatory agency, for example.

- The output is too voluminous to be browsed on-line.
- The objective of the report is to have an audit trail or to exercise some systematic control over the application.

Screen-based output (with a hard-copy function where required) is appropriate in the following situations:

- Queries about a single entity in the data base.
- Low-volume output.
- Intermediate steps in a long interactive process (as in decision support systems).

The following situations indicate the use of preprinted forms for input:

- Input transactions from personnel or third parties who do not have access to workstations.
- Legally important documents.
- Turnaround documents.

Management information systems, decision support systems, departmental systems, and the like rarely if ever rely on preprinted forms, because their input usually comes in electronic form from other systems.

The following situations are examples of the use of special-purpose equipment:

- Bar codes can be used to track the whereabouts of physical goods (packages) or documents (files of people having applied for retirement benefits). Bar codes are also used for supermarket checkout and inventory control (universal product code).
- Magnetic ink character recognition (MICR) is used by banks for check processing.
- Optical character recognition (OCR) is used with turnaround documents (e.g., invoice stub returned with payment); order entry (handwritten figures on special forms); text storage and retrieval (a use emerging with the availability of OCR equipment capable of interpreting practically any printed or typed font).
- Mark sensing (electrically or optically) can be used to analyze responses to questionnaires and grade tests using multiple-choice questions.
- Voice output is appropriate for telephone queries (bank balances or directory assistance, where a human operator processes the call but stops short of communicating the result, which is spelled out as a series of numbers by a voice response unit).
- Voice input is used in industrial environments where users cannot conveniently reach a keyboard and where the vocabulary that the computer system must recognize is small. Baggage handling in airports is the

best-known example. As bags pass operators on a conveyor belt, the operators call out the destination of each bag. A sorting system then ensures that each bag is conveyed to the plane with that destination.

- Microfilm is used for archiving large amounts of information.

GENERAL PRINCIPLES OF FORM, REPORT, AND SCREEN DESIGN

The designer of forms, reports, and screens should observe the general principles of ease of use, one clearly identified purpose, and maximum benefits at minimum costs.

Ease of Use

As with the design of dialogs described in Chapter 9, the main consideration in the design of forms, reports, and screens is ease of use. *Ease of use* has different meanings for different types of media, however. For forms and input screens (which usually mimic forms), the term means easy to prepare; for reports and output screens (which closely mimic reports), it means easy to read and understand.

In all cases, consistency is a requirement—consistency within a system and consistency with other systems, even systems outside the organization. A document to be completed by a member of the general public should use familiar words and avoid industry or organization-wide jargon.

Figure 10–1 illustrates the areas that are the subject of standards in many organizations. In a company where all or some of these areas are left to habit or chance, the project team should investigate the habits and formalize a standard, at least for use by its own members. If the standards are well devised, they will probably spread to other project teams.

Other considerations for ease of use include grouping related data and separating unrelated data so that the document has identifiable zones of information.

Clear and consistent captions and column headings are required. They should be abbreviated as little as possible. When limited space (e.g., on a screen) makes abbreviations unavoidable, they should be consistent. The abbreviation for *Supplier* should be *Supp* everywhere, not *Sup* on some forms and *Suppl* on others. Captions should never be omitted.

Aesthetically pleasing color combinations increase ease of use. However, color is not effective for conveying critical information because 7 percent of all men and 1 percent of all women suffer from partial color blindness. Colors should only emphasize or draw attention; they should never be an integral part of the information.

Where the technology permits, text items should appear in a combination of uppercase and lowercase letters. (Some line printers and older terminals may not have lowercase capability.)

Figure 10–1   **Sample Input/Output Design Standards**

Factor	Example
Size	Make all forms 8 1/2 by 11 or smaller.
Color	Send the green copy to accounting.
Data Positioning	Position important data on the left side of document or screen.
Media	Avoid preprinted computer forms; use stock only.
Codes	Tables of valid codes must always be printed on form or displayed on screen.
Dates	Use DD/MM/YY format.
Logo	Use standard logo on all external documents.
Heading	Include company name, page number, date, and report name in fixed positions.
Binding	Use three-hole paper.
End	Mark the last page of a report so that the user can check that the report is complete.
Distribution	Position distribution instructions at the bottom of the document.
Instructions	List the meaning of function keys at the bottom of the screen.
Identification	Give each form or report a companywide identification number.

Fulfilling the Purpose

Obviously, any form, document, or screen should fulfill its purpose. What is less obvious is that each form, report, or screen should have only one purpose. This purpose should be clearly identified in the requirements specification document.

Single-purpose documents are easier to change when the organization and the objectives of their users change. A report could serve two users with different purposes for a while, but if one user changes the way the report is used, it may become incompatible with the needs of the other user.

Assume, for example, a report that serves both to inform the marketing department of customer activity, by listing the amounts of invoices for each customer, and to help the accounting department post payments to the correct invoice. If the company starts a new product line, marketing may well want two columns on the report, one for each product line. This makes the report useless to accounting, interested only in the invoice total so that a clerk can match it to the payment amount.

Combining a great deal of data on a single report to serve several users or many needs of a single user makes the report harder to design and fit within the carriage width and page length of the printer. Too much data also increases volume and causes maintenance problems. With today's ad hoc reporting techniques, it is probably more economical to produce a series of simple reports rather than a single complex report.

Benefits and Costs

Good design should consider the total benefits and the total costs of each document. The main benefit, against which costs are weighed, is the avoidance of errors—transcription, interpretation, or distribution.

The main costs involved are procurement costs (paper cost, cost of designing, printing, and possibly binding or padding); production costs (computer and printer time, cost of workstations, data communication costs); and handling costs (changing paper on a printer, bursting and collating multipart, multipage reports, distributing paper).

DESIGN OF INPUT FORMS

A form may be filled in by hand, on a typewriter, or by a computer printer, in which case it is a turnaround document. Turnaround documents are often completed by hand or by typewriter before they are reentered.

The data content of a form is dictated by the application requirements. Space should not be included on the form for data unavailable to the user when the form is filled in. If additional data is to be added to the form later by another person, that data must be clearly isolated and identified with a text such as "Reserved for office use."

The size of a form should be as standard as possible and should preferably not exceed 8 1/2 by 11 inches (or A4, i.e., 210 by 297 mm, in metric countries). Half-size forms are quite acceptable. Smaller forms should be used only in special circumstances (severe constraints on storage space, such as needing a pad of forms to be carried in a pocket, or industry habits and constraints, such as charge card slips).

The number of copies of a form should be limited, as each copy of a form adds to printing and handling costs. If the form is to be entered into a computer system, then the data can be made available on-line to other users instead of a paper copy. This technique may not always be applicable. For instance, a charge card slip needs to be created in triplicate, one for the customer, one for the merchant, and one for the credit card company. In most cases, however, the need for multiple copies of forms and reports should be questioned.

A form may be supplied by a printer or copied on a photocopier from a master when needed. Copying from a master is relatively expensive and should be avoided except for small volumes of noncritical forms. Another disadvantage of this method is that colors and multipart forms cannot be handled. Also, the master is usually typed, which makes it harder to use because it prohibits some of the boxing techniques described later in the chapter.

The number of copies is in practice limited by the readability of the last copy. Depending on paper weight, the limit may be three copies for handwritten documents and four or five for typed documents. The designer must also decide whether to have the user interleave carbons, a messy and impractical choice; to have multipart sets made with carbons already interleaved; to use NCR (no carbon required) paper; or to have the user photocopy the required number of copies. On the whole, the most popular solution for multipart sets is to use NCR or snap-out carbons.

Continuous forms are most suitable for high-volume, repetitive work on a typewriter. For accurate registration, these forms must hold together well—crimped, glued, or held together by pin-feed edges (the usual solution). Continuous forms are also the most frequent solution for turnaround documents.

Single-part forms can be supplied loose-leaf or in pads, where the forms are glued together at the top or along an edge. Padding is useful for forms that are carried around, not for forms that are used by a clerk sitting at a desk.

The layout of the form itself should follow the sequence of filling it in rather than the sequence of reading it. A form is customarily filled in left to right, top to bottom. (Just imagine how inconvenient any other sequence would be for someone using a typewriter.) If several different users fill in different parts of the form, these parts should be separated. It is also a good idea to isolate the data that will be entered into the computer system from additional detail (see Figure 10–2).

Related information is grouped together in a zone. Zones are kept separate from each other by physical location, by enclosing them in lines or boxes (see Figure 10–2), or by highlighting with color or shading.

Detailed design techniques include the following:

- A descriptive title

   The title should be the first thing noticed about a form. It should be short, but detailed enough to identify the form unambiguously.

- A form number

   Unless a form is known by its number (as is the notorious Form 1040), it should be placed unobtrusively along an edge in small print. It is also a good idea to include the date of latest revision of the form.

- A preprinted sequence number

   This feature may be appropriate where it is necessary to account for all the forms, used or unused. The sequence number is often a security requirement, if the form can be used to obtain money or merchandise. Prenumbering order forms in restaurants prevents a waiter from serving an undeclared meal and pocketing the customer's money.

- Instructions

   Required instructions should be placed at the top of the form or the zone to which they apply. Very detailed instructions can be printed on the back of the form and a reference to the instructions placed on the front. Distribution instructions are best placed at the bottom.

Figure 10–2 **Typical Form for Data Entry**

Note the disposition of the zones on the form: identification data on top, data entry zone to the left, human-readable zone to the right. Boxes are used to maximum advantage. Data entry fields use dogteeth and preprinted punctuation in amount fields.

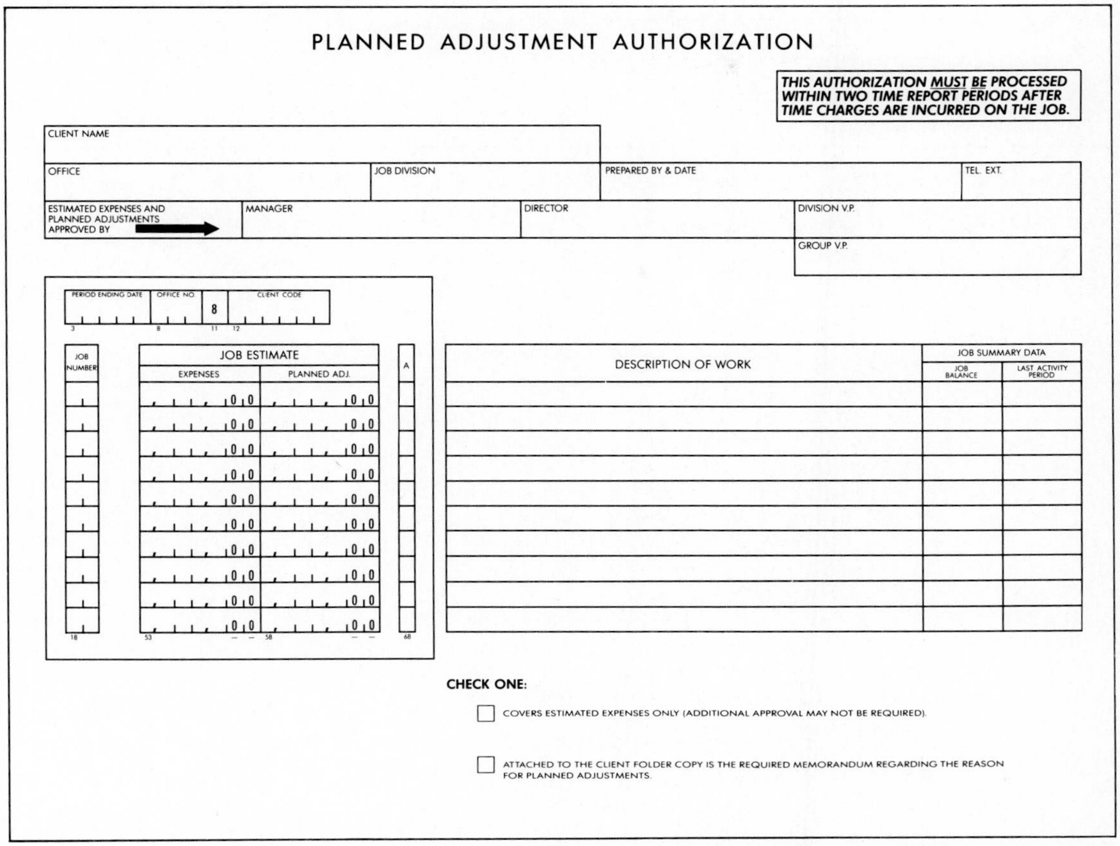

PLANNED ADJUSTMENT AUTHORIZATION

THIS AUTHORIZATION MUST BE PROCESSED WITHIN TWO TIME REPORT PERIODS AFTER TIME CHARGES ARE INCURRED ON THE JOB.

CLIENT NAME

OFFICE | JOB DIVISION | PREPARED BY & DATE | TEL. EXT.

ESTIMATED EXPENSES AND PLANNED ADJUSTMENTS APPROVED BY | MANAGER | DIRECTOR | DIVISION V.P. | GROUP V.P.

PERIOD ENDING DATE | OFFICE NO. | 8 | CLIENT CODE

JOB NUMBER | JOB ESTIMATE: EXPENSES, PLANNED ADJ. | A

DESCRIPTION OF WORK | JOB SUMMARY DATA: JOB BALANCE, LAST ACTIVITY PERIOD

CHECK ONE:

☐ COVERS ESTIMATED EXPENSES ONLY (ADDITIONAL APPROVAL MAY NOT BE REQUIRED).

☐ ATTACHED TO THE CLIENT FOLDER COPY IS THE REQUIRED MEMORANDUM REGARDING THE REASON FOR PLANNED ADJUSTMENTS.

- Clear, brief captions and headings

  Captions and headings are often the best instructions. The more frequently a form is used, the more the captions and instructions can be abbreviated. Captions should be accompanied by units of measure (hours or days, inches or feet, units or boxes of 144 units) where needed.

Figure 10–3 **Box Style**

This Is Good: **This Is Not So Good:**

NAME		DATE
STREET ADDRESS		
CITY & STATE		ZIP CODE

NAME   EMPL. NO.

1. Captions above
   the line.   _____

2. Captions below
   the line.   _____
                      NAME   EMPL. NO.

3. Captions before   NAME _____
   a line.
                      EMPL. NO. _____

- Box style

  Most forms are designed in the box style (Figure 10–3), which has been found to be the best overall. Ballot boxing, where one or several alternatives can be simply checked off, is a popular variation when only a limited number of possible values exist.

- Highlighting

  Various methods exist for highlighting parts of a form: Hatching the outline of a box, using dogteeth to indicate the required number of digits, preprinting punctuation (especially for amount fields or formatted numbers such as telephone numbers or social security numbers), or using lines of different thicknesses, shading, and color (see Figure 10–4).

- Spacing

  Spacing is an important element of usability. If space permits, the "3/5" formula enables a form to be filled in by hand or by typewriter equally conveniently. The "3/5" formula refers to 3 lines per inch in vertical spacing and 5 characters per inch horizontally. This arrangement is comfortable for most people to write in, and it corresponds to double interlines and double spacing on most typewriters. The formula also applies very well to turnaround documents.

- Alignment

  On a form that is to be filled in by typewriter, columns should be aligned so that the typist can set a small number of tabs and avoid unused stops or manual spacing of the carriage.

REPORT DESIGN

The following discussion applies to reports printed by computer either on a predetermined schedule or on demand. It does not apply to character-for-character hard copies of screens, such as those that can be requested by a terminal operator unbeknownst to the computer system to which the terminal is attached.

Figure 10–4 **Hatching, Dogteeth, and Shading**

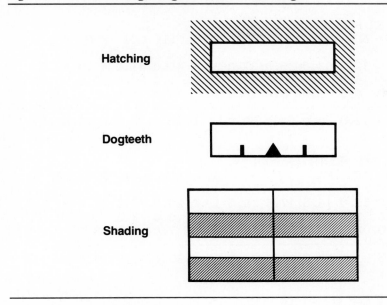

The data content of the report should satisfy the data or information needs of its recipient. To reiterate, it is probably not a good idea to design combined reports that satisfy the needs of several functions for the same or different individuals. On the other hand, the report should be as complete and informative as possible.

The following purposes of reports are typical:

- To analyze trends.
- To identify exception items for action.
- To assist in management planning and control.
- To provide an audit trail.
- To provide detailed data for inquiries against permanent records.
- To provide totals for systems control.

Providing details for inquiry is normally best done on-line. In some cases, this method may not be possible, in particular where large amounts of historical data may be involved—for instance, all the detailed transactions in a bank over several years. A more appropriate method may be to print out the data for a given period and microfilm it for economical storage and retrieval. Even though the medium is no longer paper, the data still qualifies as a report.

Figure 10–5 **Example of Trend Analysis Report, Column Format**

```
        PROJECTED SALES PER MONTH ($ 000)
        JAN  FEB  MAR  APR  MAY  JUN  JUL  AUG  SEP  OCT  NOV  DEC

SYSTEMS     27.0 29.0 30.0 32.0 33.0 35.0 37.0 38.0 40.0 41.0 42.0 43.0
SERVICES     3.0  4.0  5.0  6.0  8.0 10.0 12.0 14.0 16.0 18.0 20.0 20.0
COMPONENTS   0.0  2.0  2.0  4.0  6.0  8.0 10.0 12.0 14.0 17.0 20.0 24.0
        -----------------------------------------------------------------
TOTAL       30.0 35.0 37.0 42.0 47.0 53.0 59.0 64.0 70.0 76.0 82.0 87.0


        COST OF SALES PER MONTH ($ 000)
        JAN  FEB  MAR  APR  MAY  JUN  JUL  AUG  SEP  OCT  NOV  DEC

SYSTEMS     13.5 14.5 15.0 16.0 16.5 17.5 18.5 19.0 20.0 20.5 21.0 21.5
SERVICES     1.5  2.0  2.5  3.0  4.0  5.0  4.8  5.6  6.4  7.2  8.0  8.0
COMPONENTS   0.0  1.0  1.0  2.0  3.0  4.0  3.0  6.0  7.0  5.8  8.0  9.6
        -----------------------------------------------------------------
TOTAL       15.0 17.5 18.5 21.0 23.5 26.5 26.3 30.6 33.4 33.5 37.0 39.1


        OTHER EXPENSES PER MONTH ($ 000)
        JAN  FEB  MAR  APR  MAY  JUN  JUL  AUG  SEP  OCT  NOV  DEC

DEVELOPMENT  4.0  4.2  4.5  4.7  5.0  5.2  5.5  5.7  6.0  6.3  6.6  7.1
MARKETING    6.2  6.7  7.4  8.3  9.3 10.8 12.4 13.0 13.6 14.8 16.0 17.6
OVERHEAD     8.2  8.8  9.2  9.6 10.1 10.5 11.0 11.4 12.1 12.6 13.2 14.8
        -----------------------------------------------------------------
TOTAL       18.4 19.7 21.1 22.6 24.4 26.5 28.9 30.1 31.7 33.7 35.8 39.5
```

Figures 10–5 through 10–11 provide examples of reports that exemplify some of the uses in the preceding list. Obviously, some of these reports are better designed than others, a consideration explored further along in the section.

In general, report designers should avoid preprinted forms for computer reports because of the cost of changing forms and aligning them properly on a computer printer. The exception to this rule is documents going outside the company, such as invoices and order forms. Multipart forms, whether preprinted or not, are also expensive to handle and should be avoided. Single-part reports are often quite adequate for internal reporting, especially exception reports and reports to assist in management planning. However, preprinted forms such as invoices must often be multipart.

Recent evolutions in technology have brought to prominence the so-called laser printer, which uses electrostatic technology rather than the earlier impact

Figure 10–6 **Example of Trend Analysis Report, Bar Graph Format**

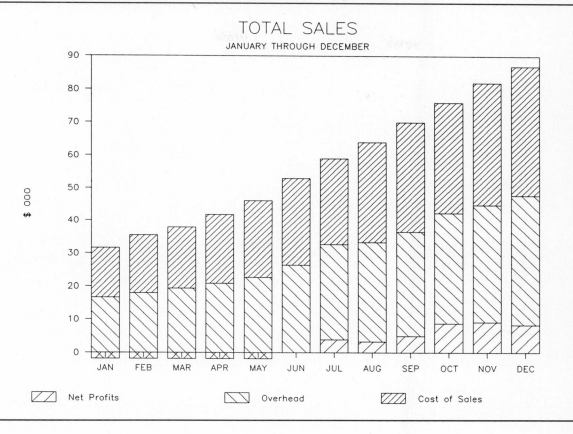

technology. Because there is no impact, there is no possibility of printing multipart forms. On the other hand, because electrostatic printers are often capable of graphics, they can be used both to present graphic information and to print such elements as boxes or the company logo while the report is being printed.

Report designers should be familiar with the possibilities and the constraints of the available technology before designing a report in detail. The size of printed reports is limited to the width of the printer—132 positions per line, plus margins, for most mainframe-attached line printers. The length of a page is arbitrary, although it has to be a whole number of inches. The most frequently used page length is 11 inches, but 12 is also often seen.

Because of the trend towards preparing reports on a large computer and then sending the data via communications lines to local, low-cost printers,

Figure 10–7 **Example of Exception Reporting, Voucher Proof List**

```
                        JOURNAL VOUCHER PROOF LIST

                               07/31/93

BATCH JOURNAL   DATE    ACCT NO        JOURNAL        DEBIT       CREDIT    DIFFERENCE
 NO     NO              MAJ MIN    ENTRY DESCRIPTION  AMOUNT      AMOUNT

 01   06-408  07/31/93  111 401  COLLECTIONS ON ACCOUNT  $12,103.76
              07/31/93  521 000  DISCOUNTS ALLOWED          $225.03
              07/31/93  112 000  CREDITS TO A/R                      $12,328.79
                                                     JOURNAL NO.  MISSING  01
      06-410  07/31/93  421 012  EXPENSE CLAIMS            $763.29
              07/31/93  111 104  EXPENSE CLAIMS                         $763.29

 01   BATCH TOTALS                                   $13,092.08  $13,092.08


 02   06-410  07/31/93  921 000  PAYROLL EXPENSE         $8,766.90
              07/31/93  212 110  ACCRUED PAYROLL                     $6,073.57
              07/31/93  212 120  INCOME TAX WITHHELD                 $1,109.43
              07/31/93  212 130  FICA TAX WITHHELD                     $480.40
              07/31/93  212 140  INSURANCE DED WITHHELD               $563.50
              07/31/93  212 150  BOND DED WITHHELD                    $300.00
              07/31/93  212 160  CREDIT UNION DED WITHHELD            $230.00

                            ENTRY DOES NOT BALANCE  $8,766.90   $8,756.90    $10.00

              07/31/93  111 601  CASH COLLECTIONS                     $375.25
              07/31/93  411 100  CASH SALES               $375.25

 02  *BATCH TOTALS               ERROR COUNT 01      $9,142.15   $9,132.15    $10.00


    **FINAL TOTALS               ERROR COUNT 01     $22,234.23  $22,224.23
```

reports are increasingly being designed for the reduced dimensions widely available on low-cost laser or dot-matrix printers, namely 8 1/2 by 11 (A4 in metric countries).

All efforts should be made to avoid routine printing of voluminous reports. The best alternative is to keep the data available on the computer and to let users, through the on-line system, query its contents or request ad hoc extracts. Another alternative is computer output to microfilm (COM), where a computer tape is fed directly into a device that produces microfilm or microfiche.

The frequency of a report depends on the frequency of the function that it helps accomplish. A weekly report to assist in the monthly closing of the accounts is of little use. The frequency of a report is also tied to its data content. The recipient of a monthly report assumes that it contains data that is complete for the month in question. If there are delays in processing the month's transactions due to transmission times, workload on clerks, and so on, then the report must be delayed as well. An incomplete report is probably no better than

Figure 10–8 **Example of Exception Reporting, General Ledger**

```
                    GENERAL LEDGER EXCEPTIONS
                    =========================

                                                    Page 1
                                        Date Prepared 09/09/92

        --------Account----------
        Number          Description         Exception Condition
        ------          -----------         -------------------

        10011           Cash                Negative Balance in asset account

        20111           Accumulated         Debit entry made to "credit only"
                        Depreciation           account: Batch 01, JE 011

        No further exceptions
```

no report at all, because it would destroy the consistency of one month's figures compared with another. The need to make sure that a report reflects all the activity of a given period, and nothing but that activity, is called *cut-off*; it is of great importance in accounting and in management information systems generally.

Most organizations have daily, weekly, monthly, and yearly cut-offs; some also have quarterly. One of the difficulties is that weekly and monthly cut-offs do not coincide, and various expedients have been adopted to counter this problem. A popular method is to align months on weeks, defining January and February as having 4 weeks, March having 5, April and May having 4, June having 5, and so on. Another method is to separate the two entirely and not try to reconcile them. In all cases, reports that detail the activity of a given period or the status on a certain date should state the period or date, preferably in the report heading.

Other elements that go in the report heading are the title of the report; the preparation date (the date that the report was actually created by the computer

Figure 10–9 **Example of Management Reporting,
Management Control Report**

PART NUMBER	REV LTR	PART DESCRIPTION	ABC CODE	UNIT PRICE	UNIT PRICE CODE	UNIT OF MEAS	ORDER POLICY CODE	OPENING BALANCE	MONTH TO DATE RECEIPTS
3663590	B	GASKET	C	1.60	$	EA	3	633	250
4782911	F	BRACKET	C	0.90	$	EA	3	660	1650
5321485	A	RESISTOR	B	0.50	$	EA	2	7830	0
8956633	B	FRAME	A	10.50	$	EA	1	350	360

PART NUMBER	CURRENT MONTH'S USAGE	ON-HAND QTY	ON-ORDER QTY	CURRENT MONTH'S IS FREQ	CURRENT MO USAGE FCST	AVE MONTHLY USAGE	MAKE/ BUY CODE	EXT VALUE AVAIL INV
3663590	242	636	250	5	260	240	M	1418
4782911	590	1700	0	2	620	620	B	1530
5321485	1020	6030	1000	8	3600	3500	B	7015
8956633	340	312	300	12	310	340	B	6426

INVENTORY SUMMARY

OPENING BALANCE VALUE $	CURRENT MONTH RECEIPTS $	CURRENT MONTH ISSUES $	TOTAL INVENTORY VALUE $	TOTAL ON-ORDER VALUE $
675,300	120,200 .	110,000	685,500	76,000

SYSTEM SUMMARY

CUST SERV LEVEL CODE	SMOOTHING FACTOR CODE	SMOOTHING FACTORS	INVENTORY CARRYING COST %	SHOP/PURCH ORDER COST
C	3	.75 .25	.23	25.80

system); the company, division, department, location, or person covered by the report; and the page number.

This heading is repeated at the top of every page. The entire report may be preceded by one or two cover pages, giving the name of the report and its distribution. These two pages are generally prepared by data processing operations, and the report designer need not worry about them.

The body of the report contains column headings and data. In general, descriptive data (account number and name, product code, and description) are on the left of the report; the numerical data concerning the account, product, and so on are to the right. An exception to this arrangement is the report style that presents two sets of near-identical data, but for two different periods (say

Figure 10–10 **Example of Management Reporting,
Summary Responsibility Report**

```
AREA NO. 60                                             APRIL, 1994
MANUFACTURING MANAGER                             REPORTS TO NO. 40


      CURRENT MONTH                                 YEAR TO DATE
  UNDER/(OVER)                                           UNDER/(OVER)
     BUDGET      AMOUNT      AREA NO. AND DESCRIPTION    AMOUNT    BUDGET
-----------------------------------------------------------------------
       (28)      5,064   61 MANUFACTURING MANAGER'S OFFICE   19,905      236
    (2,798)     13,366   62 PUNCH PRESS DEPARTMENT           48,389   (4,414)
       453      10,231   63 LATHE DEPARTMENT                 43,704     (331)
       (27)      7,619   64 DRILL PRESS DEPARTMENT           28,675      154
    (1,295)     14,946   65 MILL & AUTOMATIC DEPARTMENT      57,015     (115)
       (54)      4,164   66 PLATING DEPARTMENT               16,860      (55)
       (54)     15,000   67 ASSEMBLY DEPARTMENT              63,516     (437)
       198      14,178   68 TOOL & DIE DEPARTMENT            56,644      540
       (24)      1,855   71 PLANT ENGINEERING                 7,250       65
    (2,414)     18,399   72 MAINTENANCE                      65,498   (2,611)
       323      38,525   73 OCCUPANCY                       157,739      833
  ------------------------                          ----------------------
    (5,720)    143,347                                      565,195   (6,135)
  ========================                          ======================
```

current month and year to date) or budget and actual data. Then it may be best
to have descriptive items in the middle and numbers on either side, presented
symmetrically (see Figure 10–10). This style can also be effective for a report that
has many columns, such as a report where the months of the year are spread
across the page. (The report in Figure 10–5 could be redesigned this way.) The
body of the report also contains subtotals as appropriate.

The bottom of a report is in two parts. First, the bottom of each page, which
does not have any particular function, may be used to provide instructions or
explanations of codes. Second, the significant part, at the bottom of the last page
of the report, contains grand totals or some other unmistakable indication that
there are no more pages to the report.

Highlighting on reports is difficult. Impact printers can highlight by
overprinting. Laser printers cannot overprint, but some have multiple fonts and

Figure 10–11 **Example of Detailed (or Control) Report**

```
                                   THOMAS MANUFACTURING-NORTH LOC                          CO  003  LOC  001

                     CASH REQUIREMENTS REPORT FOR PAYMENT CUTOFF DATE 12/22/97               PAGE     13

                             DISCOUNTS LOST DATE 12/03/97


                    VENDOR   INVOICE TRAN        BK -----DUE DATE----- OVR ----------------AMOUNT DUE------------------- ST
      VENDOR NAME   NUMBER   NUMBER  TYPE  BATCH CD ORIGINAL  REVISED  RID   GROSS         DISCOUNT             NET      CD
-------------------- -------- ------- ----  ----- -- -------- -------- ---  --------------  --------------  ---------------- ---
LEKTRO EAST SERV INC.  15943320 221730  INV   0107  25 12/12/97 12/13/97        420.50          .00            420.50
                                        NET BALANCE FOR THIS INVOICE            420.50          .00            420.50       X

LEKTRO EAST SERV INC.  15943320 235822  INV   0107  25 12/23/97 12/23/97        276.00        12.00            264.00
                                 D/C    0108  25 12/20/97 12/20/97        220.50CR        .00            220.50CR
                                        NET BALANCE FOR THIS INVOICE             55.50        12.00             43.50

LEKTRO EAST SERV INC.  15943320 472813  INV   0109  25 01/03/98 01/03/98        410.50        13.00            397.50
                                 D/C    0108  25 12/29/97 12/29/97      2,175.00CR      51.25CR          2,123.75CR
                                        NET BALANCE FOR THIS INVOICE          1,764.50CR      39.25CR          1,726.25CR

                       VENDOR TOTAL PAYABLE                                     420.50          .00            420.50

                       VENDOR TOTAL NOT PAYABLE                               1,709.00CR      26.25CR          1,682.75CR

                              VENDOR TOTAL                                    1,288.50CR      26.25CR          1,262.25CR  ZZZ


     * * * * * * * * * * * * * * * * * * * * * * * * * * * * * * * * * * * * * * * * * * * * * * * *
     *                                                                                            *
     *     FINAL TOTAL PAYABLE                            1,345.35        48.30          1,297.05  *
     *                                                                                            *
     *     FINAL TOTAL NOT PAYABLE                          959.85         9.98            949.87  *
     *                                                                                            *
     *     TOTAL MANUAL CHECKS                                 .00          .00               .00  *
     *                                                                                            *
     *     GRAND TOTAL A/P FILE                           2,305.20        58.28          2,246.92  *
     *                                                                                            *
     *                                                                                            *
     *     TOTAL CASH REQUIRED THIS PERIOD                1,500.35        48.00          1,452.35  *
     *                                                                                            *
     * * * * * * * * * * * * * * * * * * * * * * * * * * * * * * * * * * * * * * * * * * * * * * * *


*** INDICATES TOTAL PAYABLE IS A DEBIT    2 VENDORS

XXX INDICATES VENDOR TOTAL EQUALS ZERO

ZZZ INDICATES VENDOR TOTAL LESS THAN TOTAL PAYABLE

  X PAYABLE THIS CYCLE
```

graphics capabilities that can help highlight. By far the best technique, because it can be used with any technology, is to isolate the data to be highlighted in a separate zone on the page—for example, in a margin not normally used or in an area preceded and followed by a number of blank lines.

The following guidelines may prove helpful in designing reports:

- Printable characters such as colons, asterisks, or the letter I should not be used to simulate columns on reports printed on stock paper. With a laser printer, overlay forms can be used. Hyphens may be used to underline column headings and to group related columns together (see Figure 10–5).

- Whenever the form is to be sent to an outside person or organization, the name and address should be located so that a window envelope can be used (see Figure 10–12).

Figure 10–12 **Placement of Name and Address on
Document to be Sent in Window Envelope**

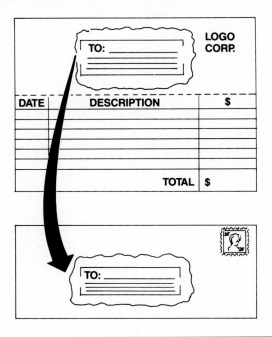

- When too few print positions are available, the column headings and captions may be abbreviated to the point of obscurity. In such cases, explanations of the abbreviations may be printed across the bottom of each page.

- A specific spacing problem is sometimes encountered on reports. There may be enough horizontal space to accommodate columns of detail numbers but not enough to accommodate the totals of these columns. In that case, the totals can be staggered on two successive lines (see Figure 10–13).

- The confidentiality of data printed on reports can be addressed by two techniques, both of which require an impact printer. The first is to have one part (often the top page) preprinted with black zones, on which printed data is nearly unreadable. The second solution is to design special carbons, where parts of the carbon paper is cut away so that some of the information does not strike through on the copy just underneath the cut-out.

- Office supplies vendors and printers have a number of ingenious, labor-saving devices that can be used to prepare envelopes and contents at the same time in self-contained mailers.

Figure 10–13 **Placement of Column Totals When Column Width is Insufficient**

```
           JAN   FEB   MAR   APR   MAY   JUN   JUL   AUG   SEP   OCT   NOV   DEC

LINE 1     54.0  58.0  60.0  64.0  66.0  70.0  74.0  76.0  80.0  82.0  84.0  86.0
LINE 2      9.0  12.0  15.0  18.0  24.0  30.0  36.0  42.0  48.0  54.0  60.0  60.0
LINE 3      0.0   6.0   6.0  12.0  18.0  24.0  30.0  36.0  42.0  51.0  60.0  72.0
           --------------------------------------------------------------------
TOTAL      63.0        81.0        108.0       140.0       170.0       204.0
                 76.0        94.0        124.0       154.0       187.0       218.0
```

SCREEN DESIGN

General guidelines for screen design are similar to those of form design (for input screens) and report design (for output screens). What varies is the specific technology of screens (size, color, graphics) and the fact that screens are an interactive and volatile medium.

Operator Guidance

One of the advantages of interactive processing is that the program can give the user constant feedback. Not only can the program check the correctness of the data as it is entered, but it can also display guidance relevant to the specific context of the conversation.

Unbuffered terminals and intelligent workstations can provide this feedback character by character as each is keyed in. Buffered terminals are somewhat less interactive, because the guidance they display can change only when the operator presses the *Transmit* key after filling in the screen.

The following guidelines can help in designing operator guidance:

- Captions and instructions must be explicit for casual users; they can be more cryptic for dedicated users. Naive users and users over which the organization has no control (general public, customers) must be handled with care. These users sometimes approach the terminal with hostility; even if they are not hostile initially, they may have very little patience with what they perceive as the computer's lack of understanding. Such systems should be

Figure 10–14 **Example of Cryptic Captions, Acceptable Only to Dedicated Users**

```
ORDER                          ORDER ENTRY                          PAGE 01

ORDNO    CUSTNO  SLSMN    RGN  COMM  ORDCT   SHPLC   SHIPDT   VIA    LINE  DLRS
XXXXX    XXXXXX  XXX      XX   XX    XXXXX   XXXXX   XXXXXX   XXXXX  XX    XX


ITEM NO          QTY   UNIT   PRICE  DOLLARS      DISCOUNTS   PACK
XXXXXXXXXX       XXXX  XX     XXXXX  XXXXXXX  XX  XX   XX     XX
XXXXXXXXXX       XXXX  XX     XXXXX  XXXXXXX  XX  XX   XX     XX
XXXXXXXXXX       XXXX  XX     XXXXX  XXXXXXX  XX  XX   XX     XX
XXXXXXXXXX       XXXX  XX     XXXXX  XXXXXXX  XX  XX   XX     XX
XXXXXXXXXX       XXXX  XX     XXXXX  XXXXXXX  XX  XX   XX     XX
XXXXXXXXXX       XXXX  XX     XXXXX  XXXXXXX  XX  XX   XX     XX
XXXXXXXXXX       XXXX  XX     XXXXX  XXXXXXX  XX  XX   XX     XX
XXXXXXXXXX       XXXX  XX     XXXXX  XXXXXXX  XX  XX   XX     XX
XXXXXXXXXX       XXXX  XX     XXXXX  XXXXXXX  XX  XX   XX     XX
XXXXXXXXXX       XXXX  XX     XXXXX  XXXXXXX  XX  XX   XX     XX
XXXXXXXXXX       XXXX  XX     XXXXX  XXXXXXX  XX  XX   XX     XX
XXXXXXXXXX       XXXX  XX     XXXXX  XXXXXXX  XX  XX   XX     XX
```

tested extensively on representative users as they are designed (see Figures 10–14 through 10–16).

- When instructions are displayed, they should be placed consistently. Only those instructions that can be used in the specific context should be displayed. For instance, if the operator is at the end of a scrolled document, the instruction that function key 5 will display the next page should not be used, because there is no next page (see Figures 10–17 and 10–18 for an illustration of how to display instructions).

- When an operator enters data in a wrong format or tries to make a choice that the program cannot process, the program should display a message to the operator. This message is unfortunately called an error message. As a result, the text of such messages often contains the word *Error* or *Wrong*. These words have a deplorable effect, especially on novice users. Error messages should be viewed as a form of context-sensitive help and worded positively. For example, instead of "Customer number error," the message

Figure 10–15 **Example of Screen with More Text,
Suitable for Intermittent Users**

```
48468389

NAME          SMITH, WILLIAM C.
ADDRESS       312 CHESTNUT
              WAUKESHA, WI 53254
TELEPHONE     (414)555-6480

ACCOUNT BALANCE       $1,212.40     PRINCIPAL TO DATE      $445.00
LOAN AMOUNT           $1,500.00     INTEREST TO DATE       $165.10
INTEREST                $322.50     TOTAL                  $610.10
TOTAL                 $1,822.50     PAYMENTS MADE                4
TOTAL PAYMENTS              12      NEXT PAYMENT DUE    09.15.94
LAST PAYMENT DUE       05.15.95
PAYMENT AMOUNT           $153.50
INTEREST RATE            $18.00
```

should say: "This customer number is not on file. Please check that you have the right one and try again, or use the Alpha Search Facility to find the customer's number if you know the name."

- Constant operator feedback should be provided. With an intelligent or an unbuffered terminal, each character should be processed as completely as possible as it is entered. If the operator enters a code or an identification key (customer number, product code, state code in an address), the translation of that code (customer name and address, product designation, spelled-out state) should be displayed as soon as it is entered. If the program can determine that a response will be long in coming, a message can be displayed warning the operator of the delay. If possible, progress should be indicated periodically. Any operator's reaction to an unchanging screen is that the message has not come through or that the computer is down.

- Everything that has been said about consistency in this and the previous chapter applies to screen design—consistency of placement, captions, emphasis, and action items.

Figure 10–16 **Example of Screen Suitable for Naive Users**

```
-------------------------------------------------------------
----------------------  E D C / 3 0 0 0  --------------------
-------------------------------------------------------------

   Which online function of EDC/3000 would you like to perform?
   (Please enter an 'X' to make a selection)


      _ EDC DATA ENTRY     - Enter transaction and report requests
                             for later processing by the
                             Engineering Data Control subsystem.

      _ EDC RETRIEVALS     - Review online information from the
                             EDC data base:  bill of materials,
                             where-used, routing, item data.
```

Figure 10–17 **Example of Direct Manipulation Interface Showing Menu Bar, Pull-Down Menu, Application Window, and Function Key Assignments**

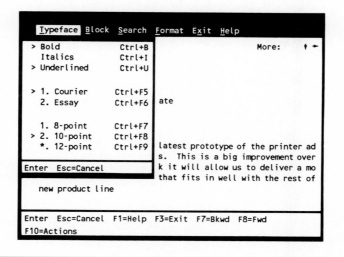

Figure 10–18 **Example of Direct Manipulation Interface Showing a Typical List Screen Design**

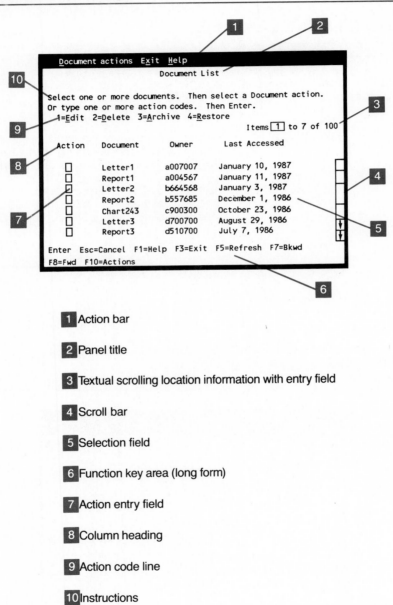

1 Action bar

2 Panel title

3 Textual scrolling location information with entry field

4 Scroll bar

5 Selection field

6 Function key area (long form)

7 Action entry field

8 Column heading

9 Action code line

10 Instructions

Highlighting, Aesthetics, and Ergonomics

Aesthetic and ergonomic factors are of great importance because of the bias of many naive users against the dehumanized aspects of computer systems and because of the widespread feelings of dedicated operators that CRT work may be hazardous or unacceptably strenuous.

The following factors should be considered when designing screens:

- The users of the system should be involved in selecting the equipment and designing ergonomically correct workstations. (If necessary, an expert in ergonomics can help.) Some of the most common factors are the height of the terminal and the keyboard, the screen glare, the combination of predominant colors on the screen (black on white, white on black, amber on black, green on black). Color should not be relied on to code hard information. Instead, color should be reserved to indicate the type of field: captions, fields that the operator can modify (data entry fields), fields containing output data, error messages, instructions, present status.

- No more than two levels of intensity and no more than three or four colors should be used. In lieu of levels of intensity, inverse video (a black-on-white field where the rest of the screen is white-on-black) or blinking fields may be used. Blinking is distracting and should be used very sparingly. If audio feedback (e.g., beeps) is used, short tones should be used for routine feedback (unavailable key or function, attempt to put alphabetic characters in a numeric field). Long, more aggressive signals are used for rare, emergency conditions, for instance, to accompany a message such as: "Ten minutes have elapsed since the last activity on this terminal. Please press a key within the next thirty seconds if you wish to remain connected to the application."

- For a sophisticated intelligent workstation that accommodates multiple sizes and fonts, no more than three fonts (normal, bold, italics) and four sizes should be used.

- Fields should be aligned judiciously. Data fields (both input and output) should be aligned vertically on the left-hand side and captions on the right-hand side. Numeric and alphabetic fields should be justified properly (see Figure 10–19). If the screen has multiple columns, the cursor normally moves from left to right, top to bottom. (The normal movement could be changed with intelligent workstation or an unbuffered terminal, but it is not advisable to do so, as the application might want to change screen types.)

Paging and Scrolling

Both input and output on screens may occupy more space than is available on the screen (normally 24 lines of 80 characters). One solution may be to get a larger terminal, but this makes the application dependent on nonstandard technology. Other solutions are to use windowing systems, available on intelligent workstations, or to provide scrolling or paging.

Figure 10–19 **Examples of Column Justification on Display Screens**

```
Product Inventory Inquiry                                      SHOW
                                                              DETAIL
 ITEM      DESCRIPTION          UNIT PRICE  U/M QTY-ON-HAND
                                                              SHOW
 00023B    Die Stocks             475.00   ea        10       USAGE
 00106A    Medium Duty Casters     45.95   ea     1,000
 01998C    Wrightson's Air Filters 35.95   ea        45       SHOW
 02004F    V278 Support Sheeting  358.86   pkg       10       VENDORS
 02013D    Forthright Gaskets      25.00   doz        3
 02015A    Ruffwood Keyseat       175.00   ea         5       SHOW
 02015B    Ruffwood Keyseat Cutter 25.00   ea         5       PURCH'S
 02045D    Keyway Bushings         45.00   pkg       24
 02073S    Carbon Steel Hex Nuts  525.00   case      10       SHOW
 02156D    Gage Block              35.00   ea         2       ON ORDR
 02178E    Pneumatic Wheel Set    234.50   ea         1
 02201F    Die Stocks             175.00   pair       3

 ITEM #   UNIT PRICE   U/M   QTY-ON-HAND   ON-HAND VALUE   USAGE/MO
 02031D    $25.00      doz       3            $75.00         15

 ON ORDER  ORDERED   QTY ORDERED   EXPECTED        VENDOR
  Yes      05/21/97       50       06/30/97  Forthright Mfg. Co       EXIT
```

```
                   ENTRY OF VENDOR INVOICES

           VOUCHER NO  999999
          PROPERTY NO  999
              UNIT NO  X_____X
            VENDOR NO  9999
          VENDOR NAME  X_____X
           INVOICE NO  X_____X
 INVOICE DATE (MMDDYY) 999999
   DATE DUE (MMDDYY)   999999
         GROSS AMOUNT  999999.99
      DISCOUNT AMOUNT  999999.99
 CHART OF ACCOUNTS NO  9999           AMOUNT  999999.99
 CHART OF ACCOUNTS NO  9999           AMOUNT  999999.99
 CHART OF ACCOUNTS NO  9999           AMOUNT  999999.99
 CHART OF ACCOUNTS NO  9999           AMOUNT  999999.99
 CHART OF ACCOUNTS NO  9999           AMOUNT  999999.99
 CHART OF ACCOUNTS NO  9999           AMOUNT  999999.99
       PAY CODE (P/H)  X
             COMMENT   X_____X
```

The windowing metaphor consists in making a rectangle on the screen available to view a two-dimensional area (such as a table, a listing, or a menu) that is larger than the window. Using function keys, the data area can be moved around underneath the window so as to show different parts of the data area through the window at any time. A screen may have multiple windows showing different data areas at the same time.

Scrolling or paging is a reduced form of windowing. Take, for example, an order that may have up to a hundred detail items. The first few lines on the screen display the information that applies to the entire order (order number, customer number, name and address, delivery date, and so on). The bottom line(s) display function key assignments and system messages. The lines in the middle display a limited number of order detail lines (say, 15 at a time). Scrolling enables the operator to press a function key to shift all the detail lines up by one, losing the topmost line but displaying a new one at the bottom. The reverse operation would shift all the lines down by one, showing a new line at the top. Paging does the same thing as scrolling, but an entire page is moved up or down at a time.

A left-right scrolling or paging function is required if the screen design calls for a data area that exceeds the width of the screen (for instance, to browse the electronic image of a report that uses the full 132 character line width of most line printers).

Scrolling and paging are practically always required for output-oriented applications, such as data base query or on-line management reporting. Many, if not most, reports or query responses require more than the standard 2,000 or so positions available on a screen. Dedicated transaction processing may also require scrolling and paging when each transaction (logical unit of work) is made up of many individual items. Office automation and departmental applications practically always require paging and scrolling because the documents processed are of arbitrary length.

Attribute Bytes: A Special Consideration for Buffered Terminals

Many buffered terminals require that the first position of each field be reserved for a so-called attribute byte, which indicates whether the field is visible, highlighted, or colored and whether the user is allowed to enter data into it. (Protection against data entry prevents the operator from accidentally overwriting captions and headings.) Some terminals can also specify via the attribute byte rules about the data to be entered: mandatory (cannot be all spaces), numeric, alphabetic, or completely filled (forcing the operator to enter nine numeric digits for a social security number, no more and no less). The attribute byte imposes a one-character interval between any two fields (captions or variable fields).

As an aside, the attribute can specify that the data in a field be hidden—not displayed at all. This feature is useful in two circumstances. First, if the operator is required to enter a password when signing on to the application, the password field should be nondisplayable. If the password can be displayed, passers-by may observe the operator's password by looking over his or her shoulder. Second, many on-line monitors use the first few characters of a screen to identify which program is to process the data that is sent when the operator presses *Transmit*. This system-oriented piece of data is of no interest to most operators and is best left hidden.

Intelligent terminals and unbuffered terminals generally do not have attribute bytes, because each character typed on the screen is processed by the program, which can decide, based on its internal logic, how the character is to be displayed or validated and how the cursor is to move over protected fields. A program communicating with a buffered terminal cannot make this decision, because the program does not receive the data until all the characters have been entered and the operator has pressed *Transmit*.

Miscellaneous Guidelines

The following guidelines may be valuable:

- If strings of alphabetic or numeric characters are more than five positions, they should be broken up in chunks of three to four characters (see Figure 10–20).

- When a new screen is sent from the computer program or an old screen refreshed with new information, the cursor should be placed in the first position of the first data entry (unprotected) field. If there are errors on the screen, the cursor should be placed in the first field containing an error (block-oriented terminals only).

- There is no need to terminate captions with colons. Abbreviations do not need punctuation, for example *BTU* rather than *B. T. U.* Punctuation should be added to numeric fields to make them easier to check. For instance, the operator should be able to enter dollar fields without decimal points and commas, but they should be displayed including the dollar sign, if there is room.

- The use of special characters, such as @, &, %, and #, should be avoided. They may not be available or compatible on all terminals. Upper- and lowercase letters should be used wherever available: text in uppercase is hard to read.

Summary

The design of input and output forms, screens, and reports should follow three main guidelines: be easy to prepare or understand, fulfill its purpose effectively, and be cost-effective.

The main factors for ease of use are clarity of the layout, sufficient space, consistent and logical sequence, instructions, and feedback. For on-line interactions, important aspects are consistency, constant feedback, and pleasant aspect of the screens with which the operator interacts.

Figure 10–20 **Splitting Long Strings into Subgroups**

NOT	BUT
ABBA423675A2	ABBA 423 675 A2
ABBD252389K4	ABBD 252 389 K4
ABCR862534M3	ABCR 862 534 M3
ABRG563487W4	ABRG 563 487 W4
ACGL190537S0	ACGL 190 537 S0

For output, the best results are obtained with one report or output transaction for each purpose. Because they reduce the number of printouts, multipurpose reports may seem more economical initially, but they are ultimately likely to be less effective.

Proper choice of medium and technology as well as adequate consideration of handling and distribution costs will maximize the cost-effectiveness of the design.

Selected Readings

The bibliography for this chapter is largely the same as for Chapter 9. Most of the books listed contain aspects of both dialog and screen design.

IBM Corporation. *Systems Application Architecture: Common User Access Panel Design and User Interaction*, 1st ed. IBM Publication No. SC26-4351, 1987.

Shneiderman, Ben. *Designing the User Interface*. Reading, Massachusetts: Addison-Wesley, 1987.

This book is mainly about the design of human-computer interactions, but it has useful guidelines and excellent illustrations that pertain to panel design (pp. 69–73 and pp. 311–351 in particular).

Martin, James. *Design of Man-Computer Dialogues*. Englewood Cliffs, New Jersey: Prentice-Hall, 1973.

James Martin's book has several examples of good screen design techniques for a variety of applications and technical environments.

Garlitz, Wilbert O. *Handbook of Screen Format Design*, 2nd ed. Wellesley Hill, Massachusetts: QED Information Sciences, Inc., 1985.

This book is a complete and reasonably up-to-date description of the main screen design techniques. It also contains chapters on the use of colors and graphics. Finally, it describes input forms design.

Review Questions

1. Which part of the user requirements document is the most directly used when designing reports, forms, and screens?

2. Which forms, reports, and screens must be mocked up or prototyped during the design phase? Which ones can be postponed until the implementation phase?

3. What types of guidelines are typically included in form, screen, and report design standards?

4. What are the three major goals of form, screen, and report design?

5. Describe the problems that might be encountered if inadequate attention were given to the following:
   a. Report data content
   b. Form makeup
   c. Number of copies
   d. Screen size
   e. Report security requirements

Discussion Questions

1. Why is the use of terminals for data entry and information display increasing at the expense of preprinted forms and computer-generated reports?

2. Review examples of forms used in everyday life (for example, restaurant order pads with a detachable receipt, credit card charge slips, individual income tax returns). Critique and improve. How would you design a screen replacing these forms, assuming that the function could be made interactive? Would alternative technologies (voice, OCR, mark sensing, bar codes, etc.) apply to these situations?

3. Identify screen design components of a PC-based product with which you are familiar, such as Lotus 1-2-3, a CASE tool, or a word processor.

4. It is often stated that if voice input and output were widely available, more executives would use computer technology. Discuss whether this is true.

Mini-Case

You are asked to prepare a mock-up of a report that will also serve as a turnaround document. A report definition form with the required data element descriptions is furnished as Figure 10–21.

The mock-up should be as realistic as possible. You should make up territory, salesperson, and customer names as well as realistic figures. The mock-up should ideally be prepared on a computer printer; if a printer is not available, use a printer spacing chart.

Figure 10–21a **Report Definition Form**

```
ACCTG                                                                 RPTDEF
BUDPREP                                                               R00262
              REPORT DEFINITION - Sales Budgeting Turnaround Rpt

PREPARED BY: Ben Dover        DATE: 15Feb88      VERSION: 2      PAGE  1
APPROVED BY: RL Turner        DATE: 18Feb88      STATUS :
```

```
PURPOSE           : Serves as a turnaround document for entry of sales budget
                    data.  Report provides prior and current year sales and gross
                    margin by quarter within customer, salesperson and territory.
                    Sales and gross margin % change between prior and current
                    years are also reported.  Budget preparers enter for next
                    year either:

                    -  Budgeted sales and gross margin amounts, or

                    -  Budgeted sales and gross margin % change from
                       current year actual quarterly amounts.

                    For current year quarters for which actual amounts are not
                    yet available, amounts are projected based on the year to
                    date change between the prior and current years.  Totals
                    are provided by customer, salesperson, territory and
                    company.  Overall totals can be balanced to control totals
                    to ensure processing accuracy.

DISTRIBUTION      : Salespersons, Territory Managers

MEDIA             : Paper

FREQUENCY OF PREPARATION:  Quarterly

NUMBER OF COPIES: 2

VOLUME OF PRINT : 250 pages

RETENTION         : 2 years

FORM              : Stock

SEQUENCE          : Territory, Salesperson, Customer

PAGE BREAK        : Territory
```

Continued

Figure 10–21b *Continued*

```
ACCTG                                                               RPTDEF
BUDPREP                                                             R00262
              REPORT DEFINITION - Sales Budgeting Turnaround Rpt
─────────────────────────────────────────────────────────────────────────
PREPARED BY: Ben Dover      DATE: 15Feb88      VERSION: 2      PAGE   2
APPROVED BY: RL Turner      DATE: 18Feb88      STATUS :
─────────────────────────────────────────────────────────────────────────


X-REF TO    DATA ELEMENT                                         NO. OF
 SAMPLE     IDENTIFICATION   DATA ELEMENT NAME OR COMMENTS      CHARACTERS
--------    --------------   -----------------------------     ----------
    1       EL00200          Territory Number                      2
    2       EL00205          Salesperson Number                   3
    3       EL00206          Salesperson Name                     25
    4       EL00220          Customer Number                      5
    5       EL00221          Customer Name                        25

                             Prior Year $ Sales to Customer
    6       EL00361          - 1st Quarter                        7
    7       EL00362          - 2nd Quarter                        7
    8       EL00363          - 3rd Quarter                        7
    9       EL00364          - 4th Quarter                        7

                             Current Year $ Sales to Customer
   10       EL00371          - 1st Quarter                        7
   11       EL00372          - 2nd Quarter                        7
   12       EL00373          - 3rd Quarter                        7
   13       EL00374          - 4th Quarter                        7

                             Prior Year $ Gross Margin for Customer
   14       EL00381          - 1st Quarter                        5
   15       EL00382          - 2nd Quarter                        5
   16       EL00383          - 3rd Quarter                        5
   17       EL00384          - 4th Quarter                        5

                             Current Year $ Gross Margin for Customer
   18       EL00391          - 1st Quarter                        5
   19       EL00392          - 2nd Quarter                        5
   20       EL00393          - 3rd Quarter                        5
   21       EL00394          - 4th Quarter                        5
```

Technique

Tools for Prototyping

DEFINITION

A prototyping tool is a set of programs that enable the project team to generate a prototype to demonstrate the actual application. The prototype typically works in a limited area and can be developed in substantially less time than it would take to build the entire application with traditional means. The purpose of prototyping is to make sure that the application will work as planned once it is actually implemented. Prototyping is therefore most appropriate when there is uncertainty.

EXAMPLES

A word processing package can show users prototypes of screen and report layouts.

A presentation tool such as IBM's Storyboard can show users the successive steps of a sample dialog, illustrating how screens are chained together, how errors are corrected, and how menus and forms are structured.

A fourth-generation language such as Focus can be used to generate an actual mini-application, with small data files, interactive screens, and executable programs. Thus, users can experiment with the conversation design to validate it or they can train on a "flight simulator."

A rule-based expert system or AI shell, such as AION, can be used to define complex processing rules and test their consequences. This type of tool is appropriate when the processing rules are so complex that the user cannot articulate them all in a single sitting. Many times, an AI shell can be useful when the user says: "I cannot explain what I need, but I will know it when I see it."

A program simulator that can generate data bases and/or transactions based on specifications entered by the design team can prototype application performance. A simulator can also exercise the teleprocessing monitor and/or the data base management system with volumes close to those that will be encountered during operations. Examples are IBM's Teleprocessing Network Simulator and DBPROTOTYPE II.

DOMAINS FOR PROTOTYPING

user interface

Prototyping is used for three purposes. The first is to ensure that the **user interface** is well designed—easy to learn and easy to use. This use of prototyping is by far the most frequent. It is no more costly than the traditional, paper-based approach for getting the users to sign off on the interface design, and it is tremendously more effective. This prototyping is part of the user interface design activity of the design phase.

performance modeling

The second most frequent use is for **performance modeling**. Performance modeling is done at a later stage of the life cycle than user interface prototyping and is used to evaluate the probable performance of a given technical design. Performance prototyping has been especially popular for evaluating physical data base design choices for prerelational data bases such as IMS. It is less useful for relational data base designs for two main reasons. First, relational designs offer fewer choices of implementation parameters; second, machines have become more powerful, thereby decreasing the amount of attention given to performance. Performance-oriented prototyping still has merit for applications where performance may be an issue and where the body of experience is insufficient to predict performance without prototyping.

functional prototyping

The third type of use, **functional prototyping**, is just emerging. This type is concerned with developing the requirements specifications (outside the user interface) iteratively. Functional prototyping will increase as the level of ambition of the applications in development increases. In one example, functional prototyping was used to develop an application to manage leased equipment being moved from construction site to construction site by a contractor. Because the contractor was also part owner of some of the sites, the accounting rules were too complex to be enumerated by one person. The prototyping approach consisted of formalizing a number of rules, setting up a prototype based on those rules, and running a number of test cases. When a test case gave a result that experience had proved wrong, the rule base was refined to cover additional rules. When all the test cases were processed correctly, the rule based was translated into English. The English version constituted the specification for the accounting part of the system.

Although some of the tools may be the same, prototyping is not the same as iterative development. Iterative development consists in delivering subsets of an application in small increments at frequent intervals (weeks rather than months or years). With iterative development, the user can start realizing some of the benefits before the entire application is ready. The high payback functions are typically implemented first, thus increasing the period over which economies can be made and consequently the total economies achieved. In iterative development, each component is developed with production in mind. The quality of the code, the documentation, the controls, the integration, and the performance are just the same as on a monolithic development project. The difference between iterative development and the traditional approach concerns primarily the delivery mode.

Prototypes of applications, on the other hand, are usually developed with the idea of throwing away the prototype and recoding it in a different language with different tools during an implementation phase. However, if a CASE tool is used for user interface prototyping, screen designs can often be reused. In the functional prototyping example cited above, it was deemed unnecessary to translate the accounting rules into a COBOL program, and the AI shell used for prototyping was integrated into the production application as well.

MECHANIZED TOOLS

By definition, prototyping requires mechanized tools. First, the very act of prototyping requires that a model system be run on a computer; a manual prototype is not adequate to demonstrate the running of a computer-based application and get significant feedback. If there are no tools, the prototype must be developed using a third-generation language such as COBOL, thus negating the benefit of quick and low-cost demonstration models.

On the other hand, the variety of tools that can be used for prototyping is immense. The considerations for picking the appropriate tool are the following:

- Availability

    Anything that can be done with standard tools on a PC (word processor, spreadsheet, micro-DBMS) is particularly effective.

- Functionality

    A user interface prototype must be able to show screens in a default sequence at least. If the application is operator-driven, this capability is not enough. For the user to give feedback, more choices need to be available. The prototype must be sensitive to data values and menu (or function key) choices. Any moderately programmable PC package (but not, for instance, a word processor) can perform the required functions.

    Other prototyping situations require more capability. Functional prototyping is best served by AI techniques. Performance prototyping requires a modeling capability that cannot be developed easily from general-purpose tools.

- Reusability

    If a prototype is extensive, it is best if the prototyping tool will accept design or implementation documentation such as screen layouts and function key assignments. This requirement militates in favor of using a CASE tool. If the entire application (or substantial parts of it) will be developed in a fourth-generation language or with an application generator, it is usually appropriate to use the same application development tool for prototyping as well.

Various categories and representative examples of tools are given in Figure 1.

Figure 1 **Characteristics of Prototyping Tools**

Objective	Tool Category	Sample Tools	Availability	Functionality	Ease of Use	Reusability
User Interface Prototyping	Word Processor	Any	+	−	+	−
	Spreadsheet	Any	+	0	+	−
	Micro-based DBMS	dBase III Rbase	+	+	0	0
	Presentation Tools	Storyboard	0	−	+	−
	CASE	DESIGN/1	−	+	0	+
	Fourth-Generation Languages	FOCUS NOMAD 2 ORACLE	0	+	−	+
	Application Generators	GAMMA TELON Pacbase Transform SAGE CSP	−	+	−	+
	High-Level Languages	REXX	+	0	+	−
Performance Modeling	Transaction Processing Model	Vendor Dependent	0	0	0	−
	Data Base Performance Model	Vendor Dependent	0	0	0	+
Functional Prototyping	AI Language	Prolog	0	0	+	0
	AI Shell for PC	AION	0	+	0	0
	AI Shell for Dedicated Hardware	KEE ART	−	+	0	−

EXERCISES

1. Prototype the medical application given as an example of menu choices and form filling in Chapter 9. For each level of menu, implement only two or three choices—choosing any other will result in a message returned to the user: "This choice not yet operational." Implement a mini-data base of 8 physicians and 15 patients. Use the tool with which you are most familiar.

2. Choose another tool that can do prototyping. Implement the same prototype. Compare the two prototypes in terms of:

   a. Cost to implement.

   b. Closeness to real application.

   c. Functional richness (and therefore probable quality of feedback).

Section V

Data Design

Section V deals with the creation of a data design, specifying the entities about which a system is to maintain data, their relationships, their characteristics, and their integrity constraints. The section covers approaches both for transaction processing systems and management information systems.

Data Modeling at Bailis, Kronberg, Kendall & Son

When the firm of Bailis, Kronberg, Kendall & Son, a New York–based financial services company, decided to replace their outdated portfolio management system, the first step of the project team was to establish a data model for the application. A working group was created, made up of the project manager, one IS analyst with a data base background, and one financial planner with stockbroking experience.

The group met for one full day a week for four weeks. For each session, an additional functional expert was brought in: marketing, international markets, futures, and income tax specialists all enhanced the team's understanding of stocks and bonds and of the services required by Bailis, Kronberg's customers.

At the end of four weeks, the group had prepared a one-page conceptual schematic of the data entities. This schematic depicted customers; contracts that these customers had signed with the firm to provide various types of services (stocks and bonds purchasing, money market accounts, portfolio management, dividend and interest collection, tax services, and so on); accounts holding the assets about which the contracts were signed; assets such as stocks, bonds, and options; and third parties involved in the various transactions, such as the person or institution from whom the stocks were purchased and the agents through which delivery was to take place.

Once this analysis had been completed, the team contacted the IS department of First Mechanics' Bank, one of the main business partners of Bailis, Kronberg. First Mechanics' Bank's IS department had recently applied data modeling to a systems plan for all the bank's loan systems (commercial loans, mortgages, consumer loans, and so on). The Bailis, Kronberg project manager wanted to cross-check the portfolio model with the model of a similar business problem.

The comparison was especially relevant because the customer base of both companies were quite similar. Both had a number of individual customers and a few medium-sized corporations, who used the brokerage firm's services to invest their pension funds and had commercial accounts with the bank.

First Mechanics' Bank's team had made a much more detailed data model, with 150 entities (compared with the 15 or so in the Bailis, Kronberg model). The bank's data modeling project had taken a team of three analysts four months to complete.

The result of the comparison was that few discrepancies were noted. The major discrepancy was in the definition of a customer. Whereas the bank had considered a customer to be either an individual or a corporation (or similar institution), treating joint accounts as an exception, the brokerage firm considered individuals and corporations as entities that were neither customers nor suppliers (or third parties to the various transactions) and created "role" entities for them. For instance, an individual could have a customer role and a supplier role. The same individual might have a role as a sole account-holder for one account and as a joint holder of another account. In addition to individuals and corporations, trusts were established as a separate category.

The Bailis, Kronberg team was very satisfied with the comparison and felt that the model developed for the portfolio system was now anchored in solid, understandable concepts. The model subsequently served as a starting point for data base design in the various portfolio management subsystems that were developed over the following three years. At the end, despite some evolutions in the design, the management information system (the last installed) was able to benefit from the ease with which all the operations processing systems were integrated with one another.

First Mechanics' Bank also benefited from the discussions with Bailis, Kronberg. They were able to develop a high-level view of the data structure of the bank, which had hitherto been missing. This high-level view later proved useful in discussions between users and IS teams by resolving elusive vocabulary misunderstandings early in the development projects for demand deposit and credit card application.

PURPOSE OF SECTION

The purpose of Section V is to show how to create a data design for a computer-based application. A data design consists of a description of the following:

- The entities about which the application needs to maintain information (Chapter 11).
- The relationships that these entities bear to one another (Chapter 11).
- The specific elements of data that are maintained for each entity (Chapter 12).
- The integrity rules that the data should obey at all times (Chapter 13).

A data design serves the following three goals. First, it should enable the users of the application to understand the underlying structure of the information. Second, it should permit data base designers to implement this data structure to yield the right balance between high performance and flexibility. Third, it should constitute a solid foundation for the future maintenance of the application by embedding in its structure only those characteristics that are unlikely to change.

The data design constitutes a static view of an application. The user interface design and the process design depict the behavior of the application; the data design depicts its structure. The data design is therefore by nature more abstract, less implementation-oriented, than the other parts of the design. This abstraction makes the data design more difficult for clerical users to understand, but easier for top management, which tends to have a bird's-eye view of the organization and its systems.

Because data design is remote from implementation considerations, it tends to provide a longer-lasting foundation for applications than the design of processes. The structure of processes depends on contingencies—both technological (such as the typical batch file update process) and organizational (such as piecemeal clerical work). In the past, however, data design has been equated with data base design, and has, as a result, been affected by technological contingencies. Section V does not teach data base design. In fact, it attempts to avoid data base design considerations altogether.

The handling of data is the hallmark of commercial information systems. Transaction processing, management information systems, and decision support systems all rely heavily on the concepts of files and data bases. Conversely, the data structures used by systems software and embedded software (in space shuttles, weapons systems, or air traffic control) rely much less on files and records, and much more on structures such as arrays, queues, stacks, and sets. These structures are what computer science tends to deal with. As a result, much of what is taught and researched in computer science is not usable in information systems unless adapted and completed.

KEY TASKS AND DELIVERABLES

The approach to data design depends on the type of system being designed. Transaction processing systems use one approach; management information systems and decision support systems use another.

Transaction Processing Systems

Data requirements analysis is difficult to distinguish from data design. Data requirements analysis starts very early in the development life cycle; in fact, it is the basis for identifying systems projects in an information plan. It is performed in the requirements analysis phase as well.

systems planning   If data requirements analysis is performed globally during **systems planning** for the entire organization or for one of its strategic business units, the output is a corporate or systems group data model. This model identifies the main entities that the information systems are likely to maintain data about.

requirements   In the development of transaction processing systems, the part of data
analysis   design that occurs in the **requirements analysis** phase is relatively simple and global. The various entities that participate in the transactions are identified: What is the transaction about? Who supplies it? From where? To whom? To where? For what return? This analysis is either based on a subset of the corporate or systems group data models or developed from scratch by creating a preliminary project data model.

Until this point in the life cycle, the emphasis is on representing entities that the users of the system are familiar with and on indicating their natural relationships. Thus, this stage has a top-down approach. Only later are the contents of the entities and the precise nature of the relationships analyzed. This later stage is what is properly called data design and takes place in the design phase, in parallel with process design.

data design   In **data design**, the two input data flows are the business functions and the preliminary project data model (entities and relationships) identified during requirements analysis. The activity of data design interacts with user interface design. The user interface designer needs to know which attributes are available and how they can be represented; the data designer needs to know which attributes are present together on screens, forms, and reports, and therefore need to be related.

The output of the data design activity is a finalized, detailed, normalized project data model. This model resides on a data dictionary in electronic form and on hard-copy documentation in graphic form. It details the physical representation of all the data elements and the users' views (not necessarily the physical representations) of the entities and relationships. This project data model then allows the data base designers to perform various volume analyses (data and transaction volumes) that will enable them to make the right physical data base design decisions. The project data model is independent of the data base management system (DBMS) used; it does not even assume that a DBMS *is* used.

Data base design activity, not covered in detail in this book, creates a logical data base design that represents the application programmers' views of the data base (also called the subschemas) and a physical data base design that represents the data base management system's view of the data base (also called the schema). The outputs of this activity become inputs to the implementation phase. The logical data base design becomes part of the programming specifications, and the physical data base design is used by the data base administration department to create the actual data base.

data base design

The flow of data design activity for transaction processing systems is depicted in Figure V–1, and the deliverables from the activity are shown in Figure V–2.

Management Information Systems and Decision Support Systems

The process of designing management information systems (MIS), decision support systems (DSS), or departmental systems is somewhat different from what was described above. For MIS or DSS, underlying transaction systems already exist and can supply the base data for the system that is being designed. These underlying transaction systems have a data model, either explicit or implicit.

If the underlying data model has not been formalized, the **requirements analysis** phase of the management information system under study must elicit it. The best method is a bottom-up approach, collecting documentation about how the existing transaction systems work—identifying data elements on files, reports, screens, and forms and building an entity-relationship model from them.

requirements analysis

The **data design** phase in this case consists in ensuring that all the information to be delivered by the new system can actually be derived from the existing data models. New entities may have to be created by storing processed forms of the base data (accumulated data, data that has been properly cut off) or by adding new data from other sources (competitive or total market data, for example, which usually are not available from transaction processing systems).

data design

If the MIS or DSS being developed needs to store its own data, the **data base design** activity would create the description of the new data base to be created. It is more probable, however, that data base design will consist of a number of requests to expand or modify the existing data bases in the underlying systems. Figures V–3 and V–4 show the alternative flow and deliverables for MIS/DSS.

data base design

Figure V–1   **Data Design Flow for Transaction Processing Systems**

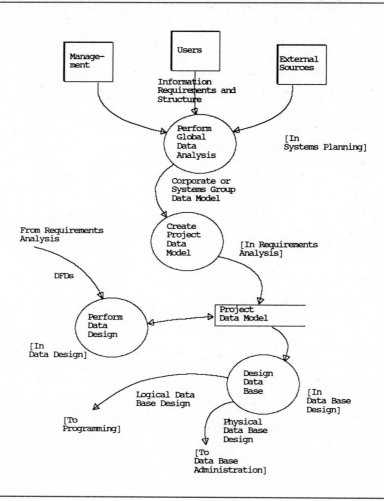

Figure V–2   **Tasks and Deliverables of Data Analysis
for Transaction Processing Systems**

Phase	Deliverable
Systems Planning	Corporate Data Model
Requirements Analysis	Preliminary Project Data Model
Data Design	Fully Normalized Project Data Model
Data Base Design	Data Definition Language for New Data Base

Figure V–3 **Data Design Flow for Management Information Systems**

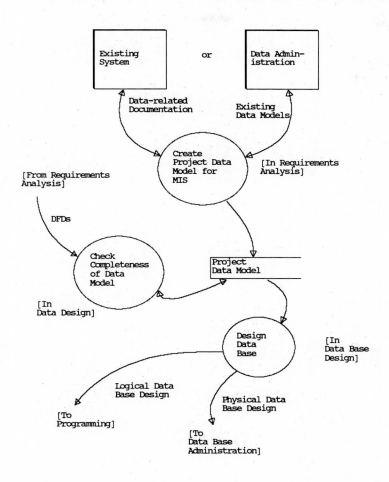

Figure V–4 **Alternative Tasks and Deliverables for Data Analysis**

Phase	Deliverable
Systems Planning	Corporate Data Model
Requirements Analysis	Data Model of Existing Transaction Systems
Data Design	Verified Data Model
Data Base Design	Data Definition Language (DDL) for Data Base Modifications

Chapter 11

Entity-Relationship Modeling

After outlining the benefits of entity-relationship modeling and providing the definitions of the terms *entity*, *relationship*, and *attributes*, Chapter 11 describes the two possible approaches to the work. The first approach is top-down analysis, used mainly for data design in transaction processing systems. It consists of four main steps: creating the initial project data model, analyzing relationships between entities, selecting attributes to be included, and assigning these attributes to entities.

The second approach to entity-relationship modeling is bottom-up, used mainly for MIS/DSS systems. It consists of three steps: analyzing the present systems forms, reports, and files; creating business function data models and user views from the existing data; and consolidating the user views into a final project data model.

In both approaches, entity-relationship modeling concludes with normalization: checking that the model conforms to a number of rules of good behavior.

Learning Objectives

- Delineate the scope of the data analysis activity, depending on the scope of the application under development.

- Analyze an initial data model to design the entities, relationships, and attributes that the users and the programmers of the application will know about.

- Update the data model to produce a final data model.

- Check that the final data model is fully normalized.

- Analyze the impact of possible future changes to forestall them whenever possible.

BENEFITS OF ENTITY-RELATIONSHIP MODELING

The key benefits of entity-relationship analysis, from management's perspective, are threefold. The analysis is a good vehicle for users to understand the system;

it provides a more solid base for future evolution; and it reduces the cost of the system by eliminating the storage of redundant data. The net result is a more responsive system.

understand the data model

If the users **understand the data model** that underlies an application, two benefits are likely to result. First, the model is more likely to be correct than if it were established by an IS professional alone. Second, the users will be able to use query and reporting tools to generate the output that is the most appropriate for their purposes, thus reducing the workload of the IS department in modifying or creating report-writing programs.

stable foundation

An entity-relationship model also provides a much more **stable foundation** than an analysis of the functions performed within the organization. Functions can be organized more arbitrarily than data, in accordance with management's wishes of the moment. For example, whether customers have a single address to which goods are delivered or several addresses is not for management to decide. On the other hand, whether billing is done daily or weekly or whether the billing function reports to marketing or accounting is much more arbitrary.

reduction of data redundancy

The third benefit of data analysis is the potential **reduction of data redundancy**. In nonintegrated applications, the same data might be stored in several different files. For instance, product information might be stored both in a manufacturing system (for storing manufacturing cost information) and in the marketing system (for storing sales prices, terms, and conditions). A customer address could be stored in the order entry application file for delivery and billing and in the accounts receivable application for collection of delinquent accounts.

The problem with data redundancy is not so much the waste of space, but the inherent loss of control over the information. In classical systems, redundancy is not carefully controlled. Thus, a customer's change of address may not be posted at the same time in both the order entry and accounts receivable files. If the new address gets changed in both applications, nothing guarantees that the new data is the same in both: Murphy's law, applied to data, says that if the same data is to be stored in two different places, at some point that information will become inconsistent. It may then become impossible, or at any rate very difficult, to determine which piece of data is correct.

Data analysis helps reduce data redundancy. Even if data redundancy is required for performance reasons, data analysis helps reduce its impact by providing a means of anticipating inconsistencies and resolving them before problems arise.

ENTITIES, ATTRIBUTES, AND RELATIONSHIPS

entities

The basic objects of data modeling are **entities**. An entity is some object that has a real existence and that is of interest to the system being designed. Examples of entities are Jane Brown; the Acme Window Cleaning Corporation for whom Jane Brown works; the route segment from New York to Dallas;

BOX 11–1

Information Modeling

Some have claimed that information systems are models of the world. They do not describe everything about the world, but they have enough of its characteristics that one can draw warranted conclusions about the world by looking at the model. (This is the very purpose of modeling.)

An example of such a model is a personnel data base. The personnel data base contains information about real-world entities (employees)—information that enables the users of the data base (the personnel department) to get answers to questions about those entities. In reality, when personnel clerks query a personnel data base, the only direct information they obtain is about the contents of the data base. The assumption is that those contents are an accurate representation of the real world that justifies conclusions about the flesh-and-blood employees.

The view that data bases are a model of the world applies to most management information systems. A set of accounts—balance sheet, profit and loss statement—is a model of the financial state of the business at the time the accounts were closed. (This example applies both to manual and computerized accounting systems.) Many so-called subject data bases are models of real-world entities such as customers, suppliers, products, inventories, employees, and so on.

In all of these examples, the data in the model may or may not be an accurate representation of the state of the world. The main objective of the whole profession of certified public accountants is to find out whether the figures in a set of accounts fairly represent the state of affairs. A data base may or may not be up to date: an employee may still be on the data base for some time after termination. A customer may not be recorded as a poor credit risk until bankruptcy

has already been declared and the company has found out about it. It is always possible, in this type of system, to seek out independent confirmation of the data base content by going out and examining the real world that is represented (see Figure 11–1).

On the other hand, many modern transaction processing systems do not model an independent physical reality. For instance, in a computerized hotel reservation system, the main entity, the reservation, is totally abstract. Its only embodiment is in the system. No amount of searching of physical reality will reveal whether it exists and has such-and-such an attribute. The customer who made the reservation may *believe* that it exists, but if the hotel reservation system does not have it, the belief may not be justified. Just imagine what happens when a customer who believes that he or she has a reservation tries to check into a hotel that is already full (see Figures 11–2 and 11–3).

More and more systems are of this nature—a trend caused by the increasing integration of technology into the operations of the organization. More and more of the data manipulated by the system only exists in the system and does not correspond to a physical reality. As a result, in these systems, users cannot examine the records post facto to determine whether they are in accord with reality. The only way to determine the accuracy of the data is to look at the way the system works to see whether the control procedures guarantee that all transactions that should be processed are processed and to ensure that the processing is in agreement with the rules. Over the past decade or so, this technique has radically changed the way auditors work. The emphasis has moved from checking the figures on the balance sheet to checking how the figures were arrived at.

Figure 11–1 **Data Base as a Model of the World**

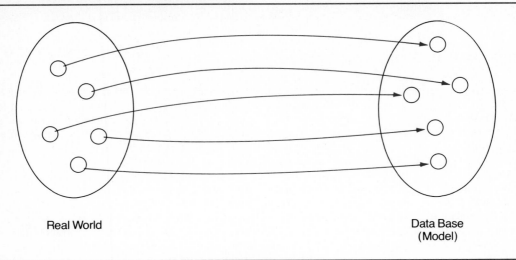

Real World   Data Base
                                              (Model)

Figure 11–2 **Overlap Between Data Base and World**

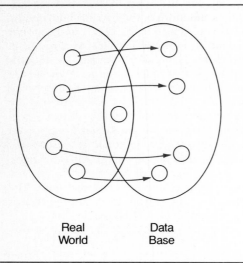

Real   Data
World   Base

Figure 11–3 **Modern Trend: Data Base and World Are Intertwined**

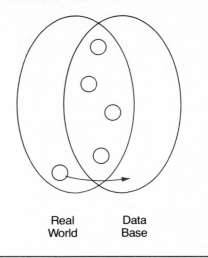

Real   Data
World   Base

American Airlines' 9:00 A.M. flight from New York to Dallas; American Airlines' 9:00 A.M. flight on February 29, 1992, from New York to Dallas; seat 17C on any airplane; seat 17C that Jane Brown occupied on American's 9:00 A.M. flight on February 29, 1992, from New York to Dallas.

Each of the above entities has properties or **attributes** that are of interest. **attributes** Jane Brown was born on August 8, 1956; she is 5'7" and weighs 140 pounds. The Acme Window Cleaning Corporation is based in Irving, Texas. Seat 17C on a Boeing 727 is an aisle seat in the nonsmoking section.

Also, there are associations or **relationships** among the different entities **relationships** that are apparent in the previous examples. The route segment from New York to Dallas is related to American Airlines' daily 9:00 A.M. flight. This daily flight is related to the actual instance of the flight on February 29, 1992. Another example is the fact that Jane Brown works for Acme. This relationship can also have an attribute: the position that Jane holds, for example.

As explained in the Technique for Section II, a relationship between two entities has a degree, or cardinality, at either end. For example, each employee holds one position and one only; a position may be held by one or more employees (or none, if it is vacant). Each passenger occupies one seat and one only; any seat is occupied by at most one passenger.

Data modeling does not work directly with entities such as Jane Brown, but with abstractions such as employees, passengers, flights, and so on. These abstractions, called **entity types**, exist because similar information is recorded **entity types** about similar entities. All persons have a date of birth; all flight legs have a departure and a destination; all employees work for some department and occupy some position. The rules for processing an entity type apply to all the instances of that entity. For example, all employees are paid; no flight leg can have the same departure and destination. Business systems are possible only because there are rules that apply across the board to all instances of an entity type.

An entity type is characterized by the **attribute types** and **relationship** **attribute types** **types** that apply to it. Attribute types and relationship types are abstractions of attribute instances and relationship instances. An example of an attribute type is **relationship types** the property "birth date" of a "person" entity type. An example of a relationship type is the "department to which an employee is assigned," where "department" and "employee" are entity types (see Figure 11–4).

Entity, attribute, and relationship types are at a higher level of abstraction than the corresponding instances. There are many levels of abstraction. For instance, a flight leg from New York to Dallas is more abstract than the flight that took place on a given day and at a given time between those two cities, but less abstract than the entity type "flight leg."

Entity, relationship, and attribute types are described in the design of a system. Entity, relationship, and attribute instances, on the other hand, do not materialize until the system is operational. The test of the proper level of abstraction—type or instance—lies in whether general rules of processing apply. If rules apply, then the object is a type rather than an instance.

Figure 11–4 **Entity-Relationship-Attribute Model**

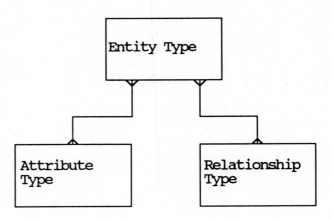

One difficulty is that many attributes and relationships can also be seen as entities. Many data modeling objects appear initially to be relationships but are revealed by later analysis to be entities. For instance, there is an obvious relationship between a part and a subassembly—the relationship of composition ("is made of"). An engine is made up of a block, pistons, valves, a camshaft, and so on. It may be necessary to record attributes about a relationship, for instance, the number of valves and the number of pistons. The thing—apparently a relationship—about which these attributes are recorded is in reality an entity, although it is a very abstract one in this case: it might be called the "made-up-of" entity.

Other modeling objects appear to be attributes, but may also turn out to be entities in some other application. For instance, a street in a customer address appears to be an attribute, but for a municipal survey application, the street in question is obviously an entity. In most cases, these difficulties can be solved intuitively. However, intuition can be dangerous, because it is often an excuse for perpetuating hidebound thinking and shallow analysis.

In other words, although the rules of data modeling appear to be quite formal and susceptible to some degree of automation, there are many gray areas. Therefore, data modeling requires more judgment than is commonly assumed.

TOP-DOWN VERSUS BOTTOM-UP APPROACH TO ENTITY-RELATIONSHIP ANALYSIS

The two main approaches to entity-relationship analysis are top-down and bottom-up. The top-down approach starts from entities and relationships that are identified intuitively or from experience, then are gradually refined. The bottom-up approach starts from more detailed information, such as the data elements used by existing systems—on forms, reports, and computer files. Then these elements are grouped according to usage and affinity, so that entities and relationships fall out naturally.

Neither top-down nor bottom-up analysis is inherently superior to the other. Generally, top-down analysis is thought to require more experience and maturity on the part of both the analysts and the users. Bottom-up analysis provides a better opportunity for inexperienced analysts to learn by practice. It is also a better method when none of the participating users has an overall perspective of the domain being analyzed.

Top-down analysis also has the reputation of being less time consuming than bottom-up. This reputation is the result of experienced personnel's tendency to work top-down rather than bottom-up; being experienced, they naturally use less time than inexperienced personnel.

Most of the books and articles on data modeling emphasize the top-down approach. So do, not unnaturally, most systems planning methodologies. Systems planning is usually done by experienced personnel who try to shorten the time of the study as far as possible so that top management's commitment does not flag halfway through the study. Experience also shows that top-down analysis is the easier of the two approaches for transaction processing systems and the more difficult for management information systems.

TOP-DOWN ANALYSIS

There are four steps in top-down analysis of an entity-relationship model: creating the initial model, analyzing the relationships in the model, selecting the attributes to be included in the model, and assigning these attributes to entities.

Creating the Initial Project Data Model

If a **systems plan** exists, it will generally contain a data model. As described in Chapter 5, this model was developed by considering the business entities and data classes required to support the business functions of the organization. This overall data model is generally documented according to the guidelines for entity-relationship models described in the Technique for Section II. Such a data model can serve as the starting point for entity-relationship modeling.

However, the global data model is usually too extensive. It is designed to meet all the data requirements of the entire enterprise or at least of a strategic business unit. The model must be reduced to the proper scope; all those data

systems plan

entities that are irrelevant to the functions covered by the application must be eliminated, which is fairly easy. The requirements specification is reviewed function by function, and the data classes required by each function are marked on the model. All those entities that remain unmarked at the end of this process can be deleted from the model; the result is the initial project data model. For example, in the design of a purchasing system, the corporate data model from Figure 3 in the Technique for Section II would be pared down as shown in Figure 11–5.

requirements analysis

If no data model exists, then it must be created from scratch during the **requirements analysis** phase. Unless JAD is used, the best technique is to write a description of the business activity that the system will cover based on the scope statement of the project and the early interview notes. Data flow diagrams (DFDs) can also be used if they have already been established. Any noun in the description is likely to be an entity; any verb that denotes a state, such as *is, has, belongs,* is likely to represent a relationship or an attribute (a relationship if both sides of the verb are nouns, an attribute if one side is an adjective or a number).

Figure 11–6 is a written description of a purchasing system. It has much more detail than does the initial model illustrated in Figure 11–5: the written description contains attributes as well as entities and relationships that are not represented on the schematic. Thus, even if an initial data model exists, it is useful to enrich the extract by going through a system description and identifying other entities and relationships. Because the system description becomes more and more detailed and accurate during the requirements analysis phase, a project data model that conforms to the description is likely to be fairly accurate at the end of that phase. However, at this point, the requirement is to establish a starting point, not a final document; if errors occur, the rest of the analysis and design process will catch them.

As work progresses in the requirements analysis phase, the data model is developed in parallel with the DFDs, so that, at the end of the phase, the two are synchronized; there should be about as many entities as there are data stores. There are exceptions: a data store may store information about more than one entity type, and an entity may appear on the DFD in several different data stores. The appearance of an entity in several data stores is often justified by the fact that DFDs reflect the dynamics of the system, whereas the data model is more static. The DFDs may depict several successive versions of the same data (such as Orders Entered but Not Picked, Orders Picked but Not Billed, Orders Billed), whereas the data model contains only one (Orders).

Entities that are not stored in any data store are likely to be outside the scope of the system being developed and should probably be removed from the data model.

JAD session

An initial data model for an application is perhaps even easier to establish in a group such as a **JAD session**. The session leader or recorder can draw boxes for entities and arrows for relationships as information is contributed by members of the group, correcting misunderstandings or imprecisions as they arise. The session leader asks questions, in particular on the nature and the

Figure 11–5 **Initial Project Data Model**

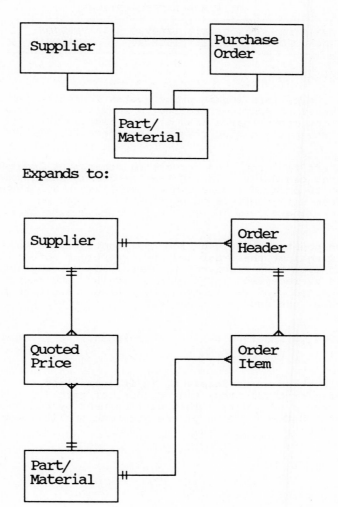

Figure 11–6 **Description of a Purchasing System**

PURCHASING   SUBURBAN PUMPS   CD-20
                                                                   PDMDS
                              DATA MODEL DESCRIPTION

PREPARED BY: ANN LYNN DATE: 12NOV90 VERSION: 2	PAGE 1
APPROVED BY: JACK CROFT DATE: 15DEC90 STATUS : D	

Once a year, suppliers submit price quotes for parts for the
following year. A supplier is free to submit a quote for any part
that is on the master parts list at that time, but no late bids are
accepted. The price quoted remains in effect for the entire year.

When parts are required, the purchasing department locates the
supplier that can deliver in the time needed at the lowest price,
grouping parts ordered from a single supplier on a purchase order.
(This process will continue to be manual, but the purchasing agents
will have on-line access to the supplier-parts data base.)

When the shipment is received from the supplier, the goods delivered
are checked against the order and any exceptions noted; the order is
transferred from "Not Received" to "Received, Not Invoiced." When
the invoice is received, it is matched against the receiving report
on the "Received, Not Invoiced" order. After resolving any
discrepancies, the order is transferred to accounts payable.

If an invoice is received before the shipment, it is held in
suspense.

As soon as a shipment is received, it is summarized in a history file
by supplier (for timeliness) and by supplier/part (quality, price,
and completeness of order). This will be used by purchasing agents
when deciding between two suppliers who both qualify from a price
viewpoint.

degree of the various relationships that are being depicted: "Can a supplier have several orders in process simultaneously?" "Can the same part be supplied by several suppliers?" "What is the relationship between a part and a substitute part? If part A can substitute for part B, does that mean that part B can also always substitute for part A?" If the group is unable to reach consensus, the session leader elicits concrete examples and counterexamples.

Although there is a danger of the discussion ranging beyond the scope of the application, the group technique is very useful in systems planning. It is also useful early in the requirements analysis phase, when it may help adjust the scope of the project to cover more (or different) problems than initially planned.

During requirements analysis, the designers emphasize the identification of entities and relationships; however, they can also begin to enumerate the essential attributes for each entity. This early attribute analysis has two benefits. If the designers document user knowledge as early as possible, they will not have to return to the users with the same questions later. Also, considering attributes may refine the entity-relationship analysis. For instance, someone in the group may identify an attribute and associate it with one entity; and someone else, with another. This difference may signal the need for a new entity or relationship. For instance, if someone associates a price with a product (the normal situation) and someone else with a customer (a special rebate or a quote), there may be two price attributes—list price and quote price. A new entity such as a quote may be needed.

Analyzing Relationships

The previous steps of the entity-relationship modeling approach are best described as analysis. The next step, the first step of the data design phase, is the first formal step in the top-down methodology. Identifying entities, relationships, and attributes remains intuitive. Consequently, two different individuals using the method just described could come up with quite different results for the same problem. The analysis of relationships is the first step towards unifying the results and applying a real methodology.

The designer applies the following six transformation rules to the initial project data model:

- Any relationship that has an attribute is transformed into an entity.

    In the university/course/student data model shown in Figure 11–7, any student who takes a course will ultimately obtain a grade in that course. What appeared initially as a relationship between the student and the course (the static verb *takes* or *has registered for* indicating a relationship) becomes an entity. Naming this entity is somewhat problematical, as there is no English noun for such a complex notion, but a combined form such as Student-Course might do. Alternatively, the entity can be named to reflect the main information that it will contain, such as Grade.

- Any many-to-many relationship is decomposed into two one-to-many relationships.

Figure 11–7 **Transforming Relationships into Entities**

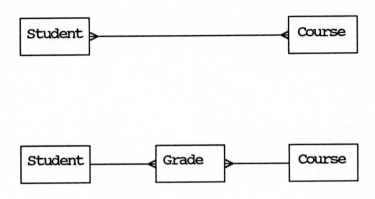

In the supplier-parts diagram of Figure 11–5, a supplier can supply many parts, and a part can be supplied by many suppliers. This structure is fairly common, but it would result in difficulties in any of today's data base systems (as well as non-data base files). In this case, a supplier-part entity must be created. This entity type will have an instance (a record or row) for each possible part that each supplier can furnish.

It is quite probable that the previous rule, that of creating an entity for each relationship that has an attribute, would have eliminated this problem. The price quoted by two different suppliers on the same part is quite likely to be different. Therefore, the supplier-part relationship has "price" as an attribute and should be transformed into an entity.

- "Or" relationships are reduced by subdividing the entity into subtypes.

In the library example of Figure 11–8, either a book is owned by the library or someone has requested that it be purchased. This example

Figure 11–8 **Subdividing Entities into Subtypes**

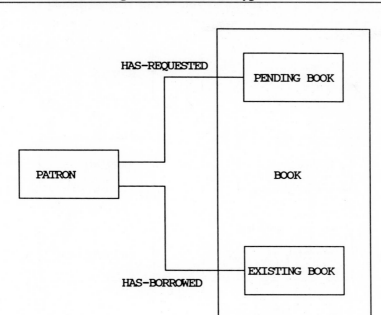

indicates that there are in reality two subtypes of books, Existing and Pending. The two entity types share many attributes and many relationships, but some are distinct. In such a case, the designer should create a subtype representation where all the common relationships are on the outer box and all the distinct relationships are on the inside boxes.

This inside-outside representation technique will not work if an entity is divided into subtypes according to more than one criterion. For instance, employees may be paid weekly or monthly; they may be married or single (significant for benefits processing). The two subdivisions are orthogonal, i.e., totally independent of each other. Some of the employee relationships depend on one of these criteria, some on another, and some are common to all employees. There are no hard rules for representing this case; two suggestions are given in Figures 11–9 and 11–10.

The preceding examples concern the one-side of relationships. If an entity has two many-sided relationships that are mutually exclusive, a superentity on the one-side of the relationship can be created. For instance, in a bill of materials, a part is either purchased from any of several suppliers or made in-house. In that case, in-house plays the same role as a supplier for some business functions, and it may be opportune to create an Extended

Figure 11–9 **Possible Representation of Multiple Subtypes**

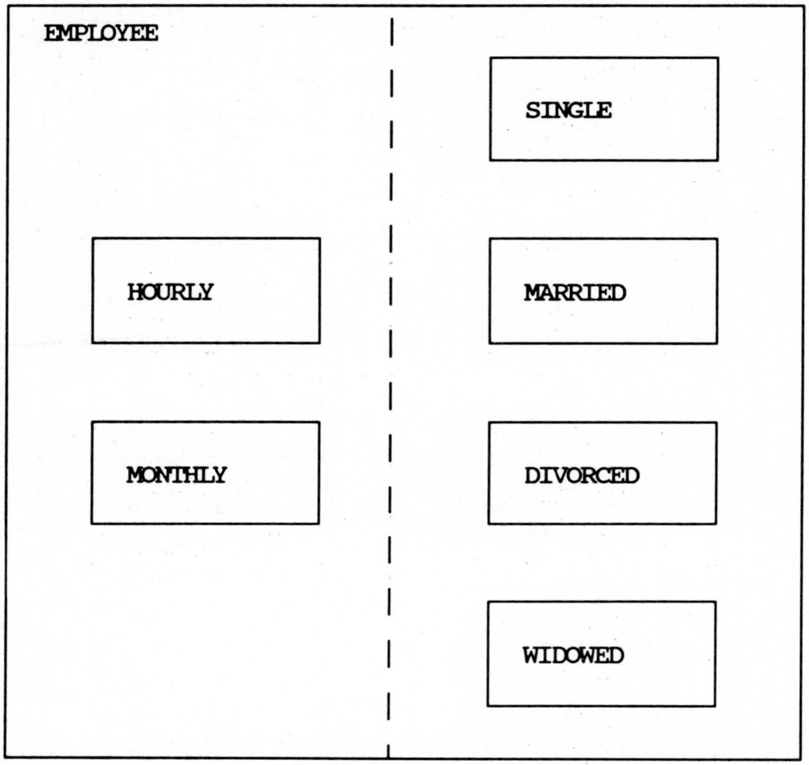

Supplier entity, whose instances will be all the normal suppliers and the in-house source. One of the attributes of the Extended Supplier entity (in reality of the Extended Supplier-Part relationship) might be the price if the company practices transfer pricing (an accounting system whereby all the goods or services furnished by one department to another are priced competitively with the market, and each department is free to purchase from or sell to the inside or the outside).

- Optional relationships may be transformed by creating superentities.

    An optional relationship (usually qualified as zero-to-one or zero-to-many) may be a variation of the subentity/superentity phenomenon. It may be that certain instances of an entity always have the relationship and others never do. In that case, if one of the attributes in the relationship indicates which is which, subdividing the entity may be possible. For instance, some

Figure 11–10 **Alternative Representation of Multiple Subtypes**

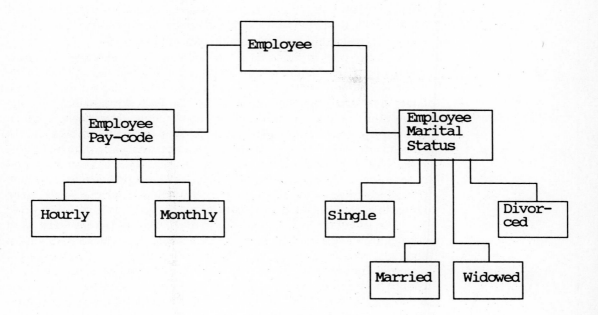

loans may be secured by collaterals, such as a mortgage, and others not. Whether there is security depends on the type of loan—mortgage, home equity, guaranteed letter of credit, and so on (see Figure 11–11). From some viewpoints, all loans are the same; from others they are different.

In other instances, the optional relationship may be accidental. At any time, each instance of the entity may or may not participate in the relationship. For example, in the library illustration (see Figure 11–8), some patrons may not have borrowed any books, and some books may not be on loan to anyone. These are legitimate zero-or-one-to-zero-or-many relationships.

- One-to-one relationships are examined for modifications.

A one-to-one relationship is an anomaly. If a relationship is truly one-to-one, then for every entity of one sort there is one and only one of the other sort. Therefore, the two entities ought to be collapsed into a single entity that combines the attributes of the two. For instance, for the relationship between a state and its constitution, most analysts would instinctively create two entities. A state is a geographical area, and a constitution, a legal document: the two entities are clearly distinguishable. From another viewpoint, however, each state must have a constitution, and no two states share the same one. In information processing, it is quite possible to consider the clauses of the constitution as attributes of the state rather than as an independent entity.

This example is farfetched. Very few business systems deal with constitutions. If they did, however, a system could deal with constitutions of countries as well as states. It becomes much less certain that constitutions of countries can be considered attributes of a country. What happens to a country such as the United Kingdom, whose constitution is not a single body of law but a series of acts and various customs and legal precedents? Could some countries not have a constitution? Or would some have two, for example, during a civil war?

In most cases, one-to-one relationships appear to be between two entities that have different natures, such as the relationship between a university and its president (see Figure 11–12). However, such relationships are really between an entity and a subset of some other entity. The quality of being a university president is not an essential one; rather, it is an attribute that a certain person holds at a given time. When a university gets a new president, the ex-president goes on existing but without the title of university president.

In practically all cases, a one-to-one relationship hides a superentity/subentity structure of some kind. It is safer to keep these one-to-one relationships as they are rather than to collapse the two entities and the relationship into a single entity, which may be difficult to uncollapse later.

- Some hierarchical relationships are represented with very specific techniques.

A hierarchy of entities exists whenever an entity (the parent) is related to another entity (the child) by a one-to-many relationship and whenever

Figure 11–11 **Creating Superentities for Optional Relationships**

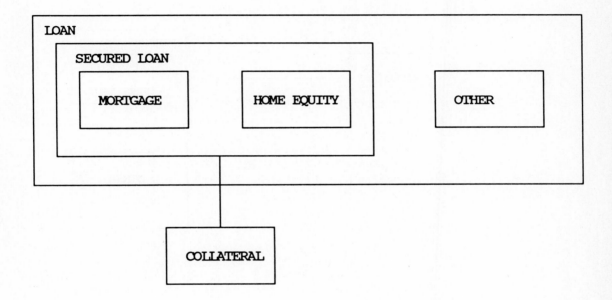

Figure 11–12 **Transforming One-to-One Relationships**

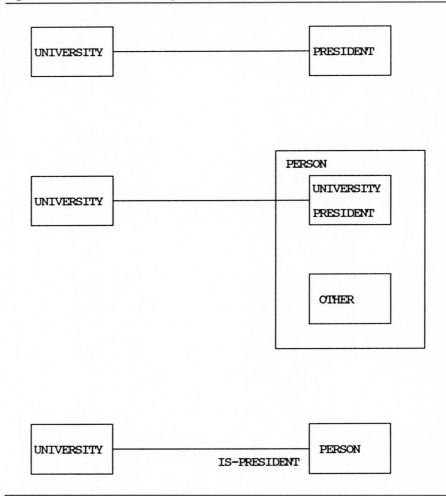

the child does not have any other parents. The child can itself be a parent of other children. A parent can have children of multiple types.

The traditional hierarchy representation is the tree diagram or Warnier chart (see the Technique for Section I). Examples are the taxonomies of biology (see Figure 11–13), hierarchies of menus (see Figure 9–19 in Chapter 9) the organization chart of an enterprise (see Figure 11–14), the bill of materials making up an assembly (see Figure 11–15). All these examples have identical or near-identical entity types at the various levels of the hierarchy.

Figure 11–13 **Sample Hierarchy: Taxonomy of Biology**

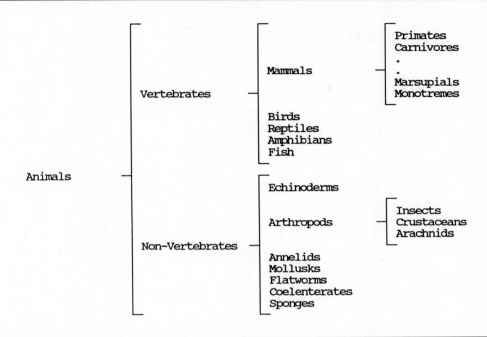

All these examples show a diagram of the entity instances rather than the entity types. For data modeling, other techniques are required to depict a single entity type that plays the dual role of both parent and child in a relationship. One solution is to connect an entity to itself, as in Figure 11–16. The relationship connector is of the one-to-many type, indicating that a parent may have many children and that each child has at most one parent. Another solution is to adopt the previous technique and transform the relationship of the entity to itself into another entity. This solution is appropriate when the relationship bears attributes, as in a bill of materials (see Figures 11–17 and 11–18). (Another reason a bill of materials should be represented as illustrated is that a subassembly may actually have several parents. For example, a nut, washer, and bolt subassembly may be used in several parts of an engine. The bill of materials is therefore not a strict hierarchy, as a child may have several parents. However, the data model representation can use the same techniques—either an entity related to itself with a many-to-many relationship, as in Figure 11–19, or a parent-child entity representing the relationship.)

Representing a hierarchical relationship by a parent-child entity has a twofold advantage. First, data about the relationship can be captured. For

Figure 11–14 Sample Hierarchy: Organization Chart of an Enterprise

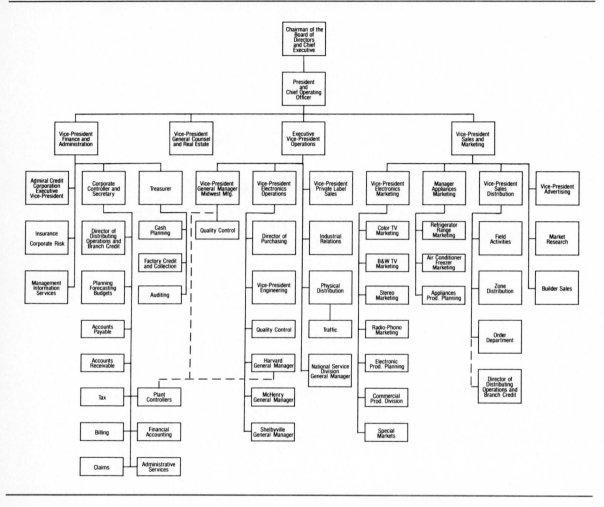

instance, in the bill of materials example, the number of parts of a certain type that enter into a subassembly can be indicated. Second, the data base designer will not inadvertently omit the possibility of navigating the data base in both directions, from product to elementary parts as well as from elementary parts to subassemblies and products.

The representation may seem somewhat artificial. It is certainly more difficult to understand intuitively than the other examples in this section. Thus, the technique is not appropriate for communicating with users. A

Figure 11–15 **Sample Hierarchy: Bill of Materials**

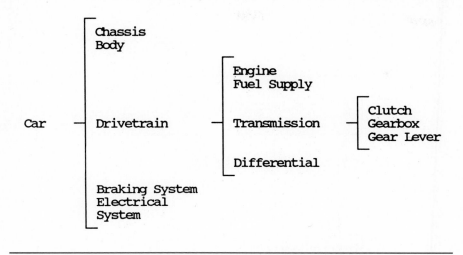

much more appropriate technique for that purpose is the relationship between an entity and itself described earlier (see Figure 11–19).

Once the designer has applied all these transformations, the data model consists of named entities and relationships that are, at worst, one-to-many. It is still in accord with the DFDs established during the requirements analysis phase. In

Figure 11–16 **Data Model for a Hierarchy**

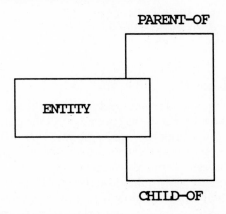

Figure 11–17 **Data Model for a Bill of Materials**

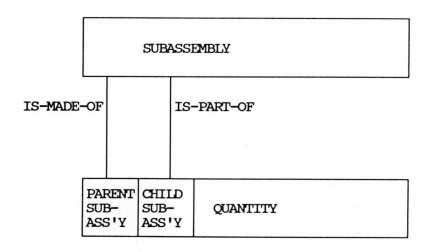

fact, this whole process could have been part of the requirements analysis phase and can certainly be done independently of user interface design and process design.

Selecting Attributes

As the design has progressed, some preliminary work on data attributes has already been done. Now is the time to enumerate all the attributes of each entity completely. This step can only be accomplished with reference to the user interface and the process design activities. For each interface—screen, report, form—the designer assigns each data element to the entity that it characterizes. Then, for each process or activity, the designer checks that all the data logically required to obtain the output data flow is present as an input data flow or in a data store.

Figure 11–18 **Examples of Entities and Relationships
in a Bill of Materials**

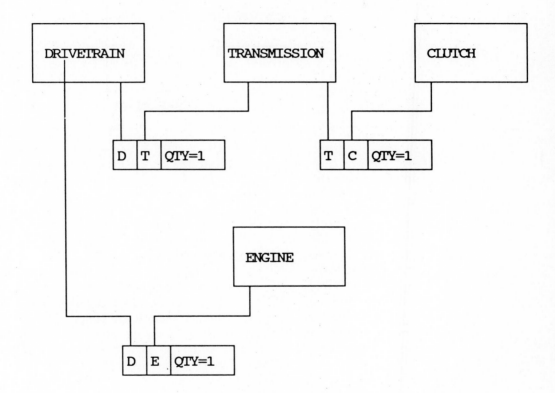

Figure 11–19 **Simplified Data Model for a Bill of Materials**

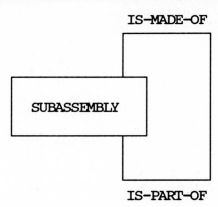

This approach is sufficient in many transaction processing systems that support clerical activities, rather than managerial, marketing, or professional ones. In other cases, there are two pitfalls to be avoided.

The first one is the inclusion of data that will not be used. Especially in marketing-oriented systems, there is a temptation to store information about a customer that might prove useful in selling, analyzing sales statistics, planning promotional campaigns, etc. Unless this information is actually used in taking orders, it will almost certainly become outdated. For instance, an insurance company might wish to store information about a policyholder's family, so as to propose new forms of coverage as the children grow older. However, in the ordinary course of paying annual premiums, the average policyholder will not report family events such as births and deaths to the insurance company. It is up to the insurance agent to maintain a relationship with those policyholders who may be of future interest. The computer application may help the agent by maintaining a sort of scratch-pad area in the policyholder file for the agent to note interesting facts. If the policyholder should change agents (as a result of a move, for example), the new agent would have to renew the scratch-pad area. This information is not guaranteed to be complete and reliable, and should probably not be used for personalized mass mailings directly to the customers.

Two criteria can be used to determine which data can reasonably be kept up to date:

- If an organization does not update a data element as a direct result of day-to-day business activity, then the value of that data element will become incorrect.

- If no person or application depends on the value of the data element to achieve a stated objective, then the value of the data element will become incorrect. If a data element on a utility's customer file is "profession" and is used only to derive statistics of electricity usage by profession, there will be a high percentage of incorrect "profession" codes on the file.

The second pitfall to be avoided is the inclusion of data that is not owned by anyone. If no one is assigned specific responsibilities for keeping the information on the data base up to date, the data base will become out of date. Each group of data elements on each record, each attribute of each entity, should be the responsibility of a specific individual within the organization. If the information is used by only one function, then the individual accomplishing that function is its owner. If several users or applications use the data, then one of them must be designated principal owner and take the responsibility for keeping the data accurate. Unless this safeguard is established, the data will become inaccurate over time. The risk of such inaccuracies is particularly high for subject data bases (see Chapter 5).

Most user departments do not view a file or a data base as a composite object over which control is shared. Therefore, the data structure may have to be presented to users as though each subject data base were divided into as many parts as there are functional groups responsible for maintaining it. The implementation may still be a single data base, but the users will have multiple views of it.

Assigning Attributes to Entities

The assignment of attributes to entities should be the most economical possible. In other words, no elementary application event or transaction should require a given element to be updated in more than one place. This technique will ultimately assure the objective of minimum data redundancy. If a given event can update the same data element in two or more places, a situation will eventually arise where one place has been updated and the other has not, thus causing an inconsistency.

Two examples of how data redundancy might occur are useful.

Inheritance of a Modifiable Attribute. An order item must contain the order number (to group the entire order together in a single delivery), a product code (to know which product has been ordered), and a quantity. Should it also contain the unit price of the product? If it does, the unit price has been *inherited* by the order item from the product.

The intuitive answer is that the order item should not contain the unit price, because it would be redundant information: the price is already recorded on the product data base in a product record. It is common information to all those order items for the given product (see Figure 11–20).

A deeper analysis would pose the question: What happens if there is a price change? Obviously, the product data base must be updated to reflect the change. But are current orders—not yet delivered, or delivered but not yet billed— affected by the change? Is the price change retroactive? If the price is guaranteed when the order is taken, then the price attribute of the order item is subtly

Figure 11–20　**Inheritance of an Attribute Value: The Unit Price**

Order No.	Line No.	Product No.	Qty.
11764	01	751A	5

Ordered on 6.3

Product No.	Description	Price
751A	2″ Widget	1.85

New Price: 1.79 on 6.5

different from that of the product entity. The price on the order is no longer the current price of the product, whatever that happens to be, but the guaranteed price for this order. It can only change if the specific guarantee represented by that specific order changes (see Figure 11–21).

Another possibility is that prices are those in effect at delivery date. Thus, undelivered orders should not contain the price, but orders delivered and not yet billed should (see Figure 11–22).

A possible way out is to maintain a price history on the product data base, with each price accompanied by its effective date (see Figure 11–23). Then, the application logic could examine the date of the order, the date of delivery, and other fields to determine which of the multiple prices on the data base is to be used when printing the invoice.

In all cases, any sales statistics data (for the MIS component of the application) must be based on the amount actually billed. This amount cannot change as product prices change but could change only as a result of the individual invoice being renegotiated with the customer.

A solution might be to include in the product data base multiple versions of the price, each with an effective date. This solution could be generalized to any modification of data attributes. The result would be the storage of the initial state of the data base together with all its modifications, each at the date at which it had occurred. Every time a piece of data was needed, the program could go back to the initial state and trace all the modifications to that piece of data. Although this solution is theoretically possible, it is hardly economical.

Figure 11–21 **Binding the Inherited Unit Price at Order Time**

Order No.	Line No.	Product No.	Qty.	Price
11764	01	751A	5	1.85

Ordered on 6.3

Product No.	Description	Price
751A	2″ Widget	1.85

New Price 1.79 on 6.5

This discussion illustrates an important point. If the multiple versions of each price were to be stored, according to entity-relationship analysis canons, the price would become an entity and would be in a one-to-many relationship with the product. Any other attribute that can change over the life of an entity could be processed the same way (see Figure 11–24). *Whether or not to do so is a totally arbitrary decision.* As a result, any attribute could potentially need to be isolated in its own entity. The difference between attributes and entities becomes very blurred.

Inclusion of an Attribute that Is a Noun, Not an Adjective. Redundancy might occur in another way. An address of a customer, employee, or supplier is usually considered as a single attribute or group of attributes, decomposed into street, city, state, zip code. The subdivision is mainly to allow the address to be printed on multiple lines. The street itself does not have any significance if taken without the city. It is obviously redundant to store both the zip code and the state, or both the address and the zip code, or both the city and the state. However, if the customer address changes, all of it changes at the same time. Never does the state change without a change of zip code and city. Nor does any element in the address change for several customers in the same elementary transaction. Or is this true?

After World War II, free municipal elections were held in France. Practically all the new municipal councils decided to honor one or more war heroes by renaming the largest streets or central squares. Left-wing municipalities usually decided to honor communist resistance heroes, such as Roger-Salengro and

Figure 11–22 **Binding the Inherited Unit Price at Delivery Time**

Order No.	Line No.	Product No.	Qty.
11764	01	751A	5

Ordered on 6.3

Order No.	Line No.	Product No.	Qty.	Price
11764	01	751A	5	1.79

Billed on 6.10

Product No.	Description	Price
751A	2″ Widget	1.85

New Price 1.79 on 6.5

Gabriel Péri; right-wingers preferred Generals Leclerc and de Gaulle. Here is a case of an elementary transaction—a street name change—affecting multiple records in the data base. Conceptually, it would be possible to devise a data base where all the addresses on the same street used the same street name record so that a change of street name could be done in a single update. This issue does not arise in most transaction processing systems, because it is so exceptional and because the customer is usually responsible for a change of address.

In reality, we do not question that the street name is an attribute of a customer, whereas we could more rigorously consider it an attribute of a geographical location (see Figure 11–25), which is an attribute of a customer. This argument is not to encourage this sort of analysis on every single data attribute. Rather, it is to show that the data structure of a system is determined by those functions and events that fall within its scope. If street name changes are forgotten in the scope, nothing serious is likely to befall the application. However, if price changes are forgotten or if the right questions are not asked about about how price changes are applied, something might be seriously amiss by the time the system is ready.

Figure 11–23 **Avoiding Inheritance by Storing Multiple Values of the Price**

Order No.	Line No.	Product No.	Qty.
11764	01	751A	5

Product No.	Description
751A	2″ Widget

Product No.	Effective Date	Price
751A	12.2.88	1.74
751A	3.6.89	1.85
751A	6.5.89	1.79

This example also illustrates the relative arbitrariness of the distinction between an attribute and an entity. A data element such as a street could be considered as either, depending on the functions or events that the designers consider to be of interest to the system.

BOTTOM-UP ANALYSIS

Bottom-up analysis is done either when the project is initially identified (during systems planning or during a feasibility study) or during requirements analysis. Normally, it is done in the latter phase, because it tends to be too time consuming in the planning stages.

Figure 11–24 **Storing Each Modifiable Attribute as an Entity**

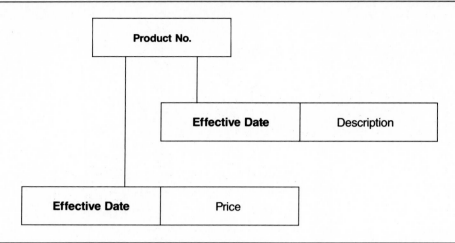

Starting Points

The best starting point for a bottom-up analysis of data structures is the existing system, if one exists. If the analysis is done during a systems planning project, the best starting point is to look at the information on **forms and reports** that the organization exchanges with the outside world—suppliers, customers, employees, regulatory agencies, industry organizations, and competitors. The analyst can then list all the elements of information on the various forms and reports and try to relate them as attributes to the entities (people, organizations) with which the information is exchanged or to the entities (transactions) represented by the form (orders, invoices, payments). Interviews with middle management will help clarify the meaning of the pieces of information on the forms and their mutual relationships. As in top-down analysis, a useful question to ask is "How many Xs can Y have?" Another is "How can the value of X change?"

Figure 11–25 **Storing Street as a Separate Entity**

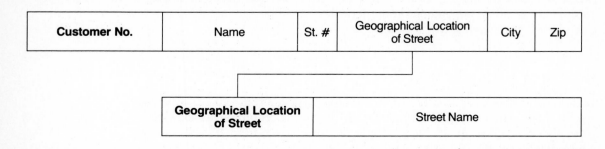

BOX 11-2

Integrating Data, Text, Voice, and Graphics

This book only covers classical data bases, containing formatted records of string and numeric variables. Many applications imaginable today would benefit from enriching the data base with other forms of information. For instance, an insurance company might like to have a data base with the data about a customer, his or her various policies, a textual description of a claim (such as an auto accident), copies of the correspondence exchanged, voice annotations made in the margins of the text by the claims adjuster, a map of the scene of the accident, and a picture of the damaged automobile.

Today, it is quite possible to store this kind of information on magnetic or optical media. There is a cost associated with the equipment required to transcribe the information—optical and audio digitizers, for instance—and an even higher cost associated with the storage of all the bits required. For instance, a voice annotation of 30 words would require 10,000 to 50,000 bits of storage, whereas the same information in text form would need less than 2,000 bits.

More of an obstacle is that efficient processing mechanisms are not available to process the relationship between two pieces of data in two different forms. Algorithms are reasonably proficient at processing two-dimensional information, such as that found on graphs, maps, and other schematics, but even these algorithms are usually not available within data base management systems designed to process one-dimensional records. Very few robust algorithms are available that can relate the content of one form of representation (say, voice or image) to another (say, line drawings or numerical data). It is very hard for a program to know that the sound made when someone says "eight" is related to a figure 8 in a photo or to the binary pattern 00001000 in a record.

Most of today's applications of the integration of classical forms of data and richer types such as voice and image are therefore in office automation, which manipulates envelopes or objects without regard to the meaning of their contents. An electronic mail system is indifferent to the content of the messages passed from one subscriber to another. Each recipient of a message must interpret its meaning and its relationship to, say, another message from someone else on a different day.

If bottom-up analysis is done as part of the analysis of a management information system, or of the MIS component of a transaction system, then the analyst should look at the transaction processing system's data stores (files, data bases) and at any existing management reports. In this case, the starting point is the **file and data base records**. The analysts can presume that each record represents an entity. If the file is a direct-access file or a data base, the name of the entity is probably closely related to the name of the key field. If the key is made up of several fields, the entity is probably related to other entities whose keys are the components of the composite field.

The analyst can also analyze data attribute (or data field) names. If two fields in two different records have the same or similar names, there may be a

file and data base records

relationship between the two entities of those two records. Or the information may be stored redundantly, as in the case of the unit price stored both in the order file and the product file. If a field in one record has a similar name to a key in another record, there is almost certainly a one-to-many relationship between the record with the key and the record with the field.

If a record contains repeating fields, each repeating field is probably a separate entity. For instance, if a file contains one amount field per month, then there should be a monthly amount entity containing the month number (date) and an amount field. Even better would be to have a period amount entity, containing the code of the period type (yearly, quarterly, monthly, weekly), the identifier of the period (month number, week number, and so on) and the corresponding amount. If an employee record contains a list of deduction codes, then there should be an employee entity with a one-to-many relationship to an employee deduction entity.

Reviewing existing management reports will probably introduce some new concepts. In particular, management tends to group figures into time periods and significant categories such as customer types, market segments, and geographical areas. Another added concept is that of trends—comparing similar figures for different time periods. In many instances, the patterns are seasonal, and the current period is compared with the same period of last year, rather than, say, this month with last month. Finally, many management reports eliminate the normal and focus on exceptions. This focus does not necessarily introduce new entities and attributes; it merely changes the emphasis.

The understanding that comes from reviewing management reports and management information needs does not necessarily add new entities, relationships, and attributes. It does, however, tend to help the analyst focus on those that are important to management. This fresh perspective on the data will also be helpful in the user interface and process design stages.

Business Function Data Models and User Views

Data design can now proceed from the collection of presumed entities and attributes collected during requirements analysis. If the bottom-up approach is used for a transaction processing system, the designer now analyzes entities and relationships for each process box on the data flow diagrams. Each box represents a business function, and each uses data elements or attributes. For instance, a process such as checking customer credit typically requires the total amount of the order that the customer is trying to place, the outstanding balance, and a list of payment incidents over the past few months or years. This analysis

business function data model

should lead to a partial data model, called a **business function data model,** applicable only to the function itself (see Figure 11–26).

user view

Next, the designer consolidates the business function data models of all the functions normally performed by one user (a single person or an entire department). The resulting data model, also called a **user view**, is a superset of all the business function data models. A problem can arise during this

Figure 11–26 **Business Function Data Model**

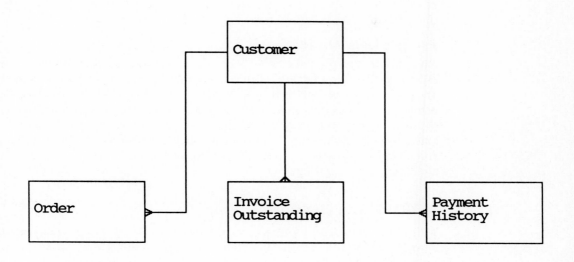

consolidation if there are contradictions among the various business function data models. Such contradictions generally indicate the presence of homonyms—pieces of data called by the same name by different individuals but having different information contents. In other cases, the designer may discover synonyms—the same data called by different names by different people.

One of the most difficult problems occurs when the existing systems and habits of the industry have created very general-purpose entities that hide the details. An example is the bank account. The word *Account* in a bank covers a multitude of different concepts. Each type of account usually corresponds to a particular product or service—checking, money market, loan, or trust, for example. Each of these has different processing characteristics, different attributes, and different relationships. In addition, accounts may have relationships between them. For instance, a loan may be guaranteed by assets that exist in another account, such as a savings account. The loan contract may specify that the amount deposited in the savings account should not be allowed to fall below the outstanding balance on the loan account. This clause is logically an attribute of the loan entity, but it is the savings processing that must enforce it. In such cases, it becomes absolutely necessary to strip away the general behavior of the entities and analyze each subtype in detail. Here is an example where bottom-up analysis is more likely to point out the right direction than top-down analysis.

Project Data Model

Once the user views have been documented, the project data model can be established by consolidating all the user views of the application and doing a top-down analysis of relationship degrees as described earlier. The end result will be the data model for the transaction systems that underlie the MIS or DSS being analyzed. In addition, there will be an analysis of management information requirements such as criteria for summarizing, accumulating amounts by periods, comparing periods for trend evaluation, and exception reporting.

NORMALIZATION

With either approach, top-down or bottom-up, the work done so far should have produced a structure of entities and relationships that obeys certain rules of good behavior. There should be no relationships of degree many-to-many; there should be no repeating groups; and each identified attribute should be associated with the entity that it characterizes in reality. No attribute bound to one entity should inherit its value from another entity through a relationship. For example, the unit price of an order item is inherited from the product entity only until the order pricing is definitively committed to. At that point, the unit price becomes bound to the order item and does not change even if there is a price increase on the product data base.

If this work has been done with sufficient understanding of the business area being modeled, the data model is almost certainly in normalized form. Although most authors consider normalization as a separate step in data modeling, we prefer to regard it as a result of applying common sense and rigorous analysis all along the process. It may be worthwhile to check that the data model actually is in normal form, however. It may be easy, especially for relatively inexperienced personnel, to overlook something.

The rules of normalization are set out in Box 11–3. They are expressed in the traditional form. As a result, they are better adapted to the process of normalizing a set of arbitrarily designed entities than to the verification of a data model established as described above. Each step of normalization corresponds to a normal form. For instance, after Step 1—the creation of a new entity for repeating groups—the data model is said to be in first normal form.

BOX 11–3

Definition of the Five Normal Forms

First Normal Form

A relation is in first normal form (1NF) if it contains no repeating groups.

Repeating groups are sometimes called multi-valued dependencies. Each attribute must have a single, well-defined atomic value, not a set of several values.

Second Normal Form

A relation is in second normal form (2NF) if it is in 1NF and all its attributes depend on the whole key; there are no attributes that depend on part of the key.

This definition only makes sense for entities that have a composite key. If the key is a single attribute, then everything that depends on the key depends on the entire key.

Dependence is defined as follows: if one attribute such as the key has a given value, then the value of the dependent attribute is wholly determined (at a given time). For instance, a unit price is dependent on the product code, not on an order quantity or a marital status.

Third Normal Form

A relation is in third normal form (3NF) if it is in 2NF and all its attributes are nontransitively dependent on the key; there are no attributes that depend on a nonkey attribute that in turn depends on the key.

This definition helps remove so-called hidden keys, attributes that appear as normal attributes in a relation, but that are in reality a key of another relation with a one-to-many relationship to the relationship being considered. An example would be the zip code and the city in an address. If the zip code is known, the city can be determined.

Boyce/Codd Normal Form

A relation is in Boyce/Codd normal form (BCNF) if it is in 2NF and all its determinants

(attributes on which other attributes depend) are candidate keys (attributes that could have been chosen as keys).

This definition is slightly more stringent than the previous one. It introduces the concept of a candidate key. As we shall see in the next chapter, a candidate key is an attribute (or a set of attributes) that identifies a relation uniquely. In some cases, there are several candidate keys for the same relation—any one of them can be chosen. It is fairly clear that what has to hold for the key actually chosen also has to hold for every candidate key not chosen.

Today, 3NF and BCNF are usually considered to be the same by adding the word *candidate* wherever the word *key* is mentioned in the definitions of 2NF and 3NF.

Fourth Normal Form

A relation is in fourth normal form (4NF) if it is in BCNF and it incorporates at most one multivalued dependency.

The problem of 4NF would arise if a relation (before being reduced to 1NF) had two or more independent repeating groups, and only one relation, incorporating both repeating groups, were separated out into a new relation. Such a separation is so counterintuitive that most authors pass over 4NF; it rarely arises in reality.

Fifth Normal Form

A relation is in fifth normal form (5NF) if it is in 4NF and all relations with three attributes or more that cannot be decomposed into two relations have been decomposed into three (or more) relations where possible.

For example, consider this company regulation: If a part used by a department can be supplied by multiple suppliers that supply some other part to the department, then that department must necessarily procure the part from each of those suppliers. The relation that says that a supplier S supplies part P to department D should then be decomposed into three independent relations, between S and D, between S and P, and between P and D. This example was inspired by Chris Date's *Introduction to Database Systems*.[1]

In summary, 3NF is usually considered to be enough. In some cases (illustrated by the zip code/city example), 3NF is not ideal, and 2NF is better. Some data bases can even contravene the 1NF principle without dire consequences. Consider, for example, the case of China, where the overwhelming majority of families have one child and one only. It would be quite admissible, for efficiency purposes, to consider that the family relation should contain all the data about the first child; only second and further children would justify creating a separate record.

For verification purposes, these four steps should be followed:

- Check that there are no many-to-many relationships.

   This check prevents repeating groups of any importance. There may still be repeating groups of data within an entity, but there will be no other entity dependent on each of these repeating groups. In other words, the repeating groups will not carry any relationships. Avoiding repeating groups with relationships is most important to reduce redundancy and make maintenance and evolution easy. On the other hand, no great risks are associated with repeating groups that do not carry relationships. For instance, if a customer may have up to four different addresses, they may be stored with the customer entity as Address-1, Address-2, Address-3, and Address-4. Some addresses would be left blank for those customers who have fewer than four.

   A customer order can be used as a counterexample. At a high level, an order item could legitimately be considered as a many-to-many relationship between customers and products. Each customer may order many products; each product may be ordered by many customers. The risks of storing an order as a repeating group of lines within the customer, however, are great. It will in particular become difficult or costly to answer questions such as "Which customer has product so-and-so on order?" In addition, if each customer could have only one order at a time, the data structure would be different than if the customer could have several orders simultaneously. The data structure of the repeating groups in the customer record might even influence the design of the product data base. The data design would become too tightly integrated and be too costly to change. Enforcing first normal form in this example would eliminate most of these problems.

- Check for inherited attributes.

   This check consists in reviewing attribute names that are the same or nearly the same in two or more entity types. If these are true attributes (that is, neither of them is an identifier such as customer number, order number, product code, or social security number), a determination should be made as to whether the value of the attribute in one of the entities is inherited from one of the other entities. Inheritance occurs when, at the creation of one entity, some attributes are copied from another entity that already exists. For example, when an order is entered, all the characteristics of the product ordered as an item on an order line are copied from the product entity.

Inheritance should occur only at the exact time when the attribute value becomes bound to the inheriting entity. The product price, for instance, should be copied to (inherited by) the order item entity when the price is irrevocably agreed on. The color or weight of an order item should be copied as soon as the actual product is shipped. After that, the color and the weight can no longer be changed by an event in the order entry system.

- Check for redundancy of attributes.

    Attribute redundancy (the same value of the same attribute of the same entity stored in several places) occurs when a single event causes the same update to be made in several entities. The meaning of *same* here is the same attribute name, the same value before update, and the same value after update. For instance, if the event were renaming 6th Avenue to Avenue of the Americas in New York, this change would have to be made to all the places where the street name was, precisely, "6th Avenue" and the city "New York."

    If this type of redundancy is found, hidden inheritance may be the problem. To resolve it, a new entity type must be created from which the existing entities can inherit the value at the proper time. If the event that would cause such an update is too rare or remote from the application, it may be decided not to resolve the redundancy.

    These two analysis techniques will check that the model is in second normal form.

- Check for derived data.

    In some cases, one attribute in an entity is a simple function of other attributes in the entity (or inherited by the entity). An example is the extended price on an order item, which can be deduced very simply by multiplying the unit price by the quantity. To store the extended price is useless and can indeed cause errors, because it can only change as the result of some other attribute (price or quantity) changes.

    In other cases, there is a more complex function. For instance, the monthly payment on a mortgage can be calculated from the principal, the length, and the interest rate. The base attributes are unlikely to change except in the event of refinancing or an adjustment in a variable rate at the end of a fixed period. Furthermore, the calculation is a resource-consuming one. Thus, it is legitimate to store the result, the monthly payment amount, even though it is theoretically redundant.

    Another case is that of the zip code. The zip code is strictly speaking a function of the city and street address, and there are publicly available data bases that can yield the correct zip code every time the address is printed.

Again, the cost of doing so may be prohibitive considering the risk and cost associated with redundant data. The person or organization whose address is stored is perfectly willing to supply the redundant data every time the address changes.

The application of this analysis will ensure that the structure is in third normal form.

Ensuring that a data model conforms to fourth and fifth normal forms is not frequently a problem. Infractions against fourth normal form arise when there are two different repeating attributes in the same entity and both have been split out into the same separate entity (which is in a one-to-many relationship with the original, owning entity). If the designer has named the relationships so as to convey their business meaning, this infraction will not occur. Nor is it probable that violations of fifth normal form will occur. In fact, if the analyst thoroughly understands what the entities are, their behavior, their real-world relationships, and their patterns of change, the data model is likely to be fully normalized before checking begins.

A simple way to express that a data model is fully normalized is the following: Each attribute in an entity depends on the key, the whole key, and nothing but the key.[2]

Analysis of Probable Changes

The final step in creating the entity-relationship model is to consider the future. This step is generally omitted, because few IS development departments worry about creating maintainable systems early enough in the life cycle. However, from experience, change analysis is the single most powerful way to make maintenance easier. Change is inevitable, both in the world and in the systems dealing with the world. Thus, a data designer should anticipate changes to the designs, because these changes are far more likely to have a major impact on the system than a simple functional change.

Generally, files and data bases are shared by many users and many programs. It is more likely for many programs to need maintenance if a data base structure changes than if a single function changes. For instance, in 1988, there was a change in the formula for computing FICA withholding on employer-provided life insurance. This instance constitutes a logic change, not a data structure change. For properly built payroll systems, the modification was not difficult to implement. Implementing a flexible benefits program where none existed before would be much more difficult, because new files and new record types would be required. In many cases, programs that do not process flexible benefits at all would still feel the impact of the new data base structure.

If the designer can anticipate that a given change will occur, both the old and the new function can be built into the system and the actual change can be made with very little disruption. However, anticipating every change in this way is not possible. Furthermore, some changes are too remote to be worth the added cost of building them into the system. Nevertheless, those systems that have been analyzed and designed with change in mind are much easier to maintain.

Changes to the **degree of relationships** should be the main objective of the analysis of probable changes, not because such changes are frequent, but because they can be very disruptive unless planned for.

degree of relationships

A typical example is a system designed so that any customer can have only one order recorded in the system. This design might result in the order header information being made part of the customer entity. But the customer may need to place another order before the first one is delivered and, therefore, have two order headers. Or the customer might want delivery on part of the order at one date and another part at another date. If this is realized after the design is completed, the data structure will need to be changed radically.

The questions that must be asked when analyzing possible changes in relationship degrees are usually of the form: "How many Xs for each Y?" "Now?" "In the future?" The objects (Xs) are typically locations (delivery address, distribution depots, manufacturing locations, departments versus office buildings) or transactions (orders per customer, parts per supplier or per purchase order). The Ys are more typically persons or organizations.

A very helpful tactic for anticipating change is to **look to the industry leaders** to see how they are organized; if they are truly leaders, they represent the future direction of the industry. Another tactic is to look at other countries. Differences in legislation lead to different forms of organization. For instance, a few years ago, branch banking was the exception in the United States, the norm in Europe and Japan. Changes in banking law have made branches more and more common in the United States. Systems built in the seventies with the assumption that the U. S. banking industry might move to branch banking have been much more resilient than those that did not make the assumption.

look to the industry leaders

The last approach to anticipating change is to **analyze what can cause changes**: management fiat, regulatory agency action, the economic environment, changes in human behavior patterns. These types of change are enumerated in the sequence of how easily the change can be made, not necessarily how easily a system can be changed to accommodate it. It is needless to justify expensive features enabling an application to change in order to accommodate a change in human nature or even a cultural change (such as computer literacy) that may take a generation to become prevalent.

analyze what can cause changes

Summary

Entity-relationship modeling consists in creating graphic representations of the data entities about which data will be stored and about the relationships between those entities. In addition, a list of the data attributes for each entity is created. This documentation (schematic and lists) is called a data model or an entity-relationship model.

In some cases, an existing corporate data model shows global entities and relationships without much detailed information. Such a model is a valuable starting point for creating an initial project data model during the requirements analysis phase. The initial project data model is suitable for communicating data structure information between analysts and users. The schematics are usually understandable without very much specialized competence.

In the absence of preexisting, higher-level data models, the analyst must build the project data model from scratch during requirements analysis. This work is often done in a group session, with middle-level user management as one of the key participants. Another approach is more akin to interviewing; the analyst collects all the documents that the organization exchanges with the outside world and identifies natural groupings of data from this knowledge.

In data design, the initial project model is refined by applying various analysis techniques to the initial model. Mainly, this work consists in making sure that all relationships are of degree one-to-many, if necessary by splitting or combining entities. Any exceptions to the one-to-many rule must be justified. Then, all the required data attributes are assigned to the various entities that have been identified.

The previous applies best to transaction processing applications. In MIS or DSS applications, bottom-up analysis is often more realistic. This has the benefit of formalizing a third level of entity-relationship model, the user view. The user view differs from the project data model in that its scope is reduced to that of one user or a series of users who perform the same functions. The user view is of most benefit in MIS/DSS applications, where different users usually have a greater variety of perspectives on the data than do the operators of a transaction processing application.

Because many systems built today have characteristics of both transaction processing and MIS/DSS, a combination of the two approaches is usually the best solution.

The analyst then creates a final project data model and checks it for adherence to third normal form. Any discrepancies are resolved or justified. Finally, the model is reviewed with respect to changes that may be expected to occur in the data structure over the lifetime of the application. If possible, these changes are reflected in the data model itself, so that should a change occur, it will be easily implemented.

The project data model derived in this fashion should have the following property: each attribute stored about an entity is truly a characteristic of that entity and that entity alone. This property eliminates data redundancy, with its attendant storage cost and risks of integrity loss.

Selected Readings

Practically all the books in this bibliography are primarily about data base design as opposed to data design, because data design has not been sufficiently recognized as a discipline independent of data base design. Data design must be done by people who understand the application; data base design must be done by people who understand data base technology. Only rarely do people have both qualifications.

Date, Chris. *An Introduction to Database Systems*, 4th ed. Reading, Massachusetts: Addison-Wesley, 1986.

This book is excellent, covering both relational and nonrelational technology. It is fairly technical, however, especially in Part Two. Recommended for a deep understanding of the issues of data design seen from the data base viewpoint.

Gane, Chris. *Rapid System Development*. New York: Rapid System Development, Inc., 1987.

This book is written from a very functional, application-oriented perspective by one of the early proponents of data flow diagrams as a tool for analyzing processes. As a result, Gane maintains proper balance and perspective.

Martin, James, and Finkelstein, Clive. *Information Engineering*. London, UK: Savant Institute, 1981.

This book is written by two of the foremost advocates of basing the analysis of systems on data structures, almost to the point of neglecting processes. Although lacking in balance, it is a good book on information engineering techniques, in particular those underlying some of the CASE tools on the market.

Inmon, W. H. *Information Systems Architecture*. Englewood Cliffs, New Jersey: Prentice-Hall, 1986.

Despite its title, this book is essentially about data design. It also covers process modeling, but in contrast to Gane's book, it is heavily inspired by data analysis. The book contains some nonstandard terminology and abbreviations, but once you have overcome the initial effort to interpret them, it has a wealth of interesting examples.

Shlear, Sally, and Mellor, Stephen J. *Object-Oriented Systems Analysis*. Englewood Cliffs, New Jersey: Yourdon Press, 1988.

The title of this book is somewhat misleading; it has nothing to do with object-oriented design and programming as embodied in certain modern languages such as Smalltalk. It is, in fact, one of the only books that deals more with data design than with data base design. It has excellent examples of how to identify entities and attributes and how to analyze cardinalities of relationships.

Ross, Ronald G. *Entity Modeling: Techniques and Application*. Boston, Massachusetts: Database Research Group, 1987.

This book is one of the most complete about data modeling. Ronald Ross is also the editor and publisher of the Data Base Newsletter, *a periodical for both data designers and data base designers.*

Review Questions

1. What is the difference between a corporate data model and a project data model? What is shown on each that is not shown on the other? Use examples to illustrate.

2. What differentiates the top-down approach from the bottom-up approach?

3. Is it always possible to dissociate a many-to-many relationship into two one-to-many relationships?

4. Draw an entity-relationship diagram for a family tree such as that established by a genealogist. (Use your own family as a starting point.) Are there entities that could conveniently be subdivided in to subentities or grouped into superentities? How is the relationship of cousin represented? Is the model likely to change in the future?

Discussion Questions

1. Why is it difficult to analyze MIS needs in a top-down fashion?

2. In relation to the genealogy exercise above, discuss whether the cousin relationship can be seen as a user view. Show that a bottom-up design is more likely to have elicited the relationship between cousins than a top-down design.

3. Using group dynamics techniques, establish an initial data model (which can contain many-to-many relationships) for a business such as a local cable TV distributor. Consider customers, locations, equipment (decoders and remote controls but not the actual cable, which we assume has been drawn already), and suppliers (TV stations).

Group the class into two projects. Let one refine the data model using relationship analysis techniques. Let the other use the rules of normalization successively from 1 to 3 (4 and 5 will probably not arise). Are there any differences in the results? Discuss why or why not, as the case may be.

Mini-Case

You are an analyst for Condor Telephone Company. You have been assigned to analyze and design a new service order entry system for Condor.

Figures 11–27 through 11–30 are documents describing the scope of the new system and some of the functions to be performed. Initially, only the service order entry part of the application is to be implemented; service scheduling and billing will come later.

Question for Discussion

1. Create a complete project data model for the service order entry project. This model will include all the entities, relationships, and attributes required to perform the functions as described. When completed, you should check that the data model is in third normal form.

Figure 11–27 **Scope of the Condor Telephone Company Service Order System**

MARKETING ORDER ENTRY	CONDOR TELEPHONE COMPANY ORDER ENTRY SYSTEM SCOPE	CD-20 SCOPE

PREPARED BY: DENNIS CASH	DATE: 27AUG88	VERSION: 1	PAGE 1
APPROVED BY: J. MALINOWSKI	DATE: 05SEP88	STATUS : F	

The Service Order Entry System processes orders from customers to perform telephone equipment and service installations.

There are six types of service requests:

- new connect
- complete disconnect
- transfer existing service to new location
- temporary disconnect
- restore service after temporary disconnect
- change to existing service/equipment.

The most frequent case is that orders are called in to the Business Office where a service representative (SR) takes the order. For existing customers, the SR asks the customer for one of his telephone numbers and looks up the customer data. If a new location is involved, the SR makes a note of it. (Each customer may have any number of locations.)

If it is a new customer, all the relevant data (name, location, service request) are first obtained. Before scheduling the installation, a credit check is performed. The SR must obtain credit data, either from another telephone company where the customer currently has or has had service, or, if the customer has never had telephone service, other credit references such as charge cards, etc. The required data is obtained from the customer over the telephone, and provisional arrangements are made for the installation.

If the service is on existing equipment, the customer records are reviewed to determine the exact location and complete description of the equipment being serviced.

Figure 11–28 **Order Entry Function Description**

MARKETING ORDER ENTRY	CONDOR TELEPHONE COMPANY ORDER ENTRY	CD-20 FUNCD

PREPARED BY:	DENNIS CASH	DATE:	27AUG88	VERSION:	1	PAGE 1
APPROVED BY:	J. MALINOWSKI	DATE:	05SEP88	STATUS :	F	

Service Representatives will respond to Customer Service Requests by
phone. To initiate a Service Order, the following data will be
captured:

-    Customer Data (name, address, historical data)
-    Service/Equipment Data (service type, equipment)

For existing customers, the Service Representative will look up the
customer data during the contact, and verify that all the information
stored about the customer is current. Any errors will be corrected
and reviewed with the customer.

For new customers, a temporary customer number will be assigned by
the system, and the Service Representative will enter all the
required data.

This function must be completed before service and equipment charges
are reviewed and credit application information is obtained.

Figure 11–29 **Credit History Function Description**

```
MARKETING                    CONDOR TELEPHONE COMPANY              CD-20
ORDER ENTRY                                                       FUNCD
                                CREDIT HISTORY
```

PREPARED BY: DENNIS CASH	DATE: 27AUG88	VERSION: 1	PAGE 1
APPROVED BY: J. MALINOWSKI	DATE: 05SEP88	STATUS : F	

For all new customers, credit application information must be obtained. The following is needed over the past five years:

- Address

- Previous telephone service

- Employer

- Major credit cards.

The system will generate a letter to any telephone company with which the customer has had service, requesting a credit check.

Figure 11–30 **Equipment Inventory Check Function Description**

```
MARKETING                     CONDOR TELEPHONE COMPANY              CD-20
ORDER ENTRY                                                         FUNCD
                              EQUIPMENT INVENTORY CHECK
```

```
PREPARED BY:  DENNIS CASH      DATE:  27AUG88    VERSION:  1    PAGE 1
APPROVED BY:  J. MALINOWSKI    DATE:  05SEP88    STATUS :  F
```

When customer data and possibly credit data has been obtained, the
following is done:

-    for new equipment, inventory is checked to see whether the
     equipment is available

-    for existing equipment, the location and the precise nature of
     the equipment to be serviced is ascertained. This is
     particularly important where the customer has several pieces of
     equipment installed at the same location

-    charges are reviewed, both the one-time service charge, the
     charge for future services (such as a reconnect of a temporary
     disconnect), and the equipment rental charge in case of a new
     equipment or permanent disconnect.

The service charge varies by type of service and type of equipment. The
charge for temporarily disconnecting a PBX is higher than for a
residential telephone; the charge for reconnecting is smaller than for
disconnecting.

References

1. Date, Chris. *An Introduction to Database Systems,* 4th ed. Reading, Massachusetts: Addison-Wesley, 1986.

2. Kent, W. "A Simple Guide to Five Normal Forms in Relational Database Theory." *Communications of the ACM* (February 1983): 120.

Chapter 12

Data Element Design

Chapter 12 describes the design of four different characteristics of data elements: names, data types, the use of data elements as keys, and the use of data elements as codes. In this part of the design, the methodology has no fixed sequence. The analyst can carry out the work in any order, although data naming should probably be carried out first.

What is critical is that data element design has to be performed by an analyst. It cannot be left to each individual programmer. Also, the analysts must observe great discipline in documenting the work. A mechanized data dictionary (see the Technique at the end of this section) is invaluable.

Learning Objectives

- Assign meaningful names to data elements.
- Group data elements in meaningful data types.
- Design the representation of data elements and coding schemes that users and programmers will be aware of, and ensure that this representation remains independent of the physical representation used on external data files.
- Use the coding schemes designed for users and other data elements to assign keys (identifiers) to entities in a manner consistent with data base design and user query and reporting requirements.
- Use tables to represent coding schemes.

NAMING DATA ELEMENTS: HOMONYMS, SYNONYMS, AND QUALIFIERS

A large part of the implementation effort of a system is devoted to programming. Whereas each programmer works alone on a single program or module, all the data definitions are shared by all the programmers. Therefore, good data-naming discipline must be followed. Data items—elements, groups, records, files—are named by analysts or data administrators in the data design phase. Most programming standards call for the programmer to use these names exclusively.

homonyms

Poor naming usually results in three types of problems. **Homonyms**, the worst problem, may have an effect even on the design of the system, because it can be a major obstacle in communicating with users. In ordinary usage, homonyms are words that look alike but differ in meaning. In data design, the term refers to using the same name for two pieces of data that are in reality different. Homonyms may occur when one department adopts a technical term as a shortcut and another department uses the same term, or a very similar one, to mean something different. For instance, the arrival date of a shipment in a data base that tracks shipping history with various transport firms might in fact consist of several dates: arrival of ship in harbor, release of goods from customs, or availability in the warehouse. If these three dates were in fact used by different departments and possibly stored in different entities, the homonym problem (ARRIVAL-DATE meaning three different things) would be severe.[1]

Homonyms can also cause problems when an attribute is the identifier or key of an entity and at the same time is used in another entity to implement the relationship between the two. For instance, a supplier number might appear in a purchase order entity and in the supplier entity. These two attributes have the same type. They do not have quite the same meaning, however. In the supplier entity, the supplier number means "identifier of the entity to which all the attributes in this entity apply." In the purchase order, it means "identifier of the supplier who placed the purchase order that is identified by the purchase order number elsewhere in this entity."

Once a case of homonyms has been found, the problem is solved by qualifying the data names, i.e., by appending to the common name a word or phrase that is different for each homonym. For example, the three arrival dates in the transportation example could be named HARBOR_ARRIVAL_DATE, CUSTOMS_ARRIVAL_DATE, and WAREHOUSE_ARRIVAL_DATE. The usual technique is to put the qualifier first and the common part last. The qualifier often refers to the entity in which the data element resides: for instance, in the supplier and purchase order example, the name for the two versions of the supplier number might be ORDER_SUPPLIER_NO and SUPPLIER_NO.

synonyms

Another problem is **synonyms.** Synonyms are two different names for the same thing. The problem is much less serious than homonyms. However, some discipline is required to make sure that all synonyms, or aliases, are recorded in the data dictionary. When maintenance is performed on a data element that has synonyms, it is necessary to search for uses of both the primary name and the synonym within the system to make sure that all the possible consequences of a modification to a data item have been evaluated.

excessive abbreviation

Very often, especially in old programs, data names are difficult to understand because of **excessive abbreviation.** Part of the reason is that early programming languages were limited to eight-character names. In addition, most programmers do not care to use long names, which are time consuming and error-prone. Some IS departments even impose the use of abbreviations because of the data entry cost associated with long names!

The arguments against verbosity and length are still valid to some extent. Most programming standards acknowledge, however, that the value of explicit naming more than makes up for the cost. As a compromise, a set of standard abbreviations is often agreed on; this solution encourages brevity without sacrificing clarity. A sample list of abbreviations is given in Figure 12–1.

The best solution for all these problems is to give the responsibility for naming standards (or even for the actual naming) to a special section within the IS department, called **data administration**. On large projects, a data adminis- **data** trator may be assigned full time during the data design phase of a project. In **administration** smaller departments or on smaller projects the function of data administrator is usually performed by one of the analysts part time. In no case should individual programmers be given the freedom to name data elements.

The coordination of data naming should be ensured by a single individual or a closely knit group, such as data administration. Coordination can prevent problems not only within the system being developed, but also in future, related systems.

DATA TYPE ANALYSIS

Data type analysis can help prevent maintenance problems because it promotes *data hiding*. The principle of data hiding is that the user of any data element should have to make as few assumptions as possible about how the data element is represented in memory or on disk. The user, whether a person or a program, should be concerned with the meaning of the data, not with its form. Unnecessary information about the data should be hidden.

Definition of Data Types

A data type is a class of data items that is homogeneous enough that all the data items of the type support the same operations. This concept of data types originated because the primitive data processing operations, those that are built into the hardware or the programming language, are constrained to work on data items that are homogeneous. For instance, it is possible to compare two variables containing numbers, perform arithmetic operations on them, and assign them new values. Assignments and comparisons may also be performed on text variables.

Another way to say that two data attributes are of the same type is to say that they have the same domain of values. This definition of a data type is slightly less powerful than the previous one. It is important, however, to specify the domain of each data type in the data model.

The following two examples illustrate the problem of incompatible data types. First, if an employee file contains the social security number of each

Figure 12–1 **Frequently Used Data Name Abbreviations**

ACCR	Accrual; Accrued
ACCT	Account; Accounting
ACCUM	Accumulated
ADDR	Address
AMT	Amount
BAL	Balance
BOM	Bill of Materials
CGR	Compound Growth Rate
CLI	Client
CO	Company
CORP	Corporation; Corporate
CR	Credit
CUM	Cumulative
CUST	Customer
DEPT	Department
DIV	Division
DT	Debit
EMP	Employee
FYE	Fiscal Year End
INVC	Invoice
INVN	Inventory
MO	Month
MTD	Month-to-Date
NO	Number
ORD	Order
PO	Purchase Order
PROD	Product
QTY	Quantity
RECD	Record
RECV	Received; Receiving
SEQ	Sequence
SER	Serial
SUPP	Supplier
TRANS	Transaction
WK	Week
YR	Year
YTD	Year-to-Date

employee stored as a number with nine digits, the hardware would allow a program to add the social security numbers of two employees and store the result. (An additional digit might be needed to accommodate a possible carry.) Most programming languages would also allow this addition. However, the result of this addition has no meaning whatever. The semantics of the application (payroll, personnel, or other) do not contain an addition operation on social security numbers.

The second example is the comparison of two fields, such as a name and a street address, that appear to have compatible types. Both are alphanumeric; in a given application, they might have the same length, say 30 characters. But to compare them, although possible from a syntactical viewpoint, makes no sense. What difference would it make to a user to know whether a customer has a street address that is the same as the customer's name?

As shown in these examples, data type analysis consists in identifying those attributes that will support the primitive operation of comparison. Two data attributes that may have the same values or that have values that can be ranked as greater or less than each other are of the same type.

If two attributes can be compared, then the contents of a variable of the type of the attribute can generally be moved into another variable of the same type. This operation is called assignment.

If the data type is numeric, then arithmetic operations may possibly be defined on it as well. As the social security number example above showed, this possibility is not as evident as one might think at first. The term *numeric* does not always mean that the variable represents a number of things, an amount, or a quantity. The term quite often refers to a variable that is arbitrarily constrained to taking on only a subset of all the possible characters in a representation scheme.

Examples of Data Types: Date

Type analysis makes no assumption whatever about how data will be represented on files, screens, forms, and reports. Thus, for example, a date is a date, regardless of whether it is represented in any of the following forms:

- January 15, 1980
- 15 January 1980
- 15JAN80
- 1-15-80
- 80015
- 15/1/1980

Date is a data type according to the definition used above. Two dates, regardless of their functional significance (date of birth, delivery date) can always be compared to see which one comes first. How a program would compare dates depends on the representation chosen. The result, however, is independent of this representation. January 15, 1980, always precedes January 13, 1981, even if the program had to deal with 1-15-80 and 81013.

Other frequent data types are listed in Figure 12–2. Most of these are simple data types that cannot be further decomposed. Entity identifiers, codes, and quantity or amount fields are typical examples. Some data types are complex;

Figure 12-2 **Frequently Used Data Types**

Type	Operations Available	Notes
Address	Assign, Compare =	Complex
Amount	Assign, Compare >, <, +, −	Precision must be indicated
Color	Assign, Compare =	Enumeration
Corporation Name	Assign, Compare =	Text
Date	Assign, Compare >, <	Math with Duration
Dimension	Assign, Compare >, <	Math if same unit
Duration	Assign, Compare >, <, +, −	See Date
Frequency	Assign, Compare =	Enumeration
Identifier or Key	Assign, Compare =	Only if same entity type
Period	Assign, Compare =	Complex (2 Dates)
Person Name	Assign, Compare =	May be complex
Precision	Assign, Compare =	Used with Amount, Price . . .
Price	Assign, Compare >, <	Math with Quantity
Quantity	Assign, Compare >, <	Math if same unit
Rate	Assign, Compare >, <	Math with Duration
Size (Surface)	Assign, Compare >, <	Math if same unit
Speed	Assign, Compare >, <	Math with Duration
Time	Assign, Compare >, <	Math with Duration
Unit	Assign, Compare =	Used with Size, Volume . . .
Volume	Assign, Compare >, <	Math if same unit
Weight	Assign, Compare >, <	Math if same unit

they are made up of more elementary data types. For instance, a date can be decomposed into year, month, day within the month, day counted since the beginning of the year, day of the week. Is a year a date? Whenever the precision required by the application is a year, then it could be considered a date. Is a month a date? Yes, if it is accompanied by a year and the precision is a month. The same reasoning applies to days within months. Every year, April 15 is the IRS income tax filing deadline. The data type of April 15, however, is not a date, because it is not clear which April 15 is referred to. April 15 without a year cannot be compared with January 15, 1990.

Thus, there can be several subtypes of date according to the precision desired. Comparison operations can be extended, provided an appropriate meaning is assigned to "equality" between two dates with different precisions. Conventionally, October 1988 might be considered to be equal to, or at least compatible with, October 2, 1988.

Time is an example of extending the precision of date. If the precision of an application demands that events be timed to the hour, minute, or second, then the date (year, month, day) is no longer enough; the time needs to be added. An example of a date in this case might be January 15, 1980, 10:55.7546 A.M., GMT. This date is equal to January 15, 1980, 2:55.7546 A.M., PDT.

The following examples illustrate typical complex data types:

- Names—first, middle, and last names.

- Addresses—number, street, city, state (or other geographical subdivision), zip code (or other postal code), country.

- Periods—start date and end date.

- Weights—a code representing the unit (pounds, ounces, grams, metric tons, etc.) and the quantity expressed in that unit.

- Amounts—currency code plus amount in that currency.

Defining Operations on Data Types

For any data type, comparison and assignment are always permitted. Other operations have more complex rules. Usually, mathematical operations such as addition and subtraction are available for many numeric data types, but not for all. Also, the operations of addition and subtraction may be defined in various ways for different types. Here are some examples of difficulties and ways to resolve them:

- Two quantities or amounts can only be added directly if they use the same unit of measure. A weight of two ounces cannot be added to a length of two yards. A weight of two ounces can be added to a weight of two pounds only if both numbers are converted to a common unit. A number of nails cannot be added to a number of machine tools. However, the dollar cost of a pound of nails *can* be added to the dollar cost of a machine tool. But if one of the cost figures is expressed in pounds sterling and the other in yens, the amounts cannot be added without prior conversion.

- A date can be subtracted from another date to yield a duration. This duration can be expressed in years, months, weeks, down to milliseconds, depending on the required precision.

- A duration can be added to a date to yield another date.

- Two durations can be added to yield another duration. A period, defined as the time elapsed between a start date and an end date, has the same unit of measure as a duration. However, two periods cannot be legitimately added unless the definition of the addition operation contains an explanation of how the addition is to be made for two periods that are not consecutive.

- A quantity can be multiplied by a unit price to yield a total cost, by a unit cost to yield total cost, by a unit weight to yield total weight, and so on. A rate or speed can be multiplied by a duration to yield total distance, output, or another result.

- Numbers that are in reality a ratio, such as unit price, rate, or speed, cannot be added. Neither can averages be added. (It is useful to remember elementary mathematics.)

- Nonnumeric data (such as names, addresses, text) and numeric data that does not represent quantities (such as entity identifiers and codes) cannot be added, subtracted, or multiplied. Other interesting operations may be defined on them. An example is concatenation, the stringing together of two partial texts to make up a longer text, often done with elementary fields such as title, first name, middle initial, a period, and last name to arrive at a single name field for printing on an envelope.

- Some attributes can require a null value, as in optional attributes. For instance, an employee file might have an attribute for storing the kind of discharge that each employee has received from the armed services. This attribute would be null for all those who had never served. Unfortunately, the term *null values* can have other meanings: does not exist, does not apply, do not know, do not care, not assigned yet, and so on. It is important to inventory all these meanings and describe the possible values of the data type accordingly.

- Multicurrency systems have to take into account the variability of the conversion factors over time. Whereas the ratio of an inch to a millimeter is constant, the ratio of the Swiss franc to the dollar is not. In many cases, currency translations must use the exchange rate in effect on the date of the transaction, which must therefore be known. If the conversion concerns the amount of an asset or a liability, the rate at the time of translation is usually used. For accounting purposes, this time means the closing date, e.g., December 31, rather than the date at which the translation was performed, perhaps some time in February.

Documentation Requirements for Data Types

The results of the data type analysis is a document or an entry into a data dictionary containing for each data type:

- The name.
- The description.
- The domain (including null values).
- The different representations on files (usually one form only), input (usually one form only, the shortest possible), and output (several forms, in particular if there are several possible precisions or if there is a need to conserve space on certain media).
- The operations—arithmetic or other—that can be performed on the type (including the notions, if any, of sequence or order).
- The restrictions, if any, on those operations (such as adding quantities only if the product codes are the same).
- The elementary data types that make up a complex data type.

If the type is a coding scheme where all the possible values are known, these values have to be specified. For example, the data type "day of week" is described as Sunday, Monday, Tuesday, Wednesday, Thursday, Friday, Saturday. An addition operation can be defined on this code: adding one day transforms a "day of week" into its successor (by definition, the first element, Sunday, is the successor of Saturday). A comparison operation yielding either equality or inequality can also be defined.

In many cases, some of the data types that are required for a new application already exist. This is almost universal when the system being designed is a management information system or a decision support system that builds on some existing transaction system or when the system is designed to replace or extend an existing computer-based system. Even in these cases, the existing data description may need to be modified to make the definition more precise, to add new representation formats, or to extend the domain (see the Technique at the end of this section).

Once all the required data types exist on the dictionary, the entity descriptions can be completed. Each attribute of an entity must have the following elements:

- Attribute name (a composite name usually containing the type name as one component).
- Data type name, pointing to all the data type characteristics.
- Additional definition.
- Representation (if the data type allows more than one).
- Unit of measure and precision (if the data type allows more than one).

KEY ANALYSIS

An important design step is the choice of data elements to be used as keys to an entity.

Purpose of Key Analysis

The key can have one of the following three objectives:

- To ensure that each instance of an entity can be uniquely identified and differentiated from any other instance of the same entity type.
- To implement relationships between two entities by storing the key of a parent entity in a child entity.
- To indicate to the data base management system (DBMS) that the data element is likely to be used as a search argument to retrieve specific instances of the entity.

An entity type really represents a set, in the mathematical sense, of entity instances—all the employees of an organization or all the customers of a

uniqueness

business, for instance. In set theory, every member of a set must be distinguishable from every other member. The use of a key is the most frequent way of guaranteeing **uniqueness** in a data base or file.

The idea is to create a key attribute and assign it a different value for each instance of the entity. Two people might have identical attributes on the personnel file of an organization. Two Edward Kennedys, both graduates from Northwestern University, might be hired by the same CPA firm on the same day. They might even have been born the same day. One might be squat and the other lanky; one might have blue eyes and the other brown, but these attributes would not be on file. A distinct employee number for each would guarantee that the two would look as different to any computer program as to friends and colleagues.

implementation of relationships

The second reason to use key attributes is for the **implementation of relationships** in relational data base systems. Two entity instances that have a relationship between them, such as a customer and all the orders of that customer, must have attributes that can be related uniquely. Thus, an order can be associated with only the customer who placed it. A reasonable way to relate the two is to store the customer number of the owner of the order in the order entity (see Figure 12–3). A data element used in this way is called a *foreign key* — the customer number stored in the order entity is a key of another, or foreign, entity.

Foreign keys are not the only way that relationships can be stored. Any functional relationship between two attributes can be used as well. For instance, a fiscal year entity might have as attributes the first and last dates of the fiscal year. These dates would be especially useful for companies that close their accounts on a date other than December 31. An accounting entry or other transaction can be related to its fiscal year by determining whether the date of the transaction falls between the two dates of the fiscal year (see Figure 12–4). (A code indicating the fiscal year could also be stored with the transaction, which could then be used as a key to the fiscal year entity.)

data retrieval

The third important reason for keys is that data base management systems often assume the existence of an identifying key and use it for efficient **data retrieval**.

Because uniqueness, implementation of relationships, and data retrieval can all be achieved through the use of keys, a great deal of confusion reigns about key design. However, each requirement can be met by other means as well:

- Uniqueness can be ensured by making certain that a combination of attributes of an entity—maybe all of them—make up a unique relation. (Some micro-based systems do this, in particular Rbase.) In addition, some entities could easily be assigned any one of a number of attributes as a key— employee number, social security number, or, in a futuristic vein, fingerprint characteristics.

- Relationships can be evaluated by relating attributes rather than keys or by using so-called pointers (a nonrelational technique).

Figure 12–3 **Relationship Implemented by Foreign Key**

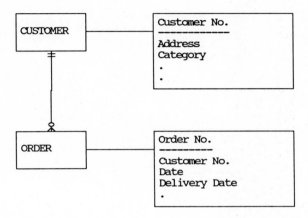

```
PREPARED BY:              DATE:          VERSION:        PAGE 1
MODIFIED BY: PER          DATE: 30NOV88  STATUS :
```

- Direct access to a record can be achieved without keys or with nonunique keys. Also, attributes that are not the primary or identifying key can be used as access keys (sometimes called secondary keys). In fact, identifying keys and access keys are nearly totally independent, at least from a logical standpoint.

The access key is properly a concern for physical data base design and thus will not be discussed further in this book. In most modern data base management systems, the access keys can be changed with very little impact on applications and files. Usually, only performance is affected.

Choosing the Identifying Key

The choice of an identifying key for an entity is usually fairly simple. The main entities within an organization already have unique keys associated with them, and there are usually many good reasons for not changing them.

If keys need to be selected for the entities in the project data model, one of the simplest and best solutions is simply to remember that an identifying key is an identifier, nothing more. *The value of the key must be unique for each*

Figure 12–4 **Relationship Implemented by a Processing Rule**

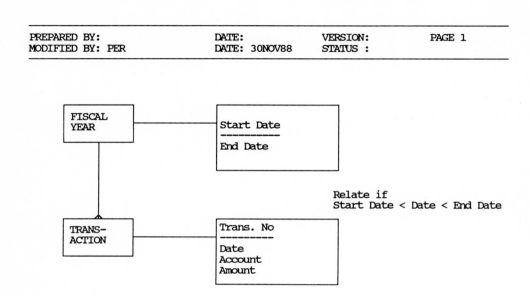

instance of the entity, and it must not change over the life of the instance that it identifies. These two criteria are easy to fulfill if the key is a simple **serial number**. In fact, some authors, in particular E. F. Codd, advocate that serial number keys, which he calls *surrogates*, be the only type of key allowed and that the DBMS be made responsible for assigning and managing all such keys.

Other techniques are possible, however. Most of them are used in a large number of installations. Two of the techniques have few problems: they are both based on concatenating a key with another attribute. A third technique, which should be avoided, consists in using a composite key with meaningful attributes.

A frequent situation is when a one-to-many relationship exists between a parent entity and a child entity, especially when the child is created by splitting out multiple occurrences of a data group (to reach first normal form). For example, a customer may have several locations where goods can be delivered. There is a strict one-to-many relationship between the customer and the location: each location must belong to one customer and only one.

The most usual (and economical) technique for designing a key for the child entity is to give the child the **parent key with a sequence number.** In the customer location example, the key of the location would be the customer number with a location number appended to it. Thus, each customer would

serial number

parent key with a sequence number

have locations numbered from 1 to N; the uniqueness would still be ensured by the fact that no two locations would have both the same location number *and* customer number (see Figure 12–5).

There are only two types of difficulties caused by this technique. First, the technique fails if the relationship is an optional one on the parent side. If a location could belong to no customer (or have a null customer number, meaning "not applicable," "do not know," or "do not care"), there would be a high risk of nonuniqueness as well as of later changes in the key value. Moreover, null values in the key are against the rules for most data base management systems. The solution here is to assign serial number keys, or surrogates, to both entities.

Second, a location could be sold or transferred to another customer, and thus, the key could conceivably change. For instance, a fast-food restaurant might transfer from one franchise to another and still be operated by the same operator. There are two solutions. The transfer can be considered as two separate transactions: one transaction deletes the location from one customer, and another transaction adds it to the other customer. Or the location entity could be assigned a unique location key that does not contain the customer number.

The next valid technique for concatenating keys, an extension of the previous technique, can be used when the entity in question has a child relationship to two other entities. This is frequently found when the entity to be identified started life as a relationship, until it was discovered that it had an attribute. The usual solution is to create the key as the **combination of the keys of both parents**. Figure 12–6, the case of a student's grade, illustrates this solution. The key to the grade entity is the combination of student ID and course code. This solution works well in this particular case because the student can get only one grade for each course. The same technique is frequently used in bill of materials processing (see Figure 11–17).

The last technique is one that should be avoided. Composite keys that have some significance other than the unique identification of the entity should not be assigned. An example of a composite key is an automobile serial number (see Figure 12–7), made up of 11 different codes.

Although composite keys are known to cause problems, they are still popular for two main reasons. First, if a key can be decomposed into components, it is easier to remember. An easily remembered key helps in filling in forms, because it eliminates having to look up the correct value in lengthy lists or catalogs. Ease of remembering is less important nowadays because many on-line systems have implemented on-line catalogs, so that customer numbers, for example, can be looked up by customer name. It can still be of importance in systems where back-office workers enter data from forms filled out in the field. With composite keys, the field-worker, typically a sales representative, may be able to remember the keys of many products without having to look them up in a printed list.

Second, composite keys may also be assigned for file sorting purposes. If a customer key contains the customer category, the geographical area, and the

combination of the keys of both parents

Figure 12–5 **Key Constituted by Parent Key with Sequence Number**

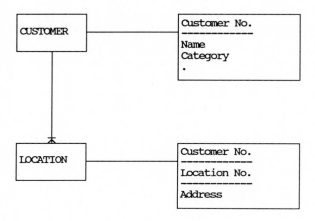

number of the assigned sales representative, then the file can be sorted on any of these criteria and significant statistics can be printed. This use of composite keys was especially important when most systems were card-based and when all the information concerning a customer had to be crammed into 80 characters. This problem justified many "trick" data representation techniques that should no longer be used today. Data storage space is no longer limited. Nor is it expensive enough to justify an identification key that contains data.

If user pressure leads the analyst to choose a composite key, each component should have an unchanging value. If the value of the key changes for an entity, most systems (and good systems practice) require that the instance of the entity identified by the old value of the key be deleted and another instance with the new value of the key be created.

Permanent values are those that cannot conceivably change over the lifetime of an entity. For a person, they include the date of birth, but not the name, and not even the sex. In many countries, the social security number contains a digit that indicates the sex of the person. A problem would arise quite needlessly if a person had a sex-change operation.

Another example of a nonpermanent value is the registration number of a motor vehicle. This number will change if the vehicle is sold, and in many

Figure 12–6 **Key Constituted by Concatenated Keys of Parents**

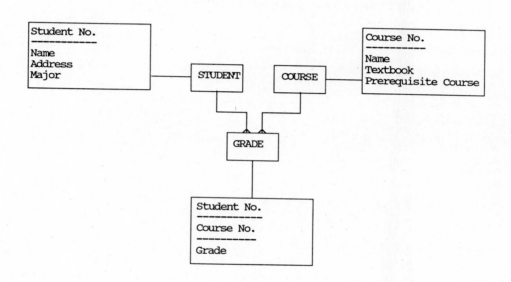

countries the same registration number can be assigned successively to different vehicles belonging to the same owner. In the United Kingdom, registration numbers can be sold and bought by individuals almost at will, and vanity plates are flourishing.

In summary, the identifying key should have the following two properties:

- The key should ensure uniqueness of identification.

- The key should not be subject to modification.

Figure 12–7 **Example of a Composite Key: Automobile Serial Number**

```
FLEET SYSTEM                SUBURBAN PUMPS                      D072
ALL SUBSYSTEMS                                                  GPDEF
            GROUP DEFINITION - VEHICLE IDENTIFICATION NUMBER
```

```
PREPARED BY: G. PILZ         DATE: 12SEP85      VERSION: 2      PAGE 1
APPROVED BY: DARRYL FIELDS   DATE: 15NOV85      STATUS : F
```

DESCRIPTION   : Unique identification number for all vehicles in the trans-
                 portation fleet. Assigned by the vehicle manufacturer.

SYNONYMS   : VIN   V.I.N.

RESPONSIBILITY: Transportation Department

MAJOR DATA ELEMENTS:

DATA ELEMENT	TYPE	LENGTH	OCCURS	MAN./OPT.	COMMENTS
NATORG	N	1	1	M	Nation of Origin
MFR	A	1	1	M	Manufacturer
MKTYPE	N	1	1	M	Make and Type
RESTRSYS	A	1	1	M	Restraint System
SERIES	X	1	1	M	Series
BODYTYP	N	2	1	M	Body Type
ENGTYP	X	1	1	M	Engine Type
CKDIGIT	N	1	1	M	Check-digit
MODYR	A	1	1	M	Model Year
ASSPLANT	A	1	1	M	Assembly Plant
SEQNO	N	6	1	M	Plant Sequential Number

Example: 1.G.1.A.Z.37.3.6.B.R.123456

---

candidate keys

In some cases, several **candidate keys**, attributes or combinations of attributes, may meet these criteria. For example, an employee might be identified by an employee ID or by the social security number. The number chosen does not much matter. What does matter is that if several candidate keys exist, they must all satisfy the integrity requirements of the entity that they identify. In particular, each candidate key must continue to be unique and not change its value.

Implementing Relationships with Keys

There are two main techniques for implementing a relationship between two entities. The first technique is used when the key of an entity consists of the concatenation of two keys or one key and a serial number. As shown in the customer location example in Figure 12–5, a one-to-many relationship that is mandatory on the parent side can be implemented by including the key to the parent entity in the key of the child entity, as part of a **concatenated key.**

The second technique is the **foreign key**. The key of the parent entity is stored as an attribute in the child entity. Because this attribute is not a key of the child but is nevertheless the key of some parent, it is called a *foreign key*. The term is also used to gloss over the fact that storing this value in both the child and the parent entities appears to be a redundancy—a piece of data stored in two places.

The foreign key technique does not cause difficulties. The data that appears to be redundantly stored is in reality two different pieces of data: the key to the parent, as stored in the child, does not have the same meaning as the key of the parent, as stored in the parent.

The foreign key technique can be illustrated by a customer order. The relationship between the order and the customer who placed it is implemented by storing the customer number in the order entity as a foreign key (see Figure 12–3). This technique is preferable to having the key to the order entity made up of a customer number combined with an order number assigned within the customer. It would be inconvenient and unnecessary to keep track of the next order number to be assigned for each customer.

In this case, therefore, the customer number is a normal attribute of the order. It is because the order must belong to one customer that null values are not allowed in the customer number of the order entity, not because the customer number is a key.

When foreign keys are used, the relationship is always implemented on the child side and not on the parent side. Implementing the reverse relationship would require multiple values of the child key in the parent. A customer entity would have to store several order numbers. This solution is contrary to the precepts of first normal form and to accepted relational data base practice. Also, if the relationship is zero-or-one-to-many, the foreign key could have a null value (a child with no parent).

Both of these techniques—concatenated key and foreign key—are quite standard and offer no particular difficulties. Other methods are possible but are much less frequently used and are liable to be difficult to apply. Two methods are described briefly here: the use of a common attribute that is not a key, and the use of a relationship between two attributes that is a relation other than strict equality.

One of the infrequent methods is relating two entities through **non-key attributes**. If a state has an integrated motor vehicle registration and parking fine collection system, motor vehicles can be identified by the serial number. Until processed, the parking tickets contain the vehicle registration number as an attribute. This attribute implements the relationship between a vehicle and its fines (see Figure 12–8). In this case, a relationship is implemented via a data attribute that is not a key of either entity.

Problems can arise because of the choice of a nonkey attribute. A motor vehicle might have a null registration number (as it is being sold or disposed of),

Figure 12–8 **Relationship Implemented by Non-Key Attribute**

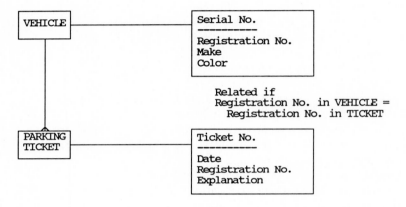

```
PREPARED BY:              DATE:            VERSION:        PAGE 1
MODIFIED BY: PER          DATE: 30NOV88    STATUS :
```

```
VEHICLE ─────────────────  Serial No.
   │                       ──────────
   │                       Registration No.
   │                       Make
   │                       Color
   │
   │                            Related if
   │                            Registration No. in VEHICLE =
   │                               Registration No. in TICKET
   │
PARKING ────────────────   Ticket No.
TICKET                     ──────────
                           Date
                           Registration No.
                           Explanation
```

or it might change license plates over its lifetime. The nonkey attribute itself is not the cause of the problem; rather, the cause is that the license plate number is not a good candidate key. The number can change or be nonnull, although it cannot be nonunique. If the candidate key is as good as the actual key, as with an employee identifier and a social security number, the choice does not matter—although the integrity checks must be enforced for candidate keys as well as for actual keys.

processing rules   Another little-used method of implementing relationships is by **processing rules** rather than by attribute values. In all the techniques based on keys or candidate keys, the equality between two attributes of the same type found in two different entities is what could implement the relationship between those two entities. Equality between attributes may not always be the best way to implement relationships, however, as shown by an example from computer-aided design. If the application is to draw floor plans of buildings, the relationship between a point on the floor plan and the building being drawn is, functionally, a yes/no relationship: either the point is inside the building or it is outside. (Consideration must be given to points that are exactly on the boundary.) The floor plan shape would most probably be represented on the

CAD data base as a series of coordinates. The point would be represented as two coordinates. To determine whether the point is inside or outside would require a complex series of comparisons. Yet the relationship is plain in another representation as a two-dimensional figure on a display (see Figure 12–9).

In summary, a relationship can best be implemented by storing in a child entity an attribute with the value of the key of the parent entity. This attribute may be a partial key of the child entity. If this technique is used consistently, then the logic of normalization works well. If not, the rules of functional dependence must be modified to incorporate candidate keys as well as identifying keys.

Documentation Requirements for Implementing Relationships

Both identifying keys and the ways relationships are implemented must be noted in a data dictionary. For each entity, the set of attributes making up the key must be identified, as must the well-qualified candidate keys, those that have the required attributes of uniqueness and nonchangeability.

The description of each relationship contains information on how the relationship is implemented and its cardinality, or degree. A good data dictionary will automatically annotate each entity in a relationship with the way the relationship is implemented. If not, all the uses of foreign keys or attributes that are candidate keys of other relationships must be identified.

The illustrations in this chapter show how relationship descriptions are depicted graphically. Figure 12–10 illustrates how the documentation might look in textual form.

CODES AND TABLES

A code is an attribute that is designed as an abbreviation, a symbol, or a placeholder for some other attribute. Abbreviating data has several advantages: abbreviations take up less space on disk, they take less time to fill in on forms, they are less prone to transcription errors, and they cost less to transmit over communications lines. Also, abbreviated codes used in keys such as product codes, customer numbers, and employee identifiers help ensure uniqueness and stability.

A good code is complete, well defined, not error-prone, expandable, concise, and convenient.

- Complete

    All the possible values must be represented. A state code that only provides for the 48 contiguous states is incomplete.

- Well defined

    If programmer, programmer/analyst, analyst/programmer, and analyst are four job classifications, then the coding guidelines must be clear enough to classify any individual within the population to be encoded.

Figure 12–9 **Relationship Between a Point and a
Two-Dimensional Surface**

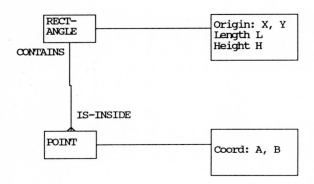

| PREPARED BY: | DATE: | VERSION: | PAGE 1 |
| MODIFIED BY: PER | DATE: 30NOV88 | STATUS : | |

Also, a well-defined code represents a single concept. A code to be applied to cities could have the following values:

0 County Seat

1 State Capital

2 Largest City

3 Geographical Center

Which code would fit Atlanta? Would a fifth code, County Seat and State Capital and Largest City, have to be created? What about other possible combinations? It would be far better to have four independent codes, each having a value of Yes or No (0 or 1).

- Not error-prone

    The code must be easy to transcribe and check. When a code is too long, it is easy to miss one of its digits or to transpose two digits. A solution is to "chunk" the code, dividing it into smaller units. An example of chunking occurs with telephone numbers. The series of seven digits is decomposed into two chunks of three and four digits.

Figure 12–10 **Documenting Keys and Relationship Implementations**

```
LIBRARY                    COUNTY OF DUSABLE                    CD-20
SYSTEM                                                          ERIMP
                    ENTITY/RELATIONSHIP IMPLEMENTATION
┌─────────────────────────────────────────────────────────────────────┐
│ PREPARED BY:  ADS        DATE:   27NOV88    VERSION:          PAGE 1  │
│ APPROVED BY:  JCG        DATE:   06DEC88    STATUS :   D             │
└─────────────────────────────────────────────────────────────────────┘
```

```
ENTITY          Patron
KEY             Patron-Number
ATTRIBUTES      Patron-Name
                Patron-Address
                Patron-Telephone-No

ENTITY          Book
KEY             ISBN-No
ATTRIBUTES      Book-Title
                Book-Author-Name
                Book-Edition
                Number-of-Copies
                Purchase-Requestor
                    IS FOREIGN KEY Patron-Number in Patron

ENTITY          Has-Borrowed
KEY             Patron-Number
                    IS FOREIGN KEY Patron-Number in Patron
                ISBN-No
                    IS FOREIGN KEY ISBN-No in Book
ATTRIBUTES      Date-Borrowed

ENTITY          Is-Waiting-For
KEY             Patron-Number
                    IS FOREIGN KEY Patron-Number in Patron
                ISBN-No
                    IS FOREIGN KEY ISBN-No in Book
ATTRIBUTES      Date-on-Waiting-List
```

Three other features that decrease the tendency to make errors in a code are to avoid mixing numeric and alphabetic digits arbitrarily, to make the code meaningful or easy to remember, and to use a self-checking digit. These features are discussed later in the chapter.

- Expandable

    A two-digit numeric code provides for 100 possibilities, a three-digit code for 1,000, and so on. A two-digit state code is adequate: it is unlikely that there will ever be more than 100 states. However, the number of products, locations, warehouses, and so on is very likely to increase. The size of the code that is chosen must be able to accommodate the increase. If the code has to be expanded to include more digits, the entire IS department could be paralyzed. A chain of department stores saw all its new development projects curtailed for nearly three years while the store code was expanded from 3 to 4 figures. A bank stopped developing new systems for 18 months when it became necessary to increase the account number from 12 to 13 digits.

- Concise

  A five-digit code for a population of 100 is probably excessive.

- Convenient

  A code that is subdivided into distinct parts, each with a meaning, may look satisfying, but may not be as convenient as a straightforward code. A subdivided code might require looking up several tables to find its meaning.

  For instance, there may be a choice between a three-digit product code and an eight-digit code subdivided into four parts: brand, product category, product, and packaging. The three-digit code is more convenient because it is shorter. The eight-digit code has more meaning and each component may be easy to remember. However, there is a risk of assembling meaningful components into a code that does not correspond to a real product.

  Just like composite keys, codes that are subdivided are usually not advisable, especially if the codes are not strictly independent. For instance, if food category 34 is canned vegetables and category 35 is frozen TV dinners, then product 01 might mean carrots in one category and beef Stroganoff in the other.

  A compromise, which is also a help in locating codes when they are being looked up, is to assign significant ranges. For instance, customers from 00000 to 19999 might be independent grocery stores; 20000 through 79000, supermarket chains; and 80000 through 99999, delis. It is difficult to ensure that the initial classification stays complete and coherent, but the device is often useful. Under no circumstance should ranges determine the processing that is to be done by a program. A distinct code is required.

A code can be meaningful (mnemonic) or not. Some interesting examples can be found in the air travel industry. Air carriers have an industry-wide symbol consisting of two letters: AA for American Airlines, PA for Pan American, TW for Trans World, and UA for United Airlines. When, in the 1960s, the newly independent ex-French colonies in Western and Equatorial Africa created an airline, they called it Air Afrique. What to do, as AA was already spoken for? The code that was chosen was RK, no more than vaguely reminiscent of Air Afrique.

Another meaningful code in air travel is the airport code: JFK for Kennedy Airport, LAX for Los Angeles, SFO for San Francisco. However, ORD for O'Hare field in Chicago (O'Hare used to be Orchard) and YUL for Montreal Dorval are not meaningful.

These examples illustrate both the attractiveness of a mnemonic code and its shortcomings. Almost invariably (with the exception of country and state codes, which have not varied much recently and are not likely to), the mnemonic code winds up having obscurities or ambiguities. If such codes are used, they should be used only as shorthand for information access. Primary keys, relationships, or processing options should preferably not be based on them.

Should keys be alphabetic, numeric, or a mix? Numeric codes have the advantage of being better adapted to turnaround documents and to international systems (Arabic numerals are more widely recognized than the 26-letter Latin alphabet). Alphabetic mode is required for all mnemonic codes.

Mixed, or alphanumeric, codes are the most economical: each digit can take 36 different values (0 to 9 and A to Z). Because each additional digit multiplies the code capacity by 36, a three-digit alphanumeric code has a capacity of 46,656, or almost half the capacity of a six-digit numeric code. By contrast, a pure alphabetic code of three digits has a capacity of 17,576. A drawback of long alphanumeric (non-mnemonic) codes is the difficulty of ensuring that offensive combinations are not assigned. Avoiding such combinations is especially difficult in an international environment. Another drawback is that codes that mix numeric and alphabetic elements freely are error-prone. For example, a code such as M1XC4D3 is much more difficult to transcribe correctly than MXCD143 or 143MXCD.

Lowercase characters are not used as separate values in codes. On data entry, it is useful to accept lowercase input, but the program should convert the input to uppercase. Special characters, such as hyphens, asterisks, underscores, commas, and periods are not part of the code. They may be included as separators on output to preserve the appearance of the code (as in telephone numbers and social security numbers). Special characters should be optional on data entry: the program should accept separators but should not require them.

A self-checking code contains an extra position with a redundant character or digit in it. The value of this extra character can be calculated from the other characters. Data entry equipment can perform the calculation as the operator enters the code and can check that the result is the same as the check digit. If it is not, then there must be a transcription error somewhere. With the advent of on-line transaction processing, self-checking codes have become much less popular. The on-line program can check all the codes entered against master files or tables and provide feedback to the operator whenever the code appears to be illegal or illogical.

Documentation Requirements for Codes

Whenever a code has been designed, it is usually appropriate to create a table to translate between the code and its meaning. In most installations, a centralized data administration or data base administration function maintains a table system and will explain the requirements. The data administrator may also locate an existing code similar to the proposed one, so that a new table will not have to be created without need.

The central table maintenance system has the following goals:

- To avoid creating codes that already exist.
- To print out or display code lists for users.
- To be read by programs that require the codes (thus avoiding embedding the codes in programs and having to change every program whenever the code changes).

A shortcoming of many existing table maintenance systems is that each table entry has only two fields, the key (or code) and the value. However, in many cases, there is a need for more than one value field. For instance, the department code might translate to a long text for reports and a short text for screens. To accommodate both, an additional table may have to be created. It then becomes difficult to keep the two tables synchronized. The lack of additional fields can also cause difficulties with a hierarchical set of tables, where one table could contain regions and another table sales territories (a subdivision of regions). Usually, the region to which each territory belongs must be known. The resulting structure looks very much like the beginning of a data base and may not be handled by a simple table maintenance system.

Summary

When entities, relationships, and the principal attributes of a data model have been defined, design decisions are made for each of the identified data attributes. Each attribute in each entity is named uniquely and related to its data type.

Each data type, unless it already exists, is described with respect to its functional definition, its value domain, its physical representation on various media, and any restrictions on the operations that can be performed. This documentation decreases the number of programming errors and data base integrity problems during implementation and operation of the system.

For each entity, a key is chosen to identify it uniquely. A good key has no meaning outside of identifying the entity uniquely (and perhaps implementing a parent-child relationship). In addition, a good key never changes its value for any given entity over the entire life of that entity.

For each relationship, an implementation is chosen. In most cases, relationships are implemented via foreign keys.

Finally, all codes are inventoried and documented. If possible, existing code tables are used to decrease the risk of inconsistencies.

Even though the cause of all this work is the implementation of a single system, one of the main purposes of data element analysis is to ensure coherence of definitions and consistency of data values across all the systems of an organization. Thus, much of this work is ideally performed by a data administration section, which covers the activities of the entire IS department, not only the current project. If there is no data administration section, then one of the analysts on the project plays the same role, covering only the project.

Selected Readings

This chapter is essentially about data element design. In the literature, it is usually treated as a subtopic of data base design or data analysis. The bibliography of the previous chapter therefore applies to this one, in particular:

Date, Chris. *An Introduction to Database Systems*, 4th ed. Reading, Massachusetts: Addison-Wesley, 1986.

Martin, James, and Finkelstein, Clive. *Information Engineering*. London, UK: Savant Institute, 1981.

Review Questions

1. Explain why homonyms present a more serious problem than synonyms.

2. What is the domain of each of the following data types?
a. Date of birth.
b. Annual interest rate for a bank loan (for example, mortgage, credit card).
c. A nation's gross national product, expressed in U.S. dollars.
d. Zip code.

3. What are the two characteristics that a primary key should have?

4. Use the example of a lending library to design a set of keys for each of the following entities:
a. Book (or title).
b. Individual copy of a book.
c. Library patron.

5. How would you implement the relationships between patrons and the books they have borrowed, the books they are waiting for to be returned, and the books they have requested to be purchased?

6. Review and evaluate various codes encountered in everyday life from the viewpoint of the characteristics of a good code described in the chapter. Consider, for example, postal codes, telephone dialing codes (international and area codes), vehicle registration numbers, social security numbers, and taxpayer identification numbers.

Discussion Questions

1. You suspect that, in an insurance company, the life insurance department and the group health insurance department use the words "policy" and "customer" slightly differently. Discuss how you would go about finding out whether there is a difference and what the difference is.

2. Analyze the following data types:
a. Instant—used to time-stamp events in a real-time data collection system.
b. Period—defined by a starting and an ending instant.
c. Duration—defined as the length of a period

Document which operations can be performed on what types, independently of their representations. Consider only primitive operations; if an operation can be performed by a succession of simpler operations, do not include it.

3. The text affirms that there must be a primary key to make each entity unique. But if two entities have exactly the same attributes and are indistinguishable from the system's viewpoint, would it be immaterial to give them an artificial identification number? Should you distinguish between two entities that have the same properties? Discuss this problem using the following examples:

a. Two employees with the same name, the same job, the same salary.
b. Two gearboxes destined for two cars of the same make and year, produced by a parts supplier and waiting in the car manufacturer's inventory to be inserted into two cars on an assembly line.
c. Two trucks of the same make, year, color, and price—but with different serial numbers—owned, operated, and maintained by the same transportation company.
d. Two 1-1/2 inch No. 8 roundheaded galvanized wood screws.

4. Review the parking ticket example of a relationship implemented using an attribute that is not a candidate key. What are the trade-offs between using the license plate number and the serial number? Consider both the likelihood of making errors and the consequence if an error is made.

Mini-Case

Complete the data element analysis for all the entities defined during the entity-relationship analysis of the Condor Telephone Company mini-case at the end of the previous chapter.

References

1. Gane, Chris. *Rapid Systems Development.* New York: Rapid Systems Development, Inc. 1984.

Chapter 13

Specification of Integrity Constraints

Chapter 13 describes the reasons for errors in a data base, two types of integrity constraints designed to prevent errors, and two transaction validation techniques to enforce integrity. The focus of the chapter is on processing rules to prevent errors, not on how to recover from them.

Learning Objectives

- Analyze the entity-relationship model and the functional requirements to find what logical rules the data must observe in order to be valid.
- Design the processes to enforce these rules.

DATA BASE INTEGRITY

The objective of imposing integrity constraints on the data base is to ensure that the data base contains as few errors as possible. If the data base is designed to model the real world (as in a personnel or customer data base), the state of the data base must change as the real world changes. If the data base *is* the real world (as in an airline reservation system), it must reflect all the activities that users believe to have been posted.

Reasons for Errors in the Data Base

Any data base will always contain some errors. (Most countries now have laws that allow the public to scrutinize records concerning themselves and have material errors corrected.) However, many errors can be avoided by having the system routinely examine all the transactions and the state of all the data on the data base to catch the most obvious mistakes—those that would make the data base absurd and those that are not permitted by management policy.

For example, if an employee file contains the marital status of each employee, there must be a transaction to modify the marital status as it changes from never married to married to divorced or widowed. The rules must not allow an unmarried person to become divorced or a widowed person to become never married (except to correct an error). Another example is that it should not be possible to delete a customer master record if there is still an order in that customer's name.

Some more subtle errors cannot be caught by today's computer programs. For example, a mail-order house might receive an order for skiing equipment in July. This order might be an error due to a mistranscribed product code, or it might be a legitimate order from a customer preparing to go on a skiing vacation in the southern hemisphere.

An analyst could imagine such errors and insert routines in the processing to catch transactions that deviate from the normal pattern. The system could then flag these transactions for manual verification before they are released. But however thorough the analyst may be, some error types will always slip through. A computer program is not capable of diagnosing those errors that the analysis did not specifically anticipate: the program has no judgment, no intuition, no common sense.

Types of Errors

Three main types of errors can arise. The first type is errors in flow: data is lost, incomplete, or not transmitted on time. The second type is errors in processing: a program has a bug or a person makes a mistake. The third type is errors in data content. It is the third type that we are concerned with here. How to prevent or minimize errors in flow and in process is treated in Section VI, which also discusses how to recover from errors.

Errors that creep into the data base are usually one of the following types:

- The data does not reflect the actual state of the world. For example, no one has recorded the fact that Bud Green got married last month. Or someone recorded Patricia McCreary as having left the company on January 15, although she did not leave until January 31. Or the M. P. Schwartz who died and is to be taken off the welfare rolls is the one who lived on 53rd Street, not the one on 35th Street.

- The data is inconsistent. Inconsistencies arise only when redundant data is stored. For example, Bud Green is recorded as being married in the personnel file but not in the departmental project control file.

- The data base is in an illegal or impossible state. This type of error occurs primarily when one entity in a mandatory relationship, such as the "1" end of a 1-to-N relationship, has been deleted. For example, there are payroll deduction records for Patricia McCreary, although the master record for Patricia was deleted when she quit. Or there are orders for products that are no longer carried. Or suppliers have been deleted although money is still owed them.

The consequences of the third type of error can range from benign to catastrophic. An order for a nonexistent product could be discovered when the bill of lading or the invoice is printed or when the customer complains about not receiving the whole order. The error may affect only the single order for that customer: no great damage is likely to result. However, a batch program might assume that the error will never occur and therefore react unpredictably when it does occur. For instance, the inventory record of some other, existing product might be posted with the quantity ordered or the accounts receivable might be out of balance. If the error materializes during an on-line session, the entire computer may come down, stopping the work of all the users who are connected to the order entry application as well as to other applications that happen to be running.

To recover from the error can also be difficult. If the error has not been anticipated, hasty action could cause further errors. If the error discovered in one invoice is thought to have invalidated the work done for all the other invoices of the same run, the error correction may be to redo the whole batch. However, if some unprinted invoices were already posted to accounts receivable, customers who properly receive only one invoice may be dunned for two.

Even more insidious can be the effect of errors in files used for management or decision support. Redundant but inconsistent data is especially insidious, because a given user will normally have access to only one of the versions. Two users who believe they are working on the same data may not understand why they have discrepancies. Errors that would easily be spotted on an individual record may get drowned in the process of summarizing and averaging.

Lack of relationship integrity is also insidious, because such an error may never be discovered. Take the example of an employee whose master record is deleted but whose deduction records remain in the system. The deduction records are normally used by the payroll application, but the program only processes deductions for current employees (i.e., those who have a master record). The persistence in the data base of deduction records is not noticeable in this application. Imagine, however, that the human resources department decides to analyze the cost of certain benefits programs paid for by deductions (flexible benefits, group life insurance, stock options). An employee might use the personnel file to extract all the deductions of a certain type without worrying about master records. No error will be encountered, but the results will be wrong. If the error occurred for only one employee, the impact will not be great. However, if the error has affected all those who have left the company over the past several years, the impact could be substantial.

There are so-called pointer audit programs that can read an entire data base and check for integrity errors such as having detail records without masters. The technique for using these audit programs is described later in the chapter.

THE REFERENTIAL INTEGRITY PROBLEM

The most important type of integrity constraint on a data base is called referential integrity. The term *referential integrity* refers to making sure that actual instances of relationships between actual instances of entities follow the degree rules documented during entity-relationship analysis.

Implementing Relationships

Relationships between entities can be implemented in a number of ways. In nonrelational data base systems, pointer chains are often used. With pointer chains, the disk address of one record is stored in another record; then the address of a third record is stored in the second record; and so on. It is possible to build different types of pointer chains, such as open-ended or circular, one-way or two-way. The data base management system is responsible for maintaining these pointer chains, and part of the job of the data base designer is to specify to the data base management system which pointers are to be implemented. As a return service, the DBMS also insures integrity. If the designer has documented to the DBMS the rule that a relationship is mandatory, then no program can violate this rule by attempting to delete a parent record without having deleted the children first.

Storing address pointers causes some inflexibility, however. In particular, the existence of pointers makes it difficult to extend the data base to encompass new entities and relationships. Also, any program that reads the data base needs to know something about the characteristics of the pointer chains; and so changing the implementation of a data base may require changing most of the programs that refer to the data base. Relational data base overcomes the lack of flexibility of traditional data bases by using foreign keys, explained in the previous chapter, to implement relationships. A foreign key in one entity provides a reference to the identifying key of another entity. In return for the flexibility allowed by the foreign key scheme, the application must check the integrity of the relationships that are not known to the data base management system.

Checking for Referential Integrity

Referential integrity is ensured when all references between data base records (or entities, in the data analysis vocabulary) are correct.

1-to-N Relationships. Most of the relationships in a well-analyzed data model are 1-to-N (where the "1" means exactly one, neither more nor less, and the "N" can stand for various possibilities—0 to N with N arbitrarily large; or 1 to N with N arbitrarily large; or either 0 or 1 to N with N limited to a theoretical maximum). For instance, in an order entry system, a customer might have any number of orders, and an order must have at least one order item, with no upper limit; in a library lending system, it might be decided that no patron can have more than nine books on loan.

Whenever one of the sides of the relationship has some imposed minimum or maximum, then every delete or create operation on an instance of the entity on that side must first make sure that the proposed operation would not violate the rule. In other words, if every X must be owned by a Y, then no transaction can suppress any Ys without first checking that they do not currently own any Xs. No transaction should delete a customer who still has products on order, a supplier who is still owed money, or departments with employees still attached. The converse, checking that maxima are not exceeded, can be illustrated by the following example: Do not let a library patron who already has borrowed nine books borrow another book; at least one book must be returned before another is borrowed.

Another check must often be performed: when a record containing a foreign key is created or modified, the foreign key points (or continues to point) to an existing record. Therefore, the value of the foreign key must be equal to the primary key of some instance of the parent entity in the data base. For example, when creating an employee record, the department number to which the employee is assigned must be the number of an existing department. If an employee is transferred from one department to another, causing the value of the foreign key to be modified, the same rule holds.

If the relationship is optional on the parent side, then the foreign key may be null. If the key is not null, it must have the value of the primary key of some existing entity. For example, an employee record might contain as a foreign key the number of the department of which the employee is in charge. Some employees are not in charge of any department and the foreign key is null. An employee cannot be put in charge of a department unless that department exists. An employee who is in charge of a department can be demoted, however, by assigning a null value to the department number in the employee record. The relationship no longer points to a department that the employee manages.

In most cases, the application of these create/delete/modify rules and the strict application of the prohibition against changing the value of a key are sufficient to guarantee referential integrity.

Referential integrity is easy to enforce in transaction processing systems developed according to a life cycle, by a project team, with appropriate standards, training, and management structures. Enforcement is much more difficult in an end-user environment, where users may not be aware of the total model of the data base. There are two solutions to this problem:

- The first solution is to use the DBMS facilities to refuse update authorization to end users. They can only read the data base; they may be able to modify a local copy that no one else shares, but they cannot modify shared files or relations.

- The second solution is to use a relational DBMS that implements referential integrity. Such a DBMS would require descriptions of how each relationship is implemented and its degree. The DBMS could then perform all the integrity checking required whenever a program attempted to create or delete a row.

Until data base systems with referential integrity checking become widely available, the technology requires that all creations, deletions, or modifications on a shared data base be implemented in an application that also performs integrity checking. This application must be specified, designed, written, tested, documented, and maintained in accordance with professional practice and cannot be left to the typical end-user environment.

1-to-1 Relationships. A special difficulty arises when a relationship is strictly 1-to-1. If the referential integrity rules were applied strictly, it would not be possible to create or delete a record. The "do not delete" rule would prevent deleting either of two related entities, because deleting one would leave the other in an invalid state. Similarly, creating one before the other is impossible, because the first one to be created would point to empty space.

The solution to this problem is to defer checking on the integrity until the entire operation (double deletion, double creation) is completed. This solution amounts to considering the double deletion or creation as an atomic operation, different in nature from the successive creation of two entities. This operation can be validated as a whole before attempting to call the data base management system to perform the creation. The logical unit of work, or business event, is what is important, not each elementary data base operation. This approach is legitimate, because the definition of logical units of work specifies that whatever happens, a unit of work is either wholly processed or not processed at all (see Section IV).

OTHER INTEGRITY CONSTRAINTS

There are many other types of integrity constraints on a data base. The most frequently encountered are the following:

- Domain constraints
    The value of each attribute must remain within the domain of that attribute, both when the attribute is modified and when the domain specification is modified.

- Nonkey dependency constraints
    The range of possible values of some attributes (their subdomains) may be dependent on the value of some other attribute, either in the same entity or in another one.

- Consistency of redundant information
    If information is stored redundantly for any reason, then any modification to one instance must be reflected in the other.

- Constraints on derived data
    If the constraint is expressed on derived data, such as an extended amount, a total, or a balance, the derived data must be recalculated or adjusted every time the base data is changed.

The domain of a piece of data is a function of the data type. The ideal solution is to have an integrated data dictionary that automatically takes care **domain checking**   of **domain checking**—making sure that each data value that is input to the system belongs to the proper domain. Otherwise, the project standards must enforce the discipline of checking the domain of every single piece of input data, whether on a screen, an input form communicated to a batch program, or a file from some other system or outside source. This solution is neither difficult nor constraining.

More difficult than domain checking is checking the data base integrity when the domain specification changes. Such a change has retroactive effect: not only does the processing rule for new elements change, but the entire data base may need to be checked for values outside the domain.

There are two kinds of domain specification changes. The first occurs when the domain is enlarged. In this case, the data base does not need to be reviewed. The second occurs when the domain is narrowed. Then the data base should be examined to determine what to do with existing records that do not meet the constraints. For instance, if the criteria for membership in a club is expanded from all-male to both male and female, no great difficulty is likely. However, if a club previously open to residents and nonresidents of a community should decide to require residence, then a number of existing members would no longer qualify. This problem can only be solved by striking their memberships or by instituting a so-called grandfather clause, which states that the criteria for membership are those in effect when membership was applied for.

Nonkey dependency constraints are similar to relationship (key) constraints, but they apply to ordinary data elements rather than to foreign keys. Suppose, for example, that employees in the "executive" category cannot have a payroll code of "hourly." This rule might have been implemented as a referential integrity constraint, using appropriate subentities for executive employees and for hourly employees. The crucial difference between nonkey dependency constraints and referential integrity constraints is that the former must necessarily be checked by the application: even a DBMS with referential integrity will not do the checking (see Figure 13–1).

In theory, **consistency of redundant information** is fairly easy to achieve. All that is required is to group in a single logical unit of work the updating of all the places where redundant information is stored. By definition, either the logical unit of work is incomplete (nothing has been committed) or complete (the redundant information has all been updated). In reality, ensuring consistency may be easier said than done. In the case of distributed processing, the redundant information might be on another computer in a remote geographical location, and the user would have to wait too long before both locations are updated. Or the remote location might not be reachable because of a breakdown in a communications link.

A special case of redundancy arises when both detail and summary records are stored. The constraint is that the summary record must at all times contain the exact total of all the detail records. A practical problem is that updating a summary record on-line each time a detail record is created or updated may cause a performance bottleneck. For instance, suppose that the application is accounts receivable and that the double-entry accounting system is implemented in the system itself. Then every payment recorded individually as a credit on the accounts receivable balance file would update the cash on hand

nonkey
dependency

consistency of
redundant
information

Figure 13-1 **Nonkey Dependency**

It is always possible to implement a nonkey dependency as a key dependency (or referential integrity constraint), but it may be an awkward solution.

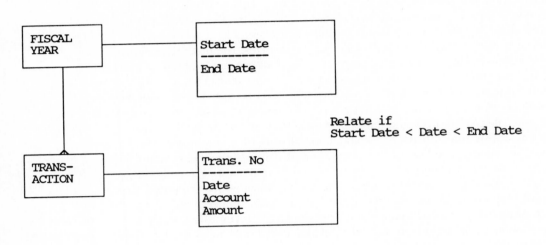

Relate if
Start Date < Date < End Date

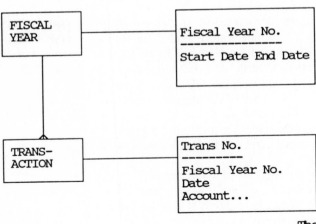

The Fiscal Year No. in
the TRANSACTION is
calculated from the Date,
with which it is
redundant

balance—a single figure on a single account. Every accounts receivable clerk would contend for the same cash balance record. What is more, by the law of logical units of work, each clerk would reserve this record at the beginning of each transaction and relinquish it at the end to ensure that no other transaction can interfere until the transaction in process is done. Thus, the system could in effect process only one transaction at a time. All operators except one would always be waiting for the cash balance record to become available. Changing the system to update the single cash balance record at the end of the day would avoid the bottleneck, but all throughout the day, the data on files would appear to be inconsistent.

A solution is to declare that the cash on hand figure is not redundant with the accounts receivables balances by making it "last night's balance" rather than "current balance." This is one example of a concept known as closing or cut-off—classifying all recorded activities by a well-defined period regardless of when the system processed the transaction. Closing is used both in accounting and in management information or decision support systems. One of the merits of cutting off is to avoid having users working on figures that keep changing as the business is conducted. It is hard to analyze trends when the figures do not stay stable for more than a few minutes at a time.

Constraints on derived data are more difficult to deal with. An example of such a constraint is the rule that a check should be rejected if the issuer's account has a debit balance. This rule requires either that redundant data be maintained (the customer's balance as well as all the transactions) or that the balance be recalculated for every transaction. Neither is wholly satisfactory. Whenever this dilemma arises, the cost of recalculating derived data every time it is needed must be analyzed versus the cost and risks of maintaining derived, and therefore redundant, data.

constraints on derived data

ILLEGAL TRANSACTIONS VERSUS TRANSACTIONS THAT CAUSE AN ILLEGAL STATE

During the design phase, constraints are specified on the state of the data base: all relationships in the data base must be of degree such-and-such; all data values in the data base must be in the proper domain; no keys in the data base can be null, and so on.

In contrast, there are two techniques for *implementing* the validation of integrity constraints. In most cases, it is reasonably easy to transform the constraint on the data base into transaction constraints, rules that any transaction must obey to be allowed to update the data base. In other cases, a technique akin to the casework approach described in Chapter 9 is better. This approach consists in trying to do all the updates required by a complex, multitransaction business event before validating the effect of the updates. If an error is discovered after all the individual updates have been performed, then the entire set of transactions is rejected.

The **transaction constraint approach** was described in the paragraphs on referential integrity above. For the degree constraint to be satisfied, it was enough to prohibit certain things from happening. (This was roughly the idea behind prohibition. It was thought that to stop a state of drunkenness from occurring, it would be enough to prevent certain transactions, namely, the sale of alcoholic beverages.)

Analyzing transaction constraints consists of describing all the legal states of the data base, listing all the events (state transitions) that can be requested, and authorizing only those that result in a legal state. Most often, this analysis is done intuitively on the basis of elementary logic and referential integrity rules:

- No attribute can have a value outside its domain.
- An entity that already exists cannot be created.
- An entity cannot be modified or deleted unless it exists.
- Children must be deleted before parents.
- Parents must be created before children.
- Children can be transferred to new parents only if the parents exist.

These rules must be applied to the business event as a whole (the logical unit of work) rather than to the individual transactions as seen by the data base management system.

The **casework approach** may be the best in applications where many different elementary transactions might occur in arbitrary sequence within a logical unit of work. In this case, analyzing each transaction separately can become onerous, because each of them might change something that would make another transaction illegal. The only disciplined way to apply the constraints transaction by transaction would be to sort the transactions into a predetermined sequence or force the operator to enter them in that order. This solution may not be the best for today's complex systems. It may be simpler to make a copy (in memory or on a working space on a disk) of all the entities touched by the update, do the update without worrying about validity, and check whether the result obeys the integrity constraint. If it does, then all the elementary transactions are correct and the working copy of the data base entities is copied back into place, with all the updates posted to it. If the result does not obey the integrity constraint, then all the elementary transactions are rejected and the working copy of the data base entities is discarded. No attempt is made by the application to determine which transaction made the difference.

Thus, an elementary transaction can create a temporary illegal state, as long as a subsequent transaction (which might also be illegal) changes the state back to a legal one. On occasion, two wrongs do make a right. This technique is usually appropriate when the logical unit of work is not completely determined in advance but rather at the initiative of the operator, as is typical of casework applications.

An extreme example of the casework approach is the data base audit program. This program reads the entire data base and examines whether it conforms to specific integrity constraints. The program is run whenever there is reason to suppose that errors have slipped through, for instance, because the validation criteria in the updating application were incomplete or because some program bug was destroying integrity. Data base audit programs can be vendor-supplied utilities, or they can be written by the development team. The former are usually limited to checking pointer integrity, while the latter can do as extensive a check as desired.

DOCUMENTATION REQUIREMENTS FOR INTEGRITY CONSTRAINTS

Many of the integrity constraints, particularly referential integrity and domain constraints, can be deduced directly from the documentation of the entity-relationship model and the descriptions of data types. Others need to be added explicitly, usually at the level of an entity or a relationship description.

Nonkey dependencies, or mutually exclusive values of two attributes, within a single entity are documented on the data dictionary within the entity description. For instance, if the flight leg entity of an airline schedule contains a flight departure time and a flight arrival time, the constraint that the flight departure time should always precede the flight arrival time is described in the flight leg entity description.

If the two attributes with a nonkey dependency are in different entities, the constraint is best documented in the description of the relationship between two entities. For instance, if a customer credit rating of "poor" entails that the customer cannot place a COD order, this constraint should be documented in the description of the customer-order relationship. When such a dependency exists between two attributes in two different entities, a relationship must always exist between those two entities.

Integrity constraints on derived data are stored with the data description of the derived data, where the derivation rule is also stored. If the derived data is not stored in an entity, it nevertheless does characterize an entity; it is in this entity that the description belongs. For instance, if a check should be rejected whenever a bank customer has a debit balance, this debit balance is recalculated whenever the check is processed. If the balance were to be stored, it would be stored in a customer account entity. Derived data of this type is sometimes called *virtual data* and considered a virtual extension of the entity.

In addition to a description of the constraints themselves, which are documented on the data dictionary, it is useful to start documenting the way in which integrity checking is performed. This documentation will be completed during the process design phase.

In general terms, the designer should document which integrity rules for each logical unit at work might be transgressed by the transaction and therefore need to be checked. In most cases, the documentation is a simple description in English (see Figure 13–2). In other cases, when the rules are more complex, the

Figure 13–2 **Sample Description of Integrity Rules**

PERSONNEL	SUBURBAN PUMPS	CD-20
PAYROLL		VRULES
	INTEGRITY RULE CHECKING	

PREPARED BY:	H. WETTERGREN	DATE: 27FEB90	VERSION: 1.1	PAGE 1
APPROVED BY:	JIMMY WEBER	DATE: 04MAR90	STATUS : D	

TRANSACTION: EMPLOYEE RECAP RECORD UPDATE

TRANSACTION TYPES: C - Create
                     M - Modify
                     D - Delete

DOMAIN CHECKING:

Check that each data element value belongs to its domain as specified in the
data dictionary.

Null values are not allowed for Create transactions.

Null values are allowed for Modify transactions (except Employee-ID).

Delete transactions contain only the Employee-ID.

TRANSACTION INTEGRITY CHECKING AGAINST DATA BASE:

Employee to be created must not already exist.

Employee to be modified or deleted must already exist.

Employee to be deleted must have a Gross-Year-To-Date equal to 0 on the data
base.

If an employee segment is to be deleted, then all its dependent segments
(skills, job history, pay history, accumulated benefits) must be removed from
the data base and copied to the personnel history file.

If an employee is created or an employee's Social-Security-Number is modified,
the new Social-Security-Number must not match any other Social-Security_number
on the data base.

TRANSACTION INTEGRITY CHECKING AGAINST EMPLOYEE-LEVEL RULES:

At the end of the processing of one employee, the employee's Gross-Year-To-Date
must exceed the sum of the employee's FICA-Withholding, Federal-Tax-
Withholding, and Benefits-Withholding. If this does not occur, all the
transactions concerning the employee are rejected.

designer should create a state transition network diagram (see Appendix 3 and Figure 13–3). These documents will eventually be incorporated into the program specifications to be developed later.

Summary

To make sure that a data base remains in a valid state as transactions are posted to it, the transaction processing programs must enforce a number of rules. The main constraints on the data base concern referential integrity—making sure that the specified degree of relationships continue to hold true. Specifically, in a 1-to-N relationship, the normal rule is that children cannot exist without a parent, whether a child has been created and not the parent or the parent has been deleted, leaving orphans.

Other integrity constraints include:

- Domain integrity: all data element values must belong to the data type's domain.

- Nonkey dependencies: the values of some data elements may be constrained by the value of other data elements.

- Redundant data rules: if the same data appears twice in the data base, they must have the same value.

- Constraints on derived data: derived data, such as a total or a balance, must be recalculated every time some transaction affects it.

There are two main approaches to maintaining integrity. The first is to assume that the data base is in a legal state prior to any transaction, and to either allow or not allow the transaction, depending on whether it will cause a transition to another legal state. The state of the data base is never checked, only the type of each transaction. This is the normal approach for transaction processing systems.

The second approach, used when the transactions are too complex or too unpredictable, is to perform the update as though every transaction were legitimate and then check the resulting state of the data base. If the state is correct, then all the transactions are accepted; if not, they are all rejected.

Selected Readings

Ross, Ronald G. *Entity Modeling: Techniques and Applications.* Boston, Massachusetts: Database Research Group, 1987.

> *This book is one of the few to address the practical ways in which data integrity can be ensured.*

Review Questions

1. What are the three main types of data content errors?
2. Define and give examples of referential integrity constraints.

Figure 13–3 **Sample State Transition Network
Diagram for Integrity Rules**

| PREPARED BY: | DATE: | VERSION: | PAGE 1 |
| APPROVED BY: PER | DATE: 01DEC88 | STATUS : | |

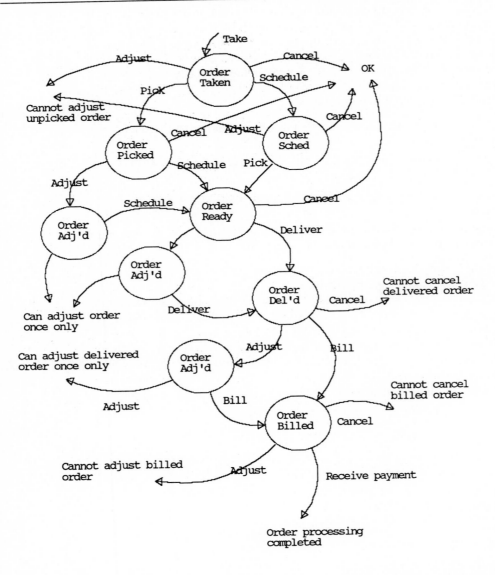

3. Define and give examples of nonreferential integrity constraints.

4. Describe the difference between the transaction constraint approach and the casework approach. Which is the most frequently used?

Discussion Questions

1. What can be done to reduce the number of errors that result when a data base is not in agreement with the actual world?

2. What can be done to minimize the risk of inconsistencies on the data base?

3. Analyze the features required for a relational DBMS to ensure relational integrity. Give examples of syntax expressing the various referential integrity rules described in the chapter. How would you solve the problem of a strict one-to-one relationship, where two entities have to be created together or not at all?

Mini-Case

For the Condor Telephone Company, translate all the referential integrity constraints on the data model developed at the end of Chapters 11 and 12 into constraints that must be met by each transaction type outlined in the scope description.

In addition, add constraints on the service requests, depending on the status of the equipment. For instance, a customer cannot reconnect equipment unless it was previously temporarily disconnected. Use a state transition diagram or similar schematic to document this constraint.

Technique

Data Dictionary

DEFINITION

A data dictionary system is a computer-based application to maintain descriptions of data used in an installation, on a project, or for a given data base.

The data dictionary produces machine-readable data descriptions for programs that manipulate the data described. Examples are COBOL Data Division statements and DDL (Data Description Language) statements for the Data Base Management System.

The dictionary also produces printed or displayed output to help analysts and programmers in the following:

- Locating in which files and programs data are used.

- Specifying the meaning of data to avoid duplication and misunderstandings.

- Describing processing rules and in particular validation rules for input data.

- Depicting relationships that reflect the data model established during design.

Most data dictionaries in use today are implementation-oriented. In other words, they have facilities for describing actual files, records, and data elements as they will be represented on the physical files and in memory. The data model (the conceptual or logical levels) may be represented as well, but only by assimilating the model to a file or set of files. The activities of data modeling are usually not well supported.

Manual, paper-based data dictionaries have been attempted, but they have not been successful.

A SAMPLE DATA DICTIONARY SYSTEM

The system flow of a sample data dictionary system is shown in Figure 1. It includes the following:

Figure 1 **Sample Data Dictionary System Flow**

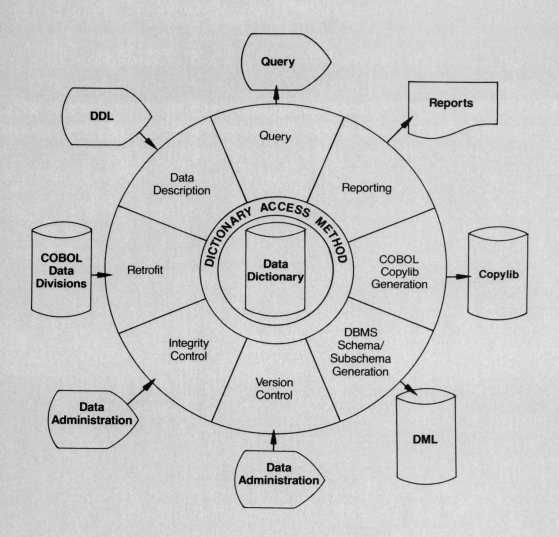

- Interactive input of data descriptions that update the data dictionary.
- Batch input of data descriptions from other sources (useful for converting existing data definitions from a DBMS, for example).
- Control reports on the update activity.
- A query and reporting facility.
- A facility for generating data definitions for the DBMS, the programming language in use, and various productivity aids.
- A generator of recompilation requests in answer to the question: "Given that such-and-such a record or element has been changed, which programs need to be changed and/or recompiled?"
- A test/production version control facility.

Figure 2 is the data model that underlies the data dictionary. The model covers not only the data definitions, but also the process definitions (programs, conversations, batch jobs) that use the data definitions. Figures 3 through 6 show sample outputs from the data dictionary.

CHARACTERISTICS OF DATA DICTIONARIES

Data dictionaries can be characterized by the type of information they contain (data elements, records, or other); how they interface to other facilities; whether they are active or passive; and how they assist in version control.

Information Content

A minimal data dictionary has facilities for describing data **elements and groups** of data elements. A data element is one that cannot be further subdivided, such as an account number, an amount, a job title, a department name, an estimated delivery date. Each data element is described only once in the data dictionary.

elements and groups

A data group is a record, a segment, or a row of a table made up of several data elements. It can also, in most systems, be a partial record made up of several elements that belong together. An address, for example, is a group made up of a number, a street, a city, a state or country, and a ZIP or other postal code. A higher-level group such as a record can be made up of a mixture of data elements and other groups.

Even if a data element or a data group is used in many different records, each of them is described only once in the dictionary. Each data element has a single name by which it is known to every designer and programmer. The data element description corresponds to the characteristics of the data type described in Chapter 12. Unfortunately, many records contain two or more data elements that are of the same type. For instance, a bank transfer contains two account numbers, the "from" account and the "to" account. These two account

Figure 2 **Data Model for a Data Dictionary**

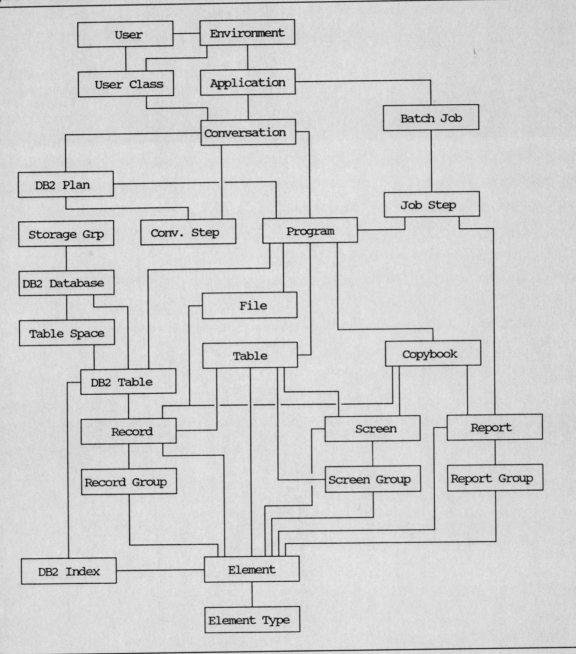

Figure 3 **Sample Element Description**

This example is taken from a data dictionary that does not support data type analysis as described in Chapter 12.

```
PERSONNEL                      SUBURBAN PUMPS                         D710
PAYROLL                                                              WMES0041
                     DATA ELEMENT - SCREEN-ERR-MSG-NUM

┌─────────────────────────────────────────────────────────────────────────┐
│ PREPARED BY:  H. WESTERGREN   DATE:  27APR89    VERSION:  1.1    PAGE 1    │
│ APPROVED BY:  JIMMY WEBER     DATE:  05MAY89    STATUS :  D               │
└─────────────────────────────────────────────────────────────────────────┘


DESCRIPTION:     MES error message number.  This field will appear in MES
                 symbolic maps and will be decoded by MES into the corresponding
                 error message field on the screen.

TYPE:            MSG-NUM  (Message Number -- see D711)


            Length             Format           Precision        Structure
            ------             ------           ---------        ---------
SCREEN-        5               ALPHA
REPORT-        5               ALPHA                                09
INTERNAL-      4               NUM                                  09
                                                                          Usage:  C
DB2 COLUMN NAME:
COBOL NAME:          SCREEN-ERR-MSG-NUM
ASM NAME:
PL/1 NAME:


HORIZONTAL LITERAL:                  Error Message Number
SHORT LITERAL:                       Err Num
FIRST VERTICAL COLUMN HEADING:       Err
SECOND VERTICAL COLUMN HEADING:      Num
THIRD VERTICAL COLUMN HEADING:


SCREEN INITIAL VALUE:     Spaces
INTERNAL INITIAL VALUE:   0 (Zero)

VALIDATION RULES
----------------

TEST TYPE:   Range
FROM:        -9999        TO:        +9999

DECODE TABLE NAME:   Table name provided in the screen definition defaulted by
                     SM with a name for the application.

                     System-level message table (for sign-on, sign-off and
                     security checking) will be WMESTMSG.
```

Figure 4 **Sample Segment Description**

REPORT NO. : RPT0760
SEGMENT   : D610.UERRMSGS
IMAGE   : INTERNAL

DESIGN/1: DESIGNER'S WORKBENCH
SEGMENT REPORTING (COBOL)

PAGE 001
12DEC93

SEGMENT CHARACTERISTICS

```
DATA LAYOUT -:   MES-ERROR-MSG-REC
  DESCRIPTION:   ERROR MESSAGE RECORD LAYOUT FOR CODES TABLE.
  DESCRIPTION:   USED BY MES TO DECODE ERROR MESSAGES.
  DESCRIPTION:   same copybook as WERMT010
         TYPE:   R
  COBOL NAME:    UERRMSGS
  COBOL PREFIX:  MEMR
  ASM NAME:
  ASM PREFIX:
  PL/1 NAME:
  PL/1 PREFIX:
  KEY ID:        (D610.WERMG002)
  ASC/DESC:      A
  TOTAL LENGTH:
```

MEMBERS

DOCUMENT ID	ITEM TYPE	ITEM NAME	FMT	LEN	PREC	US	OCCUR	BYTES	OTHER CHARACTERISTICS
D610.WERMG002	GROUP	WERMG002							
D710.WMES0041	ELEMENT	PWBSP-SCR-ERR-MSG-NUM	N	4		C		2	
D710.DAUSR004	ELEMENT	USR-LANGUAGE	A	1				1	
D710.WMES0033	ELEMENT	MES-MSG-SEQ-NUM	N	3		D		3	
D710.WMES0057	ELEMENT	MES-ERR-MSG-DATA	A	79				79	

TOTAL BYTES =   85

Figure 5 COBOL DATA DIVISION Input Generated
from Segment Description

```
RPT0210                                                01DEC88  17:20:01   PAG
                          DESIGN/1: DESIGNER'S WORKBENCH
                               CODE GENERATION
                           COBOL COPYBOOK GENERATION

   *** COPYBOOK D615.FIGE05       IS BEING PROCESSED.
   *** WARNING...Total length is ignored on D610.UERRMSGS.
   *** COBOL COPYBOOK FOR D615.FIGE05        HAS BEEN GENERATED WITH WARNINGS. ***



   COPYBOOK GENERATION PROCESSING TOTALS:
                   Number of copybooks requested            :   1
                   Number of copybooks generated successfully :   0
                   Number of copybooks generated with warnings :   1
                   Number of copybooks generated with errors :   0




     01   WSER-UERRMSGS.
   *************************************************************************
   * RECORD UERRMSGS                            GENERATION DATE 01DEC88   *
   *                                                                      *
   *   ERROR MESSAGE RECORD LAYOUT FOR CODES TABLE FILE.                  *
   *   USED BY MES TO DECODE ERROR MESSAGES.                              *
   *   SAME COPYBOOK AS WERMT010                                          *
   *                                                                      *
   *************************************************************************
       05   WSER-WERMG002.
          10   WSER-PWBSP-SCR-ERR-MSG-NUM
                                         PIC S9(4)      COMP
                                                        VALUE ZEROES.
          10   WSER-USR-LANGUAGE         PIC X          VALUE SPACES.
          10   WSER-MES-MSG-SEQ-NUM      PIC 9(3)       VALUE ZEROES.
       05   WSER-MES-ERR-MSG-DATA        PIC X(79)      VALUE SPACES.
```

Figure 6 **Sample Cross-Reference or Where-Used Report**

```
                              SUBURBAN PUMPS
                        DATA DICTIONARY REPORTING
                        CROSS-REFERENCE WHERE-USED

12DEC91                    FOR ITEM S0000015 element              PAGE 001


S0000015  element  ITEM-NUM
     AIN11001  group  *** DESCRIPTION REQUIRED
          AINIM10   screen   INVENTORY INQUIRY ITEM LIST
               AINILIST   step   ITEM LIST
                    AINI   conversation   INVENTORY INQUIRY
          AIN2P20   screen   ITEM INVENTORY SELECT
               AIN2LIST   step  AIN2 LIST
                    AIN2   conversation   ITEM INVENTORY MAINTENANCE
     AIN1M20   screen   INVENTORY INQUIRY MULTI-WAREHOUSE
          AINIWLIST   step   MULTI-WAREHOUSE ITEM LIST
               AINI   conversation   INVENTORY INQUIRY
     AIN0D010   record   INVENTORY-ITEM-TABLE
          AIN0D010   db2 table   INVENTORY ITEM TABLE
          AIN0D010   copybook   INVENTORY-ITEM-TABLE
          TIN0D010   db2 table   INVENTORY ITEM TABLE
          TIN0D01   db2 table   INVNETORY ITEM TABLE
          TEMMTEMP   db2 table   INVENTORY ITEM TABLE
     AIN0G001   group  ITEM-WHSE-AVAIL-KEY
          AIN0R010   record   INVENTORY-ITEM-WHSE-AVAIL
               AIN0R010   copybook   INVENTORY-ITEM-WHSE-AVAIL
                    AIOMOD   program   DB2 TABLE I/O MODULE
               SCE10001   copybook   WAREHOUSE-ITEM-RECORD
                    SCE1C060   program   WAREHOUSE INVENTORY LIST
                    AIN2C010   program   ITEM INVENTORY PROMPT
                         AIN2PRPT   step  AIN2 PROMPT
                              AIN2   conversation   AIN2
                    WCG5I051   program   WCG5
                    ATESTC01   program   TEST CONVERSATION
                    ATESTC02   program   TEST DESCRIPTION
                    TEMMTEMM   program   TEST TEMM PROGRAM
     SCE0D011   record   ORDER-ENTRY-LINE-TABLE
          SCE0D011   db2 table   ORDER ENTRY LINE TABLE
          SCE0D011   copybook   ORDER-ENTRY-LINE-TABLE
     SCE1M40   screen   ORDER ENTRY LINE ITEM
          SCEMLINE   step   LINE ITEM
               SCEM   conversation   ORDER ENTRY MAINTENANCE
  *****
```

numbers need different names and are usually considered to be two distinct data elements by the data dictionary. Very few data dictionaries existing today recognize the notion of type.

Some facilities (usually in connection with productivity aids such as report writers, program generators, fourth-generation languages, and application generators) style themselves data dictionaries, but can describe data elements only within records. If both the customer master record and the order header contain the customer number, these facilities require that the length and type of the customer number be fully described in both places. Each customer number could be named something different, such as CUSTOMER_NUMBER and CUST_NO, thus causing undocumented synonyms. Conversely, two different elements could be called by the same name in two different records without the so-called data dictionary objecting. In reality, such a facility is not a data dictionary but rather a facility to store record descriptions, on a par with COBOL copy libraries.

Minimal data dictionary facilities are present in practically all data base management systems. In addition to element and record descriptions, these dictionaries also describe other DBMS entities: file structures (the hierarchy of records going into a physical data base such as IBM's IMS); views (the results of join and project operations performed on a relational data base and presented for manipulation to a user); and so on. Because these facilities usually cannot extend their reach beyond the data base that they document, they have difficulty meeting some of the main objectives of data dictionaries.

In addition to field and record descriptions, a useful data dictionary should contain descriptions of **files, data bases, and programs** that use those files and data bases. (For this discussion, reports and screens are assimilated to files.) Thus, the data dictionary can be queried about where an element or a group is used so that the impact of a change can be analyzed. This characteristic is especially useful during the design and implementation stage of development, when data descriptions are not yet complete and definitive. On a large system, a data dictionary helps ensure that all the team members are kept up to date on seemingly minor design decisions.

files, data bases, and programs

In addition, those dictionaries that contain file and screen descriptions can support the generation of programming language statements required to use the screens in on-line conversations and the files in batch programs. This simplifies the task of the programmers by eliminating a tedious, uninteresting, and error-prone job of copying paper descriptions and translating them to the appropriate syntax.

Interfaces

All productivity aids such as fourth-generation languages and application generators require data descriptions, just as COBOL requires a Data Division in every program. Ideally, each data dictionary should generate the data descriptions required by each productivity aid. However, each productivity aid uses its own conventions and formats. Therefore, most data dictionaries simply provide access to the data dictionary structure, so that each installation can create programs that will format the data definitions to be accepted by those productivity aids in use at that installation. Many data dictionaries have active user groups, a good source for such programs.

Programs to format data descriptions for a productivity aid can be created only if the productivity aid in question accepts data description input in batch mode from files. If data descriptions can be entered only interactively, via a screen, then it is not very useful to have the data dictionary generate this input.

Active versus Passive Dictionaries

Dictionaries have the most merit if they are the only possible source for data descriptions. If COBOL programmers are free to choose between dictionary-generated Data Division statements and hand-coded ones, a programmer will sometimes resort to coding by hand because it is quicker, because the data dictionary has not been updated, or because the programmer has not learned about the benefits of a data dictionary. The hand-coded version may then differ from the data dictionary version of the data, negating the main benefit of the dictionary—to be an exhaustive description of all the data in an installation or on a project.

So-called *passive dictionaries* do not address this problem. *Active dictionaries* address it by forcing the programs to refer to the data dictionary whenever a data description (length, format, precision) is required. (A good example of an active dictionary is Cullinet's IDD, the data dictionary used by the IDMS data base management system.) Even for active dictionaries, the solution is only partial; it only applies to DBMS operations and not to classical files.

Another approach would be to have the data dictionary integrated with the program development system, particularly the compiler. This approach would cause a recompilation when the data dictionary is changed and force the compiler to use only the data dictionary as a source for describing data. This approach has not yet been implemented on large-scale, commercially available systems. In most cases, the only way of forcing the programmers to use the data dictionary is through procedural means.

Version Control

The last main feature of a data dictionary is the support of several versions of the same data. This feature is required because changes cannot be made instantaneously. When a record description changes, a team is set up to modify all the programs that use the record. Some programs will be changed today, others tomorrow, and some at the end of next month. The change cannot be implemented in production until all the programs are changed and the files that contain the modified record are converted to the new format. In the meanwhile, one of the programs affected by the change may need some urgent modification—perhaps because of a bug. That program will therefore need to be recompiled with the old version of the record description. Similar considerations apply during the design of a large system. Changes may be proposed by one group, evaluated by another, and finally accepted or rejected by whoever has that authority. In the meanwhile, those not immediately touched by the evaluation of the modification must continue to work with the old version of the data.

A good data dictionary therefore needs a version control facility with two or more versions of the data descriptions for test and production, together with a convenient means of transforming test data descriptions to production and vice versa.

WHERE USED IN THE LIFE CYCLE

Most data dictionaries are designed to be used during the implementation and maintenance phases of the life cycle. In these phases, programmers incorporate data definitions into programs and productivity aids, data base administrators maintain the data base descriptions, and maintenance analysts query the data dictionary as one step in evaluating where a proposed change would have an impact.

Attempts have been made to use the same dictionaries in the design phase of a project to record data design decisions both for user approval at the end of design and to carry over to the implementation phase. Attempts have also been made to use data dictionaries to support entity-relationship modeling. In both cases, problems have arisen. The main difficulty is that during data modeling and data design some of the characteristics of data captured by a good implementation-level data dictionary are not known. Physical representation format is one of these characteristics.

The current trend is for CASE tools to provide their own data dictionary or data description facilities and for the contents of the design-level dictionary to be transportable to an implementation-level dictionary. The ability to transport data from the design level to the implementation level also implies that existing data descriptions can be transported from the implementation-level dictionary for reuse by design teams who are creating systems that use, at least in part, existing data. This feature, however, is not widely available in CASE tools.

Some experts predict the emergence of a new type of dictionary-based tool, called a *repository*. The repository would store all the information that is needed to manage the software (and perhaps even the hardware) resources of the entire installation, including data descriptions as well as program and batch job descriptions. The repository would integrate design documentation with source and object code of programs and, increasingly important as distributed data processing gains hold, where data and programs reside. In the case where the same system is distributed to many different sites, the repository would keep track of what version is running at each site, what corrections and changes have been implemented where, and so forth.

Figure 7 **List of Independent Data Dictionaries**

Company	Product
Manager Software Products, Inc.	Datamanager
IBM Corporation	Data Dictionary DB/DC

EXISTING TOOLS

Figure 7 is a list of implementation-level data dictionaries that are not integrated with a specific DBMS.

Figure 8 is a list of data base management systems with fairly complete associated data dictionary systems.

Figure 9 is a list of CASE tools with a reasonably strong data dictionary component.

CRITERIA FOR USE

The implementation and enforcement of a single data dictionary by the entire IS department is a major undertaking. It implies reorganizing part of the department to create a data administration function with new job descriptions, possibly hiring experienced data administrators, and training all the analysts and programmers in the use of the data dictionary. Such a step should not be undertaken without top IS management commitment.

If a data administration function as such does not exist for the IS department, each major development project must provide its own data administration function by acquiring the data dictionary software and designating project team members to keep the data dictionary up to date and enforce its use. Even if no data dictionary software is available in the department, a minimal system providing most of the functions required during development of a single project can easily be developed. The project team can use whatever data description facilities are available in a CASE tool. Alternatively, the team can use

Figure 8 **List of Data Base Management Systems with a Strong Data Dictionary Function**

Company	DBMS Product
Computer Associates	Datacom/DB
Cincom	Supra
Software AG	Adabas
Cullinet	IDMS

Figure 9 **List of CASE Tools with Data Dictionary Component**

Company	CASE Product
Andersen Consulting	Foundation
CGI	Pacbase
Index Technologies, Inc.	Excelerator
Knowledgeware, Inc.	Information Engineering Workbench
Knowledgeware, Inc.	Gamma
Pansophic Systems, Inc.	Telon
Sage Software, Inc.	APS
Texas Instruments	Information Engineering Facility

a fourth-generation language to create a data dictionary that will accept data element, record, screen and report descriptions; print them out; and generate DBMS, COBOL, and other tool output.

Selected Readings

Ross, Ronald G. *Data Dictionaries & Data Administration*. New York: AMACOM, 1981.

This book is the most useful reference on data dictionaries.

EXERCISES

1. Review and critique the data dictionary functions of tools that you have available:

    a. CASE tool

    b. Micro-based DBMS (dBase III, Rbase)

    c. Fourth-generation language (Focus, Oracle)

2. Design a minimal-function data dictionary to cover the entity-relationship and data element design components of this book. Evaluate the effort to program and test such a system on a micro-based DBMS such as dBase III.

3. Use a CASE-based data dictionary function to document one of the data structures established when you studied entity-relationship modeling (see Technique for Section II). Create a complete set of paper reports from the dictionary. Contrast the use of paper output and on-line query.

Section VI

Process Design

Section VI describes the third and final component of design, that of the system processes. How to design programs that satisfy the user's functional requirements is explained in Chapter 14. Chapters 15 and 16 describe how to ensure that these programs also satisfy the control and performance requirements, respectively.

Finally, Chapter 17 describes how the design is translated into a plan for implementing the system, how to analyze its costs and benefits, and how to gain management approval for proceeding.

The New York State Retirement System

In the early 1980s, the state of New York needed a new system to manage its retirement program. The new retirement system would take two and one-half years to develop. It would contain 800 COBOL modules with a total of several hundred thousand lines of code, and the development team would number between 40 and 50 analysts and programmers.

The system would handle all state employment retirement functions, from the membership application through the retirement itself, the payment of pension and other benefits, and the final disposition by death or other termination. The system would write 200,000 pension checks per month and handle employees from 2,000 different state agencies.

The project team had several challenges. First, the users of the system were to be the retirement case officers themselves—the operational decision makers—rather than clerks; the users would therefore place greater demands on the human interface of the system. Second, because the system was to be so large, the team would have difficulty coordinating the designs of the various subsystems. Third, the underlying technology was unfamiliar: the system would be one of the first of its size to use relational data base for transaction processing.

The first challenge to be addressed was designing a system for the case officers rather than for data entry clerks. The job characteristics of these professionals were the following:

- The two major events in the life of a retirement plan member were the initial registration (at employment time) and the retirement itself. Each of these events could open up a series of processing steps lasting up to six months. A single officer would be assigned to the case for the entire six months.

- Frequently, the case officers would have to interpret regulations and make judgments according to a sense of fairness. At the end

of a case, the officer's supervisor would review the work and approve the decisions made by the case officer before clearing the case for final disposition.

- The regulations and the processing were so complex that new case officers required an apprenticeship period, with more supervision and more on-line help available than more experienced officers.

- Each case officer would handle many cases concurrently. The caseload of each officer would therefore have to be managed.

- The main problem of the previous system was to control all the paperwork, making sure that each member's file was complete, that copies of relevant documents could be found, and that the necessary letters were sent to members. The new system would therefore require a strong office automation component.

The designers created a human interface based on a dialog structure illustrated in Figure VI–1. The first screen is a sign-on screen: the user enters an identification and a password so that the system can establish access to the caseload of the user. Next, a case selection screen prompts the operator for the case to be worked on. Depending on the type of case (such as membership application, transfer, or retirement), the system displays a guide to the different activities that the user can choose. From this point on, the user is free to select any of the activities by picking one of the case-general or application-specific screens.

Case-general screens include activities required for all cases regardless of their type: opening, reviewing, and closing a case; maintaining a list of things to do or a list of personal notes that the case officer makes as the case progresses; and so on. The application-specific activities depend on the type of event processed: the forms to be filled out, the calculations to be made, and the decisions to be taken are different for each type.

At any point, the user can suspend the processing to invoke help functions; execute queries against the member data base, the caseload, or existing correspondence; or adapt and combine standard paragraphs into a letter informing the member of decisions or requesting more information.

The second challenge was to coordinate the team's design and development of a large number of program modules. This challenge was primarily met by creating a highly standardized application architecture. For the on-line part of the system, four standard screen styles were designed (see Figure VI–2). Every screen had to conform to one of four styles: case open/close; form with one line per data item; report with a header and detailed lines; and text used for help and word processing.

Another element for standardizing the on-line part of the system was to provide five different styles of on-line programs for the following processes: data entry and update; queries; displaying lists for browsing; opening and closing cases; and selecting a case activity. Each style of on-line program had its specific structure so that the programmer had only to complete the needed details—which screen was to be displayed, which record was to be read on the data base, and so on.

Finally, batch architectures were also standardized (see Figure VI–3). In the structure shown, batch transactions are received from the retirement system's 2,000 employers, each with its own system to track employment, transfers, terminations, and retirements. These transactions are first validated, then posted to the permanent data bases. Reporting is done either from an activity file or from the permanent data base, depending on the content of the report. Various logs and control reports are issued at critical points in the processing for manual balancing and reconciliation.

The third challenge was the use of relational data base technology for high-volume transaction processing. The project team selected DB2, IBM's relational DBMS, but not before the team had developed and run a performance benchmark to ensure that the software could process between five and ten transactions per second. During the rest of the project, the benchmark results helped the team evaluate whether a design decision would have a negative effect on performance. In the final implementation, the system required a somewhat larger processor than initially anticipated; however, this was mostly due to requirements that arose after the benchmark was conducted. Today, the performance of the system is generally satisfactory and improving with every new release of the software.

PURPOSE OF SECTION

The purpose of Section VI is to explain how to design the programs that implement the functions of the system and that fulfill the control and performance requirements established during the requirements analysis phase. The section concludes with a chapter on the cost/benefit analysis performed at the end of the design.

The section emphasizes the role of the system's technical architecture in making the design easier. The technical architecture consists of three layers. The first is made up of the hardware, the systems software, and the distributed processing approach of the entire installation. This layer is

Figure VI–1 **Dialog Structure**

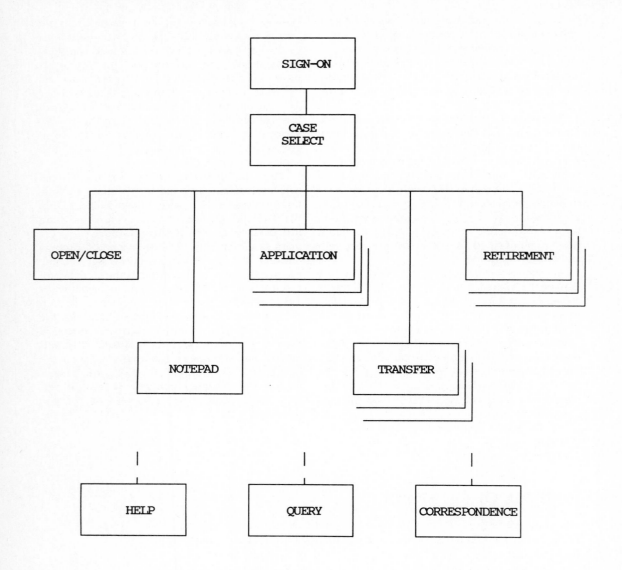

Figure VI–2 **Standard Screen Styles**

```
SCREEN NO                  NEW YORK STATE                    DATE
                           RETIREMENT SYSTEM          CASE NUMBER
OPERATOR NAME              SCREEN TITLE               CASE NAME

              CASE NUMBER:  999.99.9999
                     NAME:  XXXXXXXXXX X. XXXXXXXXXXXXX
                  ADDRESS:  XXXXXXXXXXXXXXXXXXXXXXXX
                            XXXXXXXXXXXXXXXX, XX 99999-9999
                   STATUS:  XXXXXXXX
       LAST ACTIVITY DATE:  99XXX99
                    NOTES:  XXXXXX  XXXXXXX  XXXXXX XXXXXXXXXX
                            XX X XXXXXXXX



PF1=HELP  PF3=END  PF4=TOP  PF5=BOTTOM  PF6=RIGHT  PF7=LEFT  PF8=NEXT
PF9=BACK  PF10=PRINT  PF12=CANCEL
MESSAGE TEXT: _____
```

```
SCREEN NO                  NEW YORK STATE                    DATE
                           RETIREMENT SYSTEM          CASE NUMBER
OPERATOR NAME              SCREEN TITLE               CASE NAME

              XXXXXX:  _____

            XXXXXXXX:  _____
                       _____
                       _____

                 XXX:  ____

       XXXXXXXXXXXXXX:  _

          XXX XXXXXXX:  _____

PF1=HELP  PF3=END  PF4=TOP  PF5=BOTTOM  PF6=RIGHT  PF7=LEFT  PF8=NEXT
PF9=BACK  PF10=PRINT  PF12=CANCEL
MESSAGE TEXT: _____
```

```
SCREEN NO                  NEW YORK STATE                    DATE
                           RETIREMENT SYSTEM          CASE NUMBER
OPERATOR NAME              SCREEN TITLE               CASE NAME

   XXXXXX  XXXXXXXXX  XXXXXXXXXXXXX       XXXXXX  XX  XXXXXXXXXXXXX
   ------  ---------  ------------------  ------  --  ------------------
    9999   9,999.99   XXXXXXXXXXXX        XXXXXX  X
    9999   9,999.99   XXXXXXX             XXXXXX  X
    9999   9,999.99   XXXXXXXX            XXXXXX  X
    9999   9,999.99   XXXXXXXXXXXX        XXXXXX  X   99-XXXXXXXXXXXXX
    9999   9,999.99   XXXXXXXX            XXXXXX  X
    9999   9,999.99   XXXXXXX             XXXXXX  X
    9999   9,999.99   XXXXXXXXXXXXXX      XXXXXX  X
    9999   9,999.99   XXXXXXXXXXXX        XXXXXX  X
    9999   9,999.99   XXXXXXXXXXXX        XXXXXX  X

PF1=HELP  PF3=END  PF4=TOP  PF5=BOTTOM  PF6=RIGHT  PF7=LEFT  PF8=NEXT
PF9=BACK  PF10=PRINT  PF12=CANCEL
MESSAGE TEXT: _____
```

```
SCREEN NO                  NEW YORK STATE                    DATE
                           RETIREMENT SYSTEM          CASE NUMBER
OPERATOR NAME              SCREEN TITLE               CASE NAME

 Adfghjklzx Cvbnmqw

 Ert yuiop asdfgh jk Klzxcvbnmpo Iuytrewqlkj hgf dsamnbvcxz plok mi
 IJNUHB-Y, gv tfcrdxe:

 SZW:      Aqwazsexdr, cftvgy bhu njimkolpqwer tio y upaaas df
           ghjklzxcvbn mpoiuytr.

 EWQ:      Lkjhgfdsam nbz bvcx pl okm  Ijnuhbygvtfc tf CRD.  Xrdeszw, waq
           qazws xe dcrf vtgby:  tgbyhnujm ujmik olploktijn uhb ygvtfcr
           dxes zwaq(p) oli kujmyhn tgbrfvedc wsxqaz (mnbvcxzlkj
           hgfdsapoiu; exhaustively ytrewqd zxcv bnmasd fghj kl qwe

PF1=HELP  PF3=END  PF4=TOP  PF5=BOTTOM  PF6=RIGHT  PF7=LEFT  PF8=NEXT
PF9=BACK  PF10=PRINT  PF12=CANCEL
MESSAGE TEXT: _____
```

Figure VI–3 **Standard Batch Architectures**

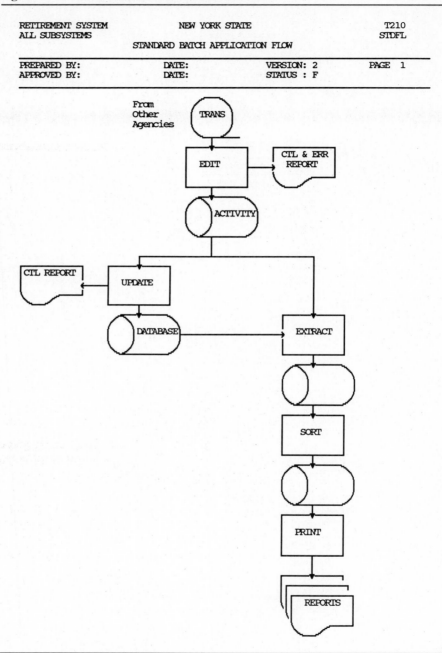

RETIREMENT SYSTEM   NEW YORK STATE   T210
ALL SUBSYSTEMS   STDFL
                        STANDARD BATCH APPLICATION FLOW

PREPARED BY: DATE: VERSION: 2   PAGE   1
APPROVED BY: DATE: STATUS : F

described as the production environment in Chapter 6. The second layer is made up of the development environment—a subset of the standards and tools used by the IS development personnel across applications. The third layer, known as the application architecture, is made up of the overall structure of the on-line and batch processes, the common style of user interfaces, and the standard program designs adopted by the project team. The New York State retirement system illustrates one particular application architecture well adapted to the casework style of user interface.

Some IS departments do not establish a technical architecture at each of these three levels. Instead, many installations let the project team choose its own tools, which can result in excessive tool proliferation. Other installations do not encourage an application architecture and allow each project team member to solve the same design problem in different ways. This practice wastes time spent devising solutions and makes maintenance more difficult. This section therefore concentrates on frequently used architectural elements in transaction processing systems.

KEY TASKS AND DELIVERABLES

Based on data flow diagrams, conversation designs, and the data model for the application, program design identifies all the programs required to accomplish the processing specified. The design is documented on a system flowchart that depicts the sequence of batch programs, the relationships between on-line programs, and the interfaces between programs through messages and files.

The next level of documentation concerns the decomposition of the largest programs into modules, i.e., the appropriate units of work for estimating and assigning work to individual programmers. A structure chart, a Warnier or Jackson diagram, or HIPO documentation depicts the control structure of the program.

Controls design consists of analyzing and documenting the risks that must be controlled, assessing their potential impact, and selecting the appropriate control techniques. A controls memorandum documents the analysis and serves as a supplemental input to the program design activity, so that control functions can be incorporated in the appropriate modules. Because many of the risks that the controls are designed to cover arise only as the programs are being designed, controls design and program design must be conducted with some degree of parallelism or iteration.

Performance analysis consists in estimating the resource consumption of the processes and the data bases and the impact on the performance requirements. Where required, the process and data designs are modified. The output from this activity is a document summarizing the estimated resource requirements of the application to be used as input to the cost/benefit analysis.

Once the design is completed, all the outputs from the user interface, data structure, and process design tasks flow into the final activity of the design phase: installation planning, economic analysis, and management approval. Only at the end of the design can the project team develop the plans for building the system, testing it, training the users, converting files, and starting live operations. These plans help determine the total development cost and the cost of operating the manual part of the system. The performance design determines the cost of operating the automated part. An economic summary is provided to management, weighing the development and operating costs against the benefits determined during the feasibility study and the requirements analysis, possibly modified by decisions made in the design phase. Management can then decide whether to go ahead with the installation of the system: this is the last major go/no-go decision point in a project.

Figure VI–4 **Data Flow Diagram for Process Design**

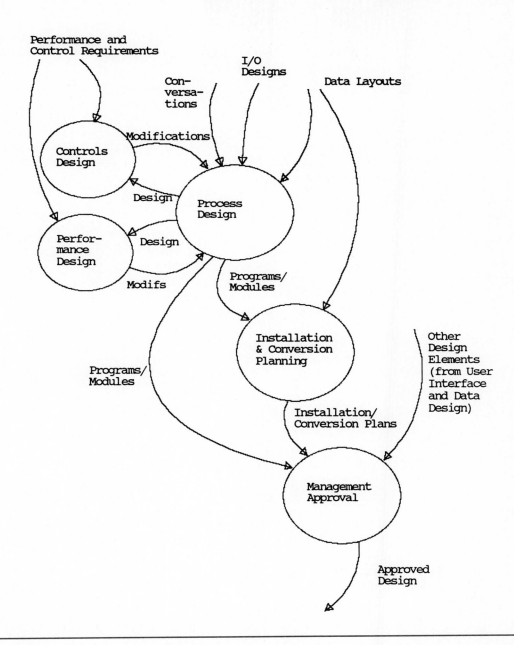

Chapter 14

Program Design

This chapter describes how to design on-line and batch programs. Included are examples of on-line programs of increasing complexity, from the simple inquiry to on-line update. Backup, recovery, and restart are discussed in detail. Also described is the standard batch architecture, consisting of a succession of programs to validate transactions, update data bases, extract data, and prepare reports. A discussion of interfaces explains how to communicate data between systems. Finally, there is a description of the need for cut-off processing.

Learning Objectives

- Understand the principles of on-line program design.
- Describe the considerations underlying the design of single-exchange and multi-exchange conversations for inquiry, data entry, and update.
- Be aware of the need for restart and recovery procedures in on-line systems and of the main methods of implementing them.
- Describe the standard batch processing architecture for validating, updating, and reporting, as well as some of the common variations on this standard.
- Understand the process of extracting and printing report data and apply it to specific cases.
- Be aware of the impact of the requirements to interface to other systems and to do cut-off processing.

ON-LINE VERSUS BATCH PROGRAM DESIGN

The main distinction between systems architectures of today is between batch and on-line processing. The architectural difference is that in on-line processing, a number of processes go on at the same time, and the sequence of activities is unpredictable. It is generally impossible to reproduce the exact sequence of events that led to a given result because many operators interact with the system simultaneously and independently. (Consequently, some bugs in on-line systems are extremely hard to find if they depend on a coincidence of several independent events happening in a specific sequence.) To each user corresponds a thread of control; the on-line monitor intertwines these threads to maximize the use of resources and minimize response time, while ensuring the integrity of shared data. This type of process is called *transaction-driven* or *event-driven*.

In traditional batch processing, only one thread is going on. Each record of the principal input file is read, processed completely, and replaced by the next record in sequence. Contrary to on-line processing, two successive executions of the same batch program with the same input files will yield identical results, unless there has been a change in the hardware or the systems software.

Sometimes, the very nature of the problem dictates a batch solution. For instance, to produce a management report with detail lines, subtotals, and grand totals, all the detail lines in a group have to be processed before the subtotal is printed; then the next group is processed with its subtotal, and so on, until the end of the file when the grand totals are printed. The input file is in the same sequence as the report, and the technique used is called control break processing. Processes that depend on the input file being in a specific sequence are called *file-driven*.

At other times, the problem calls for batch processing but the sequence is less significant and there is no control break processing. Take, for instance, the processing of insurance premiums. A file of policyholders is read, and each policyholder is billed for a premium that depends on the specific policy, neither on the previous one nor on the next one. The process appears file-driven in the sense that there is an input file and a single thread of control; nevertheless, this processing is much more akin to on-line processing than the previous example and is therefore better qualified as event-driven.

Another example of transaction-driven batch processing can be found in the insurance industry. Assume an insurance company with 2 million policies, all billed every six months. Rather than read the entire file of 2 million policies every day to extract only those policies that fall due (on the average 1 in 180 or so), the company could create a file for each day of the year that contains the numbers of the policies that fall due on that day. It could use the day's file as input, and therefore read only the full data base records for the specific policies contained on the input file—an average of less than 26,000. This method is possible because the processing is not dependent on sequence—just as in event-driven processing. The same type of logic is also applied in utility billing and bank statement preparation. In these cases, the activity is spread over the period of a month.

For on-line programming, the design strategy is transaction-oriented. Each transaction type is considered as a separate entity, and all the functions required to complete the transaction are analyzed within that transaction.

For batch processing, the design strategy is not to group functions by transaction but by type of data transformation they accomplish. Thus, validation functions are grouped together for all transactions, as are data base updating, report extraction, and report printing functions. Within each transformation type, the processing is then broken down by transaction.

These transaction and transformation strategies are due to Ed Yourdon.[1] Each strategy is normally assigned to on-line and batch systems, respectively. However, it is possible, although uncommon, to organize on-line processing along data transformation lines and batch processing along transaction lines (see Box 14–1).

ON-LINE PROGRAM DESIGN

On-line program design is largely determined by the user's view of the user interface. Some technical decisions remain to be made, however, including decisions on how to use the functions of the teleprocessing (TP) monitor. How to implement these decisions is naturally dependent on the specific TP monitor and is therefore beyond the scope of this text.

A day in the life of a user of an on-line system is depicted in Figure 14–1. The first step is the initialization of activity though a sign-on procedure, which starts a session. In traditional, mainframe-based, centralized transaction processing systems, a session is made up of multiple conversations, each corresponding to a unit of work that stands on its own (a business transaction). Each conversation is made up of several exchanges between the program and the operator. On some days, the user may see a system crash: the work will be interrupted while the cause of the crash is located, the data is recovered, and the processing restarted.

Session Sign-On

As a user signs on to the application, a number of activities must take place. First, it is necessary to *identify* the user: name, account number, terminal location, for example. Then, if the application is sensitive, it may be necessary to *authenticate* the identification. An example is the PIN or Personal Identification Number that users of automatic bank tellers are asked to key in before any transactions are accepted; this number is akin to the password used in many on-line applications. The third step is to *authorize* the user to perform certain functions. Authorization can be given by reference to a file containing the facilities that each user is allowed to request. Or the system can, by default, allow the user access to all the functions of the application. A user authorization file might also contain some of the user's characteristics, such as personalized tailoring of screens (color preferences, for example) and the characteristics of the terminal used (number of lines, monochrome versus color).

Technically, sign-on (or log-on) processing can be done by the operating system, by the application, or by a combination of both. Usually, a system-wide

BOX 14-1

Strategies for Program Design

The strategies for program design that underlie the content of Chapter 14 come from two sources, Edward Yourdon[1] and David L. Parnas.[2]

Yourdon's contribution is to distinguish two substrategies for designing programs: transform analysis and transaction analysis. Briefly, in transform analysis, processes are factored according to their action on the data: validate, calculate, post, print. In transaction analysis, processes are factored according to the business functions that they accomplish: for instance, in an order entry program, new orders, back-orders, credit checking, and order status inquiry. Depending on the approach chosen, the top level of the program (the mainline) will generally have a file-driven or an event-driven structure. The modules called by this top-level structure will be factored according to the strategy—either by transform or transaction function.

Parnas's work, published earlier than Yourdon's, does not distinguish between these two substrategies. Instead, Parnas points out the qualities that good modular design should have. The design should group functions into modules (a unit of work for a programmer or a maintainer) that have high cohesiveness and low coupling. These qualities will increase the maintainability of a program made up of such modules and therefore decrease its total life cycle cost.

A highly cohesive module is one that contains processing instructions that are closely related to each other, that accomplish a single goal, and that are likely to change or stay unchanged as a unit. These characteristics preclude grouping functions solely on the basis of their being performed at the same time, for example, the processing of control totals and the closing of files at the end of the program, which should be in separate modules.

Parnas also advocates low coupling. Two modules have low coupling if each does not depend on the internals of the other. High coupling occurs if a single design or implementation decision affects both of the modules: if the design decision is changed, both modules will change. For instance, the design team may decide to incorporate into the customer number a check-digit of a certain type, say Modulo-11. If the checking is done in two different modules in the system (e.g., in an order entry module and in an accounts-receivable payment posting module), an error in the algorithm or a decision to change the number to Modulo-10 would be reflected in two different places, causing both debugging and maintenance changes.

Another, more universal, example of high coupling is the sharing of data structures—record layouts, data base relationships and pointers, program working storage. Very few IS professionals realize that COBOL is conducive to high coupling because it encourages programmers to share data structures among multiple programs. When a data structure changes, one, many, or all programs that use the data structure may be affected. The worst problem is that some programs appear to see parts of data structures without needing to see them. For instance, a module that changes customer addresses may see the entire customer data base record, including, say, billing conditions. If the billing condition data elements were to change, the address change module would probably not notice; it might simply be recompiled with the new record layout. However, it is impossible to predict this reliably without further analysis.

Conflicting assumptions about the meaning of individual data items can cause many bugs. Conflicting assumptions occur especially frequently for codes such as status information, for fields that may have a null value, and for fields that have a choice of formats (such as a date or an amount whose precision could vary). A problem arises when a module that uses the information is unaware of all possible values the data element can take and is therefore surprised when the data element contains a value which appears illegal or meaningless. When such an error occurs within the working storage of a single program, it may be relatively easy to find the source of the error because no other program is involved. When the problem occurs on a file, the culprit may be much more difficult to find, especially if the file can be updated through end-user facilities such as relational data manipulation languages.

There is always a temptation to factor into a single module functions that have the same purpose, the same name, and even similar algorithms but are performed on different data structures. Two functions that fit this description could be the sorting of an array or a table in memory and the sorting of an external, sequential file. Two business-related functions would be insurance processing for homeowner and automobile insurance. In both examples, the objective and the general logic of the process is the same. However, the actual implementation is likely to be quite different. Reading and writing files of arbitrary length is not at all the same as manipulating an array of known length in main memory; and the premium calculation, the claims processing, and the management statistics about two different kinds of insurance are likely to take into account a vast number of different elements. To factor them into a common module would require multiple processing switches directing the procedure to account for such

items as the driver's record (for auto insurance) or the neighborhood (for homeowner insurance). Too many of these switches would increase the coupling of the module and decrease its cohesiveness.

Thus, each module should see only the data that it uses. Parnas calls this "information hiding." Later authors have pushed the argument further, stating the requirement as: "Each module should hide one design decision, and one only." Therefore, any change to a design decision should be limited to one module.

This doctrine cannot be strictly enforced. Some design decisions are all-encompassing and cannot be confined to one module. In addition, many design decisions are made subconsciously and are not seen as decisions. For instance, the decision to represent an amount as packed decimal rather than floating-point is probably so natural to a commercial application programmer that it does not appear to be a decision. In CICS, the design of the work area that enables data to be held in memory over the course of a multiple exchange conversation must be known to all the screen processing modules. And it is illusory to think that programmers and end-users can be insulated from knowledge of file layouts and that all I/O must go through centrally controlled modules. End-user computing, decision support, and ad hoc query would then become cumbersome, if not impossible.

sign-on process will perform all the identification and authentication interactively, and the application will perform the authorization processing without user interaction. In this way, a user can switch back and forth between applications with different authorization requirements without having to provide identification and authentication every time.

If the operating system performs identification and authentication, the project team building an application need not design these functions. On the other hand, the team must make sure that the authorization processing that the application is to perform obeys the constraint of the system sign-on facilities.

Figure 14–1 **User View of On-Line System Functional Hierarchy**

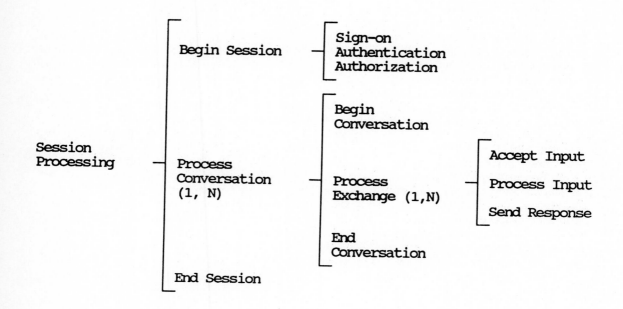

Additional authorization processing may be performed by the DBMS at program execution time, for instance, when the data base contains sensitive information that certain users are not allowed to see. For instance, a payroll clerk might be allowed to see salaries of everyone in the data base except managers and above.

The authorization file, if it exists, must obviously be well protected. Protection is even more critical for the file containing authentication data such as passwords. In addition to being password-protected, with access reserved for security personnel, these files are often encrypted, so that a computer operator will be unable to gain access to its data through a utility program that bypasses the operating system.

In some cases, the application or the operating system will monitor each user, so as to cause an automatic sign-off after a certain interval of inactivity. Thus, if a user leaves the workstation, passers-by cannot easily gain access to a restricted application.

Depending on the architecture of the transaction processing monitor and the application, resources may need to be allocated to the operator at application sign-on time. For instance, the application may maintain running control totals of transactions by type, so as to have a check at the end of the day against a preestablished total and against the transaction files processed in batch during the night. If a single, application-wide control total is maintained, it may have to be shared by a large number of users and therefore constitute a bottleneck. A better technique may be to assign a control total work area to each operator and consolidate all the operator totals at the end of the shift.

Conversation Design

This section covers only the design of programs interacting with block-mode terminals. In this operating mode, a user fills in an entire screen (usually a form-oriented layout or a menu choice) and presses an *Enter* or a *Transmit* key. The system then processes all the data on the screen and sends a response to the user at the terminal.

Programs running on an intelligent workstation and programs interacting with character-mode terminals are covered under cooperative processing in Box 14–7, at the end of this chapter.

Single-Exchange Inquiry Conversations. Some business transactions require only one exchange between the operator and the system—for example, an inquiry to list all the open orders for a customer whose customer number is known. The programming technique for this type of transaction is simple. The logic of the inquiry dictates that certain tasks be performed in a certain order: validate the format of the data entered by the operator, read the data base record(s) requested, and format and send the response. If there is a format error or if the record requested does not exist on the data base, an error message is sent instead of the formatted screen. Such a transaction can usually be processed within a single module.

Very few inquiry transactions are as simple as this one. In general, the data structures are more complex, requiring several successive inquiries to get the answer. These inquiries can be strung together independently, as illustrated in Figure 14–2, which shows a series of single-exchange, unrelated conversations that nevertheless accomplish a single objective.

Forms of processing other than inquiry, such as data entry and on-line data base update, are also more complex. Even though they may be single-exchange, they have file access and data integrity control requirements that require special consideration.

Conversational Inquiry. A more functional way of implementing the three single-exchange inquiries of Figure 14–2 would be to design a three-step,

BOX 14–2

Distributed Processing

The design of a distributed application, one where data and processes are distributed over multiple processors that run independently of each other, is beyond the scope of this book; only elementary considerations and illustrations of some of the difficulties associated with distributed processing will be covered.

A simple form of distributed data processing is one where the on-line activity is done at remote locations (close to the customer or the warehouse) during the day and where results are consolidated centrally at night. No communication between sites is required to complete a given on-line transaction. The problems associated with this type of distributed processing are fairly simple to solve: It is sufficient to design efficient data uploading and downloading mechanisms and effective controls so that all data that should be transmitted actually will be. A typical design consideration is whether to download to each site in the morning the entire data base required by that location or only the records that have changed as a result of the night's activity.

The problems become more complex when a transaction at a given site requires access to data from another site. A typical design consideration in this case is whether the user or operator must know where to look for the data or whether the system will keep track of it. The latter is the ambition of distributed data base management systems, which are not universally available today. Another consideration is how the transaction will be handled if the remote site that has the data is unavailable because of hardware or network failures. Can the application work in degraded mode? This question is much more critical than with a single-site application because the probability of some link's failing in a distributed network is much higher. (The risk of the *entire* network's failing is much lower, however.)

The most difficult case to design for is one in which a given transaction requires that several locations in the network update data locally and that these updates be synchronized: either all the updates are performed or none of them are. This synchronization is generally considered to require a procedure called *two-phased commit*. A "commit" is the action that an on-line user takes to indicate to the system that the business transaction being processed is essentially complete and correct and that it can be posted to the data base. This technique ensures that transactions do not get partially posted and, thus, that they do not endanger the integrity of the data base.

The two-phase commit procedure consists of a transaction at a given site asking all the other sites involved in the transaction whether they are ready to commit (phase 1). When a positive acknowledgment has been received from each one, the transaction sends the order to perform the actual commitment (phase 2).

Two problems are associated with the two-phase commit. One, it is time- and resource-consuming. Even a two-second response time is unlikely to be achieved if a telecommunications network is concerned (rather than a local area network, for example). Two, there are no standard protocols that allow different DBMS software to cooperate in two-phase commit transactions. Therefore, either a homogeneous network where all the DBMS systems come from the same vendor and have a two-phase commit protocol must exist, or a custom protocol must be developed. The latter is costly; the former is hard to find.

Figure 14–2 **Single-Exchange Inquiry Application Flow**

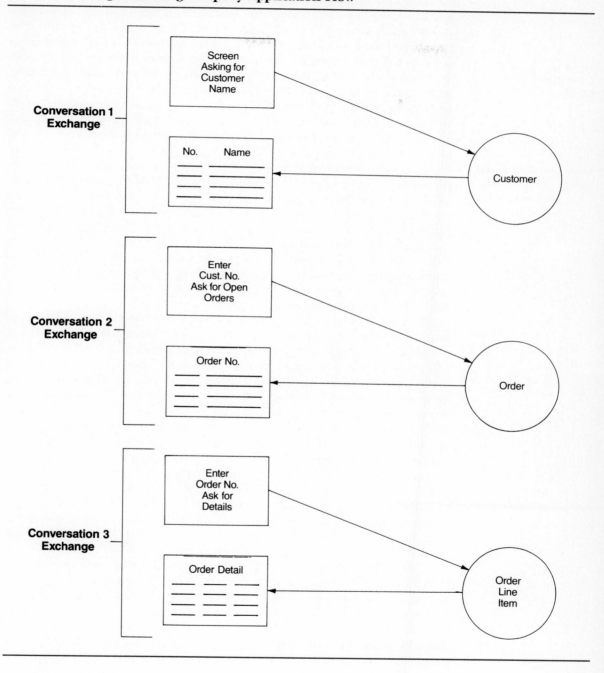

conversational inquiry, as shown in Figure 14–3. In this design, the user does not need to remember and reenter the customer number from the first to the second exchange and the order number from the second to the third. The design does complicate the program somewhat, however. Now the program must keep track of data between two operator actions. Depending on the teleprocessing monitor, this can be done in either of two ways. In **conversational mode,** the teleprocessing monitor does not automatically release resources when a message is sent to the terminal. Therefore, the whole conversation can be written as a single module, as shown in the pseudo-code in Figure 14–4, using its own working storage to transmit customer and order numbers from one part of the conversation to the next.

In **nonconversational mode** (or pseudo-conversational mode), the teleprocessing monitor cannot send several messages from the same program. As soon as a message is sent, the program that sends it terminates, and the teleprocessing monitor waits for a new message to appear. No data in working storage is kept between the two successive programs. In this case, the programmer must write three distinct programs and use the teleprocessing monitor's facilities (for instance, a temporary file) to pass data from one to the other. This method is obviously more complex, because the programmer must manage the acquisition and release of temporary storage areas (on files or in memory). Figure 14–5 illustrates the sample pseudo-code.

Why use nonconversational mode for conversational activities, then, as it is much more complex? There are two answers. First, there may not be a choice: the most popular teleprocessing monitors, IBM's CICS and IMS/DC, are both essentially nonconversational. Second, and more important, conversational mode can have severe performance implications. In general, the processing between an operator pressing *Enter* and receiving a response takes a few seconds or even less. For the operator to respond to the message takes considerably longer: 10 to 15 seconds for typical end-user work; 30 to 60 seconds for on-line data entry and data base update; 5 minutes to an hour if the operator leaves the terminal to get a cup of coffee or go on lunch break. Any resources used by a conversation, main storage in particular, will then be unavailable to the rest of the system for the duration of the operator's absence. Most teleprocessing monitors were created when storage was at a premium and therefore take measures to conserve its use. Today, many systems use virtual memory or memory-swapping techniques; the resource consumption of idle tasks is therefore a less critical issue than before.

The trend is towards less expensive memory and intelligent workstations, which should make conversational mode become more attractive. However, this evolution is likely to take a long time. Most mainframe-based systems today are still being developed using nonconversational monitors.

Inquiry with Terminal Paging. A common case of conversational inquiry arises when the response to an inquiry may not fit on a single screen. For example, suppose an inquiry screen requests the operator to enter a customer's

conversational mode

nonconversational mode

Figure 14–3 **Multi-Exchange Inquiry Application Flow**

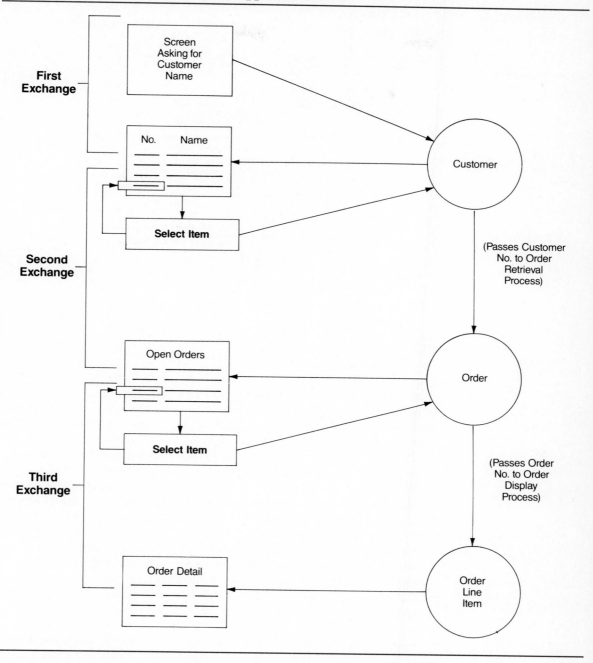

Figure 14–4 **Multi-Exchange Inquiry Pseudo-Code (Conversational)**

```
SALES                           SUBURBAN PUMPS                   CD-20
ORDER ENTRY                                                     Q1453
                              ORDER DATA BASE QUERY

 ┌──────────────────────────────────────────────────────────────────────┐
 │ PREPARED BY:  F. LAGARDERE    DATE:  27SEP90     VERSION:  1   PAGE 1  │
 │ APPROVED BY:  J. WEBER        DATE:  05OCT90     STATUS :  D          │
 └──────────────────────────────────────────────────────────────────────┘

Dowhile Operator_Signed_On
         Write_To_Terminal Prompt_For_Customer_Name
         Read_From_Terminal Partial_Customer_Name
         Dowhile Customer_Name Matches Partial_Customer_Name
                 Get_From_DBMS Customer_Number
                               Customer_Name
                 Move_To_Next_Line Customer_Number
                               Customer_Name
         Enddo
         Write_To_Terminal Customer_Number_Screen
                           Prompt_For_Customer_Number
         Read_From_Terminal Selected_Customer_Number
         Dowhile Selected_Customer_Number Matches Order_Header_Customer_No
                 Get_From_DBMS Order_Header_Data
                 Move_To_Next_Line Order_Header_Data
         Enddo
         Write_To_Terminal Order_No_Screen
                           Prompt_For_Order_Number
         Read_From_Terminal Selected_Order_Number
         Get_From_DBMS Order_Data for Selected_Order_Number
         Move Order_Data to Order_Detail_Screen
         Write_To_Terminal Order_Detail_Screen
         Read_From_Terminal When_Operator_Done
 Enddo
```

name and returns a list of customer numbers for that name. If the name is Brubaker, a single screen may suffice to hold all the Brubakers in the data base, but if the name is too common, such as Smith, it may not. A similar problem probably arises when displaying the order.

This problem can be resolved by scrolling or paging. Scrolling is invoked by a function key that causes the program to drop the topmost line on the screen, roll all the remaining lines one line up, and thereby provide room for one fresh line at the bottom. An alternative to scrolling is paging, which consists of keeping the screen header intact and refreshing all the detail lines, 10, 16, 20, or whatever there is room for at a time (see Figure 14–6).

Two techniques are possible for paging. The inquiry program can prepare all the data at the initial request, display the first page, write the entire result of the inquiry to some temporary storage medium, and let a general-purpose paging routine take over if the user wishes to navigate from page to page. This technique is costly in hardware resources, but less costly to develop and maintain.

The alternative is that the inquiry program reads only the data base records required for the first page. If the user requests page two, the same inquiry

Figure 14–5 **Multi-Exchange Inquiry Pseudo-Code (Nonconversational)**

```
SALES                          SUBURBAN PUMPS                    CD-20
ORDER ENTRY                                                      Q1453
                            ORDER DATA BASE QUERY

PREPARED BY:  F. LAGARDERE   DATE:  27SEP90      VERSION:  1     PAGE 1
APPROVED BY:  J. WEBER       DATE:  05OCT90      STATUS :  D
```

```
Module 1
            Read_From_Terminal Partial_Customer_Name
            Dowhile Customer_Name Matches Partial_Customer_Name
                    Get_From_DBMS Customer_Number
                                  Customer_Name
                    Move_To_Next_Line Customer_Number
                                      Customer_Name
            Enddo
            Write_To_Context_Data_File Customer_Number_Screen_Data
            Write_To_Terminal Customer_Number_Screen
                              Prompt_For_Customer_Number

Module 2
            Read_From_Terminal Selected_Line
            Read_From_Context_Data_File Customer_Number on Selected_Line
            Dowhile Customer_Number Matches Order_Header_Customer_No
                    Get_From_DBMS Order_Header_Data
                    Move_To_Next_Line Order_Header_Data
            Enddo
            Write_To_Context_Data_File Order_Header_Data
            Write_To_Terminal Order_No_Screen
                              Prompt_For_Order_Number

Module 3
            Read_From_Terminal Selected_Line
            Read_From_Context_Data_File Order_Number on Selected_Line
            Get_From_DBMS Order_Data for Order_Number
            Move Order_Data to Order_Detail_Screen
            Write_To_Terminal Order_Detail_Screen
```

program reads the next few records, and so on, until the user is satisfied. This technique is more economical of hardware resources, because a number of accesses to the data base may be avoided (if the user finds the answer on the first page) and only the data base keys required to start the following page need to be passed from one exchange to the next. It takes more time to program, however, especially if there are many types of multipage inquiries, because the paging routine has to be rewritten for each inquiry type.

On-Line Data Entry. On-line data entry is practically always implemented with a multi-exchange conversation because one of the main objectives of data entry is to validate the input and have the operator correct errors as they occur. The error correction cycle requires saving the data that has already been entered so that the user needs to reenter only the erroneous data and not the entire transaction.

There are two types of on-line data entry: intelligent data entry at the source and media conversion. With intelligent entry at the source, the operator has all the information required, or can get it easily, and can correct practically any type of error on-line. In media conversion, the operator has only a document of the

Figure 14–6 **Terminal Paging**

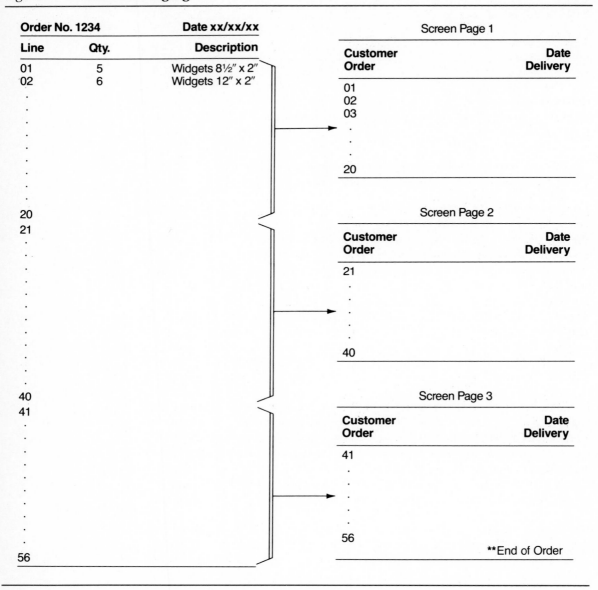

transaction at his or her disposal. If errors were committed when the document was created, the operator has no way of knowing what the correct information should be. The difference between the two is therefore in the amount of validation performed. Intelligent data entry implies as much validation as possible; media conversion tries to catch only transcription errors by the operator.

The architecture most commonly used for either form of data entry is depicted in Figure 14–7. This schematic shows that each exchange consists of accepting the input data, validating it for errors, and storing it on a transaction file. The transaction file will later be used in a batch job to update master files and to do whatever other processing is required. At the end of the conversation, the program acknowledges to the operator that the work is completed and the transaction written to the output file.

Hard-copy output may be required for different reasons—for instance, to print out a receipt, a confirmation, or a temporary justification to a waiting customer. Such output is generally deferred until after the conversation. During the conversation, the program accumulates the data necessary to print the report. At the end, it communicates the data to a report-writing program that can print the output while the operator starts a new transaction. This technique is called spooling or asynchronous printing. The TP monitor may not be able to accommodate spooling, in which case the operator will be slowed down by waiting for the printing to be completed before starting the next transaction. No hard-copy output should be necessary for media conversion. Proof lists, if required, are a batch function.

A slight problem may arise in this architecture. If data is stored as it is validated and the user either decides to abandon the transaction or discovers an error in already entered data, it may be difficult to correct or eliminate those records already written to the transaction file. It must be possible to update records already written, thereby introducing many of the complexities of on-line update into the program. A better alternative is to create a "cancel" record that can be inserted or sorted before the erroneous records, thus signalling to the batch processing routine that these records are not to be processed.

On-Line Update. On-line updating is quite similar to on-line intelligent data entry, with the added requirement to post the transaction to one or more master data bases. There are three alternative architectures for on-line updates: immediate posting, end-of-conversation posting, and asynchronous (or post-conversation) posting (see Figures 14–8 through 14–10). In all three cases, validation and reporting are similar to data entry: validation is usually done immediately, as data are entered, and on-line reporting, if any, is asynchronous. When the posting is performed is different for each of the three approaches. In immediate posting, the data base is updated and transaction records for batch processing created as soon as a correct screen is received. In end-of-conversation posting, the processing takes place once all the screens of the conversation have been validated and the operator is satisfied that the logical

Figure 14–7 **Data Entry Application Flow**

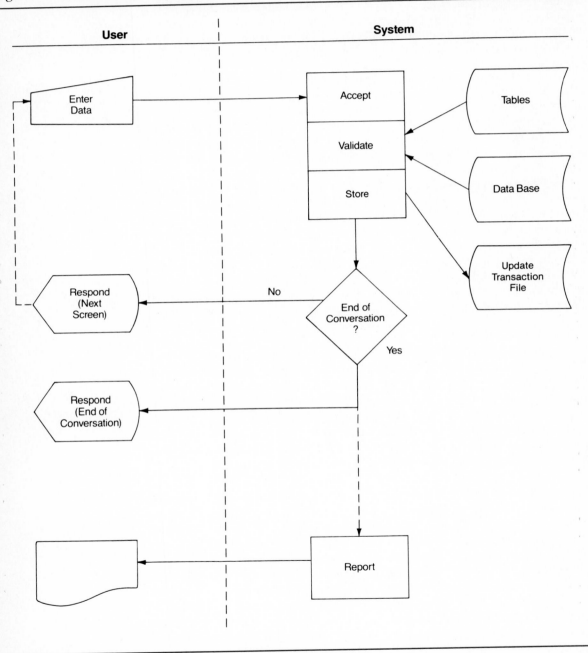

Figure 14–8 **On-Line Update Application Flow
with Immediate Posting**

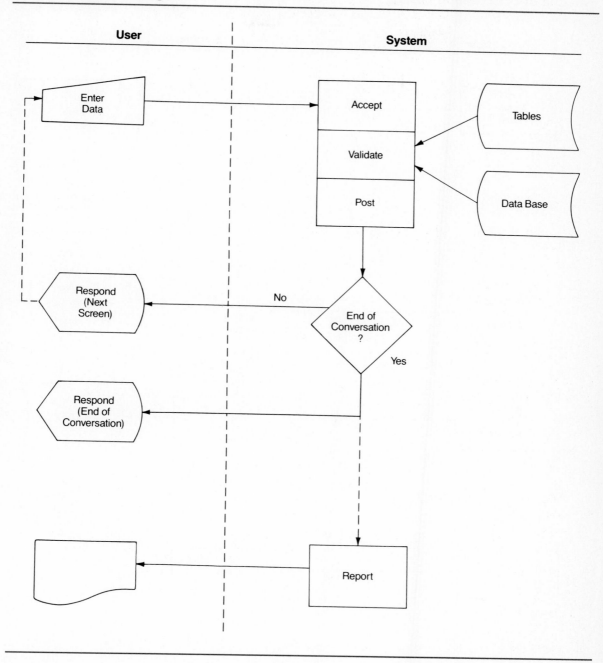

Figure 14–9 **On-Line Update Application Flow
with End-of-Conversation Posting**

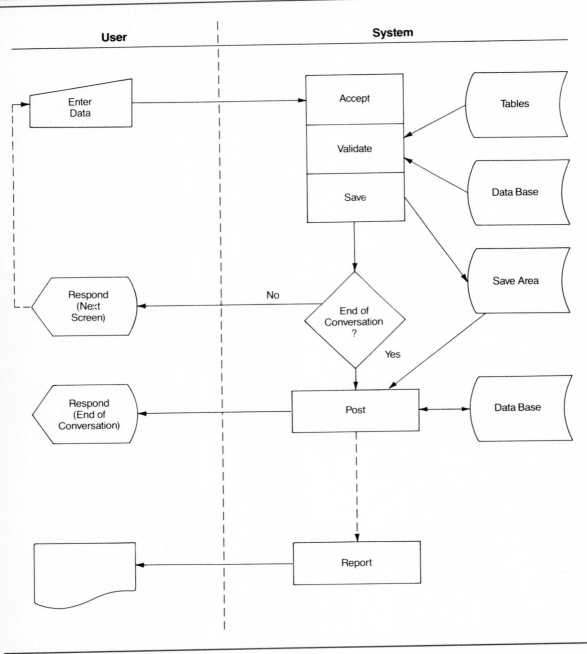

Figure 14–10 **On-Line Update Application Flow
with Deferred Posting**

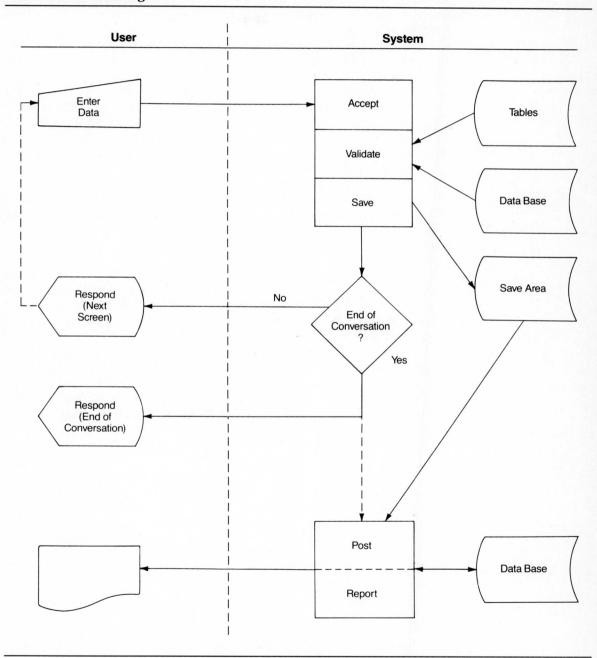

unit of work is complete. The operator is notified when the posting is complete. Asynchronous posting is similar to end-of-conversation posting, except that the operator may start a new activity before being notified that the previous transaction has been posted.

The biggest problem with on-line posting is that each data base record to be updated must be reserved for the duration of the updating process, lest some other user try to update the same information simultaneously. How this might occur with an automated teller machine are shown in Section IV. Another example might occur when an airline passenger is told at 12:10 that a seat is available and lets a few minutes pass before making the reservation, say at 12:17. In the meanwhile, another passenger may have taken the same seat from a different agent by reacting more quickly, say, only a minute after being told at 12:12 that it was available.

The advantage of immediate posting is that the reservation of the record to be updated and the actual updating usually occur within a very short time, often less than a second. This short span decreases bottlenecks occurring when some other user wants to update the same information (or, depending on the DBMS, information that is stored in its general vicinity). Another advantage is that transactions are simpler to design.

Immediate posting is not always possible, especially when the validity of the transaction depends on the state of several master data base records or when the sequence of updates is at the operator's discretion, as in most customer-contact applications, such as airline reservations. The resulting applications are more complex to design.

Asynchronous posting can be advantageous when the application can tolerate slightly deferred updates and some rejected transactions that appeared correct when entered. Because less processing takes place on-line, the response time can be improved. Also, the system may be operated in degraded mode if the master data base should not be available (for example, it is being backed up, restored, or converted to a new format).

To illustrate the difference between immediate posting and end-of-conversation posting, consider what happens in the following order entry situation. In this system, reservations for the ordered quantities are made against an inventory file. If one item is not available, the entire order is put in as a back order. To avoid overreservations, back-order items are not reserved against inventory.

In immediate posting, each order line is processed completely as it is entered, and the ordered quantity is reserved for the item if it is available. If an item is unavailable, all the previously processed order lines must be backed out and the corresponding reservations undone.

In end-of-conversation posting, each item is first checked for availability, but no reservation is made. At the end of the conversation, if all the items are available, all the reservations are made and the order is declared good. There is some risk that another order might have decreased to zero the quantity available between the time the availability was checked line by line and the time the reservation was actually made. If so, the order would be rejected even though it appeared acceptable initially. The only way to avoid late rejection would be to block the product records for each item ordered so that no other user could interfere with them between checking the availability and making the reservation. For a large order entry system with perhaps hundreds of orders being processed at the same time, this solution is not reasonable, and immediate update is probably preferable.

In other cases, blocking the records is of lesser consequence and end-of-conversation posting is the preferred alternative. It may be the only alternative if the sequence of exchanges within the conversation is variable and if the transaction cannot be validated until all the exchanges have been completed. It may also be the only possibility when the data base integrity constraints specify that two entities depend on each other—for instance, that all departments must have at least one employee and all employees must work for at least one department (see Chapter 13). In this case, the creation on the data base of a new department and at least one employee must be an "atomic" action: either both are created or neither. If the creation takes two successive exchanges and there is a system error or hardware failure between the two, the data base might well wind up in an illegal state.

Backup, Recovery, and Restart in On-Line Systems

On-line systems are particularly vulnerable to hardware and software failures, because these interrupt an activity in the middle, and it is very difficult to know where to restart. In single-threaded batch jobs, recovering from failures is easier, because the process can normally be restarted from the beginning.

The difficulties caused by recovery and restart procedures were long a major deterrent to on-line updates. For many years, prudent designers advocated updating in batch; the most that should be done on-line was so-called memo update. Memo update consists in having a scratch-pad area in each record that can be updated to provide a running value; this value is erased at the end of the day and recalculated by the batch update program running overnight.

Most TP monitor and DBMS combinations now have good enough restart and recovery facilities that memo update is no longer a requirement. The advantages of on-line update are great enough to justify the slight additional effort required to use these vendor-provided restart and recovery facilities.

There are still many decisions on restart and recovery to be made by the designer. The main incident to be guarded against by restart and recovery procedures is the failure of the system at an arbitrary point during the on-line session. When the system fails, there is no way to tell how much work has been actually completed and recorded on the data base or other external files. Because the contents of memory may be lost, any work that has been done only in memory is deemed not to have been done at all.

The principle of all restart and recovery procedures is to place the external data base and other files in a known state of integrity (recovery), inform the users of the system of this state, and ask them to resume processing at this known point of integrity (restart).

backup copy

The simplest way to accomplish these tasks is to take a **backup copy** of the data base every night; if the system goes down, the copy is restored and the users are asked to reenter all the day's transactions. This way of ensuring recovery is not popular with users. Imagine how a user might react when the system loses power or has a bug at 4:55 P.M.! Manual reentry can, however, be used for very low-volume applications, where no single user is likely to enter more than a few transactions every day. For instance, an on-line time-reporting package where each individual worker enters time-sheet data once a day or even once a week might use this kind of restart recovery.

Instead of every day, the data base might be backed up several times during the day to minimize the work lost in case of failure. This solution usually fails because of the volume of data to be backed up. Some data bases are so large that it takes all night to back them up.

A more usual practice is to take a daily copy of the data base and then accumulate all the modifications posted to the data base on a separate log. The log will contain each modified record as it looks *after* the update. The technique is called **after-image logging** (see Figure 14–11). Whenever the data base is updated, the log must be written to first, and the transaction must wait for the actual physical I/O to be completed.

after-image logging

If the system goes down, the backup copy can be restored, and a special recovery program can read all the after-images and write them to the data base. Validation and other processing should be unnecessary, as anything written to the log has gone through all the validations already. When the log has been completely posted, the data base is in the same state as when the system went down.

There is still a problem, however. Those conversations that were stranded in the middle may have been partially completed (because some updates were already made), but the working storage component of the transaction program is lost. If the program maintains a running total, say, to provide a control total or a credit check, the operator entering that transaction would have to reconstitute the state of memory before continuing. Accordingly, many log systems are designed so that incomplete business transactions, or logical units of work, are not restored using after-images.

This result is easy to achieve if the TP monitor is truly conversational, i.e., it knows when a conversation starts and when it ends. The most popular TP monitors, however, are pseudo-conversational. With these monitors, the same result can be achieved if all updates are done in an end-of-conversation routine, rather than exchange by exchange. From the standpoint of data base recovery, all the significant activity then takes place in the end-of-conversation routine. Since after-image recovery process recovers those exchanges that were completely processed when the system failed, the data base can be returned to a consistent state. This characteristic is one of the reasons why end-of-conversation posting is popular.

Figure 14–11 **After-Image Logging and Forward Recovery**

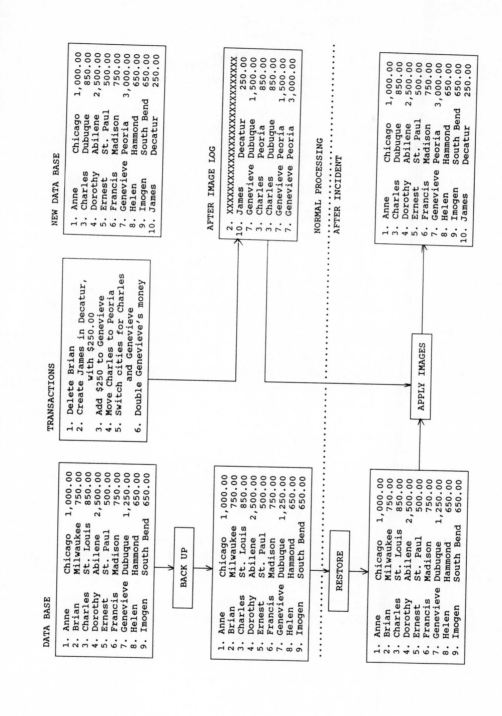

before-image logging

The same effect as forward recovery using after-images can be achieved differently and sometimes more economically. Instead of storing the modified images of the data base records, the log stores the images of the records *before* they were updated. This is called **before-image logging**. These images can be used to roll back the data base: the log is read in reverse sequence and the before-images are substituted, gradually working backwards to the point where each transaction in process at the time of the crash has been undone (see Figure 14–12). This technique saves the time required to restore the data base from a backup copy. Still required is knowledge of the starting point of each business transaction; thus, multi-exchange conversations in nonconversational systems still pose a problem.

An additional refinement is installed in systems where on-the-fly recovery is required. This term refers to recovery to the point where the operator does not have to reprocess anything at all, except possibly the contents of the screen being filled in at the time.

transaction restart

On-the-fly recovery is made possible by logging transactions as well as either after- or before-images. When the data base has been restored to a known state, an automatic **transaction restart** facility can bring the system up to date by simulating the word done by the operators at the time of failure, up to the point where there is no more data on the log. Then, each user takes over, very close to the point where the work was interrupted (see Figure 14–13).

The designer must understand the various recovery methods, know which tools are available either in the DBMS or the TP monitor to implement recovery, and be able to choose the appropriate method based on cost of implementation versus risk and cost of possibly lost work. Also, restart and recovery considerations help govern the choice of update method in a nonconversational system.

BATCH PROCESSING

On-line processing has gradually overshadowed batch since the mid-1970s. On-line applications have taken over practically all transaction processing. Many management information systems also rely heavily on on-line query or on-line ordering of reports. Some practitioners even surmise that batch processing will eventually disappear because it is an unnatural way to conduct business.

While batch has decreased in importance relative to on-line, it is still far from defunct. Many applications where the processing is initiated by a date rather than by an arbitrary event (such as bank statements or parking sticker renewals) are better done in batch and will continue to be. Why should an operator intervene in a process that can be completely automated?

Other processes require substantial amounts of data to be read before the result can be obtained. Much management control reporting is of this nature. Other applications include taking backup copies of files for restart and recovery purposes, reviewing a data base to audit its integrity, materials requirements planning for a production run, and so on. These applications are file-driven; they may be executed on-line, but many of them are not because they are too costly.

Figure 14-12 **Before-Image Logging and Backout Recovery**

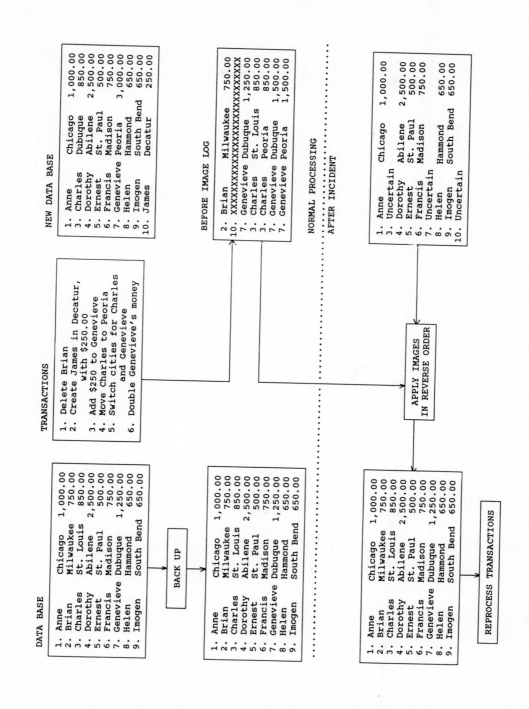

Figure 14-13 **Transaction Restart**

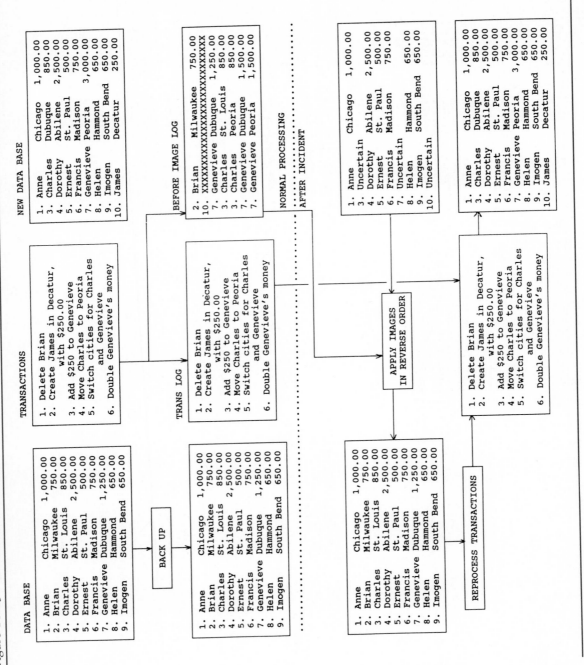

In any case, whether or not file-driven programs are executed on-line, the technique used to design them is the same—and it differs substantially from transaction processing.

Standard Batch Architecture

The standard batch application architecture evolved in the late 1950s and early 1960s and has changed little since then. Figure 14–14 shows its three main components: validation, update, and report separated by sorts.

There are many variations on this architecture. Some batch applications need to update multiple master files or data bases, and the central run may be duplicated. Others have multiple reporting runs. Validation may not be required for date-driven or file-driven processes. Sorting transactions before posting may not be necessary. The essence of the architecture is still the same.

Validation

Batch transaction validation is quite similar to on-line validation. There may be an additional level of validation, called batch control. Batch control consists of grouping transactions together in batches and checking that each batch is complete. The number of transactions is counted or the transaction amounts are totaled and noted on the batch header. When the program has processed an entire batch, it can determine whether the total accumulated during the processing corresponds to the one noted on the batch header. If not, the program signals the discrepancy.

Each transaction is validated, field by field, to determine whether the value of the field belongs to the domain.

Next, all the integrity constraints applying within each transaction record are validated, then those that apply across multiple records, and finally those that apply to the state of the data base (for example, a nonexistent entity cannot be modified or a parent cannot be deleted without deleting the children, and so on—see Chapter 13).

Invalid transactions are generally rejected and an error report generated. In some systems, the invalid transactions are kept in a suspense file that can be corrected on-line (or in batch, for that matter) and resubmitted for the following validation run. In some cases, when a transaction against a master record is invalid because of the state of the master record, the master record can be modified and the invalid transaction recycled without change the next day. It will automatically become valid when the master record changes.

In some cases, the validation against the master data base or master file is not done until the update run. This method is typical of sequential master files, where access for validation requires the transactions to be sorted in the same sequence as the master file.

Some validation programs do not reject transactions; rather, the problematic transactions get posted to the master file, to a suspense account, for example. One of the integrity criteria of an accounting system is that the total amounts of

Figure 14–14 **Standard Batch Architecture**

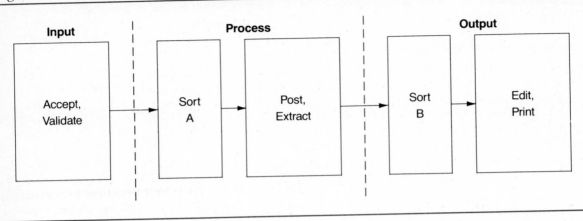

credits and debits must always balance. It is therefore difficult to reject a credit transaction of, say, $187.65, especially if there is no debit transaction of the exact same amount (an accounting entry may have multiple debits and/or multiple credits). If the accounting entry itself is out of balance, a dummy transaction is generated to a specific suspense account to make up for the difference. Error correction does not consist of modifying the transactions and resubmitting them; rather, it consists of creating new accounting entries that will balance those in the suspense accounts.

Update

In the standard batch architecture, the valid transactions are sorted in the same sequence as the master file or the data base to be updated. The master file and the transactions are both read sequentially, and each transaction is posted to the corresponding master file records before these are written out to a new generation of the master file. If there are no transactions for a given master record, then the master record is written to the new master unchanged. As each master record and each transaction is processed, all the information needed to prepare the reports of the application are extracted to a report file. This file, which consists of one record per report per item (master or transaction) to be reported on, will later be sorted by report number, and within report number, by sequence within the report. Sequential update is a classic example of a file-driven process. Boxes 14–3 and 14–4 describe two popular sequential update architectures.

There are many variations on this architecture. The main variation is that sequential processing can be replaced by direct-access update. In this case, the transaction file does not require sorting, and each transaction is posted as it arrives. The master file or data base is not rewritten to a new generation; it is

BOX 14–3

Process-driven Design

Most of Chapter 14 deals with the identification of which programs will make up an application, which functions will be performed by each of these programs, and how the programs relate to each other through data interfaces. The question of how each program is structured is usually left to the implementation phase. There are two exceptions: (1) when the program designer is inexperienced and needs to check that the program he or she designed will actually work and (2) when the program is so complex that it has to be decomposed to estimate its complexity and to incorporate it into the implementation plan.

The traditional way of structuring a program is to group related processing functions into related modules: A mainline module acts as "traffic cop" and passes control to each subordinate module in turn.

A typical example of process-driven design is found in on-line conversational transactions, where processes are grouped by their objectives: validation, update, reporting.

Another typical example is in the standard sequential file update structure (see Figure 14–15). Functions are grouped mainly according to the file operations performed, and the central pivot of the program is the comparison of the sort key of the master file and the transaction file.

A third typical example is represented by the report printing program (see Figure 14–23).

The key elements are the determination of control breaks and page breaks.

In the standard sequential file update and the report printing program, it is easy to spot what appear to be illogical structural elements. For example, in the file update, the reading operation takes place just after the writing operation (and there are two initial file read operations in the housekeeping section). In the report printing, precautions must be taken so that control breaks are not processed at the start of the program when no detail lines have yet been printed.

These seemingly illogical structures are, of course, highly logical; the program would not accomplish its functions if they were not there. Experienced programmers do not think twice about them and incorporate them naturally in their programs, as required. Experience has told them that these structures are the best way to make a process-driven program work. Novice programmers, on the other hand, usually have trouble the first few times they encounter these situations. They have to simulate the flow of records from the input files before understanding that structures that appear more natural at first have bugs in them.

In the authors' experience, process-driven design is not problematic in most transaction-driven or event-driven applications. It is less well adapted to file-driven applications.

---

updated in place. The validate run and the update run can often be combined (see Figure 14–17). In direct-access update, the process is transaction-driven.

Many reports require every master file record to be read because the criteria for including data are independent of the transaction file. For these reports, the transaction-driven update run cannot be used. A separate, file-driven run must read the entire file or data base sequentially to prepare the report records.

Figure 14–15 **Pseudo-Code for Process-driven Update**

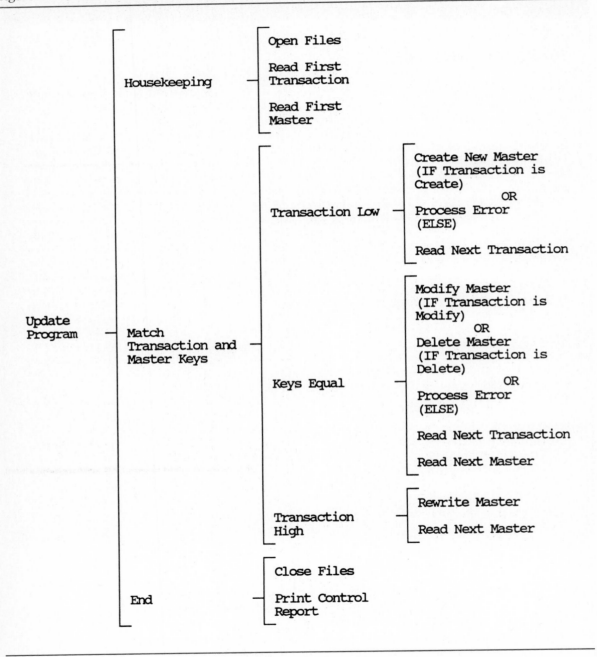

BOX 14–4

Data-driven Design

Process-driven design of programs (see Box 14–2) is the norm in the United States. Data-driven design is much more common in Europe; Jean-Dominique Warnier generalized its use in France starting in the 1960s, and Michael Jackson popularized it in the United Kingdom in the 1970s. Since then, both Warnier and Jackson methods have been acknowledged in the United States and have been adopted by some advocates.

The premise of data-driven design is that the program structure should match the data structure. Warnier's view is that the output structure should dictate the program structure, which in turn dictates the input structure. In Jackson's slightly different view, the correspondence or lack of correspondence (called structure clashes) between input and output structures determines the program structure.

Designing a program, thus, consists of designing a hierarchical data structure. The structure of the program does not depend on which entities are on which files. If a program has two transaction files or updates two master files (which are in the same sequence), the program looks no different than if it had a single file. (As an example, the two programs described in Box 14–3 are shown designed according to Warnier's principles in Figures 14–16 and 14–24.)

As an exercise, the reader should try to modify the update program so that the add and modify transactions are in two different files. The reader will quickly realize that the process-driven program's structure changes much more than the data-driven one.

Is data-driven design better than process-driven design, then? Not necessarily. In transaction-driven processes, the two do not yield substantially different results, mainly because the data structures are not complex. In sequential update, data-driven design has the reputation of being easier to debug and of being less dependent on file organizations. However, sequential update has gone out of fashion. In reporting problems, data-driven design also provides clearer and more logical structures, although, if the data structure is straight, with no fan-out at lower levels, its advantage over process-driven design is minimal. (Report writers have the least trouble with this type of structure.) For more complex data structures, such as the one represented in Figure 14–24, data-driven design is most certainly advantageous from a debugging standpoint. (This argument applies to reporting as well as to other file-driven processing, such as the daily cut-off processing of an on-line data base). There is still disagreement on whether data-driven or process-driven programs are easier to maintain. It is possible to find cases of maintenance requests that would wreak havoc with either of the structures.

A random-access update followed by a sequential read of the master file or data base for extraction of reports is well adapted to relational data base technology, where the master relation does not necessarily have to be maintained in key sequence.

The report extraction process just described works well for routine production reports such as proof lists, routine management reports, and

Figure 14–16 **Pseudo-Code for Data-driven Update**

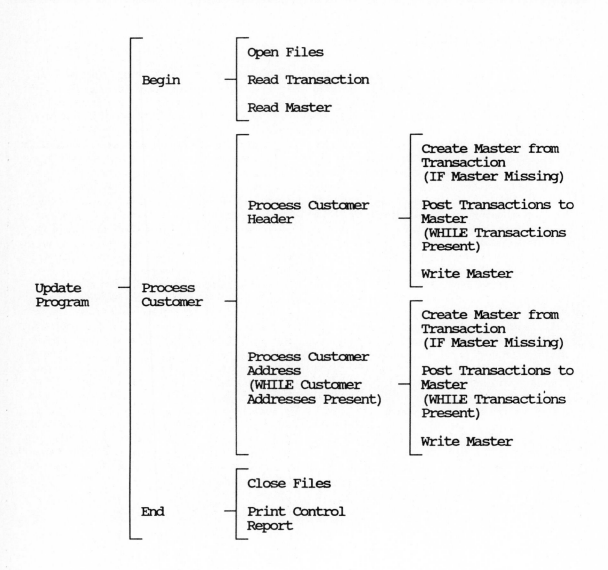

BOX 14–5

Object-oriented Design

A new programming and program design paradigm is becoming increasingly popular: object-oriented programming and design. Object-oriented programming has its origins in a modeling language called SIMULA, in the late 1960s. The ideas of SIMULA were picked up by a team at Xerox PARC (Palo Alto Research Center) and incorporated into a language called Smalltalk. The conciseness, reliability, and maintainability of complex Smalltalk programs have made object-oriented programming and design the subject of much research and some passionate debate.

Object-oriented design and programming purport to eliminate the controversy between process-driven design and data-driven design by combining the two. A Smalltalk object is a piece of data to which is attached all the processing that the data can undergo. For instance, a number is stored together with the rules of addition, multiplication, printing, rounding, and so on that apply to it. The programmer can never have

access to the data other than through one of these processes, also called methods.

Chapter 12, which contains a long discussion of abstract data types, points out that it makes no sense to compare, much less add or subtract, data of incompatible types. Such a view of data types is very close to the Smalltalk view of an object.

Very little experience exists with object-oriented programming and design in transaction processing and MIS applications. The main successes of object-oriented approaches have been in the creation of powerful generic (non–application dependent) user interfaces, such as the desktop interface initially created by Xerox for a system called the Star, now incorporated into Apple's Macintosh and acknowledged as the standard for office automation and personal computing. Other successful applications have included graphic processing software and simulation applications.

Figure 14–17 **Alternative Batch Architecture**

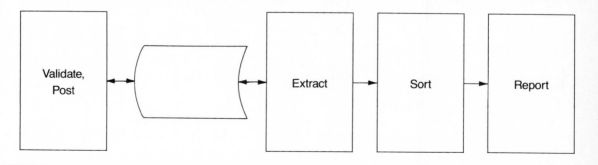

documents that are to be sent to outside entities. The process does not work as well for ad hoc reporting using a report writer. Most report writers can produce only one report per pass of the master file. In this case, each report is a distinct run, consisting of either a single run of the report writer (if the report is in the same sequence as the file) or a dual run with a sort interposed (see Figure 14–18).

The extract run parallels the hierarchical structure of the file or the hierarchical view of the relations making up the master records. (In structured programming, every program is a hierarchical, or tree, structure. Data-driven design, as explained in Box 14–4, chooses to use the hierarchical view of the data as the program structure.) For each detailed record in the master file, the current headers are maintained in memory. These headers change only when a control break is encountered. For example, if the file contains detailed sales records and is sorted by sales region, product, and customer category, then the layout of the work area that is passed to each extract module contains a complete *information set*: sales region data, product data, and customer category data as well as the detailed sales record (see Figure 14–19). The header information may be on the master file, or it may have to be looked up on a direct-access file or data base. When all the detailed sales records for a given customer category within a product within a region have been exhausted, the next customer category information set is fetched and delivered with the first of the detailed records within that category.

In relational data base technology, the same effect can be obtained by using the base relation containing the detailed sales data and by joining customer category, product, and sales territory relations to it.

In some cases, the extraction criteria require that a collection of detailed records be examined to determine whether or not to extract. Perhaps someone has requested a report showing all orders with more than 20 items. Then, the entire order (header and detail lines) would have to be read to find out how many lines it contains. The extract program must then provide sufficient space to contain all the records in a detailed group. Only when all the records in the group have been read can the extract modules be called (see Figure 14–20). When the hierarchy is a complex one, as in the employee data base shown in Figure 14–21, this approach is the standard one.

If just one report requires that multiple detailed records be contained in the work area passed to the extract module, then all the reports in the run must be extracted with the same work area structure. A sample structure of an extract run using the information set approach is illustrated in Figure 14–22.

Reporting

Once all the report records have been extracted, they are sorted in sequence by report number, and, within report number, in whatever sequence the report is in. This process determines the overall structure of the report printing program as illustrated in Figure 14–23.

Writing report programs is fairly simple: there is generally only one input file and one output file. Maintaining running totals and tracking control breaks

Figure 14–18 **Ad Hoc Reporting Architecture**

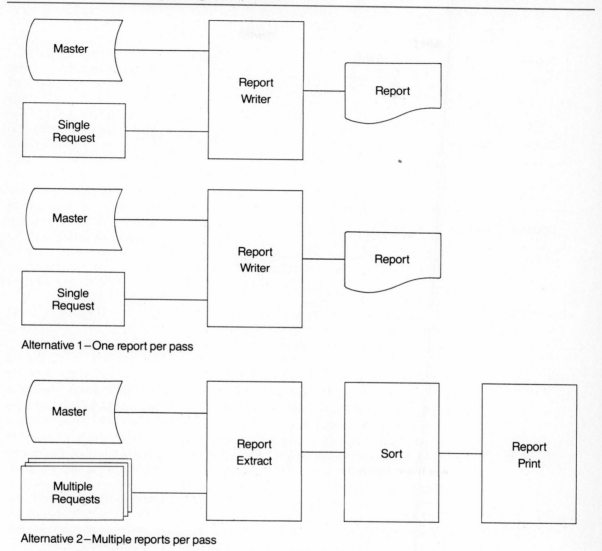

Alternative 1–One report per pass

Alternative 2–Multiple reports per pass

Figure 14–19 **Information Set for Simple Hierarchy**

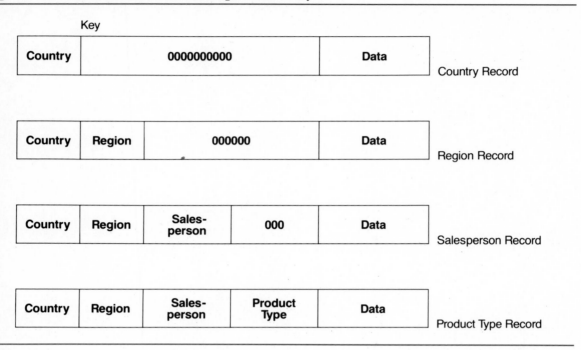

is not very complex. As a result, report programs or modules are often given to beginning programmers, while validate and especially update/extract runs are given to more experienced personnel.

The only difficulty in report writing is keeping track of page breaks. In Michael Jackson's terms, there may be a structure clash between the output (physical pages of reports) and the input (control groups in a hierarchy, with an arbitrary number of lines in each detail group). If the hierarchy is complex, as in Figure 14–24, page breaks can become quite difficult to manage.

Some common styles of reports require special techniques either for extraction or for printing. Three of these special techniques are calculating totals before printing details, responsibility reporting, and printing multiple columns in phone-book style.

Total Before Detail. When each detail report line contains the percentage of the total control group represented by that detail line, the total of the control group has to be calculated before the detail is printed. The simplest way of dealing with this requirement is to extract two detailed records for each line to be printed and add a sort criterion with a value of 0 in one of the records and 1 in the other. This sort field must be inserted just after the argument that serves

Figure 14–20 **Information Set with All Detail Records in Storage**

Country	Region	Sales-person	Product Type	
U.S.	N.W.	147	01	
U.S.	N.W.	147	13	
U.S.	N.W.	147	15	
U.S.	N.W.	147	17	
U.S.	N.W.	147	24	
U.S.	N.W.	147	37	
U.S.	N.W.	147	63	
U.S.	N.W.	147	64	
U.S.	N.W.	147	65	
U.S.	N.W.	147	69	

Country Record

Region Record

Salesperson Record

Product Type Records

as the basis for the total (see Figure 14–25). When the report program reads a record with 0 in the field, it totals it; when a 1 record is encountered, the total is already known, and the line can be printed.

Responsibility Reporting. Responsibility reporting consists in creating a report for each organizational entity (cost center, profit center, section, etc.) at a certain level of detail (say, by account) and then rolling up the organizational entity into the next one, while maintaining the same level of detail reporting.

Figure 14–21 **Information Set for Complex, Fanned-Out Hierarchy**

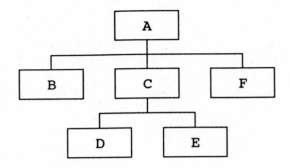

RECORDS:

Level 1 key	Level 2 key	Level 3 key	Data
A 1	000	000	Root data
A 1	B 1	000	1st B segment
A 1	B 2	000	2nd B segment
A 1	B 3	000	3rd B segment
A 1	C 1	000	1st C segment
A 1	C 1	D 1	1st D segment
A 1	C 1	D 2	2nd D segment
A 1	C 1	E 1	1st E segment
A 1	C 2	000	2nd C segment
A 1	C 2	D 1	1st D segment within 2nd C
A 1	C 2	E 1	1st E segment "
A 1	C 2	E 2	2nd E segment
A 1	C 2	E 3	3rd E segment
A 1	C 2	E 4	4th E segment
A 1	F 1	000	1st F segment
A 1	F 2	000	2nd F segment
A 1	F 3	000	3rd F segment
A 1	F 4	000	4th F segment
A 2	000	000	2nd A segment

Figure 14–22 **Structure of Extract Program**

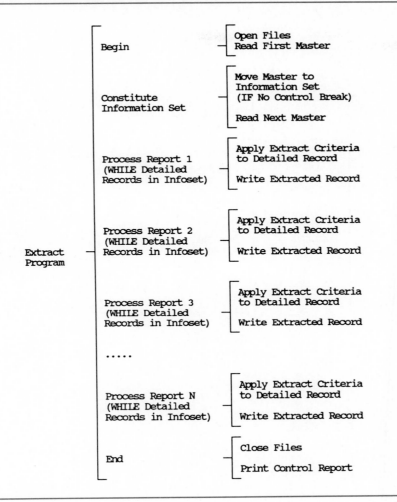

This type of report is best handled by a specialized extraction technique. It requires maintaining a hierarchical file of the organizational entities, as illustrated in Figure 14–26. When a detail record to be extracted is encountered, the extract program creates one report record with the original department or section number in it. This process will create a report line at the lowest level. In addition, one report record is created for each entity that is directly above the detail one in the hierarchy, with the corresponding entity number replacing the detail department or section number.

Figure 14–23 **Structure of Report Printing Program**

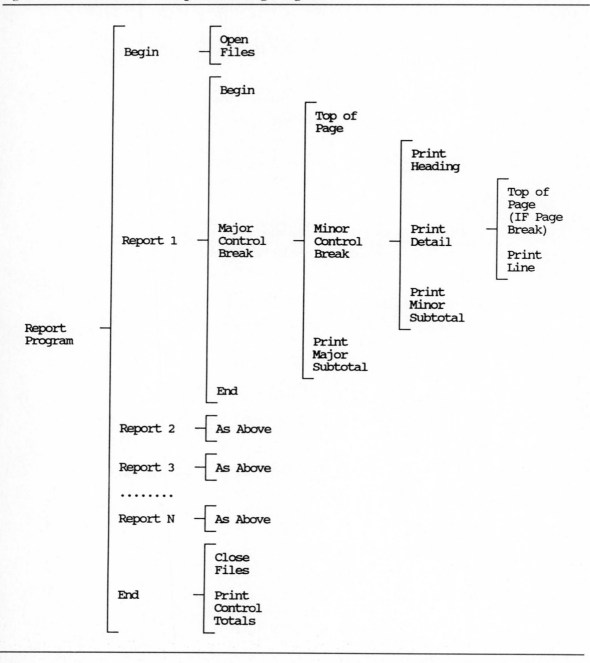

Figure 14-24 **Complex Report Structure**

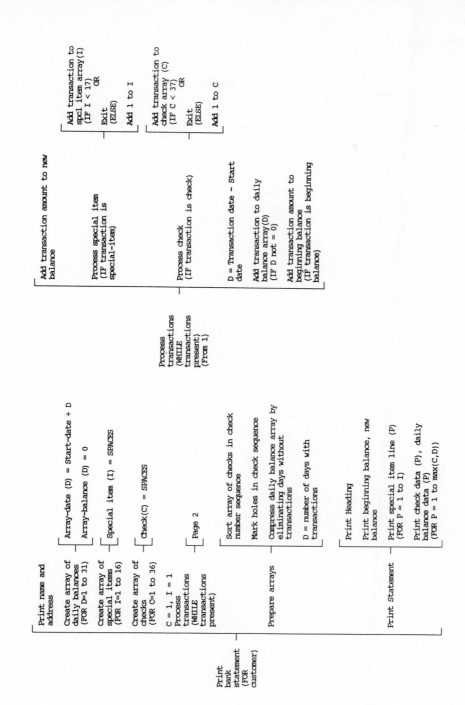

Figure 14–25 **Total before Detail**

```
MARKETING                      SUBURBAN PUMPS                      D220
STATISTICS                                                         R394
                       SALES CONTRIBUTION REPORT MOCKUP
┌─────────────────────────────────────────────────────────────────────────┐
│ PREPARED BY:   ANNE LYNN      DATE:  27AUG90    VERSION:  4      PAGE 1   │
│ APPROVED BY:   JACK WEBER      DATE:  05SEP90    STATUS :  D              │
└─────────────────────────────────────────────────────────────────────────┘



         CONTRIBUTION TO SALES BY PRODUCT TYPE AND SALESPERSON
                       PERIOD: MAY 19XX


Salesperson 147:   JOHN Q. DOE

                         Product 01         123,250      22.0%
                         Product 13          61,600      11.0%
                         Product 20          76,550      13.7%
                         Product 72         175,740      31.4%
                         All others         122,860      21.9%
                         --------------    ----------    ------
                         All products       560,000     100.0%
                         ==============    ==========    ======
```

The report records are sorted by organizational entity as the major key. The report-printing program will then encounter all the records required for each organizational entity, in sequence by entity.

Phone-Book Style. When a report only requires a small number of print positions (usually less than 40), the number of pages required to print it can be reduced by half or more just by repeating the column multiple times across the page (see Figure 14–27).

The temptation is to print the report line by line so that the elements are in sequence from left to right, top to bottom. This format is by far the easiest for the programmer. It is also by far the most inconvenient for the reader, especially if the report is to be used as a reference, such as a phone book in which the reader searches for an item by using the alphabetical sequence.

The desirable sequence for reading such a report is top to bottom, left to right. This arrangement implies that the reporting program must accumulate all the data required for an entire page before starting to print the first line. An added complication occurs at the end of the report, when the information to be printed does not fill an entire page. Special logic must then be provided to balance the length of each column.

Figure 14–26 **Hierarchical Responsibility Reporting**

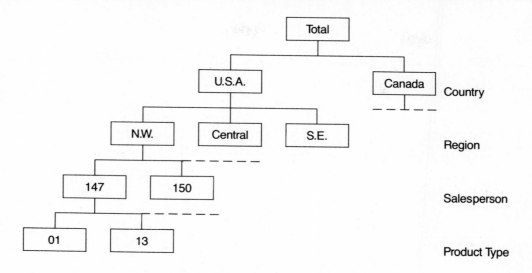

The problem is to print an analysis of sales by product type at each level, salesperson, region, country, and grand total.

From a detail record such as the sample below…

U.S.A.	N.W.	147	01	$123.25

extract the following…

Country	Region	Sales-person	Product Type	Data	
—	—	—	01	$123.25	for grand total.
U.S.A.	—	—	01	$123.25	for country total.
U.S.A.	N.W.	—	01	$123.25	for region total.
U.S.A.	N.W.	147	01	$123.25	for salesperson total.

Figure 14–27 **Phone-Book Style Report**

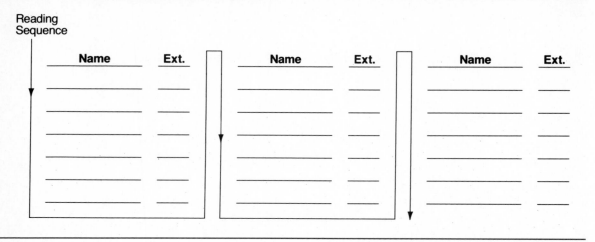

INTERFACES TO OTHER SYSTEMS

Interfaces to other systems are frequently part of the design of the system. Interfaces are of three types: shared master files, interface files, and interface messages.

shared master files

Shared master files or data bases present no particular problem except when several different programs or applications can update the same data. Then, carefully designed audit trails are required, because understanding the concurrent interaction of multiple independent programs can become very difficult. If the master file is a data base, a good audit trail is usually sufficient. If the master file is a traditional file, then it cannot be updated simultaneously by several programs running at the same time. Care must be taken in the design so that the file will never be needed by another program during the update run.

interface files

Interface files are files written and closed by one system and then opened and read by another system. A typical example would be the accounts receivable information produced by an invoicing application. The use of one application to generate transactions for another application is one of today's prime sources for batch processes, along with reporting and file backup. No particular design considerations are required here.

interface messages

Interface messages achieve the same goal as interface files, but are generally on-line. They are used when one application has to request another application to process some transaction without delay. An example can be found in international banking, where money transfers and other transactions are carried on the S.W.I.F.T. interbank network. Some commercial banks have applications that produce requests for international transfers. If the bank's computer is connected to the network on-line, a message can be sent by this

BOX 14–6

Impact of Fourth-Generation Tools and Prototyping

If a fourth-generation tool is used to prototype an application, many design considerations do not apply. A prototype does not normally require the attention given to integrity and performance that an operational application needs. Moreover, most good fourth-generation tools have design decisions built into them. These decisions concern the structure of the application, the controls, and the general performance criteria.

These built-in decisions eliminate some design work; on the other hand, they reduce the number of options available to a designer. This lack of options is not much of a problem for prototyping. In contrast, problems arise when such a tool is used to develop a full-fledged transaction processing application, where several users share the same data and when there is a mix of on-line and batch preprogrammed and ad hoc activities (as is often the case in departmental applications).

One technique used by a fourth-generation language to avoid having two people update the same record simultaneously is simply to cancel one of the transactions when there is a collision and to request one operator to start over again.

This solution is perfectly acceptable as long as the problem happens very infrequently. However, it cannot be used when volumes increase and users start requiring the same records more and more frequently. Another technique used by some fourth-generation tools is that a full pass of the master file is required for every report extracted. This technique is acceptable for small master files that can be read quickly or for situations with very few reports. It can become prohibitively expensive when volumes are high.

Even if a fourth-generation language is used for prototyping only, there may be a temptation to make the prototype the basis for the operational system and to carry over some of the design decisions (and even code) from the prototype. This carry-over might be tantamount to a "creeping decision" to use a tool adopted only for prototyping purposes to implement the operational system.

In summary, a fourth-generation tool simplifies program design, but it also reduces the designer's degree of freedom to satisfy integrity and volume requirements.

application. (In other banks, transactions to be sent on the network are accumulated all day on an interface file, which is read by the system at the end of the day using interface files rather than messages.)

Interface messages are also used when one application needs data from another application, perhaps on another computer, as in distributed processing.

Message interfaces present two design requirements. The first is that the sending application must make sure that the receiving application has actually received the message and acknowledged it. In certain cases, it must also wait for the response. If the receiving application "times out," i.e., does not acknowledge receipt within a specified time, the sending application must decide what to do—abandon the transaction or use a backup procedure to write it to a file for later processing.

The second requirement is that, as with shared master files, a carefully designed audit trail must be built. When exchanging sequential files, the file itself constitutes a good audit trail (although file control totals, as described in the next chapter, are still required). When exchanging messages, both the sending and the receiving systems must log these messages so that discrepancies can be researched and accounted for.

CUT-OFF PROCESSING

Cut-off processing is the processing required to synchronize two applications that use the same data but have different rhythms. For instance, taking deposits and disbursing funds in a bank; preparing and selling hamburgers in a fast-food restaurant; making automobiles in a Detroit factory; drilling, pumping, and refining oil in an oil company are essentially continuous activities. The accounting for these activities has a yearly rhythm (for audited financial statements to stockholders), a quarterly rhythm (for some regulatory reporting), a monthly rhythm (for internal accounting reports), and perhaps even a daily rhythm (for customer and cash requirements accounting in a bank).

The data supplied by transaction processing to management information systems and decision support systems must be cut off. Management reports or summary files that feed decision support systems have their data neatly classified by period; once a transaction has been assigned to one period, it cannot normally be reassigned to a different period.

It is not possible here to give exhaustive descriptions of all the cut-off processing requirements that a corporation may have. Some of these requirements, however, are often encountered and are often mishandled by inexperienced analysts. The discussion will be limited to the daily cut-off between the on-line system and the batch activities. Weekly, monthly, and yearly cut-offs are subject to similar considerations.

Assume that the application is a demand deposit accounting application in a bank, and that there is a requirement to process daily statements. Moreover, the account balance and all the transactions of the last two weeks are maintained on-line for customer inquiry purposes.

If the on-line system is only available during office hours, the cut-off process is relatively simple. At five o'clock, the on-line system is shut down; a batch process is started to extract transactions for the daily statements; and fresh balances and transaction histories are reloaded to the data base. The data base has to be re-created because it is not economical to carry more than two weeks' transaction history. Therefore, every day, the oldest transactions are dropped and the most recent ones are added.

This form of cut-off is the easiest to design. However, even in a simple case such as this one, there are several important requirements. One is to design the system so that the on-line processing can start even though the batch programs may not have been completed. A frequently used control step is to check, during the on-line start-up process, that the date of creation of the data base is equal to the system date less one. Although this control step is useful, it must be possible to override it to handle unexpected delays in the overnight batch process.

Another important requirement is to design the system so that it is possible to run two cut-off processes in a row. If the batch process could not be run on one night, it must be possible to run two cut-off processes in succession on the following night.

An example of a more complex (and less common) requirement is illustrated by a bank that acquires a series of automated teller machines, requiring the system to be up 24 hours a day, 7 days a week. The extraction of statements must not disrupt the on-line processing. The cut-off process will have to be run by the transaction processing monitor concurrently with other transactions, so that any possible simultaneous updates can be controlled. The requirement to reload the data base with a fresh transaction history is more difficult to meet. The procedure in this case is to create a fresh copy of the data base, switch from the old copy to the new copy, and reprocess any transactions that came in while the fresh copy was being prepared and that therefore were posted only to the old copy. This is very similar to recovering on the fly.

RECENT TRENDS IN BATCH PROCESSING

On-line systems are more and more often run well beyond office hours. Automated teller machines must be available twenty-four hours a day; so must airline and hotel reservation systems and often also computer-integrated manufacturing systems. In such systems, batch programs cannot be assumed to run under a single thread of control because they must share the master files or data bases with the on-line system. One solution often adopted is to write the batch functions as though they were "operatorless" on-line transactions.

Summary

The main architectural characteristic of programs is whether they are on-line or batch. On-line programs are event- or transaction-driven; batch programs are generally file-driven, although they may also have transaction-driven characteristics in some cases.

On-line programs should provide for sign-on activities and the actual transactions to be carried out. Sign-on activities are required to authenticate the user and to authorize him or her to work with the application. The designer must know the operating environment of the application to decide which part of the sign-on is done in the application and which is done by the operating system or other general facilities.

Conversations fall into several patterns. The most frequent patterns are single-exchange inquiry, multiple-exchange inquiry, on-line data entry, and on-line update. Single-exchange inquiry is the simplest and presents no general design problems. Multiple-exchange inquiry is more complex; the program

BOX 14-7

Cooperative Processing

Cooperative processing is the name given to a reduced form of distributed processing. It refers mainly to the case where the user's workstation handles part of the application and another processor—usually a PC, but possibly any other size computer—handles the other part.

Cooperative processing has two main purposes. The first is to present the user with a better interface, which uses the modern techniques of graphic interfaces, pointing devices, windows and WYSIWYG (What You See Is What You Get). The second main purpose is to reduce the load of processing on shared resources, in particular, the processor that has access to data.

The conventional view of cooperative processing is therefore to separate the application into two parts: a user interface part, running on a PC, and a data server part, running a DBMS on a mainframe, a mini, or another PC. Little is known about the long-term effects of cooperative processing on user satisfaction, on maintain-

ability, and on cost-effectiveness.

However, two considerations come to mind. One is that the best on-line help is data sensitive. To achieve data sensitivity, the data should be at the workstation rather than on another processor, contrary to the objective of data sharing. The other consideration is that multiple-exchange conversations need to be known to the data server if proper control over the shared data is to be maintained. (The alternative is to go to two-phase commit, but the cost hardly seems worth the advantage.) The division of the application into conversations and exchanges is part of the user interface, which therefore must be known both to the workstation and the data server.

Thus, even though the general guideline is to separate user interface and data manipulation, compromises must be made to preserve the integrity of the application. Experience is insufficient yet to determine where these lines of compromise should be drawn.

must provide for data to be kept in memory or on disk between two successive exchanges. The techniques for doing this depend on the functions and the architecture of the TP monitor being used. On-line data entry introduces the additional notion of validating, posting, and, if required, reporting on the transaction. The designer must choose at which point in the conversation these activities take place: at each exchange, at the end of the conversation, or after the conversation is finished. In on-line update, additional consideration must be given to the best way of ensuring that the updated data base remain in an acceptable state of integrity.

Backup, restart, and recovery must be provided for. The designer chooses between the various methods—backup with after-images or backout with before-images being applied to a point of integrity. The designer also chooses whether to provide on-the-fly restart of transactions.

Batch processing generally uses a standard architecture of validation, sorting, update/extract, sorting, and reporting. Validation is very similar to on-line validation in that it is transaction-driven. Updating can be file-driven (in a sequential update, more and more infrequently encountered) or transaction-driven (in direct-access update). Extracting and reporting is always file-driven. The standard reporting architecture calls for reading the master file (or the master relation) once, extracting all the information required for all the reports in the same pass. Some special considerations apply to particular kinds of reports: processing totals before details, responsibility reporting, and printing a report in phone-book style.

Interfaces to other systems also have to be designed. They are of three types: shared data bases, files created by one application and used by another, and messages sent from one application to another. Of the three, sending messages between systems is the least frequent and requires the most care in design.

A particularly frequent requirement for interfacing to other systems results from the need to perform cut-off processing, i.e., assigning transactions to periods that are significant to MIS and DSS users. The need arises whenever there is an interface between two applications or two parts of an application that do not have the same processing cycle, on-line, daily, weekly, monthly, quarterly, or yearly. Most important, cut-off processing must provide flexibility in the overlap of these cycles.

Selected Readings

Martin, James. *The Design of Man-Computer Dialogues*. Englewood Cliffs, New Jersey: Prentice-Hall, 1973.

As described in Chapter 9, this book, although fairly old, still has extremely useful information, both on user interface and program design.

Blackman, Maurice. *The Design of Real-Time Systems*. London: John Wiley & Sons, 1978.

This is a very complete book for on-line systems.

Date, Chris. *An Introduction to Database Systems*, 4th ed. Reading, Massachusetts: Addison-Wesley, 1981.

This book has an explanation of recovery and restart as well as two-phase commit.

Jackson, Michael. *System Development*. Englewood Cliffs, New Jersey: Prentice-Hall International, 1983.

Michael Jackson is perhaps best known for his work on how to design the internals of a program. This book extends his work to the design of application architectures. His methods in this field have not reached the same degree of recognition as in program design; nevertheless, his book is very interesting and has a number of novel approaches. It is recommended for those who want to explore the subject to great depth.

Review Questions

1. Explain the difference between a single-exchange conversation and a multi-exchange conversation:
    a. From the user's viewpoint.
    b. From the viewpoint of program design.

2. Compare development effort and resource consumption of the two types of terminal paging:
    a. Preparing all the data at the initial request and letting a generalized paging module display those pages that the operator is interested in.
    b. Preparing only the data strictly necessary to answer each request for a fresh page as the user makes it.

3. Describe the advantages and disadvantages of performing some functions after the end of the conversation (asynchronously).

4. Describe the recovery and restart process involved in restoring the data base and posting after-images to it. Describe the process using the current state of the data base and backing out the updates to a known point from before-images. Contrast the two in terms of performance, user impact, and risk to the integrity of the data base.

5. Is batch processing likely to disappear?

6. What are the components of the standard batch (sequential update) architecture? How does the batch architecture change if the master file is not processed sequentially?

7. Why is it usual to extract data for reports in a first program and then print the reports in a second program?

8. Describe the three main ways of interfacing to other systems. Which is the easiest to control?

9. Name some reasons for the need for cut-off processing.

Discussion Questions

1. Contrast nonconversational and conversational modes of processing. Why is conversational processing likely to increase over the next few years?

2. What additional work does the use of nonconversational mode impose on the program designer and the programmer?

3. Discuss scrolling and paging applied to intelligent workstations (given that the text of the chapter only refers to block-mode terminals). In particular, discuss whether scrolling is preferable to paging, or vice versa:
    a. For the user.
    b. For the developer of the workstation portion of the program.
    c. For the developer of the host portion of the program.

4. What are the merits of transaction restart on the fly? In what type of application would you expect to see it used?

5. How does distributed processing affect restart and recovery procedures?

6. How does the use of fourth-generation languages affect program design?

Mini-Case

Figure 14–28 depicts a conversation flow for order entry for the Condor Telephone Company. This conversation implements the ordering of telephone equipment and services for private individuals.

The conversation flows as follows: a menu choice has permitted the user to display a screen requesting either a customer number (in practice, one of the customer's telephone numbers) or a customer name (if the number is not available). The name may be partially entered. If the number is known, the order header panel is displayed by the program. If not, the program displays a list of names with their respective telephone numbers matching the partial name entered on the first screen. The operator picks one and continues with the order header screen as before.

When the order header is entered, each order line is entered in turn. There can be no more than ten lines per order. (Remember, these are residential customers.)

Finally, when the order is all entered, the operator presses a function key and the order is finalized; the program goes on to display the menu choices again.

Questions for Discussion

1. Design the on-line conversation (excluding the menu choices) implementing this function. The following assumptions are made:
   a. The environment is nonconversational: you must design the data to be held from one exchange to the next.
   b. Each order line concerns an item of equipment or a service. If it is an item of equipment, then the inventory must be checked for availability and updated by subtracting the item from stock.
   c. If it is a service, the service department schedule must be checked. If the service request can be accommodated, it must be entered on-line on the schedule. Last-minute adjustments to the schedule are frequent, however, and it is not unusual to overbook the service department on a given day.
   d. No back ordering of unavailable equipment is possible. The customer must call again to reorder when the item is in stock.
   e. The phone company covers a township with 65,000 inhabitants in an area that is popular with corporate transferees.

2. Your design should cover validation, file look-up, error processing, file update, and printing a hard copy of the order for customers who are physically present (less than 5 percent of the total number of orders).

Figure 14–28 **Order Entry Conversation
at Condor Telephone Company**

```
MARKETING                  CONDOR TELEPHONE COMPANY              U525
ORDER ENTRY                                                      CNV016
                       CONVERSATION FLOW - ORDER ENTRY
─────────────────────────────────────────────────────────────────────
PREPARED BY: KATHY KRALL    DATE: 15JUN93        VERSION: 1     PAGE 1
APPROVED BY:                DATE:                STATUS :
─────────────────────────────────────────────────────────────────────

                    (PER CONV.)
  DEFAULT FLOW       OCCURS       SCREEN NAME      ALTERNATE SCREEN   FUNCTION KEY
────────────────    ──────     ──────────────     ────────────────   ────────────

SCN0050             1          MENU               SCN0051            Line 1
                                                  SCN0052            Line 2
                                                  SCN0053            Line 3
                                                  SCN0054            Line 4


SCN0060             1          ORDER ENTRY PROMPT  SCN0099           F11

SCN0061             1          ORDER ENTRY HEADER  SCN0061           F14
                                                  SCN0099            F11

SCN0062             1-99       ORDER ENTRY HEADER  SCN0063            F3
                                                  SCN0062 (Previous) F7
                                                  SCN0062 (Next)     F8
                                                  SCN0098            F11

SCN0063             1          ORDER CONFIRMATION  SCN0050            F3
                                                  SCN0060            {Enter}
                                                  SCN0061            F14

Suspend-and-resume screens:

SCN0098             0-99       PRODUCT QUERY       Resume             F3

SCN0099             0-1        CUSTOMER QUERY      Resume             F3
```

Although many orders are for new customers, you should consider that the customer has already been created on the data base; this step is not necessary during order processing.

References

1. Yourdon, Edward, and Constantine, Larry L. *Structured Design*. Englewood Cliffs, New Jersey: Prentice-Hall, 1979.

2. Parnas, David L. "On Criteria to Be Used in Decomposing Systems into Modules." *Communications of the ACM*, (April 1972): 221–227.

Chapter 15

Controls and Security

Chapter 15 examines the importance to management of controls over information systems and the main sources of errors. Also described are general controls and application controls. The general control objectives recognized by industry are described. Next, specific examples illustrate the most frequently used transaction processing control techniques for transaction origination, data entry, processing, reporting, data base, and system interfaces. Finally, privacy issues and the rights of the individual are discussed.

Learning Objectives

- Recognize the importance of controls in protecting the organization from the risks associated with a system failure.

- Understand general systems controls as a set of overall controls and standard operating procedures in the IS department.

- Understand application controls as specific features built into computer systems to protect the application from inherent risks as well as risks associated with the system's hardware and software.

- Recognize three typical sources of computer system errors: human errors, technical failures, and natural forces.

- Describe the generally accepted application control objectives useful in identifying overall risks related to the organization and transaction processing risks related to the application.

- Apply transaction processing control techniques that pertain to how transactions flow through a typical data processing system.

- Give examples of transaction processing control techniques, including controls over transaction origination, data entry, and processing.

- Become aware of societal concerns regarding privacy and the rights of individuals when designing information systems.

MANAGEMENT CONTROL OVER INFORMATION SYSTEMS

As information and information systems become more significant in the long-term success of an organization, management must have greater assurance that the IS function is properly controlled. The importance of having adequate controls can best be appreciated by understanding likely results of inadequate controls:

- Normal business operations may be curtailed with the resultant loss of revenues and customer goodwill. If the disruption is so serious that normal operations are suspended for an inordinately long period of time, then permanent termination of operations may follow.

- Erroneous management decisions may be made because of inaccurate or untimely information supplied.

- Excessive costs may be incurred when information systems are less efficient or effective than possible.

- Fraud and embezzlement are made easier.

- Legal or regulatory penalties are possible from late or misleading information.

Organizations have learned to deal with such risks by making sure their IS function is well controlled. Proper controls over IS functions fall into two categories, general controls and application controls.

general controls

General controls are the controls and standard operating procedures in place in the IS department governing all aspects of the unit's operations. They typically cover such areas as the organization structure, personnel policies, physical security, and information access.

application controls

Application controls are specific features built into computer systems to protect the organization from risks inherent in the application itself or in processing by the computer system's hardware and software.

To ensure adequate protection against risks, management should at least enforce the following rules:

- Adequate overall written control procedures should be provided for all general controls. Systems development documentation should describe the appropriate application controls.

- Management should verify that controls are used in daily operations by having periodic compliance tests made under the supervision of audit personnel.

- Periodic reviews of IS controls should be made by a qualified third party. Control reviews are usually performed by external auditors during the course of the annual audit. A more in-depth review may be warranted in many instances, especially in those organizations whose information systems are in one of the three strategic quadrants described in Chapter 1.

- Finally, management should be responsible for maintaining or supplying information to such people as investors who rely on information to make decisions and individuals who expect protection for their rights to privacy. Litigation may be the price paid for lack of diligence.

SOURCES OF ERRORS

Controls are made a part of computer-based information systems to protect the organization from risks associated with a system failure. Controls can not only **prevent** errors but also **detect** and call attention to errors that do occur in order to **correct** them quickly. Corrective action will normally consist of reversing the effect of the error on data bases, transactions, or reports, and then examining the design specifications for systems controls to determine changes necessary to prevent similar errors from occurring again.

prevent

detect

correct

To understand how to prevent, detect, and correct errors, it is useful to analyze the three most usual sources of errors: human errors, technical failures, and natural forces (see Figure 15–1).

Human Errors

As illustrated in the figure, human errors resulting in system errors occur when authorized users make mistakes or when unauthorized users accidentally or intentionally gain access to the system. For example, a clerk taking telephone orders for software could capture information incorrectly, fail to ask for needed information, or enter information into the system more than once. The clerk could enter an incorrect product code, for example, and the customer would receive the wrong software package. The clerk could fail to enter the customer's telephone number, resulting in an incomplete customer data base record. Finally, if in the backup procedures (used when the computer system is down), clerks write orders manually and save them for later entry to the computer, a clerk could inadvertently enter the same order twice or forget an order.

Errors can also occur when unauthorized users gain access to the system either accidentally or intentionally and introduce errors. For example, a disgruntled employee familiar with the order entry system described above could enter fictitious orders or alter existing orders.

Technical Failures

Technical failures occur when a system's hardware or software do not function as expected. Although hardware malfunctions from time to time, computer program bugs are the most common type of technical failure. Even though a program has been well tested and in operation for some time, errors can still arise when circumstances not encountered before cause a new path to be taken with unforeseen, erroneous results. Ted Glaser, a principal designer of the IBM

Figure 15–1 **Generic Causes of Errors**

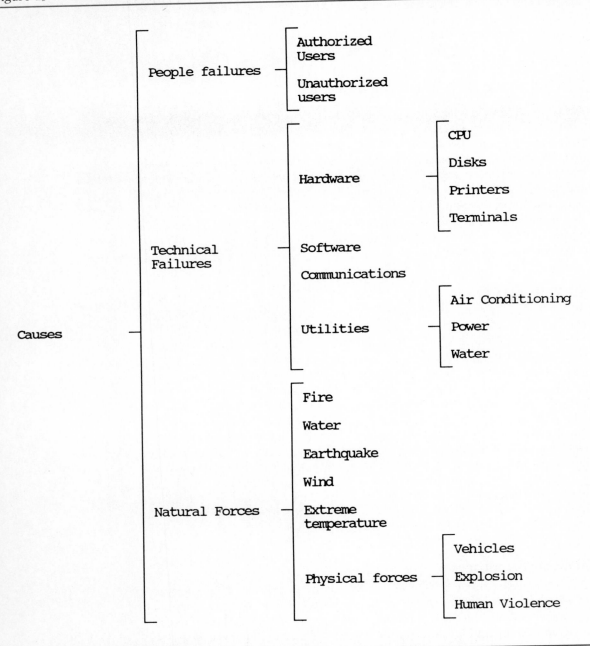

705, one of the earliest computers, was fond of saying that "there is no such thing as a completely debugged computer program. What we call a debugged computer program is simply one that has not experienced an error in a reasonably long period of time."[1]

Natural Forces

System errors, or more accurately system disruptions, are often the result of natural forces such as fire, earthquakes, or flood. Organizations have learned to protect themselves against business disruptions caused by natural forces. This protection becomes particularly important as organizations become more dependent on computer-based systems to conduct normal business operations. Imagine the effect on our daily lives if such computer-based systems as electric power dispatching and control, air traffic control, and supermarket checkout systems suddenly ceased to function.

A case in point was the fire that destroyed much of an Illinois Bell telephone switch in Hinsdale, Illinois, in May 1988. Not only did the fire leave numerous residences and businesses without telephone service, but it also disrupted data transmission networks over long-distance lines in the western suburbs of Chicago. Most of the damage was caused, not by the fire, but by the water used to extinguish it. Similar incidents could have occurred in computer rooms.

GENERAL SYSTEMS CONTROLS

General systems controls are the set of overall controls and standard operating procedures in the IS department, while application controls are specifically designed for a particular application. General systems controls include organizational and administrative controls, systems development controls, and controls over computer operations. Their primary functions are to ensure that the IS organization operates as planned, provide a firm base for application controls, and safeguard information and system resources. General systems controls usually incorporate a set of policies and procedures in such areas as the following:

- The organization structure should clearly define the functions within IS responsible for the development, maintenance, and operation of information systems. The systems development and operations functions should be clearly separated from each other—for example, to lessen the likelihood of erroneous or fraudulent changes to transactions or programs. Responsibilities of users for entering transactions and verifying application controls should also be set forth; IS personnel should be prohibited from carrying out such activities.

- Standard operating procedures for performing the various functions within the IS organization should be clearly defined, documented, and maintained.

- Personnel policies for positions within the IS organization should be developed and adhered to. For example, adequate screening procedures should be established to ensure that only those persons with the necessary qualifications are hired for or promoted to the various positions within the IS organization. Orientation of new employees should include all security practices applicable to the employees' positions as well as the organization's policies on personal and professional ethics.

   Terminated employees should be removed from sensitive positions immediately and should relinquish confidential or proprietary documents (e.g., customer lists, program listings) along with keys and identification cards. Physical and system access privileges should be restricted in keeping with the turnover of responsibilities to a replacement. Some of the best documented examples of system sabotage have been committed by recently terminated employees.

- Physical security procedures should be established to minimize losses caused by such physical threats as fire, storms, floods, and access by unauthorized persons.

   Adequate fire detection and fire suppression equipment is critical. Although most computer equipment will not burn, fire or heat can cause severe damage. The computer room and the data set libraries, in particular, should be closed to all except those who have responsibilities directly related to computer operations or data storage management. Visitors, vendors, and others who have reason to be in restricted areas temporarily should be properly authorized and escorted at all times by a responsible member of the IS department.

- Information security should be provided by software that restricts access by unauthorized persons to information residing within the computer system. The software should provide positive identification (authentication) of each person logged on for system access and should monitor the activities of that person throughout the time that the terminal is connected and active. Usually there are several levels of access controls implemented in a system. An on-line computer system, for example, might restrict any sort of access to those persons who are able to supply a valid password to the system when logging on. From that point on, various system functions would be made available to the terminal based on an internal authorization list. Some users would be authorized to inquire against the file, some would be authorized to inquire and post certain transactions, and some would be authorized to perform all system functions.

- Finally, contingency plans permit operations to continue when they are disrupted for any reason. Most installations store duplicate copies of programs and data off-site. Thus, duplicates can be made available to an alternate processing facility so that system operations can be quickly resumed. The contingency plan should be tested by realistic exercises at least twice a year.

BOX 15-1

Turning a Computer into a Better Vault

Just as the outlaws of the Old West spurred security companies to design better vaults, modern-day electronic bandits are inspiring the development of advanced computer security gadgetry. The most sophisticated new equipment includes biometric machinery-products that verify the identity of would-be computer users by analyzing their unique physical characteristics. Among the offerings is an eye-scanning device that detects the unique blood vessel patterns in the retina, a sort of "eye signature." Made by EyeDentify, an Oregon firm, it is designed to restrict access to computer databases. To use a computer equipped with the scanner, you first have to look through a scope. The scanner then takes a reading of your retina. It grants computer access only to authorized users whose blood vessel patterns have been recorded and stored in its electronic memory. Other biometric devices work on the same principle. For example, Palo Alto-based Identix Inc. produces devices that use fingerprints to control access to computers. Your fingerprint is read by a rectangular sensor about the size of a large index card. A Boston company, Ecco Industries, manufactures voice-based identity verification equipment. How far can biometric technology go? Some companies are experimenting with lasers to scan people's cells for genetic characteristics to determine who should be granted computer access. Other access control equipment relies more on the way people do things rather than on their biology. For example, there are devices that read signatures based on writing patterns, speed and pen-to-pad pressure. Similarly, there is an identity verification gadget designed to distinguish a "keyboard signature"—an individual's typing speed, acceleration patterns and finger-to-key pressure. In addition, there are systems that rely on identification cards, much like the banking industry's automated teller machines.

While these new devices are becoming more popular, the use of passwords is still the most common means of controlling computer access. Many companies assign a password—typically a one-word code—to their computer-using employees. To gain access to computer data, employees type these passwords on the computer keyboard. However, the password system also has been advanced. There are circuit-bearing "smart cards" for traveling employees who use a personal computer to communicate with the company's main computer. These cards flash the password needed to gain access to the main computer. What's more, they flash new passwords continuously, a feature designed to thwart intruders who try to gain computer access by guessing or stealing the code. Typically, the passwords change one to four times a minute. Such access controls are sufficient for many companies, but some corporations—firms involved in top-secret U.S. Defense Department contracting, for example—provide an extra layer of protection. They install cryptographic ciphers, equipment that turns English into a gibberish-like code.

The devices, used when sensitive data is transmitted from one computer to another, are intended to thwart industrial spies who try to intercept messages. Another device translates the code back to readable form. Meanwhile, the work goes on to develop even more sophisticated computer protection. "Companies are still trying to build a better vault," said Richard Rueb, executive director of the Newport Beach based Information Systems Security Assn.

White, George. "Battle Against Computer Crime Out of the Trenches" LOS ANGELES TIMES Los Angeles, CA; v107, n248, Section 4, August 7, 1988, Copyright The Times Mirror Company; Los Angeles Times. All Rights Reserved. 1988 Los Angeles, CA.

As information systems become more critical to the strategic mission of organizations, general systems controls become increasingly complex and important. A complete discussion is beyond the scope of this text, but additional information can be obtained from the sources cited in the selected readings.

APPLICATION CONTROLS

General systems controls and application controls are not mutually exclusive. Application controls are built on the foundation provided by the general systems controls. Once a specific set of control requirements for a particular application has been determined, the analyst will see which of those requirements are already provided by the general systems controls. Requirements not already met will be incorporated into the set of requirements for the new system in the same way as any other system processing, data, or reporting requirement and treated exactly the same way: designed, programmed, tested, and implemented.

Application controls deserve separate consideration from other user requirements for two main reasons. First, users tend not to think of control requirements when they are interviewed in the requirements analysis phase. Second, systems techniques introduce sources of errors that users may not be aware of. The IS professional therefore has a special responsibility to provide for complete and reliable control mechanisms.

Specification of Application Controls

Application controls are built into information systems to protect the organization if the system fails to operate properly. The thrust of controls design, therefore, is to first identify risks associated with the system and then specify adequate controls to protect the organization against them.

With a knowledge of the organizational and application characteristics as well as a knowledge of the processing system, an analyst can identify specific risks (see Figure 15–2). Once the risks are reviewed with appropriate users (including audit personnel), an analyst can identify control requirements and from them specify control techniques for the design specifications of the system. When controls are designed, experienced systems analysts will consult with both internal and external auditors for two principal reasons:

- To make use of their expertise in the identification of risks and related controls requirements.
- To reduce the likelihood of having control deficiencies pointed out by the auditors reviewing the new system in operation.

Application Control Objectives

Over the years, a set of generally accepted control objectives has been developed by various organizations and professional bodies such as the American Institute of Certified Public Accountants and the Institute of Internal Auditors. An example

Figure 15–2 **Specification of Control Techniques**

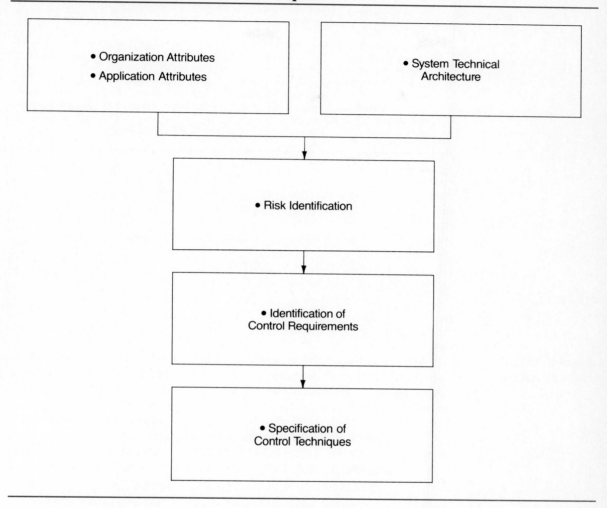

of broadly stated control objectives used by one organization is shown in Figures 15–3 and 15–4. Figure 15–3 contains overall application control objectives, useful for identifying risks related to organizational and application characteristics. Figure 15–4 contains transaction processing control objectives, more useful for identifying risks related to the way the computer system operates.

Overall Application Control Objectives. A list of overall control objectives might consist of such items as the following. **Authorization** refers to the fact   **authorization**

Figure 15–3 **Overall Control Objectives**

Authorization should be according to criteria established by the appropriate level of management.

Transactions (or business events) should be *classified* to permit preparation of

- Financial statements in conformity with generally accepted accounting principles and management's plan.
- Internal operating reports according to management's plan.

Report and data base contents should be periodically *substantiated* and *evaluated*.

Access to assets and proprietary data should be allowed only according to management's criteria.

Company operations should result in *efficient* and *effective* utilization of resources.

that responsibility and authority for tasks are often delegated to specific positions within the organization. For example, a salesperson in a department store may be authorized to approve a personal check up to $50, but a supervisor's approval is required for larger amounts. Systems controls enforcing the authorization policy should prevent the acceptance of checks over $50 when, for example, a clerk does not enforce the policy. The controls should also detect any infraction in order to inform the clerk and avoid future errors.

classification

Proper **classification** of transactions is necessary for accurate systems information. For example, both sales and adjustments contain monetary amounts, but systems information will not be accurate if sales are somehow misclassified as adjustments.

substantiation and evaluation

Periodic **substantiation and evaluation** of information contained in systems reports and data bases assures that the information is accurate and reliable. For example, certain data bases become inaccurate because they do not lend themselves to updating through the natural course of events. A personnel data base might contain different attributes on each employee. Information such as employee address or postgraduate courses taken may not be accurate at some point if the employee has no convenient way of notifying the employer when such items change. To make sure such information is accurate, organizations

Figure 15–4 **Transaction Processing Control Objectives**

Business events should be *recognized* and submitted for acceptance on a timely basis.

All and only those business events meeting management's criteria should be accurately converted to transactions and *accepted for processing* on a timely basis.

All accepted transactions and/or recognized business events should be *processed* accurately, on a timely basis, according to managements's policies.

Results of processing should be *reported* accurately and on a timely basis.

Data bases should accurately reflect the results of processing.

Interfacing events between systems should result in transactions that are reflected by each system in the same processing period.

often distribute to each employee yearly reports of information on the personnel data base and ask for any necessary corrections. Ex-spouses are often removed as life insurance beneficiaries through just such a process.

As more and more confidential or proprietary data is contained in computer data bases, **access** to information assets and proprietary data should be restricted to those persons authorized by management. For example, one of the most valuable assets of a mail-order house is its list of potential customers to whom catalogs and product descriptions are sent. Management would want to be sure that its customer list did not fall into the hands of a competitor. In addition, a mail-order house that advertises in newspapers and magazines typically codes responses to evaluate the effectiveness of ads in various media. Summary information showing the relative returns from ads would also interest a competitor and should therefore be protected by restricting access to such information. access

Efficient and effective utilization of resources is even more important as the competitive environment intensifies. Management has a right to expect that systems controls will help realize this objective. For example, large electric power companies employ hundreds of clerks to answer customer inquiries on account status and process orders using on-line computer systems. Many such systems provide by-product information to help ensure efficiency and effectiveness. Standard times are established for handling various types of on-line transactions. Actual times taken to handle transactions are developed by the system, as well as totals of the various types of transactions. If, for example, certain transactions take more time than what management expected, ways to correct the departure from standard are devised, such as additional training for clerks. This technique falls under the general category of computer monitoring, and certain ethical issues should be considered before the technique is used. For example, if someone is monitoring the time employees take to process system transactions, the employees should be informed of the monitoring and the reason for it—to identify the need for further training. efficient and effective utilization

Transaction Processing Control Objectives. The control objectives related to the system technical architecture, or transaction processing control objectives, have to do with the way transactions flow through a typical data processing system, such as the one illustrated in Figure 15–5. Figure 15–6 superimposes the transaction processing control objectives from Figure 15–4 on a typical data processing system's transaction flow to show how each control objective relates to the transaction flow.

- When an event occurs that should be recorded as a system transaction, the first requirement is that it be recognized. For example, if you purchase a quart of milk at the local convenience store but the clerk decides to pocket your money rather than ringing up a sale on the cash register, an unrecognized business event has occurred. Or, if you call your insurance agent to say you have purchased a new car and the agent forgets to transmit

Figure 15–5 **Typical Transaction Processing System Flow**

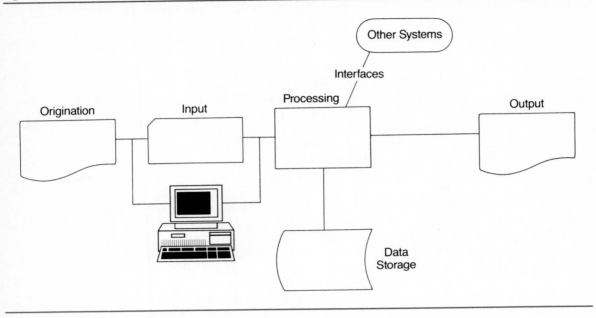

the new information to the home office, a business event occurred that was not properly recognized.

- Only business events meeting management's criteria should be accepted for processing. Not all recognized transactions are accepted for further processing by a computer-based information system, only those that meet a predetermined set of criteria. Reasonableness tests on transaction amounts are often set by management to avoid the processing of incorrect transactions. For example, a reasonableness test on a transaction recording the issue of inventory items from stock may relate that quantity to the average quantity issued over some time period in the past. Thus, if ten were the average quantity, a transaction containing an issue quantity of 1,000 would not be accepted for processing until it had been reviewed and either accepted or corrected.

- Transactions that are accepted for processing should be processed on time, accurately, and according to management policies. Processing rules that conform to management policies are embodied in the system's specifications. Controls are necessary to verify that management objectives are being met. It is not unusual to read stories in the business press of companies who have been victims of inadequate transaction processing controls in their computer systems. The typical story is one of customer bills going out late or payments being improperly credited to customers accounts as a result of

Figure 15–6 **Transaction Processing Control Objectives**

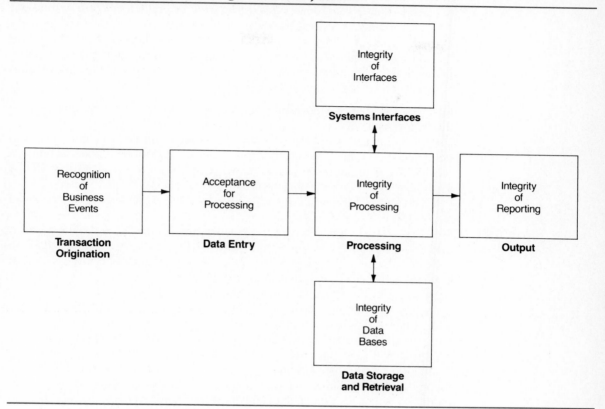

a "computer glitch" and the resultant cost to the company in clean-up efforts and a tarnished image.

- Reporting results on time and accurately is important because management relies on information to control operations and make decisions. Standards for accuracy and timeliness will vary by application. In some cases, management may be willing to sacrifice some degree of accuracy in exchange for obtaining information sooner. Once standards are set for accuracy and timeliness, however, the transaction processing controls must see that they are met.

- Data base controls assure that changes to the data base can be explained by the known effect of transactions accepted for processing. Controls are necessary to protect against program bugs that cause unwanted changes to occur, against changes caused by a person who has managed to gain unauthorized access to the data base, or against a technical failure of some sort.

- The higher the level of management, the more likely it is that information needed for decision making is drawn from several information systems. All too frequently, however, individual subsystems were designed and installed over a period of many years with imperfect interfaces between them. The purpose of interface controls is to ensure that information passed between systems is accurately received so that there is consistency in information between related functional subsystems.

Business risks are systematically identified by an analysis that can best be thought of as a subset of the process of determining functional requirements. Lists of overall control objectives such as the one illustrated in Figure 15–3 can help uncover control requirements otherwise overlooked. Other techniques include involving audit personnel as well as persons with specific knowledge applicable to the industry and application.

For example, the text referred earlier to a mail-order business that placed a high value on its customer list maintained in a computer data base. When analyzing control requirements, the business was interested in finding a way to make sure that the customer data base would not fall into the hands of a competitor and that, if it somehow did, management would know it as soon as possible. It had already established traditional physical security controls over copies of the data base and password control over access through on-line terminals. It also developed an encryption routine, a program that made the data base contents unintelligible unless translated by the encryption program. Even with these measures, management wanted to know if security had been breached by having employees, for example, copy and sell the data base and the encryption program specifications. The solution was to intersperse records on the data base containing fictitious names and the home addresses of various members of management. If the head of the internal audit department, for example, received from a competitor a mail solicitation at his or her home addressed to the fictitious name "Robert T. Kendall," he or she would know that a competitor had somehow obtained an unauthorized copy of the company's data base.

EXAMPLES OF TRANSACTION PROCESSING CONTROL TECHNIQUES

In selecting transaction processing control techniques, analysts are able to use experience gained from establishing effective controls over computer-based information systems. While business functions change from system to system, basic transaction processing flows tend to resemble the one illustrated in Figure 15–5. Examples of specific control techniques used in practice are discussed under the headings of functions listed in Figure 15–6.

Controls over Transaction Origination

Controls over transaction origination provide assurance that all business events that should be entered in a system are recognized. These controls usually tend to be manual controls rather than controls built into the computer system itself. They include such techniques as written procedures explaining the way source documents are to be prepared.

A common technique is to use prenumbered forms and have all forms accounted for in numerical sequence as either properly completed and containing a transaction or voided. Most people use this same technique to balance their personal checkbooks.

Another common technique is to log all incoming mail and phone calls to ensure that all requests originating outside the corporation are ultimately taken care of. To be effective, requests should be logged as soon as received by someone not charged with responding to them.

Controls over Data Entry

Data entry is entered into a computer system in one of two modes: in batch mode (wherein a number of transactions are accumulated and entered at the same time) or in real time (transactions are entered into the system as they occur). Batch entry can be either off-line (with transactions keyed into computer-readable formats before entry into the system) or on-line (with transactions entered directly into the system). Real-time entry of transactions is always associated with on-line entry. Illustrations of the three basic forms of data entry are shown in Figure 15–7. The three main control techniques applying to data entry are transcription error controls, batch controls, and validation controls.

Transcription errors can occur as the clerk prepares the manual document or as the data entry clerk enters it onto the data entry equipment or on-line terminal. These errors are minimized by techniques such as check digits and double data entry (where two operators enter the same data independently and the data entry equipment signals an error if the two do not agree).

**transcription errors**

A check digit is a digit added on to a code such as a customer number. Its only purpose is to guarantee that the code has been transcribed correctly. It is calculated as a function of the rest of the code the first time the code is assigned (when the customer number is created). Thereafter, it becomes part of the customer code itself. There are several algorithms that yield good check digits. The quality of such an algorithm consists in detecting whether a single digit has been altered or two contiguous digits have been transposed.

Batch control techniques can help minimize the loss or duplication of transactions. Batch control techniques are used to provide assurance that all data to be entered into the system is actually entered. User departments break transactions down into "batches" of numbers of transactions (say, 100) and establish control totals on the batches before submitting them to the data entry department. A control total is generally a "hash" or meaningless total of a numeric field on the source document such as the amount field. Sequential numbers are assigned to individual batches as the batches are prepared and entered into a log in the user department. As batches of source documents are

Figure 15–7 **Three Types of Data Entry**

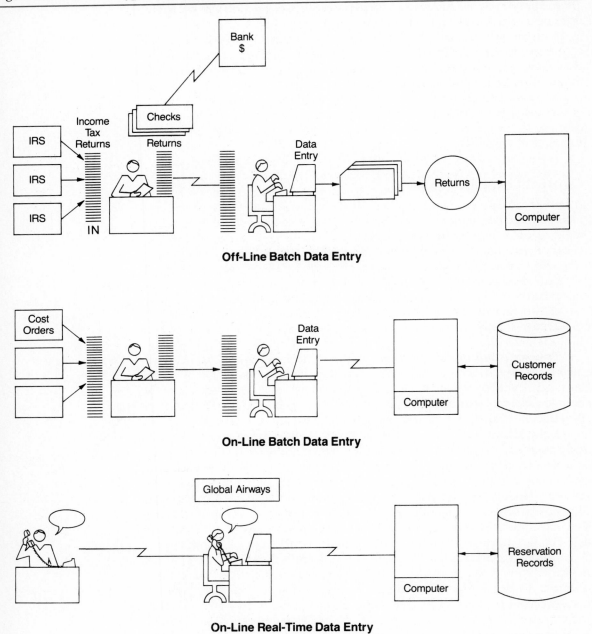

Off-Line Batch Data Entry

On-Line Batch Data Entry

On-Line Real-Time Data Entry

entered into the computer system, the data entry program adds the individual control field amount in each transaction and compares the total to the total for the batch as computed by the user department. If the two totals do not agree, the entire batch is rejected and returned to the user department, which traces the error, corrects the batch, and submits it for reentry. A batch control report lists batches in sequence by batch number. Thus, users can verify that all batches submitted were entered. The batch control report also lists the details, i.e., each transaction, the batch total, and the total calculated out-of-balance batches. With this information, the user department can track down the error, correct it, and resubmit the batch. The entire process is illustrated in Figure 15–8.

Validation of transactions is required regardless of whether data is entered in batch mode. Complete validation attempts to ensure that transactions with invalid data do not even enter the system, much less endanger the integrity of the data base. The types of validation performed were described in Section V. In particular, it is necessary to check that every elementary data field has a value belonging to its domain and that the referential integrity of the data base would not be compromised if the transaction were executed. **validation**

The following are examples of domain checking: determining that amounts have numeric data; seeing that these numeric data stay within reasonable ranges (an age less than 10 or greater than 85 for a new employee might be questioned); making certain that coded fields take on only possible values (sex must be either male or female); and ensuring that consistency is respected (a male patient should not be admitted to a maternity ward).

Referential integrity involves such tasks as making certain an existing customer is not created; requiring that a customer must already exist before it can be modified; preventing the placement of an order by a nonexistent customer or for a nonexistent product; and preventing the deletion of a customer if there are still orders to be filled.

In on-line systems, as much validation as possible is built into the transaction processing conversation. The operator must have access to the information needed to enter all the required information correctly. As each data element is entered, or as each exchange of a full screen is processed by the on-line program, the program verifies all the constraints and responds to any errors with a message highlighting the error: an error message in a reserved area of the screen; a visual cue, such as displaying an erroneous field in red or high-intensity mode; or a discreet audio beep.

Where possible, a batch validation program applies tests to all data fields. Every field on each transaction is subjected to the appropriate validation tests. Transactions with invalid data are rejected by the system and listed on an error report, which is returned to the user department for correction and subsequent reentry.

When validating transactions, all fields must be tested for errors, rather than rejecting the transaction based on the first error encountered. The latter procedure might require several cycles before all errors are found and a transaction accepted.

Figure 15–8 **Batch Balancing Flow**

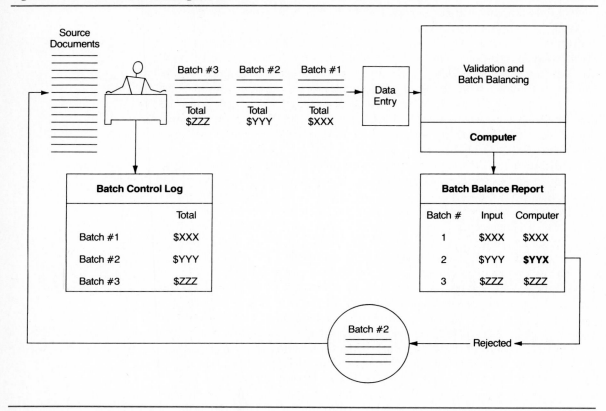

Controls over Processing

The overall purpose of processing controls is to provide assurance that transactions are processed correctly and that system files or data bases accurately reflect the results of that processing. In the past, these controls were established to assure that card files were complete and in the correct sequence and that operators did not make errors of manipulation. An operator could easily misplace a card and cause a processing error. When card files were replaced with tape files, these controls seemed unnecessary: it is impractical to excise a record from a magnetic tape—and even more difficult to remove a portion of a disk permanently enclosed in a disk drive. Unfortunately, however, operator errors continued to plague correct processing even on tape systems. Yesterday's tape could easily be taken instead of today's; they do look alike from the outside. Moreover, a new culprit had been added: the program. Because the program can remove records or alter them in subtle ways under the influence of bugs, processing controls are now more required than ever.

The nature of processing controls differs depending on whether a sequential or direct processing method is used.

Sequential Processing Controls. In a sequential processing system, transactions are accumulated and sorted into the same physical sequence as the master file. Each master record is read, and if a transaction is present for it, processed. If no transaction is present for a master record, processing may still take place, usually initiated by the passage of time (e.g., end of month). If there is no master file record for a transaction, the transaction is rejected as an error unless the transaction is to insert a new master record. Three types of controls are typically used with sequential file processing.

- **Run-to-run controls** assure the accuracy or completeness of information received by a program. For example, following validation, the program that validated the transactions develops control totals of valid transactions by transaction type. Control records are written at the end of the transaction file containing the control totals by transaction type. The file processing program accumulates a similar set of control totals as the transaction file is read. When all transactions have been read, the program compares the control totals at the end of the transaction file with the total accumulated by the file processing program. Any difference signals an error, usually caused by a program malfunction (Figure 15–9).

  run-to-run controls

- **File balancing controls** assure that records are not lost because of processing and that changes in critical fields in the file are a function of the known effect of valid transactions entered. Control fields in the file are selected; totals are accumulated on them during each processing cycle and written in control records at the end of the master file. At the completion of each processing cycle, the beginning balance of a file control field is added to the net transactions processed and compared with the independently developed ending balance of the control field. An out-of-balance condition signals an error. Figure 15–10 illustrates the way this technique is employed for an accounts receivable file. At the end of a processing run, the beginning balance in the accounts receivable file is obtained from the control record. Sales transactions posted are added to it, and cash transactions processed are subtracted from it. The total should equal the ending accounts receivable balance obtained by accumulating accounts receivable balances from individual accounts.

  file balancing controls

  In addition, a standard technique is to maintain a control record at the end of the file containing these totals. Any program that reads the file (not only the update run) can therefore validate that the file is not corrupted and that the program itself processed all the master records correctly.

- **Generation data sets** are a common file backup technique for sequential data files. In Figure 15–10, for example, the updated accounts receivable file is considered the "child"; the input master file is considered the "parent"; and the version of the master file combined with a transaction file to create

  generation data sets

Figure 15–9 **Run-to-Run Controls**

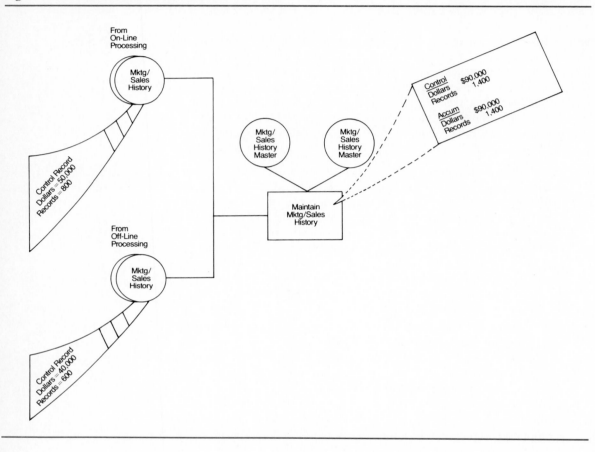

the parent is considered the "grandparent." Most systems maintain three generations of data sets to protect against the inability to use the current version of the master file. For example, in the above illustration, assume that in the next file maintenance cycle it was not possible to read the child version of the master file then being used as the input master file. The backup procedure could re-create the child by rerunning the program that originally created it using the parent version of the file together with the associated transaction file. The grandparent version of the file is held in case the parent file cannot be used or in case an error in the parent file is discovered when the child file just created is read for some other purpose. Usually at least one copy of all backup files is stored in another location to protect against disaster at the primary computer center.

Figure 15–10 **File Balancing Controls**

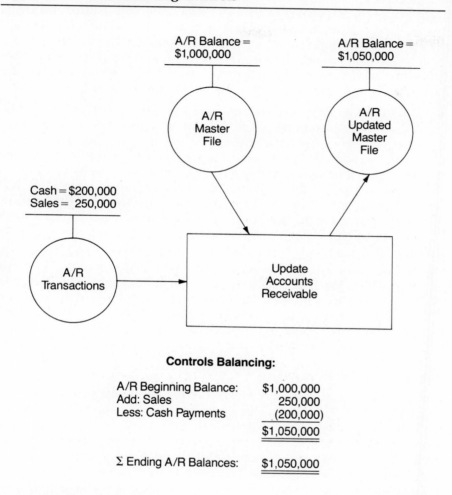

Controls Balancing:

A/R Beginning Balance:	$1,000,000
Add: Sales	250,000
Less: Cash Payments	(200,000)
	$1,050,000
Σ Ending A/R Balances:	$1,050,000

Direct File Controls. In direct file processing, transactions are processed in the sequence of their arrival. Master files are updated only if a transaction is processed against them. In contrast to sequential file processing, the entire master file is not re-created during each processing cycle. In direct file processing, analysts are typically working with a data base management system in which updates occur in place. In other words, the updated master file is written in the same physical location on the disk as the original version. Thus, the old version of the master file is destroyed.

Processing controls are more complicated in a direct processing environment. For this reason, some systems are designed to update in place on a memo basis only and capture transactions thus entered for later updating sequentially after the close of business. Many demand deposit applications in banks, for example, are still handled this way. The most common controls in a direct file processing application are system logs and data base balancing. These are also described, from a restart/recovery viewpoint, in Chapter 14.

system log

- A **system log** is used to record file processing activity so that the file can be re-created if necessary. The most common techniques record an image of every updated master record before and/or after its update. Also recorded are the transaction data, the date and time the change was made, and the program and on-line user who made the change. The log is written on a secondary storage device, often in two copies to guard against loss, and backed up as well. System logs are used to re-create the data base by reposting transactions against a copy data base from a point in time when the data base was known to be correct.

data base balancing

- **Data base balancing** is done from time to time to be sure that changes in the data base control fields (e.g., accounts receivable balance) are the result of beginning data base balances plus or minus the known effect of valid transactions. In contrast with sequential file processing, the entire data base may not be re-created each processing cycle. Periodically, however, the entire data base is read and control totals taken. Re-creation of the file to correct errors, if necessary, would be done using the system logs.

Controls over Reporting

Controls over reporting primarily verify that reports are correctly printed and delivered on time. Many IS departments have a control group to review output for accuracy and completeness before it is delivered to the user. For instance, if a continuous report were being printed as the printer ran out of paper, the control group would see that printing had resumed where it was interrupted and that no pages were missing. The control group would also ensure that system output is delivered on time to authorized users and would control access to output until it has been turned over to the users. User departments are generally responsible for verifying application control totals and batch control totals and for correcting validation errors.

Data Base Controls

Data base controls are generic controls established to protect the organization from loss or misuse of information in permanent files. These controls include the following:

- Integrity checks, most often performed during transaction processing, but on occasion during a separate run.
- Files and procedures for recovery and restart.

- Control over access to the data base.

- Physical protection against destruction or theft.

These controls are explained elsewhere in this chapter and in Chapters 13 and 14.

Systems Interface Controls

Systems interface controls resemble the data entry controls except that data entering one computer system is the output of another computer system. Control totals should be established on transactions passed from one system to another to prevent a loss of data in the exchange.

In addition, validation tests may need to be added. Even though transferred data was validated when it first entered a computer system and has been controlled since then, there may be different error tolerances between systems and, therefore, a revalidation of certain fields may be necessary. An example is that of a weekly file produced for a monthly run; between the first and the last week of the month, the contents of the master file might have been changed and the data from the first week might no longer be associated with a master file record. The validation does not necessarily point out errors in the transactions only; an error in a transaction may only be symptomatic of an error in a master file.

Another, more frequent error may occur when an interface file is produced by a third party, as in electronic data interchange. A customer may produce an order file or a vendor an invoice file. In all probability, the customer's or vendor's systems and files are not synchronized with those of the organization.

PRIVACY ISSUES AND THE RIGHTS OF THE INDIVIDUAL

IS professionals need to be aware of individual and privacy rights, because the systems design largely determines how these rights can be protected.

Individual rights relate to the responsibility of organizations to be sure stored information is given freely, accurately, and confidentially. Everyone routinely supplies information to various organizations: banks, tax authorities, applications for consumer credit, and so on. Then why is the issue of privacy of greater concern with computer-based information systems than with paper-based systems? According to Deborah G. Johnson[2] concern has increased because more and more organizations maintain computer data bases and thus can exchange information on individuals so much more easily than with paper documents. An error in the information exchanged is a matter of concern. Because organizations base decisions about individuals on information contained in computer data bases, an individual could be harmed if the information is not correct. For example, the individual could be denied credit, turned down for employment, or perhaps even arrested.

The issue is complicated because with multiple exchanges between computer-based systems, erroneous information is not restricted to a single organization but could be multiplied many times over. Imagine the difficulty an individual would have correcting an erroneous credit rating report if the report had been shared with countless organizations. It would be difficult even to find out which organizations were keeping records on the individual.

Organizations could be held responsible in the courts if an individual could prove harm as a result of decisions made on erroneous information. Systems analysts have certain ethical responsibilities to society that should dictate the way systems are designed. Systems professionals also have a responsibility to their organizations to design systems that minimize the likelihood of lawsuits.

Another issue arises mainly in government organizations. Information from different sources could be pooled and conclusions drawn about individuals that might threaten their civil liberties. In particular, there is a fear that law enforcement agencies might obtain revealing data about personal habits, religious beliefs, or other knowledge that would not qualify as evidence in the courts. Some agency could use this information to interfere in citizens' private lives, much as Big Brother in *1984*.

A Special Advisory Committee on Automated Personal Data Systems to the Secretary of Health, Education, and Welfare identified five principles that established a code of fair information practices. The Committee worded the principles as follows:

- There must be no personal record-keeping systems whose very existence is secret.

- There must be a way for an individual to find out what information about him is on record and how it is being used.

- There must be a way for an individual to correct or amend a record of identifiable information about him.

- There must be a way for an individual to prevent information about him that was obtained for one purpose from being used or made available for other purposes without his consent.

- Any organization creating, maintaining, using or disseminating records of identifiable personal data must guarantee the reliability of the data for their intended use and must take precautions against the misuse of the data.[3]

These principles have become widely accepted as the foundation for much social policy and possible legislation on privacy. Systems analysts should keep the principles in mind when designing data bases and their related controls.

The attention given to privacy and individual rights varies from country to country. In some countries, legislation has been enacted; in other countries, legislation is pending. Thus, the issue is particularly thorny when an application transfers personnel data from one country to another, causing a so-called *transborder data flow*. Because the area is in a state of evolution, analysts should be sure they are current.

Summary

Management and IS professionals must be certain that the organization's information systems include the necessary controls to protect the organization from risks. Such risks range from erroneous decisions made because of incorrect information to loss of assets and the interruption or cessation of operations.

Errors are usually attributable to one of three sources: human errors, technical failures, and natural forces. Controls are instituted to prevent errors and to detect errors that do occur so that corrective and preventive measures can be taken.

General controls are the set of controls and standard operating procedures in the IS department. They serve as the foundation for application controls. Application controls are tailored to the specific requirements of each application and incorporated in the system's specifications, much the same as other functional requirements.

Once risks are identified for a particular application and its organizational setting, application controls can be specified. Audit personnel can be helpful in this process and should be consulted.

Two sets of application control objectives are used to help identify specific control techniques: a set of overall application control objectives and transaction processing control objectives. Each set of control objectives has a set of associated control techniques that practitioners have used to satisfy the objectives.

Finally, the issues of privacy and individual rights focus attention on the risks organizations may face because of inaccurate or misused information they maintain on individuals.

Selected Readings

Davis, G., Adams, D., and Schaller, C. *Auditing and EDP*, 2d ed. New York: American Institute of Certified Public Accountants, 1983.

In this authoritative and recent book, controls are seen from the external auditor's viewpoint.

Johnson, D. *Computer Ethics.* Englewood Cliffs, New Jersey: Prentice-Hall, 1985.

This book covers ethical issues for IS professionals, including codes of the various professional societies, privacy, power, liability for malfunctions in computer programs, and issues of computer program ownership.

Review Questions

1. Describe the difference between general systems controls and applications controls. The two are not mutually exclusive. How do they relate?

2. When do human errors result in system errors?

3. What are common types of technical failures?

4. Why is it increasingly important for organizations to protect themselves against disruptions of their computer systems by natural forces?

5. Explain the approach taken in designing application controls.

6. Why do experienced systems analysts consult with both internal and external auditors when controls are designed?

7. Briefly summarize the overall application control objectives.

8. Briefly summarize the transaction processing control objectives.

9. Explain how and why user departments use batch control techniques over data entry operations.

10. Which data validation test would apply to the following examples?
   a. A transaction that listed bananas at $390 per pound.
   b. A transaction containing an "o" instead of a zero in a quantity field.
   c. An undergraduate student attempting to register for a graduate-level course.
   d. A student undergraduate classification of "5" where the permissible classifications are "1" (freshman), "2" (sophomore), "3" (junior), or "4" (senior).

11. Describe the purpose of the following transaction processing control techniques:
   a. Controls over transaction origination.
   b. Controls over data entry.
   c. Controls over processing.

12. Summarize the control techniques over sequential file processing and direct file processing.

13. What are the privacy and individual rights issues related to designing computer-based information systems?

Discussion Questions

1. Software may provide information security by restricting access to computerized information on a need-to-know basis. Consider a bank with four departments: new customer accounts, checking, savings, and loans. What controls would you recommend on departmental employees' ability to read and/or modify data base information? (For example, should a checking department employee be able to read savings account information? Modify savings account information?)

2. Compare and contrast file processing controls for sequential processing and direct processing controls. Discuss why direct processing controls are more difficult than sequential processing controls.

3. Imagine that you have become associated with a new organization that needs to establish general systems controls over all aspects of its IS department's operations. Outline the areas that should be considered and recommend appropriate controls.

4. For the same organization, outline general application control objectives and transaction processing control objectives for an on-line point-of-sale system designed for a discount retail store. Assume that a perpetual inventory system interfaces with the point-of-sale system.

5. Discuss the possible ramifications to individual privacy of multiple exchanges of data base information between computer-based systems.

Mini-Case

Genesee Supply Corporation. Assume that you are an independent consultant engaged by Genesee Supply Corporation to assist it in the design of an order entry, billing, and accounts receivable system. Genesee is a medium-sized distributor of industrial supplies with sales of approximately $80 million per year and 185 employees. The company has had a minicomputer installed for several years. Applications include the present order entry, billing, and accounts receivable system (installed about ten years ago), payroll, inventory control, financial planning and reporting, and sales analysis. The MIS department is headed by Ricardo Diaz. He has two programmer/analysts and four operations personnel in his department. The controller, Marsha Hunt, is in charge of all accounting operations, including billing and accounts receivable.

During the course of your project, you interviewed both Ricardo and Marsha in order to understand the general systems controls in place at Genesee Supply and the applications controls in place for the present order entry, billing, and accounts receivable system. The results of the interviews will be used as one of the inputs into the process of specifying the controls required in the new system. Their responses to your questions to describe the general systems and applications controls, respectively, were as follows:

Ricardo (re: general controls): "I believe that controls can choke an organization. People become too involved in controls and end up not doing their jobs. We have very low turnover and our employees are loyal and motivated. If something is wrong with a system, they will notice it. They are familiar enough with our routines to fix errors when they occur. Every year our external auditors review our operations and submit their suggestions. However, we never have adequate resources to implement the suggestions. I go over the auditor's recommendations with the president and explain to him how we're covered, and then we don't worry about controls for a while. I can tell you this: we've never lost a file, we've never had a program bug we couldn't fix, and we've never had a fraud or embezzlement. That's more than a lot of companies can say."

Marsha (re: application controls): "I happen to be a fanatic on accuracy. Every transaction that is entered into the system is proofread from a report prepared by the computer back to the transaction document to be sure there were no errors. The data entry clerk does proofreading for new accounts added to the master file and for each transaction, cash, bills, etc. As far as balancing the file is concerned, we keep a control account balance of accounts receivable. After each posting run, we reconcile the change in the control total to the total amount of bills for that day less the total amount of cash and adjustments for the day. Cash flow is a problem for us, so you can be sure we're paying attention to receivables controls!"

Question for Discussion

1. In each case, what additional information (if any) do you feel you should obtain?

References

1. Personal communication with the author.

2. Johnson, Deborah G. *Computer Ethics*. Englewood Cliffs, New Jersey: Prentice-Hall, 1985.

3. Hare, W. H., chairman. "Records, Computers and the Rights of Citizens, A Report of the Secretary's Advisory Committee on Automated Personal Data Systems." Washington, D.C.: U.S. Department of Health, Education and Welfare, 1973.

Chapter 16

Designing for Performance

Chapter 16 describes how to design systems to meet the most frequently specified performance requirements, while minimizing the cost associated with these requirements. First, the main measures of performance are defined. Next, practical ways of attaining stated requirements are described. Finally, techniques for estimating systems resource requirements, which ultimately translate into costs, are covered.

Learning Objectives

- Understand the definition of the three most generally used measures of performance: response time, throughput, and availability.

- Describe some of the most frequent ways of designing a system to ensure that the performance requirements are met.

- Be aware of the various steps involved in estimating the resource requirements of an application as it is being designed.

DEFINITION OF PERFORMANCE

An example can illustrate how difficult it is to define the meaning of "meeting performance requirements." In the example, three transportation systems basically perform the same function: they move people from one point to another. However, the three must meet widely varying performance requirements. The performance of a 747 airplane is described by its capacity to carry 385 passengers at 550 miles per hour for a maximum distance of 6,000 miles without refueling. The performance of a sports car is described by the horsepower rating of its engine, its maximum speed, its acceleration, and quite secondarily its fuel consumption. The number of passengers is also a secondary consideration. The performance of the Queen Elizabeth II is characterized by the time it takes to cross the Atlantic Ocean, the number of passengers it carries, but perhaps more importantly, the ratio of service personnel to passengers and the availability of luxuries.

In business systems, performance measures will also vary widely. Nevertheless, some traits are shared by all systems and can serve as a basic definition: an application that performs well is one that accomplishes its operational objectives within given time and resource constraints. This chapter concentrates on the time and resource constraints; it does not concentrate on the operational objectives such as functionality, ease of use, reliability, maintainability, and speed of implementation, which are application dependent.

Meeting the time and resource requirements is just as important to the success of the system as is meeting the functional needs. For example, a small insurance company was replacing a card-based system in the early 1970s with a system based on sequential processing of tape files. The system had been entirely designed, programmed, and tested. As the time for system testing approached, the team decided to call in a consultant to help estimate the time that would be required for the application to run. The consultant found that the daily update would take 16 hours of processing time on the existing equipment and that the monthly billing run would require 125 hours of processor time. Design changes, which would take about three months to implement, would reduce the figures to 11 and 25 hours respectively. Even these figures were considered excessive, and the system was abandoned. The new computer was returned to the vendor, and the two principal designers of the system found jobs elsewhere.

In early days, performance requirements were mainly considered to be made up of quantifiable volumes of input and output to be processed. Today, much more attention is given to the performance requirements of the users of the system. For instance, the psychological effect of excessive on-line response times is considered on a par with the economical effects. If the response time to a transaction is too long, the operator loses concentration and requires more time to enter the next transaction. Excessive irritation at frequent delays can also cause increased fatigue. As hardware becomes less and less costly compared with the cost of human resources, the balance of performance preoccupation shifts from optimal use of hardware to optimal use of personnel.

USUAL MEASURES OF PERFORMANCE

The three most commonly used measures of performance are response time, throughput, and availability.

Response Time

Response time is the first measure of computer system performance that usually comes to mind, just as speed is for transportation. It is also the most frequent subject of complaints by users because it is the most noticeable characteristic.

Response time is defined as the time that elapses between the initiation of an activity and the availability of the result. In an on-line system, the response time is usually the time taken by the computer to process a single exchange.

More specifically, the user response time on a block-mode terminal is the time elapsed between the operator pressing the *Transmit* key and the first character of the response appearing on the screen. (Sometimes, the last character of the response is used instead.) In a batch system, the expression "response time" is rarely used; instead, the turnaround time is defined as the time elapsed between the user making a request for processing (such as an ad hoc report) and receiving the output (such as the printed report being delivered to the user's office).

Both of these response times are viewed from the user's perspective. They may include components over which the IS department has no power, such as mail-room delays for the delivery of printed reports or delays encountered on the public data transmission network for on-line transactions from a remote terminal. Often, an IS department considers response time and turnaround time to include only the part of the time spent in the department. (This part is often called the *system response time*.) This difference in definition is obviously a source of conflict; the response or turnaround time objectives that are set in the requirements specifications are those that the users see.

On-line response time is made up of several components, as illustrated in Figure 16–1. Figure 16–2 illustrates the components of batch turnaround time. When the operator presses the *Enter* key, the data in the terminal buffer is sent over a communications line to the computer. The telecommunications access method readies the data in a buffer and signals to the teleprocessing monitor where the message comes from. The teleprocessing monitor determines which user program is to process the message, usually by looking at a code at the start of the message or because it knows that the terminal was previously attached to an unfinished conversational program. The user program performs work, such as validation, calculations, etc., and it probably also requests data from the DBMS (or from a classical file access method).

Once the user program has finished its processing, the reverse sequence is gone through. The teleprocessing monitor deactivates the program and signals to the telecommunications access method that there is a message in a buffer waiting to be sent to the terminal. When the first (or, alternatively, the last) character of the message has negotiated its way back to the terminal through the transmission network, the time elapsed since the operator pressed *Enter* constitutes the response time.

The previous discussion applies to block-mode terminals. Character-mode terminals have an additional category of response time, called character or screen response. This is the time it takes for each character to appear on the terminal once it has been keyed in. In many systems, this time is so short that it appears instantaneous, but in others, it can become substantial. If the operator systematically types faster than the system can display characters on the screen, the application may become unusable.

The response time is a function of the volume of information or processing at each stage and of the speed or capacity of each component. For instance, a **volume** of 2,000 characters per message takes longer to transmit than one of

volume

Figure 16–1 **Components of On-Line Response Time**

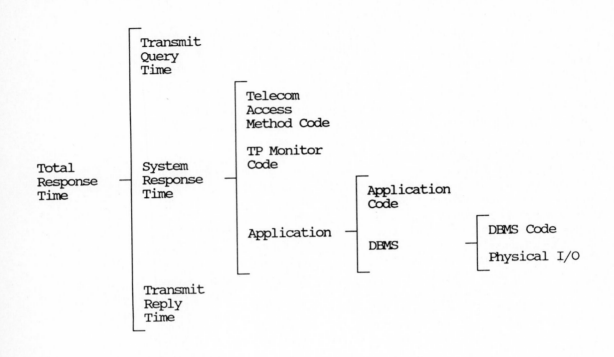

200. It does not necessarily take longer to process at the access method, TP monitor, user program, or DBMS stages, however. Obviously, a short message requiring 80 data base records to be read will use more data base access time than one requiring 10 records to be read.

    Another factor is the speed with which each stage is processed. This speed is a function of the **capacity** of the resource. In business data processing, transmission lines vary in capacity from 1,200 bits per second to hundreds of millions of bits per second. Transmission speed is a function of technology and distance; the hundreds of millions cannot be achieved over long distances with the present state of the technology. On the other hand, DBMS speeds depend on the disk technology—the faster a disk rotates and the quicker the reading arm travels, the shorter the response time—but also on the functions performed by the DBMS and the organization of the data base. If the data base does not have an index to the field that is used as a search argument, a more extensive search

capacity

Figure 16–2 **Components of Batch Turnaround Time**

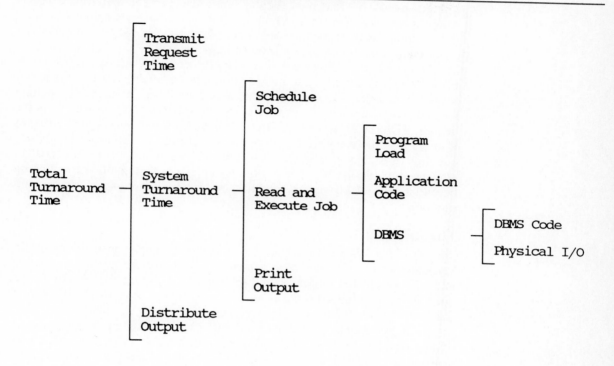

is needed and response times go up. This fact has often been cited as an argument against relational data base management systems in the past; the problem can be overcome by proper design and also by the DBMS adding more efficient searching mechanisms.

What is less obvious is that it is not enough to add up the processing time used by each resource at each stage to process the transaction. Whenever a resource is shared by several users, one user may have to to wait for the previous user to be finished with the resource before being able to use it. This is called **queuing,** by analogy to customers waiting in line at a supermarket or a service station. The art of performance design is to strike a compromise between short queues and economy of resource. A comparison with a supermarket can illustrate the need for a compromise. If management's objective is to avoid customer waiting time altogether, enough checkout lanes and enough cashiers would need to be present at all times to handle the largest possible crowd. As

queuing

crowds are not permanently present, most of the registers and most of the cashiers would be idle most of the time. Management therefore effects a compromise: customers must wait in line part of the time and cashiers must be idle at other times. Statistics enable management to know how many lines to provide and what the average customer wait time will be.

Similarly, in on-line systems, rules of thumb provide guidance on how much resource to provide to keep queuing times at a tolerable level. A branch of mathematics called queuing theory has established that the time spent waiting for a resource varies as the inverse of its free capacity ($1 - u$, where u is the degree of utilization of the resource). This yields a graph such as the one in Figure 16–3. The curve in the figure has a characteristic elbow beyond which queuing rises dramatically for very little additional utilization. The goal of response time design is to get as close to the elbow as possible without going beyond it, thus establishing the optimal compromise between performance and economy.

Throughput

Throughput refers to the capacity of the system rather than to its speed. Throughput can be defined as the amount of work that the system can process in a unit of time. In on-line systems, this capacity is generally expressed as the number of transactions per second or per hour; in batch systems, it is usually the number of jobs per 24-hour period or per month.

In the requirements analysis stage, the system throughput requirement is usually stated as follows: "The system must be capable of performing all the processing associated with so many orders per day or paychecks per month."

One of the problems associated with throughput is that there is no universally satisfactory method of measuring it across applications. Capacity cannot be expressed in a single unit which might assume that one order is equal to 1.75 paychecks or .05 management report.

The throughput of an on-line transaction processing system is a function of the number of operators doing work and the time it takes each operator to process a transaction. As long as response times stay acceptable, most of the operator time is devoted to what is conventionally termed *think time*. This is the time that elapses between the first character (or the last, depending on which convention is used for response times) of a response appearing on a terminal and the user pressing *Enter* for the next transaction. For dedicated operators, the think time is everything that is not response time; it is composed of time spent thinking about what to do, getting the information required, and keying it onto the terminal. For intermittent operators, think time also includes time spent away from the system on other tasks. Breaks and other brief periods of inactivity must also be taken into account.

Typical think times range from 10 seconds for trained users doing interactive work, such as end-user computing or on-line programming, testing, and debugging, to 60 seconds for complex on-line transaction processing, such as order entry in the presence of a customer.

Figure 16–3   **Queuing Time as a Function of Utilization**

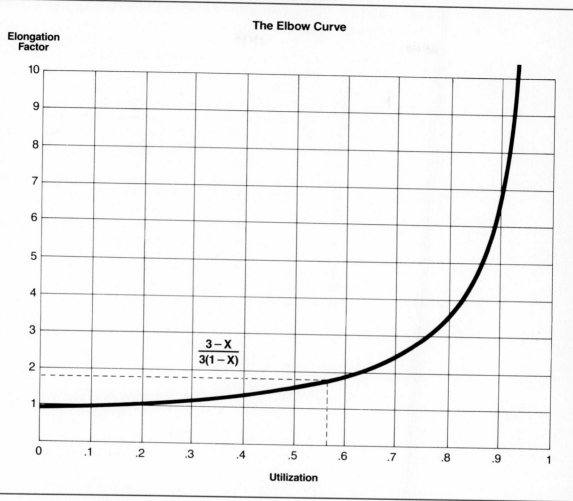

As suggested in the discussion of response times, when many users share
the same resource, response times go up. This increase results from each user
consuming a certain percentage of the available resource over the cycle of
response time plus think time. When this percentage is added up for all of the
users sharing the resources, the total utilization of the resource is obtained. If
this utilization does not reach the elbow on the curve in Figure 16–3, the
response time is made up mainly of processing time. If it goes beyond the elbow,
response times are degraded. Apart from the consequence on the productivity
of the user, high response times add to the total time required by each operator
to enter a transaction. If the operator has a think time of 60 seconds, then,

degrading the response time from, say, 2 seconds to 33 seconds will increase the time required by 50 percent. Such an increase would mean that the same workload would require 50 percent more operators, 50 percent more terminals, etc. If the cumulative resource usage of all the operators combined exceeds the available capacity, the relationship with response times becomes immaterial.

For batch systems, the throughput is generally expressed in number of batch jobs per time period. This unit of measure is a problem because the variability of batch jobs is much greater than that of on-line transactions, ranging from seconds to hours or even days. Stating the performance requirements during the analysis phase and making sure they are met during design can be done in one of two ways. The first is to assume that, because batch tends to be a decreasing part of the requirement, any resource (such as a mainframe processor) capable of handling the on-line load can also handle the batch load. This method is the most frequently used and the least satisfactory.

The alternative is to estimate batch processing requirements based on input/output requirements. When the process design is completed, file volumes are known and total input/output requirements can be estimated. Instead of concentrating on whether the processor resource is available, as is usually done in on-line systems, the analyst can determine whether the I/O subsystem can handle the workload. There are rules of thumb relating the I/O subsystem capacity to the size of processor normally needed for a balanced configuration. If the I/O subsystem capacity needs to be increased for the batch processing load, it is probable that the processor capacity needs to be increased accordingly.

Availability

Not only must the system be capable of processing the requisite number of transactions within a given response time, but it must also be able to do so when required. Availability is especially important for on-line transaction processing systems that are integrated into the operations of a company. If an airline reservations system fails, passengers can no longer be checked in at the gate and flights are delayed. If a bank's ATM system has frequent outages, customers will no longer rely on it. If a computer fails on board the space shuttle, the flight may have to be canceled. The failure of even a small part of the air traffic control system could have dire consequences.

The availability of a system is generally expressed as a percentage. The time that the system will be available to process work is divided by the time period that is of interest—24 hours a day, 7 days a week for an ATM or an airline reservation system; 8 hours a day, 5 days a week for an on-line order entry system manned from, say, 9 to 5 on weekdays.

Availability is tied to schedule and reliability. If the daily schedule calls for the on-line system to be operational at 9 A.M. and it takes 30 minutes to start it, then all the elements required for the start-up phase (the data base, for example) must be ready at 8:30. If the data base needs to be backed up and the backup takes 3 hours, then the backup process must start no later than 5:30 A.M.

Here is where reliability comes in. If the schedule dovetails so nicely that the entire 24-hour cycle is accounted for, as it is with the 100 percent availability requirement of airline systems, for example, then the reliability of the system is what determines availability. The reliability of a system is characterized by two statistical measures: the mean time between failures (MTBF) and the mean time to recover (MTTR). The mean time between failures can be quite short as long as the mean time to recover is also short. For instance, a system that is capable of recovering from program incidents on the fly, by backing out uncommitted transactions and restarting them, has a short MTTR, and an application with a fairly high frequency of program failures can have acceptable availability.

HOW TO DESIGN FOR PERFORMANCE

Designing for performance is done in three steps: identifying the performance requirements, estimating the likely performance consequence of each design decision, and choosing the design decision that minimizes total cost while meeting the performance requirement.

Understanding the most frequent solutions to performance problems depends on some general characteristics of the design decisions. First, a performance design decision usually falls into one of the following classes: changing the design so that it uses fewer resources, increasing the resources available, or relaxing the performance requirement.

Second, to satisfy the principle of maximum return when design changes are contemplated, most of the work is done on those parts of the design where the performance impact is the greatest.

- If a transaction response time is predicted to be excessive, it is usually not useful to optimize the application code. The telecommunications access method, the teleprocessing monitor, and the DBMS frequently consume ten times more CPU time than the application code. Therefore, improving the application code even by a factor of two is likely to have very little impact on the response time (which is mainly made up of I/O time and transmission time) and even on the total CPU consumption.

- It is better to concentrate on the 20 percent of transaction types that typically make up 80 percent of the total volume than to work on rarely executed transactions.

Although many sources of performance problems exist, the following discussion addresses the most frequent sources of problems and their suggested solutions for each of the three classes of performance measures: response time, throughput, and availability.

Response Time Problems

The two greatest contributors to response time problems in on-line environments are message transmission times and data base I/O times. Message transmission time is only relevant for remote terminals. Terminals that are within 2,000 feet of the host machine can usually be attached locally, and transmission speeds are so high that there is no need to worry about their impact on response times. There are various ways to minimize the impact of **message transmission times**:

- Decrease transmission volumes by not transmitting repetitive or useless information.

    This solution implies technology at the terminal that automatically transmits only the part of the screen that has changed or that can store screen formats (text, instructions, headings, etc.) so that they do not need to be transmitted from the host.

- Increase transmission capacity by increasing line speeds.

    Today, the maximum recommended speeds are 4,800 bps over switched lines, 19,200 bps over leased lines, and 56,000 bps over digital transmission facilities. When using a third-party network, such as a value-added or packet-switched network, transmission speeds vary with many other factors, in particular with the number of nodes where the message has to be received in its entirety before it can be forwarded to the next node. The number of nodes traversed can actually vary from transmission to transmission.

    In some cases, transmission capacity may be increased by adding more transmission lines to reduce line sharing between multiple terminals.

- Relax the performance requirement.

    This solution may seem like admitting defeat, but that is not necessarily the case. First, many response time requirements identified in the analysis stage are unreasonable. For instance, some studies have shown that subsecond response time increases productivity; such short response times are certainly more pleasant for the users. However, with today's transmission technology, it is probably useless to hope for subsecond response times over an analog network. Many transaction processing applications have been quite successful with 2- to 5-second response times.

    Another consideration is that users expect response times to be high for what is perceived to be difficult or nonroutine transactions. Quite high response times are therefore acceptable for a small number of transactions that perform complex tasks.

    The worst feature of high response times is that the user does not know when to expect the response to arrive. In fact, the user generally does not even know whether the system is operational while waiting for the response. A proven measure to minimize the impact of poor response times is to give the user immediate feedback, such as: "Your query is noted. Processing will take some time. Please stand by." Even better is to display an estimated percentage of completion of the task at regular intervals. This solution is usally confined to intelligent workstations.

A final consideration is that in dedicated-operator processing, such as data entry, telephone order processing, or reservations, consistency of response time is the most important factor. An occasional longer wait than normal breaks the operator's rhythm and concentration. It would be better to have all response times be 2 seconds, rather than 1.5 seconds 80 percent of the time and 3 seconds 20 percent of the time.

The impact of **high I/O times** can be minimized by the following steps:

high I/O times

- Decrease the volume of I/O operations performed.

    The volume of I/O may be decreased by redesigning the data base to introduce a controlled amount of redundancy (by storing parent data in the child records, for example) or by providing more indexes. Another solution is to keep larger volumes of data in main storage. As the price of main storage continues to drop, this solution will become more and more attractive.

    A different strategy can be to cut a complex, high-I/O transaction into several smaller transactions, each requiring substantially less I/O (see Section IV).

- Increase I/O capacity by using faster disks or channels or by spreading the I/O over more resources (decreasing resource sharing and queuing).

    The effect of this type of measure is limited by the fact that disk performance tends to span a very narrow range. The main cause of disk performance problems is "seek time," the time it takes for the read/write arm to move to the track where the data is. Seek time usually varies within a range of no more than 1 to 2 on a given category of equipment.

- Relax the performance requirement.

For batch turnaround times, the time required to get the request to the IS department, schedule the work, print the output, and transmit the report back to the user usually overshadows processing times. The same applies for end-of-period processing such as the monthly or yearly accounting and management information applications. Organizational measures are the ones that are the most likely to be effective.

Throughput Problems

Where the performance problem is one of total throughput rather than response times, the measures to be taken are somewhat different. (Throughput depends on the total capacity of the system, and capacity problems tend to cause high response times. The reverse may not be true: high response times are not necessarily caused by capacity problems.)

For a throughput problem, the performance bottleneck must be identified. The bottleneck is caused by a single resource that cannot handle the total processing load—the one whose consumption would exceed 100 percent with the estimated workload. Often, removing one bottleneck causes another bottleneck to appear. However, it can be difficult to guess which resource will cause the next bottleneck before the prior bottleneck is actually removed.

The bottleneck is likely to be the central processing unit, the main memory, or both. In either case, for on-line systems, it is not easy to solve the problem by redesign, nor is it realistic to expect the user to decrease the volume of activity. Therefore, most solutions will entail getting a larger processor or main memory. The requirement for upgrading the processor or the memory must be defined before the economic evaluation of the application takes place (see Chapter 17); the cost impact can be very high.

For batch processing, the system may be redesigned so that total throughput can increase. The main step to be taken is to avoid nonproductive work. Several examples in other chapters have pointed out designs that minimize the number of times a file is read sequentially. Reducing the total volume of output by reporting only exceptions or reducing the reporting frequency might be other steps to be taken.

Availability Problems

The last measure of performance to be considered is availability. There are two main ways to increase availability. One is to decrease the MTBF (mean time between failures), the other is to decrease the MTTR (mean time to recover).

reduction of the MTBF

Reduction of the MTBF can be achieved through the following types of measures:

- Design the application to be independent of schedules.

    If the cut-off process is designed so that the on-line application can restart regardless of the state of the daily batch processing, the number of availability incidents due to late starts will be minimized.

- Design the application for continuous operation so that it does not have to be stopped to do cut-off processing.

    This solution may not be possible in all environments. In particular, few data base systems are capable of maintaining the data base description while the on-line system is running, continuing to update the data base.

- Increase software reliability through good design, programming, testing, and debugging practices.

    Improving software reliability is easier said than done. However, some interesting results have been obtained by various approaches to develop zero-defect software. These approaches rely on continuous monitoring of quality throughout the entire process so that bugs are not allowed to arise.

- Increase hardware reliability by duplicating critical components.

    This is the approach chosen by several manufacturers of so-called fault-tolerant equipment, who make machines that continue to operate in the presence of failures. A well-known example was the system of computers on board the Apollo flights, where four computers all processed the same data, and a fifth processor continually monitored the four to make sure that they were obtaining the same results. In the commercial world, Tandem and Stratus are the best known for fault-tolerance equipment.

Reduction of the MTTR can be done by resorting to the following types of measures:

reduction of the MTTR

- Use the duplication technique described in the previous paragraph to achieve a shorter MTTR, rather than MTBF, by providing for spare parts on site.

  The spare part concept can extend to the entire processor: if a company has two processors, one doing more essential work than the other, then one of the processors can serve as backup for the other.

- Decrease the time to recover from a malfunction by designing the recovery process adequately.

  This technique is described in Chapter 14.

ESTIMATING RESOURCE REQUIREMENTS

The resource requirements of an application must be estimated for two main reasons: to verify that response time (or turnaround) requirements can be met and to check whether there are enough hardware resources available in the installation to execute the new application. Ultimately, the resource requirements of an application translate into hardware and systems software costs. Although these costs are decreasing relative to total systems costs, they are still substantial.

There are two ways to estimate resource requirements. The first, **the analytical approach,** is to decompose the application into its components and to estimate what is required for each component. This approach is the easiest, given enough data about the environment. It is also the most uncertain, especially with innovative applications or recently released systems software. The description of the analytical emphasizes the general logic to be followed. The specific details of the calculations and the base resource consumption figures are dependent on the particular hardware and software in use. The details also change rapidly over time, as new hardware and software technology becomes available. Possible sources of current performance data are vendors, industry associations, specialized firms, and the press.

the analytical approach

The alternative to the analytical approach is **benchmarking**, or prototyping, the application. Benchmarking consists of creating and running an application with the same volumes, I/O, and processing characteristics as the application being designed. This approach works quite well in modern DBMS-oriented applications because the resource consumption is more a function of the data base structure and activity than of the complexity of the application code. At the stage reached before the economic evaluation of the application, the data design is usually much more firm than the process design. Benchmarking also requires less knowledge of the internals of the systems software (such as TP monitor and DBMS). Benchmarking is much more expensive than the analytical approach,

benchmarking

however, and it may also require specialized software to simulate a large population of terminal users and a high-volume data base.

The following example describes a simple order entry application such as the one for Condor Telephone Company (see the mini-case in Chapter 14). In the example, the conversation consists of two exchanges: an order header exchange (used to enter the customer number, order number, delivery dates, etc.) and a detail line exchange (used to enter an average of 3.7 order item lines per order).

The following assumptions are made:

- An input screen contains an average of 200 characters.

- An output screen contains an average of 1,200 characters.

- Each order detail screen requires 45 disk accesses, as specified in Figure 16–4.

Transmission Time

In the simplest case, the transmission time is equal to the number of characters transmitted (here, 1,400) divided by the effective line speed in characters per second. The effective line speed is always somewhat slower than the rated line speed because of transmission overhead, such as parity bits and control characters, and electronic switching delays. It is prudent to assume that the effective line speed is between 60 and 75 percent of rated line speed.

Thus, a line speed of 9,600 bits per second might correspond to an effective line speed of 700 to 1,000 characters (each composed of eight bits) per second. For a volume of 1,400 characters, the time required would be between 1.4 and 2 seconds (see Figure 16–5).

If the network topology requires that the data transmission should flow over several nodes, the transmission times must be calculated for each segment and added up, as each node must receive the message completely before passing it on. Some applications call for a protocol converter between the user and the processor. The protocol converter is used for connecting two equipments that do not use the same transmission disciplines (because they are from different manufacturers, for example). If the application had a protocol converter to which the terminal was connected via a dial-up line of 1,200 bps and if the protocol converter was attached to the host via a 9,600 bps line, the total time required would be between 7 and 10 seconds (see Figure 16–6).

Transmission via satellite has the same requirement. Although transmission speeds are much higher, the transmission does not bounce off the satellite like a mirror; the message is received and retransmitted. This buffering adds an overhead of about 250 milliseconds to any transmission time. In addition, the satellite is usually far enough from the earth that the speed of transmission (the speed of light, 186,000 miles per second) is a factor. Communications satellites are in orbit about 22,000 miles above ground, thereby imposing a minimum trajectory of 44,000 miles for any message, tacking on another 250 milliseconds

Figure 16–4 **Disk Accesses Required to Process a Four-Line Item Order Exchange**

```
MARKETING                    SUBURBAN PUMPS                    CD-20
ORDER ENTRY                                                   DASDA
                          DISK ACCESS ESTIMATE

┌────────────────────────────────────────────────────────────────────┐
│ PREPARED BY:  PETER NG      DATE:  13DEC94    VERSION:       PAGE 1   │
│ APPROVED BY:  JEANNE ZMUD   DATE:  13DEC94    STATUS :                │
└────────────────────────────────────────────────────────────────────┘
```

	Primary Index	Secondary Index	Record	Total
Alpha search for customer no:				
- max		20	12	
- avg		6	4	10
Read 2 customer records	1		2	3
Search for product no:				
- avg		6	6	12
Read 4 product records	4		4	8
Write 6 order records	6		6	12
Grand Total				45

or so. This phenomenon can sometimes be observed in overseas phone calls, or even on domestic television when the image is carried via satellite and the sound through ground telephone lines.

Even though satellite transmission channels are very fast, typically exceeding a million bits per second, the half-second incompressible overhead makes satellite transmission unsuitable for applications with many short exchanges; it is much better suited to applications such as file transfer, where there are long bursts of data transmitted in one direction.

Figure 16–5 **Calculation of Transmission Time**

```
MARKETING                        SUBURBAN PUMPS                    CD-20
ORDER ENTRY                                                        TCEST
                        TELECOMMUNICATIONS TIME ESTIMATE
┌─────────────────────────────────────────────────────────────────────────┐
│ PREPARED BY:   PETER NG       DATE:   13DEC94     VERSION:      PAGE 1     │
│ APPROVED BY:   JEANNE ZMUD    DATE:   13DEC94     STATUS  :                │
└─────────────────────────────────────────────────────────────────────────┘
```


              Line Speed: 9600 bits/second

        Character Length: 8 bits

              Line Speed: 9600/8 = 1200 characters/second

  Useful Line Speed Factor: 60% to 75%

     Practical Line Speed: 1200x60% to 1200x75%

                     say: 700 to 1000 characters/second

 Time to Transmit 1400 Characters: 1400/1000 to 1400/700

                     say: 1.4 to 2.0 seconds

In some applications, the time required to establish the connection must also be added. For instance, credit card authorization terminals are used by many retail stores. These terminals are not permanently connected to the authorization center; the costs would be staggering. Instead, a code in the magnetic stripe on the back of the card indicates to the system how to reach the authorization center. The terminal waits for the dial tone, dials the number, waits for the phone to ring and be "picked up" by the authorization center computer at the other end before transmitting the card number and the amount to be

Figure 16–6 **Calculation of Transmission Time—Multi-Node Network**

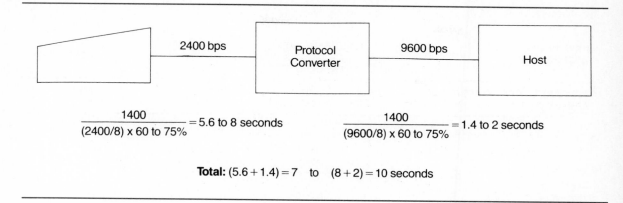

$$\frac{1400}{(2400/8) \times 60 \text{ to } 75\%} = 5.6 \text{ to } 8 \text{ seconds} \qquad \frac{1400}{(9600/8) \times 60 \text{ to } 75\%} = 1.4 \text{ to } 2 \text{ seconds}$$

Total: $(5.6 + 1.4) = 7$ to $(8 + 2) = 10$ seconds

authorized. This sequence takes several seconds and is the main component of the response time of that particular application.

Processor Time

Most of the processor time is devoted to teleprocessing monitor and data base management systems functions. Figure 16–7 shows some representative estimates of the number of machine instructions executed for various functions. These estimates, called path lengths, vary enormously from manufacturer to manufacturer and for each systems software component; they also vary over time, as new releases of the software add new functions and therefore new overhead. (The figures in Figure 16–7 should not be used in a real situation.)

In transaction processing systems, a conservative estimate is that application logic adds 20 percent to the number of instructions required by the systems software.

Once the number of instructions per transactions has been estimated, the time it takes the CPU to execute these instructions can be calculated. Many manufacturers supply instruction execution rates, expressed in MIPS, or millions of instructions per second, for their various models. For those manufacturers that do not, the press publishes estimates. These execution rates are by necessity rough approximations only. As some types of instructions take longer to execute than others, the average rate depends on the particular mix of instructions. This mix varies with the software environment, the operating system, and even the hardware: some models may be optimized for engineering and scientific applications, and others for program development, batch, or transaction processing.

The MIPS rating of processors can therefore be used to estimate execution times only in a given hardware and software environment. In a different environment, the MIPS rating of the hardware could change by as much as 20

Figure 16–7 **Number of Machine Instructions per Function**

```
MARKETING                    SUBURBAN PUMPS                      CD-20
ORDER ENTRY                                                     PATHL
                              PATH LENGTHS

┌─────────────────────────────────────────────────────────────────────┐
│ PREPARED BY:  PETER NG       DATE:  13DEC94    VERSION:`    PAGE 1     │
│ APPROVED BY:  JEANNE ZMUD    DATE:  13DEC94    STATUS :                │
└─────────────────────────────────────────────────────────────────────┘
```

	Operating System	TP Monitor	DBMS
Sign-on	50,000		
Read message	10,000	10,000	
Load program		4,000	
Read DB record by primary index	5,000		35,000
Read DB record by secondary index	5,000		75,000
Read next DB record	5,000		20,000
Update DB record	10,000		20,000
Create DB record	10,000		45,000
Write record to log	2,000	4,000	
Write message to terminal	10,000	10,000	

percent; and the instruction count is certain to vary by much more than that. The MIPS rates illustrated in Figure 16–8 cannot reliably be used to compare the power of the machines among themselves, or to other machines whose MIPS rating is provided in the press. MIPS has been translated to "meaningless indicator of processor speed." The uncertainty on MIPS ratings is at least ±30 percent. In addition, the uncertainty on the estimated number of instructions is very high.

In the case study, the total processor time comes out to 0.25 seconds on a 4381-22 processor from IBM.

Figure 16–8 **MIPS Ratings of IBM Mainframes**

Model	MIPS
9375-40	0.5
9375-60	1.3
4381-21	2.2
4381-22	3.3
4381-23	4.8
4381-24	8.1
3090-120E	7.5
3090-150E	10.1
3090-180E	15.6
3090-200E	31.2
3090-300E	46.3
3090-400E	61.5
3090-600E	79.0

Source: *Computerworld*, September 21, 1987.

Disk Access Time

To calculate disk access time, it is first necessary to estimate how many disk accesses are required. Each transaction does a certain number of file or data base operations. In the example of the order entry application, each order line must be written to disk, and each perpetual inventory record to be updated must be read, then written back to disk. In addition, the teleprocessing monitor generates a number of I/O operations of its own to retrieve context data saved from the previous exchange, load processing programs, and log transactions and data base images.

The DBMS does more than one I/O operation for each file access requested by the application. Usually, the DBMS will read one or several index entries to find the address of each input record to be read, and it will create index entries for the records to be written. Sometimes, a verify operation is requested after a record is written. What was just written to disk is read and compared with the original, so that hardware errors can be detected while they are still easy to correct.

In relational data bases, if there is no index on the attribute that serves as the selection argument, the entire relation may have to be read. If the volume is low, the relation may be kept in memory; if not, lengthy disk access times can be anticipated. In the example, if the order entry system were to be implemented using relational technology, indexes would in all probability be available, thus bringing the relational data base performance closer to that of a nonrelational one. In other cases, it may be impossible to obtain enough knowledge to estimate the number of disk accesses reliably. The prototyping approach may then be the only viable alternative.

Thus, knowledge not only of the application logic but also of the data base organization and the internals of the teleprocessing monitor is required to estimate the number of disk accesses. An example is shown in Figure 16–9.

Once the number of accesses is known, the time for each access must be determined as a function of the performance characteristics of the disk device. A disk access consists of three phases: seek, latency, and data transfer. Seek time refers to the average time needed for the arm that bears the read/write mechanism to be positioned on the disk cylinder. Latency refers to the average time required before the beginning of the record to be read rotates to a position where it is exactly under the read/write mechanism. On the average, if the movements of the arm are randomly distributed with regard to record locations, latency is one-half of the time it takes the entire disk to rotate one full rotation. (However, for a verify operation, it is one full rotation minus the length of the record, because the disk has to come full circle before the read/write head can read the record it just wrote.) Finally, the data transfer time is the time actually spent reading or writing data; it is a function of the length of the record and the speed of the disk.

As Figure 16–10 shows, the estimated disk I/O time for the order entry application is about 3.5 seconds.

Calculation of the Response Time

In on-line systems, all the activities within a transaction are executed in strict sequence. Therefore, all the components of response time have to be added together. There is one exception: asynchronous processing as described in Chapter 14 does not enter into the response time calculations.

In the case study, the total response time was calculated to be 5.15 to 5.75 seconds. This calculation, however, assumed that all the resources were available and that there was no waiting or queuing. Even under the best of circumstances, it is prudent to allow at least twice the CPU time and a 20 percent factor on the other times. This factor corresponds to a CPU utilization of 60 percent and to network and I/O utilizations of about 30 percent. A conservative estimate for the response time for the application in the example is therefore 7 seconds (see Figure 16–11).

Although the calculations used to arrive at 7 seconds may seem rigorous, the result is in reality not very reliable—certainly not within a second or two. However, the result can be used to determine whether the order of magnitude of response time is compatible with what is expected. In addition, each of the components of the response time has been analyzed, so that it is easy to concentrate on those components that make up the largest portion—in this case disk I/O times and network transmission times.

Total On-Line Resource Consumption

If the throughput of the application is of concern, then the resource usage must be computed for each transaction by component (including any asynchronous

Figure 16–9 **Calculation of Number of Disk Accesses**

```
MARKETING                        SUBURBAN PUMPS                    CD-20
ORDER ENTRY                                                        DASDA
                             DISK ACCESS ESTIMATE

 PREPARED BY:   PETER NG     DATE:   13DEC94      VERSION:         PAGE 1
 APPROVED BY:   JEANNE ZMUD  DATE:   13DEC94      STATUS :
```

	Primary Index	Secondary Index	Record	Total
Read customer table	1		4	5
Read product table 4 times	4		36	40
Read Total				45
Write 6 order records	6	36	24	66
Write to log			9	9
Write Total				75

processing but excluding wait times) and must be multiplied by the transaction rate. If there are 60 users, each entering a transaction every 50 seconds, a transaction rate of 1.2 transactions per second would result. If the CPU usage was estimated to be 0.25 processor second per transaction, as in the example, the total processor utilization would be less than 40 percent—a perfectly acceptable figure if no other activity is going on in the system. In fact, the processor would have enough capacity to accommodate 3 transactions per second, achieving a maximum utilization of 75 percent (generally thought to be the rule-of-thumb figure for most transaction processing systems).

Figure 16–10 **Calculation of Estimated Disk I/O Times**

```
MARKETING                    SUBURBAN PUMPS                    CD-20
ORDER ENTRY                                                   DASDA
                           DISK I/O ESTIMATE
```

PREPARED BY: PETER NG	DATE: 13DEC94	VERSION:	PAGE 1
APPROVED BY: JEANNE ZMUD	DATE: 13DEC94	STATUS :	

```
IBM 3380

    Avg. Seek Time                              16     ms

    Avg. Latency                              8.33 ms

    Read time for 1 block of 6,000 characters   2     ms
                                             --------
        Total per access (no write check)    26.33 ms


    Rotation time for write check            16.67 ms
                                             --------
        Total per access (with write check)  43.00 ms


    Total disk time

        45 x 26.33 + 75 x 43  =  3,500 ms  or  3.5 seconds
```

Other Resources

Once the required CPU capacity has been determined, the memory required to
run the application can be estimated. Again, rules of thumb are available to
account for operating systems, teleprocessing monitor, and DBMS requirements.
To these must be added the application requirement—usually a minor factor
nowadays. If the system has virtual memory (as most mainframes do), the real
memory required for the application code is usually about one-half the size
of the amount of virtual memory required. An example is detailed in Figure
16–12.

Figure 16–11 **Calculation of Total Response Time**

```
MARKETING                       SUBURBAN PUMPS                      CD-20
ORDER ENTRY                                                         RTEST
                         TOTAL RESPONSE TIME ESTIMATE

PREPARED BY:   PETER NG      DATE:   13DEC94      VERSION:          PAGE 1
APPROVED BY:   JEANNE ZMUD   DATE:   13DEC94      STATUS :
```

```
                                    Service     Elongation      Total
                                      Time         Factor        Time
                                    -------     ----------      -----
              Transmission            1.4          1.2           1.7
                                 to   2.0                        2.4

              CPU                     0.25         2.0           0.5

              Disk                    3.5          1.2           4.2
                                                               -------
                     Total                                       6.4
                                                           to    7.1

                                           say,                  7.0 sec
                                                              ==========
```

Similar calculations would have to be made for the I/O components and the network. As these calculations depend on the topology of the network and on the architecture of the processor and the operating system, no further details are given here.

Resource Consumption in Batch Processing

Calculating the resource consumption of a batch process follows the same logic as for on-line systems, with a few minor exceptions. Network time is usually not applicable; however, printing time and time spent reading and writing batch-

Figure 16–12 **Calculation of Memory Requirements**

```
MARKETING                        SUBURBAN PUMPS                    CD-20
ORDER ENTRY                                                       MEMEST
                          REAL MEMORY REQUIREMENTS ESTIMATE
 ┌───────────────────────────────────────────────────────────────────────┐
 │ PREPARED BY:  PETER NG       DATE:  13DEC94    VERSION:        PAGE 1   │
 │ APPROVED BY:  JEANNE ZMUD    DATE:  13DEC94    STATUS  :                │
 └───────────────────────────────────────────────────────────────────────┘


        Operating system base:    6.0 MB

   Teleprocessing monitor base:   2.0 MB

                     DBMS base:   4.0 MB

   Application programs:
          2.4 MB virtual / 2 =    1.2 MB

   Workarea per user:  .17 MB

   Number of users:   30

              Total workarea:     5.1 MB
                                 --------
                 Grand total:    18.3 MB
                                 ========
```

oriented peripherals such as magnetic tape must be added. In general, operating system overhead figures for batch are more difficult to obtain, and estimates may not be very reliable.

Calculating elapsed times (turnaround, the batch equivalent of response time) becomes more difficult. Contrary to on-line programs, batch programs may overlap sequential file operations with processing. Direct access file operations cannot be overlapped with processing but could overlap sequential file operations.

As a consequence, the elapsed time of a batch program is somewhere between a maximum (represented by the addition of CPU time, direct access time, and sequential file time) and a minimum (represented by the largest of the overlappable components—either CPU plus direct access time, or file processing time for the largest sequential file). The calculation of batch turnaround time is shown in Figure 16–13.

Summary

Many performance problems can only be solved through proper design of the applications. Others can be solved by increasing the resources used to run the application. Both types of problems must be addressed in the design phase of the application rather than at implementation time, when it is too late to solve them.

The main measures of performance of an application are response time (called turnaround time for batch processing), throughput, and availability. All of these measures relate to processing capacity; the way of solving problems is to decrease the amount of resources consumed by the processing, increase the amount of capacity available, or relax the performance constraint. In any case, the greatest effort should be expended on those parts of the process where the payback is likely to be the highest, i.e., where the resource consumption is the highest.

Response times can probably best be reduced by increasing the transmission speed to and from remote terminals and by designing the data base so that the number of I/O operations is minimized. It may also be possible to divide complex transactions into simpler transactions, each with a shorter response time. Finally, excessive response times may be made more tolerable by simply informing the user of the progress of the transaction.

Problems with batch turnaround time are usually best solved by organizational measures, because most of the delays are likely to be in waiting for a job or printed output to be transmitted to the next stage of processing.

Many of the design hints described in earlier chapters (Chapter 14 in particular) have the objective of reducing resource consumption, thereby enabling the available capacity to meet the throughput requirements.

Availability can be increased by various means: proper scheduling and cut-off processing, reduction of the mean time between failures (increasing reliability), and reduction of the mean time to recover (decreasing recovery times).

Estimating resource requirements is an important part of performance design. It serves to check that both response time and throughput performance requirements can be met.

Response times are calculated by adding the time required by each resource—line transmission, processor, and disk access—and then calculating a queuing factor, which is a function of the utilization of each resource involved.

Resource utilization is calculated by multiplying the amount of the resource used for each activity by the number of times the activity is executed in an

Figure 16–13 **Calculation of Batch Turnaround Time**

MARKETING ORDER ENTRY		SUBURBAN PUMPS TOTAL BATCH TURNAROUND TIME ESTIMATE		CD-20 BTEST

PREPARED BY:	PETER NG	DATE:	13DEC94	VERSION:	PAGE 1
APPROVED BY:	JEANNE ZMUD	DATE:	13DEC94	STATUS :	

System time for batch program:

    CPU + direct access time   5.00 min

    Transaction file input   .75 min

    Master file input   4.50 min

    Master file output   4.50 min

Pessimistic hypothesis of no overlap:
        (no allowance for other jobs)
        5.00 + .75 + 4.50 + 4.50   14.75 min

Optimistic hypothesis of total overlap:
        max {5.00, .75, 4.50, 4.50}   5.00 min

Assuming the transaction and master
files are on the same data path:
        max {5.00, .75 + 4.50, 4.50}   5.25 min

interval. If resource utilization is less than 100 percent, then the throughput requirement may be met. However, high utilization may cause long response times beyond the required maximum.

Selected Readings

Most of the available literature is about performance modeling, rather than benchmarking and performance improvement. For the two latter topics, the reader is referred to current magazine articles in such publications as *Datamation*, *Byte*, and, most importantly, *EDP Performance Review*.

Sauer, Charles H., and Chandy, K. Mani. *Computer Systems Performance Modeling*. Englewood Cliffs, New Jersey: Prentice-Hall, 1981.

> *This book is a representative example of most of the literature on the analytical approach to performance prediction. It requires some mathematical background, in particular in probability theory.*

Review Questions

1. Describe briefly the three main measures of performance. What is the functional requirement that underlies each unit of measure?

2. What are the three courses of action open to an analyst when the design does not meet some performance requirement?

3. Describe some possible ways to make excessive response times meet the requirements.

4. Describe some possible ways to resolve availability problems.

5. Summarize the process of calculating response times in an on-line environment. Explain how the result ties in to the calculation of throughput.

Discussion Questions

1. At what points in the life cycle is performance-related work performed?

2. Why is it important to do detailed performance analysis at the end of the design? What are the risks incurred if this activity is glossed over?

3. Discuss the response time requirements for different types of applications (transaction processing, query, DSS, office automation) and different types of users (dedicated, heads-down operators; frequent professional or managerial users; infrequent professional or managerial users; members of the public).

4. In some cases, an application is implemented in stages, with volumes only gradually increasing. This kind of growth is typical when the system has to be installed and users have to be trained in multiple locations. Although the first few months of operation show satisfactory response times, a problem may arise when there is a gradual degradation of response times as volumes increase and resource utilization creeps past the elbow in the curve. Discuss approaches to deal with this problem.

Mini-Case

Condor Telephone Company. You have just performed the response time calculations for the order entry application example described in this chapter, and your preliminary results show response times of upward of 7 seconds for many of the exchanges of the application. You are attending a meeting of the project steering committee and have informed the committee of these figures.

The reactions of various members of the committee range from benevolent to vocal:

Ed Schramm, VP of administration, to whom the IS department used to report before being attached to a newly created chief information officer: "That is way too high! All the on-line applications that I have seen have response times of 2 seconds. You can read any book you want on the subject, they all say that 2 seconds is the absolute maximum for human operators. You must bring the time down dramatically."

Barbara Cahill, CIO: "This application is not heads-down data entry. I admit that 7 seconds sounds high, but we don't have the budget to buy the hardware required to bring the response times down to 2 seconds. I would guess that we can fine-tune the design and reduce the times to about 5 seconds, which ought to be enough."

Grant Hougham, head of the Customer Service Department (the main user of the application): "I don't understand. I was sitting at the same table as two of your programmers the other day, and they were telling me that a scientific study had proved that response times below 1 second got the best productivity and user satisfaction. They also told me that our installation was well on its way to achieving that goal for on-line program development. Why can't my people in the field offices, who take customer orders over the phone, get the same kind of service?"

The committee does not reach consensus. The meeting breaks up with the chairman asking you to prepare an evaluation of what it might take—redesign, additional hardware resources, or whatever else—to reach each of these three goals.

Questions for Discussion

1. For each of the three goals, prepare a strategy and an assessment of the following:
   a. The probability of success.
   b. The economic impact.

2. Pick one of the three goals as your preferred choice; prepare to defend it and to marshal arguments against the other two alternatives.

Chapter 17

Installation Planning, Economic Analysis, and Management Approval

Chapter 17 describes the activities required to complete designs for management's approval. The end products of user interface design, data design, and process design must be sufficiently detailed to allow realistic estimates of the effort, cost, and time necessary for implementing the system. In addition, the chapter describes how to plan the installation and how to present anticipated costs and benefits of the system to management. Finally, the chapter describes the process of deciding whether to proceed with the installation of the system, cancel it, or postpone it.

Learning Objectives

- Understand the criteria used to determine when design is complete.
- Understand why the management checkpoint after systems design is the most important checkpoint in the entire systems development life cycle.
- Describe the planning activities involved in developing plans for testing, user training, file conversion, and detailed installation.
- Become aware of the importance of preparing cost/benefit analyses at this stage.
- Know the components of a cost/benefit analysis.
- Understand the structure of the overall economic summary.
- Understand how intangible benefits are treated in the cost/benefit analysis.
- Recognize the contents of the management report as well as the order of presentation.

- Appreciate the preparation activities and presentation skills appropriate for the management review meeting.

COMPLETING THE DESIGN

Although management can review a system at many points during the development life cycle, the most important checkpoint is at the end of design, prior to implementation. At this point the system can be described in sufficient detail for users to understand what the new system will do for them. The technical design has also reached the stage where IS professionals can prepare a reliable estimate of the time needed to implement it. With this information, an economic analysis that will set forth the costs and benefits of proceeding with implementation can be prepared. Experience shows that approximately 25 to 30 percent of the total project effort is expended in the project steps through this point (see Section I). If management decides not to continue with implementation, the major portion of the project effort will have been avoided.

If the users do not understand the functions and features of the new system before implementation, they may ask for changes after programming has begun. At this point, changes are more costly. If the project steering committee decides that a proposed change should be postponed until after implementation, the new system will not function as the users expect. Thus, users will not likely accept the new system. James McKeen reports that systems projects in which more time was spent making sure users understood the requirements were more likely to be implemented within their budget and accepted by the users.[1]

If the IS department attempts to estimate the time required to implement the system before technical design has been completed, time and cost estimates may be inaccurate. Management has a right to be upset when told that an approved system implementation project is going to require considerably more time and money than originally estimated. In some instances, management's reaction to such news has been to press the IS department to meet the original targets, creating a "crisis" project characterized by overtime for the project team and by a compromise on quality. Crisis projects are also the ones most likely to result in operational disasters.

The design can be considered complete, therefore, when the project team prepares the following end products in sufficient detail to estimate realistically the effort, cost, and time needed to implement and operate the proposed system.

functional specifications report

The **functional specifications report** summarizes the system's functional design for final management review and approval. It describes the following components of the system:

- Processing functions
- Reports
- Screens
- Input forms
- Procedures (manual and automated)

The **technical specifications report** summarizes the system's technical design for final management review and approval. It covers both computer and manual processing and includes the following:

technical specifications report

- Application architecture
- Design of the data base and files
- Major program logic
- Testing and conversion procedures
- Hardware and systems software requirements

PLANNING THE INSTALLATION

An important step is to identify the effort required to install the system. For each of the tasks, the required skill level, estimate of effort, and timetable must be included. Some of the major components in the installation plan are the test plan, the user training plan, the file conversion plan, and the detailed installation plan.

The Test Plan

Testing is an essential step in the development of a new system. It provides assurance that the system will operate in accordance with its design specifications. A program is not considered complete until it has been thoroughly tested, and a system is not considered complete until its constituent programs have been tested together as a system.

The test plan outlines the procedures for all types of testing, including unit tests, integration tests, system tests, and acceptance tests. Standards for using program libraries and test files are identified. Any special software required for testing is identified as well. This software might include such programs as test data generators for volume testing and programs that can automatically compare test results with anticipated results.

Users should be involved at this stage to ensure that any acceptance testing criteria important to them are considered in the test plan. For example, users may wish to have assurance that the system operates in accordance with specifications when large volumes of transactions flow through the system. Users may also wish to have the system pilot tested in a small, controlled environment prior to making it available to the larger community for which it has been designed. Pilot testing is particularly appropriate when a critical system, one that affects many users or locations, is contemplated. A hospital system designed to perform real-time monitoring of intensive care patients' vital signs would no doubt benefit from careful pilot testing—first in a simulated setting and next with one or two patients.

The User Training Plan

Because users who are expected to use the new system must accept it, the proper training of users on the new system is critical. In addition, users should understand the way the new system will help to achieve an organization's goals and objectives. This understanding can make users more receptive to the necessary training.

Before training begins, a plan must be prepared. The training plan should identify the time required both to prepare training materials and to plan and conduct training sessions.

The usual approach to training is one of "training the trainers." Resources are used to train a cadre of personnel from the user departments and/or from the organization's internal training department. The personnel trained in the initial training sessions then conduct training sessions for the other users. This approach is preferable; it minimizes the drain on project team resources, and users prefer training sessions conducted by persons who are recognized as users or professional trainers.

The Conversion Plan

The conversion plan explains the method of converting to the new system. The plan consists of two key elements: the method of preparing initial system master files and the approach to shifting operations from the old to the new system.

system master files

System master files or data bases are often converted from master files maintained by existing computer systems. In such cases, all that is necessary is that the project team be sure the format and content of the new files are consistent with system specifications. In some cases, the existing files can be used without change. In most cases, however, a file conversion program is written to translate files from the existing system into the format required by the new system. Validation and file maintenance programs from the new system should be used to perform at least a portion of these tasks, if possible. This procedure will assure that the new system's beginning files will have passed through the same validation and control routines as will be used by the new system.

Usually, the new system will require some additional data, which must be collected and added to the converted files before the system is operational. During this phase, synchronization is very important in both sets of files—the old ones, which are still operational and therefore continue to change, and the new ones, which are not yet part of the standard change process. All changes posted to the existing file must be logged and processed before the new files can be operational.

If files are not available on an existing computer system, the first option is to use programs from the new system. Additions to the file could be created and passed through the new system's validation and file maintenance programs. This approach is almost always the preferred approach unless for some reason it cannot be used. For example, if the project team is approaching the date of conversion with the file maintenance program behind schedule and on the critical path, it may be more expedient to write a special file conversion program. In any case, controls over the conversion will have to be established to insure the accuracy and reliability of the beginning system master files.

The project team should also decide on **the basic approach to conversion** at this time. Some of the factors that the team should consider are whether to run the new system in parallel with the old and whether to convert to the new system in phases.

the basic approach to conversion

Parallel Operations. Fundamentally, the project team must be sure that the conversion approach selected protects the organization from an intolerable interruption in operations in the event the conversion does not go well. The most conservative approach is to continue to run the old system after converting to the new system, running both systems in parallel. The results of the new system's operations are reconciled to the results of the old system. When the members of the project team have confidence that the new system is operating as planned, they will recommend to the project steering committee that operation of the old system be suspended. If the new system has too many problems, operation of the new system will be suspended, and the old system will be used until the problems with the new system are corrected.

Running the new system in parallel with the old provides the most protection in the event the conversion has to be suspended. Parallel operations also require a significant effort from the project team and users. Project team members are typically very busy at this point, attempting to make final adjustments to the new system and "putting out fires." Users are also attempting to adjust to the changes in their routines that the new system has created. Thus, running two systems requires an additional resource commitment that must be recognized and planned for.

If a parallel operation is chosen during conversion, the outputs of the new system may not be directly reconcilable with results of the old system. For example, the system control scheme or the way certain calculations are made may be different. In addition, the new system and the old system will usually not match business functions on a one-to-one basis. For such reasons, procedures must be established to reconcile the results of the new system with those of the old system. If possible, computer programs should be written to perform such reconciliations automatically.

Sometimes, in parallel operations, difficulties occur that necessitate suspending the new system's operation. Organizations generally try to avoid this undesirable occurrence by planning a thorough system test of the new system and allowing ample time for all parties to be satisfied with the new system's operations before beginning the conversion.

Phased Conversion. Converting the system in phases is another way of reducing risk during the transition period. If the system is to be installed at several locations, it can be pilot tested at a selected location. In addition to giving the project team an opportunity to observe the system in operation in a controlled environment, pilot testing can help promote user acceptance. If users at the pilot location are pleased with the new system, word will usually spread to their counterparts at other locations within the organization. Bad news about the new system will probably spread even faster. For these reasons, the site for the initial conversions in a phased approach should be selected with care. The site for a pilot test should be one where management and support personnel are anxious to learn about the new system.

Another option for a phased conversion is to convert a large system in modules. For example, an integrated system for inventory control, accounts payable, and purchasing using electronic data interchange (EDI) for purchase orders and invoices might be converted in the sequence illustrated in Figure 17–1.

The Detailed Installation Plan

The detailed installation plan is the way the project team estimates the amount of effort and the elapsed time required to install a new system. The plan lists the segments, tasks, and work steps required for the system installation phase. For each task, required skill levels are specified. The work plan should be sufficiently detailed to be used in the cost/benefit analysis prepared at this point in the project. A more detailed plan for controlling the installation project is prepared after management's approval to proceed with the installation.

Sample work plans containing checklists of project segments, tasks, and work steps are usually included in commercially available standard development methodologies. Such checklists should be used only as a guide, however. Standard work plans must almost always be tailored to the specific requirements of each project. Some steps will probably be added, and others will probably be deleted. In addition, as illustrated in Figure 17–2, some commercially available software packages aid analysts in developing work plans. Some of the packages have data bases compiled from the experience gained from working with other projects. These data bases can aid in estimating the effort required on specific work tasks. The detailed installation plan for a system might well contain all of the segments illustrated in Figure 17–3. A bar chart (Figure 17–4) summarizes the estimated workdays and time frame for each segment of the project and gives management an overview of the sequence and timing of the major segments of project effort.

COST/BENEFIT ANALYSIS

A cost/benefit analysis is performed at this stage in the project. The system's functions and features have been designed in sufficient detail to permit the benefits of the new system to be identified, and the technical design has been completed to the point where its installation and operating costs can be estimated with acceptable accuracy.

The preparation of cost/benefit analyses is so common now that it almost constitutes a standard practice. In some situations, however, a key member of

Figure 17–1 **Example of Phased Conversion**

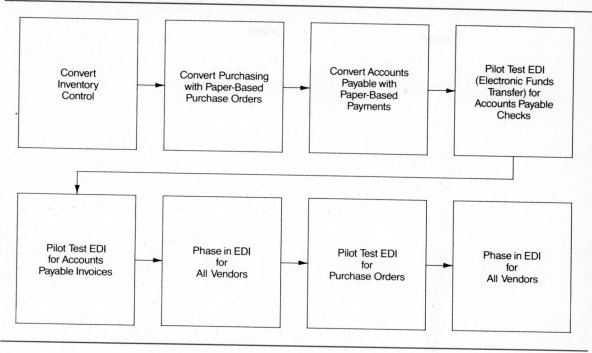

management may suggest that this step be omitted, usually on the grounds that the system is so important that it must be implemented no matter what the cost. If possible, the project team should press for a cost/benefit analysis anyway. Even though cost may not be a crucial issue, management should be aware of the costs and benefits before proceeding. In addition, members of management are replaced from time to time, and the project team is well advised to press for a review of costs and benefits to protect itself from criticism by successor management.

For example, in one company, the IS department had adopted as standard practice the preparation of cost/benefit analyses and postimplementation audits. Top management, in this case, was preoccupied with other issues and had left the details of IS operations to middle management. Later, the business environment turned sour, and top management turned its attention to finding ways of reducing costs. It found that IS expenditures had increased markedly over the period and asked that the current level of expenditures be justified. Because the head of IS had prepared cost/benefit analyses over the years, he was able to demonstrate quickly that although expenditures had indeed gone up, they were more than justified by the cumulative savings in affected user departments.

Figure 17–2 **Description of Software Package
Used to Prepare Work Plans**

```
SYSTEMS                     SUBURBAN  PUMPS                      CD-20
PLAN                                                            PMFF&F
                FUNCTIONS/FEATURES  OF  PROJECT  MANAGEMENT  SOFTWARE

┌──────────────────────────────────────────────────────────────────────┐
│ PREPARED  BY:   J. WEBER      DATE:   27AUG88    VERSION:   1.1    PAGE 1 │
│ APPROVED  BY:   JACK CROFT    DATE:   05SEP88    STATUS  :   D           │
└──────────────────────────────────────────────────────────────────────┘
```

The following functions and features for project management software are to be
used as a guideline for evaluating commercially available packages and
selecting the one that best fits the needs of Suburban Pumps for the
implementation of the systems plan.

1.   Work plan preparation

    o   A hierarchy of phases, tasks, and detailed activities compatible with
         our systems development methodology

    o   Enough flexibility to accommodate changes in the methodology

    o   An existing data base of estimating factors which we can use in the
         absence of our own

    o   A means of updating the estimating factors based on historical data

    o   Critical path (or PERT) analysis

    o   What-if functions to assist in rescheduling in case of project
         overruns

    o   Presentation of printed output by project, subproject and individual

    o   Bar chart (GANTT chart) presentation of overall work program

    o   Variable degree of detail in reports (summarized by phase, task,
         subtask...)

2.   Time reporting

    o   ....

    o

Components of the Cost/Benefit Analysis

A cost/benefit analysis includes the costs of operating the old and new systems
and the costs of installation.

**operating costs
of the present
system**

Operating costs of the present system are obtained by adding all
costs associated with the operation of the present system, including personnel,
hardware, software, communications, other IS department costs, and other costs
incurred by user departments.

Figure 17–3 **Standard Activities of Installation Phase**

```
PERSONNEL                        SUBURBAN PUMPS                      CD-20
PAYROLL                                                             IPLAN
                               INSTALLATION TASKS

PREPARED BY:   GLORIA HUNTER   DATE:   15JAN90    VERSION:  1       PAGE 1
APPROVED BY:   JACK WEBER      DATE:   22JAN90    STATUS :  F
```

PROJECT ORGANIZATION
         Organize and manage project
         Establish standards
         Establish project training program
         Administer training

DETAILED DESIGN
         Complete design of screens and reports not done during design
         Complete data base design
         Design and document programming work units
         Prepare common test data for unit tests
         Perform structured design reviews

USER PROCEDURE DEVELOPMENT
         Develop user and IS operations manual contents
         Plan training program
         Produce user and operations manuals
         Produce training materials
         Conduct training

SITE PREPARATION
         Plan site modifications (user and IS)
         Procure required hardware, software and supplies (e.g., preprinted forms)
         Supervise construction, delivery, and installation

CONVERSION PREPARATION
         Complete conversion plan
         Develop conversion procedures
         Convert files
         Plan system test

PROGRAMMING
         Code
         Unit test
         Document
         Conduct structured review
         Supervise programming

SYSTEM TEST
         Perform integration test
         Perform system test
         Check results and issue change requests
         Implement changes if approved

CONVERSION
         Convert system
         Monitor production
         Transfer to routine production

ACCEPTANCE
         Measure degree of compliance with requirements specification
         Negotiate and implement required changes
         Formalize user acceptance

Figure 17-4 Sample Bar Chart Summary

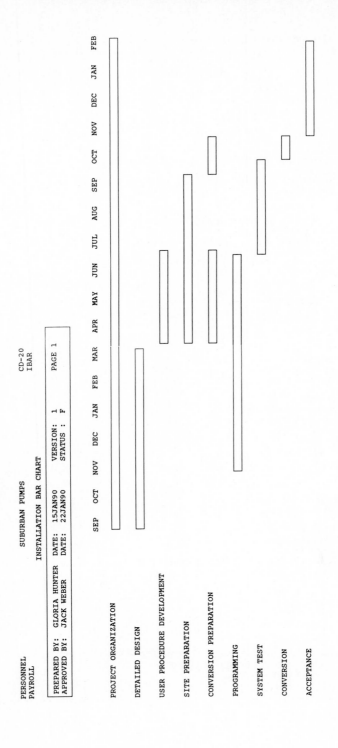

Operating costs of the proposed system are obtained by estimating the costs of operating the proposed system. The same categories are used for these estimates as were used in determining the costs of the present system. Because the proposed system costs are estimates, user departments should be involved in the prediction of those costs under their control. For example, an estimate that the new system will operate with 80 percent of the clerical staff required under the present system has more credibility with management if it is made by user personnel rather than IS personnel.

operating costs of the proposed system

Estimates of operating costs for the proposed system will often include net changes in revenue (usually increases) associated with the system's installation. For example, suppose a resort condominium complex proposed the installation of a marketing system to attract previous renters. The objective is to increase by 5 percent the percentage of renters who return in subsequent years. The increase would offset the costs of operating the proposed system.

Installation costs are the one-time costs associated with installing the system. They include personnel costs as reflected in the installation work plan, incremental hardware costs for program testing and conversion, and any other resources required to move from the present system to the proposed system.

installation costs

OVERALL ECONOMIC SUMMARY

Present system costs, proposed system costs, and installation costs are projected in an overall economic summary, as illustrated in Figure 17–5. The overall economic summary should be presented in a format familiar to management. The project team should involve others in the organization who can give guidance on the proper format. The illustration in Figure 17–5 is a simple payback analysis, which is used by many companies.

Some organizations may adopt more sophisticated analysis techniques such as return on investment (ROI) or net present value to analyze capital investment proposals. Using ROI, an organization simply divides the average annual benefits by the average investment. Figure 17–6 shows the overall economic summary from Figure 17–5 using ROI rather than payback analysis. ROI analysis assumes that the benefits from the investment in the new system are realized evenly over its useful life.

Present value is widely used as a capital investment analysis technique and receives complete coverage in finance courses. If present value analysis were used for the overall economic analysis of the system of Figure 17–5, it would appear as illustrated in Figure 17–7. What has been done is to multiply the cost and benefits for each year of the useful life of the project by a factor obtained from a table of present values. Present value tables discount amounts by a factor that takes into account both time and interest rate. For example, the value today of a dollar to be received one year from now is $.909, assuming 10 percent could be earned on money invested today for one year. (The value of a dollar today is one dollar.) Net present value is the difference between costs and benefits computed on a present value basis.

Figure 17–5 **Sample Overall Economic Summary**

```
PERSONNEL                    SUBURBAN PUMPS                      CD-20
PAYROLL                                                          ECONS
                         OVERALL ECONOMIC SUMMARY

┌─────────────────────────────────────────────────────────────────────┐
│ PREPARED BY:  GLORIA HUNTER   DATE:  15JAN90    VERSION:  1   PAGE 1  │
│ APPROVED BY:  JACK WEBER      DATE:  22JAN90    STATUS :  F           │
└─────────────────────────────────────────────────────────────────────┘



Benefits/Costs                   1991 1992 1993 1994 1995 TOTAL  AVG
                                 ------------------------------------
    Tangible benefits approximation

       Cost avoidance opportunity 160  160  160  160  160   800  160
       Cost reduction opportunity  10   10   10   10   10    50   10
       Quantifiable intangible benefits 30 30 30  30   30   150   30
                                 ------------------------------------
          Total quantifiable benefits 200 200 200 200 200  1000  200



    Cost approximation

       Development costs          180    0    0    0    0   180   36
       Continuing costs (net increase) 30 30  30   30   30   150   30
                                 ------------------------------------
          Total costs            210   30   30   30   30   330   66



    Net continuing benefit (cost) *  170  170  170  170  170   850  170
    Less taxes (50%) *               85   85   85   85   85   425   85
    Net after tax benefit (Cost) *   85   85   85   85   85   425   85
    Depreciation *                   40   40   40   40   40   200   40
    Estimated cashflow approximation 109  109  109  109  109   545  109

    * Does not include development cost
```

Figure 17–6 **Sample Overall Economic Summary Using ROI**

```
MARKETING                      SUBURBAN PUMPS                    CD-20
ORDER ENTRY                                                     ECONS
                  COST/BENEFIT OF SUMMARY SALES REPORTING MODIFICATION
┌──────────────────────────────────────────────────────────────────────┐
│ PREPARED BY:  MARYANN UNGER  DATE:  08JAN92    VERSION:  1    PAGE 1    │
│ APPROVED BY:  GLORIA HUNTER  DATE:  22FEB92    STATUS :                 │
└──────────────────────────────────────────────────────────────────────┘


                                                      Amount
                                                      ------
   1.   One-time Change Costs
   ------------------------------------------------

          Personnel expense -

               50 workdays analyst               6,000
              100 workdays programmer            8,000
               30 workdays clerical                960

          Machine hours cost -

               20 CPU hours                      12,250

          Equipment and supplies -

                  Paper and office supplies         100
              25 reels magnetic tape               625
                                                ----------
                  Subtotal                        27,935
                                                ----------


   2.   Recurring Costs and Savings
   ------------------------------------------------

          Clerical savings - Annual -

               25 workdays/month                (9,600)

          Supplies                               (100)


   3.   Intangible Costs and Benefits
   ------------------------------------------------

          Information available earlier (not
               quantified)                          (0)

                                                ----------
                  Subtotal                        (9,700)
                                                ----------

   4.   Payback Period
   ------------------------------------------------

          27,935/9,700 = less than 3 years


   5.   Return on investment over 4 years
   ------------------------------------------------

          9,700 * 4 - 27,935 / 27,935 = 40%
```

Figure 17–7 **Sample Overall Economic Summary**
Using Net Present Value

```
MANUFACTURING              SUBURBAN PUMPS                    CD-20
QUALITY CONTROL                                              ECONS
                        OVERALL ECONOMIC SUMMARY

 ┌────────────────────────────────────────────────────────────────────┐
 │ PREPARED BY:  JOE DAVIS      DATE:  15MAR93    VERSION:  1    PAGE 1 │
 │ APPROVED BY:  PIERRE FAVIER  DATE:  04APR93    STATUS  :            │
 └────────────────────────────────────────────────────────────────────┘
```

CLASSIFICATION	Period 1	Period 2	Period 3	Period 4	Period 5	Period 6
Continuing cost and benefits (assuming 7% inflation)						
Present system		1,480	1,584	1,694	1,813	1,940
Proposed system		1,353	1,448	1,549	1,657	1,774
Net reduction (increase)		127	136	145	156	166
Installation costs	280	21	0	0	0	0
Net savings (costs)	(280)	106	136	145	156	166
Estimated savings using present value method						
Present value of savings (cost) based on 10% cost of capital	(280)	96	112	109	106	103
Total net present value	248					
Cumulative savings (cost)	(280)	(174)	(38)	107	263	429
Cumulative present value	(280)	(184)	(71)	38	144	248

Estimated payback period: 3-4 years

Most companies have an assumed interest rate factor that is used for evaluating investments based on the company's opportunity cost—the amount the company feels it could earn if this particular investment were not made. In such cases, the company's opportunity cost is the basis for selecting the interest rate used in present value calculations. In any event, if the net present value technique is to be used for the overall economic summary, the project team should consult the company's finance or budget department to obtain the appropriate rate. By doing so, the team will be assured of using assumptions that are consistent with those used in other capital investment analyses reviewed by management.

The finance or budget department can also supply the project team with the standard assumptions it uses for such factors as inflation, wage increases, standard volume increases, and the like. Using standard assumptions about the future will result in financial projections in the project report that are consistent with what management is accustomed to seeing in financial projections. In some cases, management is more comfortable seeing the overall economic summary expressed with a range of values, i.e., as most likely and least likely scenarios rather than as specific estimates.

Experience has shown that the overall economic summary should not be extended beyond a period of about five years. Beyond that, the accuracy of the estimates becomes less reliable, particularly in the present environment of rapid competitive and technological change.

Questions often arise about the proper way to show IS department costs if the organization charges costs for development and/or operations back to the using department. Differences in the figures can arise depending on whether incremental costs or allocated costs are used. For example, if a relatively small system were to be installed on a large CPU with ample additional capacity, the incremental cost to the organization to operate the new system might be very low. If, however, the IS department allocated costs to user departments, the user departments would have to account for the allocated costs in their budget. Depending on the method of allocation, the costs to the user departments could be considerably higher than the incremental costs to the organization. The procedure usually followed by the project team in such cases is to prepare two overall economic summaries, one using incremental costs and the other using allocated costs.

When the overall economic summary is prepared, it is often possible to place economic values on intangible benefits (or costs), employing various estimating techniques. For example, if a proposed billing system is designed to produce bills five days sooner than the present system, it should be possible to estimate the net effect of a speedup in cash flow and a possible reduction in write-offs for uncollectible accounts. If the system is expected to increase market share, the net effect of such an increase should be estimated. However, such estimates should have the strong support of users so that they will have credibility with management.

After all quantifiable costs and benefits have been identified, additional benefits often remain that are too difficult to quantify. Examples of such intangible benefits are more timely management information, better customer service, and more accurate information. Such intangible benefits should be separately identified and discussed as a part of the overall economic summary, for they can have a significant bearing on management's decision to proceed with the installation of the proposed system.

PRESENTING THE ANALYSIS TO MANAGEMENT

Presentation of the analysis of the project effort usually takes two forms: a written report of the work performed to date and a meeting at which the report is presented and discussed in order to reach a decision on a future course of action.

The Management Report

The management report is prepared to summarize the relevant considerations affecting management's decision of whether to proceed with the installation of the system. It usually contains the following items:

- An executive summary presents a summary of key system objectives, features, and benefits, including the bottom line of the economic analysis, a high-level contrast of the new system with the old system, and the project team's recommendation for the next steps to be taken.

- A summary of system functions and features—drawn from the more detailed functional specifications report—should present key differences between the present and proposed systems in more detail than did the executive summary.

- A summary of the system's technical architecture, processing, data base design, and security and control design—drawn from the more detailed technical specifications report—should be presented in terms understandable to the management audience being addressed.

- The overall economic summary is included.

- The bar chart contains a summary of the installation schedule.

- In a discussion, the costs and benefits of installing the system are weighed against other options that should be considered. A typical case is one where management can choose to stay with the present system, install the proposed system, modify the present system in some way, install only certain modules of the proposed system, or postpone the installation. The project team should identify and discuss other viable options that management may wish to consider before making a decision.

The project team should be sure that the final report addresses the five elements of feasibility (technical, operational, economic, schedule, and motivational).

The Management Review Meeting

After management has read the report, analysts meet with the project steering committee to reach agreement on the proposed course of action. The level of management approval required will vary from organization to organization and from project to project. With some projects, only the steering committee's approval is required to proceed with the installation.

The written report should have been distributed to those persons attending the meeting well enough in advance to give them a chance to absorb its contents. The presentation itself is shared between users and IS personnel. Users cover the functions, features, and benefits of the proposed system and that portion of the economic analysis for which they will be responsible. IS personnel cover the technical features of the proposed system, the installation plan, and that part of the economic analysis for which they will be responsible.

It is worthwhile to hold a practice session of the presentation before knowledgeable persons who have not been closely associated with the project. Members of the audience should play devil's advocate, critiquing the project team's presentation. They should attempt to anticipate the questions management will ask to see how effectively the project team is able to respond. Finally, they should evaluate the relevancy and readability of visual aids.

After the project team has decided who will be giving the presentation, they should agree that any questions from management will be answered by the person in front of the group at that time. Presenters should refer questions they are unsure of to the project team leader, who may either answer the questions, or refer them to another project team member. It is disconcerting to ask a question of a presenter only to hear the answer come from someone sitting on the sidelines.

At the conclusion of the presentation, the project team should seek formal approval of its recommendation. Management may approve the installation of the proposed system; it may choose one of the other options identified by the project team; or it may suggest new options the project team will be asked to evaluate. When approval is given to move ahead with the proposed system, the project has reached the beginning of the implementation phase (see Section VII).

FREEZING THE SPECIFICATIONS

Once installation is approved, the system's specifications should not be changed. If the project team has done a thorough job, user requirements have been carefully identified, and the need for changes to the specifications should be unlikely. Some changes cannot be avoided, however, and analysts must decide whether to include them in the new system specifications or to add them after the initial conversion. Changes imposed on the system from the outside—changes in tax law or legal reporting requirements, for example—cannot be postponed.

The further along the project team is in the installation the more costly it is to make changes. If they cannot be avoided, and are significant enough, analysts can revise the installation schedule and economic summary; management can review the changes and consider their effect.

Summary

The design is considered complete when the users understand and are satisfied with the functions and features of the proposed system, and when the IS professionals are satisfied with the system's technical feasibility. At this point, IS professionals can comfortably estimate the time and resources required to implement the system. The functional specifications report and the technical specifications report should be complete at this point.

Planning the installation includes preparation of plans for testing the system, training the users, converting files, and developing a detailed installation plan to control the work of the project team. Various conversion strategies and options include the pros and cons of running the new system parallel with the old. A fallback plan is necessary in the event that the new system does not function well enough to continue it. Also valuable are phased conversions and pilot tests.

A cost/benefit analysis should be prepared regardless of whether management feels it is necessary. Even if the new system need not be cost justified, management should be made aware of its cost. In addition, managers sometimes move on, and their replacements may ask for the cost/benefit analysis of a converted system.

The cost/benefit analysis should use the organization's usual techniques for analyzing capital expenditures. The most common techniques are payback, return on investment, and net present value. The typical components are current system operating costs, proposed system operating costs, and the costs of installation. The project team should also use the standard assumptions of the organization for such factors as inflation and wage increases. Extending the economic analysis beyond five years is probably not wise because of the effect of business and technological change on factors used in the analysis.

Intangible benefits should be identified separately and presented to management as additional factors in deciding whether to install the new system.

The project team should submit to management a written report that summarizes work completed and recommends the next steps. After reviewing the report, management will decide whether to accept the recommendations.

If approval of the implementation phase is obtained, the system's specifications should be considered frozen. If subsequent changes become necessary, the target dates or resource requirements approved by management may have to change. Depending on the magnitude of the changes, reapproval of the project may be required.

Selected Reading

Gildersleeve, T. *Successful Data Processing Systems Analysis*, 2d ed. Englewood Cliffs, New Jersey: Prentice-Hall, 1985.

This text contains a detailed section on alternative techniques for preparing cost/benefit analyses. In addition, it has a useful discussion on ways to place values on intangible benefits.

Review Questions

1. Why is the management checkpoint at the end of design considered the most important of all the management checkpoints in the systems development life cycle?

2. Describe the end products of systems design.

3. What are the main components of the installation plan?

4. What is the purpose of testing? When is testing complete?

5. To what extent should users be involved in preparing the test plan?

6. How is user training related to their acceptance of the system?

7. What are the two key elements of the conversion plan?

8. Describe the procedure(s) for preparing the initial system master files.

9. Compare the advantages and disadvantages of parallel system conversion.

10. Describe two options for a phased conversion approach.

11. Why should the project team press for cost/benefit analyses for new systems?

12. How is the overall economic summary prepared? What is the maximum time frame recommended for the summary? Why?

13. How should intangible benefits of the new system be treated in the cost/benefit analysis?

14. What is the purpose of the management report?

15. How should the project team prepare for the management review meeting?

16. How flexible are the system specifications once management approval has been secured?

Discussion Questions

1. Why is the approval of the major portion of project expenditures delayed until after completion of the technical design?

2. Discuss the opportunities for user involvement during installation planning, economic analyses, and management approval.

3. What is the difference between tangible and intangible benefits? Provide examples of each. For the intangible benefits, is it possible to attribute economic benefits to them? If not, how would you cover them in the cost/benefit analysis?

4. Why is the project team's recommendation to management presented "up front" in the executive summary of the management report?

Mini-Case

Techline University. Techline University is planning to install a new student registration system. Although Techline has served its students with an on-line registration system for quite some time, the new system design will provide notable improvements. For example, the new system will permit students to request classes by using a touch-tone telephone. Currently, they have to wait in long lines for a data entry clerk to key in class request data.

Another design improvement is that the system will check the student schedule for time conflicts. In addition, the new system will provide reports for better administrative planning, for example, predicting the need for additional classes long before the need arises.

Question for Discussion

1. The project team is preparing a conversion plan. Make recommendations for the following:

    a. A procedure for creating the new system's master file.

    b. A recommended approach to conversion.

References

1. McKeen, James. "Successful Development Strategies for Business Application Systems." *MIS Quarterly* (September 1983): pp. 47–65.

Program Structure Charting

DEFINITION

A program structure chart is a specialized version of a hierarchical diagram (see the Technique in Section I) that depicts the relationships among the functions executed by a program. Program structure charts afford a more graphical view of a program than does code or pseudo-code. Program structure charts can easily be prepared to show less detail than code or pseudo-code. It is therefore a tool that can be used by analyst and programmer alike, regardless of the prevailing division of responsibilities.

EXAMPLE

Figure 1 shows a program structure chart that contains examples of the three main logical constructs of a structured program: sequence, iteration, and condition. The sequence is implicit in the disposition of the diagram, which is read left to right, top to bottom. The iteration construct is illustrated by an UNTIL clause. The condition construct is illustrated by four IF clauses.

WHERE USED IN THE LIFE CYCLE

Program structure charts are used in the late stages of design and in programming. During design, program structure charts are prepared to display the functions performed by each program and their relationships. The charts can serve to verify that the design is exhaustive, i.e., that all the functions identified during the requirements analysis are performed. They can also help check that the design is consistent and, in particular, that the data required to perform each function can be made available to the program. Finally, the program structure charts serve as the basis for estimating the programming effort and assigning work to analysts and programmers during program specification and program-

Figure 1 **Illustration of a Program Structure Chart**

```
                      ┌ Begin
                      │
                      │                              ┌ Process type 1
                      │                              │ (IF Record-type = 1)
   Program          ──┤  Process file             ──┤           OR
                      │  (WHILE not end-of-file)     │ Process type 2
                      │                              └ (ELSE)
                      │
                      └ End
```

ming. During the design phase, only high-level charts are prepared. Iteration and condition constructs are only indicated when they are essential to the understanding of the chart.

During programming specification and programming, program structure charts are used to specify the way a program functions in successively greater detail, until all the control functions (iterations and conditions) are described. Generally, a first level of detail is prepared by an analyst for the programming specification; then a programmer takes over and documents to the lowest detail. The limit between the two is determined by installation standards or, in many cases, by the experience level of the programmer.

FORMAL RULES

A program structure chart consists of a number of *statements* tied together by three constructs: *sequence*, *iteration*, and *condition*. The tool on which the illustrations in this chapter are based depicts statements in Warnier-style hierarchies, left to right, top to bottom. Each statement can be accompanied by an iteration or a condition specification in parentheses under the statement (see Figure 1). Each bracket to the right of a statement represents the span of control of the iteration or the condition and contains all statements that are executed inside the loop or are executed when the condition is true.

There are three forms of loops: UNTIL, WHILE, and FOR (see Figure 2). An UNTIL loop is performed by executing the loop, then testing for the condition

Figure 2 **Iteration Constructs**

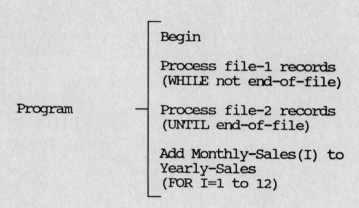

```
           ┌─ Begin

              Process file-1 records
              (WHILE not end-of-file)

Program  ─┤   Process file-2 records
              (UNTIL end-of-file)

              Add Monthly-Sales(I) to
              Yearly-Sales
           └─ (FOR I=1 to 12)
```

specified in the UNTIL statement. If the condition is true, the execution continues in sequence; if false, the loop is performed again. An UNTIL loop is always executed at least once.

A WHILE loop is similar to an UNTIL loop, but the condition is tested before the statements in the loop are executed. If the condition is true, the loop is executed; if false, the loop is skipped and the next statement in sequence is executed. A WHILE loop may not be executed at all, unlike the UNTIL loop.

A FOR loop is controlled by a variable inside the loop, so that the loop is executed a specified number of times (at least once). An additional construct can be simulated with the FOR statement, namely, a FOR EACH iteration. This iteration specifies that the loop is to be performed for each occurrence of some item on a file, in a table, or in an array. The most useful way to use FOR EACH is to document a loop that is repeated for each row in a relational table. The FOR

EACH statement can then be qualified further with a WHERE statement similar to the WHERE statement in SQL, the most popular relational data manipulation language (see Figure 3).

The conditional statements that are allowed are the simple IF and the repetitive IF (or CASE) statement. Each may be used with an ELSE condition. Figure 4 illustrates the use of IF and ELSE.

When using program structure charts in the programming phase, the rule normally followed for creating brackets is that the parent of a bracket (the statement to the left of it) is necessarily qualified by a loop or a condition. An exception may be made if there is a lengthy sequence of unqualified statements that are logically tied together: an owning bracket may then be created with a statement to the left of it, which simply names the function that the related statements accomplish. A statement with an iteration condition attached to it must always be the parent of some lower-level bracket.

Subprograms and common routines cannot be represented on the same program structure chart as the the statements that call these subroutines. A fresh structure chart should be created for each subprogram. If the subprograms are few and simple, a possible artifice is to create a bracket (the last one on the second level) to contain them (see Figure 5).

When using program structure charts in the design phase, the rules are less stringent. In particular, lower levels may be omitted, as may iteration and condition clauses that do not add to the understanding of the functions performed by the program. For instance, such iteration clauses as UNTIL End-of-File following a READ statement are not necessary. A program structure

Figure 3 **The FOR EACH Construct**

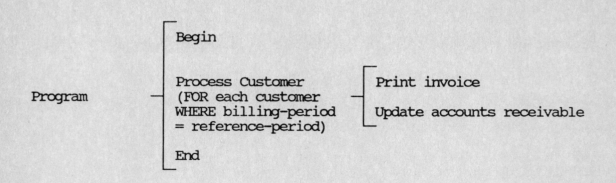

Figure 4 **IF and ELSE Constructs**

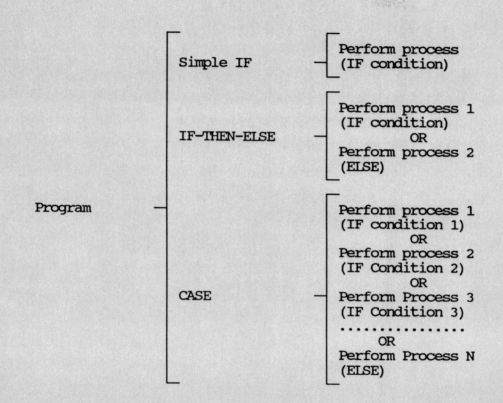

Figure 5 **Subprogram**

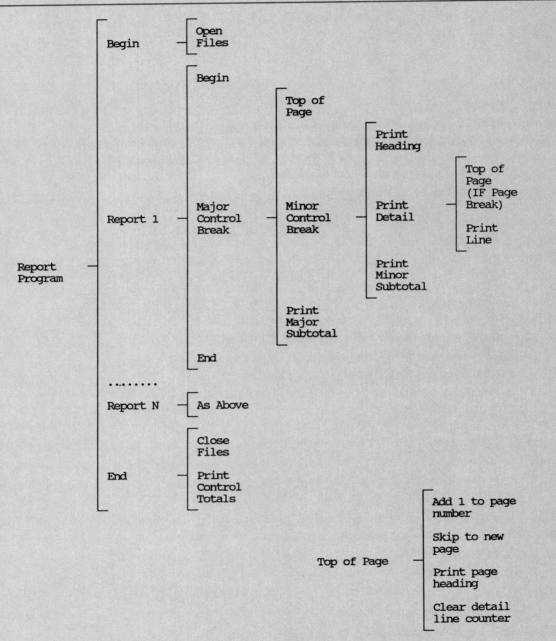

Figure 6 **Jackson-style Program Structure Chart**

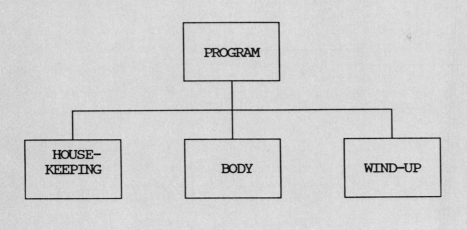

chart in the design phase is to be considered an unfinished structure chart, to be detailed in a later phase.

EQUIVALENT TECHNIQUES

Two main forms of documentation are equivalent to the Warnier-style program structure charts described here. One is the Jackson-style chart. This is a hierarchy of boxes containing the program functions marked with a symbol to signify iterations and conditions (see Figure 6). In addition, some methods recommend adding indications of data used and created by each function (see Figure 7).

The second form of documentation is pseudo-code (see Figure 8).

As explained in Section I, these two alternative techniques are both hierarchical in nature and have about the same expressive power as Warnier-style charts. The main disadvantage of the Jackson-style chart is that it is more difficult to describe iterations and conditions fully. The main disadvantage of pseudo-code is that it does not depict the overall structure of the program quite as graphically.

Figure 7 **Jackson-style Program Structure Chart
with Data Used/Created**

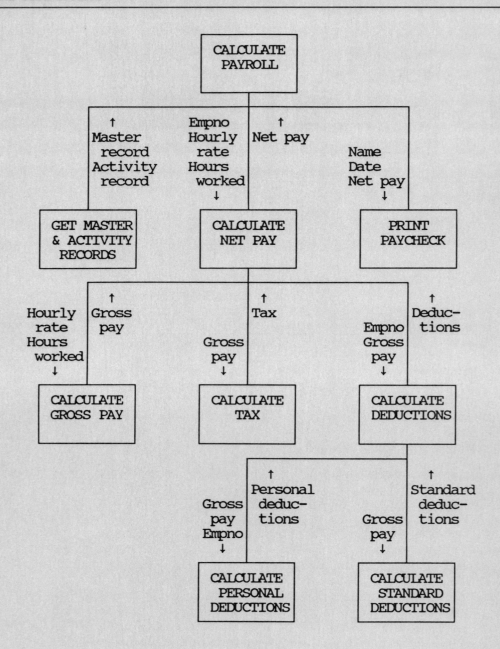

Figure 8 **Pseudo-Code**

```
open master_file activity_file history_file
dowhile records on activity_file
      get activity_record
      get corresponding master_record
      do net_pay_calculation
            gross_pay = hourly_rate * hours_worked
            tax = gross_pay * tax_rate
            net_pay = gross_pay - tax
            deduction_total = 0
            dowhile personal_deductions
                  deduction = gross_pay * deduction_rate
                  write deduction, deduction_code to history_file
                  deduction_total = deduction_total + deduction
            enddo
            dowhile standard_deductions
                  deduction = gross_pay * deduction_rate
                  write deduction, deduction_code to history_file
                  deduction_total = deduction_total + deduction
            enddo
            net_pay = net_pay - deduction_total
      enddo
      print name, date, net_pay on paycheck
enddo
close master_file activity_file history_file
```

EXERCISES

1. Create program structure charts for a program that counts paragraphs, lines, words, and characters in a text file and prints the totals out at the end of the program. Use two or three different documentation techniques. Compare and contrast the various techniques.

 2. Create a detailed program structure chart for each program in the Condor order entry application described in the mini-case of Chapter 14.

3. Create a detailed program structure chart from the pseudo-code examples given in Figures 14–15 and 14–16. Once each detailed chart is created, simplify it so that it corresponds to a level of detail appropriate for the design phase rather than the programming phase.

Section VII

Implementation

This section covers the remainder of the systems development life cycle, once the planning, analysis, and design phases have been completed. Chapter 18 describes the tasks of analysts and programming supervisors during the programming phase. Chapter 19 covers the various stages of testing: unit tests, integration tests, systems tests, and acceptance tests. Chapter 20 describes how to convert the files for the new systems and how to prepare the users for the day when the new system goes into operation. Finally, Chapter 21 describes how systems are maintained and enhanced during the rest of their life cycles, until they are replaced by new systems.

IBM's Multiples Marketing Program

A glass and concrete building outside Atlanta houses IBM's Multiples Marketing Program. This organization assists IBM customers who are installing a system—hardware, software, or both—at a large number of sites.

The Multiples Marketing Program could help manufacturers of agricultural or automotive equipment to install ordering and inventory systems in their dealerships around the country. It could help insurance companies to install workstations at their agents' offices or airlines to place reservation systems at travel agencies. In fact, it could be used by any corporation that has distributed processing requirements for many sites or that is installing a system linking it to its customers.

The program is called "Multiples Marketing" because it deals with multiples of systems—one hundred at a minimum—and because it emphasizes advice to the customers of the program on how to market their systems to their own customers or users. The need for a well-thought-out approach to marketing is evident in many cases. For example, if a car manufacturer wants to place a system at its dealers, any dealer is free to refuse to install the system. If the dealer is or feels coerced, the installation will not be a success. Even if the users are internal and therefore not free to refuse, a poorly presented system increases the risk of failure.

The program therefore offers customers assistance in developing a marketing plan to sell the system to its prospective users. Techniques to make the prospective users want to use the system are developed. Responsibility for marketing the system is assigned to the organization that is the most closely associated with the user. This is often the marketing or the sales organization when the system is being distributed to customers.

Project planning and control assistance is also given. In IBM's words, the two phases are: "plan the work" and "work the plan." The Multiples Marketing Program provides assistance in the first phase, establishing a project schedule by adapting and detailing the Master Project Schedule shown in Figure VII–1. The project control process is also designed. However, executing the plan and controlling it remain the responsibility of the customer.

Systems installation is prepared by planning for the logistics of installing new hardware at all the locations. The plan calls for the user to do as much of the installation work as possible and for the role of the central installation team to be limited to problem situations. This approach reduces the bottleneck that would be caused by a central installation team flying around the country and spending several days at each site.

An administration group is created centrally to handle all the logistics of ordering equipment, monitoring delivery schedules, and tracking problems. For large numbers of installations, the responsibility of logistics should not be assigned to the systems development team, which will be occupied with technical problems during the installation.

The program also offers help in setting up other support functions, such as training, documentation creation, and a response line or help desk. The overall objective of these functions is to help the end users of the system develop two essential attributes for the success of a system: self-sufficiency and ownership.

By far the most interesting aspect of the Multiples Marketing Program, however, is the usability lab. Two usability lab rooms are installed in the same building as the rest of the program. The rooms have a workspace for an operator and an observation center separated from the workspace by a one-way mirror. The observation center is equipped with video and audio recording equipment, as well as with two computer terminals. One terminal shows exactly what is being shown on the screen in the workspace; on the other, an observer can log events as they happen.

A usability lab session usually lasts about a

week, during which two to four volunteer users, one at a time, test the system (or a prototype of it) under conditions that are as realistic as possible. The user is instructed to "think aloud" as he or she is doing the work. This running commentary provides a valuable guide for the observation team to pinpoint why difficulties arise. The last day of the week is reserved for evaluation. The observation team and sometimes the users come together to summarize what problems were encountered and what is required to solve them.

The usability lab has proven extremely valuable to those organizations that have used it. Some have even set up their own labs in-house. According to several users, the usability lab has made all the difference between a smooth installation with good user acceptance and a problem-fraught one where the central help desk is smothered by irate customer calls or where users reject the system after experiencing early frustration and failure.

Figure VII–1 **Multiples Marketing Program Master Schedule**

Master Project Schedule

Application Software	Plans & Req'mnts	Design FS +	Devel. Proto-type	Develop Programs		System Test	User Pilot Test	PKG	Buffer	Ship	
Milestone	1	2	3	4	5	6	7	8		9	
Usability Evaluation	Plan	Develop Script	Usab. Test								
User Documentation	Plan & Design	First Draft / Review	Second Draft		Re-view	Print	User Test	Buffer	Ship		
User Training	Plan & Design	Develop Training Course			Test/ Review	Up-date	User Test	Buffer	Train End Users		
System Installation	Plan	Site Planning	Develop Install. Guide	Usability Test	Up-date Guide	Re-view	User Pilot Test	Install Hardware / Install Application			
Support Center		Plan	Design		Train		User Test	Support Users			
Marketing	Determine Goals	Develop Plan	Organize to Plan		Set Timetable		User Test	Set Expectations			
Administration	Plan	Design System & Create Data Base			Train		Implement System				

PURPOSE OF SECTION

The purpose of this section is to round out the topics of analysis and design by summarizing the part of the life cycle that comes after the design has been completed and approved. Instead of covering the full detail of such familiar activities as programming and testing, the section illustrates some of the main types of problems that arise during programming, testing, installation, and maintenance. These illustrations will help explain many of the design practices described in earlier chapters.

Many of the problems encountered after the design of a system is complete result from the need for IS professionals to work as a team rather than as individuals. Whereas programming is essentially a solitary exercise, systems development cannot be: systems are too large to fall within the scope of a single individual. Although most IS professionals may have been trained to solve the technical problems that they are faced with, they may not have been exposed to the problems of teamwork. They may have had little experience with imperfect communications; noninstantaneous access to information; frictions with users, with management, and within the team.

To help address these problems, this section describes some of the management techniques that have been found useful on large projects.

KEY TASKS AND DELIVERABLES

Detailed program design and coding is the first of the activities to take place once the design has been completed. This activity can be viewed as the last point at which design decisions are made. Usually, all the important design decisions have already been made, either because they have been explicitly made during the design phase, or because there is a department-wide standard that dictates how details will be implemented in each program. Only those decisions that have no impact on the team as such are left to individual programmers.

The next activity is testing. The first tests of a program or a module are run by the programmer writing it: this is called *unit testing*. Later, several modules or programs making up a larger unit, such as a subsystem, are integrated and tested: this process is known as *integration testing*. Finally, the entire system — both its automated and its manual parts — is tested with the participation of the users. This is called *system testing*. Normally, after a satisfactory system test, the system is put into service. In some cases, the first weeks or months of service are also considered to be part of the test of the system: this process is called *acceptance testing*.

A very effective view of testing is to consider it as part of a quality control scheme, as depicted in Figure VII–2. This schematic shows the main phases of the development cycle and the corresponding phases of tests. Quality control appears in three different ways. First, the arrow pointing from each phase back to itself indicates the need to check that the document produced at the end of the phase is internally consistent and has been prepared according to the rules,

Figure VII–2 **Testing and Quality Control**

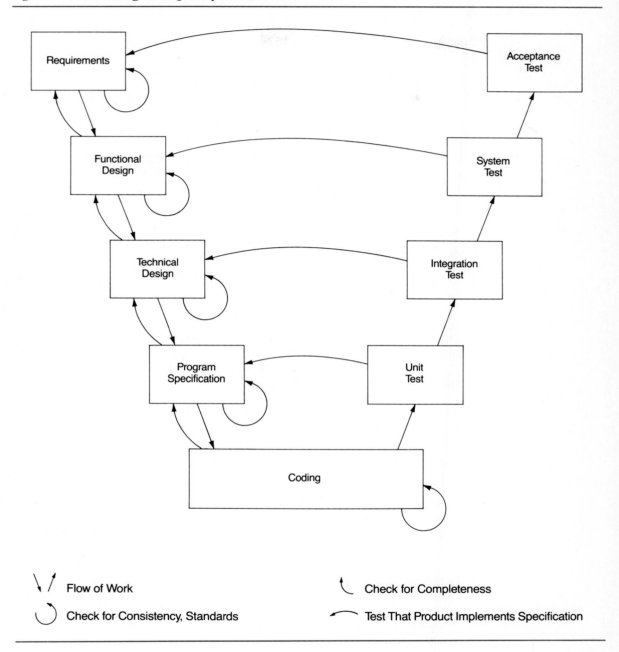

Figure VII–3   **Test Phases and Objectives**

Test Phase	Objective
Unit Test	Check that each module or program behaves as specified in the programming specification
Integration Test	Check that the system behaves as specified in the technical specification (process design)
System Test	Check that the system behaves as specified in the functional specification (user interface design)
Acceptance Test	Check that the system behaves as specified in the requirements specification

methods, and standards of the phase. The arrow pointing to each previous phase indicates the need to control that all the decisions made in that previous phase have been carried over to the next phase—that nothing has been forgotten or deformed. The arrow pointing from each test phase to the corresponding development phase indicates that the objective of the test is to verify that the component, subsystem, or system being tested actually implements the specification produced in the development phase.

The term *installing the system* refers to two kinds of activities: building the data bases required for the system to operate (conversion) and preparing the manual component of the system (user procedures and training). These activities can be performed in parallel with programming and testing.

The key deliverable of the implementation phase is an operational system, which includes the following components:

- Programs and program documentation from the programming step.

- Test plans, test results, and user sign-offs from the testing steps.

- User and operations documentation, training materials, and a trained body of users and operators from the implementation step.

- Master files and data bases, if applicable, from the conversion step.

Maintenance, the last phase in the systems development life cycle, is what happens to the system after it has become operational. It includes changes to the programs as well as to the user procedures. The inevitable changes to organizations and the way they conduct business must be reflected in the organization's business systems. More importantly, the systems of an organization should never be allowed to impede changes that the organization wishes to make. As a result, maintenance is a critical activity of the IS department. In fact, many IS departments have more than 75 percent of their analysts and programmers assigned to maintenance.

The key deliverable from the maintenance phase is a system that continues to be operational: all the programs, tests, and other documentation must be kept up to date as the system evolves.

Chapter 18

Program Specifications and Programmer Supervision

Chapter 18 describes various programming team organizations, management styles, and planning methods. It then covers the programming specification, the documentation package prepared for a programmer by an analyst. Finally, structured walk-throughs and programming supervision activities are detailed.

Learning Objectives

- Understand the most frequent forms of organization of the programming team, the way it is supervised, and the way it relates to the rest of the project team.
- List the contents of a completed program specification and describe who is usually responsible for preparing each part.
- Recognize the role of structured walk-throughs and describe how a walk-through is planned, performed, and followed up.

ORGANIZING AND MANAGING THE PROGRAMMING EFFORT

On most projects, programming and related activities consume large amounts of time. Therefore, programming management is a critical aspect of the wider concept of project management.

The principles of programming management are no different from the principles of project management: plan the work, identify the resources to do it, monitor its execution, and evaluate the result. But because of the technical specialization of programmers, programming management is usually not the responsibility of a single person. The planning and evaluation phases are by necessity done by the overall project manager. Usually, a programming supervisor with authority over all the project's programmers assigns and monitors the work.

If the project is large enough, the programming supervisor may be assigned to the project full time. In this ideal situation, the programming supervisor is integrated into the team structure, understands the project's overall context, and can develop a sense of ownership. A "we and they" attitude between analysts and programmers is less likely to develop.

On smaller projects, the programming supervisor may only be assigned part time to the project. This situation is more difficult to manage. The analysts will tend to suspect that the programming supervisor, and by association the entire programming team, have divided loyalties. Also, the reporting relationships and communications between analysts and programmers tend to become more formal.

These difficulties may be solved by assigning the required number of programmers directly to the project team and having an analyst—usually the most technically oriented—play the role of programming supervisor. This solution is often adopted by IS departments organized along application lines rather than by technical specialty. However, the arrangement is not without drawbacks. The main one is probably that the programmers lack permanent leadership, from the perspective of their technical specialization as well as their careers. Also, the analyst chosen to play the role of programming supervisor is generally chosen for his or her technical know-how and may not have the leadership and administrative qualifications to be a full-time programming supervisor.

Another form of organization is the chief programmer's team advocated by IBM in the 1970s. In this approach, the programming, and indeed most of the design, is done by small, autonomous teams of about six people. Each team is headed by a chief programmer, who determines the architecture of the programs assigned to the group and writes most of the difficult code. The chief programmer is assisted by another highly qualified technician, who knows almost as much as the chief programmer, who codes whatever the chief programmer does not code, and who can take over at a moment's notice. Other team members include a secretary, who takes care of documentation and administration, and a program librarian, who is responsible for source code, object code, test data, job control, and version management.

Chief programmer's teams have never encountered a great deal of success in commercial information systems departments, possibly for two reasons: it is hard to find the required number of people talented enough to be chief programmers; and in the commercial environment, it is difficult to subdivide a problem into units that are independent enough to be tackled by a small team working largely on its own. Such units were easier to find in the batch environment, where large, complex programs used to be the rule. Now, with the emphasis on on-line transactions, the programs tend to be rather small, with a high degree of uniformity in how they are invoked from a menu and are tied to each other in conversation structures.

The structured walk-through, or peer review as the technique is also called, is another idea from the 1970s. It has had more success than chief programmer's teams, but is not practiced nearly as universally as it ought to be. During a structured walk-through, the work of one programmer or one small team is reviewed by other people who have not been involved with the work. The reviewee "walks through" a completed unit of work (for example, a section of code or an entire program), explaining how it is supposed to work, while the reviewers try to point out problems such as errors, omissions, or nonstandard practices. Structured walk-throughs can very effectively increase code quality and decrease the number of bugs. They are difficult to implement, however, because most people's work habits do not make it easy for them to bare their work to others and to receive criticism, however constructive. Nor is it easy for most people to give constructive criticism. The rule of structured walk-throughs that is the most difficult to follow is the one that forbids reviewers from suggesting solutions to the problems found; that is the province of the programmer who did the work initially.

The use of structured walk-throughs can make the technical role of the programming supervisor somewhat less critical; when properly applied, it certainly promotes team cohesion.

Structured walk-through techniques originated in programming. They have later been extended to encompass both design and requirements analysis activities as well. How a walk-through is conducted in the programming phase is explained later in this chapter; it is easy to adapt the rules to other situations.

PLANNING THE PROGRAMMING EFFORT

However the programming effort is organized, the main difficulty with managing the programming portion of a project is making sure that the work gets done on time. In *The Mythical Man-Month*,[1] Fred Brooks points out that time and personnel resources are not interchangeable. In fact, one of his laws states, "Adding people to a project which is late makes it later." (Incidentally, this law holds for the entire project, not only for the programming phase.) To prevent the project from becoming late in the first place requires monitoring progress very closely, so that underlying causes of problems can be corrected before major delays occur.

An almost universal characteristic of programmers is their incurable optimism. Most programmers believe that the next program they write will be bug-free, or almost, and that it will only require a few tests. As a result, when asked how far along they are, programmers tend to respond: "I am almost (or 90 percent, or 95 percent) finished." The impression is often that the last 10 percent of a program takes as long to finish as the first 90 percent. The remedy for this is to create frequent measurable milestones: no module should take longer than about two weeks to write and debug fully. (Milestones should not be based on coding alone because it is easy to cut down the time spent on coding at the expense of time spent testing.) At the end of the two weeks, the module is either done or it is not. If another week goes by before completion, there is a problem, as the variance is then 50 percent. In this way, systematic problems can be diagnosed and corrected within the first few weeks of the programming effort.

The following maxim is also useful to remember. Underestimating the time required for a unit of work will result in late delivery. Overestimating, however, will not make the delivery early; it will make the worker perform below full capacity. Even with a mix of over- and underestimating, the project will tend to slip, because there is no automatic compensation between the two. Frequent milestones will help for two reasons. First, it is easier to give reliable estimates for short tasks than for long tasks. Second, people can work above capacity for a short time without side effects, thereby catching up when minor delays occur for a single milestone.

THE PROGRAMMING SPECIFICATION

The analyst documents the work to be done in a program specification, which is communicated to the programmer. The specification, based on the process design done in the design phase, is created in the implementation phase. As described in Section VI, the amount of detail in the design phase is sufficient when the implementation can be planned and a cost/benefit analysis can be completed with reasonable precision.

In the implementation phase, the detailed design must be continued to a level sufficient for the programmer to understand it. Also, the design must add ancillary functions that are not of direct day-to-day concern to the user, such as table updating programs, file printouts for audit trails, and other utilitarian functions. (These functions must all have been identified in the design phase for planning purposes, but their content were not been detailed at that time.)

Level of Detail

A difficult question is the degree of detail required in the specification, i.e., the division of labor between analyst and programmer. A specification can be more or less detailed, more or less close to the actual code that will implement it. In fact, just as the design documents created earlier, the programming specification can be viewed as an arbitrary point on the continuum between requirement and operational system. The difficulty is that if the specification is not detailed enough, the programmer will flounder; if it is too detailed, the programmer will feel reduced to a role of coder who simply transcribes into programming language what the analyst has specified in a variety of English that strangely resembles COBOL (see Figure 18–1 for an example).

A problem is that the right level of detail varies with the experience and competence of each individual programmer. Generally, the programmer to be assigned to a specification is not known when the specification is created. Therefore, the role played by the programming supervisor is critical in directing analysts to a level of detail that is appropriate for the general population of programmers to be assigned to the project.

Figure 18–1 **Program Specification That Is Too Close to Code**

```
MARKETING                    SUBURBAN PUMPS                    T235
ORDER ENTRY                                                   OE12010
                    PROGRAM DEFINITION - CREDIT CHECKING

PREPARED BY:  FRANK GERMAIN  DATE:  01MAR89    VERSION:  1    PAGE 3
APPROVED BY:  SHEILA MANN    DATE:  05MAR89    STATUS  :
```

2.1.3.7   If the customer-rating code is equal to 7, do credit-processing as outlined in paragraphs 2.1.4.g through 2.1.4.k.

2.1.3.8   If the customer-rating code is equal to 8, do credit-processing as outlined in paragraph 2.1.4.l.

2.1.3.9   If none of the above, perform program error processing as described in paragraph 2.9, with error message number 78 (see attached list of error messages). Then exit the execution of the program with a return code of 0016 (hex 0010).

2.1.3.10   Once the credit has been checked, test the order reject switch. If it is on, process the next order; if it is off, go to Section 3.

2.1.4   Detailed processing rules.

2.1.4.a.   Add the order total calculated in paragraph 1.2.3 to the current balance of the customer.

2.1.4.b.   Add the order total calculated in paragraph 1.2.3 to the 30-day-or-more balance of the customer.

2.1.4.c.   If the balance calculated in 2.1.4.a exceeds the credit limit of the customer, perform order reject processing as described in paragraph 2.7 with error message 12. Add 1 to the control counter for number of orders rejected. Set the order-rejected switch and return.

           If the balance calculated does not exceed the credit-limit, then add one to the control counter for number of orders accepted.

2.1.4.d.   If the balance calculated in 2.1.4.b exceeds the credit limit of the customer, perform order reject processing as described in paragraph 2.7 with error message 13. Add 1 to the control counter for number of orders rejected. Set the order-rejected switch and return.

           If the balance calculated does not exceed the credit-limit, then add one to the control counter for number of orders accepted.

2.1.4.e.   If the balance calculated in 2.1.4.a exceeds the credit limit of the customer category obtained by look-up of the customer category table of credit limits described in paragraph 1.3.2, perform order reject processing as described in paragraph 2.7 with error message 12. Add 1 to the control counter for number of orders rejected. Set the order-rejected switch and return.

           If the balance calculated does not exceed the credit-limit, then add one to the control counter for number of orders accepted.

As programmers code and test the programs assigned to them, they complete the specification with the results of their work to the level of source code and test results. The specification of a finished program is invariable (unlike the state of the specification prepared by the analyst for the programmer).

Content

The specification of a completed program contains the following:

- The context of the program: its place and objectives in relation to other components of the system.

    The context specification takes the form of a schematic (see Figure 18–2) that shows which other programs calls this one; which programs this one calls; and which files, screens, or other I/O are read and written. A short statement (see Figure 18–3) states the objectives of the program.

- The I/O interfaces: file, record, and element descriptions from the data dictionary, as well as screen and report mock-ups (see Figure 18–4).

- The calling interfaces: input and output parameters as well as return codes for the calling sequences that call this program and the parameters and codes this program uses to call other programs (see Figure 18–5).

- The functions of the program: the processing to be done to accomplish the objectives, including the handling of exceptions and errors (see Figure 18–6).

- The unit test plan: a list of each test case, cross-referenced to the function description to be tested and to the input and output test data (see Figure 18–7).

- The program design in graphic or pseudo-code form.

    In some installations, the design may be omitted if it is established by the programmer and if it is fully documented in the code, i.e., if the COBOL program actually reflects the pseudo-code accurately and understandably (see Figures 18–8 and 18–9).

- The source code of the final version of the program.

- The unit test input and results, cross-referenced to the test plan (see Figure 18–10). This part of the specification is further detailed in Chapter 19.

- A checklist of milestones and review sign-offs (see Figure 18–11).

In most cases, the analyst is responsible for at least the first four items on this list—context, I/O interfaces, calling interfaces, and functions. The programmer is always responsible for the last three—source code, test results, and checklist. The middle two—design elements and test plan—are the responsibility of the analyst in some installations and of the programmers in others. A test for checking whether the programmer has a good understanding of the program is to have the programmer prepare the test plan. The analyst can then check the

Figure 18–2 **Sample Context Specification**

PERSONNEL   T235
PAYROLL   CPR505
                      MODULE DEFINITION - PAYROLL CALCULATION PROGRAM

PREPARED BY: WENDY SMITH   DATE: 24MAR89   VERSION: PAGE 1
APPROVED BY: JOE DAVIS   DATE: 24MAR89   STATUS :

PROGRAM NAME: CPR505 - PAYROLL CALCULATIONS

ONE-TIME MODULE INSTR. COUNT:

RECORD IDENTIFICATION	NUMBER OF EXECUTIONS	RECORD NAME	CALL TYPE	CPU INSTR/EXEC
{D610.RC01005}	1200–1400	Valid Time Report Trans.	INPUT	
{D610.RC01006}	1	Control Record	INPUT	
{D610.X01}	7000–10000	Employee Data Base	DATABASE	
{D610.RC01010}	1200–1400	Pay Records	OUTPUT	
{D610.RC01006}	1	Control Record	OUTPUT	
{D320.CPR505C}	1	Control Report	PRINT	

ENVIRONMENT

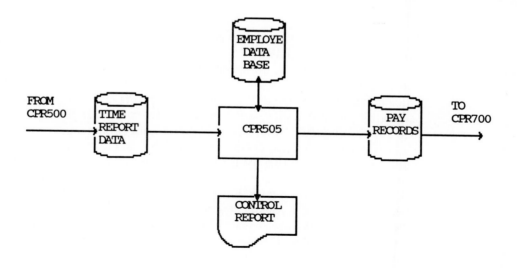

Figure 18–3 **Sample Program Objective Statement**

```
PERSONNEL                                                        T235
PAYROLL                                                          CPR505
                MODULE DEFINITION - PAYROLL CALCULATION PROGRAM

PREPARED BY: WENDY SMITH      DATE: 24MAR89      VERSION:        PAGE 2
APPROVED BY: JOE DAVIS        DATE: 24MAR89      STATUS :
```

ABSTRACT DESCRIPTION

This program calculates the bi-monthly pay of all engineers and technicaians, who submit a monthly time report. The time report data is used to reimburse expenses and keep track of vacation days. The program reads permanenet employee data from the employee data base and updates the data base with accumulated pay data, vacation and sick days taken, and deductions.

The output from the program is a file containing the data required to print the employees' pay slip and make the payments.

---

programmer's understanding of the program by reviewing the test plan for completeness and relevance.

The design section of the specification is the least important one, at least if the guideline of not exceeding two weeks' worth of work in a single program or module has been observed. If the program is substantially more complex and cannot be subdivided, this section takes on much more importance and may need to be completed by an analyst or by a senior programmer.

Traditionally, all these documents have been typed or handwritten pages, put together in a three-ring binder, and maintained as the primary maintenance documentation of the system. An emerging approach is to use electronic documentation for large parts, if not all, of the specification. This trend started with the emergence of data dictionaries in the 1970s. Data dictionaries made it possible to exclude the detailed I/O interfaces of the program from the specification; only the file (or screen/report) names were given. Programmers could obtain up-to-date details by consulting the data dictionary.

Electronic documentation can easily be extended to other parts of the specification. The concept of the data dictionary can be enlarged to that of a *repository* for all the elements of the system: data descriptions, source code, test files, and textual documentation.

Figure 18–4 **Sample I/O Interface Specification**

```
ACCTG                                                              RPTDEF
BUDPREP                                                            R00262
             REPORT DEFINITION - Sales Budgeting Turnaround Rpt
────────────────────────────────────────────────────────────────────────
PREPARED BY: Ben Dover      DATE: 15Feb88      VERSION: 2      PAGE   2
APPROVED BY: RL Turner      DATE: 18Feb88      STATUS :
────────────────────────────────────────────────────────────────────────


X-REF TO     DATA ELEMENT                                      NO. OF
 SAMPLE      IDENTIFICATION   DATA ELEMENT NAME OR COMMENTS    CHARACTERS
--------     --------------   -----------------------------    ----------
      1      EL00200          Territory Number                     2
      2      EL00205          Salesperson Number                   3
      3      EL00206          Salesperson Name                    25
      4      EL00220          Customer Number                      5
      5      EL00221          Customer Name                       25

                              Prior Year $ Sales to Customer
      6      EL00361          - 1st Quarter                        7
      7      EL00362          - 2nd Quarter                        7
      8      EL00363          - 3rd Quarter                        7
      9      EL00364          - 4th Quarter                        7

                              Current Year $ Sales to Customer
     10      EL00371          - 1st Quarter                        7
     11      EL00372          - 2nd Quarter                        7
     12      EL00373          - 3rd Quarter                        7
     13      EL00374          - 4th Quarter                        7

                              Prior Year $ Gross Margin for Customer
     14      EL00381          - 1st Quarter                        5
     15      EL00382          - 2nd Quarter                        5
     16      EL00383          - 3rd Quarter                        5
     17      EL00384          - 4th Quarter                        5

                              Current Year $ Gross Margin for Customer
     18      EL00391          - 1st Quarter                        5
     19      EL00392          - 2nd Quarter                        5
     20      EL00393          - 3rd Quarter                        5
     21      EL00394          - 4th Quarter                        5
```

Figure 18–5 **Sample Calling Interface Specification**

```
PERSONNEL                                                      T235
PAYROLL                                                        CPR50534
              MODULE DEFINITION - PROCESS SAVINGS BONDS
```

```
PREPARED BY: WENDY SMITH    DATE: 24APR89    VERSION: 1        PAGE 3
APPROVED BY: JOE DAVIS      DATE: 27APR89    STATUS :
```

```
                    CALLING INTERFACE SPECIFICATION
-----------------------------------------------------------------------

CPR50534 is called using the following interface

RECORD
IDENTIFICATION   RECORD/ELEMENT NAME          I/O   REMARKS
--------------   -------------------          ---   -----------------------
{D610.RC01024}   EMPLOYEE RECORD              I/O
                     EMPLOYEE ID               I    Used to access data base
                     SAVINGS BOND DEDUCTION    O    Amount of this month's
                                                    deduction.  If refund,
                                                    amount is negative

{D610.RC01035}   BOND PURCHASE ORDER RECORD    O    Created if bond to be
                                                    purchased.  If not, left
                                                    blank.

{D610.RC01099}   CONTROL RECORD              I/O
                     BOND-PO-COUNTER          I/O   Incremented by one if bond
                                                    purchase order issued.
                     BOND-PROCESSING-COUNTER  I/O   Incremented by one

{D610.RC01098}   RETURN-CODES                  O
                     PROGRAM RETURN CODE            OK or PROGRAM-ERROR
                     REASON-CODE                    OK or DATA BASE ERROR

DBIO is called using the following interface

{D610.DBIOFUNC}  DBIO FUNCTION CODE            I    RU for READ TO UPDATE

{D610.HR0071}    SAVINGS BONDS RECORD        I/O
                     RECORD TYPE               I    Set to SAVINGS-BONDS
                     EMPLOYEE-ID               I
                     SAVINGS-BONDS-OPTION      O    NONE, STOP, or OK
                     CURRENT-PRICE             O
                     ACCUMULATOR              I/O

{D610.DBIORET}   DBIO RETURN CODE              O    OK or NOT-FOUND.  (If
                                                    other value, return
                                                    control to calling
                                                    module).
```

Figure 18–6 **Sample Program Function Specification**

```
PERSONNEL                                                    T235
PAYROLL                                                      CPR50534
               MODULE DEFINITION - PROCESS SAVINGS BONDS

PREPARED BY: WENDY SMITH      DATE: 24APR89      VERSION: 1        PAGE 2
APPROVED BY: JOE DAVIS        DATE: 27APR89      STATUS :
```

ABSTRACT DESCRIPTION

This module determines whether an employee is taking a savings bond deduction.
If so, a purchase is made by updating the savings bond accumulators and
writing a bond purchase record.

The stop bond indicator is checked. If the bond purchase option is
terminated, then the remaining balance in the indicator is refunded to the
employee.

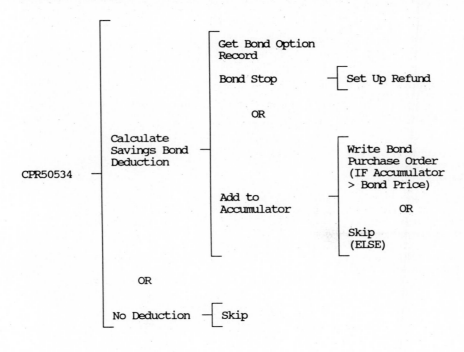

Figure 18–7 **Sample Test Plan**

```
MEDICAL RECORDS                GENERAL HOSPITAL              T915
ADMISSIONS                                                  APR0100
                                  TESTING PLAN

┌──────────────────────────────────────────────────────────────────┐
│ PREPARED BY:  CRAIG MINDRUM   DATE:   27DEC92    VERSION:   PAGE 1 │
│ APPROVED BY:                  DATE:              STATUS  :         │
└──────────────────────────────────────────────────────────────────┘


No.  Point                           Disposition                     Cycle
---  ----------------------------    ----------------------------    -----
1.   The admission updates should
     process inpatients (I) and
     outpatients (O).  All other
     codes are invalid

2.   Admission clerks must be able
     to go back and correct data
     before it is stored on the
     Medical Records Data Base

3.   Make sure the patient's age is
     calculated correctly from year
     of birth and today's date on
     confirmations.

4.   Check that only valid IDs can
     inquire/update the Medical
     Records Data Base (these are
     separate authorities; however,
     update implies inquiry).

5.   If no admissions are made
     during the day, test that
     processing occurs normally.

6.   Check that the Medical Records
     Data Base is updated for the
     admitted patient's account
     number and that patient's only.

7.   Test that the confirmation
     printout formats correctly
     relative to page breaks.
```

Figure 18–8 **Sample Pseudo-Code**

			T213
	MODULE PSEUDOCODE		DRQA3333

PREPARED BY: JANE WASSIN	DATE: 12.12.95	VERSION:	PAGE 1
APPROVED BY:	DATE:	STATUS :	

```
perform housekeeping
if number of records requested = 0
    then set severe return code
         set error message to no records requested
elsif parent entity id = spaces and
         child entity id = spaces
         then set severe return code
              set error message to parent or child entity id required
     elsif user language = low-values or
              user language = spaces
              then set severe return code
                   set error message to user language not specified
         endif
     endif
endif
if not severe return code
    then
    case code = get unique or
         code = get unique update or
         code = get unique delete
         then do get-unique-processing
    case code = get next or
         code = get next update
         then do get-next-processing
    case code = get many or
         code = get many update
         then do get-many-processing
    case code = update row
         then do update-row-processing
    case code = insert row
         then do insert-row-processing
    case code = copy child
         then do copy-child-processing
    case code = delete many
         then do delete-many-processing
    case code = delete row
         then do delete-row-processing
    case code = internal-function
         then do internal-function-processing
    case other
         then set severe return code
              set error message to invalid function
    endcase
 endif
 perform wrap-up
```

Figure 18–9 **Sample Self-documenting COBOL Program**

```
003580          A1000-MAINLINE-PROCESSING.
003581          **************************************************************
003582          *                                                            *
003583          *   A 1 0 0 0 - M A I N L I N E - P R O C E S S I N G        *
003584          *   ------------------------------------------------         *
003585          *                                                            *
003586          **************************************************************
003587              PERFORM A0600-HOUSEKEEPING.
003588              IF DRIO-NUM-REC-REQUESTED EQUAL ZERO
003589                  SET   DDEA-NUM-REC-REQ-ZERO TO TRUE
003590                  SET   DRIO-SEVERE-RC TO TRUE
003591              ELSE
003592                  IF DRIO-PART-DD-ENT-ITEM-ID = SPACES AND
003593                     DRIO-CHLD-DD-ENT-ITEM-ID = SPACES
003594                      SET DRIO-SEVERE-RC TO TRUE
003595                      SET DDEA-PAR-OR-CH-ID-REQ TO TRUE
003596                  ELSE
003597                      IF DRIO-USER-LANGUAGE = SPACES  OR
003598                         DRIO-USER-LANGUAGE = LOW-VALUES
003599                          SET   DRIO-SEVERE-RC TO TRUE
003600                          SET DDEA-LANGUAGE-NOT-PASSED TO TRUE
003601                      END-IF
003602                  END-IF
003603              END-IF.
003604              IF NOT DRIO-SEVERE-RC
003605                  PERFORM A5000-APPLICATION-PROCESS
003606              END-IF.
003607              PERFORM A9600-WRAP-UP.

003931          A5000-APPLICATION-PROCESS.
003932          **************************************************************
003933          *                                                            *
003934          *    A 5 0 0 0 - A P P L I C A T I O N  P R O C E S S        *
003935          *    -----------------------------------------------         *
003936          *    THIS PARAGRAPH IS THE MAIN PROCESSING DRIVER. IF AN     *
003937          *    INVALID FUNCTION EXISTS, NO PROCESSING IS DONE.         *
003938          *                                                            *
003939          **************************************************************
003940              IF DRIO-GET-UNIQUE OR
003941                 DRIO-GET-UNIQUE-UPDATE OR
003942                 DRIO-GET-UNIQUE-DELETE
003943                  PERFORM A5100-GET-UNIQUE
003944              ELSE
003945              IF DRIO-GET-NEXT OR
003946                 DRIO-GET-NEXT-UPDATE
003947                  PERFORM A5200-GET-NEXT
003948              ELSE
003949              IF DRIO-GET-MANY OR
003950                 DRIO-GET-MANY-UPDATE
003951                  PERFORM A5300-GET-MANY
003952              ELSE
003953              IF DRIO-UPDATE-ROW
003954                  PERFORM A5400-UPDATE-ROW
003955              ELSE
003956              IF DRIO-INSERT-ROW
003957                  PERFORM A5450-INSERT-ROW
003958              ELSE
003959              IF DRIO-COPY-CHILDREN
003960                  PERFORM A5500-COPY-CHILD
003961              ELSE
003962              IF DRIO-DELETE-MANY
003963                  PERFORM A5600-DELETE-MANY
003964              ELSE
003965              IF DRIO-DELETE-ROW
003966                  PERFORM A5700-DELETE-ROW
003967              ELSE
003968              IF DRIO-INTERNAL-FUNCTION
003969                  PERFORM A5800-INTERNAL-FUNCTION
003970              ELSE
003971                  SET DDEA-INVALID-FUNCTION TO TRUE
003972                  SET DRIO-SEVERE-RC TO TRUE
003973              END-IF.
```

Figure 18–10 **Sample Unit Test Results**

```
MEDICAL RECORDS              GENERAL HOSPITAL               T915
ADMISSIONS                                                  APR0100
                               TESTING PLAN
┌──────────────────────────────────────────────────────────────────────┐
│ PREPARED BY:  CRAIG MINDRUM  DATE:  27DEC92   VERSION:  1    PAGE 1    │
│ APPROVED BY:  F. FUJIWARA    DATE:  05FEB93   STATUS :  F             │
└──────────────────────────────────────────────────────────────────────┘
```

No.	Point	Disposition	Cycle
1.	The admission updates should process inpatients (I) and outpatients (O). All other codes are invalid	Tested	2 3
2.	Admission clerks must be able to go back and correct data before it is stored on the Medical Records Data Base	Pass-the last input screen automatically prompts clerks to make sure there are no more additions/corrections before updating data base.	
3.	Make sure the patient's age is calculated correctly from year of birth and today's date on confirmations.	Tested	6
4.	Check that only valid IDs can inquire/update the Medical Records Data Base (these are separate authorities; however, update implies inquiry).	Tested	4 8 9
5.	If no admissions are made during the day, test that processing occurs normally.	Tested. If there has been no activity, operators are not prompted to run batch.	10
6.	Check that the Medical Records Data Base is updated for the admitted patient's account number and that patient's only.	Tested	4
7.	Test that the confirmation printout formats correctly relative to page breaks.	Tested	6

Figure 18–11 **Sample Checklist of Milestones and Review Points**

PERSONNEL   SUBURBAN PUMPS   CD-20
PAYROLL   BCRIT

                         ORGANIZATION/FUNCTION MATRIX

PREPARED BY: WENDY SMITH   DATE: 10NOV91   VERSION:
APPROVED BY: JOE DAVIS   DATE: 15NOV91   STATUS :   PAGE 1

| | | | | | -----DATES----- | | | | |
Program/Module	Analyst	Pro-grammer	Spec	I/O Design	Test Plan	Coding	Clean Compile	Unit Test	Doc Complete
CPR50510	Smith	Gretry	12.02 OK	11.29 OK	12.04 OK	12.05 OK	12.09 OK	12.13	12.14
CPR50520	"	Gretry	12.02 OK	11.29 OK	.....	.....			
CPR50530	"	Fuller	12.02 OK	11.29 OK					
CPR50531	"	Fuller	12.09 OK	11.29 OK					
CPR50532	"	Fuller	12.09 OK	.....					
CPR50533	"	Schreiner	12.09 OK						
CPR50534	"	Schreiner	12.09 OK						
CPR50535	"	Schreiner	12.09 OK						
CPR50536	"	Schreiner	12.09 OK						
CPR50539	"	Schreiner	12.09 OK						
CPR50540	"	Unassigned	12.16						
CPR50550	"	Unassigned	12.16						
CPR50551	"	Unassigned	12.16						
CPR50552	"	Unassigned	12.16						
CPR505 (Integration)		Unassigned	12.16						

Language and Style

The language and style in the specification varies from the very formalized (record layouts) to almost natural English. The essential objective of the program specification is to communicate what the program is to do—its functions—and in which context—its interfaces.

Once the code is written and tested, the functional, informal description of the program may appear to be redundant, because the behavior of the program is fully determined by the code. However, the functional description should still be carefully maintained to give maintainers as many clues as possible to what the program does as well as why it does it, relating each function to the objectives of the system. It is best if the functional description of the program is couched in a language that is as close to everyday English as possible, with the fewest possible assumptions about how the program is to work. To illustrate this guideline, Figure 18–12 contains two versions of a functional description. The first version is by far the better. The second version adds nothing of value; all the information can readily be ascertained from the source code.

Some researchers have created specification languages, highly symbolic representations of a program's functions. The advantage claimed is that because such a specification language can be checked by computer for correctness and completeness, it contributes to the quality of the system. Another claimed advantage is that, ultimately, it will be possible to generate code from the specification, so that the error-prone process of programming can be eliminated altogether.

In most installations, specification languages are partly realized today: tools such as screen painters and report writers can be checked for correct syntax and can generate both control blocks and some executable code. However, specification languages cannot substitute for English-language descriptions of functions and data elements, whose purpose is to communicate an understanding about the design and implementation of a program from one human to another.

Programs versus Modules

Throughout the preceding, the word *program* was used. This use is appropriate for simple programs such as straightforward on-line transaction processing and the most frequent types of reports. Such programs can usually be completed within the two-week guideline. More complex programs have to be subdivided into smaller units of work, however. Each unit of work should stand on its own and should be capable of reaching a measurable milestone in the same length of time as one of the simpler programs. In other words, the unit of work must be capable of being compiled and tested independently of any other unit of work. Such a unit is generally called a module, and it is the basis of a practice called modular programming (the criteria for good modular design were described in Chapter 14).

A module is in general called by another module, which passes to it a number of parameters. The called module changes some of the data in these

Figure 18–12 **Contrasting Styles of Specifications**

There are 8 different credit check codes. Depending on the code, the logic for
checking creditworthiness is slightly different.

Code 1: This is the code which applies to wholesale customers with good credit
history. Each customer has a specific dollar limit which is specified on the
customer file. If the amount of what the customer owes to which is added the
value of the order being processed exceeds the limit, the order is refused.

Code 2: This code is for customers with poor payment history. The limit
specified on tyhe customer file will generally be smaller. However, instead of
using the total amount of what the customer owes, only that portion which is
aged more than 30 days is used. (The current order amount is added to this
balance before comparison).

Code 3: Similar to code 1 except that the limit is not founmd in the customer
record. Rather, the limit is found in a table (see TA00203) which gives the
limit for each category of customer: the category is found on the customer
file.

   . . . . .

2.1.3.7   If the customer-rating code is equal to 7, do credit-processing as
           outlined in paragraphs 2.1.4.g through 2.1.4.k.

2.1.3.8   If the customer-rating code is equal to 8, do credit-processing as
           outlined in paragraph 2.1.4.1.

2.1.3.9   If none of the above, perform program error processing as described
           in paragraph 2.9, with error message number 78 (see attached list of
           error messages). Then exit the execution of the program with a
           return code of 0016 (hex 0010).

2.1.3.10   Once the credit has been checked, test the order reject switch. If
           it is on, process the next order; if it is off, go to Section 3.

2.1.4   Detailed processing rules.

2.1.4.a.   Add the order total calculated in paragraph 1.2.3 to the current
           balance of the customer.

2.1.4.b.   Add the order total calculated in paragraph 1.2.3 to the 30-day-or-
           more balance of the customer.

2.1.4.c.   If the balance calculated in 2.1.4.a exceeds the credit limit of the
           customer, perform order reject processing as described in paragraph
           2.7 with error message 12. Add 1 to the control counter for number
           of orders rejected. Set the order-rejected switch and return.

           If the balance calculated does not exceed the credit-limit, then add
           one to the control counter for number of orders accepted.

2.1.4.d.   If the balance calculated in 2.1.4.b exceeds the credit limit of the
           customer, perform order reject processing as described in paragraph
           2.7 with error message 13. Add 1 to the control counter for number
           of orders rejected. Set the order-rejected switch and return.

           If the balance calculated does not exceed the credit-limit, then add
           one to the control counter for number of orders accepted.

parameters and passes control back to the calling module, often with a *return code*, which indicates whether the module successfully completed its function or, if not, the type of error encountered. During the execution, the called module may in turn call other modules, passing them parameters and receiving return codes (see Figure 18–13).

The description of program specifications applies equally to module specifications. From the programmer's standpoint, there is no difference between the two, except for some minor difficulties in testing (see Chapter 19).

A program that is made up of several modules requires an additional level of documentation, however. The main additional document is a module map, which shows the hierarchy of modules and calling patterns. This schematic is often a structure chart modified by penciling in module boundaries around the functions represented by the lines (Warnier) or boxes (Yourdon, Jackson, HIPO) of the chart (see Figure 18–14). The module map can be transformed into a chart that no longer shows the program structure, as in Figure 18–15. The rules for a module chart are slightly different from a structure chart; the module chart does not need to be strictly hierarchical. In fact, one of the arguments in favor of modular programming is that it is possible to write general-purpose or multipurpose modules, which may be called from any point in the program. Thus, the strict hierarchical rule that a child can have only one parent does not apply to modules.

Another addition to the documentation is the call interface descriptions. The parameters that each module is to receive and the completion codes that it can return must be documented. This documentation must be centralized and available to any programmer who wishes write a program that will call the module. (It is very similar to a file/record description on a data dictionary. Moreover, it serves the same purpose; and changes to a call interface have the same sort of multiprogram impact as changes to a file or data base design.)

STRUCTURED WALK-THROUGHS

In addition to quality control practices such as standards and proper supervision, structured walk-throughs are believed to have a major impact on quality in programming. A structured walk-through is a peer review of any activity—programming, design, requirements analysis, or other—to pinpoint errors, weaknesses, and omissions while they are still easy to correct.

This section will deal with structured walk-throughs during programming and unit testing. This is the area where the practice first emerged in the 1970s, as part of the "structured revolution."

Participants

A walk-through is performed by one or more peers of the author of the product to be reviewed. For a program, the peers are programmers; normally, they should be at least as experienced as the author, but they should not be in the author's direct chain of command.

Figure 18–13 **Graphical Representation of Modular Structure**

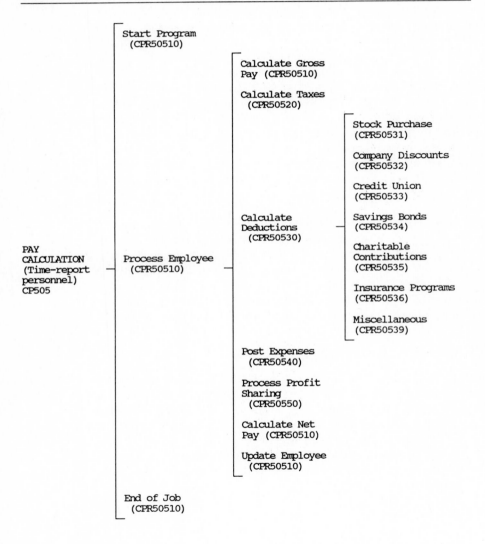

PAYROLL   T213
PERSONNEL   CPR505
            PROGRAM/MODULE CHART - PAY CALCULATION

PREPARED BY: BRUCE BAUER   DATE: 27FEB89   VERSION: 1   PAGE 1
APPROVED BY: JOE DAVIS   DATE: 05MAR89   STATUS :   OF 1

                    Start Program
                    (CPR50510)

                                    Calculate Gross
                                    Pay (CPR50510)

                                    Calculate Taxes
                                    (CPR50520)
                                                        Stock Purchase
                                                        (CPR50531)

                                                        Company Discounts
                                                        (CPR50532)

                                                        Credit Union
                                                        (CPR50533)

                                    Calculate   Savings Bonds
                                    Deductions   (CPR50534)
                                    (CPR50530)
                                                        Charitable
PAY   Contributions
CALCULATION   Process Employee   (CPR50535)
(Time-report   (CPR50510)
personnel)   Insurance Programs
CP505   (CPR50536)

                                                        Miscellaneous
                                                        (CPR50539)

                                    Post Expenses
                                    (CPR50540)

                                    Process Profit
                                    Sharing
                                    (CPR50550)

                                    Calculate Net
                                    Pay (CPR50510)

                                    Update Employee
                                    (CPR50510)

                    End of Job
                    (CPR50510)

Figure 18–14 **Alternative Graphical Representation of Modular Structure**

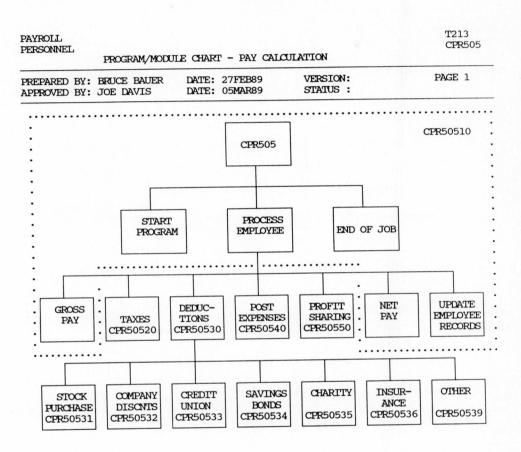

Figure 18–15 **Walk-through Control Sheet**

```
   _____                SUBURBAN PUMPS              A455
   _____              WALK-THROUGH CONTROL SHEET    _____
 ┌─────────────────────────────────────────────────────────────────────┐
 │ PREPARED BY: _____  DATE: _____  VERSION:     PAGE 1         │
 │ APPROVED BY:               DATE: _____  STATUS :                    │
 └─────────────────────────────────────────────────────────────────────┘
```

Coordinator's checklist:

☐   1.   Confirm with author that material is ready and stable

☐   2.   Issue invitations, assign responsibilities, distribute materials

      Date: _____   Time: _____   Duration: _____

      Place: _____

Responsibilities	Participants	Can attend?	Received materials?
_____	_____	_____	_____
_____	_____	_____	_____
_____	_____	_____	_____
_____	_____	_____	_____

Agenda:

☐   1.   All participants to follow the set of rules (see A552)

☐   2.   New project: first walkthrough

☐   Old project: item-by-item checkoff of previous point sheet

☐   3.   Creation of new point sheet

☐   4.   Group decision to be taken

☐   5.   Forward copy of this form to management after completion

Decision: ☐ Accept as is   ☐ Revise   ☐ Revise and redo walkthrough

Some reviewers may play specific roles, reviewing the program from different vantage points. One role is that of standards enforcer, who has responsibility for pointing out areas where standards are not being followed. (Remember, however, that a standard is the way that something should be done unless there are valid reasons to do otherwise—standards are not absolutes.) Another role is that of future maintainer, played by a programmer adopting the viewpoint of a person who will maintain the program.

The customer should also be represented. In programming activities, the customer is typically the analyst; in technical design, the customer can be the functional analyst; in functional design and requirements analysis, the customer is a representative of the users. Often, in technical design, DP operations are represented as well.

The author of the product to be reviewed participates by presenting the product to the reviewers and by making sure all the comments are understood.

One of the participants is designated to take notes and produce a detailed list of points after the walk-through. This role is very time-consuming and probably precludes any actual review work during the meeting. This role should therefore rotate among reviewers from walk-through to walk-through.

Finally, the meeting leader's role is among the most important. This role is similar to that of the leader of a Joint Application Design session (see Chapter 8). The meeting leader should be the most highly qualified and respected of the participants but should not be in their direct line of hierarchy. His or her role is to introduce the meeting, keep it on track, and make sure that it is followed up.

Preparation of the Walk-through

The walk-through meeting needs preparation: the participants and their roles must be identified; the meeting must be scheduled; materials must be distributed in time to be reviewed before the meeting.

Normally, the programming supervisor is responsible for identifying the participants. Some care must be taken to distribute the roles evenhandedly so that no one has the feeling of doing too much or too little, or of being saddled with the thankless job too often.

The meeting is fairly easy to schedule because the participants usually have few schedule constraints and because the meeting is short. Ideally, a walk-through takes less than an hour; it should never exceed 90 minutes. The meeting should be scheduled with the first clean compile and before unit tests have proceeded too far. A clean compile is of great help to the reviewers because it provides neat, legible documentation, including cross-references. If testing has proceeded too far along and if the review reveals a need for heavy modifications, all the tests will have to be redone.

Before the meeting, each reviewer should receive all the materials required: a copy of the program specification, a compilation listing, and any other materials that help explain the context of the program. The author is responsible for packaging the product to be reviewed. As the walk-through should take no more than an hour or so, the amount of materials to be reviewed is strictly limited. A guideline is that about 100 lines of code can be reviewed in a single meeting. In an installation that has strong standards, a somewhat higher number of lines of code can be reviewed. If more than the allowed quantity of code is to be reviewed, the programmer may have to divide the program into separate parts, each of which stands relatively well on its own. (This is a desirable practice in any case: divide to conquer!)

Each participant should review the distributed materials before the meeting. Generally, preparation time of one hour is adequate for a one-hour walk-through. If a single participant comes unprepared, the others may feel that they are wasting precious time while the unprepared person is brought up to speed.

Conduct of the Meeting

The leader starts the meeting. If any participants are unfamiliar with the ground rules or need reinforcement, the leader explains how the review is conducted.

The author of the program then describes the product to be reviewed. For a program, the description progresses level by level, then line by line. Each control structure, such as a *dowhile-enddo* or an *if-then-else-endif*, is reviewed before the code inside it is tackled.

As the author walks through the code, the reviewers ask questions and make comments. This is the substantive part of the walk-through. It is important that the meeting leader make the reviewers speak out and keep the meeting from turning into a confrontation. Disagreements may occur, but it is critical to keep them on a nonemotional level.

For two reasons, the purpose of the walk-through should be error detection, not correction: first, the meeting must be kept short; second, the author's sense of ownership should not be challenged. If the author sees an immediate solution to the problem, it can be proposed to the group. Alternatively, the author may request that a reviewer outline an idea for a solution. If the discussion becomes too detailed, the meeting leader should stop the discussion and ask that the interested parties continue it after the meeting.

Follow-Up

The follow-up to a walk-through consists in documenting its results and implementing solutions to the problems identified during the meeting. The documentation is the primary responsibility of the meeting leader. It has two parts: first, evidence that the walk-through was conducted (see Figure 18–16) and second, a detailed list of points to be addressed based on the notes taken by the designated reviewer. These detailed notes are normally given only to the author, although in some installations, they are given to the other participants as well. It is usually not a good idea to send the notes to the programming supervisor or to anyone who has the responsibility of reviewing programmer performance. Structured walk-throughs should encourage the viewpoint that

Figure 18–16 **Sample Walk-through Point Sheet**

```
MARKETING                      SUBURBAN PUMPS                    A557
ORDER ENTRY                                                      OE550
                          WALKTHROUGH POINT SHEET

 ┌─────────────────────────────────────────────────────────────────────┐
 │ PREPARED BY:  J. WEBER       DATE:  27AUG88     VERSION:  1   PAGE 1  │
 │ APPROVED BY:                 DATE:              STATUS :  I           │
 └─────────────────────────────────────────────────────────────────────┘

CREDIT CHECKING MODULE


No.        Point                          Disposition            Review
---        ----------------------------   -------------------    ------

1.         Working-storage prefix is not
           standard.


2.         CASE statement without an "ALL
           OTHERS" part.


3.         Calculation of aged balance
           will be incorrect in leap
           years.

4.         Test data to be extended to
           test leap years.


5.         Unnecessary code in line 132-
           150.  Case of Credit Code = 7
           has been eliminated in line 45.

6.         If Credit Code is tested before
           Customer Category, program
           would be simpler (to maintain).


7.         Error in logic line 165:  NOT
           (A OR B) means NOT A AND NOT B.


Disposition to be reviewed in next walkthrough.
```

errors committed during development are normal, that a peer review is one of the best ways of detecting them, and that the programmer should be judged only by the end result.

The author of the program is naturally responsible for implementing solutions to all the problems found during the review. Evidence that all the problems are covered can be furnished to the initial reviewers in a subsequent review or in an annotated copy of the points discovered during the review. In any case, the programmer should keep a written log of the disposition of each of the points raised (see Figure 18–17).

THE ROLE OF THE PROGRAMMING SUPERVISOR

Because the programming effort is such a large part of the project, one of the most important roles of the programming supervisor is to identify problems early. Three types of problems tend to arise frequently:

- The programming team does not have the required resources: poor response times, infrequent turnaround on tests, inadequate technical assistance.

- A particular programmer does not perform well, through lack of training, personal characteristics, or incapacity.

- A particular programmer may perform well in isolation, but has a problem functioning in a team.

The programming supervisor is responsible for monitoring these problems. For the first one, lack of machine or technical assistance resources, the programming supervisor must first determine whether there is a real problem or whether the complaints of poor service cover some other, hidden phenomenon such as lack of training or poor organization.

The programming supervisor must negotiate agreements on the levels of service to be provided by the supplier of the resources—normally some other group in the IS department, but on occasion a service bureau or a consultant. This service level agreement should cover such items as on-line response times and system availability, compile and test turnaround with results accessible on-line, frequency of library maintenance, availability of disk data space, turnaround for printed output, and access to specialists when problems arise.

The performance objectives in this agreement should ideally be monitored continuously. In many cases, however, they are measured only when there is a complaint. Measuring often makes the cause of the complaint disappear—for instance, when programmers complain of long response times, they can usually be measured the next day and found to be quite acceptable. The problem is only partly psychological; many disturbances are transitory and disappear by themselves. The most consistent psychological factor is that one freak problem is taken to be systematic. A programmer who has to wait too long for a compilation twice in a row might be tempted to see the degradation as permanent. The next

Figure 18–17 **Disposition of Points Raised**

```
MARKETING                      SUBURBAN PUMPS                 A557
ORDER ENTRY                                                   OE550
                          WALKTHROUGH POINT SHEET

 PREPARED BY:  J. WEBER      DATE:  27AUG88     VERSION:  2    PAGE 1
 APPROVED BY:                DATE:              STATUS :  F
```

CREDIT CHECKING MODULE

No.	Point	Disposition	Review
1.	Working-storage prefix is not standard.	Pass. Too costly.	OK
2.	CASE statement without an "ALL OTHERS" part.	ALL OTHERS included.	OK
3.	Calculation of aged balance will be incorrect in leap years.	On investigation, old formula proved correct (see test).	OK
4.	Test data to be extended to test leap years.	Included.	OK
5.	Unnecessary code in line 132-150. Case of Credit Code = 7 has been eliminated in line 45.	Deleted.	OK
6.	If Credit Code is tested before Customer Category, program would be simpler (to maintain).	Pass. Too costly. Additional comments inserted	OK
7.	Error in logic line 165: NOT (A OR B) means NOT A AND NOT B.	Pass. Error was in specification (analyst has corrected).	OK

time a compile takes too long, the previous incident will reinforce that impression, even if turnaround has been consistently good for several days. Regular monitoring and publication of the results help prevent such exaggerations.

When a programmer fails to perform as expected, the problem is more difficult to resolve. The programming supervisor must be a good people manager to handle all the problems that can occur.

Sometimes, the problem can be easy to solve. If a programmer repeats the same mistake, the problem may simply be a lack of training.

More difficult is the case of a programmer with personal or family difficulties. Some people are unable to perform well under pressure when this happens; others take refuge in their jobs and use them as an outlet for the pressure they feel, thus being even better than usual. Many large corporations have a counseling service for employees with problems; the programming supervisor should become familiar enough with these services and with some practical examples of situations where the service has helped to be able to direct programmers who need assistance to the appropriate counselor.

Summary

Programming management does not differ significantly from other aspects of project management. A variation is often introduced by the role of the programming supervisor, who performs part of the programming management (usually the assignment of the work and the supervision of its execution, but not the planning and the evaluation).

The programming supervisor may be attached to a project full time; this is the form of organization that causes the fewest problems. A programming supervisor who splits his or her time between several projects runs the danger of being viewed as having conflicting loyalties. Having no programming supervisor and having programmers report directly to the analysts on the project team is unsatisfactory because it endangers the long-term prospects of the programmers. Chief programmer teams, introduced in the 1970s, have not tended to solve these problems in commercial installations.

Programming management relies on dividing the work into units that can be planned, assigned, executed, and followed up individually. These units should take no longer than about two weeks, so that programmers do not work too long without measurable milestones of progress.

Throughout this chapter, the word *program* is often used when the more correct technical term should perhaps be *module*. A module is a portion of a program that is developed, compiled, and unit tested as a single unit of work. Several modules that make calls to each other, passing parameters and results, usually make up a program. In this way, a large program that would take too long to write can be divided into manageable pieces that obey the rule of two-week milestones. Whatever applies to programs in the chapter also applies to modules.

The programmer works from a program specification, which includes descriptions of the context of a program, its interfaces to files and to other programs, the functions to be executed, the test plan, the actual design and implementation of the program, the test results, and a checklist of milestones and review sign-offs. This specification is begun by the analyst and completed by the programmer. Where the frontier goes between the two is installation dependent.

Although formal specification languages are useful for eliminating some of the programming work, most program specifications are written in natural language. Thus, the programmer and, later, the maintainers can understand not only what is being done, but also why functions are being performed.

Once the program is written, but before it is tested, a structured walk-through of the program may take place. A structured walk-through is a review of the program by a number of the programmer's peers, under the leadership of a meeting leader who plays the role of facilitator and sees that the rules are followed. A structured walk-through is similar to a joint application design session, but it is much shorter, ideally only an hour. It is therefore much easier to organize and conduct.

During the session, the reviewee explains the work to the group, which in turn asks questions and points out errors. Some reviewers can be designated to play specialized roles, reviewing the work from a specific vantage point such as the enforcement of standards and the ease of later maintenance. The focal point of the review is to identify problems, not necessarily to solve them on the spot.

During the session, notes are taken on the problems encountered and on the comments made, so that the author of the product can later follow up and implement solutions to all the points raised.

Throughout the programming phase of a project, the programming supervisor is responsible for solving any problems that may arise on the programming team, such as insufficient technical resources, the failure of programmers to perform adequately, and behavior that is detrimental to the team effort.

Selected Readings

Brooks, F. *The Mythical Man-Month*. Reading, Massachusetts: Addison-Wesley, 1975.

This book has become a classic on project management. Brooks managed the creation of IBM's Operating System (OS/360), which required a thousand work-years of effort, in the 1960s. This book describes the errors that he learnt from.

Weinberg, G. *The Psychology of Computer Programming*. New York: Van Nostrand Reinhold, 1971.

Weinberg's book is one of the earliest works on the nontechnical aspects of programming. This book has been extremely influential in promoting the thought that programmers do not work in a social vacuum (although they.

might want to). It coined the term egoless programming. *Although some of the examples are somewhat dated, the principles and the practical advice contained in this book are remarkably valid almost 20 years later.*

Yourdon, E. *Structured Walkthroughs*, 2d ed. Englewood Cliffs, New Jersey: Prentice-Hall, 1979.

This well-written and consistently useful book is the main reference on structured walk-throughs by one of the best-known authors on structured techniques in systems development.

Review Questions

1. Why has the chief programmer concept been difficult to put into practice in most companies?

2. What is the purpose of a structured walk-through?

3. From a programming management standpoint, what is the value of restricting the size of programming assignments to about two weeks?

4. Why must the programming supervisor be careful to direct programming specifications to the correct level for each programmer?

5. What are the usual contents of a complete set of program specifications?

6. In complex programs, what are the guidelines for defining a module?

7. What is the right time to schedule a structured walk-through? Why?

8. What are the key roles played by the various participants in a structured walk-through?

9. What three problems are identified most frequently in the programming phase of a project?

Discussion Questions

1. Discuss the pros and cons of alternative forms of organizing teams for the programming phase of a project.

2. Given the numerous problems that could confront a programming supervisor, why is it said that his or her main difficulty is in assuring the work gets done on time?

3. Discuss the pros and cons of using a specification language.

4. Discuss the pros and cons of giving the notes from a structured walk-through only to the author of the program. Could there not be, for example, some training value to other programmers if the results of the walk-through were shared with them as well?

Mini-Case

Walton Products. Walton Products is in the programming phase of a new order entry system to be installed in each one of its 70 U.S. and Canadian branch offices. Carl Martin, the programming supervisor on the project, is determined not only to bring the project in on time and within budget, but also to deliver code of a higher quality than Walton Products had ever seen before. To help him accomplish these objectives, he decided to introduce the practice of conducting structured walk-throughs of each program. Carl had heard a speaker discuss structured walk-throughs at last month's DPMA meeting, but had no other experience in employing the technique.

He told Marge Krawlik that her program would be the guinea pig for this new technique and asked her to be ready to discuss it with the rest of the programming team on the next Friday. Carl then sent the following memo to the other six programmers on the team:

> I would like each of you to plan to attend a structured walk-through of Marge's program this coming Friday. The meeting will be held beginning at 8:30 in the staff conference room and will continue until we are collectively satisfied that her work is of the highest quality obtainable. The success of the order entry system is critical to the future success of Walton and we must all work together to see that our product is the best that we can produce as a team.

Marge wondered why she had been singled out. She felt that Carl suspected that her work was not up to par but that he did not want to deal with the issue personally. Her worries were intensified when other members of the programming team jokingly commented that they could not wait until Friday when they would have a chance to go over her program with a fine-tooth comb.

Questions for Discussion

1. How successful is the walk-through on Friday likely to be?

2. How likely will members of the programming staff be to want to adopt structured walk-throughs as a shop standard?

3. What steps could Carl have taken to increase his chances of a successful meeting?

References

1. Brooks, F. *The Mythical Man-Month*. Reading, Massachusetts: Addison-Wesley, 1975.

Chapter 19

Testing

Chapter 19 first outlines the importance of proper testing practices. It then describes unit testing (the tests run by a programmer on a single program) and integration, system, and acceptance testing (the tests run on a collection of programs and procedures). The chapter concludes with a description of other, less frequently used methods to find errors in a system.

Learning Objectives

- Understand the different components of testing productivity: sharing test data, reusing test data for maintenance, testing with the objective of finding bugs, using a test plan and precalculating results, referencing the test to a specification, and using proper tools.

- Describe unit testing in terms of objectives and responsibility, planning the test cases and test cycles, preparing test data, and running and exploiting the test.

- Describe integration, system, and acceptance testing in terms of objectives and responsibility, planning the test cases and test cycles, preparing test data, and running and exploiting the test.

- Be aware of other methods for removing defects from programs, such as program proving and statistical testing.

THE IMPORTANCE OF TESTING

Proper testing practices are necessary to deliver a product that fulfills the user's requirements and runs without major incidents. Proper testing practices can also reduce the cost of the systems development project and contribute significantly to higher productivity.

Testing vies with coding for the most time-consuming activity in systems development. Often, unit testing is counted as part of coding, because they are done by the same person and are therefore difficult to distinguish. In that case,

BOX 19–1

Why Is Testing Necessary?

Early in the history of computing, it was realized that however much effort was put into the coding of a program, it would still malfunction on occasion. Testing became a major part of computer programming almost immediately.

Testing has been the main way of finding errors or defects in a system, so as to remove them before the system goes live. There are two basic causes for errors. First, if a requirement is considered as a problem and the program or system as its solution, the two do not have a common structure. The very languages in which the problem and the solution are expressed are totally dissimilar—from natural language to a series of binary bits. The number of transformations between one and the other leaves the door open to errors at every stage.

The second factor is the very large number of interacting system elements to keep track of: data elements, processing modules, interfaces, data structures, and program structures. No single human brain can manage the ensuing complexity; as a result, errors cannot be totally eliminated by simply thinking about the implementation or reviewing it.

coding is probably the most expensive part of the cycle. But if unit testing is included with other kinds of testing—integration, system, and acceptance tests—then testing is the most expensive and therefore has the most potential for cost reductions.

This potential is even higher because of the poor testing discipline that prevails today. The following are the main areas where testing productivity and quality could be improved in most installations:

- Sharing test data among team members.
- Reusing existing test data to test modifications during maintenance.
- Testing to find bugs rather than to prove that the program or system works.
- Testing from a test plan and precalculated results rather than from operational or randomly generated data.
- Testing against a documented specification.
- Using proper tools: test data generator, output file comparators, testing harness, symbolic debugger, static analysis tools, etc.

Some of these elements exist in most installations; in very few installations are they all present. Most of the emphasis tends to be on finding causes of errors once the errors are discovered (*debugging*) and altogether too little on planning the tests so that they will be exhaustive yet of manageable size. This emphasis is probably partly because debugging is much more fun than planning. Most IS professionals feel intense satisfaction when they understand some improbable concurrence of conditions that lead to an unexpected result. Of all the activities of the life cycle, debugging is the most like puzzle solving—both challenging and rewarding.

UNIT TESTING

Objectives and Responsibility

The objective of unit testing is to check that each individual unit of work—program or module—that makes up the system is a correct implementation of its specification. It is generally done entirely by the programmer, who plans the test, creates test data, executes the test, and evaluates the results. The programming supervisor and possibly the analyst will later review the programmer's work to verify that the testing of the program has been done properly.

The resources available to the programmer to perform this work consist of the programming specification and a testing environment with whatever tools are required to create test data files, run the test, print the results, and find bugs. In addition, the programmer may be able to use a common test data base (already loaded with test cases) and programs that have previously been written and tested.

Planning the Tests

When planning tests, most analysts and programmers tend to ignore the real objective of a test. The objective is not to check that something functions as planned. The objective is to find where the program does *not* function as planned. Many programmers declare their programs tested based on a small number of test cases, all within the normal range of data. But most program bugs arise when input data values are exceptional, when users take unexpected actions, or when combinations of conditions produce strange effects. In addition, performance and control requirements are part of the systems specification: they also need to be tested. To test that response time is acceptable, a useful technique is to run higher and higher volumes through the system, noting at what point performance becomes unacceptable.

As a result, it has been said that a test that does not uncover a problem is not a successful test. Therefore, the last test of a program or a system is always unsuccessful.

To start testing, the programmer uses the programming specification to create a test plan. The test plan usually contains a number of test cycles. For each test cycle, a number of test cases or conditions to be tested are created. For instance, for an order entry system, several different orders are created, each order being designed to test one or more conditions. One order might test that the logic works for single-line orders. Another order would be required to test multiple-line order logic using a single screen (no paging), while a third might have more lines than can fit on the screen to test the paging logic. For reasons of economy, many conditions may be tested in each test case. For instance, the one-line order might be for a residential customer and one of the multiple-line orders might be for a corporate customer. As many independent conditions as desired may be tested in a single test case (see Figure 19–1).

Each of the test cases is initially developed from the programming specification, and each condition is cross-referenced to the specification. Cross-referencing consists in annotating the specification with the case number and the condition number (see Figure 19–2). When all the different elements of the specification have been cross-referenced, the basic test plan is complete.

One verification remains to be made. The test plan should also be cross-referenced against the program itself to check that each branch of the code is exercised at least once. Traversing each branch is not so much to assure that all the instructions written get executed at least once as to ensure that the test plan does, indeed, cover all the conditions that can arise and that the analysis of the test plan against the specification was complete. If the analysis was complete, and there are still branches of the program that are not traversed during the tests, then those branches will logically never be traversed under any circumstances and can be suppressed from the program. This might be a sign that the programmer has misunderstood part of the specification.

Next, the test plan is finalized by grouping the test cases into test cycles. Test cycles are designed to get as much output as possible from each test run so that many errors can be found for each test shot. (Remember that the primary objective of testing is to find the errors in the program, not to check that the program runs correctly.) For a simple program or module, a single cycle may be enough, but generally, several are required. For instance, one of the conditions to be tested may include the absence of transactions: the program should run correctly even though it has nothing to do. This test must obviously be done in a separate run. Another frequent case to be tested arises when the program checks the input file control totals. At least two runs are necessary, one with a correct control total and one with an incorrect control total on the input file. On-line query programs have as many cycles as there are different transaction cases to be tested. A document must be prepared noting the composition of each cycle (see Figure 19–3).

Preparing Test Data

When the program to be tested is an on-line transaction taking input from the screen and writing output to a sequential file or querying an existing data base, the input test data preparation is fairly easy. The test cases in a cycle are documented on paper, and the programmer (or a clerical operator) uses them as a script for executing the test.

In most cases, however, the program requires input from one or more files (or data bases). Normally, these files do not exist, and the programs that create them as output are probably not yet completely written and tested. Therefore, the programmer must create files or relations on data bases that contain the

Figure 19–1 **Test Case Control Sheet**

```
MEDICAL RECORDS                GENERAL HOSPITAL                    T935
ADMISSIONS                                                        APR0100
                            TEST CASE CONTROL SHEET

 ┌───────────────────────────────────────────────────────────────────────┐
 │ PREPARED BY:  CRAIG MINDRUM  DATE:  27DEC92      VERSION:      PAGE 1   │
 │ APPROVED BY:                 DATE:               STATUS :              │
 └───────────────────────────────────────────────────────────────────────┘



DATA ELEMENT          TEST CASE 1          TEST CASE 2          TEST CASE 3

Patient name
Room number           1                    2                    2
Bed Number                                 11                   11 (error)
Patient Address
Patient City
Patient State
Patient Zip
Patient Phone
Patient Soc Sec
Division              01                   03                   07
Patient Birthday      Feb 22, 1899         March 1, 1899        March 29, 1999 (err)
Admitting Priority    A                    B                    C
Patient Sex           M                    F                    F
Smoker                Y                    N
Married               Y                    N                    Y
Occupation
Employer
Business Phone
Birthplace
Maiden Name           None                 None                 None (error)
Spouse Name           Jones                Jackson (error)      Jackson
Father Name
Mother Name
Religion

(Arbitrary values to be picked where not filled in)
```

Figure 19-2 **Annotated Program Specification**

MARKETING	SUBURBAN PUMPS	T235
ORDER ENTRY		OE12010
	PROGRAM DEFINITION - CREDIT CHECKING	

PREPARED BY:	FRANK GERMAIN	DATE:	01MAR89	VERSION:	1.T PAGE 3
APPROVED BY:		DATE:		STATUS :	

Test case

2.1.3.7   If the customer-rating code is equal to 7, do credit-   007
          processing as outlined in paragraphs 2.1.4.g through
          2.1.4.k.

2.1.3.8   If the customer-rating code is equal to 8, do credit-   008
          processing as outlined in paragraph 2.1.4.1.

2.1.3.9   If none of the above, perform program error processing as   199
          described in paragraph 2.9, with error message number 78
          (see attached list of error messages). Then exit the
          execution of the program with a return code of 0016 (hex
          0010).

2.1.3.10 Once the credit has been checked, test the order reject   All
          switch. If it is on, process the next order; if it is off,
          go to Section 3.

2.1.4   Detailed processing rules.

2.1.4.a. Add the order total calculated in paragraph 1.2.3 to the   001,101
          current balance of the customer.   102,104
                                                                      003
2.1.4.b. Add the order total calculated in paragraph 1.2.3 to the 30- 002,103
          day-or-more balance of the customer.

2.1.4.c. If the balance calculated in 2.1.4.a exceeds the credit   001
          limit of the customer, perform order reject processing as
          described in paragraph 2.7 with error message 12. Add 1 to
          the control counter for number of orders rejected. Set the
          order-rejected switch and return.

          If the balance calculated does not exceed the credit-limit, 101
          then add one to the control counter for number of orders   102
          accepted.

2.1.4.d. If the balance calculated in 2.1.4.b exceeds the credit   002
          limit of the customer, perform order reject processing as
          described in paragraph 2.7 with error message 13. Add 1 to
          the control counter for number of orders rejected. Set the
          order-rejected switch and return.

          If the balance calculated does not exceed the credit-limit, 103
          then add one to the control counter for number of orders
          accepted.

2.1.4.e. If the balance calculated in 2.1.4.a exceeds the credit   003
          limit of the customer category obtained by look-up of the
          customer category table of credit limits described in
          paragraph 1.3.2, perform order reject processing as
          described in paragraph 2.7 with error message 12. Add 1 to
          the control counter for number of orders rejected. Set the
          order-rejected switch and return.

          If the balance calculated does not exceed the credit-limit, 104

Figure 19–3 **Test Cycle Control Sheet**

```
MEDICAL RECORDS              GENERAL HOSPITAL                 T925
ADMISSIONS                                                    APR0100
                         TEST CYCLE CONTROL SHEET
┌─────────────────────────────────────────────────────────────────────┐
│ PREPARED BY:  CRAIG MINDRUM  DATE:  27DEC92    VERSION:     PAGE 1     │
│ APPROVED BY:                 DATE:             STATUS :                │
└─────────────────────────────────────────────────────────────────────┘
```

Cycle 6: Confirmation processing

Purpose: Test for proper processing and printing of patient admission
          confirmations.

No.	Condition	Test cases
A.	Proper printing break processing	001,002 003
	Only one confirmation should print for every patient admitted. Page breaks should occur properly.	
B.	Patient age calculation	001,002 003
	Correct patient age to be calculated from birth date.	
C.	Admission date and time generation	001,002,003
	Admission date and time generated from system timer. This requires that part of the test be run without the system date/time simulator.	
D.	Patient number generation	001,002,003 101,102,103 201,202
	Patient numbers are generated by the system on a consecutive number basis. This test requires shutting the system down and restarting it in the middle of the cycle twice: once cleanly and the other time in the middle of a transaction.	
E.	Proper admitting division classification	001,002,003
	The proper division, corresponding to the division code entered, will be printed on the confirmation.	
F.	Correct patient type processing	001,102
	The patient type of Inpatient or Outpatient will be printed correctly.	
G.	Proper report formatting	001,002,003
	The report will be formatted according to the report sample provided as D220.RPT0055.	

required conditions, using a a specialized program, called a test data loader. There are generic test data generators on the market, whose only purpose is to help programmers create test files (see Figure 19–4). Other solutions include using fourth-generation languages, application generators, or even regular programming languages to create a mini-application to load the required files (see Figure 19–5). In both cases, a specialized program takes a sequential file with alphanumeric characters only and transforms it into the required file or data base structure, with data in the format required by the program to be tested (for example, alphanumeric, binary, floating point, or decimal). In principle, every field on the test file to be created must be specified by the programmer on the input file. Some test data generators have features that can generate random values or calculate values (for instance, by generating transaction numbers that increase by one for every new record). These features may sometimes be useful for reducing the effort required to create complete test data.

In some cases, there may be a data base of shared test data that can be used. A test data base usually exists for system and acceptance test purposes. It may also be a copy of an operational data base for the system being replaced. In the latter case, the programmer may use this copy as the basis for creating a test data base or file. Normally, the data on a shared test data base need to be adapted to the test conditions for each individual program. The best procedure is to extract those test data from the shared test data base that are relevant, copy them to a temporary file, and modify them as required using a test data generator, an application generator, or some other utility (see Figure 19–6). The programmer always works on a copy, never on the original data.

In modular programming, the program may not have input and output files. Rather, it receives messages from the calling module and sends messages to subordinate modules. It is of course possible to postpone testing until the entire set of modules has been written, making up a program that has only external file I/O. Testing in this manner is generally counterproductive, both because of the waiting involved and because it is tantamount to doing integration testing at the same time as unit testing.

The solution to this problem is stub testing. Instead of waiting for the calling module to be available, the programmer can create a stub, a simple program that makes a call with the appropriate parameters to the program to be tested. These parameters can be hard-coded into the stub or read off a file prepared with a test data generator (see Figure 19–7). By the same token, stubs can simulate modules called by the program to be tested. A called stub posts updates to the parameters passed to it and returns control to the calling module without doing any actual productive work (see Figure 19–8).

Before executing any tests, a last activity must be completed: calculating the expected results of the tests. Every expected output for every test case in every test cycle must be calculated and documented *before* the test is run. This discipline is required because the human brain tends to anticipate positive results: when checking the result of a calculation, a programmer quite fre-

Figure 19–4   **Test Data Generation**

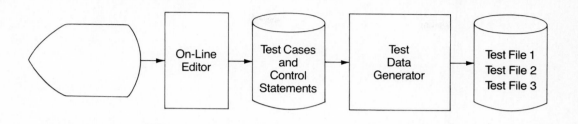

quently makes errors that make the result seem right. Also, precalculating results can allow this data to be loaded to a file and the comparison between actual and expected output can be mechanized with a file comparator, thus providing much greater accuracy.

Executing the Test

Executing a batch test is not a great problem. It is no different than submitting a compilation, except that more job control statements have to be prepared. (In good installations, much of this job control preparation is automated to relieve the programmers of the burden of being experts on job control.) With modular

Figure 19–5   **Loading Test Data with a 4GL**

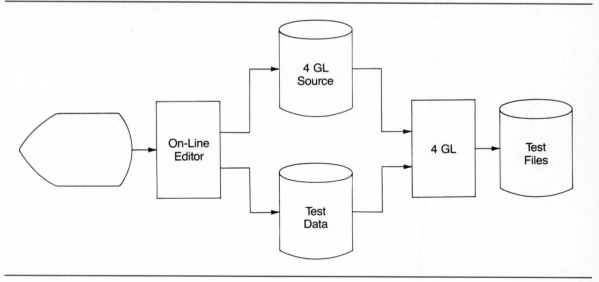

Figure 19–6　**Loading Test Data from a Shared Test Data Base**

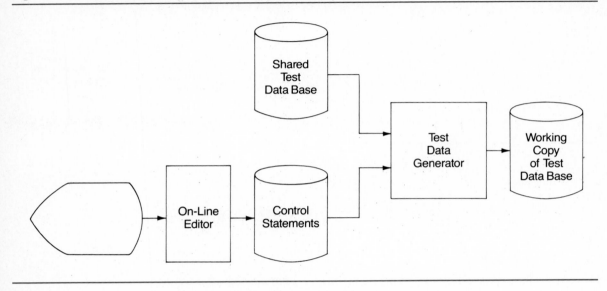

Figure 19–7　**Stub Testing: Calling Stub**

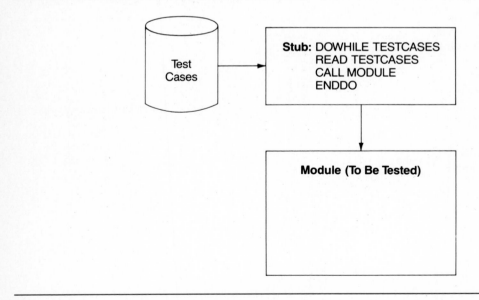

Figure 19–8 **Stub Testing: Called Stub**

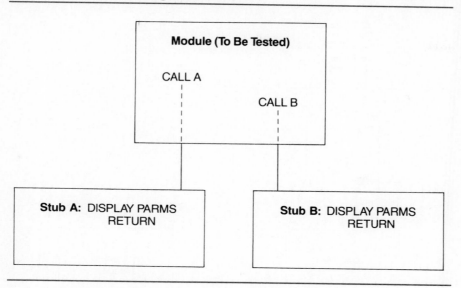

programming, the module itself as well as all the required stubs must also be linked together, requiring some additional knowledge of job control.

The test run is made up of a series of steps: loading the test data, executing the program, and printing the results (see Figure 19–9). Whether the test data is reloaded for each execution of the test is a compromise between execution time and storage space. However, if the test run modifies the input data in place or when the test data is wrong, there is no choice: the test data must be reloaded.

The problem is more difficult with on-line programs. On-line programs do not stand alone; rather, they are executed in the environment provided by an on-line monitor. Some on-line monitors have associated batch simulators. These make it possible to treat each test cycle as a batch process by simulating the on-line environment to the program. The program believes that it communicates with a screen; in reality, the screen images are intercepted by the simulator, which turns them into batch test files (see Figure 19–10). The advantage of this procedure is its repeatability.

Without a batch simulator, the test must be performed on-line, which is much more time consuming for the programmer. On-line testing usually requires a test version of the on-line monitor, so as to avoid any risk of interference with production work. Also, some monitors require that all the programs that are to be run be linked to the monitor before it is started up. This requirement implies a great deal of planning and discipline. Moreover, in most environments, the programmers share the on-line monitor. The environment in which the test is executed therefore has an element of randomness, making it extremely difficult to trace causes of some errors.

Figure 19–9 **Test Run**

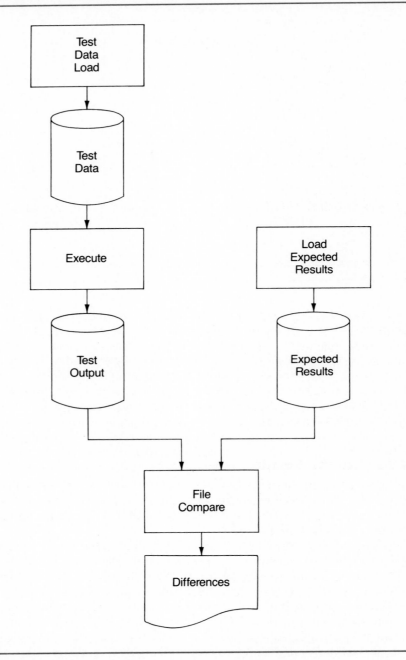

Figure 19–10 **Batch Terminal Simulator**

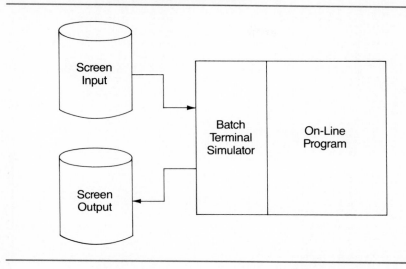

Another element of randomness is that the person who executes the test may do things in a slightly different sequence, committing different errors of data entry on different executions of the test cycle. This problem can be avoided by the use of a tool known as a transaction capture facility, which records every keystroke by an operator and reproduces the sequence later on.

Checking screen output against the expected results is more difficult than for output files, because screen contents are volatile. Unless the program writes a copy of the screen to a file, an automated comparator cannot be used.

Evaluating the Results

Test results are normally in the form of output files, reports, screens, or updated data on data bases. To be exploited by the programmer, these results must be printed out, made available for on-line browsing, or compared with the expected results and the differences printed out.

When the results are not as expected, other forms of output may be generated. The best known is perhaps the storage dump (see Figure 19–11), which presents an unformatted printout of the contents of memory when an execution is interrupted because of some serious problem—for instance, trying to perform a numerical operation on nonnumeric data. For many reasons, a dump is the least desirable result of a test run. First, it is difficult to use. Second, as it usually interrupts the execution of the test, subsequent test cases must wait until the next execution. Third, it is often the sign of a serious problem in the program.

Figure 19–11 **Sample Page of a Dump**

```
00037300  18A0D203  A028B78F  E0149240  18E09644  CAD5D250  COD6C0D5  D207CACD  61A51870  *.K.......NK..O.NK.. *
00037320  D203702C  C1301810  58F00010  9180F3D0  47E0B4D2  58F0F3D0  05EF47F0  B4EA0700  *K..A....O....3..K.03....O.. *
00037340  45F0B468  0037734C  00000000  C992D1C5  C6C6C0F2  0A0658D0  D0045880  B6D0181C  *.O.Y........IKJEFF02....K... *
00037360  41101000  0AA1FFF  58E0D00C  980CD014  07FE90EC  C084D203  6064B77F  58206010  *....... ..........K... *
00037380  60104740  B5165870  60585970  B6C44720  B5325970  B6BC4770  B5585020           *....... ..........K... *
000373A0  COC09240  COEDC239  COEDC0EC  D21EC0CD  B60458E0  COC850E0  COC0D203  C127B797  *....... .K...M..H...DK.A *
000373C0  45E0B5E0  12224780  B5DA5020  COC85800  60585900  B6C44720  B5765900  C127B797  *....... .K.....H....D...K.A *
000373E0  B5989240  COEDC240  4110C0C8  COE6C0E5  D217COCD  B70B58A0  COC850A0  4780B58C  *.......VK.W.VK........H...K.A *
00037400  45E0B5E0  4110C0C8  41000000  89000018  16100A3E  58706058  5970B68C  4780B5BC  *....D....O.K.A....P..K.A *
00037420  5970B6C4  47D0B5DA  50F0C0C0  D203C127  B7979240  CODFD246  COE0C0DF  D21CC0CD  *...D.....O...K.A....K.A.. *
00037440  B74B4560  B5E098EC  C08407FE  90ECC048  58A0601C  D73FA014  A014D203  A028C127  *...K..AK...AK..A...K.A..0 *
00037460  9654A014  D203A02C  C12CD203  A030C130  B7979240  C134D203  000374A0  000000  *....K.....AK....3...03....PATCH AREA . DSN* *
00037480  00109180  F3D047E0  B62858F0  F30005EF  47F0B63E  45F0B63C  000374A0  00000000  *....3...03...O...O...PATCH AREA . DSN* *
000374A0  C9D2D1C5  C6C6C0F2  0A0698EC  C04407FE  D7C1E3C3  C840C1D9  C5C14060  40C4E2D5  *IKJEFF02....K....PATCH AREA . DSN* *
000374C0  C5C3D7F0  F140F8F5  4BF2F4F2  B660B662  B664B666  B66CB66A  B670B672  000000  *ECP01 85.242.....PATCH AREA . * *
000374E0  B674B676  B678B67A  B67CB67E  B680B682  B684B686  B688B68A  B68CB68E  B690B692  *..........AFTER COMPARE.SWAP. R2. ZTCBPTRN* *
00037500  B694B69A  B69CB69E  B6A0B6A2  B6A4B6A6  B6A8B6AA  B6ACB6AE  B6B0B6B2  *........O PUTGET MESSAGE. R15. BEFORE DE* *
00037520  B6B4D200  C0CD7001  00000002  00000064  00000096  00C50110  00000140  *......TACH. ZTCBPTR . ENTER DSNECP01. R* *
00037540  C1C6E3C5  D4D7C1D9  C561E2E6  C1D76B40  D9F26B40  E9E3C3C2  D7E3D9D5  *....6..NO C INPUT. MXRPLEN. AFTER DET* *
00037560  D640D7E4  E3C7C5E3  40D4C5E2  E2C1C7C5  6B40D9F1  F57E40C2  C5C6D6D9  C540C4C5  *....ACH. R15.LEAVE DSNECP01TRYAGAINZ* *
00037580  E3C1C3C8  6B40E9E3  C3C2D7E3  D9407E40  D5D6D0C4  40C4E2D5  C5C3D7F0  F16B40D9  *....INPUT. CIB US 0050008009001000* *
000375A0  F67E40D5  D640C340  C9D5D7E4  E3D9D3C5  D7F0F1E3  D9E8C1C7  C1C9D5E9  *....llOT200DSNECP01.00.DSNEMSG 8* *
000375C0  C9D5D7E4  E340C3C9  C240E4E2  F0F0F5F0  F0F8F0F0  F9F0F0F0  F1F0F0F0  *....5.350.......A * *
000375E0  F1F1F0E3  F2F0F0C4  E2D5C5C3  D7F0F14B  F0F06B40  F0F8F0F0  F1F0F0F0  *....K........N......O * *
00037600  F54BF3F5  F0000090  00C00C5B0  4510B008  0AA1A8C1  50D0C004  9801D014  *....K......N.....K....N. * *
00037620  50C0D008  18DCD507  6190B1B4  4770B028  47F0B030  58206020  9240C050  *.......K....N......K....N. * *
00037640  D282C051  C050D73F  20142014  D2032028  60989654  20149604  20204130  *.K.......K.....O.....O * *
00037660  2021D203  202C6124  D2032030  6128D203  2034612C  D2032038  6130D503  *....K...........Q.......O * *
00037680  2028B1BC  4770B088  94EF2014  B1C04770  B0A294EF  0CF09480  181C4110  *....PATCH AREA .......Q.H * *
000376A0  202C9680  202C9680  B0B4D503  D5032028  B1C04770  94EF2014  9680202C  *....K....0......K.Q.H * *
000376C0  181258F0  00109180  F3D047E0  47F0B0E2  45F0B0E0  00037704  00037704  *....O......0.....0...0 * *
000376E0  00005021  000042E1  F30047E0  B1405820  6090D213  000C58F1  100043E1  *....O......03......O.Q * *
00037700  D203C0F0  B1DC4130  C0504110  COF09480  100055031  0000A0A  1FFFF8E0  *....K...........Q......0 * *
00037720  F0305058  58E01008  C0F09480  101C4110  100009630  10000A0A  1FFFF8E0  *....0........0......N. * *
00037740  00005021  000042E1  D7C1E3C3  C840C1D9  C5C14060  40C4E2D5  C5D4E2C7  40F8F5  *....PATCH AREA . DSNEMSG 85* *
00037760  D7C1E3C3  C840C1D9  181C4110  B1C04770  B0A294EF  1FFFF8F5  04F04F8F5  *....350...........PATCH AREA . DSNEMSG 85* *
00037780  D00C980C  D01407FE  C6C6C0F2  C5C14060  40C4E2D5  C594E2C7  B19B192  *....DSNECP00101010401310..T100.....DSNE* *
000377A0  4BF3F5F0  B178B17A  B18CB18E  B188B18A  B18CB18E  B19B192  *....T101 STUB .. ENTEREDT200 * *
000377C0  B194B196  B198B19A  B1A4B1A6  B1A8B1AA  B1A00000  *....DSNET20I * *
000377E0  C4E2D5C5  C3D7F0F0  F1F3F1F0  F4F0F1F0  F1400000  00014000  *....0040..DSNE004E PROBABLE* *
00037800  00000000  40404040  40404040  40404040  00250030F  C4E2D5C5  *.......SUBSYSTEM ERROR DETECTED IN CSE* *
00037820  E3C5D5C5  E4E24000  C5C3E3C5  C440C9D5  40C3E2C5  C4F0F4C5  *....CT. SUBSYSTEM FUNCTION RE* *
00037840  C9C2E8E8  15680E02  E4C2E2E8  E2E3C5D4  C3E3C9D6  6B40D9C5  *....TCODE. REASON CODE 00500061.* *
00037860  C5400000  C5400000  F0F5C140  E4E3C5D4  E2E3C140  D5406DC2  *....DSNE005A EXECUTION IS INTERRU* *
00037880  E2E3C5D4  C3E3C9D6  40C9E240  C9D5E3C5  D9D9E440  40F0F5C5  *....PTED. ENTER C TO CANCEL. OR A * *
000378A0  D5C94006  E3C8C5D9  40D9C5D7  D3E840E3  D640D9C5  E2E4D4C5  *....NY OTHER REPLY TO RESUME THE * *
000378C0  40E2E4C2  C3D6D4D4  C1D5C44B  F0F0F6F1  40C3E8C9  D3D30000  *....SUBCOMMAND.0061..DSNE006A * *
000378E0  40E6C9D3  D340E3C5  D9D4C9D5  C1E3C540  E3C8C540  E2E4C240  *....C WILL TERMINATE THE SUBCOMMAND* *
00037900  40E6C9E3  C8404005  E4E3C3D6  D4D4C9E3  E3C5C440  C3C8C1D5  *....WITH UNCOMMITTED CHANGES BACKED* *
00037920  D5C5C440  E4D7404F  E4E3F0F0  F8F04BC4  E2D5C540  F0F0F8C9  *....UP.OUT080.DSNE008I REPLY W* *
00037940  C1E24060  F6B40C3C5  40E4E3C3  D6D4D740  D9C5E2E4  D4C5C440  *....AS . DSNE009I REPLY WAS C. EXECUT* *
```

The dump used to be the main tool of debugging; fortunately, it is increasingly replaced by more powerful tools. One series of such tools is implemented by the compiler, which, as an option, may be able to print out the names of the routines as they are executed together with the contents of critical data areas. This feature is called a trace option. If the compiler does not have one, the programmer can fairly easily introduce trace points to display messages or selected data. These trace points must be removed before the final test of the program.

Another compiler option is to print a cross-reference between data areas and program code, indicating which parts of a program use a given data element or record, thereby potentially modifying it. The cross-reference is very useful for forming hypotheses about why a data area contains unexpected values (see Figure 19–12).

Even more sophisticated is the tool known as a symbolic debugger, which enables a program to be executed on-line, with a window on the terminal reserved for programmer interaction. The programmer may cause the program to execute in step mode, one instruction at a time, inspecting the contents of data areas and the instructions affecting them as the test is proceeding. The programmer may also modify erroneous data areas (and in some cases, program instructions) to enable the rest of the program to execute.

When a discrepancy between the test result and the expected result is found, the program or possibly the test data is corrected and the test cycle is repeated until all the results are correct. To aid in controlling this process, the test plan is annotated with the results from each execution of each cycle, together with the actions taken (see Figure 19–13).

After the final test, a walk-through or a review by the programming supervisor or the analyst checks the completeness and the accuracy of the tests. At this point, the unit test data should be "frozen" and kept until the program needs modification, when it may serve as the basis for regression testing— testing not only that a modification works, but also that what has not been modified continues to work. Because additional bugs are likely to be discovered during integration, system, and acceptance testing, the unit test data will probably be used very soon after the unit test is completed.

Test walk-throughs are organized very much like programming walk-throughs, as described in Chapter 18. A test walk-through is organized at the completion of the testing plan, at the completion of testing, or both.

INTEGRATION, SYSTEM, AND ACCEPTANCE TESTING

Integration, system, and acceptance testing have objectives similar to unit testing; they all seek to demonstrate that a given specification—technical design, functional design, or user requirements—is met by the implementation of the system. They are all quite different from unit testing, however, in that they are generally conducted by separate testing teams. Both technical and functional analysts may participate, but tests are best conducted by people who have not

Figure 19-12 **Sample Cross-Reference Listing**

AN "M" PRECEDING A DATA-NAME REFERENCE INDICATES THAT THE DATA-NAME IS MODIFIED BY THIS REFERENCE.

DEFINED	CROSS-REFERENCE OF DATA NAMES	REFERENCES
3031	DB2-INDEX-CONTAINS-ELEMENTS	
206	DB2-TABLE-NAME	
207	DB2-TABLE-TYPE	
409	DC-DATE-CONVERT-AREA . . .	3635
420	DC-ERROR-MESSAGE	
411	DC-GREGORIAN-DATE-RETURNED	
414	DC-GREGORIAN-DAY	3638
413	DC-GREGORIAN-MONTH . . .	3637
412	DC-GREGORIAN-YEAR. . . .	3636
417	DC-JULIAN-DATE-NOT-NUMERIC	
410	DC-JULIAN-DATE-SENT. . .	M3634
416	DC-JULIAN-DATE-VALID	
419	DC-JULIAN-DAYS-EQUAL-ZERO	
415	DC-RETURN-CODES	
418	DC-TOO-MANY-JULIAN-DAYS	
155	DCLDRQA3333.	M3625
80	DD-ENT-TYPE-ID	3180 3215 3240 3265 3290 3315 3340 3365
83	DD-SEARCH-ARG-1.	3180 3215 3240 3265 3290 3315 3340 3365
84	DD-SEARCH-ARG-2.	3180 3215 3240 3265 3290 3315 3340 3365
85	DD-SEARCH-ARG-3.	3180 3215 3240 3265 3290 3315 3340 3365
86	DD-SEARCH-ARG-4.	3180 3215 3240 3265 3290 3315 3340 3365
87	DD-SEARCH-ARG-5.	3180 3215 3240 3265 3290 3315 3340 3365
459	DDEA-ALREADY-EXISTS. . .	M4619 M4802
450	DDEA-CHILD-ID-REQUIRED .	M4956
436	DDEA-DD-EXPLANATION-ANALYSIS	M4989
438	DDEA-DD-RETURN-CODE. . .	M3625 M4796 5970
460	DDEA-END-OF-ENTRIES. . .	M4404 M4420 M4471
453	DDEA-ENT-AND-MODEL-ID-REQ.	M4713
455	DDEA-ENT-ID-OR-DESC-REQ	
448	DDEA-ENT-ID-REQUIRED	
458	DDEA-ENT-NOT-FOUND . . .	M4011 M4039 M4518 4795 M4848 M4872 M4893 M5241 M5293 M5345 M5579 M5662
446	DDEA-INVALID-CHILD-ID. .	M4266 M4454 M4600 M4949
443	DDEA-INVALID-ENT-ID	
442	DDEA-INVALID-FUNCTION. .	M3971
444	DDEA-INVALID-MODEL-ID. .	M4966
445	DDEA-INVALID-PARENT-ID .	M4015 M4043 M4047 M4183 M4338 M4596 M4763 M4931
461	DDEA-LANGUAGE-NOT-PASSED	M3600
447	DDEA-MODEL-DOES-NOT-EXIST	M4759
451	DDEA-MODEL-ID-REQUIRED .	M4974
457	DDEA-NOT-AUTH.	M4062 M4067 M4076 M4284 M4289 M4487 M4514 M4615 M4755 M4844 M4868 M4889 M4913
456	DDEA-NUM-REC-REQ-ZERO. .	M3589 M4604
452	DDEA-PAR-AND-CH-ID-REQ .	M4019
454	DDEA-PAR-OR-CH-ID-REQ. .	M3595 M4159 M4315 M4823
449	DDEA-PARENT-ID-REQUIRED.	M4939
462	DDEA-PARENTS-EXIST	
441	DDEA-SQL-COMMAND-TIMEOUT	
439	DDEA-SQL-ERROR	
463	DDEA-TABLE-ROW-TOO-LONG	
495	DDID-INT-ID	
493	DDID-INT-ID-ABSTIME	
485	DDID-INT-ID-BATCH	
487	DDID-INT-ID-BATCH-SEQ-NOS. .	491
472	DDID-INT-ID-DATA	M3625
473	DDID-INT-ID-DAY.	474

Figure 19–13 **Testing Log**

```
MEDICAL RECORDS                GENERAL HOSPITAL                    T940
ADMISSIONS                                                         APR0100
                                   TEST LOG
PREPARED BY:  CRAIG MINDRUM  DATE:  27DEC92       VERSION:          PAGE 1
APPROVED BY:  HARRY ENDERBY  DATE:  27NOV93       STATUS : F
```

CYCLE NO	DESCRIPTION	MILESTONES: CYCLE COND DEFINED	TEST DATA PREPARED	EXPECTED RESULTS PREPARED	RESULTS: TEST 1	TEST 2	TEST 3	TEST 4
1	Load Initial Patient Number	04SEP93	20SEP93	22SEP93	ABEND	EOJ, no report	OK (24OCT93)	
2	Inpatient Processing	04SEP93	20SEP93	22SEP93	ABEND	processed invalid patient	OK (27OCT93)	
3	Outpatient Processing	04SEP93	26SEP93	28SEP93	data format error	ABEND	accepted invalid division	
4	Admission Update	04SEP93	26SEP93	28SEP93	conversation control problem	slow response time	OK (26OCT93)	OK (01NOV93)
5	Daily Admission Extract	05SEP93	26SEP93	28SEP93	OK (17OCT93)			
6	Confirmation Processing	05SEP93	02OCT93	17OCT93	ABEND	invalid date processing	report format errors	OK (17NOV93)
7	Periodic Reporting	05SEP93	02OCT93	17OCT93	some reports not generated	OK (06NOV93)		
8	On-Line Inquiry Processing	06SEP93	02OCT93	21OCT93	slow response time	OK (08NOV93)		
9	On-Line Update Processing	08SEP93	07OCT93	23OCT93	slow response time	invalid ID allowed to update	ABEND	OK (03DEC93)
10	Management Reporting	09SEP93	07OCT93	23OCT93	EOJ, no reports	incorrect math	OK (22NOV93)	

been too closely involved with design and implementation decisions. This precaution is less imperative for integration testing than for acceptance testing.

Definitions

integration testing

Integration testing consists in testing that programs and modules communicate with each other in accordance with the technical design specifications developed in the design phase. This means that calling and called modules agree on the contents of the messages that are passed back and forth and that output files from one program can actually be used as input files to the next. The integration is gradual. The test team starts with one module to which it adds a few other modules, then some more, increasing the scope gradually until the entire system has been put together. On small, relatively simple systems, integration testing can be conducted as part of the system test.

system testing

System testing exercises not only the computer system itself but also the manual procedures, restart and recovery, and human-machine interfaces, which must all operate according to the functional specifications. The basis for the system test data is selected live data that is adapted and extended to make it as complete as possible. The objective is not to generate large volumes but to have representative samples. Users must be involved in the system test.

acceptance testing

Acceptance testing is the final hurdle before the users declare the system ready to go. For small, simple systems, this may occur at the end of system testing. On larger systems, a separate acceptance test with user-prepared test data and realistic volumes is conducted. One of the most popular ways of conducting acceptance testing has been parallel testing: running the old and the new system at the same time and checking that the results are the same. Parallel testing is becoming less popular. Running in parallel is becoming more and more expensive as systems grow in size. Comparing the outputs of the old and the new system is also becoming increasingly difficult, because many modern systems implement changes in the business process and create new information.

In other cases, acceptance testing may simply be the first few weeks of operation, during which the project team is on call and during which a fallback to the old system may still be possible. In this case, user acceptance frees the project team for other duties and gives final production status to the new system.

Planning the Tests

Planning integration, system, and acceptance testing starts earlier than the planning for unit testing. The strategy for each, and indeed whether they are separate tests or just separate objectives of the same test, is determined in the installation planning segment at the end of the design phase.

The approach to detailed planning is similar to that described for unit testing. Test cases are identified based on the specification being tested against and cross-referenced to it. Test cases and cycles are determined based on the functions of the system and the natural cycles of the business. There is likely to be a greater number of cycles in system testing than in unit testing, however. A typical financial accounting and control system might require as many as 20 or 30 system test cycles. Some of the functional requirements that have to be tested in separate runs are file loading; budget preparation; daily posting; monthly, quarterly, and yearly closing, each with a preliminary and a final run; error corrections; and restart and recovery.

Preparing Test Data

The volume of test data increases with each subsequent testing cycle. One imperative of integration and system testing is to keep the data as low in volume as possible, while still remaining complete. Keeping the volume low reduces the time required for preparing expected results and checking the actual output.

The system test data should be prepared in such a way that it can be saved and can serve as regression test data for successive versions of the system in maintenance. To serve in regression testing, the test data must be complete; it must also be documented so that future maintainers understand the purpose of each test case. (One frequently used technique is to include a description of the case in text areas of the data records. For instance, instead of putting "John Smith" in the name field of a customer record, one might put "Residential customer with $250 credit limit.")

Acceptance tests require higher data volumes than system tests because one of the objectives is to stress test the system, i.e., to evaluate whether it meets volume requirements. If parallel testing is adopted, the normal daily volumes will be encountered. It may then be necessary to add artificially created transactions to test peaks. For instance, the New York Stock Exchange may want to test a future system based on the volume of transactions experienced on October 19, 1987, rather than on a run-of-the-mill day. Artificially high volumes can be created using random test data generators or just plain duplication, as the objective of this test is not to evaluate the functional output; rather, the expected result that serves as the yardstick of a successful test is response time or throughput.

For other integration, system, and acceptance tests, files with expected results must still be prepared before executing the test. Using live data here has the advantage of possibly decreasing the time required to create the expected results files. It must be emphasized again and again that live data alone cannot be expected to constitute complete coverage of all the test cases.

Executing the Tests

The greatest difficulty in executing integration, system, and acceptance tests comes from the large volumes of on-line transactions, which require human resources, terminals, and computer power to be available in large quantities. The problems with unpredictability of the environment and nonrepeatability of the exact sequence of steps continue to exist. For large-scale on-line systems, a batch terminal simulator facility is extremely useful.

The testing cannot be entirely based on simulators, however. Both the reaction of users to terminal dialog and the behavior of the communications network (including human operations, troubleshooting, etc.) must be addressed before acceptance testing is over.

Evaluating the Results

In general, the same comments apply as for unit testing. The role of walk-throughs of integration testing and especially system testing, both plans and results, is even more important than for unit testing.

New questions arise in connection with program changes made necessary by problems found during integration or system testing. These changes must be analyzed and controlled at least as rigorously as for maintenance. When a change is made, each modified program must be unit tested afresh. In fact, as the error is probably in the specification, the test plan must usually be revised. When the program is unit tested, the integration or system tests must be redone. There are two approaches: one is to run all the test cycles again (time consuming but reassuring); the other is to rerun only those cycles that are predicted to be affected (less safe, but more economical). No one approach is superior; in fact, the best is probably to make the decision every time the case arises, based on an assessment of the actual costs and risks involved (see Figure 19–14).

Normally, the question of debugging tools arises much less in integration, system, and acceptance testing than in unit testing. Testing in later phases is not designed to debug programs; abnormal results such as memory dumps needing advanced program tracing or on-line debugging should not arise. Most of the diagnostics required can be performed by looking at printed output, possibly going so far as to browse a file or data base with an on-line query facility.

There is, however, a dearth of tools to deal with the great administrative complexity of the execution of the test cycles and the modifications made necessary by bugs. The best that can be done today in most environments is probably a mix of manual bookkeeping and PC-based tools such as spreadsheets. Even though it is time consuming to prepare expected results and to keep scrupulous track of all the test runs, omitting these steps is likely to be even more time consuming.

OTHER DEBUGGING TECHNIQUES

Although testing and walk-throughs are the most common techniques for removing defects from systems, other techniques exist. The two most important are static program analysis and statistical testing. Two others are described in Box 19–2.

Static program analysis consists in using a series of automated tools to analyze the structure and content of a program, beyond the syntax checking done by the compiler. For instance, the analyzer can point out data items that are not referenced and code that cannot be reached. It can find *dowhile* loops that

Figure 19–14 **Strategies for Testing After Bug Correction**

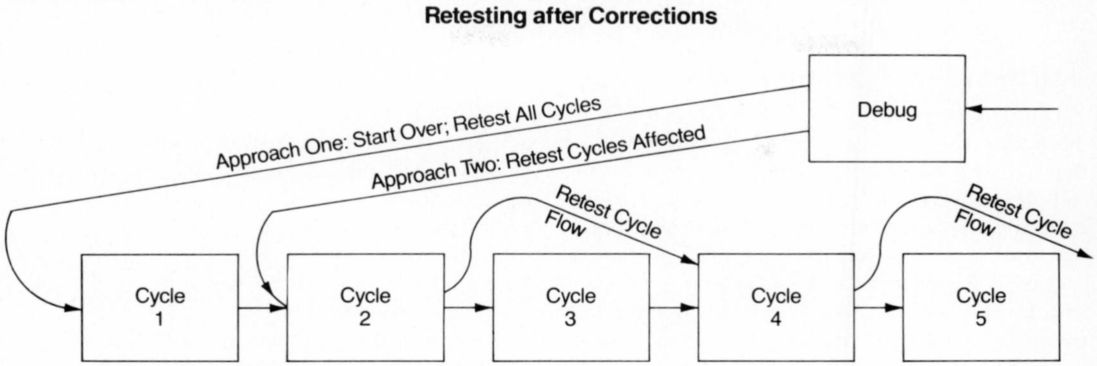

Retesting after Corrections

might never terminate and show errors in logic by a procedure known as pretty-printing—indenting code so that the various logical blocks of the program stand out clearly (see Figure 19–15). It can also help enforce standards by extending the syntax checking to incorporate coding rules that are edicted by the installation. Static program analyzers exist in large numbers for Fortran; there are few available for commercial languages such as COBOL and PL/I.

Statistical testing proceeds from another idea altogether. As the objective of testing is to remove bugs, testing should continue until only a small number of bugs remain. (It is, according to popular wisdom, impossible to eliminate bugs altogether.) This logic is flawed because it is impossible to tell how many bugs remain in the program—or is it? Statistical testing is an effort to predict, at all points during the test, how many bugs are left. An independent team injects a controlled number of known errors into the program, in addition to the unknown bugs already there. This process is called seeding. The proportion of seeded bugs discovered by the testers indicates the proportion of unseeded, or natural, bugs. For instance, if a program is seeded with 20 errors, and testing has discovered 45 errors, 15 of which were seeded, the 30 unseeded bugs discovered represent, on the average, 75 percent of all the unseeded bugs. Therefore, there remain, statistically speaking, 10 bugs to be discovered.

Statistical testing of this type requires a completely separate testing team: the authors of the program would soon recognize the majority of the seeded errors if they were to do the testing. Moreover, it requires a separate seeding team, which has to exercise considerable ingenuity in inventing errors to be seeded. Finally, if the statistical foundation for the method is to work, no unit testing by the author of the program can be allowed. The technique has been used together with so-called clean-room methods in systems programming; it has not gained popularity in commercial programming.

BOX 19–2

Alternative Testing Techniques

Techniques for locating and removing errors or defects are constantly being improved. One important current of research in recent years has been the attempt to treat programs as mathematical entities susceptible to proof: if mathematical techniques can prove a program correct, then it should not be necessary to test it. Another research theme can be described as the clean-room approach: as in semiconductor manufacturing environments, no "polluting particles" (read: errors) are allowed to creep into the system during the development process.

These two techniques do not dispense with testing. Proving that a program functions correctly falls short for two reasons. First, it is only possible to prove that the program does what it is supposed to do, not that it does what the user actually needs. Second, it is only possible to prove that programs behave correctly, not the human beings who use the system. So although program proving may help locate some bugs, it is of little help in assuring that the system will achieve its objectives and that its human interface is good. One can only prove that the program performs the task right, not that it does the right task. An additional, practical difficulty is that the proof itself is generally long and cumbersome; if it is done by hand, the proof itself becomes error-prone.

The clean-room approach could theoretically eliminate testing altogether if it is applied successfully at every stage. The phrase "no defects allowed" means literally that. However, for the two reasons outlined above, some errors will continue to creep in and testing remains necessary. In the clean-room approach, however, testing is used much the same way as in statistical quality control: it serves as the measure of the quality of the product and as a criterion for accepting or rejecting the product. If the product is rejected, it is reworked. Some successful experiments have been conducted combining the clean-room approach with the statistical testing approach.

Summary

Testing makes sure that the system performs in accordance with its specifications, i.e., that it does what it is supposed to do and does not do what it is not supposed to do. Modern systems require that testing be done at four levels: unit testing, integration testing, system testing, and acceptance testing.

Unit testing is usually performed by the programmer who has coded an individual program or module. When the programmer is satisfied that testing has been completed successfully, the results are reviewed by the programming supervisor and possibly by the analysts for their concurrence. The programmer prepares a test plan before beginning the unit test, building test cases cross-referenced to the program specifications. Test cases are grouped into test cycles to test a number of cases in a single test run.

Test data must be created containing information necessary to test the conditions identified by the test plan. Specialized programs are available to assist

Figure 19–15 **Sample "Pretty Printed" Program**

```
005665          A8200-UPDATE-ROW.
005666          ****************************************************************
005667          *                                                              *
005668          *          A 8 2 0 0  -  U P D A T E - R O W                   *
005669          *          ---------------------------------------            *
005670          *       THIS PARAGRAPH UPDATES DB2 TABLES                      *
005671          *                                                              *
005672          ****************************************************************
005673              MOVE WS-CONVERTED-DATE TO RELAT-LAST-UPDAT
005674                          DRIO-DR-UPDATE-DATE(OCCURS-INDEX).
005675              MOVE WS-TIME TO RELAT-UPDATTIME
005676                          DRIO-DR-UPDATE-TIME(OCCURS-INDEX).
005677              IF (WS-HOLD-REL-TYPE NOT EQUAL
005678                  IND-DTE-REL-TYPE OF DCLDRQA3333) OR
005679                  (WS-HOLD-SEQ-NUM NOT EQUAL
005680                  IND-DTE-SEQ-NUMBER OF DCLDRQA3333)
005681          *****    EXEC SQL
005682          *****        UPDATE WDD0D020 SET
005683          *****            DR_REL_TYPE= :DCLDRQA3333.IND-DTE-REL-TYPE,
005684          *****            DR_SEQ_NUM = :DCLDRQA3333.IND-DTE-SEQ-NUMBER
005685          *****          WHERE
005686          *****            DRPARENT_INT_ID   = :DRPARENT-ENT-ID
005687          *****        AND ENTITY_DIVISION   = :DRIO-ENTITY-DIVISION
005688          *****        AND ENTITY_ENVIR      = :DRIO-ENTITY-ENVIR
005689          *****        AND DRPARENT_ENT_TYPE = :DRIO-PART-DD-ENT-TYPE-ID
005690          *****        AND DRCHILD_INT_ID    = :DRCHILD-ENT-ID
005691          *****        AND DRCHILD_ENT_TYPE  = :DRIO-CHLD-DD-ENT-TYPE-ID
005692          *****        AND DR_REL_TYPE       = :WS-HOLD-REL-TYPE
005693          *****    END-EXEC
005694              PERFORM SQL-INITIAL UNTIL SQL-INIT-DONE
005695              CALL 'DSNHLI' USING SQL-PLIST38
005696              IF SQLCODE < 0 GO TO A6130-DB2-ERROR ELSE
005697              IF SQLCODE > 0 AND SQLCODE NOT = 100
005698              OR SQLWARN0 = 'W' GO TO A6130-DB2-ERROR ELSE
005699              MOVE 1 TO SQL-INIT-FLAG
005700              END-IF.
005701          *****EXEC SQL
005702          *****    UPDATE DRQA333333 SET
005703          *****IND_DTE_REL_TYPE = :DCLDRQA3333.IND-DTE-REL-TYPE,
005704          *****IND_DTE_SEQ_NUMBER = :DCLDRQA3333.IND-DTE-SEQ-NUMBER,
005705          *****IND_DTE_KEY_ORDER = :DCLDRQA3333.IND-DTE-KEY-ORDER,
005706          *****        RELAT_LAST_UPDAT = :RELAT-LAST-UPDAT,
005707          *****        RELAT_AUTHCREAT  = :LT-RELAT-AUTHCREAT,
005708          *****        RELAT_AUTHREAD   = :LT-RELAT-AUTHREAD,
005709          *****        RELAT_AUTHUPDAT  = :LT-RELAT-AUTHUPDAT,
005710          *****        RELAT_AUTHDELET  = :LT-RELAT-AUTHDELET,
005711          *****        RELAT_UPDATTIME = :RELAT-UPDATTIME
005712          *****      WHERE
005713          *****        DRPARENT_ENT_ID   = :DRPARENT-ENT-ID
005714          *****    AND RELAT_DIVISION    = :DRIO-ENTITY-DIVISION
005715          *****    AND RELAT_ENVIR       = :DRIO-ENTITY-ENVIR
005716          *****    AND DRCHILD_ENT_ID    = :DRCHILD-ENT-ID
005717          *****    AND IND_DTE_REL_TYPE = :WS-HOLD-REL-TYPE
005718          *****END-EXEC.
005719              PERFORM SQL-INITIAL UNTIL SQL-INIT-DONE
005720              CALL 'DSNHLI' USING SQL-PLIST39
005721              IF SQLCODE < 0 GO TO A6130-DB2-ERROR ELSE
005722              IF SQLCODE > 0 AND SQLCODE NOT = 100
005723              OR SQLWARN0 = 'W' GO TO A6130-DB2-ERROR ELSE
005724              MOVE 1 TO SQL-INIT-FLAG.
```

the programmer in developing test files or data bases. Among these are test data loaders and test data generators. The programmer is responsible for specifying the data to be included in each field of each test data record, even though some of the tedium of developing test data can be performed by the specialized programs.

Shared test data bases are often used. In these cases, the programmer must still ascertain that the test data covers all of the conditions to be tested.

The final step before beginning a test is the calculation of predetermined output from each test case and test cycle. This step not only ensures that errors are not overlooked, but also makes it possible to place expected results in computer-readable form so that a file comparator can compare test results against expected results. A file comparator program makes this comparison much more accurate than a manual comparison.

Although executing the test in a batch environment is fairly straightforward, conducting a test of on-line programs is more difficult. If the on-line monitor has an associated batch simulator, it can facilitate the testing process. If not, the programmer must perform the test on-line—a time-consuming process. In addition, evaluating test results can be a laborious and error-prone process, unless testing tools and techniques such as a transaction capture facility or automated comparisons of test result screens with expected result screens are used.

When test results differ from expected results, additional tools are available to assist in debugging. The storage dump, once the most common tool, is being replaced by such compiler features as trace options, cross-references between program data areas and code and symbolic debuggers.

Integration testing verifies that modules work together correctly by joining them together gradually, testing their operation at each step, until the entire system has been assembled.

System testing tests the entire computer system together with the surrounding manual procedures, restart and recovery procedures, and human-computer interfaces to be sure all components function in accordance with the specifications. User involvement is required during system testing.

Acceptance testing is the final step in the process. This step, which requires heavy involvement by the users, attempts to run the system under volume and stress conditions as close to the expected operating environment as possible. The acceptance testing team is often composed of personnel who have not been too close to the system's design and installation in order to achieve maximum objectivity in evaluating the acceptance test results. When the acceptance testing team is satisfied that the system will perform as planned, the acceptance testing step is considered to be complete and ready for implementation. An alternative technique is to consider the first few weeks following implementation to be the acceptance test with the project team standing by to deal with problems as they occur. This latter technique is usually employed only if the old system can be easily reintroduced in the event serious problems are experienced with the new system.

Selected Readings

Dunn, Robert. *Software Defect Removal*. New York: McGraw-Hill, 1984.

> *This book is a quite complete treatment of testing and debugging methods. It gives practical advice on how to use many of the tools and techniques described. And last, but not least, the book is well-written and a pleasure to read.*

Cho, Chin-Kuei. *An Introduction to Software Quality Control*. New York: John Wiley & Sons, 1980.

> *Cho describes in more detail than the previous book some of the more recent testing methods based on sampling approaches. He also refers to correctness proofs.*

Review Questions

1. List some of the areas where testing quality could probably be improved in many IS departments.

2. Explain the purpose of each of the four testing phases:
   a. Unit testing
   b. Integration testing
   c. System testing
   d. Acceptance testing

3. What is stub testing? Under what circumstances would it be used?

4. What is the value of using a batch terminal simulator for testing on-line programs? What are their operating characteristics?

5. Why do many IS professionals consider the storage dump to be the least valuable of the possible outputs from a test?

6. What is the value of having a trace option in the compiler? A symbolic debugger?

7. Why should test data volumes be kept low in the integration and acceptance testing phases?

8. What are static program analyzers?

9. Explain the concept of statistical program testing.

Discussion Questions

1. Under what circumstances should the use of a test data generator be considered?

2. What are the advantages and disadvantages of using a common test data base?

3. Discuss the pros and cons of conducting formal walk-throughs for the planning and evaluation of the integration and system testing phases.

4. What is the value of having key participants in the acceptance testing phase who have not been closely involved in the systems design?

Mini-Case

Crawford Corporation. Heather Paulson has just been hired as the director of MIS for the Crawford Corporation. One of the primary reasons for her employment is that the president of Crawford is not satisfied with the overall quality of the MIS operation. Projects never seem to come in on time and within budget, and users are constantly complaining that the computer systems are not operating satisfactorily.

The systems and programming group consists of 40 professionals. Stuart Hendren has seniority over the three programming supervisors in the MIS department. He has been with Crawford for over 20 years, having started as a computer operator before becoming a programmer and now a programming supervisor. Stuart has been in the habit of using live data in test data bases for new systems that he and his team develop as well as those that they maintain. Heather's training was in an environment where test data bases were constructed for various test phases along the lines discussed in this chapter. She has decided that one of the first things that must be changed in the department is the practice of testing with live data. Stuart is a man of strong opinions, known to be reluctant to accept suggestions from anyone.

Question for Discussion

1. If you were Heather, what approach might you take in trying to convince Stuart of the advantages of using specially prepared test data bases rather than live data for each phase of testing?

Chapter 20

Installing the System

Chapter 20 covers the remaining activities that must be performed before the system can be delivered to its users. After an introduction on preparing users for change, the chapter describes how to document the user procedures and train the users, how to document the data processing operating procedures, and how to convert the files to be ready for use by the new system. The chapter concludes with a discussion on the cutover and follow-up activities after the initial weeks of operations.

Learning Objectives

- Describe the various types of user and operations documentation prepared during systems implementation.

- Understand how to prepare for and conduct end-user planning.

- Be aware of the issues to be resolved with DP production before the application can be put into production.

- Understand the issues raised by the need to convert the files some time before cutover and maintaining both old and new files.

PREPARING USERS FOR CHANGE

Today, increasing emphasis is placed on the behavioral aspects of systems implementation. Many failures or operational problems encountered in the past were caused by insufficient user preparation. In addition, today's systems tend to reach a much wider spectrum of users.

The diminishing cost of hardware makes it possible to design systems that are much more responsive to human needs. In the implementation phase, this orientation must be followed up by reemphasizing the nontechnical activities. The Multiples Marketing Program owes much of its success to the central tenet that to be a success, the system must be adopted and owned by its users rather than pressed on them by some external agent.

marketing plan

The **marketing plan** for the system should therefore be aimed at establishing in the user's mind, first, that there is a need for a system, and second, that the system being implemented meets that need. This effort should start at the very beginning of the systems development cycle.

user participation

User participation throughout the development cycle is another key to adoption. The more the users participate, the more they will feel ownership when the day comes to start running the system live. Many IS departments now tend to involve users in the early stages, when analyzing requirements and designing the user interface. Later, they consider that users cannot contribute anything during the technical design and programming phases and do not involve them again until the system test, or worse, the acceptance test. This approach is to be rejected; the participation must be permanent.

prototyping and iterative development

Permanent participation can be achieved in two different ways. One of the most popular today is the combination of **prototyping and iterative development**. If the user interface design phase is interspersed with delivery of operational systems components, the users continue to feel permanently involved. In addition, their training is gradual enough that they do not feel the shock effect of a more massive change. End-user development can be seen as the ultimate form of iterative development. All other things being equal, systems developed by end users have a much higher acceptance rate than do those developed by the IS department.

Prototyping is always possible, at least in the user design phase. Iterative development, however, may not be appropriate in all cases. Many systems developed to gain a competitive edge or to change the way in which management uses information are too complex for iterative development. They must be designed first, in their totality; once designed, a critical mass must often be implemented as a unit. For example, implementing a frequent-flier program in only certain parts of the country or for only certain flights or ticket types may not be possible. The part of the system that accumulates mileage may be implemented a little before the part that handles the awards, but not by a wide margin: a really frequent flier can tot up enough miles in a month to be eligible for a companion ticket.

In many cases, these systems are complex enough that a number of activities performed by users can be staggered all along the project. Typical user participation in the installation might include the following:

- Planning and preparing test data for the system test and the acceptance test.

- Preparing training materials and conducting user training.

- Detailed forms design and procurement.

- Converting files, particularly correcting errors discovered in existing files before conversion.

- Planning physical installation of equipment in user locations: terminals, printers, telecommunications equipment, electrical cabling, and remodeling.

User participation in system and acceptance testing is critical. This is the best possible vehicle for training a core set of users to become self-sufficient as early as possible. In general, the system test will reveal a number of operational difficulties; if users can be made to diagnose and resolve these difficulties, they will understand the system much better, develop ownership, and be trained to meet unanticipated difficulties and changing requirements.

USER PROCEDURE DEVELOPMENT AND USER TRAINING

User procedure development concerns the manual aspects of the system. The general flow of manual work has already been identified in the requirements and design portions of the project. Now is the time to create the documentation explaining how this flow is to be implemented.

On-Line versus Paper-based Documentation

User procedures can be documented in various forms. The current tendency is to provide more and more documentation on-line for users who interface through the system via workstations. Explicit prompting, help screens, and other design features explained in Section IV can help. Perhaps the biggest advantage of on-line documentation is that it largely eliminates the administrative task of distributing corrections and updates to bulky users' manuals and making sure that they actually get updated.

Where users do not have access to workstations, the user documentation must be paper-based. It is then important to reduce its bulk and make information in it easy to find. The documentation must also be easy to modify when the procedures change: a loose-leaf organization with pages numbered within chapters is probably the best. This makes the manual easy to update and to disseminate selectively, each user receiving only those parts of the documentation required for his or her specific tasks.

Types of Manuals

There are three generic types of user documentation: reference manuals, training documentation, and task guides. Traditionally, the **reference manual** has been the main type of documentation. A reference manual typically contains a description of all the components of a system: manual procedures, input forms, output reports, screens, equipment, and so on. The description of each component outlines its purpose, its relationship to other parts of the system, the possible values of the data, and some guidelines for interpreting the report or filling in the form. Manual procedures are described as flows of documents, starting with who prepares each document and in what way, how it is transmitted from one department or section to the next, what is done to it at each stage, and how it is finally disposed of (see Figure 20–1).

reference manual

Figure 20–1 **Sample Reference Manual Page**

```
PERSONNEL                    SUBURBAN PUMPS                    U715
PAYROLL                                                        RFMAN
                    REFERENCE MANUAL INDEX -- PAYROLL SYSTEM

 ┌──────────────────────────────────────────────────────────────────────┐
 │ PREPARED BY:  RON TURNER    DATE:  15MAR91    VERSION:  1.1   PAGE 1   │
 │ APPROVED BY:  J. WEBER      DATE:  01APR91    STATUS :  D             │
 └──────────────────────────────────────────────────────────────────────┘


                    INDEX TO REFERENCE MANUAL
                    ===========================


              TOPIC                 SECTION      ITEM        ENTRY
---------------------------------- ---------- ---------- ----------
General System Description             10

    Policy Guidelines                             .10
    Description and Use of Output                 .20
    Source Document Information                   .30
    Description of Transactions                   .40
    Flow of Transactions and Data                 .50
    General Input/Output Schedule                 .60

Detailed Procedures                    20

    Processing Daily Time Reports                 .10

        Filling in Time Reports                               .10
        Receiving Time Reports                                .20
        Logging in Time Reports                               .30
        Batching Time Reports                                 .40
        Transmitting Time Reports                             .50

    Time Report Transcription                     .20

        Keying Data                                           .10
        Correction of Errors                                  .20
        Balancing and Controls                                .30
        Filing Instructions                                   .40

    Weekly Adjustments Preparation                .30

        Adjustment Claims Processing                          .10
        Completing Input Forms                                .20
        Transmittal to Data Entry                             .30
        Data Entry                                            .40
        Data Validation                                       .50
        Balancing and Controls                                .60
        Output Processing and Distribution                    .70

List of Exhibits                       30
```

The reference manual is usually organized in sequence by component type and component name: first all the input forms by form number, then all the reports by report name, etc.

The complete reference manual for any but the smallest system is therefore likely to be extremely bulky and difficult to use. In fact, many installations have found that users do not refer to the reference manual at all, preferring to ask other employees or call the IS department when they have difficulty. As a result, some IS departments do not prepare reference manuals.

Instead, they tend to rely on **training documentation**, hard copies of overhead foils, handouts, and the notes taken by each participant. Training documentation is certainly needed, but it should not substitute for other forms of user documentation. Training documentation distributed at a given session is a picture of how the system works at a point in time. Usually, updated overheads are not sent out to already trained personnel. Moreover, training documentation usually treats only the basic cases. The trainers rely on users understanding how to process more complex tasks through a combination of experience on the job and formal documentation.

The most widely used form of documentation today is not a reference manual, but a **task guide**. Less complete than a reference manual, the task guide lists the most frequent tasks or situations that a given employee may encounter and explains how to deal with them. Exceptions and advanced topics are relegated to the reference manual, which still remains a necessity, although large parts of it can be replaced with on-line help. Rather than describing the flow of work from one position to another and detailing the role of each link in the chain, the task guide concentrates on what a single individual is called on to do. This approach is very appropriate in on-line systems, where manual procedures are less often based on forms transmitted from one employee to another and where each on-line user performs a fairly complete and complex set of tasks. For example, a task guide for a bank teller might be organized as illustrated in Figure 20–2.

Most users find that a good task guide is sufficient for everyday work. The reference manual is still needed, but only to resolve exceptions. In the bank teller example, for instance, the reference manual might be the source for how an international wire transfer is handled, a transaction not frequent enough for each teller clerk to know about. Often, only one or two users have a reference manual, and other workers come to them when the task guide does not explain how to perform a task under specific conditions. The same function is handled by a central help desk when the users are dispersed in multiple locations.

training documentation

task guide

Contents of Procedure Manuals

The procedure manuals must contain a description of all the tasks that are required to run the system. The main categories of procedures are summarized as follows.

Figure 20–2 **Sample Task Guide**

```
PERSONNEL                       SUBURBAN PUMPS                    U716
PAYROLL                                                          TGUID
                        TASK GUIDE INDEX -- PAYROLL SYSTEM

 ┌──────────────────────────────────────────────────────────────────────┐
 │ PREPARED BY:  RON TURNER    DATE:  15MAR91    VERSION:  1.1   PAGE 1   │
 │ APPROVED BY:  J. WEBER      DATE:  03APR91    STATUS :  D             │
 └──────────────────────────────────────────────────────────────────────┘


                        INDEX TO TASK GUIDE
                        ====================


               TOPIC                    SECTION      ITEM      ENTRY
------------------------------------    ----------  ---------- ---------
Who should read this manual                10

Project members                            20

    What data do I need to fill in a time
        report?                                       .10
    How do I submit a time report when
        traveling?                                    .20
    How do I report sick time and vacation
        time?                                         .30
    How do I report overtime?                         .40
    What happens if I miss a deadline?                .50
    Can I submit a time report electronic-
        ally, from my PC?                             .60
    Expense and per diem guidelines                   .70
    How am I notified of errors and how
        do I correct them?                            .80
    What if I am assigned part time to
        multiple projects?                            .90

Project Managers                           30

    How to interpret project cost control
        reports                                       .10
    Possible errors and how to correct them           .20
    Adjusting through time report
        corrections                                   .30
    Adjusting through weekly claims adjust-
        ment forms                                    .40
    Closing a project                                 .50
    Opening a new project                             .60
    Assigning personnel to projects                   .70
        Full-time                                                .10
        Part-time                                                .10
```

User procedures cover functional tasks performed by users, such as processing documents, filling out forms, and distributing or using reports in batch systems; interactions with terminals for data entry, error correction, and reentry; and conversation flows in on-line systems.

user procedures

Computer operations procedures cover tasks performed by DP personnel, including scheduling the application, manipulating tape and disk files, processing output such as bursting and collating printed reports, and so on. In the on-line environment, computer operations procedures also cover network supervision, control, and troubleshooting. Vendor-provided documentation is usually available to describe the operation of the processor, its peripherals, and its terminals.

computer operations procedures

Security procedures ensure that only authorized personnel gain access to the application and its data and that only security personnel modify the authorizations.

security procedures

Performance procedures describe how to monitor actual response times, turnaround, throughput, utilization, and the performance of both user and DP personnel.

performance procedures

Control procedures ensure that valid and complete data enter the system and are processed accurately and without loss. Controls are ultimately the users' responsibility; however, many controls are actually performed by DP personnel to monitor the automated portions of the system.

control procedures

Recovery/restart procedures are required to restore the system to normal use after the system has had an emergency or abnormal termination. Most of the activities concerned with recovery/restart are performed by DP operations personnel, in particular restoring files from backup copies and transaction logs and restarting the on-line system. However, users must also know about restart, in particular where activities must be reprocessed. For instance, if an invoice has to be reprocessed, the printed output from this reprocessing must be destroyed to avoid sending two identical invoices to the same customer for a single order.

recovery/restart procedures

Fallback procedures cover the steps to be taken if the system is anticipated to be unavailable for a long while. Fallback processing can be provided by manual procedures or by transporting the processing to a fallback site (another computer in a different location, ready to take over). One of the oft-cited advantages of distributed systems is that one site may be out of service without affecting the others. Moreover, the surviving locations may be able to absorb the workload of the failing site.

fallback procedures

Backup procedures concern the routine copying and storage of files, program libraries, supplies, and documentation so that they will be available if needed, in particular for fallback purposes.

backup procedures

User Training Planning

Planning for training is primarily driven by three considerations: who is to be trained, what training they need (learning objectives), and what resources will be required.

The role and level of the personnel to be trained determines the general scope of the training. Training for management can often be reduced to an informal presentation of an hour or two. Clerical personnel may need formal training in the new system, a period of practice, and possibly an introduction to new workstations and new control techniques.

In some cases, the initial training is not dispensed to users, but to other trainers, who will then deliver their knowledge to the users. This approach, known as *training the trainers*, can be very effective when large numbers of people are to be trained. Moreover, trainers from either the corporation's training department or the user's own department are likely to be more effective, do a more professional job, and be better accepted by the trainees than a training team of IS professionals.

The resources required depend on the number and types of people to be trained, as well as the information content of the training. Usually, when classes are conducted, a maximum instructor-to-student ratio of 1:7 to 1:20 is aimed for, depending on the difficulty of the subject matter.

Self-study training can sometimes be used when the classroom approach is not appropriate. This technique is especially valuable when the ultimate user is a customer or when large populations of casual users have to be trained. Both printed programmed instruction manuals and computer-based training are possible tools.

The best option may be to incorporate into the system itself a training mode that gives the user access to the system and to a controlled set of transactions or other activities and that lets the user interface with the system. The only difference between training and real modes is that operational files are not updated and output documents are marked as being facsimiles. This approach is expensive, however, and it must be designed into the system. The great advantage is that it can be used long after conversion to train new operators, for whom it may be difficult to schedule classroom teaching.

Training Development and Conduct

In many large corporations, an internal training department can help develop training materials. In other cases, the project team may have to do without assistance. If so, the developers of the training materials should be aware of some general guidelines for effective training, such as the theory/examples/practice approach.

Suppose that the system is for rental agents for a large housing authority. One of the training objectives is to learn to use a waiting list form. The agents will first be told what data is on the form and how to process it (theory). Then they will be shown how several sample situations are treated on the form (examples). Finally, they will be paired off, with one agent playing the role of an applicant and the other filling in the form (practice).

The rental agents example concentrates on the acquisition of a skill. In modern systems development, the additional need for attitude formation is increasingly recognized. The best approach to teaching attitude is probably to keep in mind how the system is likely to benefit its users. An acronym to help training developers focus on this need is WIIFM, which stands for "What's In It For Me?"—a question that is subconsciously asked by all users during training. Providing answers to WIIFM can be done by stressing throughout the training how the training and, by association, the system will help the trainee do a better job with less effort, improving the company or the user's department at the same time.

Those who conduct training sessions should be aware of the following major considerations:

- The trainees are adults, often older, more experienced, and more mature than the instructors. An effort must therefore be made not to appear patronizing or overbearing. It is perfectly normal for an instructor to know less than the audience in the domain of expertise of the audience. In fact, better results will be achieved if the instructor can draw on the participants' expertise and experience to make the training more relevant.

- The role of the trainer should not be that of a lecturer. Much more will be learned in a friendly, informal atmosphere, where everybody participates in the discussion. The trainer should act somewhat like the impartial leader described in Chapter 8, encouraging all to participate while preventing the most vocal participants from monopolizing the discussion. In addition, the trainer must keep the group on track and provide continuity.

- The trainees also have a role to play. They can contribute their own experiences and discuss different points of view in a constructive manner, helping the group stay on track and encouraging others to participate.

- Successful presentations are those where the presenter has physical presence and the material is well structured. Some presenters have the required physical presence almost naturally. Others must work hard to achieve it by paying attention to those factors that communicate the presenter's interest in the subject and the audience: eye contact, spontaneous gestures, varied movements, and proper use of the voice.

  The structure of the presentation refers to the way the introduction sets the tone and the expectations, the pacing of the delivery, good transitions between major subjects with summarizing and questions, and an appropriate ending that relates the topic to its objectives or to other parts of the course.

- During the presentation (or sometimes after a formal presentation), there will be discussions. These can be initiated by the trainer asking the audience a general question or directing a specific question to an individual. The audience will also ask questions, especially once they feel at ease with the instructor. The most difficult part is to get the discussion started; the next most difficult thing may be to stop it.

  During the discussion, the trainer should be careful to respond positively to audience statements by reinforcing good responses ("That's a good point") and by avoiding flat disagreement, keeping the discussion open even if the participant's response was inappropriate.

OPERATIONS PROCEDURES DEVELOPMENT

DP operations procedures have already been mentioned as part of the overall documentation to be developed during implementation. Specifically, the computer operations procedure manual is written exclusively for DP operations. Most of the others—security, control, performance, recovery/restart, fallback and backup procedures—have aspects that apply to DP operations.

Writing procedures for DP operations and training the operators to run the computer part of the application are not very different from user procedure writing and user training. The main difference is that DP operations handles applications from many different functional areas and cannot be expected to have a very deep understanding of the purpose and the functional architecture of each application. In addition, internal control principles should preclude DP operations from making business decisions normally made by the users.

As a result, the flow of an application should be as uniform from day to day and as automated as possible. Uniformity and automation are easily achieved with on-line applications, where the main role of DP operations is to start up the system in the morning and take it down at night. In addition, DP operations is responsible for recovery and restart, but if the recovery/restart procedures have been designed in accordance with the precepts in Chapter 14, this responsibility becomes largely routine.

Batch processing is more difficult. Part of the task of simplifying the running of the application is achieved by good design. For instance, no program should be allowed to request a response from the system operator. Any options, parameters, and dates that vary with each execution of the program should be entered by a user in a parameter file at the start of the run. If the operator's attention has to be drawn to some exceptional condition, such as an input file being out of balance, the program should be interrupted and the rest of the job abandoned, either by causing a program error (not a halt) or by returning an abnormal return code to the operating system. In the latter case, this return code may signal to the operating system that some other program, required for recovery, is to be run, simplifying the operator's task even more.

Some actions can be taken to automate operations once the programs have been designed, coded, and tested. Properly used, the operating systems job control facilities may chain programs and jobs together so that they can run to their normal end without the operator's intervention. In addition, restart points and procedures must be identified. For instance, one tactic may be to keep all the work files intact until the end of the batch process. Thus, the process can be restarted at any point in a series of programs and only the work that failed is redone. If a file is updated randomly, it may be necessary to back out the updates before restarting or restart the process against a backup copy, as in an on-line environment. In other cases, a program may be so long that there would not be time to reexecute it in its entirety, should it fail towards the end. For instance, an overnight program that takes 10 hours under normal circumstances might fail because of a program error, a hardware problem, or an operator mistake after 9 hours. To run the program over again would bring the total time required to 19 hours (plus the time required to fix the cause of the failure) on that night: it would probably not be done on time. In such extreme cases, the programmer, in cooperation with DP operations, must introduce *checkpoints* into the program. A checkpoint is a pause in a program where its state (working storage, file buffers, etc.) is recorded on an external medium. An associated restart facility enables the operating system to load the checkpoint from the external medium, position all the files at the point where they were at the checkpoint, and restart the program. If a checkpoint is taken every one or two hours, the time required to recover from failures is decreased correspondingly.

DP operations must also make sure that output gets directed to the appropriate medium. This concerns tape files and files on other removable magnetic media, whether sequential master files, backup copies of data bases, or interface files sent to customers, suppliers, or other locations. Clear operator instructions and proper use of the operating systems file and library control facilities help distribute output correctly. Printed output must be sent to the proper printer and instructions for mounting the proper continuous form, if required, must be developed. Each DP operations department tends to have its own techniques and standards for printing and processing reports.

Finally, as explained in Chapter 15, the control and security procedures must be developed. An example will illustrate what requires to be documented. For any sequential master file, a minimum of three generations should always be kept to ensure that the current version can be re-created if it is lost. Thus, for a daily application, a master file created on Monday must be kept through the end of processing on Thursday, three days later. A file created on Thursday must be kept until the end of processing on Tuesday, or even Wednesday if the Monday should happen to be a holiday—up to six days. The most widely used technique is to have the operating system create an expiration date for the file a given number of days after the date on which it is created. The number of days between creation and expiration is called the *retention period* of the file. A proper retention period ensures that no error of manipulation will accidentally destroy the file while it might still be needed. In the example, the daily file would require the retention period to be six days. For a monthly application, a retention period of 100 days would probably be prudent, given the variability of the number of days per month and the fact that the scheduling of monthly applications often varies by a few days.

FILE CONVERSION

In many cases, the application requires a new data base, new master files, new records in existing files or data bases, or new fields in existing master records.

When most applications were conversions from manual systems, the strategy was to start a file creation process several months before the scheduled application cutover date. Thus, the master file would be loaded and ready when required. During those months, user personnel would prepare data entry forms for each record to be created—customer, product, supplier, personnel—in addition to their normal duties. Data entry personnel, often the future data entry clerks of the application being developed, would enter the data on computer-readable media. To populate the master file, operations would run a mini-application (see Figure 20–3), which would have to be ready, programmed, and debugged at a fairly early stage.

This strategy created a heavy transient workload on users, data entry, and DP operations alike. Some of the workload could be reduced by using temporary personnel and resorting to outside service bureau processing; the cost was still substantial.

Nowadays, this way of converting files is still encountered on occasion. Much more frequently, most of the information required to create the new master file or data base already exists on some electronic medium. For instance, a new utility billing system created today will usually replace an existing one that has a fairly complete customer file. The conversion from one to the other may be a simple restructuring exercise. In this case, all the data for the new data base exists on old master files, but the new data base has a different structure (for instance, because it is a data base rather than a sequential tape file). The problem is then easy to resolve: a program is developed to read the old files and create the new. This program can be run the day before cutting over to the new system (see Figure 20–4).

Even in this simple case, it is prudent to have a dry run some weeks before cutover. In general, the integrity requirements for a data base will be much higher than for a sequential file, and the conversion program should identify any related problems. For instance, in converting a customer file, some customer records might contain sales representative numbers of salespersons who have left. An obsolete sales representative number might not be of any functional consequence if the customer is inactive, but the data should be cleaned up before the new data base is created. All these problems should be identified and corrected on the old files before the final conversion run is made (see Figure 20–5).

Sometimes, however, the file conversion cannot take place overnight, on the day before cutover. With large files, the process might be too long. More probably, the existing files do not have all the data required. There are three approaches to solving this problem. The first and most common is to convert the existing files a few weeks before cutover and have users complete the new file during the transition period. The problem with this approach is that the old file continues to live and be updated during the time that the new file is being completed. Stringent controls must be put in place to ensure that all the updates to the old master are reflected in the new one as well, so that the two are

Figure 20–3 **Typical File Creation Application**

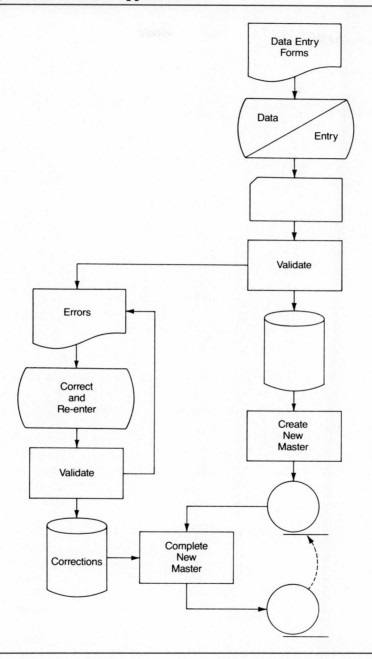

Figure 20–4 **One-Time Conversion of Files from Existing Files**

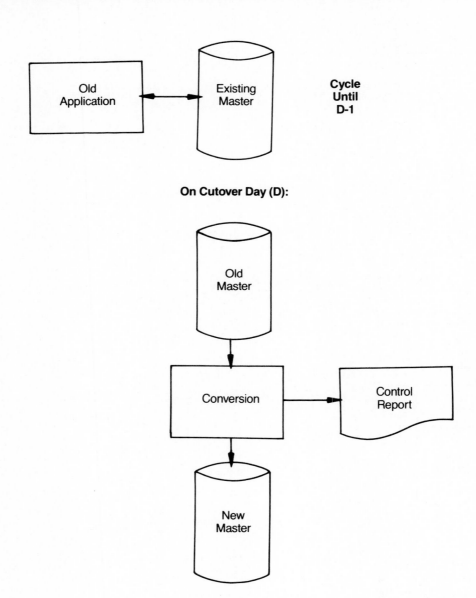

Figure 20–5 **Conversion of Files from Existing Files after Cleanup**

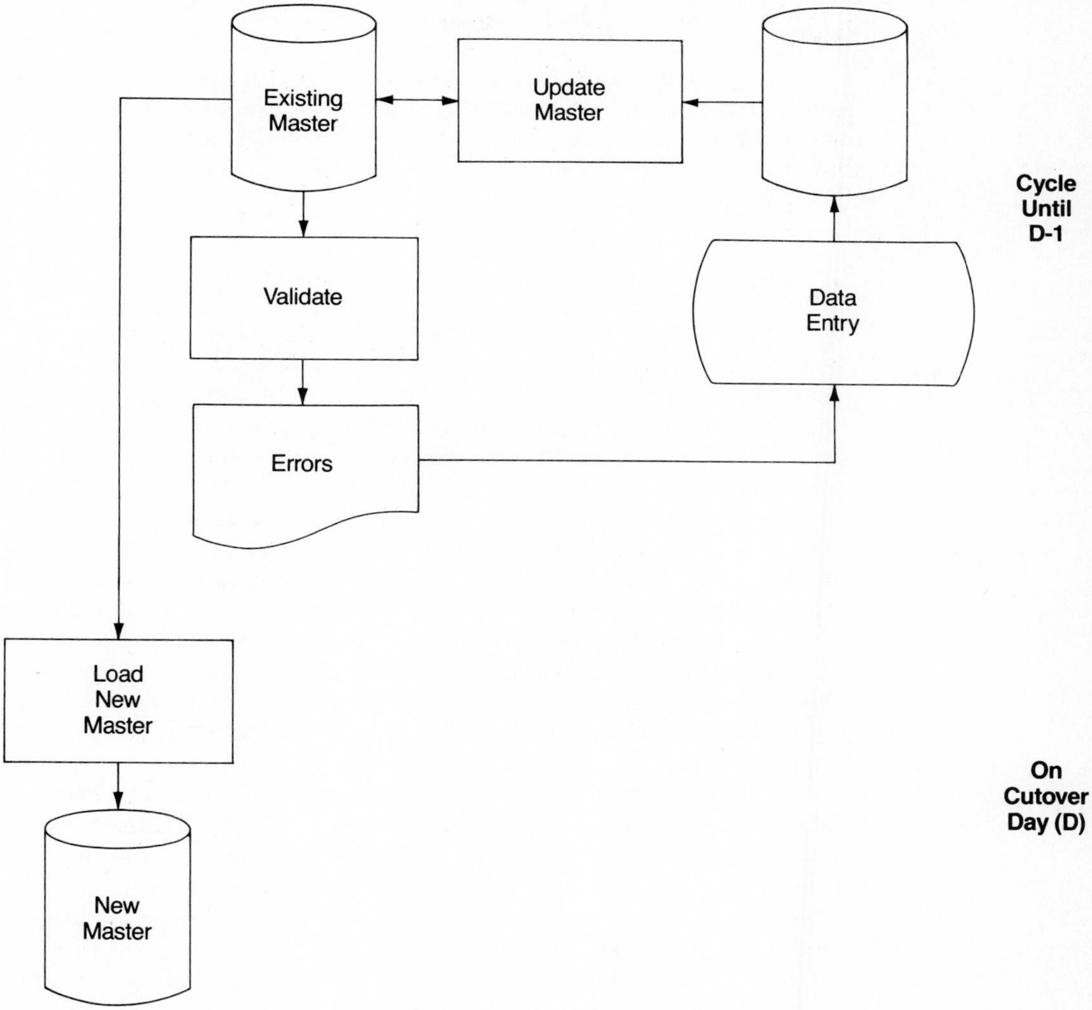

synchronized on cutover day. The shorter the period between the initial file conversion and cutover, the easier it is to ensure synchronization (see Figure 20–6).

The second approach is to modify the existing system to accommodate the supplementary information without necessarily processing it. The data is simply stored on the master file records. This approach eliminates the problem of maintaining two versions of the same file for several weeks or months. Naturally, the cost of modifying the old application may be prohibitive, as one of the main reasons for replacing applications is that they have become hard to modify (see Figure 20–7).

The third approach can be taken when the new data is not required on cutover day but can be completed as new transactions come in. For instance, if the new customer address file should have a nine-digit zip code instead of the five-digit zip code that existed on the old file, this change can probably be implemented gradually.

CUTOVER AND FOLLOW-UP

On cutover day, the new system is brought up instead of the old one. If it has been possible to test the system on one or two pilot sites, the risks are not too great. Most of the practical difficulties have probably already been shaken out, and the remaining problems are not likely to be catastrophic. The installation team already has experience in answering user questions and allaying their concerns.

If the system is started without the benefit of a pilot test, the situation is likely to be different. All the resources and fortitude of the team will be required to solve the problems, answer the unexpected questions, and make last-minute changes. If system testing has been properly performed, most of the really serious problems have been resolved already, and temporary solutions can be found for the remaining ones; but it will be hard work, and the pressure is high. This pressure is likely to continue for several months; in most cases, about half the total installation team should be available for three to six months after cutover.

During this time, it is critical to display discipline in change management. Each problem must be documented and each change request from users acknowledged. For each problem, it is best to find a temporary solution so that as few changes as possible are made to the computer system under pressure, when maintenance analysis is likely to be too quick and testing is likely to be superficial. The ideal way to handle such changes is to group them into a controlled release, due some months after the initial installation. Chapter 21 describes how the process of change can be controlled.

Summary

User procedures document the manual aspects of a system, including human-computer interfaces. Such documentation may be either manual or paper-based, but on-line documentation is easier for users to access from their workstations. It also eases the burden of preparing and distributing updates.

Of the three types of user documentation, task guides are most common today. They are less complete than reference manuals and are also organized differently. Reference manuals are complete descriptions of systems compo-

Figure 20–6 **Gradual Conversion of Files from Existing Files**

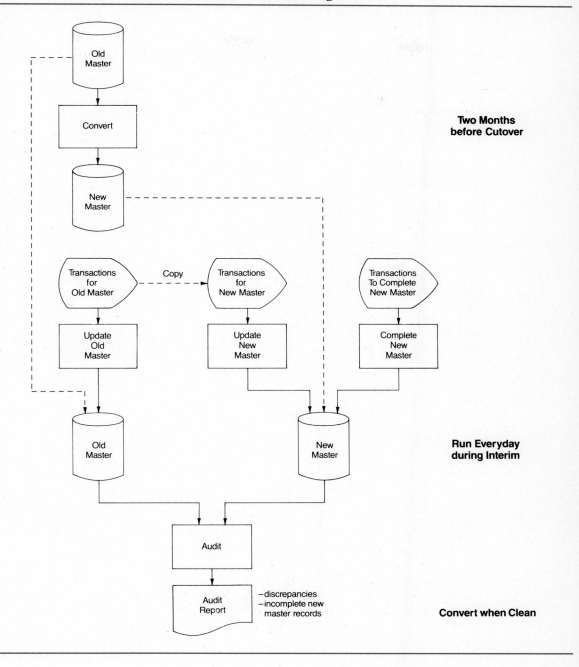

Figure 20–7 **Modifying Existing File Design before Conversion**

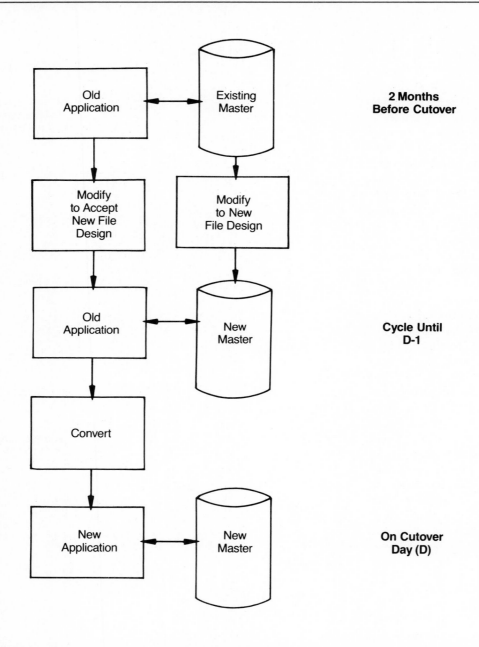

nents (e.g., forms, reports, procedures) presented in sequence. Task guides, on the other hand, list the tasks most likely to be encountered by an employee and explain how each is handled. Rather than prepare complete reference manuals, some IS departments save the training materials for the new system's operations and use them in place of a formal reference manual. Training manuals do not replace a formal reference manual satisfactorily. Task guides available to all employees coupled with reference manuals available to a few of the most experienced employees provide a good balance for most situations.

Other types of procedures that require formal documentation include computer operations, security procedures, performance procedures, controls, recovery/restart, and fallback and backup procedures.

A successful implementation requires that users be well trained in the new systems operations. Considerations in developing a plan for training users include: (1) who is to be trained, (2) what training they need, and (3) what resources will be required. Management users of the system require less training than personnel who will be working more closely with the system. When large numbers of users must be trained, training the trainers is effective and does not unduly burden the project team. Building a training component into the system itself is often the most effective strategy in the long run. If the organization has a training department, the project team should use it to help develop training materials and conduct training sessions.

Some of the major considerations for the conduct of training sessions are (1) to treat the trainees as adults, (2) to avoid the role of a lecturer, (3) to encourage participation by the trainees, (4) to aim for structured presentations delivered by trainers with an appropriate physical presence, and (5) to manage discussions during the training sessions.

Developing procedures for DP operations is facilitated if guidelines are followed during design that lead to streamlined operations in the first place.

Most systems today involve the creation of new system files or data bases from existing electronic media rather than from manual records. Even though today's systems simplify the effort, file conversion still requires careful planning to ensure that the new system begins with correct data in its master files.

Following cutover to the new system, the project team must be available to deal with inevitable problems. Such problems can be minimized with well-planned and executed testing and training. In most cases, however, about one-half the installation team will need to be available for a period of three to six months for post-cutover problem resolution.

Review Questions

1. What are some of the advantages of on-line documentation?

2. Distinguish between the three types of user documentation manuals.

3. What functional tasks might you expect to find covered in a well-designed set of user procedures?

4. To what technique does the phrase "training the trainers" refer?

5. What is the advantage of incorporating training into the system itself?

6. What is a program checkpoint?

7. What are the three primary approaches to file conversion?

8. What are some of the techniques used to minimize post-cutover changes to the new system?

Discussion Questions

1. Under what circumstances might it be more appropriate to distribute reference manuals rather than task guides to users?

2. Why do users often prefer to be trained by other users or professional trainers rather than by IS personnel? When might users prefer to be trained by IS personnel?

3. Cite as many situations as you can where a self-study approach to training might be the most appropriate option.

Mini-Case

Northwest Distributors. Northwest Distributors operates a mail-order business in tools, hardware, and home supplies from its offices in Seattle. Two years ago, it engaged the firm of Harwood and Hancock (H&H) to assist with the design and installation of a new customer information system. Northwest's existing system had been in operation for over ten years and was becoming increasingly difficult to maintain properly. In addition, the mail-order business was getting much more competitive each year, and Northwest's marketing manager, Ron Zayots, was dissatisfied with the demographic data in the present system's files.

The new system's design expanded the customer data base by adding several new fields, and the system itself contained several new functions and reports that Ron wanted.

The development project had been a difficult one. H&H had agreed to do the work for a fixed fee, and the project had taken more time than Dick Zimmer, the H&H project manager, had estimated. Dick was concerned that unless shortcuts could be found in the project's remaining tasks, he would come in well over budget and might find his job on the line.

Two of the major tasks remaining are training user personnel and developing a strategy for building the new data base. Dick has decided to recommend the following approaches for these two tasks at the upcoming meeting of the project steering committee:

- Northwest is to take responsibility for training users on the new system and for developing all training materials and procedure manuals. Dick is going to argue that this strategy will be better accepted by the users and will assure all concerned that Northwest employees understand the new system.

- Required new fields will be added to the file by Northwest personnel following conversion.

Dick has discussed these ideas with Ron Zayots. Ron told Dick to expect some resistance at the steering committee meeting from Ron himself as well as from Janis McDonald, the supervisor of customer service operations. Ron wants the new file to contain the new data fields right from the start. He said the new system would not be considered complete or H&H's work complete until the new fields are in the customer master file. Janis McDonald was not pleased with Dick's approach, because she maintains that her personnel deserve to be trained by professionals, not by amateurs, and that her people are so busy already that they want to minimize the time for training on the new system. She is familiar with on-line documentation from her previous employer and wants to know why such a technique could not be implemented with Northwest's system.

Question for Discussion

1. What suggestions do you have for Dick as he prepares for the steering committee meeting?

Chapter 21

Maintenance

After an introduction to the maintenance problem, Chapter 21 explains the various possible causes for maintenance. It describes an approach to the organization of maintenance by grouping modifications into versions, releases, and temporary fixes to the system. Next, it describes the actual process of maintaining a system: filling out a change request, organizing the maintenance team, and performing the modifications. Last, the chapter refers to how existing systems that are being maintained are integrated into the systems plan, thus closing the cycle of systems development.

Learning Objectives

- Understand the importance and the difficulty of solving maintenance problems.

- Describe the six major causes of maintenance and their frequency in different stages of the life of a system.

- Describe the differences between system versions, system releases, and temporary fixes to systems.

- Describe how maintenance requests are initiated through a change request form.

- Be aware of the possible ways to organize the maintenance team to support version and release control.

- Understand how the maintenance work is actually performed.

THE MAINTENANCE PROBLEM

Most mature installations devote approximately three-quarters of their analyst and programmer resources to maintaining existing applications. For an application lasting 20 years, not an unusual figure, maintenance can cost from two to five or more times the original amount spent on development (see Figure 21–1).

Figure 21–1 **Cost of Maintenance**

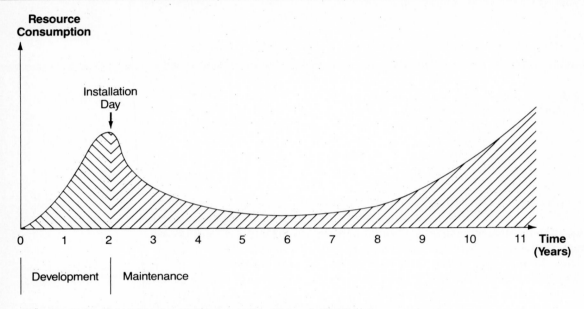

The cost of development and maintenance is the area under the curve.

Maintenance is considered an unglamorous job, and maintenance workers are easily discouraged. Often, too, management compounds the problem by assigning the best workers to development and average or mediocre ones to maintenance, where, in fact, greater intelligence and technical know-how is required.

Yet little attention has been paid to maintenance in the literature and in available products. This situation is starting to change. A number of books have been written, research on maintenance problems has been initiated in many universities, and several tools have emerged since about 1985 that can help maintenance programmers produce better quality work.

Perhaps one reason maintenance has so long been neglected is that the latest development techniques have always promised that they would all but eliminate the maintenance problem. When structured programming emerged in the 1970s, its promoters argued that the elimination of GOTO statements would make all programs understandable and therefore maintainable. Today, the supporters of object-oriented programming and design claim that one of the main benefits of their approach will be to reduce maintenance efforts.

The claims made on behalf of these methods have merit. Some of the design techniques described in this book are also justified mainly by their effect on maintenance. However, few if any serious studies have actually quantified the maintenance benefits of new methods of design and programming. Because systems last for up to 20 years, by the time such a study was completed, the technique that it applies to would be out of date.

Most maintenance problems are not related to design and programming style but rather to management difficulties and poor testing practices. Certainly, all software houses that distribute systems or application software to a large number of customers have found that it is more cost effective to maintain systems in versions and releases than to implement changes day by day, as they are requested. These software houses also have advanced testing practices; they use independent testing teams and regression testing techniques for system modifications. They are also more willing than most corporate IS departments to assign high-quality people to the maintenance and support jobs.

TYPES OF MAINTENANCE

Figure 21–2 lists some of the most frequent causes of maintenance. Maintenance and enhancements are treated together, although some authorities distinguish between them. These causes can be plotted against the curve of the cost of maintenance (see Figure 21–3). As can be seen, in the early days of operation of the system, bugs and minor functional enhancements dominate.

The minor functional enhancements continue to be a factor throughout the life of the application. Solving a problem usually creates (or reveals) a new problem. If a management report on causes of personnel turnover helps reduce turnover, the report is no longer required in its present form. It must be modified or replaced by another report that helps solve some other current problem, such as lack of training effectiveness, recruiting difficulties, or absenteeism.

Then, after a few years, additional causes for maintenance appear: major functional enhancements that are the result of gradual external changes. These new needs do not appear immediately for two reasons: first, some of them have been anticipated at the design stage and can easily be implemented (they become minor instead of major). Second, some problems accumulate gradually, with the users working around the system to meet new requirements, for instance, by supplementing computer-prepared reports with manually prepared graphs or PC-based spreadsheets. At some point, the work-around becomes too cumbersome for the users, who then request a major enhancement to streamline these nondesigned, nonarchitected, spontaneously generated layers of minor modifications.

Technical causes of maintenance follow a similar pattern. The evolution of the technical architecture of the installation for the first few years can be anticipated and built into the application. Later, more substantial changes are necessary to keep the application up to date. For instance, migrating to a new operating system or a new data base management system may require substantial rewriting of the application. New design and programming methods may

Figure 21–2 **Generic Causes of Maintenance**

Changing reporting needs

New hardware and software

Changing business operations

Changing business environment
    (customers, suppliers, regulatory agencies)

Cumulative effect of maintenance

also justify technical rewriting of parts of an application. For example, an application written 15 years ago in assembler may have to be rewritten in COBOL, just because the IS department no longer has enough personnel with assembler language competence. (A drawback of changing development methods to make applications more maintainable is that numerous changes in style make it more and more difficult for maintenance programmers to understand the programs they are to maintain, which have all been created with different standards, styles, and tools.)

Figure 21–3 **Causes of Maintenance over Time**

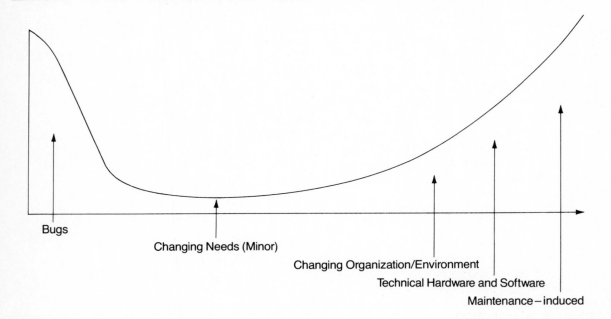

Towards the end of the life of a system, previous maintenance becomes a major cause of new maintenance. Keeping a program or an application well structured is extremely difficult when it is modified several times in succession. Too many patches on a garment may make the original fabric and style all but invisible. The resulting degradation of the program structure does not increase the number of maintenance requests, but it does increase the unit cost per request. It can also result in fewer maintenance requests actually being accepted. Many requests get turned down with the following justification: "The program is too old; it works fine now, but we don't dare touch it any more." When this justification is invoked frequently, there is good evidence that the entire application ought to be redeveloped.

VERSIONS, RELEASES, AND FIXES

Software houses, and now more and more in-house IS departments, organize the maintenance efforts so that changes are implemented in successive versions of the system, successive releases of each version, and, if required, fixes distributed between releases.

In general, new **versions** of a system are created for major changes, either functional or technical. What distinguishes a version is that it must be tested as thoroughly as the initial implementation: integration test, system test, and acceptance test. Generally, the test data must be redesigned or substantially overhauled. Substantial user documentation revisions are required, and users may have to be partially retrained. A new version is therefore a large effort and should not be undertaken more than once every two to five years.

versions

New **releases** of a system incorporate minor modifications at periodic intervals, usually about every six months. This period is a compromise between the cost of a new release and the frustration of users who might have to wait a year or more for relatively minor requests to be honored. Testing is also thorough, but generally, the existing test data can be used with only minor modifications. Thus, the test results can largely be checked automatically by comparing test results to those saved from the previous release. Testing using the existing test data to verify that unchanged parts of the system continue to function as before is called regression testing; it is a fundamental requirement of proper maintenance and one of the main arguments for implementing maintenance in releases rather than continuously. Documentation changes must also be made; however, they are usually minor and can be distributed as addenda or as loose-leaf replacements. Retraining is the exception rather than the rule.

releases

Finally, some modifications cannot wait for the next release. They may be required to correct bugs discovered during operations, or they may be due to sudden changes in the environment, for instance, the critical need to match some competitor's offering immediately (as one suspects happened in 1988, when one frequent-flier program's offering of triple miles was matched within a few weeks by two of its competitors). In these cases, **temporary fixes** are applied to the

temporary fixes

system immediately. Often, no documentation change is required: if the fix was for a bug, chances are that the documentation described the way the system was supposed to operate rather than the incorrect way in which it actually worked. Testing is necessarily summary; it would be too expensive to conduct an entire regression test cycle every time a fix is posted.

This kind of fix must be strictly temporary; it has to be put in as a separate request to be addressed in the next release as well, so that it can then be properly analyzed, designed, programmed, tested, and documented.

The lack of rigorous testing of temporary fixes implies a high risk of errors caused by the fix, just as the use of untried drugs to treat a medical condition often induces unanticipated side effects, some of which can be more serious than the condition that the drug was supposed to cure. The following precautions should be taken:

- No temporary fix should be made to the automated part of the system if there is a manual bypass available.

- An honest effort should be made to test the effects of the fix on those parts of the system that are the most likely to be adversely affected. The practice of using live data to test the fix (in particular the practice consisting of rerunning the same data that caused the bug to appear) is not to be condoned. Properly designed test data, including the case that made the bug appear, should be used; test results should be precalculated; all test output should be checked. Ideally, at least the entire unit test cycle for each module that is modified should be updated to incorporate the new test case and rerun. If there are too many cycles, this requirement may be somewhat relaxed, but the lack of complete testing should at least be documented.

- Because the risk of errors is so high, a fallback procedure must be planned, so that the temporary fix can easily be reversed if necessary.

- Temporary fixes should be withdrawn and reimplemented for the next new release as a permanent modification.

PROCESSING CHANGE REQUESTS

At the heart of the maintenance process is the change request. This form is filled in by the user liaison person, an IS professional with the responsibility for maintaining contact with the various users. (The help desk is part of the user liaison's responsibilities, although it is usually manned by junior personnel on a rotating basis.) The change request form should accommodate both enhancements and reports of problems and errors (see Figure 21–4). The change request may be initiated by a user or potential user, by DP operations, or by the user liaison.

Each change request is assessed as to its completeness, urgency, and probable cost. A form is not complete unless its explanation of what is requested or why it is requested allows the maintenance group to evaluate its importance

BOX 21-1

Configuration Control

The distribution of systems over multiple locations has created the need for a new discipline, called configuration control. Maintenance requires changing the system, so that each component—program, data base design, hardware, documentation—may exist in different versions in different locations. Configuration control consists in keeping track of these different versions and planning for their implementation at each site, while avoiding incompatibility problems.

Examples of problems that may arise are the following:

- A bug is discovered in a program. The correction of this bug is different in version 1 than in version 2. To distribute the correction to all the users of the program, it is necessary to know which users have version 1 and which ones have version 2.

- A data interface between a distributed site and a central site is changed. Therefore, a program change is necessary at every site. However, there is no way to guarantee that all the changes will take place at the same time. During the period where both interfaces must exist, some solution must be devised for their coexistence. The central site must accept both interfaces and know which distributed site uses which.

- A new site is created. If the software has hardware dependencies (for instance, if version 1 does not support laser printers but version 2 does), the right components for the new hardware configuration must be assembled, tested for compatibility, and shipped.

- An existing site wishes to change hardware. It must first upgrade its software environment to a baseline that supports both the current and the planned hardware, regardless of functionality changes. (This upgrade is called *positioning*.)

These types of problems have long been known to computer manufacturers who distribute systems software in the current version to their customers and then ship updates to fix bugs or to migrate to new releases.

The same problems also exist in nondistributed systems, in cases where there is a high degree of integration between subsystems on the same site. A case in point is with subject data bases. As the design of a subject data base changes, the systems that share the data base must evolve in concert.

Finally, configuration control problems may arise when changes to the design of a system are requested and authorized during development. If the design of an interface changes after one of the programs using it has been developed, that program must be modified. The problem is to make sure that all the programs or modules affected by a change are synchronized when integration testing starts. If they are not, integration testing will probably discover the discrepancies, but at a much greater cost.

Very few configuration control tools exist in today's commercial environment. The use of data dictionaries with proper version control can help; but for the actual source and object code of programs, most installations have a manually controlled series of separate programming libraries for different versions of the programs and the data structures. The proper libraries are selected at compile time, with the objective of creating object code libraries that contain compatible versions of each module. If there is no compilation phase, as in many fourth-generation languages, a step replacing the compilation must be performed to make sure that the proper versions of source programs are made available in production.

Figure 21–4 **Change Request**

<pre>
                  CONDOR TELEPHONE COMPANY   A825
                                                     CHREQ
                       CHANGE REQUEST

  PREPARED BY: Alan Forlink   DATE: 4 JUNE 1994   VERSION: PAGE 1
  LOCATION: Marketing Springfield area   STATUS : Submitted
</pre>

Priority (check one):

__ High   xx Med __ Low   Date required: <u>End 1994   </u>

Short description: <u>Separate billing address for residential customers </u>

Description: <u>Some residential customers have a need to have their monthly</u>

<u>telephone bills sent to a different location than where the equipment is</u>

<u>installed. Since we already do this for corporate customers, it should be</u>

<u>easy to provide for residential customers as well.   </u>

Reason required: <u>Customer requests (Privacy, convenience) in increasing</u>

<u>volume over the past five years.   </u>

To be filled in by analyst:

Program/Procedure affected	Est effort	Version	Assigned	Deadline
Order Entry Procedure	25 days			
POE735	5 days	3.5		
Convert existing customers?	60 days			

and its cost; incomplete forms are sent back to the initiator. If the form is complete, the request is classified as a candidate for a bypass solution, a temporary fix, an enhancement in the next release, an enhancement in a future version, or it is refused. In some cases, the request may be refused because the change has already been made, unbeknownst to the originator of the request. In other cases, it is refused because it is not deemed to be cost-effective or because it is in contradiction with some other, accepted change.

This initial classification is based on a very high-level evaluation of the request. In many cases, this evaluation is performed in a committee of IS department management and lead analysts so that each member can contribute detailed knowledge of some aspect to the discussion, and so that priorities and resources can be distributed evenly over applications. Typically, such a committee meets once a week. A weekly schedule does cause a problem for emergency requests, which must be fixed without delay. An exception procedure is then required which, however, does not preclude the requested change or problem report from being reviewed at the next maintenance committee meeting.

Because the initial classification is made without much analysis, it is subject to later change. In particular, if a problem is classified as urgent and subject to a temporary fix, a bypass solution may be devised to avoid a modification to the automated part of the system. In other cases, a seemingly minor modification may turn out to have major ramifications once it is studied in detail, and the corresponding request may be changed from a "next release" to a "next version" or "refused" classification.

Once the request has been classified, its originator is notified of the disposition and the request is turned over to the maintenance team for action at the appropriate time.

ORGANIZATION OF THE MAINTENANCE TEAM

The maintenance team is now responsible for analyzing each change in detail. The team's responsibilities include the following:

- Identifying all programs, files, procedures, and documentation requiring to be changed.
- Documenting how the change is to be implemented.
- Estimating the time required to implement the change.
- Performing an economic analysis of the change: implementation costs, operation costs, savings.
- Coding the change.
- Testing the change.
- Modifying the procedures and the documentation.
- Training users and DP operations, if required.

- Converting files that need to change.
- Coordinating the actual implementation of the change with other changes.

These responsibilities constitute a miniature of the entire life cycle of a project. Quite some time will elapse between the analysis and design of a change and its actual availability; therefore, a version and release approach to maintenance will require freezing the change requests some time prior to the planned availability of the release. Any new request arriving after the freeze date will be scheduled for the following release.

A technique that has been used successfully to deal with this timing issue is to divide the maintenance team into two subteams, which work on alternative releases. For instance, the first team will be implementing changes while the second team accepts and analyzes change requests. When the first team has implemented its release, the change requests for the second team are frozen, and it starts implementing those requests that have already been received, while the first team starts receiving fresh requests. The synchronization of the two teams is depicted in Figure 21–5.

In this scheme, the requests for change that arrive during the initial implementation cycle can already be assigned to a maintenance cycle before release 0 of the system has even been implemented, so as to ensure that release 1 is ready no more than three to six months after release 0 (see Figure 21–6).

Fred Brooks, in *The Mythical Man-Month*, recommends that the second version of any system should be a complete technical rewrite of the first version, without any functional enhancements at all.[1] His reasoning is that lack of experience and design compromises in the initial version combine in practically every case to make the first version a poor-quality product. By concentrating exclusively on correcting implementation errors in version 2, a high-quality basis for further evolutions can be obtained. Brooks also adduces the reason that most people tend to go overboard in version 2 and produce a system that incorporates every idea that was even considered in the initial implementation, but rejected because of time pressures. His reasoning is that if the idea or function did not deserve implementation then, it probably does not now. The only way to prevent overdesigning version 2 is to impose the strict discipline of avoiding innovation altogether.

Brooks was writing from the perspective of a software vendor; the strategy that he recommends is probably most relevant for systems that are distributed to many sites.

PERFORMING THE WORK

Because the substance of the work associated with a new release starts when the change requests are frozen, all the existing requests can be reviewed together. Those that affect similar areas can be grouped and assigned to a single person, thus minimizing the chances of two analysts simultaneously trying to change the same program. Normally, consolidation will somewhat reduce the total estimate

Figure 21–5 **Synchronizing Releases**

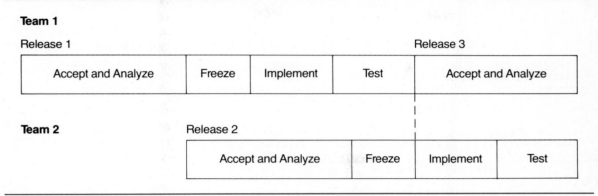

of the work to be done. This reduction can serve as a security margin for making sure that the next release is delivered on time.

Next, an economic analysis is made for each change request (see Figure 21–7). The economic analysis may result in some changes being rejected or delayed, if they turn out to be less profitable than others. This could free up some resources, which could in turn be used to unfreeze a few selected changes that may have come in after the initial deadline. These changes should be

Figure 21–6 **Overlapping Development and First Releases**

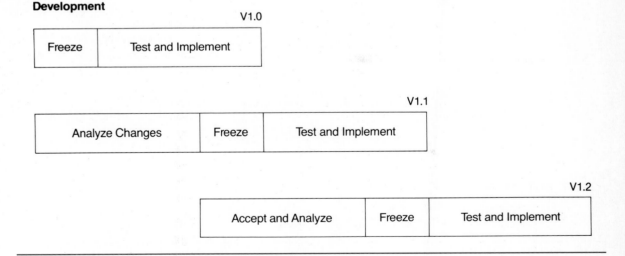

Figure 21-7 **Economic Analysis of Maintenance**

```
MARKETING                    SUBURBAN PUMPS                    CD-20
ORDER ENTRY                                                   ECONS
            COST/BENEFIT OF SUMMARY SALES REPORTING MODIFICATION
 ┌──────────────────────────────────────────────────────────────────────┐
 │ PREPARED BY:  MARYANN UNGER   DATE:  08JUN94    VERSION:  1   PAGE 1   │
 │ APPROVED BY:  HANS ABKORP     DATE:  22JUN94    STATUS :             │
 └──────────────────────────────────────────────────────────────────────┘


                                                      Amount
                                                      ------

1.   One-time Change Costs
-----------------------------------------------

        Personnel expense -

            50 workdays analyst               6,000
           100 workdays programmer            8,000
            30 workdays clerical                960

        Machine hours cost -

            20 CPU hours                      12,250

        Equipment and supplies -

                Paper and office supplies        100
            25 reels magnetic tape               625
                                             ----------
                    Subtotal                  27,935
                                             ----------

2.   Recurring Costs and Savings
-----------------------------------------------

        Clerical costs - Annual -

            5 workdays/month                   1,920


3.   Intangible Costs and Benefits
-----------------------------------------------

        Customer satisfaction  -  translating
            possibly to 1000 added local calls
            per month:  yearly                (4,000)

                                             ----------
                    Subtotal                 (2,080)
                                             ----------

4.   Payback Period
-----------------------------------------------

        27,935/2,080 = more than 13 years
```

selected not so much on their absolute merit as on the synergy that they may have with other, scheduled changes.

The work is then assigned to analysts and, later, to programmers; it proceeds much as in the regular life cycle.

In some cases, a detailed analysis will reveal that the modification is much more complex than initially thought. A change in classification or resources allocated may then be necessary. If, as a result of the detailed analysis, the cost of a modification increases substantially beyond what was initially evaluated, a fresh economic evaluation may be justified.

In truth, few installations actually perform cost/benefit analyses for maintenance work. In most cases, maintenance is performed on the basis of qualitative judgment ("sounds like a good idea"). One of the merits of the release and version approaches is that cost/benefit analyses are consolidated and can therefore be made more significant. Ordinarily, it is also much easier to perform an accurate analysis of the economic impact of a change than of an entirely new system because there are not nearly as many factors of uncertainty.

RELATIONSHIP WITH SYSTEMS PLANNING

The maintenance process feeds information to the systems planning process. Systems planning usually takes place at an initial point, with updates being made to the systems plan at more or less regular intervals—ideally once a year, in conjunction with the business planning cycle of the organization.

Some information about maintenance costs is useful for systems planning. The amount of resources allocated to each existing system for new releases and especially for new versions and the cost/benefit history of the application will help indicate to the systems planners when the economic life of an application is approaching its end. Thus, the effort to redevelop the application from scratch can be planned well in advance.

Summary

Maintaining installed systems is a major cost of operating a mature IS department. It is not unusual to find three-quarters of the programmer and analyst resources devoted to maintaining installed systems rather than to developing new applications.

Of the various types of maintenance, minor functional enhancements are to be expected throughout the life of the system. Major functional enhancements tend to appear after the system has been in operation for a few years, as do maintenance requirements caused by technical reasons. As a system ages, previous maintenance performed becomes a major reason for new maintenance, as the system becomes so "patched" that maintenance is increasingly difficult for anyone to perform.

Some in-house IS departments are adopting the policy of versions and fixes used by software houses. Fixes are installed as problems are corrected, and new versions are released when major modifications are made. Each new version incorporates all fixes installed since the last version was released. Careful attention must be given to procedures for testing fixes and new versions.

The change request form and accompanying procedures provide a systematic way of recording user requests for changes and for classifying them, assigning priorities to them, and managing their execution.

Maintenance teams install changes in a process that is similar to the development life cycle in miniature. Some IS departments will have two maintenance teams working on the same system at one time. When one team is implementing changes on a given release of the system, the other team is analyzing change requests and planning for their implementation in a subsequent release.

Although many departments do not attempt formal cost/benefit analyses on each maintenance request, the adoption of the release and version technique permits change requests to be grouped, thus reducing overhead costs.

Finally, the maintenance process should be structured so that it provides a continuous feedback to the systems planning process. Thus, systems planners are made aware of when an installed system is approaching the end of its useful life and is becoming a candidate for replacement.

Selected Readings

Margin, J., and McClure, C. *Software Maintenance: The Problem & Its Solutions.* Englewood Cliffs, New Jersey: Prentice-Hall, 1983.

This book is James Martin's view of maintenance. Although it has been less influential than many of James Martin's other books, it is still worthwhile reading.

Parikh, G. *Handbook of Software Maintenance.* New York: John Wiley & Sons, 1986.

Girish Parikh is the best-known author today specializing in maintenance. This book is one of the most representative of his views, but there are several others that are also valuable.

Review Questions

1. What are some of the most frequent causes of maintenance?

2. What are some of the indications that a system is becoming too difficult to maintain and should be replaced?

3. What is the distinction between a program fix and a new version?

4. What are some of the precautions that should be taken if temporary fixes are made to a system in actual operation?

5. What are some of the benefits of using formal change requests for maintenance?

6. Why does Fred Brooks, in his book *The Mythical Man-Month*, recommend that the second version of a system be a complete technical rewrite?

7. What information should be communicated from the systems maintainers to the systems planners?

Discussion Questions

1. What techniques can be employed in the systems design and programming phases to make the resultant system more easily maintainable?

2. Give several examples of the phenomenon that "solving a problem creates (or reveals) a new problem."

3. What are the pros and cons of organizing maintenance efforts into two teams as suggested in the chapter?

Mini-Case

CJ Automotive Supply Corporation. CJ Automotive Supply Corporation is a large automotive parts supplier and distributor located in Detroit, Michigan. Its IS department has been an integral part of the company's operations since 1962 when a computer was installed to perform various accounting-related applications. The IS operation has grown to the point where it now includes applications in all functional areas of the business including an up-to-date computer-integrated manufacturing application and an electronic data interchange (EDI) application between CJ Automotive and its major customers. The company has two large mainframe computers, several minicomputers, and hundreds of PCs. Most of this hardware is tied together on a sophisticated computer network.

Like most companies that have been running computer applications for a considerable number of years, CJ Automotive finds that it must devote a substantial portion of its programmer and analyst resources to maintaining existing computer resources. Dave Lambert, the director of MIS at CJ, is concerned about the ever-rising cost of maintenance. He is concerned about not only the percentage of resources he must devote to the area, but also the difficulty of keeping maintenance personnel motivated. Turnover of maintenance personnel is twice that of personnel working on new development. Exit interviews show that most maintenance personnel who leave consider their work to be tedious and removed from the leading edge of technology.

You are an independent consultant in the information systems field. Dave has called you and asked you to come to his office so that he could determine whether you would be able to help him devise a plan to reduce his costs of maintaining the existing applications.

Questions for Discussion

1. What questions would you want to ask Dave about the environment surrounding the maintenance function at CJ Automotive?

2. What suggestions could you put together for ways to make the maintenance assignment more interesting and challenging?

References

1. Brooks, F. *The Mythical Man-Month*. Reading, Massachusetts: Addison-Wesley, 1975.

Writing User Documentation in Playscript

DEFINITION

User reference manuals incorporate procedures written in *playscript*, a technique devised to make user procedures easy to understand and to use. The manuals also contain descriptions of input forms and output reports, including screens.

It is immaterial to the use of playscript whether the system is mechanized or not. The objective is to create reference materials for manual procedures or for the manual part of mixed manual/automated procedures.

EXAMPLES

Figure 1 shows a sample procedure written in playscript. After a heading indicating the subject of the procedure and to whom it applies, a series of steps is listed together with the person responsible for carrying out those steps.

Figures 2 and 3 show samples of a form and a report, together with the explanations on how to use them. Figure 2 depicts a form with descriptions and explanations included on the sample form itself. Figure 3 depicts a report on one page, cross-referenced to a page of explanations and descriptions.

WHERE USED IN THE LIFE CYCLE

These techniques are used in the installation phase of the life cycle, when the project team is preparing user documentation required for the operation of the system.

FORMAL RULES

Writing procedure manuals does not follow formal rules per se. The guidelines that follow will help make written materials as usable as possible.

Figure 1 **Sample Playscript Procedure**

PROCEDURE
=========

SUBJECT: Use of Company Cars

Policy: If you require transportation for company business, use a company-furnished auto.

The driver is responsible for traffic violations

Responsibility	Action
Employee	1. Fills out Form 302, "Request for Company Car," giving destination and business purpose.
	2. Obtains approval of department head.
	3. Presents Form 302 to Transportation Department.
Transportation Department	4. Provides fully serviced car for use of employee.
	5. Explains regulation son use of car, including purchase of gasoline, or oil for any long trips.
Employee	6. If gasoline and oil are required, pays for such supplies and has Form 528, "Fuel Requisition", filled out in duplicate by the station attendant.
	7. Upon return to the office, parks vehicle within the plant compound.
	8. Returns keys to Transportation Department, or,
	8a. if after working hours, to Security Guard.
	9. If the vehicle requires mechanical attention, reports such requirements on Form 302.
	10. Reports any accidents, however minor, to Insurance Department at once (Extension 7277).

Figure 2 **Sample Forms Description**

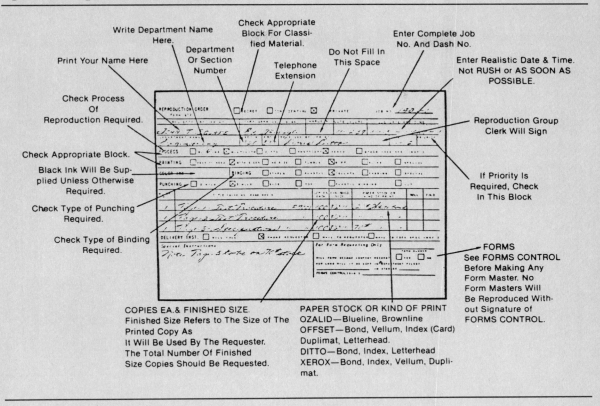

Write Department Name Here.
Print Your Name Here
Department Or Section Number
Check Appropriate Block For Classified Material.
Telephone Extension
Do Not Fill In This Space
Enter Complete Job No. And Dash No.
Enter Realistic Date & Time. Not RUSH or AS SOON AS POSSIBLE.
Check Process Of Reproduction Required.
Reproduction Group Clerk Will Sign
Check Appropriate Block.
Black Ink Will Be Supplied Unless Otherwise Required.
Check Type of Punching Required.
If Priority Is Required, Check In This Block
Check Type of Binding Required.
FORMS See FORMS CONTROL Before Making Any Form Master. No Form Masters Will Be Reproduced Without Signature of FORMS CONTROL.

COPIES EA.& FINISHED SIZE. Finished Size Refers to The Size of The Printed Copy As It Will Be Used By The Requester. The Total Number Of Finished Size Copies Should Be Requested.

PAPER STOCK OR KIND OF PRINT OZALID—Blueline, Brownline OFFSET—Bond, Vellum, Index (Card) Duplimat, Letterhead. DITTO—Bond, Index, Letterhead XEROX—Bond, Index, Vellum, Duplimat.

The primary use of playscript is for the procedure reference manual, which gives a complete overview of how the system works (see Chapter 20). In addition to a reference manual, a task guide may be created, describing how an individual user can perform typical activities rather than how a procedure flows through the organization.

General Rules of Procedure Writing

The following rules are intended to make it easier to read, understand, and follow a procedure:

- Avoid special words and jargon; use plain English instead.
- Use action verbs; avoid words that do not add to the description of the action. Be straightforward; avoid qualifiers.
- Write in the present tense.
- Use short sentences and avoid parentheses.

Figure 3 **Sample Report Description**

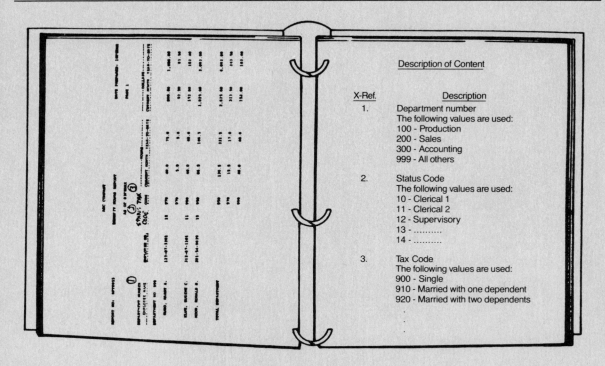

Description of Content

X-Ref.	Description
1.	Department number The following values are used: 100 - Production 200 - Sales 300 - Accounting 999 - All others
2.	Status Code The following values are used: 10 - Clerical 1 11 - Clerical 2 12 - Supervisory 13 - .... 14 - ....
3.	Tax Code The following values are used: 900 - Single 910 - Married with one dependent 920 - Married with two dependents

- Do not put too much into the procedure. It is intended only to describe what is done, by whom, and when—not why.

- Break the system down into logical cycles of related activities, with specific start and end points. Write one procedure for each cycle, even if it crosses department boundaries.

- Include all the activities from the cycle in the procedure, from beginning to end. Figure 4 shows some examples of cycles.

- Organize the procedure steps in time sequence.

- Know your reader. Write the procedures specifically for the people who are to execute them. Send to each only those procedures that are of interest.

- Without including a long discourse of the objectives, the philosophy, or the conceptual background of the procedure, do include a brief statement—a sentence or two—on the relevant policy and purpose of the procedure.

Figure 4 **Typical Business Cycles**

Area	Cycles
Purchasing	From purchasing to receiving From receiving to payment From receiving to stock
Fixed assets	From authorization to installation Maintenance
Personnel	From employment to work start Transfer or promotion From termination decision to exit
Production	From production authority to shop work From shipping to invoicing
Accounting	Accounts payable Accounts receivable Payroll

The Playscript Approach

Playscript is a way of documenting a procedure that clearly identifies who does what. It is called playscript, because it can be compared to a play, where each character's name is placed next to the character's lines.

Figure 1 can serve as a reference for understanding the elements of a playscript procedure. At the left of the page, the "actor"—the person or organizational entity responsible for executing some action—is defined. If the action is handled entirely by an individual, his or her title is specifically given. If the action is the responsibility of a department, the department name can be given. The example assumes that the transportation department has its own criteria for determining who is to do actions 4 and 5 and that the employee to whom this procedure is addressed does not need to know which transportation department employee to ask for.

Next, there is a sequence number, which makes it easier to check that all steps have been performed and to cross-reference one part of the procedure to another. For each sequence number, there is one action and one only. It is described in a brief and clear sentence that starts with an action verb in the present tense. If the action is subject to a condition, the condition is described first, then the action (see actions 6 and 9 in Figure 1).

A guideline for the layout of a playscript document on an 8-1/2 by 11 sheet is given in Figure 5.

When procedures are revised, it is useful to indicate which paragraphs have been modified and which have been added. An example of how this can be done is shown in Figure 6.

Figure 5 **Layout Guidelines**

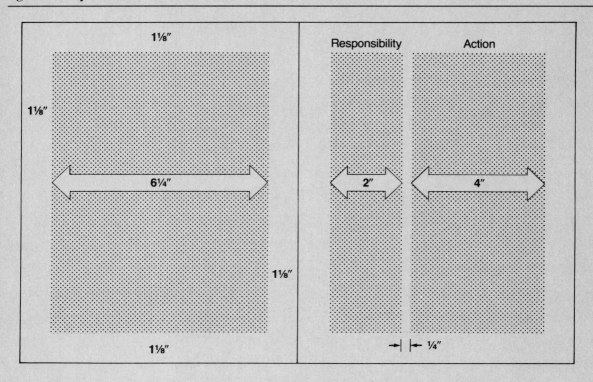

Common Variations

Often, the arrival of a document starts a procedure. The document may have

multiple origins

multiple origins, as shown in Figure 7. Multiple origins are represented by indicating multiple actors, separated by the word *or*, and adding a letter to the activity number, such as 1a, 1b, 1c, for each description.

sidetrack

On occasion, it may be useful to **sidetrack** from the main procedure to explain what happens in exceptional cases. The technique used is to indent all the steps in a sidetrack to the right from the step that initiates it and to number the steps by adding a letter to the step number. This is illustrated in Figure 8. Only the first step in the sidetrack has the condition applied to it. Once that initial condition is met, all the sidetrack steps are executed.

There should be no more than 10 or 12 steps in a sidetrack. If there are more, a separate procedure should be created. Also, sidetracks within sidetracks should not exist.

Figure 6 **Revised Procedure**

```
                              PROCEDURE
                              =========


SUBJECT:  Use of Company Cars

Policy:  If you require transportation for company business, use a company-
furnished auto.

The driver is responsible for traffic violations

Responsibility         Action
--------------         ------------------------------------------------------
Employee               1.   Fills out Form 302, "Request for Company Car,"
                            giving destination and business purpose.

                       2.   Obtains approval of department head.

                       3.   Presents Form 302 to Transportation Department.

Transportation
  Department           4.   Provides fully serviced car for use of employee.

                       5.   Explains regulation son use of car, including
                            purchase of gasoline, or oil for any long trips.

                     **6.   Checks the validity of the employee's driver's
                            license.

Employee              *7.   If gasoline and oil are required, pays for such
                            supplies and requests a stamped receipt from
                            the station attendant.

                       8.   Upon return to the office, parks vehicle within the
                            plant compound.

                       9.   Returns keys to Transportation Department, or,

                            9a.  if after working hours, to Security Guard.

                      10.   If the vehicle requires mechanical attention,
                            reports such requirements on Form 302.

                      11.   Reports any accidents, however minor, to Insurance
                            Department at once (Extension 7277).


    *   Revised
    **  New
```

Figure 7 **Multiple Origins**

```
Responsibility        Action
--------------        -------------------------------------------------------
Customer              1a.  Sends proposed change in writing to the Project
                           office

 - OR -

Flight Department     1b.  Sends a complaint memo to liaison engineer to
                           approve and forward to Project Office

 - OR -

Engineering
  Department          1c.  Notifies the Project Office by submitting a formal
                           Engineering Change Proposal (ECP).

Project Office        2.   Okays change request

                      3.   ...........
```

**multiple
conditions**
A procedure step may have **multiple conditions**, each with a different action, somewhat like a CASE statement in structured programming. This is illustrated in Figure 9.

flowback
A **flowback**, indicating the return of a document to its originator or to a previous user, with the expectation that it will come back corrected, is illustrated in Figure 10. **Outflows** and **Inflows** are similar but refer to documents that leave the procedural flow to join another separate procedure or the reverse.

outflows

inflows

Documentation of Forms and Reports

The two main alternatives for documenting forms and reports are shown in Figures 2 and 3. Both forms and reports can be documented either way; there is no special reason to use the same page for a form and separate pages for a report, as shown in the example.

MECHANIZED TOOLS

Obviously, a good word processor is best for this technique. As a second-best solution, a spreadsheet package can be used.

Figure 8 **Sidetrack**

```
Responsibility        Action
--------------        ------------------------------------------------------
Employee              1.   Records hours worked during the week.

                      2.   Gives attendance record to immediate supervisor on
                           Friday afternoon.

Supervisor            3.   Reviews and approves as appropriate.

                      4.   If the employee has less than one day of absence,
                           approves and sends Attendance Record to timekeeping
                           before 9 A.M. on Monday

                        4a.  If the employee has one or more days of absence,
                             sends Attendance Record to the Department Manager
                             for approval.

Department Manager      4b.  Approves absence in accordance with absence
                             policy.

                        4c.  Sends Attendance Record to timekeeping before 9
                             A.M. on Monday.
```

EQUIVALENT TECHNIQUES

Techniques other than playscript can be used. In particular, graphical techniques, such as procedure flowcharting, data flow diagramming, decision tables, Warnier charts, and so on, are available.

A procedure flowchart is best described as a data flow diagram modified to incorporate implementation details, such as who does what, the media on which the information resides (reports, forms, etc.), and conditional flows. The flowchart is thus better adapted to explaining procedures than data flow diagrams. It is however ill accepted by most users, who tend to prefer text.

A data flow diagram is probably best used at a higher level than the individual procedure descriptions. It could be used to show the relationships between a number of related procedures.

Decision tables are useful when there are a great many different conditions to be evaluated for a relatively limited number of actions. They are best used to clarify the text rather than to substitute for it, as most people are unfamiliar with the format. If decision tables are a critical part of the procedure, the users must be trained to understand them.

Figure 9 **Multiple Conditions**

```
Responsibility          Action
---------------         -------------------------------------------------------
Help Desk               1.    Receive call from user with problem

                        2a.   If user has forgotten password, initiate a password
                              reset procedure.

                        2b.   If user has equipment malfunction, pass call to
                              equipment control.

                        2c.   If user is a novice and the problem is a routine
                              one, explain proper procedure and refer user to
                              tutorial.

                        2d.   If user is novice and the problem is non-routine,
                              have user reproduce problem while describing
                              symptoms over the phone.  If problem recurs,
                              document it on a problem reporting form and
                              transmit to the development team.

                        2e.   If user is experienced and the problem is routine
                              or documented on the "known problems list", give
                              solution and refer user to reference manual
                              chapter.

                        2f.   If user is experienced and problem is non-routine
                              during sign-on, pass call to network administrator.

                        2g.   If user is experienced and problem is other non-
                              routine, pass call to product expert.
```

EXERCISE

1. Convert the procedure descriptions given in Figures 11, 12, and 13 into playscript.

Figure 10 **Flow-Back**

```
Responsibility        Action
--------------        -------------------------------------------------------
                      .
                      .
                      .
Property              6.    Checks form for returnable property items.
Accounting
Officer                 6a.  If form is not made out correctly, sends back to
                             originating department manager, requesting full
                             information in writing.

                      7.    Holds form until return date
                      .
                      .
                      .
```

Figure 11 **Transfer and Budget Adjustment Procedure**

<u>Subject: Handling Transfers and Budget Adjustments of Personnel</u>

It shall be company policy and practice to transfer employees from one department to another when the work needs so require such transfer. Transfer requests shall be initiated by the releasing department supervisor and be properly substantiated by department requesting to fill specific needs.

Transfers of personnel shall not be made without prior adjustment of the current personnel budgets and work load records maintained currently in the Accounting and Finance Division, Budget and Planning Section.

The Personnel Department shall have the responsibility to secure the receiving department's supervisory signature on all transfers. Personnel shall set the effective date of transfer, and this shall be added to Form 457, Transfer Request, in the spaced provided. Copy 2 shall be sent to department receiving personnel so transferred, while copy number 1 will be filed in the personnel folder.

All budget and work load records shall be adjusted from a copy of Form 457, which shall be sent to the Budget and Planning Section of Accounting and Finance.

Approval of both the releasing and the receiving departments' supervisors shall be necessary before the request for transfer can be effective.

The Department Personnel Records, but not the Personnel Department Folder, shall be sent to the receiving department, along with its copy of Form 457. All other affected personnel records shall be posted to reflect the transfer, particularly in the receiving department, as receiving department records must be up to date and each employee shall be currently charged to the correct burden or cost-center account.

It is company policy to keep such employees' record folders in a locked personnel records cabinet. Only supervisors shall have access to, or refer to, these records.

Figure 12 **Invoicing Control Procedure**

Verification That All Materials Shipped Are Invoiced

1.   The Invoice Clerk receives the invoices from Data Processing and
      the sales slips from the Pricing Clerk.

2.   Each invoice is matched with the correct sales slip. Attached to
      each sales slip are two copies of the Bill of Lading (the original
      and number 4 copy).

3.   To verify invoicing of truck shipments, the Invoice Clerk must
      construct a control sheet which is a listing of all the Bill of
      Lading numbers in sequential order.

4.   At the same time that each invoice is matched to the corresponding
      sales slip and Bill of Lading (refer to Number 2), the Invoice
      Clerk writes the date of the corresponding invoice next to the Bill
      of Lading number on the control sheet, thus indicating that the
      shipment has been properly billed. If there is a Bill of Lading
      without a matching invoice, or vice versa, the Invoice Clerks
      contacts the Pricing Clerk for an explanation.

5.   The original Bill of Lading is then attached to the two white
      copies of the invoice and mailed to the customer.

6.   The number 4 copy of the Bill of Lading is attached to the yellow
      copy of the invoice and the sales slip, and filed in an open file
      until the invoice is paid; then it is filed in a paid file.

7.   The green copy of the invoice is the reference, or control, copy
      and is filed numerically in the control binder.

Figure 13 **Customer Credit Clearance**

Customer Credit Clearance Policy and Procedure

Initiation of   1.0 Field Salespeople shall initiate requests
Credit Clearance   for credit clearance.   If adequate credit
Requests   information is not available from normal
                            sources (D&B rating and reports or past
                            experience), Finance and Administration
                            will contact the customer directly for
                            additional information.

Customer Credit   2.0 A Customer Credit Limit List, indicating
Limit List   preapproval of various amounts of credit
                             for established customers, shall be
                             issued to Field Salespeople each quarter
                             by Finance and Administration.   The
                             published limits, up to a maximum of
                             $25,000, represent conservative amounts.

Review of Sales   3.0 Salespeople shall review each potential
Orders   sale against the Customer Credit Limit
                             List.   All orders under $1,000 for
                             customers not on the list do not require
                             credit approval.   Orders over $1,000 for
                             customers not on the list will be
                             accepted and acknowledged only after
                             clearance.

Approvals   4.0 The Manager, Finance and Administration,
                             will approve all orders which are
                             acceptable from a credit basis.
                             Exceptions will be reviewed for approval
                             by the General Manager before an order is
                             accepted.

Appendix 1

Value Chain Analysis

THE VALUE CHAIN

All organizations consist of a collection of value activities that are performed to design, produce, market, deliver, and support their products or services. Value activities can be viewed as building blocks by which an organization creates products or provides services valuable to its customers. An organization's value activities can be listed systematically using the value chain framework. Developing the value chain and analyzing value activities in detail provides the analyst with an understanding of how an organization performs its activities, how activities interact, and what the relative importance of each activity is.

VALUE CHAIN COMPONENTS

The value chain consists of primary and support activities and added value, as illustrated in Figure A1–1. Primary activities are activities involved in the physical creation of the product or service, its sale and delivery to the buyer, and the support after the sale. Support activities complement the primary activities by providing such functions as human resources, procurement, technology development, and administrative support. Added value, sometimes called margin, is the difference between the collective cost of the value activities and the amount customers are willing to pay for the organization's product or service. In a profit-making organization, added value is the equivalent of pretax profit. In a not-for-profit organization, added value represents the benefits achieved less the total cost of creating such benefits.

Primary Activities

There are five generic categories of primary activities involved in any industry:

- Inbound logistics includes activities associated with receiving, storing, and disseminating materials and other inputs necessary to create the product or service. Examples are warehousing and inventory control.

Figure A1–1 **Value Chain**

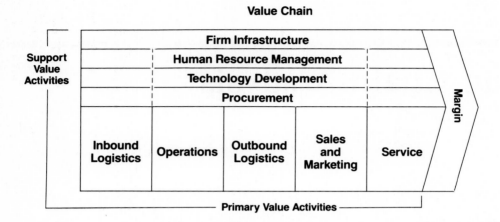

* Operations activities are associated with transforming inputs into the final product form. Examples are such activities as machining, assembly, and packaging.

* Outbound logistics activities are associated with collecting, storing, and distributing the product to customers. Examples are activities such as finished goods warehousing, order processing, and delivery.

* Marketing and sales activities are associated with methods of persuading buyers to purchase a product or service and providing them with the means to do so. Examples are activities such as advertising, sales efforts, and retailing.

* Service activities are associated with providing after-sales services such as installation, repair, or follow-up services, which enhance or maintain the value of the product or service delivered.

Each cell can be broken down into distinct activities. Figure A1–2 illustrates how operations activities might be listed for a manufacturer of chocolate bars.

Support Activities

Support activities can be divided into four generic categories:

* Procurement activities are associated with the acquisition of all inputs necessary to produce the product or provide the service. Examples include

Figure A1–2 **Value Chain of Chocolate Manufacturer**

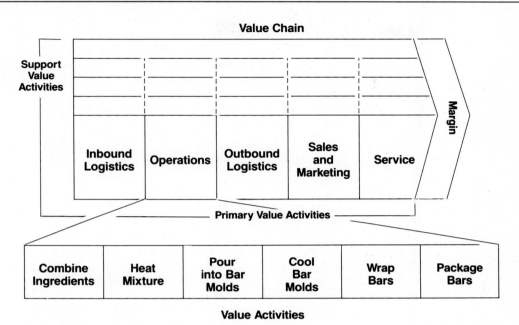

Value Activities

activities such as purchasing raw materials, searching for new supplier sources, and monitoring supplier performance.

- Technology development activities are associated with the design and creation of the product or service. Examples are activities such as product design, technology selection, or development of a new service line.

- Human resource management activities are associated with all aspects of hiring, training, evaluating, and rewarding personnel. Examples are activities such as hiring, administering benefit programs, or conducting training programs.

- Firm infrastructure activities are those activities that collectively support all elements in the value chain. Examples are activities such as general management, planning, finance, and legal.

The dotted lines for the support activities in Figure A1–1 reflect the fact that procurement, technology development, and human resource management are often associated with specific primary activities as well as supportive of the entire value chain. Firm infrastructure is not associated with specific primary activities but supports the entire value chain.

APPLYING VALUE CHAIN ANALYSIS

Figure A1–3 is a completed value chain for a commercial airline company, ASAP. The information necessary to prepare such a value chain is usually gathered through interviews with user personnel. Analysts familiar with a particular industry are able to determine quickly whether the lists of activities in each category of the value chain are complete, since similar activity lists will be found in the value chains of companies in the same business.

Although the identification of value chain activities is sometimes difficult, the basic principle is to look for the following types of activities:

- Activities that have a high potential for increasing the added value of an organization's product or service.

- Activities that represent a significant or growing portion of cost within the organization.

Functions such as operations or marketing contain broad activities that must be further subdivided into several levels of narrowing activities in order to assist an analyst's understanding. The level to which activities should be subdivided depends upon the purpose for which the value chain is being created. For example, high-level value chains are often used to compare and contrast firms in the same industry. A more detailed value chain could point analysts to areas in which opportunities to reduce costs or increase added value exist.

In any situation, value chains help analysts identify areas for further study and possible improvement. For example, ASAP's value chain may suggest questions such as the following:

- How is baggage handled? Can the activity be automated?
- Are self-ticketing machines used?
- What benefits might be derived from a higher investment in personnel training?
- How is scheduling performed?

In the ASAP example, if scheduling were selected as an activity that would benefit from further study, it would be analyzed using either a hierarchical technique (see the Technique to Section I) or data flow diagram (see the Technique to Section III). For example, a data flow diagram for the scheduling activity is illustrated in Figure A1–4. Note that the data flow diagram has broken down the scheduling activity, identified all inputs and outputs, and identified interfaces with other activities. Interfaces can be within or outside the organization.

- Internal interfaces such as sales and load data come from ASAP's sales function. Passenger service provides information concerning customer service and requests for new service. Maintenance provides the aircraft maintenance schedule. Human resources provides training and monitors governmental or union rules.

Figure A1–3 **Completed Value Chain for Airline Company**

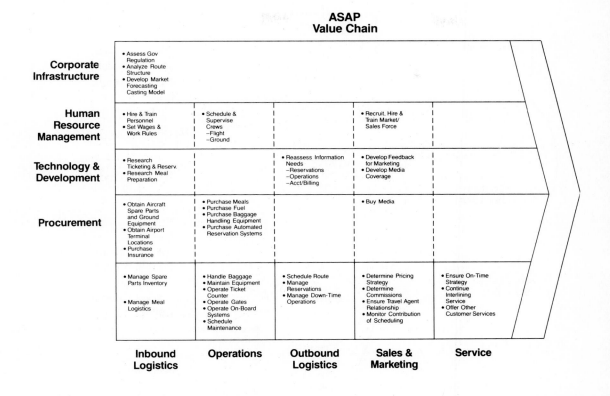

The completed schedule contains information required by other functions. Marketing needs the schedule to develop sales strategies, maintenance needs the schedule to plan maintenance schedules, human resources needs the schedule to schedule flight crews and ground personnel, and information services must update its files for the on-line reservation system.

- In this example, there is only one external interface. ASAP's selection of routes and departure times depends in part on the actions of its competitors. Thus, information on competitor's routes and schedules is used in the determination of ASAP's route frequency and times.

Analysis of activities, their inputs and outputs, and their interfaces can help uncover operational inefficiencies. Changing how an activity is performed or deleting unnecessary steps can enhance efficiency and reduce cost. Sources of customer dissatisfaction can also be identified. For example, if customer requests were missing from ASAP's scheduling activity, an analyst would

Figure A1–4 **Data Flow Diagram of ASAP Scheduling Activity**

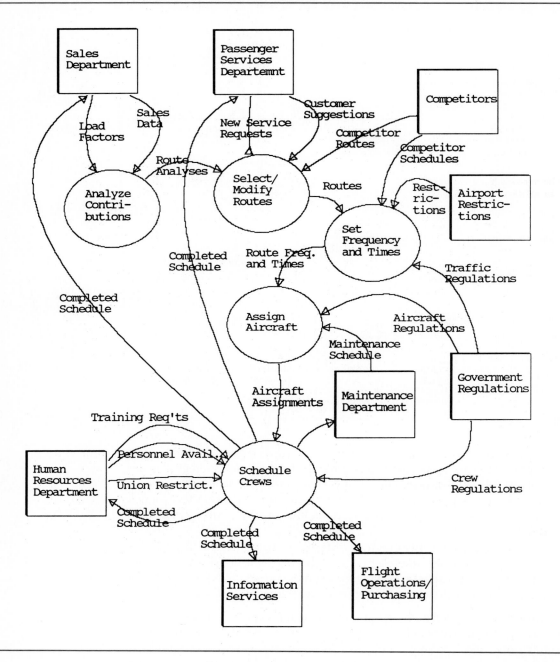

probably recommend that it be used as an input to the process of selecting routes and flight times.

Review of the data flow diagram for ASAP's scheduling activity might prompt questions such as the following:

- Is the sales data captured by marketing adequate for analyzing routes?
- Is ASAP receiving a large number of customer complaints?
- How effectively does ASAP monitor the scheduling and pricing actions of its competitors?
- Are ASAP's maintenance costs in line with industry standards?
- Which scheduling activities can be improved by automation?

Answers to these and other questions would help analysts generate recommendations to improve ASAP's business. Recommendations for change would then become a part of ASAP's business plans.

COST ANALYSIS TOOLS

Three cost analysis tools form a systematic framework for cost analysis:

- Cost maps
- Cost drivers
- Asset maps

All three draw information from the value chain. Cost maps associate cost with the value activities, and asset maps associate assets with the value activities. Cost drivers are factors that influence the cost of an activity, causing it to increase or decrease.

Cost Maps

Cost maps express the cost of each activity in terms of percentages of the total cost. The cost map for ASAP is illustrated in Figure A1–5. Preparing a cost map requires that costs be distributed to specific value activities. In practice, this often requires a redistribution of costs from the way they are kept in the accounting records because, in many cases, costs are not classified precisely according to activities. For example, the salary of an aircraft maintenance manager may be classified as "management salaries" when in reality 85 percent of the salary should be associated the maintenance activity.

Activities on the cost map may be further aggregated or disaggregated in accordance with the following guidelines:

- Disaggregate, or separate, activities that represent significant or rapidly growing percentages of cost
- Aggregate, or group, activities that represent small, stagnant, or decreasing percentages of cost

Figure A1–5 **ASAP Cost Map**

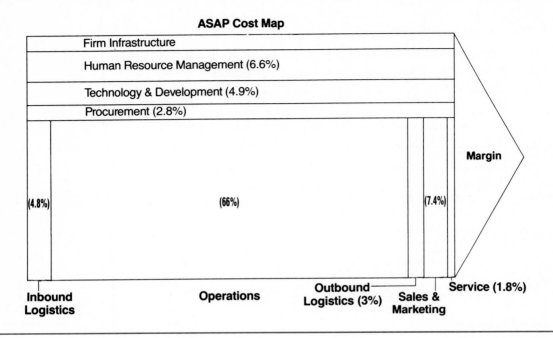

Applying these guidelines to ASAP, the operations activity, which represents 66 percent of the costs, would be separated into its six components, as illustrated in Figure A1–6.

Cost maps are useful for identifying high-cost activities as targets for cost reduction efforts. For example, 20 percent of ASAP's operations costs are spent in the operation of on-board systems. Significant savings could result if this activity could be performed more efficiently.

Cost maps are also useful for making comparisons between competitors in a particular industry. Although the information to make precise comparisons is not always readily obtainable, much of it is public information. What is not available publicly can be obtained or imputed through observation or other means. For example, the number of maintenance employees and their average wage may have been disclosed in a newspaper article concerning a competitor's labor contract negotiations. This information, combined with knowledge of the number of airplanes in the competitor's fleet by type and age may be enough to estimate their maintenance costs with a sufficient degree of accuracy.

An organization derives important information about itself by classifying its costs according to activities. Very often, organizations may find that certain activities cost them much more than was thought. Usually, there is a tendency to

Figure A1–6 **ASAP Cost Map with Breakdown of Operations Activity**

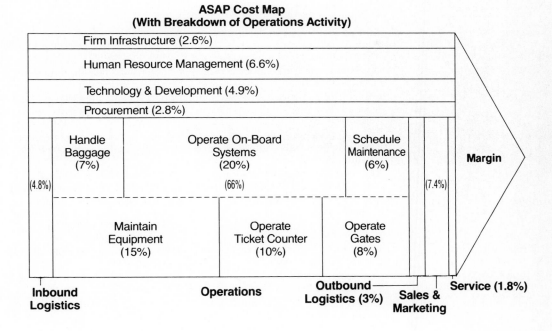

focus cost improvement efforts on primary activities. A cost map, however, may indicate that support activities represent a larger portion of total costs than was thought and are thus a more logical target for cost reduction efforts.

Cost Drivers

Cost drivers are factors that influence the cost of an activity. One way to reduce costs is to work on changing cost drivers. Cost drivers affect the unit cost, not the total cost, of an activity. Cost drivers can cause unit costs to increase or decrease. Categories of generic cost drivers, together with examples of each, are illustrated in Figure A1–7. The generic categories are useful as a starting point for identifying cost drivers for an activity.

Scale. The cost of value activities often exhibits different levels of efficiency at different volume levels. For example, if the same item is requested by several

Figure A1–7 **Generic Cost Drivers**

Generic Cost Driver	Description	Examples
Scale	Cost of activities are often subject to different efficiencies at different volumes.	Longer production runs, buying in bulk.
Learning	Cost of an activity can decline over time due to learning that increases efficiency.	Work is better scheduled and organized once worker is familiar with job details.
Capacity Utilization	Fixed costs can create a penalty for underutilization.	Selling excess facilities and skills.
Linkages	The cost of an activity is frequently affected by how other activities are performed.	Inspection and after-sale service linkages with suppliers.
Interrelationships	Cost can be affected by interrelationships with other SBUs within a firm.	Sharing an activity such as order processing between two SBUs.
Integration	The level of vertical integration in an activity may influence its cost.	Owning a service instead of contracting out, e.g., payroll.
Timing	When an activity is performed can affect its costs.	Raw materials may be cheaper at certain times of the year. Being the first in the market helps establish a brand name.
Discretionary Policies	Policy choices that a firm makes will affect activities' costs.	Service policies, wages paid, quality policies.
Location	The geographic location of an activity can affect its cost.	Differing cost of labor, raw materials, energy, and transportation.
Institutional Factors	Usually outside firm's control. This cost driver can influence the cost of an activity very heavily.	Government regulations, unionization.

different departments, purchasing them together in one order from a single vendor could result in lower unit cost because of price concessions from the vendor and a reduction of effort within the purchasing department.

Learning. The cost of an activity can decrease over time as a result of organizational learning that increases efficiency. For example, when a new product is manufactured, production rates are lower and scrap rates higher at first because employees are not familiar with the processing steps and make more mistakes. As they become more familiar with the process, they produce items faster and better, thus reducing the item's unit cost.

Capacity Utilization. When a value activity has a substantial fixed cost, a penalty is paid for underutilized capacity. Resources not utilized represent the loss of potential revenues. For example, every empty seat on an ASAP flight represents revenue lost forever. Controlling underutilization requires studying

patterns of usage and taking steps to minimize fixed costs. In the ASAP example, it may be possible to increase utilization by either filling empty seats with passengers flying on incentive fares or by using smaller planes on routes on which current capacity is chronically underutilized.

Linkages. The cost of an activity is frequently affected by the way another activity is performed. Such connections between activities are called linkages. Two broad types of linkages exist: internal (within the organization's value chain) and external (within the value chains of other organizations, for example, buyers or suppliers). Linkages create the opportunity to lower the combined cost of linked activities. ASAP's inventory management system is an example of an external linkage acting as a cost driver. ASAP's suppliers keep an inventory of spare parts in anticipation of orders from ASAP, parts that would otherwise need to be held in ASAP's inventory. ASAP also keeps an inventory of the same parts in case the suppliers are out of stock when maintenance needs to be performed. The inventory levels for both ASAP and its suppliers could be reduced if the suppliers were aware of ASAP's demand patterns. Because spare parts for aircraft can be expensive, exploiting the linkage between ASAP and its suppliers could produce substantial savings.

Interrelationships. Any form of sharing among strategic business units (SBUs) represents an interrelationship. The most significant form of interrelationship is when a value activity can be shared with other SBUs. In ASAP, there are two SBUs: cargo and passenger service. Maintenance for the planes used by both SBUs are performed by the same maintenance unit. Sharing resources is a potential means of achieving economies of scale, decreasing the learning curve, and increasing capacity utilization.

Integration. Activities can be performed by an organization's own employees or by external vendors. Integration (performing an activity in-house) may be more cost-effective for some activities and deintegration (engaging external vendors to perform all or part of an activity) may be the better choice for other activities. This choice is commonly called the "make or buy" decision. For example, meals aboard ASAP's flights are prepared by an external caterer. ASAP could operate a catering service of its own and integrate the preparation of meals into its operations if it would be beneficial to do so.

Timing. The cost of a value activity is often affected by the timing of its acquisition or performance. For example, ASAP's fuel may be purchased at a lower cost during certain times of the year, or at times when the price is at a low point because of excess supplies. Many companies will purchase computer time from third parties during nighttime hours, when it is offered at the lowest price.

Location. The location of a value activity can affect its cost in several ways. The prevailing cost of employees, office space, raw materials, and energy can vary widely by country or by region within a country.

Institutional Factors. Institutional factors (e.g., governmental regulations, taxes, labor laws) are the final major cost driver. They can be significant factors for some industries. Favorable institutional factors such as tax incentives can lower costs. Unfavorable factors such as tariffs can increase costs. For example, strict government regulations for the maintenance of aircraft have a heavy cost impact on ASAP.

Identifying cost drivers and their effect is not always an easy task. Three methods are usually employed in practice:

- Quantitative Measures. One method often used is to measure the efficiency of an activity using quantitative nonmonetary measures such as yield, scrap rates, and labor hours to probe the sources of cost changes in a value activity. For example, if it were determined that the average time to take a customer's reservation by telephone was too high, steps could be taken to reduce it, possibly by investing in additional employee training.

- Internal Experience. Another method is to examine an organization's internal experience. Analyzing cost levels at different levels of activity may help to clarify scale economics.

- Interviews with Experts. Individuals who have extensive knowledge of a value activity can answer "what if" questions about the effects of changing various cost parameters. For example, the head of ASAP's marketing and sales department could answer such questions as:

    What if we exclude travel agents and sell tickets directly to passengers?
    What if we increase or reduce the permanent sales force?
    What if we establish a marketing link with a national carrier?

    Answers to such questions can help an analyst determine if there are integration, capacity utilization or linkage cost drivers for the marketing and sales activities. Decision support systems are often very helpful in analyzing questions like these.

Figure A1–8 shows the cost drivers for some of ASAP's major activities. By knowing what drives the cost of an activity, ASAP's staff can take steps to reduce the cost. For example, if learning is a cost driver in some of the operations activities, then hiring more experienced personnel or starting a more comprehensive training program should be considered. Locating its reservations clerks and supporting computers in a low-cost region of the country may drive down the costs of the reservations activity.

Cost drivers are key in helping an organization analyze its costs. Cost maps associate costs with value activities and highlight high-cost activities. Cost drivers help the analyst understand factors affecting costs so that steps can be taken to control them.

Asset Maps

Asset maps are similar to cost maps. However, instead of assigning costs to value activities, assets are assigned. On the asset map, assets for each value activity are

Figure A1–8 **Cost Drivers**

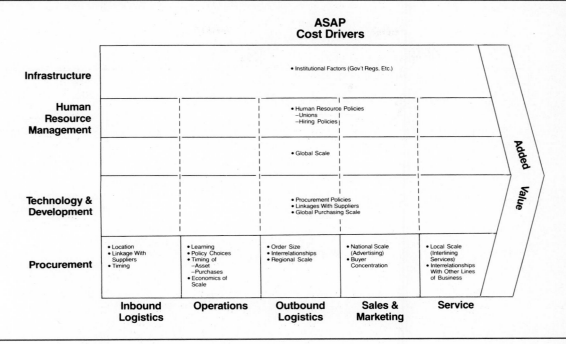

assigned as a percentage of total assets, both fixed and current. Figure A1–9 is the asset map for ASAP.

Assets should be assigned to the activities that employ, control, or greatly affect their use. Like costs, information on the value of assets can be extracted from the accounting records. Asset accounts must usually be regrouped to correspond to activities. For example, ASAP's motor vehicle asset account would be assigned to several activities. Luggage trucks would be assigned to baggage handling, fuel trucks to equipment maintenance, and food trucks to managing meal logistics.

Like cost maps, asset maps are most commonly used for comparison with competitors. The main objective in comparing asset maps is to highlight any unusual allocation of assets in competitor organizations. This could provide some insight into the competitors' strategies. If ASAP discovers that a competitor who normally purchases its airplanes suddenly leases several new ones instead, it may mean that the competitor is planning to replace the new planes in a short period of time or that it is trying to conserve its capital for some reason.

Figure A1–9 **ASAP Asset Map**

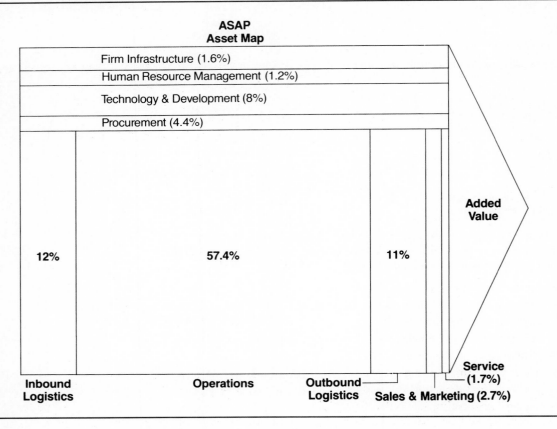

SUMMARY

The objective of value chain analysis is to help an organization better understand its activities and costs and search for ways to enhance its position in the competitive arena. The value chain and analysis of value activities are the base on which the other tools are built. In building value chains, primary and support value activities are identified, categorized, and analyzed. Costs and assets are assigned to value activities in building cost and asset maps. The costs of each activity are expressed as a percentage of total costs and total assets, respectively. To reduce costs, the behavior of costs must first be understood. Identification of cost drivers for each value activity assists in the process of understanding cost behavior. Taken collectively, the tools discussed in this appendix can be of great help to analysts searching for opportunities to apply information technology.

Appendix 2

Typical Job Descriptions

FUNCTIONAL ANALYST

A functional analyst works closely with users to ensure that a new system is designed to meet users' needs. The functional analyst defines user requirements and prepares functional specifications (described in Chapter 8). Also, the functional analyst performs these tasks:

- Reviews the technical design to ensure that user requirements are incorporated in it.
- Participates in developing security, control, and user procedures and produces user manuals.
- Trains user personnel.
- Aids in systems testing (planning, executing, and reviewing) and in tasks related to conversion.
- Monitors actual operations following conversion to the new system.

TECHNICAL ANALYST

A technical analyst advises functional analysts during the development of user requirements and then ensures that user requirements are converted into a workable technical design. Also, the technical analyst performs these tasks:

- Develops security, control, and user procedures and helps produce user manuals.
- Performs systems testing and tasks related to conversion.
- Serves as liaison between users and technical personnel.
- Monitors actual operations following conversion to the new system.

PROGRAMMERS AND PROGRAMMING SUPERVISORS

A programmer is responsible for coding, testing, and debugging the programs that make up the new system. A programmer also participates in structured design reviews (described in Chapter 18). In a small environment, one person may perform the functions of both technical analyst and programmer, although the tasks should be performed as distinct tasks to ensure good design and programs. A programming supervisor coordinates the entire programming effort and is responsible for its timely completion. He or she assigns work to programmers and supervises the day-to-day activities of anywhere from five to eight programmers. The more experienced programmers will do more program design and be more likely to work on the more difficult programs, for example, updates. Beginning programmers are more likely to work on simpler tasks such as reports.

DATA ADMINISTRATOR

A data administrator serves in an organization that has centralized control over data. If an automated data dictionary is used, the data administrator controls it and helps the project team gain its benefits. The data administrator also has these tasks:

- Sets standards for data definitions.
- Assists the project team in defining data in conformance with standards.
- Ensures adequate documentation of data definitions.

DATA BASE ADMINISTRATOR

A data base administrator is generally found in organizations using data base management software and the data base approach. In addition to overseeing the day-to-day administration of data bases and the changes to them, the data base administrator performs these tasks:

- Designs data bases and installs data base software.
- Assists in the use of data base software facilities and features.
- Makes periodic analyses of the operational efficiency of applications using data base software.

SYSTEMS SOFTWARE SPECIALIST

A systems software specialist is seldom assigned as a full-time member of a project team. Rather, the specialist is a full-time support person to all members of the IS department. During a development project, a specialist performs the following tasks for a specific software product:

- Installs and maintains the software product (operating systems, automated programming aids, etc.).

- Resolves any problems experienced by the project team with system software.
- Transfers completely tested programs to production libraries.
- Aids in the analysis of program and hardware efficiency.

USER REPRESENTATIVE

The most important function of a user representative on a project team is to make sure the other project team members understand the needs of the users for whom the new system is being developed. In addition, a user representative provides information on the company and industry. This information will explain the business issues that the project team should address in the design of the new system. A user representative also performs these tasks:

- Defines systems specifications from a user's perspective (i.e., a functional as opposed to a technical perspective).
- Approves detailed report, screen and form layouts, data base contents, and processing requirements after obtaining input from other users when necessary.
- Aids in gathering data for the conversion effort.
- Trains other user personnel in the use of the new system.

COMPUTER OPERATIONS PERSONNEL

Like the systems software specialists, computer operations personnel are typically not full-time members of a project team, but they do provide key support functions. They help design the operating procedures of a new system to conform to the computer environment in which the new system will operate. In addition, computer operations personnel will do the following:

- Provide data control and conversion support.
- Execute program tests and distribute results.
- Operate the new system when it is put into production.

Appendix 3

State Transition Diagrams

State transition diagrams are used to represent the behavior of so-called *finite-state machines*. Finite-state machines are data entities, business transactions, or system components (such as conversations) that can take on any one of a finite number of states. These states have specific transactions that cause the entity to make a transition from one state to another. State transition diagrams are widely used in systems software; they are applicable to many other fields but are generally not understood by many analysts.

An example of a state transition diagram is given in Figure A3–1. The schematic represents the state of a person relative to a corporate retirement plan and the various transactions that can affect that state. The possible states are represented by circles labeled with the designation of the state, and the transitions by the labeled arcs between states. The figure shows that a person who is fully vested and 65 years old or more can apply for benefits and become retired. A person who is not fully vested and leaves the company is eliminated from the plan.

Another example of the use of a state diagram is given in Figure A3–2. This graph represents part of a parser of a COBOL compiler. (A parser is the part of a compiler that recognizes elements of the language in the source code and validates that these elements obey the language's syntax.) Most of the circles are not labeled; this is because the intermediate states are only useful as partial steps towards verifying that an entire COBOL statement is correct. Note that errors (unauthorized transitions) are assumed to be processed by a subroutine, which is not represented on this diagram.

Figure A3–3 represents a lower level of parsing for the COBOL compiler, that which isolates a word and determines whether it is a reserved COBOL word, a valid data name, or a numeric or text literal. The state machine represented by this diagram can thus be used by the one represented in Figure A3–2.

An alternative format for state transition diagrams is the fence diagram, illustrated in Figure A3–4. This figure reproduces the retirement plan example, but with states being represented by vertical lines and transitions by arrows drawn between lines.

Figure A3–1 **State Transition Diagram for Retirement System**

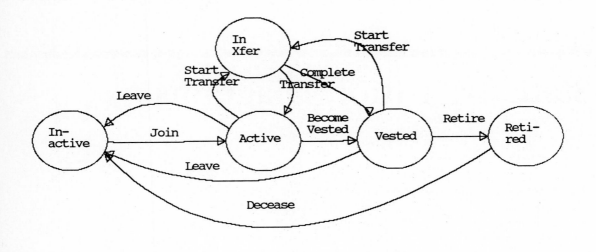

Figure A3–2 **State Transition Diagram for COBOL Parser (Partial), Version 1**

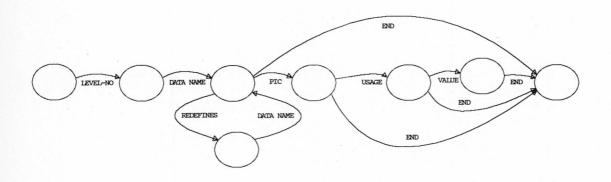

Figure A3–3 **State Transition Diagram for COBOL Parser (Partial), Version 2**

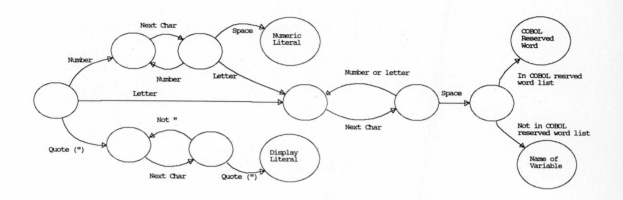

Figure A3–4 **Fence Diagram for Retirement System**

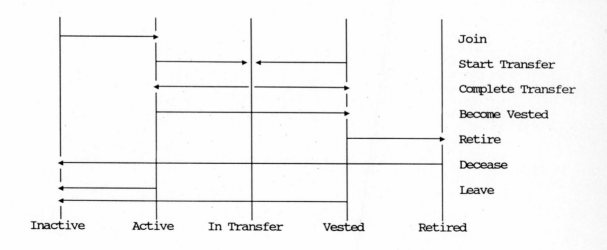

Both types of diagrams are excellent communications tools. For rigorous analysis, another form of representation, the state transition matrix (see Figure A3–5), may be useful. This matrix represents states along one dimension and inputs (or attempted transitions) along the other. In this matrix, each cell must be filled in with the next state reached (or an error indication) and the other actions to be taken, such as the creation of an output message.

State transition diagrams are useful whenever the entity to be analyzed can take on five or more states and when the logic for accepting and processing transactions is complex and depends heavily on the state variable. For instance, whereas yesterday's transaction systems guided the operator heavily through a menu-driven, form-filling dialog, today's transaction systems tend to give much more freedom to the user in selecting the next course of action. Consequently, many more unpredictable sequences of events may arise; finite-state machines are excellent for analyzing how these events should be processed.

A limitation of state transition diagrams is that they appear to be able to represent only one variable. When the entity being processed has two independent variables, either two independent state transition diagrams (with two separate sets of transitions) are required or the state variable must be transformed into a single two-dimensional variable. This was implicitly done for

Figure A3–5 **State Transition Matrix**

Transition:	State: 0	1	2	3	4	5	6	7	8	9	10	11
Number	1		1						7			
Letter	7		7						7			
Quote	4					6						
Not Quote						4						
Next Character		2			5			8				
Space			3						9			
In Table										10		
Not In Table										11		
Final				F			F				F	F

the retirement illustration, where the states of vestedness and the age were combined (e.g., "fully vested" and "over sixty-five").

One of the advantages of finite-state machines is that they are quite easy to program in a generalized way, so modifying the state transition logic only requires updating a table in memory, representing the state transition matrix.

Appendix 4

Computer Graphics

INTRODUCTION

In his landmark book, *The Visual Display of Quantitative Information,* Edward R. Tufte gives the following reasons why a graphical display of quantitative results is often much more effective than a numerical display:

> Modern data graphics can do much more than simply substitute for small statistical tables. At their best, graphics are instruments for reasoning about quantitative information. Often the most effective way to describe, explore, and summarize a set of numbers—even a very large set—is to look at pictures of those numbers. Furthermore, of all methods for analyzing and communicating statistical information, well-designed data graphics are usually the simplest and at the same time the most powerful.[1]

Information from today's computer systems is often presented in the form of graphs. Current display technology and software tools have made it relatively easy to accommodate a user's preference for a graphical display of output in place of or in addition to numerical displays. Graphical presentation of computer output is most often found in decision support systems (DSS) and executive information systems (EIS).

Writing of the importance of graphical presentations for EIS, John F. Rockart and David W. De Long said:

> The availability of new presentation formats—particularly graphics—has an important impact on the way executives think about information. But graphics is not the only formatting advantage provided by the computer. The CEO at one major food distributor took advantage of the computer's ability to combine tabular, text, and graphic data on the same page to satisfy his idiosyncratic way of looking at data.
>
> Most commonly, graphics are used for standard performance reports or to present the results of ad-hoc queries. The president of Banco Internacional found that a graphic display of profits versus goals and forecasts provided a picture over time and revealed dynamics of the business he had not previously recognized.

Derwyn Phillips, Gillette's executive vice president, implemented his EIS largely to review performance reports graphically. Phillips believes that executives can get too caught up in minor variances when looking only at numbers. The key is in seeing trends, he says, not minor blips, and graphs help management do that.[2]

In a DSS or EIS environment, it is frequently a single user who decides on output format designs, depending on his or her individual preferences. In some cases, the IS analyst may not be involved in the process at all. There will, however, be many opportunities for the IS analyst to assist users in selecting a graphical presentation format. Thus, it is important for IS analysts to be aware of good design principles for the presentation of quantitative information in a graphical format.

TYPES OF GRAPHS

There are several types of graphs encountered in practice. Each is discussed briefly and illustrated in Figures A4–1 through A4–9.

- Pie charts are used to show the proportions of components to the whole. The graphic can give a much better sense of the relative importance of a given component than if one merely views a table of numbers. This is illustrated in Figure A4–1. Figure A4–2 is an "exploded" pie chart, used to draw the attention of the viewer to one of the components.

- Line graphs are used to plot the interaction of two variables on x and y coordinates as illustrated in Figure A4–3. It is customary to plot the independent variable along the x-axis and the dependent variable on the y-axis. Figure A4–4 overlays another line graph on the first so that the user can easily compare two different years.

- Time series graphs are commonly used to show how a parameter varies over time. Time is the independent variable and is thus shown along the x-axis. Figure A4–5 is an example.

- Bar graphs are often used in place of line graphs, for example highlighting changes in magnitude (see Figure A4–6). Bar graphs can also be in stacked format, as shown in Figure A4–7.

- A specialized form of bar graph is the histogram (see Figure A4–8). This type of graphic shows a frequency distribution of the dependent variable. (Ordinary bar graphs are often also incorrectly called histograms.)

- Scatter diagrams are used to plot x-y coordinates of two variables that are believed to correlate statistically with each other. Once the scatter diagram is prepared, the viewer can choose between various standard statistical techniques to determine the degree of correlation (see Figure A4–9).

Figure A4–1 **Simple Pie Chart**

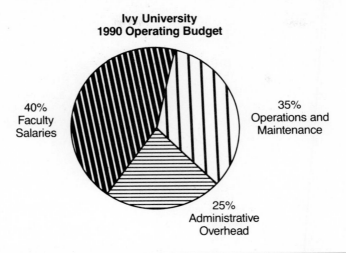

Figure A4–2 **Exploded Pie Chart**

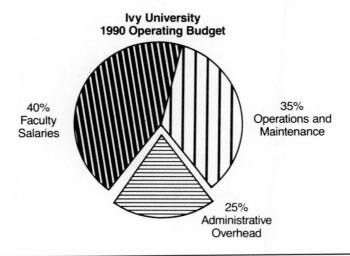

Figure A4–3 **Line Graph**

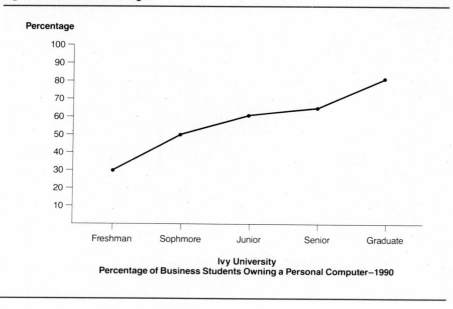

Ivy University
Percentage of Business Students Owning a Personal Computer–1990

Figure A4–4 **Line Graph with Two Variables**

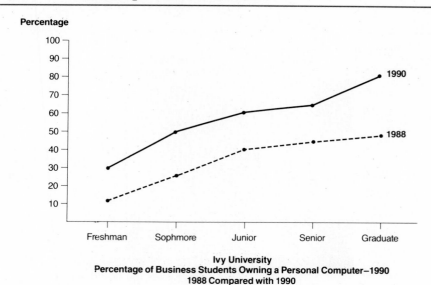

Ivy University
Percentage of Business Students Owning a Personal Computer–1990
1988 Compared with 1990

Figure A4–5 **Time Series Graph**

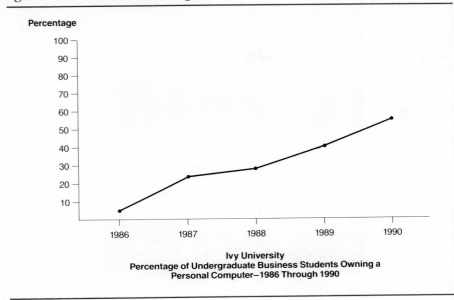

Ivy University
Percentage of Undergraduate Business Students Owning a
Personal Computer–1986 Through 1990

Figure A4–6 **Bar Graph**

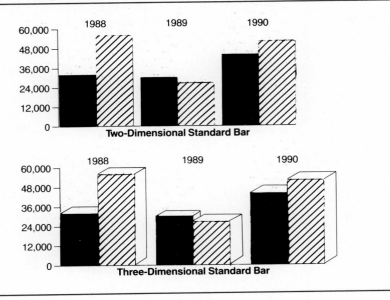

Figure A4–7 **Stacked Bar Graph**

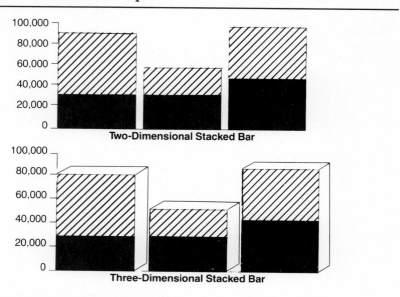

Figure A4–8 **Histogram**

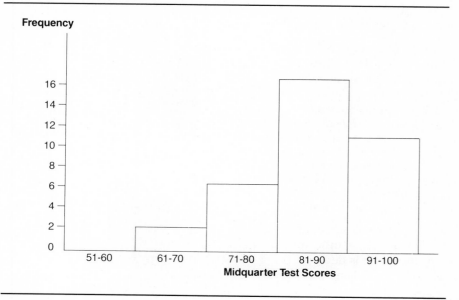

Figure A4–9 **Scatter Diagram**

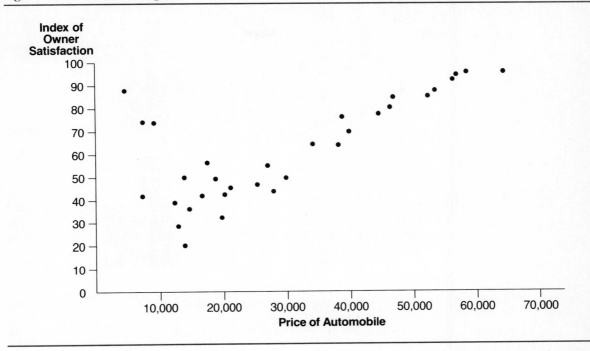

GRAPHICAL EXCELLENCE

The design of a graph is an important factor in whether it will communicate effectively. Edward Tufte lists five general principles of graphical excellence that apply equally well in the more specific case of computer graphics design:

> Graphical excellence is the well-designed presentation of interesting data—a matter of *substance*, of *statistics*, and of *design*.
> Graphical excellence consists of complex ideas communicated with clarity, precision, and efficiency.
> Graphical excellence is that which gives to the viewer the greatest number of ideas in the shortest time with the least ink in the smallest space.
> Graphical excellence is nearly always multivariate.
> And graphical excellence requires telling the truth about the data.[3]

The last point bears some elaboration. A graphics designer can either deliberately or inadvertently miscommunicate the meaning of data behind a graph by the way the graph is designed. Designing a graph that is an accurate representation of the underlying data is called graphical integrity.

GRAPHICAL INTEGRITY

Tufte identified six principles of design that will help ensure graphical integrity:

The representation of numbers, as physically measured on the surface of the graphic itself, should be directly proportional to the numerical quantities represented.

Clear, detailed and thorough labeling should be used to defeat graphical distortion and ambiguity. Write out explanations of the data on the graphic itself. Label important events in the data.

Show data variation, not design variation.

In time-series displays of money, deflated and standardized units of monetary measurement are nearly always better than nominal units.

The number of information-carrying (variable) dimensions depicted should not exceed the number of dimensions in the data.

Graphics must not quote data out of context.[4]

Figure A4–10 is an illustration of a graph that violates some of these principles. Figure A4–11 is an example of a graph that presents the same underlying data with integrity. Tufte's book contains many wonderful illustrations and should be read by anyone with an interest in the subject of graphical displays.

References

1. Tufte, Edward R. *The Visual Display of Quantitative Information*. Cheshire, Connecticut: Graphics Press, 1983, p. i.

2. Rockart, John F., and De Long, David W. *Executive Support Systems—The Emergence of Top Management Computer Use*. Homewood, Illinois: Dow Jones-Irwin, 1988, p. 141.

3. Tufte, *Visual Display*, p. 51.

4. Tufte, *Visual Display*, p. 77.

Figure A4–10 **Graphic Lacking Integrity**

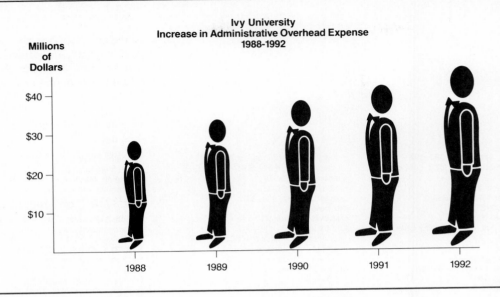

Figure A4–11 **Graphic with Integrity**

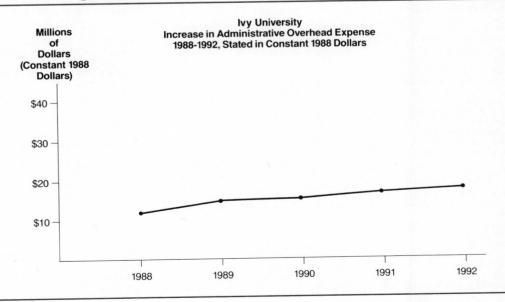

Index